The Self-Sufficient Gardener

A Complete Guide to Growing and Preserving All Your Own Food

JOHN SEYMOUR

DOLPHIN BOOKS
Doubleday & Company, Inc.
Garden City, New York
1980

The Self-Sufficient Gardener was conceived,
edited and designed by Dorling Kindersley Limited,
9 Henrietta Street, London WC2

Originally published in Great Britain
by Faber and Faber Limited, London

Library of Congress Cataloging in Publication Data

Seymour, John, 1914 –
    The self-sufficient gardener.
    Includes index
    1. Vegetable gardening. 2. Fruit-culture.
3. Vegetables – Preservation. 4. Fruit –
Preservation. I. Title.
SB321. S53   1979   635   78-19223
ISBN 0-385-14671-X

The Self-Sufficient Gardener

Contents

Introduction

When I was a boy in the countryside – fifty years ago and more – people really did garden for self-sufficiency, but it would not have occurred to them to do otherwise. People were self-reliant because they had to be: it was a way of life. They were doing what generations had done before them; simply carrying on a traditional way of life. Money was a rare commodity: far too valuable to be spent on things you could grow or make yourself. It was spent on tools or fabric for clothes or luxury foods like tea and coffee. They would have laughed at a diet of store-bought foods – such an extravagance. Even in my own childhood rural towns were far apart and roads were often bad. Many were not passable in winter snows or muddy spring thaws. To have a few chickens, a pig in the sty and a vegetable patch, was simply common sense. These country gardens were enormously productive. They were bursting with fertility derived from the compost heap and the manure of the animals.

As people grew richer and food became cheaper, and as farming became increasingly mechanized, sending more and more countrymen into the cities to earn their livings, so these small-scale food-producing gardens declined in popularity. During World War II "victory gardens" gained favor, but the fashion died and soon the roses took over from the rhubarb. Gardens acquired a new role, that of a status symbol. Neighbors compared the greenness of the lawn, the diameters of their dahlias and the size of their patios. The supermarket trolley replaced the wheel barrow and vegetables were bought canned, frozen and dried.

But now, once again, the pendulum is swinging the other way. As food, and everything else, is becoming more expensive, there is coming about a great renaissance of gardening for self-sufficiency. People find that they are saving a significant part of their salaries by doing it, that their food tastes better and does them more good, and that their children are healthier. They themselves benefit from some hard work in the fresh air, and from being involved with the benign cycle of the seasons and with the satisfying process of helping nature create beautiful and nourishing food out of what is apparently nothing.

In the United States plots of land for food-growing are sought with great eagerness. And where a few years ago, in Europe, there were plenty of allotments with nobody working them, now there is a waiting list everywhere for allotments. Everywhere gardening is losing its image as a retired person's sport; young people are learning

to do it and lively minds are getting to work on new techniques.

Organic gardening

Alongside this re-emergence of the desire to grow food has come an awareness that the earth's supply of mineral-derived energy is limited. Simplistic gardening with chemical fertilizers is becoming a thing of the past as the new generation of gardeners is learning to do without the petrochemicals on which gardening has become dependent, and to rely solely on nature's very own methods. People are re-discovering the value of waste organic matter — animal and vegetable. Methods of making compost and of keeping animals in the garden are again being treated as matters of crucial importance.

The whole question of chemical versus organic gardening is still, at the present time, a major controversy. In my view the best proof is in the eating. My own garden is far from perfect. I sow more than I can reap, like most serious gardeners, and end up with too many weeds, not enough time to hoe them, and occasionally crops that I am ashamed of. But on the whole my garden is lush and fertile, and I grow a great deal of produce in it. Orthodox gardeners, who use chemicals on their gardens, come and look at my crops sometimes and refuse to believe that I put no inorganic fertilizer on them. But I don't: not an ounce of artificial nitrogen has gone on my land for thirteen years now. And even when the weeds do overwhelm me, I am often surprised that there seems to be fertility enough for them and my crops. This year my onions, carrots and parsnips, which were all interplanted with each other, were neglected and overrun with weeds. And yet out of the mess, I have dug large and beautiful carrots and parsnips, and the onions, all hanging in strings now, are twice as big as my fist, luscious and firm.

I am not advocating the cultivation of weeds. But rather than douse them with some "selective weed spray" (which is only selective up to a point of course — if a chemical damages one form of life you can be sure that it will do at least some damage to many other forms of life), I would rather have a few weeds and maybe a slightly smaller crop.

I am surprised when I read the advice of many gardening writers that their readers should apply this or that amount of "complete fertilizer", or of some proprietary high-nitrogen chemical, or that the soil should be doused with herbicides, pesticides, or fungicides ("cide" means kill and no

gardener should forget that fact). I wonder whether these writers have tried gardening without chemicals. Applied nitrates definitely harm the soil in the long term, although it must be admitted that they have a dramatic effect on the growth of crops in soil that is already hooked on them — that is to say soil which therefore has no nitrogen-fixing capacity of its own. However, the main point that needs to be made is that some of the best garden — and farm — crops in the world are grown without any of these expensive and dangerous aids at all. The highest yield possible with any crop can be, and very often is, achieved without chemicals.

But here there is a trap that many a would-be organic gardener has fallen into. "I am 'organic'; I don't put any artificial fertilizers on my land", they say. But neither do they put anything else! Nothing will come out of nothing, and if you continue to take crops out of your soil and put nothing back you will eventually grow — well, next to nothing. If you see a garden, which is held to be organic, filled with nothing but miserable insect-eaten crops surrounded by weeds, it is probable that you have encountered this negative approach. Some advocates of organic gardening also put forward eccentric notions like planting crops according to the phases of the moon, sprinkling tiny amounts of obscure substances on the soil, and so on. Plant seeds will germinate and plants will grow when temperature, humidity, and nutrients are right for them. The organic philosophy has no need of these irrational and superstitious notions. The organic approach is based on sound fact and science, and its practice can be seen to be effective and correct.

The organic philosophy is well summed up as adherence to the following six laws: first, the gardener must work with nature and not against it; second, nature is diverse and therefore the gardener must practise diversity; third, the gardener must husband other forms of life — animal or vegetable — in environments as close as possible to those for which they evolved; fourth, the gardener must return to the soil as much, or nearly as much, as he takes from it; fifth, the gardener must feed the soil and not the plant; sixth, the gardener must study nature as a whole and never any part of it in isolation.

Garden animals

It is, of course, possible to live on vegetables alone. In fact, it is theoretically possible to live on peas, beans and potatoes, if you have enough of them. However, those gardeners who are not vegetarians will find that on even the smallest pieces of land, they can keep rabbits, chickens or both. Any animals you have will make a major contribution to the fertility of your garden, and if you add rabbit and chicken meat, and eggs, to your vegetable and fruit produce you can certainly be a self-sufficient gardener in the true sense, and you will be coming close to providing yourself with the varied diet that is now fairly commonplace in the West. Dairy products and the meat of large animals will be almost the only things that you need to buy.

Many people feel that animals will tie them down; they won't be able to take a vacation, or even go away for the weekend. But what if they team up with neighbors, and either keep birds and animals cooperatively, or else agree to take turns at looking after each others'? To feed a few rabbits and a few hens, and collect the eggs, is the work of minutes a day.

The advantage of keeping birds and animals is immense. As well as the food they provide, almost more important is the fertility they give to the garden. Detailed instructions for keeping garden animals are given on pp. 230 to 239.

I have organized the chapters of this book in which I discuss the cultivation of vegetables and fruit (see pp. 113-190) on the basis of the natural families and orders into which plants have been grouped by botanists. I have done this because there are very close relationships between plants of the same family and you will find that if you think of plants in terms of their relations, you will eventually get a very real feeling for the characters of the different plants.

For example, you grow potatoes and tomatoes for quite different reasons: the former for its underground tubers and the latter for its fruit. You could, of course, grow them successfully for years without realizing that they are very closely related. But once you have them classified in your head as members of the *Solanaceae*, or nightshade family, you immediately see and feel their close relationship and take an interest in it. And, of course, you soon find that potatoes and tomatoes suffer from all the same diseases and respond well or ill to much the same sort of treatment.

It is also fun to spot the similarities which make, for example, apples, strawberries and roses close relations. It is useful to know that pears are closely related to hawthorns, and plums to sloes, for it is well worth grafting scions, or fruiting spurs, of fruit trees on to the root stocks of their wild, and therefore more hardy, relations. A sense of the specialness, similarities, and differences, of different kinds of plants adds enormously to the pleasure of gardening; it gives an insight into plants and engenders in the gardener the sort of sympathy that good husbandmen should have – the sympathy which is best described by the phrase "green fingers".

Finally, let me stress that self-sufficient gardening needs commitment. It requires the determination to produce as much good food as is humanly possible on whatever area of land is at your disposal. Every patio, every flat roof, every window sill, should be looked upon as a possible food-producing area. New methods of organic gardening which produce high yields in small spaces should be considered. More than this, self-sufficient gardening requires a commitment to understanding your plants, your soil and the workings of nature: its seasons and its cycles. I have given over a chapter of this book to explain the workings of the seasons. Other chapters discuss the growing of the individual varieties of vegetables, fruit and herbs in detail. In the remainder of this introduction I shall try to explain about the soil and the cycles of nature as I understand them. But before I move on to these topics, I should like to introduce you to the deep bed method of gardening.

THE DEEP BED METHOD

Unless you have a very large area of land at your disposal, the key to success as a self-sufficient gardener is to be able to grow a lot in a small space. Of the new techniques for growing more vegetables in smaller areas, the most important in my view is what I call the Deep Bed Method, which is being developed in California by several

Americans, several Chinese immigrants and an Englishman called Alan Chadwick. The method is derived from age-old techniques that have been practiced in France and China, but which have never been widely adopted in the West.

The essence of the method is to dig deeply and then never tread on the bed. This means your plants are growing in very loose, deeply dug soil; their roots will go down instead of sideways. You therefore get bigger plants, and can grow them closer together. The Deep Bed Method is discussed in detail on pp. 106 to 112. Throughout the chapters on the Cultivation of Vegetables and Fruit (pp. 113-190), I have included instructions for growing each crop by the Deep Bed Method, wherever this differs from conventional practice.

A deep bed should produce about four times the yield by weight that a conventional bed will produce. A deep bed of 100 square feet (9 sq m) can produce from 200 to 400 lbs (90-180 kg) of vegetables a year. According to the US Department of Agriculture's statistics the average American eats 322 lbs (145 kg) of vegetables a year. Thus one tiny bed — just pace out 20 feet by 5 feet (6 x 1.5m) on the floor to get an idea of the size of it — can keep one adult in vegetables.

From what I have seen of deep bed gardens and from my first hand experience on my own land, I can say that the claims made for this method are by no means exaggerated. I think it highly likely that more and more serious vegetable gardeners will adopt this method. If your aim is to grow as many vegetables as you can in the space available to you, then I urge you to study the technique and try it.

NATURE'S CYCLES

Early in the evolution of living things the animal and vegetable kingdoms diverged along different paths. Since then they have evolved in co-existence, each dependent on the other. Plants are essential to animals, for only plants can store the energy of the sun by photosynthesis, and fix the free nitrogen in the air into compounds from which both they and the animals can draw energy.

A DEEP BED
You can create a deep bed by digging to a spade's depth and loosening the soil to a further spade's depth. You must incorporate a large amount of manure and never tread on the bed. The very loose soil will allow the roots of your crops to penetrate deep down, instead of spreading sideways as they do in conventional beds. You will get bigger vegetables and you will be able to grow them closer together.

At the same time plants could not exist without animals. Nearly all flowering plants – which means nearly all the higher plants – are dependent on animals, especially birds and insects, for pollination. Without animals they could not reproduce. But beyond this, there is a benign cycle between plants and animals at all stages of their lives. Plants inhale carbon dioxide, which would kill animals in too great a quantity, and exhale oxygen without which animals cannot live. Animals inhale the oxygen and exhale the carbon dioxide which is needed by plants.

Animals consume plants and, quite simply, transform plant tissue into more complex matter. Simple plant protein is converted into more complex animal protein. Animals void such food as they cannot directly absorb, and this falls on the earth making instantly-available food which is taken up again by plants. Plants feed animals, and animals feed plants. This is the basic cycle of nature without which life on this planet would cease to exist.

As well as the animal-plant cycle, there are other natural cycles, which define the ceaseless circulation of the elements within the earth's atmosphere. Two of these are of the utmost importance to gardeners: the water cycle and the nitrogen cycle.

The water cycle

The water cycle is the simpler of the two. Put briefly, water is evaporated from the sea, the lakes, the rivers and the soil by the sun and it is also transpired by plants and animals. It is carried about the atmosphere by winds, precipitated in the form of rain or snow, some of which falls back into the sea, but much of which falls on the land.

If it falls on good soil, with plenty of humus in it, it soaks in. Some of it remains in the soil, held like water in a sponge. The rest sinks down deeper, until it reaches impervious rock. It then makes its way down any slope it can until, perhaps, it emerges on the surface lower down a hill, runs down to a stream, and eventually it gets to the sea.

Now such water as remains in the soil may possibly reach the surface and be evaporated again, or it may be taken up by a plant, in which case it will probably enter the roots of the plant. It will ascend the plant, carrying whatever soluble chemicals there are dissolved in it, for it has taken these things up from the soil. Some of this water will make part of the plant's tissues, and deliver the nutrients it has in solution to the various cells of the plant. The remaining water, which is not taken into the plant tissue, will be transpired through the stomata of the leaves, the small apertures in the leaves' skin.

Without this movement of water from the soil below it to the sky above it, a plant could not eat, nor could it grow. Plants depend entirely on water to bring them their food. This does not mean that you have to swamp your plants with water. Most land plants need moist soil, not waterlogged soil, to keep them healthy and growing. If their roots are immersed completely in water for any length of time, ultimately they will die.

The nitrogen cycle

Nitrogen is an essential ingredient of all plants and animals. The air is a mixture of oxygen and nitrogen; but the two elements are not in compound, simply in mixture. This means that the nitrogen is what is called "free nitrogen", meaning that it is still free to combine with another element, or elements, to form a compound. But the higher plants cannot use free nitrogen: they must have it combined as a compound with at least one other element. For example one part of nitrogen combined with three parts of hydrogen produces ammonia which, when it has undergone further changes, can be used by plants.

Fortunately certain bacteria, and certain algae, are capable of "fixing" nitrogen, in other words making it available to higher forms of life in the form of a compound. Also the tremendous power in a flash of lightning can fix nitrogen. (It has been conjectured that nitrogen fixed by lightning made possible the first forms of life on Earth.) And nitrogen can also be fixed artificially by the same process as lightning uses. Nitrogen can be combined artificially with hydrogen to form ammonia. The ammonia can then be combined with oxygen and other chemicals to make such substances as ammonium sulfate, urea, ammonium nitrate, sodium nitrate and calcium nitrate, all of which are used as artificial nitrogen fertilizers.

Nitrogen fixation by artificial means requires one constant: an enormous expenditure of power. Therefore, as power becomes more expensive, and more difficult and dangerous to produce, the nitrogen fixed free by bacteria becomes more and more valuable. Fortunately, by employing perfectly simple and well-tried methods of gardening, you can encourage nitrogen fixation by natural means and grow crops as good as any that ever have been grown with artificial nitrogen, with nitrogen fixed by natural agencies alone.

If you study the illustration and caption below, you will see that much fixed nitrogen simply goes around in a short circle – plants, micro-organisms, plants, micro-organisms and so on – and in good soil conditions, little nitrogen is released into the air. But any that is released to the air comes back again, eventually, fixed by nitrogen-fixing bacteria.

Other fixed nitrogen goes in a rather longer circle – plants, animals, micro-organisms, plants, animals and so on. No chemist or biologist has ever been able to explain this, but animals are capable of transforming plant matter with a very low nitrogen content into manure with a fairly high nitrogen content in a matter of hours. Keeping animals in your garden is extremely good for your soil and your vegetables. If you have animals, or if you can import animal manure from elsewhere, you will never be short of fixed nitrogen to feed your crops.

There are some important facts about the nitrogen cycle that gardeners need to know. First, all dead animal or vegetable tissue put in or on the soil will eventually release its nitrogen for the use of plants. But, and this is of great importance, it may do so very slowly, because of what is called the nitrogen/carbon ratio. If there is not enough nitrogen to balance the carbon which forms a large part of the body of every living organism, the putrefactive bacteria, which break down organic matter and release nitrates for the higher plants to use, will have to borrow nitrogen that is already in the soil. This means that, temporarily, they will rob the soil of nitrogen. However, eventually they

THE NITROGEN CYCLE

The power in a flash of lightning can fix nitrogen – take it from the air and leave it in the soil in a compound form which can be absorbed by plants. More often nitrogen is fixed by bacteria in the soil, some of which live in nodules on the roots of leguminous plants. Plants turn nitrogen into protein. Animals eat plants and produce more complex protein. Animal waste and the dead bodies of plants and animals return the protein to the soil. Bacteria work on this protein, once again producing nitrogen compounds which will feed plants, and nitrogen which returns to the air.

will complete their work and release into the soil the nitrogen they have borrowed, and also the nitrogen they have got from the organic matter they have eaten.

Now, in practice this means that if you dig or plow in material which is low in nitrogen, such as straw, sawdust, or plants which have already gone to seed, you should either put some highly nitrogenous substance in with it to feed the bacteria which are to break them down, or else be prepared to wait a long time before that soil is again very fertile. Leguminous plants like alfalfa or clover, turned into the soil before they have flowered, are sufficiently high in nitrogen to break down almost immediately and release their nitrogen in a matter of a very few weeks — the warmer the weather, the quicker the process. Straw from sweet corn, and old plant residues that have seeded, will take a year or even two.

One lesson to be learned from this is: only dig in green manure crops if they are young and succulent. If any plant has already seeded, which means that most of its nitrogen has gone into its seed, put it on your compost heap. This is the value of your compost heap: it rots down organic matter, so that the matter can give its fixed nitrogen back to the soil, without robbing the soil in the process. This is why extra nitrogen, ideally in the form of animal manure, should be added to the material in your compost heap to help the rotting process. Organic matter will rot down in your compost heap even if you don't give it more nitrogen, but the process will take a long time.

The other lesson that the nitrogen cycle teaches is that a gardener should grow as many plants that belong to the family *Leguminosae*, the pea and bean family, as he can. As I have explained, the members of this family have nodules on their roots containing bacteria which fix nitrogen. Quite apart from this, leguminous plants are extremely nutritious and very high in protein. In fact it would be difficult on an all-vegetable diet to live without them: the "pulses", as the seeds of peas and beans are called, are the best form of vegetable protein you can get.

THE SOIL

A spadeful of soil may look a very simple, innocuous substance. But it is, in fact, of such enormous complexity that it is doubtful if mankind will ever fully understand it. First of all, if it is good soil, it is filled with life. In every teaspoonful of soil there are millions of bacteria — bacteria of numerous species as well as algae, microscopic

animals, the mycelium of fungi, and viruses. In larger quantities of good soil you are sure to find worms and the larvae of numerous beetles and other insects. It has been calculated that there are from five to ten tons of living matter in every acre of soil.

The interrelationships of these various animals and plants are of great complexity. There are long and involved food chains, and subtle mutually beneficial arrangements. There are chemical processes of such complexity that no scientist has ever been able to duplicate them in his laboratory. For example, there are five species of bacteria that we know of which can fix nitrogen from the air and convert it into the type of amino acid which can

make protein for plants and ultimately people. Two other species of bacteria have the baleful effect of turning useful nitrites and nitrates, that could have been used by plants, into free nitrogen gas again; three species can turn ammonia into nitrites; another can turn nitrites into nitrates which plants can use; and a huge array of bacteria, fungi and actinomycetes turn protein and other dead organic matter into ammonia. That simple spadeful of soil is a chemical factory of a sophistication that no human chemist has ever been able even to approach.

The origins of soil

Fundamentally, soil is rock that has been pulverized by such agents as heat and cold, water and wind, and, very importantly, has been subjected to the eroding effect of lichens, bacteria, algae and other living creatures. The hardest rock in the world, as long as it is exposed to light, is being gradually gnawed away by plant life.

For the purposes of the gardener, although a geologist might disapprove, it is enough to say that most of the land surface of the Earth consists of a layer of soil lying on top of rock. Between

The Ecology of the Soil

All terrestrial life comes from the soil and returns to it. And all terrestrial death comes to life again through the soil, because decomposing organic matter contains nearly all the nutrients that plants require. The good gardener will respect this natural cycle and thereby ensure that the soil in his garden is always living and life-giving.

SOIL LAYERS *Every soil can be divided into three distinct layers: topsoil, which in a fertile soil is rich in humus (decayed organic matter); subsoil, which is composed mostly of rock particles; and rock from which the basis of all soil is formed. Minerals are found in all layers.*

PLANTS *The roots of different plants and trees push outward and downward to varying extents. Where many species grow together nourishment is drawn from all layers of the soil through their roots.*

ANIMALS *The complexity and interaction of animal life in the soil performs two crucial functions: the breaking down and returning to the soil of organic matter; and the aeration and loosening of the soil which enables roots to spread deep and wide, and oxygen, nitrogen, rainwater and other useful elements to penetrate deep down. It is the delicate balance between a myriad species which keeps soil healthy, productive and free from disease.*

ANT NEST *The building of an ant nest aerates the soil, but it may kill the plant above.*

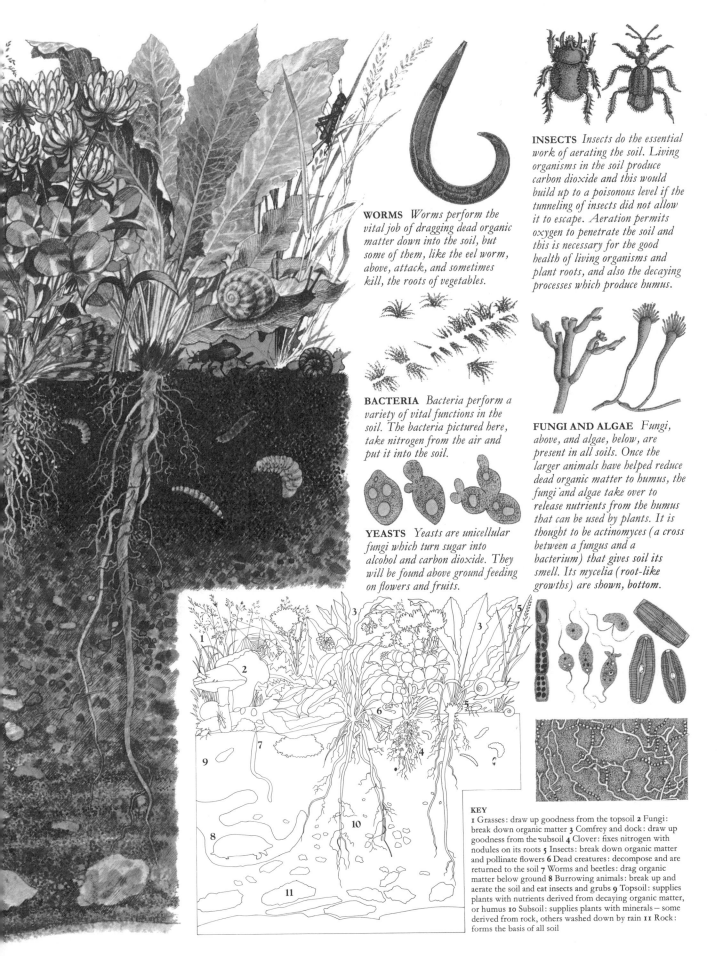

WORMS *Worms perform the vital job of dragging dead organic matter down into the soil, but some of them, like the eel worm, above, attack, and sometimes kill, the roots of vegetables.*

INSECTS *Insects do the essential work of aerating the soil. Living organisms in the soil produce carbon dioxide and this would build up to a poisonous level if the tunneling of insects did not allow it to escape. Aeration permits oxygen to penetrate the soil and this is necessary for the good health of living organisms and plant roots, and also the decaying processes which produce humus.*

BACTERIA *Bacteria perform a variety of vital functions in the soil. The bacteria pictured here, take nitrogen from the air and put it into the soil.*

FUNGI AND ALGAE *Fungi, above, and algae, below, are present in all soils. Once the larger animals have helped reduce dead organic matter to humus, the fungi and algae take over to release nutrients from the humus that can be used by plants. It is thought to be actinomyces (a cross between a fungus and a bacterium) that gives soil its smell. Its mycelia (root-like growths) are shown, bottom.*

YEASTS *Yeasts are unicellular fungi which turn sugar into alcohol and carbon dioxide. They will be found above ground feeding on flowers and fruits.*

KEY
1 Grasses: draw up goodness from the topsoil **2** Fungi: break down organic matter **3** Comfrey and dock: draw up goodness from the subsoil **4** Clover: fixes nitrogen with nodules on its roots **5** Insects: break down organic matter and pollinate flowers **6** Dead creatures: decompose and are returned to the soil **7** Worms and beetles: drag organic matter below ground **8** Burrowing animals: break up and aerate the soil and eat insects and grubs **9** Topsoil: supplies plants with nutrients derived from decaying organic matter, or humus **10** Subsoil: supplies plants with minerals — some derived from rock, others washed down by rain **11** Rock: forms the basis of all soil

the two is an intermediate layer known as subsoil, which is rock in the process of being broken down by natural forces. Some soils are the direct products of the rock underneath them; others were brought to where they are by other forces. They may have blown there, like the loess soils of North America and China, been carried there by glaciers, like much of the soil in North America and much of the soil north of the Thames in Britain, or been washed there by water, like many soils in river valleys.

Types of soil

To the practical gardener the origin of his soil is of interest, but not vitally important. What is important to the gardener is the nature of his soil, wherever it came from: whether it is light, meaning composed of large particles like sand; heavy, meaning composed of very small particles like clay; or something in between. It is important to know: whether it is that rare commodity, organic soil, which means it is composed of decaying vegetable matter; whether it is acid or alkaline – sand is inclined to be acid, clay alkaline; whether it is naturally well drained or not; what lies underneath it – soil above chalk or limestone is very likely to be alkaline.

Fortunately, whatever your soil is like, you can improve it. There is scarcely a soil in the world that will not grow good crops of some sort if it is properly treated. Excess acidity is easily remedied by adding lime; excess alkalinity by adding compost or manure. Waterlogging can always be cured by drainage. Trace element deficiencies can be cured simply by adding the missing trace elements.

Humus

Above all, everything about your soil can be improved by the addition of one thing: humus. Humus is vegetable or animal matter which has died and been changed by the action of soil organisms into a complex organic substance which becomes part of the soil. Any animal or vegetable material, when it dies, can become humus.

Humus has many beneficial effects on the soil. All the following have been established experimentally by soil scientists – they are not just the optimistic conjectures of a humus-enthusiast: humus protects soil from erosion by rain and allows water to percolate gently and deeply; it reduces erosion by wind; its slimes and gums stick soil particles together and thus turn a very fine soil, or clay, into a coarser one; it feeds earthworms and other useful soil organisms; it lowers soil temperature in summer and increases it in winter; it supplies nutrients to plants, because it contains all the elements that plants need and releases them slowly at a pace that the plant can cope with; it enables the soil to hold water like a sponge, and minimizes the loss of water by evaporation; it ensures that chemical changes are not too rapid when lime and inorganic fertilizers are added to the soil; it releases organic acids which help to neutralize alkaline soils, and help to release minerals from the soil making them available to plants; it holds the ammonia and other forms of nitrogen in the soil in an exchangeable and available form – without it nitrogen is lost quickly because of the action of denitrifying bacteria; it keeps down many fungal diseases and the notorious eel worm.

Clearly one of your main aims as a gardener should be to increase the humus content of your soil as much as possible. Soils ranging from the heaviest clay to the purest sand can be improved and rendered fertile by the introduction of sufficient humus. There is no soil that does not benefit from it, and there is no crop, that I know of, that is not improved by it.

Now, any organic material that you put into the soil will produce humus. Compost, green manure, farmyard manure, peat, leaf-mold, seaweed, crop residues: anything that has lived before can live again. Bury it in the soil and it will rot and make humus. Leave it on top of the soil; it will rot, the worms will drag it down deep under the soil and it will still make humus.

Humus is the firm basis of good gardening. It is possible to grow inferior crops on humus-deficient soil by supplying all your plants' chemical requirements, mainly in the form of nitrates, out of a fertilizer bag, but if you do this your soil will progressively deteriorate and, ultimately, blow or wash away, as the topsoils of so much of the world's surface, abused by mankind, already have.

CHAPTER ONE

The Illustrated Index of Vegetables, Fruits and Herbs

*Containing the edible roots,
stems, leaves, flowers, seeds,
pods and fruits that constitute
the produce of the kitchen garden.*

The Edible Parts of Plants

I was once extremely hungry in a jungle and almost overwhelmed by plant life. However, I could not find a single edible plant. I was made to realize that for human beings few of the thousands of plants that grow on this planet are edible. Most of them are far too tough. Humans cannot digest cellulose which is the basis of much plant tissue. Of the comparatively few plants that humans can eat, most are only edible in part. The larger and more complex edible plants have, just like animals, evolved separate and specialized organs which are quite different from each other and which serve quite different purposes. We, and other herbivorous and omnivorous animals, eat different parts of different plants, on the basis of what tastes best and does us good.

For the purposes of the gardener the main parts of plants can be classified as: roots, stems, leaves, flowers, fruit and seed. Most plants have all of these parts. There are some oddities that don't, like cacti which don't have leaves — their stems serve instead. The tissues of which the various organs are composed are different in kind, and the botanist can tell, quite easily, whether an organ is, for example, a stem or a root. The non-botanist is in for a few surprises. This is because some plants have developed some of their organs for very particular purposes — storing nourishment through the winter, for example — and the resulting organ is often a unique and strange-seeming example of its type.

Many of the plants we eat, particularly root and stem vegetables, are naturally biennial. The plant uses a swollen root or stem to store in its first year of growth much of the energy which it will use in its second year to produce flowers and seeds. Gardeners harvest these biennial plants after their first year of growth, so as to get the full benefit of this stored up nourishment before it is dissipated. This is why lettuces should not be allowed to "bolt", and why many vegetables should not be permitted to go to seed. If you leave a beet or carrot, for example, in the ground for more than one year, the edible roots will become tough, and shrink as the energy stored in them is used to make the plants flower.

Roots

When analyzing plants it seems sensible to start at the bottom, with roots. Most roots have the specialized function of absorbing from the soil the non-organic nutrients that plants need to grow and survive. These include: water, in which all the other nutrients have to be dissolved; nitrogen; potash; phosphates; and all the many trace elements which are essential to plants. Roots force themselves far down into the soil in their search for water and nutrients. Fortunately for humans, some plants also use their roots for storing food as well as gathering it. Gardeners are able to harvest this stored food to keep themselves going in the lean times of winter or drought.

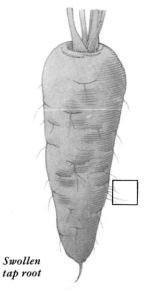

ROOTS
Most edible roots are swollen tap roots. Laterals, or side roots, grow from the tap root, and toward the ends of these are the microscopic root hairs which feed the plant by absorbing moisture and nutrients from the soil.

Swollen tap root

Edible roots are nearly all tap roots. A tap root is the main support root of the plant, out of which grow the searching side roots and their absorbent root hairs. A number of common vegetables are swollen tap roots. These include carrots, parsnips, radishes, rutabagas, turnips and beet. Red beet is the beet that is eaten: sugar beet stores the plant's energy in the form of sugar and is grown commercially for that very reason. Most plant energy is stored in the form of starch, but energy can only be transported about a plant in the form of sugar. This is because starch is not soluble. This fact is important to the gardener. If you want the sweetness of certain vegetables — new potatoes and sweet corn are cases in point — you must harvest the crop when the energy is still in the form of sugar and not wait until the plants grow older and the sugar has been stored away as starch. If you make wine, you will find that you need certain enzymes to turn the starch into sugar, for only sugar, and not starch, can be turned into alcohol by yeast.

Stems

There are some very unusual stems. Potatoes, for example, although they grow underground and are swollen to store food, are not roots but stems.

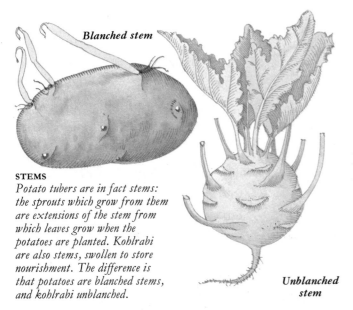

Blanched stem

STEMS
Potato tubers are in fact stems: the sprouts which grow from them are extensions of the stem from which leaves grow when the potatoes are planted. Kohlrabi are also stems, swollen to store nourishment. The difference is that potatoes are blanched stems, and kohlrabi unblanched.

Unblanched stem

Potatoes have all the morphological characteristics of stems. They don't put off lateral roots and the "eyes" in them are in fact growth buds from which normal stems and leaves develop when the potatoes are planted below ground. Exposed to the light potatoes immediately develop chlorophyll – turn green – as most stems do, so that they can engage in photosynthesis.

Photosynthesis is not only the very basis and mainspring of the gardener's art, but it is the one process that keeps every single living being, animal or vegetable, alive on this planet. It is the miraculous process – no scientist has ever been able to duplicate it – that uses the energies of the sun to make carbohydrate or starch, which is the basis of all plant and animal energy. Photosynthesis is carried out by chlorophyll – the green matter of plants – and in the total absence of light no green plant can live. Non-green plants, like fungi, only live as parasites or saprophytes on the living or dead tissue of other organisms. They lack chlorophyll and cannot derive their energy from the sun.

Many stems are very tough – consider the stem of an oak tree – because they have to support the upper parts of the plant in the air. Some stems are pleasant for us to eat only if they are blanched, that is kept from the light so they do not develop chlorophyll and stay white instead of turning green. Potatoes are like this, and so are celery stems, seakale and chards, which are the stems of cardoons. The stem is the edible part of a rhubarb plant: the leaves are actually poisonous. Kohlrabi and celeriac are both stems, swollen so that they can store food. Notice the leaf buds and the scars left by leaves on the stems of kohlrabi.

Leaves

Leaves are often edible, and some of them have evolved to become storehouses of energy, just like the specialized roots and stems. For example, onions, leeks, garlic and shallots are really layered clusters of leaf bases adapted to store food throughout the winter. The leaves of hearted cabbages behave in much the same way, and other plants, like lettuces, are halfway along this line of evolution: toward tight clumps of leaves which store energy through the winter, so that, if you allow it to, the plant gets away the second year to produce a flowering head and early seed.

"Monocots" and "dicots" All plants are either monocotyledons (monocots) or dicotyledons (dicots). The difference lies in the seed, the leaves and the mode of growth. The seed of a dicot – a bean, for example – is made up of two halves. You can see this for yourself: a broad bean will readily split in two if you just press into it with your fingernail. A monocot seed, on the other hand, is self-contained and cannot be split.

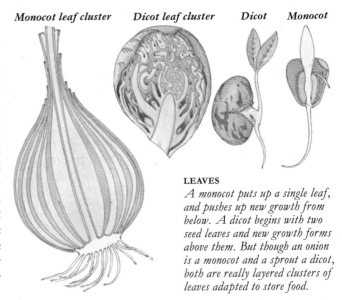

Monocot leaf cluster   *Dicot leaf cluster*   *Dicot*   *Monocot*

LEAVES
A monocot puts up a single leaf, and pushes up new growth from below. A dicot begins with two seed leaves and new growth forms above them. But though an onion is a monocot and a sprout a dicot, both are really layered clusters of leaves adapted to store food.

Dicots produce two seed leaves. Thereafter the stem grows upward and new leaves issue from a growing point at its tip, or from growing points at the tips of branches. Monocots grow in a completely different way. They begin by pushing up a single leaf – a blade of grass or an onion is a good example. Thereafter they continue to grow by pushing from the seed upward. The first leaf is pushed up and to one side and new ones push their way up beside it. Dicots add new growth above existing growth, while monocots push existing growth upward adding new growth beneath it. Most vegetables are dicots, but some notably onions, leeks, asparagus and sweet corn, are mono-cots. An easy way to distinguish between the two is to look at the leaves. If they have almost parallel veins, the chances are they are monocots, but if the veins of the leaves splay out away from each other, they are almost certainly dicots.

Flowers

Flowers are the next step upward in a plant, and they are not as a rule an important food for humans. But they are important to the plant, of course, for they ensure its posterity.

Sex reared its beautiful head in a new and elaborate form millions of years ago in the Jurassic Age, when insects and plants developed their amazing symbiosis. The plants provide nectar and other delights to attract the insects, and the insects unwittingly cross-fertilize the plants by going from one to the other carrying pollen, from the male organs of one flower to the female organ of another. The extraordinary elaboration of devices to attract the right insects, and ensure that they collect pollen on their bodies, and do not self fertilize the flower they are visiting, but instead fertilize the next flower, has been the life study of many botanists, including, notably, Charles Darwin. It is a very good thing to keep bees — particularly if you have fruit trees, for not only do you get honey from them but they pollinate your trees and flowering plants.

Some flowers are pollinated by the wind. Corn is one of them, and because of this you should plant your sweet corn in a wide block and not in one long row. You must try to make sure that when a wind blows from any direction it blows pollen from one plant to another.

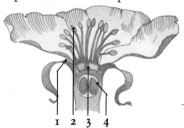

FLOWERS
Flowers are essential to the reproduction of plants. Their nectar 1 attracts insects who pick up pollen from the male part 2 of one plant and carry it to the female part 3 of the next. The ovary 4 of a flower after it has been fertilized is the fruit.

1 2 3 4

There are not many flowers which are edible. The main ones are cauliflower and broccoli, which are immature flowers. If you leave these to continue growing instead of eating them, they will produce inedible mature flowers, just as an aban-doned cabbage will. Globe artichokes are flowers, although only a small part is actually edible. Nasturtium seeds make good substitutes for capers, and some herb flowers are good for flavoring and coloring. But, if you had to live exclusively on flowers, you would get very thin indeed. Seed and fruit, which come from the re-productive part of flowers are more important to the self-sufficient gardener.

When the female element of a flower has been pollinated the flower forms a fruit. The fruit grows and produces seed within it. The seed is spread far and wide by a number of amazingly ingenious methods which plants have evolved so as to propagate their species. A gardener who wishes to enjoy his craft will study all these things, for a knowledge of them will increase enormously the pleasure he gets from his labors. The more you learn about plants, the more you will wonder at the extraordinary cunning and elaboration that selection has evolved for their survival and perpetuation.

Fruits

To a botanist, fruit is the ovary of a flower after it has been fertilized. Fertilization causes the ovules, which are inside the ovary, to turn into seeds and the ovary itself to turn into a fruit. Some fruits don't bear much resemblance to what a store-keeper would call fruit. A whiff of dandelion fluff is a fruit, and so are all nuts. Tomatoes, eggplants, peppers, beans and pods full of peas are all fruits; an individual pea and a bean threshed from its pod for drying are seeds.

To a cook and a gastronome, and to most people in fact, fruit means the sort of sweet succulent fruit which is eaten as a dessert. I have used this common classification in ordering this book. The only exception I have made is rhubarb, which though eaten as a dessert is not naturally sweet and is grown like a vegetable, which in fact it is.

Botanically a blackberry or raspberry is not one fruit but a cluster of fruits. Each tiny globe that goes to make up such a "berry" is a complete fruit. The word berry means something different to a botanist. A tomato is a true berry, because its seeds are embedded in soft pulp. Grapes, goose-berries and oranges are also berries. The fruits which contain single stones — plums, cherries and peaches — are called drupes. Fruits like apples and pears are called pomes. Only the core of a pome is a cluster of true fruits; the edible part surrounding the core is just a layer of stored food. Each tiny pip in a strawberry is a single fruit. They are all held together by a succulent mass. If you take the trouble to cut open pomes, berries and drupes at various stages of their growth you will see how all this works. Every part of the fruit is in embryo in the flower and you can follow the development of each part of the flower as it becomes a fruit.

Generally speaking, fruits contain little nourishment, and most of the little they have is in the form of sugar. All the stored energy of the plant is going to go into the seed, not the fruit. If you tried to live on fruits alone, you would soon become seriously undernourished. Fruits tend to be rich in certain vitamins, however, particularly vitamin C, and this makes them valuable to humans. Many years ago a learned doctor said: "Apples have no nutritive value whatever and it does not matter whether you eat them or not." He was completely mistaken, but then he did not know about vitamins. William Cobbett made the same mistake when advising his cottagers not to grow fruit trees. He thought they were good for nothing but giving children belly-aches.

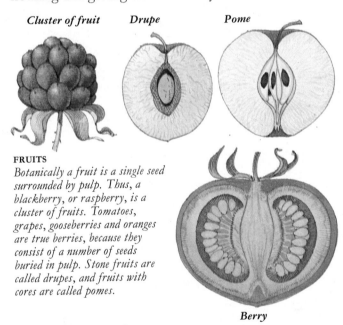

Cluster of fruit   *Drupe*   *Pome*

Berry

FRUITS
Botanically a fruit is a single seed surrounded by pulp. Thus, a blackberry, or raspberry, is a cluster of fruits. Tomatoes, grapes, gooseberries and oranges are true berries, because they consist of a number of seeds buried in pulp. Stone fruits are called drupes, and fruits with cores are called pomes.

All the members of the squash tribe are fruits. Some, like melons, seem to have developed their large, water-filled fruit so that they can store water. They come from parts of the world with short rainy seasons. The stored water gives the seeds a head start — one good watering — to enable them to stay alive until the next rains. Other fruits have undoubtedly developed to attract animals. Apples, plums, peaches and cherries have all evolved in this way. Man has taken many of these slightly succulent and somewhat sour wild fruits and, by artificial selection, evolved improved varieties, containing a lot of sugar, extra flavor, plenty of succulent flesh, and not too much acid. If you compare the wild crab apple with a Golden

Delicious you will understand what has happened. Most cultivated fruits have been improved out of recognition.

Seeds

If it were not for edible seeds humans could scarcely survive. Some seeds have to pass through the guts of an animal in order to germinate. So it is important for plants that their fruit should be eaten. Many seeds are not strictly edible; humans eat them but they pass through them intact without doing them any good. It is the fruit that they benefit from.

Other seeds, especially the cereals, such as wheat, rice and corn, are eaten for direct nutrition and it is these seeds that keep humanity alive in many parts of the globe. Before an annual plant dies it puts all the nourishment it has into its seeds, which are to carry its life on into future generations. Thus seeds are generally far more nutritious than any other parts of plants and, if you grind them or cook them and make them palatable, they will give you the energy to keep alive. Without seeds a vegetarian would live on a very sparse diet indeed: it would be scarcely adequate to sustain life.

Seeds of certain plants, notably leguminous ones, are quite rich in protein. Pea and bean seeds of all kinds are very important. A vegetarian can enjoy a near perfect diet if he eats plenty of soybeans, some other vegetables and a little comfrey, which is almost the only edible plant that contains vitamin B12. The great thing about seeds is that they are easy to dry and store.

Herbs

Many herb seeds are used to flavor food, for the essential oils and other virtues of herbs are often concentrated in their seeds. Many of the more aromatic herbs come from dry warm regions. Their aromatic oils have evolved largely to protect them from over-dessication in dry hot weather. The small leaves of many of them — often mere needles — are that size and shape to prevent moisture being transpired by the plant too fast.

Some of the delicious flavors and aromas of culinary herbs are there for reasons that are not fully understood yet: attracting and repelling various insects may well be one of them. But plants are endlessly fascinating and mysterious, and happily it is improbable that we will ever know all there is to know about them. It should be enough for us that thyme and rosemary smell and taste as they do, without worrying why.

Roots

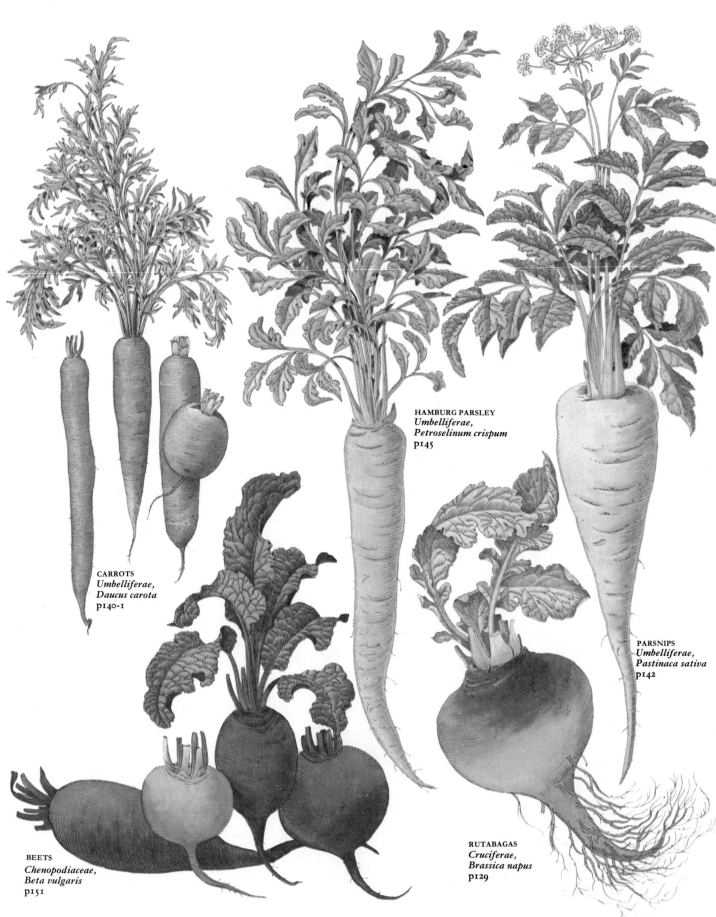

HAMBURG PARSLEY
Umbelliferae,
Petroselinum crispum
p145

CARROTS
Umbelliferae,
Daucus carota
p140-1

PARSNIPS
Umbelliferae,
Pastinaca sativa
p142

BEETS
Chenopodiaceae,
Beta vulgaris
p151

RUTABAGAS
Cruciferae,
Brassica napus
p129

Index of Vegetables

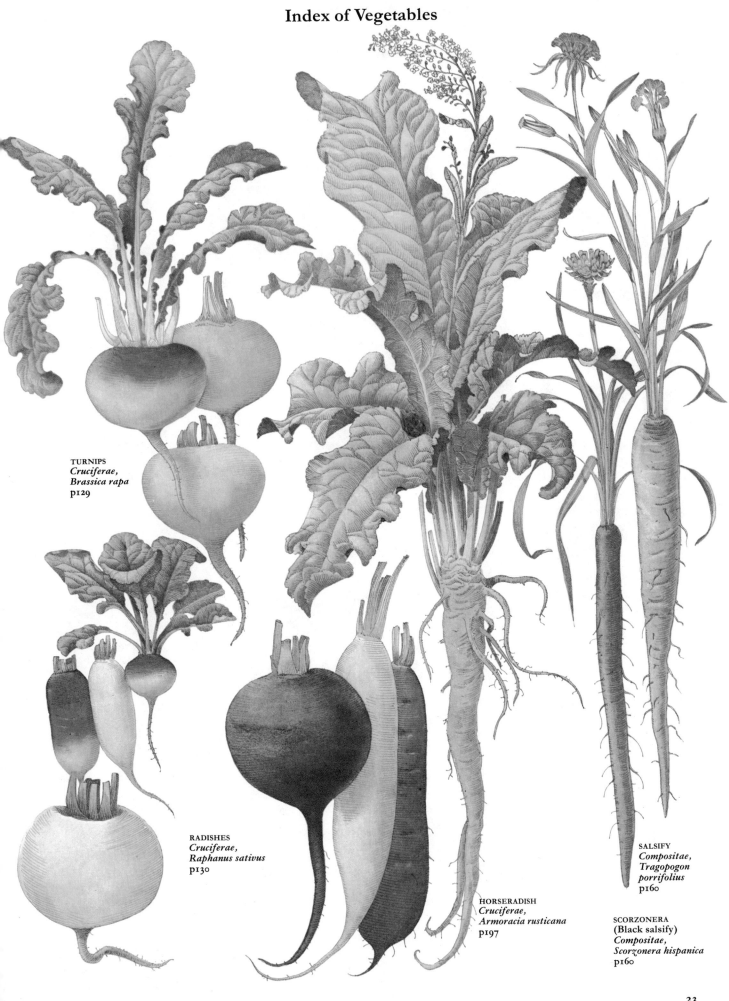

TURNIPS
Cruciferae,
Brassica rapa
p129

RADISHES
Cruciferae,
Raphanus sativus
p130

HORSERADISH
Cruciferae,
Armoracia rusticana
p197

SALSIFY
Compositae,
Tragopogon
porrifolius
p160

SCORZONERA
(Black salsify)
Compositae,
Scorzonera hispanica
p160

Stems

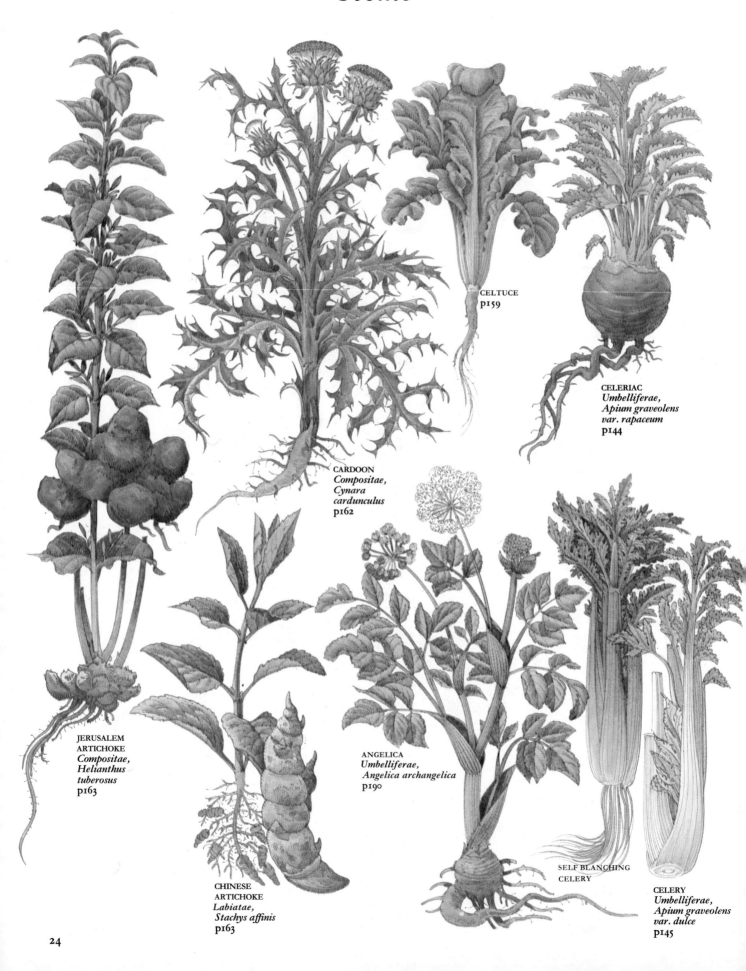

CELTUCE
p159

CELERIAC
Umbelliferae,
Apium graveolens
var. rapaceum
p144

CARDOON
Compositae,
Cynara
cardunculus
p162

JERUSALEM
ARTICHOKE
Compositae,
Helianthus
tuberosus
p163

ANGELICA
Umbelliferae,
Angelica archangelica
p190

SELF BLANCHING
CELERY

CELERY
Umbelliferae,
Apium graveolens
var. dulce
p145

CHINESE
ARTICHOKE
Labiatae,
Stachys affinis
p163

Index of Vegetables/Herbs

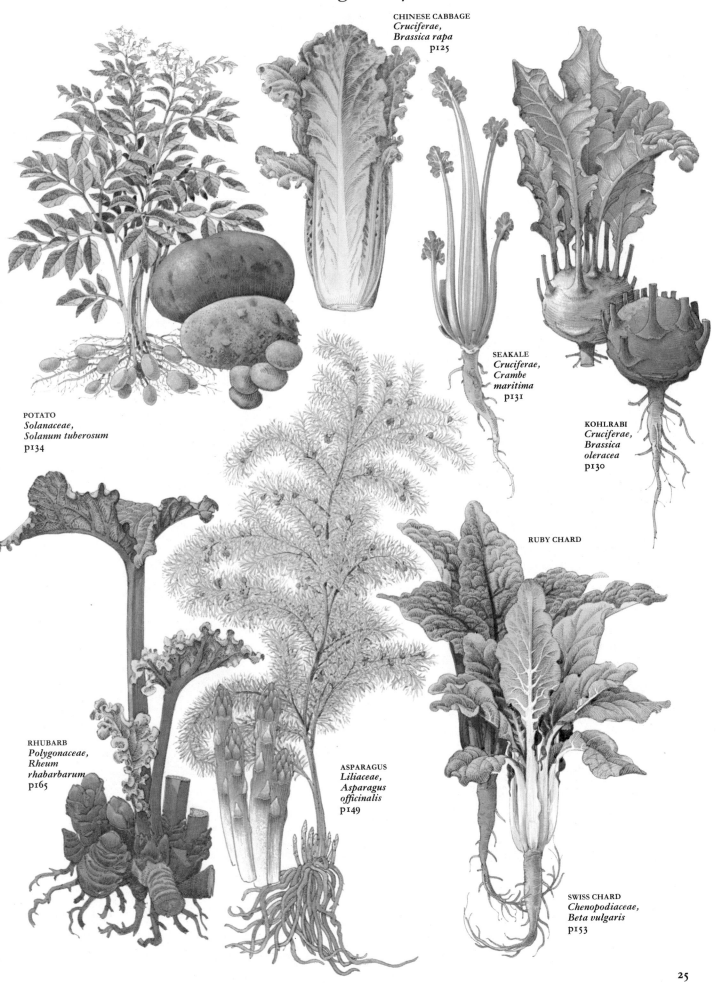

CHINESE CABBAGE
Cruciferae,
Brassica rapa
p125

SEAKALE
Cruciferae,
Crambe
maritima
p131

KOHLRABI
Cruciferae,
Brassica
oleracea
p130

POTATO
Solanaceae,
Solanum tuberosum
p134

RUBY CHARD

RHUBARB
Polygonaceae,
Rheum
rhabarbarum
p165

ASPARAGUS
Liliaceae,
Asparagus
officinalis
p149

SWISS CHARD
Chenopodiaceae,
Beta vulgaris
p153

Leaves

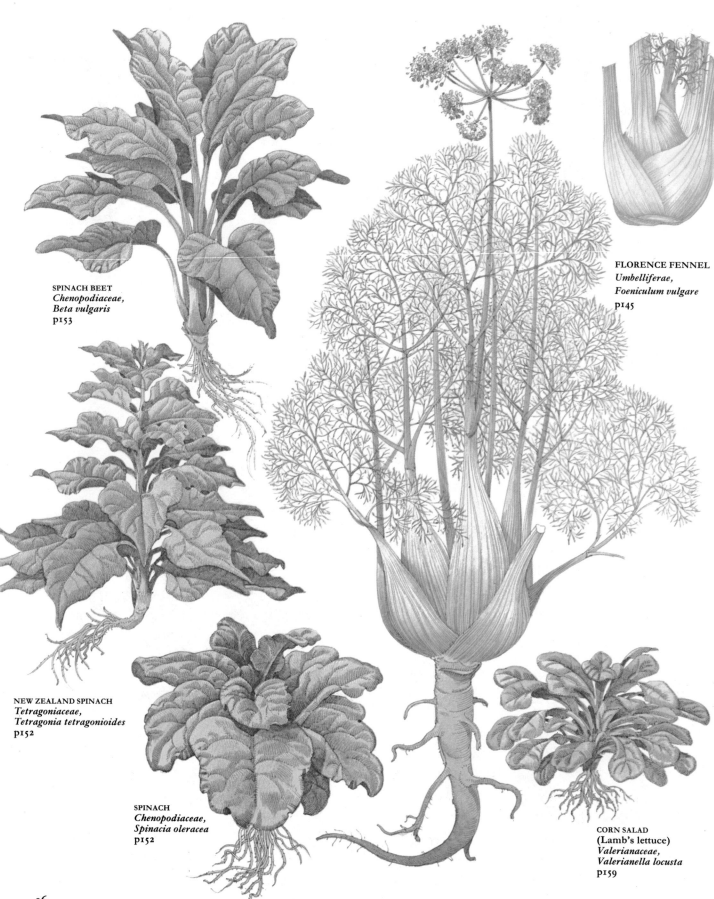

SPINACH BEET
Chenopodiaceae,
Beta vulgaris
p153

FLORENCE FENNEL
Umbelliferae,
Foeniculum vulgare
p145

NEW ZEALAND SPINACH
Tetragoniaceae,
Tetragonia tetragonioides
p152

SPINACH
Chenopodiaceae,
Spinacia oleracea
p152

CORN SALAD
(Lamb's lettuce)
Valerianaceae,
Valerianella locusta
p159

Index of Vegetables

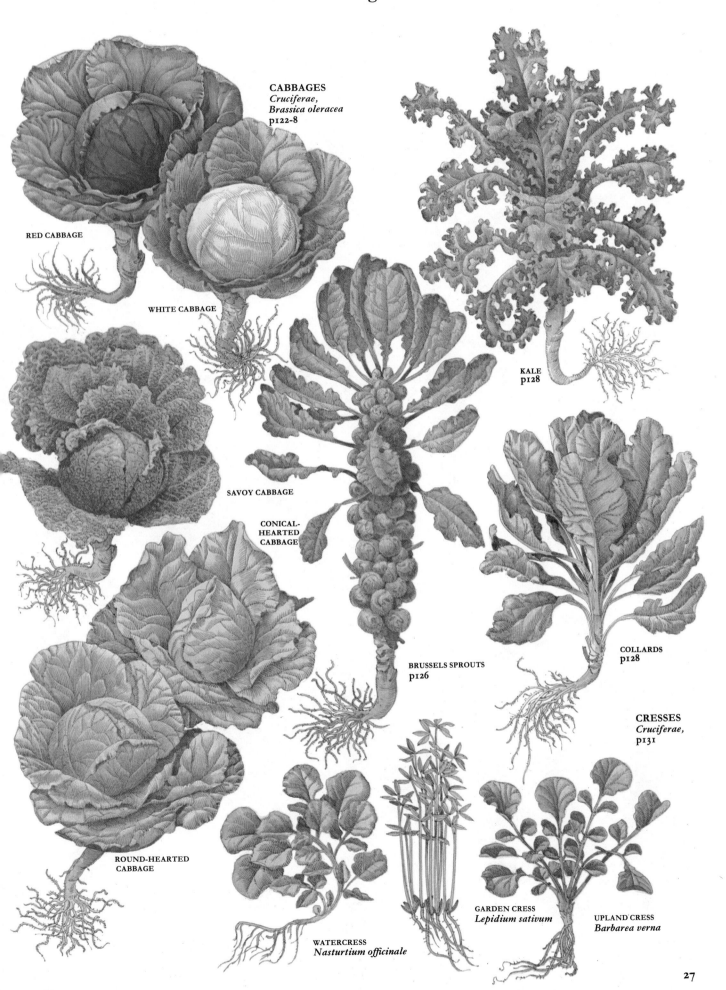

CABBAGES
Cruciferae,
Brassica oleracea
p122-8

RED CABBAGE

WHITE CABBAGE

KALE
p128

SAVOY CABBAGE

CONICAL-
HEARTED
CABBAGE

COLLARDS
p128

BRUSSELS SPROUTS
p126

CRESSES
Cruciferae,
p131

ROUND-HEARTED
CABBAGE

WATERCRESS
Nasturtium officinale

GARDEN CRESS
Lepidium sativum

UPLAND CRESS
Barbarea verna

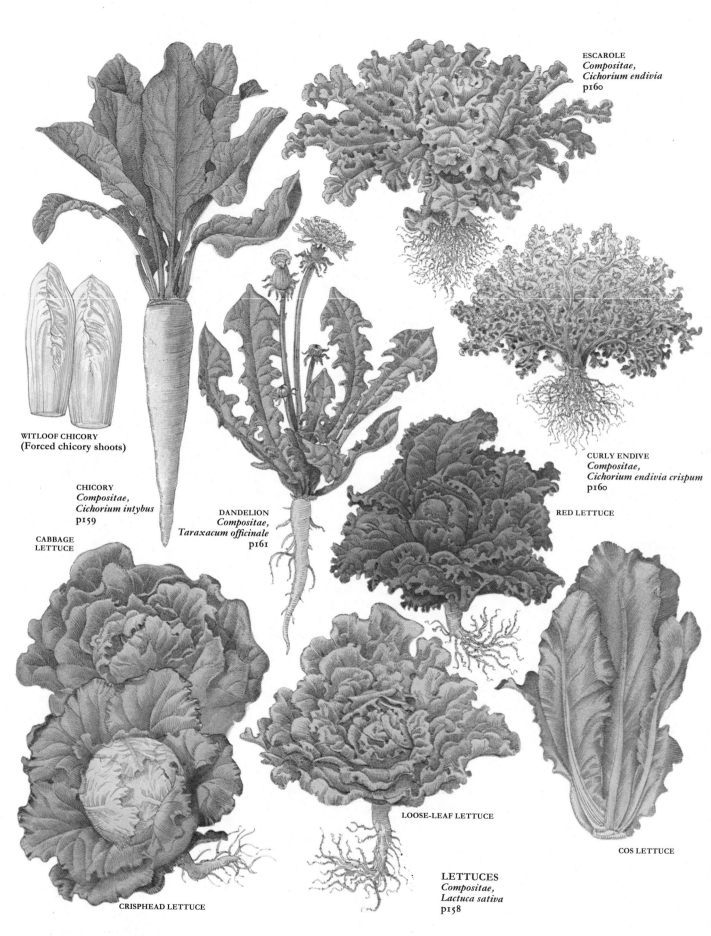

ESCAROLE
Compositae,
Cichorium endivia
p160

CURLY ENDIVE
Compositae,
Cichorium endivia crispum
p160

WITLOOF CHICORY
(Forced chicory shoots)

CHICORY
Compositae,
Cichorium intybus
p159

CABBAGE
LETTUCE

DANDELION
Compositae,
Taraxacum officinale
p161

RED LETTUCE

LOOSE-LEAF LETTUCE

COS LETTUCE

CRISPHEAD LETTUCE

LETTUCES
Compositae,
Lactuca sativa
p158

Index of Vegetables

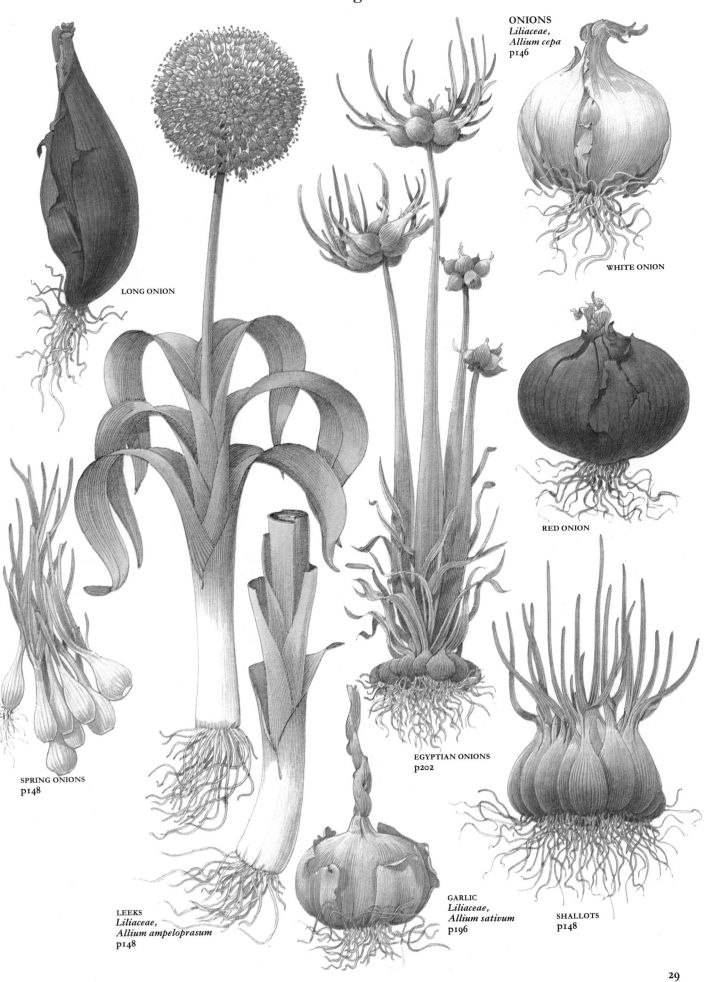

LONG ONION

ONIONS
Liliaceae,
Allium cepa
p146

WHITE ONION

RED ONION

SPRING ONIONS
p148

EGYPTIAN ONIONS
p202

SHALLOTS
p148

LEEKS
Liliaceae,
Allium ampeloprasum
p148

GARLIC
Liliaceae,
Allium sativum
p196

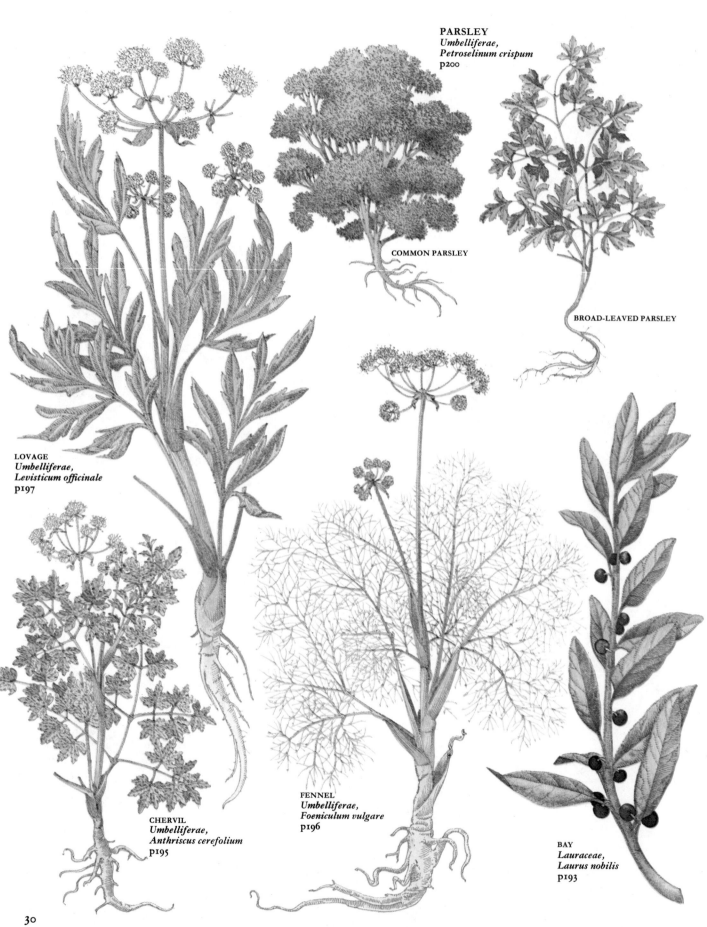

PARSLEY
Umbelliferae,
Petroselinum crispum
p200

COMMON PARSLEY

BROAD-LEAVED PARSLEY

LOVAGE
Umbelliferae,
Levisticum officinale
p197

CHERVIL
Umbelliferae,
Anthriscus cerefolium
p195

FENNEL
Umbelliferae,
Foeniculum vulgare
p196

BAY
Lauraceae,
Laurus nobilis
p193

Index of Herbs

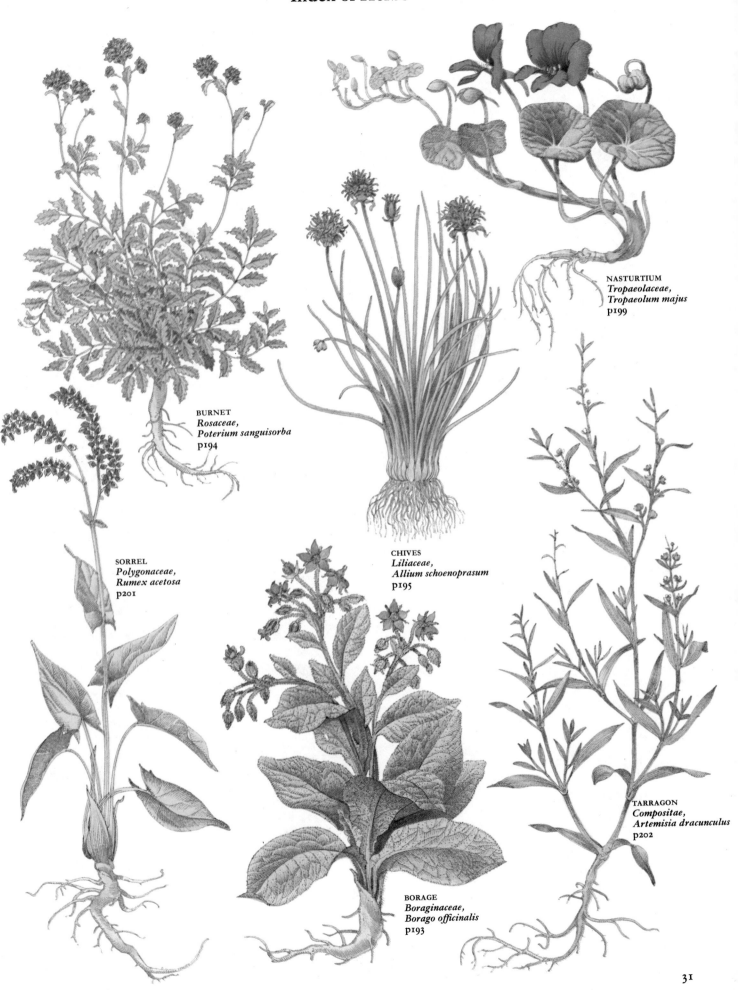

NASTURTIUM
Tropaeolaceae,
Tropaeolum majus
p199

BURNET
Rosaceae,
Poterium sanguisorba
p194

SORREL
Polygonaceae,
Rumex acetosa
p201

CHIVES
Liliaceae,
Allium schoenoprasum
p195

TARRAGON
Compositae,
Artemisia dracunculus
p202

BORAGE
Boraginaceae,
Borago officinalis
p193

Leaves

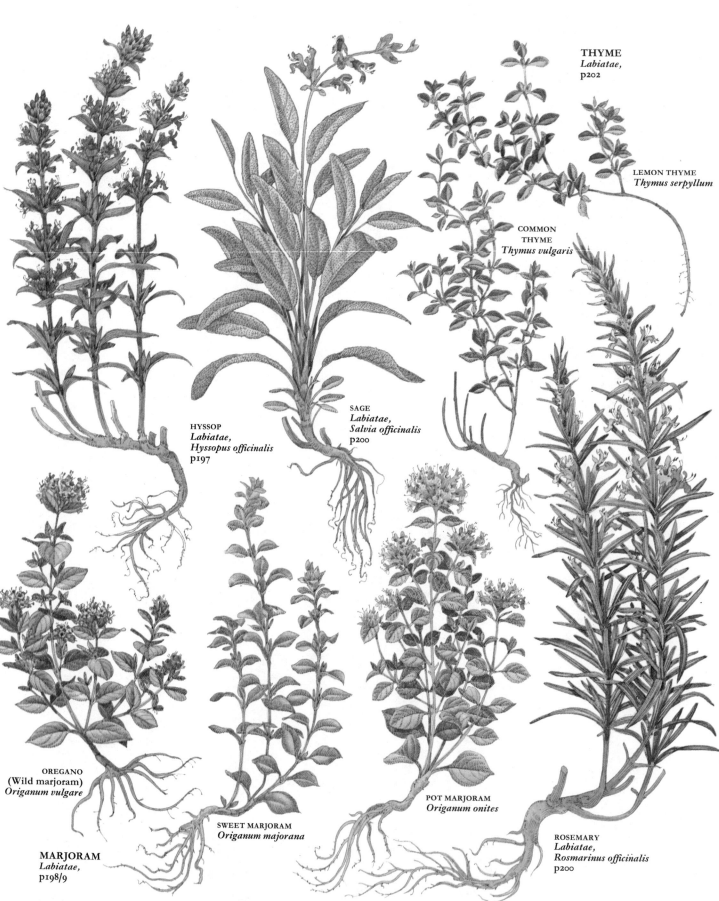

THYME
Labiatae,
p202

LEMON THYME
Thymus serpyllum

COMMON
THYME
Thymus vulgaris

HYSSOP
Labiatae,
Hyssopus officinalis
p197

SAGE
Labiatae,
Salvia officinalis
p200

OREGANO
(Wild marjoram)
Origanum vulgare

SWEET MARJORAM
Origanum majorana

POT MARJORAM
Origanum onites

MARJORAM
Labiatae,
p198/9

ROSEMARY
Labiatae,
Rosmarinus officinalis
p200

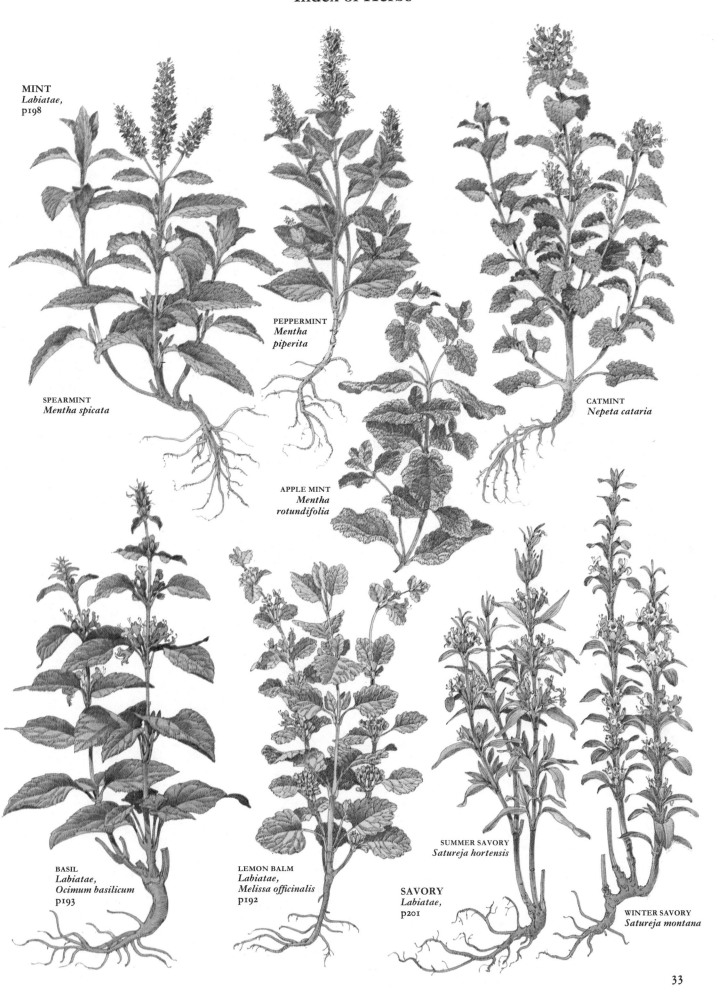

MINT
Labiatae,
p198

PEPPERMINT
*Mentha
piperita*

CATMINT
Nepeta cataria

SPEARMINT
Mentha spicata

APPLE MINT
*Mentha
rotundifolia*

BASIL
*Labiatae,
Ocimum basilicum*
p193

LEMON BALM
*Labiatae,
Melissa officinalis*
p192

SUMMER SAVORY
Satureja hortensis

SAVORY
Labiatae,
p201

WINTER SAVORY
Satureja montana

Flowers and Vegetable Fruits

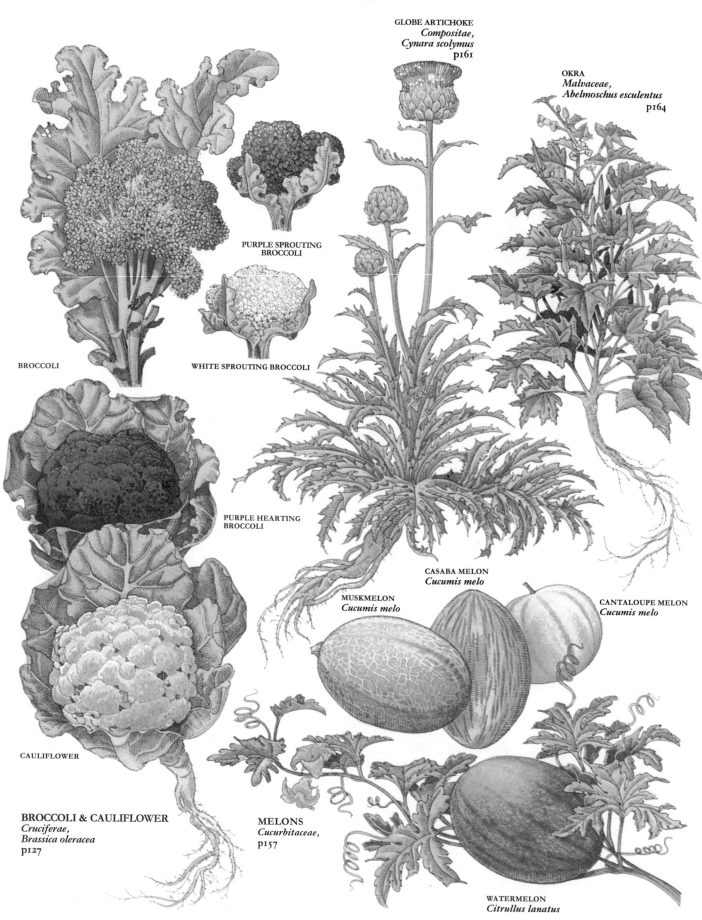

GLOBE ARTICHOKE
Compositae,
Cynara scolymus
p161

OKRA
Malvaceae,
Abelmoschus esculentus
p164

PURPLE SPROUTING
BROCCOLI

WHITE SPROUTING BROCCOLI

BROCCOLI

PURPLE HEARTING
BROCCOLI

CAULIFLOWER

CASABA MELON
Cucumis melo

MUSKMELON
Cucumis melo

CANTALOUPE MELON
Cucumis melo

BROCCOLI & CAULIFLOWER
Cruciferae,
Brassica oleracea
p127

MELONS
Cucurbitaceae,
p157

WATERMELON
Citrullus lanatus

Index of Vegetables

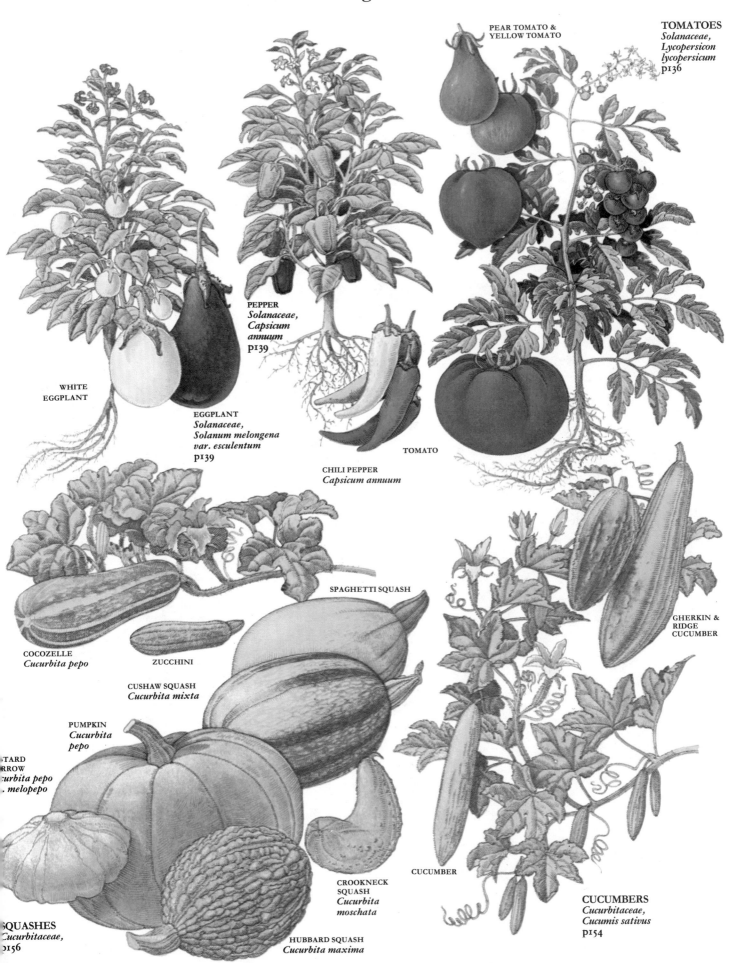

PEAR TOMATO &
YELLOW TOMATO

TOMATOES
*Solanaceae,
Lycopersicon
lycopersicum*
p136

PEPPER
*Solanaceae,
Capsicum
annuum*
p139

WHITE
EGGPLANT

EGGPLANT
*Solanaceae,
Solanum melongena
var. esculentum*
p139

TOMATO

CHILI PEPPER
Capsicum annuum

SPAGHETTI SQUASH

GHERKIN &
RIDGE
CUCUMBER

COCOZELLE
Cucurbita pepo

ZUCCHINI

CUSHAW SQUASH
Cucurbita mixta

PUMPKIN
*Cucurbita
pepo*

STARD
RROW
*urbita pepo
. melopepo*

CUCUMBER

CROOKNECK
SQUASH
*Cucurbita
moschata*

CUCUMBERS
*Cucurbitaceae,
Cucumis sativus*
p154

SQUASHES
Cucurbitaceae,
p156

HUBBARD SQUASH
Cucurbita maxima

Seeds and Pods

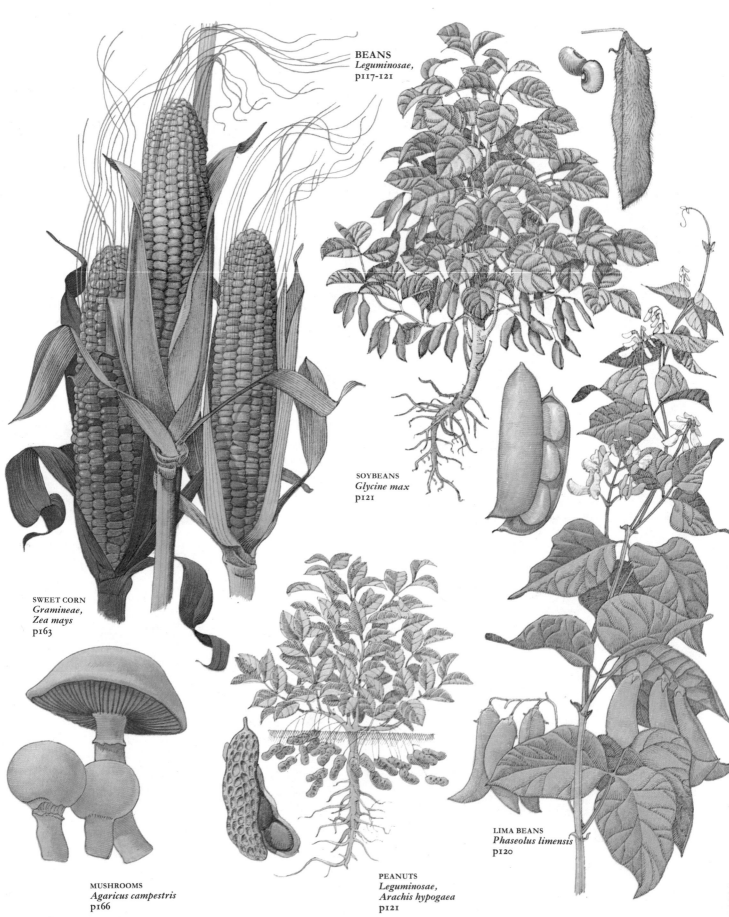

BEANS
Leguminosae,
p117-121

SOYBEANS
Glycine max
p121

SWEET CORN
Gramineae,
Zea mays
p163

LIMA BEANS
Phaseolus limensis
p120

MUSHROOMS
Agaricus campestris
p166

PEANUTS
Leguminosae,
Arachis hypogaea
p121

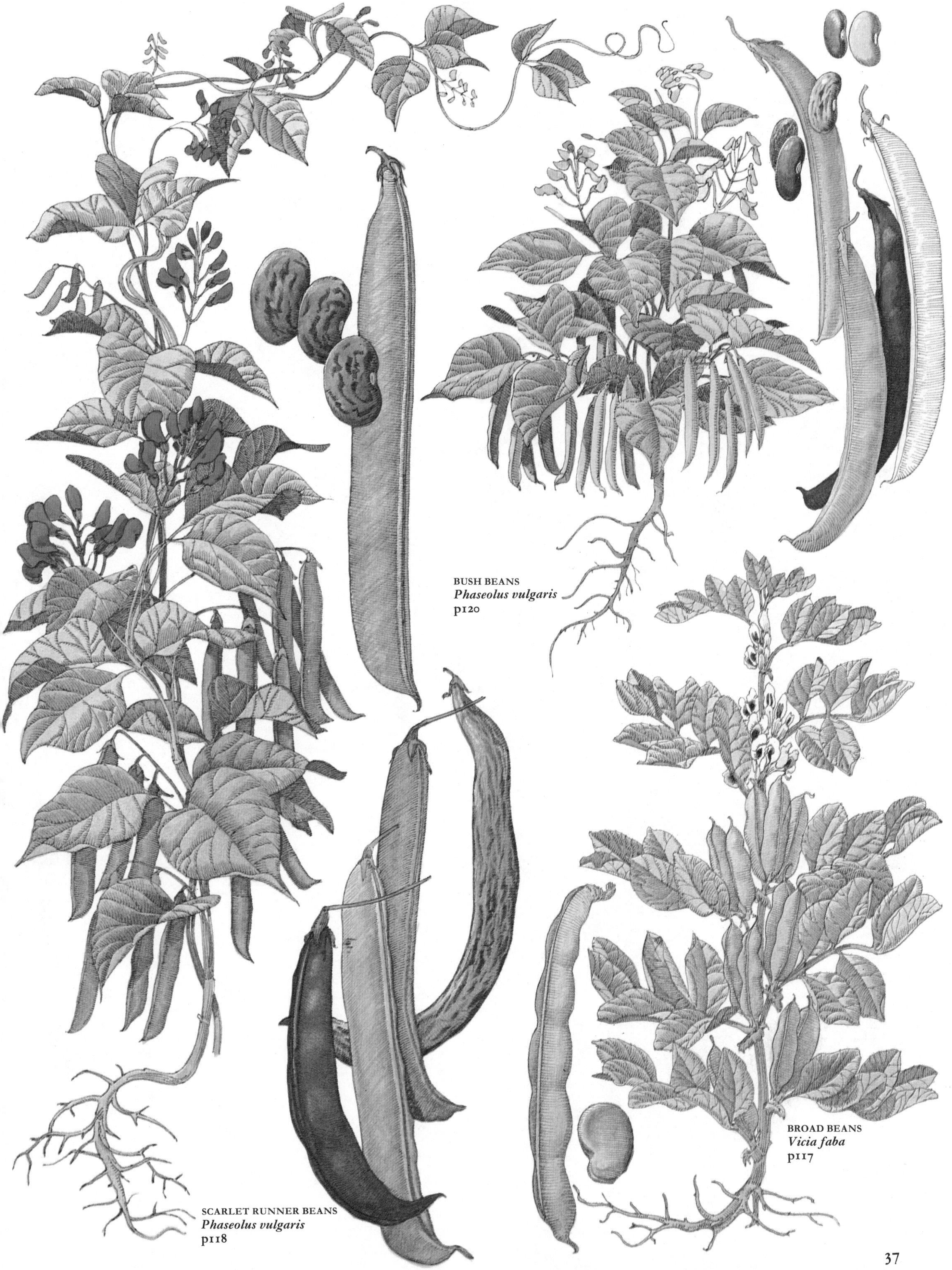

Index of Vegetables

BUSH BEANS
Phaseolus vulgaris
p120

SCARLET RUNNER BEANS
Phaseolus vulgaris
p118

BROAD BEANS
Vicia faba
p117

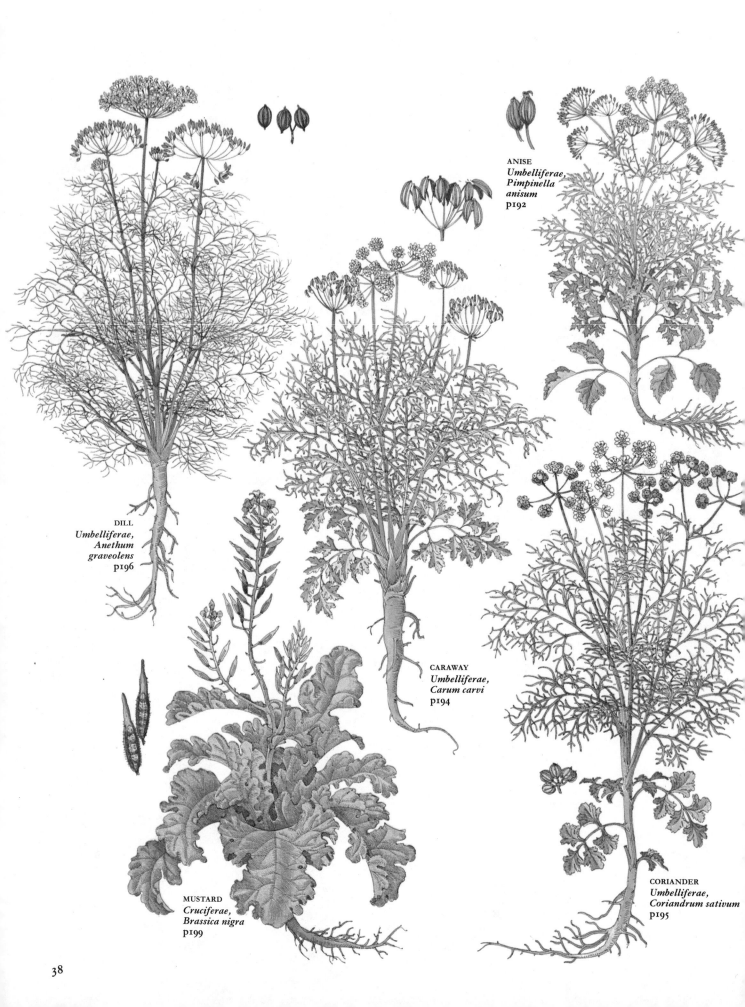

ANISE
Umbelliferae,
Pimpinella
anisum
p192

DILL
Umbelliferae,
Anethum
graveolens
p196

CARAWAY
Umbelliferae,
Carum carvi
p194

MUSTARD
Cruciferae,
Brassica nigra
p199

CORIANDER
Umbelliferae,
Coriandrum sativum
p195

PEAS
Leguminosae,
Pisum sativum
p114-6

SUGAR
PEAS

PURPLE
PODDED
PEAS

LENTILS
Leguminosae,
Lens culinaris
p116

GREEN PEAS

ASPARAGUS PEAS
Leguminosae,
Lotus tetragonolobus
p116

Fruits

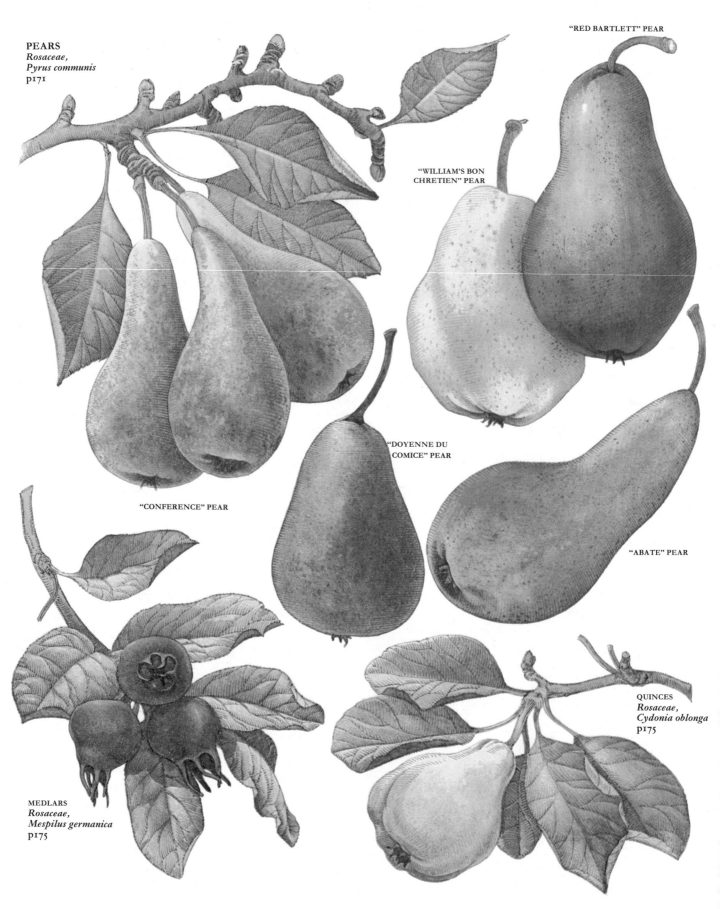

PEARS
Rosaceae,
Pyrus communis
p171

"RED BARTLETT" PEAR

"WILLIAM'S BON
CHRETIEN" PEAR

"DOYENNE DU
COMICE" PEAR

"CONFERENCE" PEAR

"ABATE" PEAR

MEDLARS
Rosaceae,
Mespilus germanica
p175

QUINCES
Rosaceae,
Cydonia oblonga
p175

Index of Fruits

"GOLDEN DELICIOUS"
APPLE

"GRANNY SMITH" APPLE

"RED DELICIOUS" APPLE

APPLES
*Rosaceae,
Malus pumila*
p168

"BRAMLEY" APPLE

"COX'S ORANGE PIPPIN"
APPLE

"ALLINGTON PIPPIN"
APPLE

"RUSSET" APPLE

"JONATHAN" APPLE

PLUMS
Rosaceae,
Prunus domestica
p174

GREENGAGES
Prunus domestica
insititia

APRICOTS
Rosaceae,
Prunus armeniaca
p173

DAMSONS
Prunus domestica
insititia
p174

Index of Fruits

PEACHES
Rosaceae,
Prunus persica
p173

NECTARINES

MORELLO CHERRIES
Prunus cerasus

CHERRIES
Rosaceae,
p172

SWEET CHERRIES
Prunus avium

RED GRAPES

GRAPES
Vitaceae,
Vitis vinifera
p188

OLIVES
Oleaceae,
Olea europaea
p187

WHITE SEEDLESS GRAPES

EUROPEAN
RED
GRAPES

BLACK GRAPES

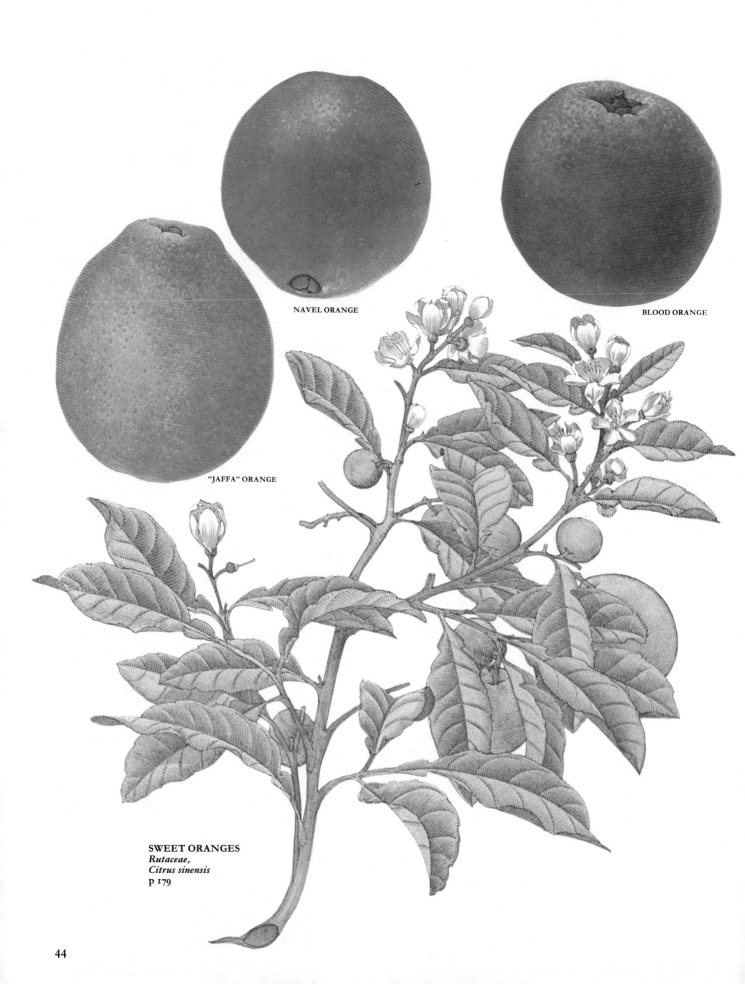

NAVEL ORANGE

BLOOD ORANGE

"JAFFA" ORANGE

SWEET ORANGES
Rutaceae,
Citrus sinensis
P 179

Index of Fruits

MANDARINS
Rutaceae,
Citrus reticulata
p 179

TANGERINE

KUMQUAT
Rutaceae,
Fortunella margarita
p 180

CLEMENTINE

SEVILLE ORANGE
Rutaceae,
Citrus aurantium
p 179

GRAPEFRUIT
Rutaceae,
Citrus x paradisi
p 181

LEMONS
Rutaceae,
Citrus limon
p 181

LIME
Rutaceae,
Citrus aurantiifolia
p 181

LOGANBERRIES
Rosaceae,
Rubus ursinus var. *loganobaccus*
p176

RASPBERRIES
Rosaceae,
Rubus idaeus
p175

BLACKBERRIES
Rosaceae,
Rubus macropetalus
p176

STRAWBERRIES
Rosaceae,
Fragaria x Ananassa
p177

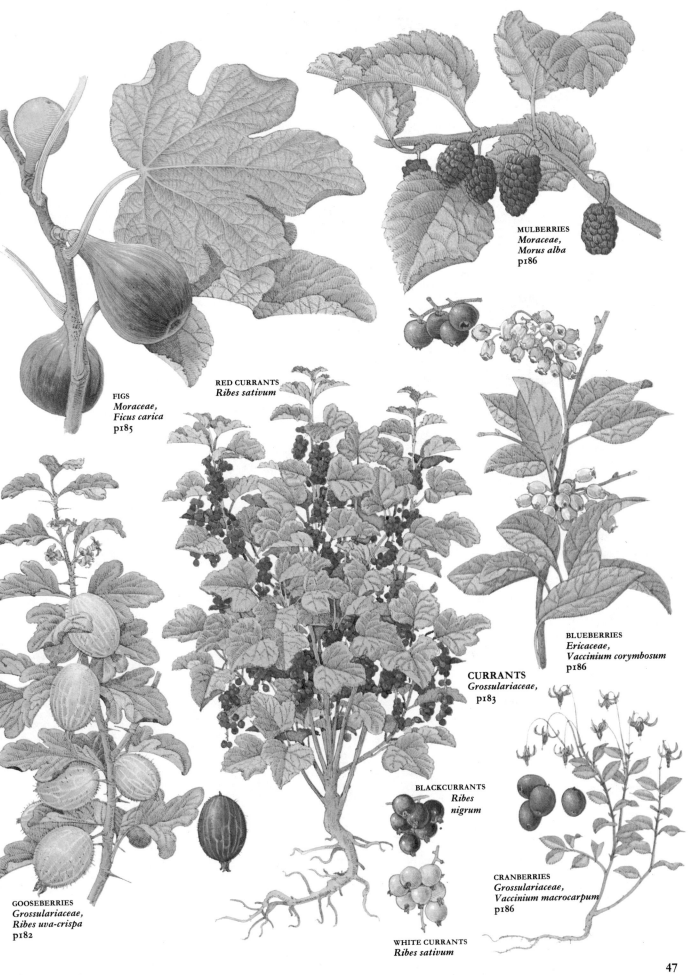

MULBERRIES
*Moraceae,
Morus alba*
p186

FIGS
*Moraceae,
Ficus carica*
p185

RED CURRANTS
Ribes sativum

BLUEBERRIES
*Ericaceae,
Vaccinium corymbosum*
p186

CURRANTS
Grossulariaceae,
p183

BLACKCURRANTS
*Ribes
nigrum*

GOOSEBERRIES
*Grossulariaceae,
Ribes uva-crispa*
p182

CRANBERRIES
*Grossulariaceae,
Vaccinium macrocarpum*
p186

WHITE CURRANTS
Ribes sativum

Green Manure Crops

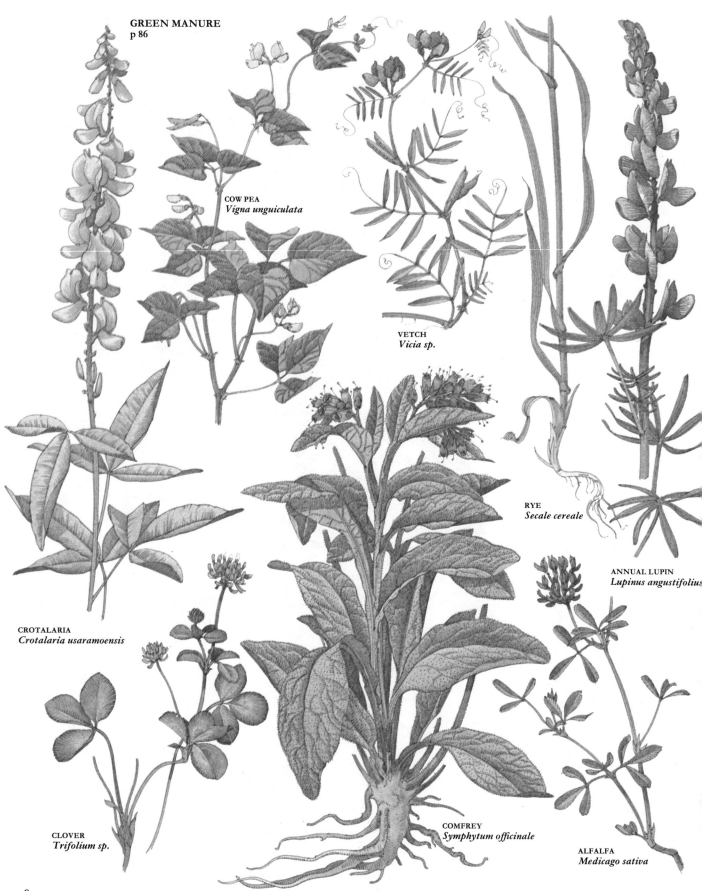

GREEN MANURE
p 86

COW PEA
Vigna unguiculata

VETCH
Vicia sp.

RYE
Secale cereale

ANNUAL LUPIN
Lupinus angustifolius

CROTALARIA
Crotalaria usaramoensis

CLOVER
Trifolium sp.

COMFREY
Symphytum officinale

ALFALFA
Medicago sativa

CHAPTER TWO

Gardening through the Year

*Containing the cycle of the
seasons, the effect of the seasonal
changes on the garden, and a calendar
of tasks for the diligent gardener.*

Gardening through the Year

A man may live in a city all his life and scarcely be aware of the seasons: he knows it is winter when he comes out of his house and finds a new fall of snow on the sidewalk; he knows it is summer because he can feel the heat of the sun. But as soon as that man starts a vegetable garden the seasons become all important to him: they dictate the tasks he must perform each month and they bring with them their own peculiar weather, which sometimes helps, sometimes hinders. If a gardener forgets some vital operation at any time of the year he will find he will suffer for it later on – perhaps twelve months later – when he has to go without some useful crop or buy it from the market.

A philosophical gardener will say to himself: "there is no bad weather!" The rain that stops him doing his spring digging is good for his early seed-beds; the drought that is shriveling his summer lettuces is giving him a chance to get out with the hoe and win the battle of the weeds.

There is no bad season: every season presents the gardener with a challenge and an interest of its own. All weather is good for somebody, or some plant, somewhere. The gardener cannot change these things. He must accept the challenge of learning to understand the seasons and of adapting himself to work within their never-ending cycle.

On the following pages the seasonal activities in a typical food-producing garden in a temperate climate are described in detail. The illustrations show how the same garden changes through the year. A key to these illustrations is provided below.

WINTER

During the spring, summer and fall you may feel you are under pressure. There is always an imperative: weeds to combat, seeds to sow, plants to plant, summer pruning to do, food to harvest and so on. When you have got the last of the root crops harvested in the fall you may well heave a sigh of relief and feel you can relax.

Now you can stand back and take stock, congratulate yourself on what has gone right and not lose too much sleep over what has gone wrong. Now is the time to tidy up, lay paths, build sheds, put up a new greenhouse, repair tools and prepare for next year's food-growing campaign. But don't

KEY TO SEASONAL GARDEN
The garden which is illustrated on the following pages contains four plots for annual vegetables. These plots are cultivated according to a four course rotation, so the vegetables grown in each vary from year to year. In the year illustrated the plots are allocated as follows: **1** *Plot A – Miscellaneous* **2** *Plot B – Roots* **3** *Plot C – Potatoes* **4** *Plot D – Peas and beans/brassica. You will notice that in winter and spring some vegetables from the previous year's rotation are still growing. The garden also includes:* **5** *Seedbed* **6** *Holding-bed* **7** *Perennial vegetable bed* **8** *Cold frames* **9** *Soft fruit bed* **10** *Standard fruit tree* **11** *Bee hives* **12** *Greenhouse* **13** *Cordon fruit trees* **14** *Compost heap* **15** *Rhubarb* **16** *Herb bed.*

forget that now is also the time to feast. The winter is when beer mug and cider flask should circulate among those who have earned this merry-making by their toil.

But even if life is less demanding now than at other times of the year, winter also has its tasks. In a temperate climate a quarter of your main garden will be growing *brassica*, and as much of the rest of it as possible should be down to green manure. I dig in rye grass, which gives good bulk, and common vetch, which provides nitrogen.

It is nearly always better for the ground to be covered with some crop in the winter: this prevents soil erosion, and locks up the soluble nutrients temporarily so that they are not washed out by winter rains. Mulching serves much the same purpose. Mulch the asparagus bed heavily: a friend of mine covers his thickly with seaweed every winter and gets a splendid crop, because asparagus likes salt as well as protection from hard frost; also mulch other perennial crops like globe artichokes and rhubarb.

When the frost grips the soil and makes it hard enough to bear a heavy weight, use the wheelbarrow to carry compost from the piles or bins out on to the land, where it will do more good than it would if it rotted away where it was. Out on the land it will feed and sustain the earthworms, which are the gardener's best friend. Pull rotten leaves off Brussels sprouts and other big *brassica* plants, and put them into the very middle of the compost heap.

In the late fall, dig up unproductive heavy clay so that the frost can get at it and break it down. But remember that in an organic garden you can improve the heaviest and most stubborn clay with yearly dressings of compost or manure. After a few years of this treatment, it will not be so necessary to dig it up every winter; the soil will break down naturally anyway in the spring.

In winter you should dig your deep beds (see p. 106) after first spreading a dressing of compost on top of them. Test the soil with a testing kit, if you think you need to, and apply lime to next year's legume plot if the pH is below 6.5.

Winter is also a good time to cut brush for peas and beans, because the leaves are fallen from trees and hedges. Look for slender branches with some twigs still on them and cut lengths four feet (1.2 m) long. Hazel sticks are the very best.

In February sow onion and leek seeds in seed boxes and keep them in a warm place indoors. Onions grown from such a planting will ripen early and dry off well for winter storing; the leeks will grow as thick as your arm for use in the early fall. If you want to force early rhubarb, put some barrels or steel drums over the plants and bury these completely under manure with plenty of straw in it. The heat will force on rhubarb for eating in early spring. In late March set seed potatoes to sprout in boxes in a shed or greenhouse: they need light, but must never suffer frost.

In the greenhouse be sure to provide extra ventilation on sunny or warmer days. There should be some ventilation all the time except in hard freezing weather. The air in a greenhouse should always be buoyant.

Cauliflowers for harvesting in early summer will be growing in flats or seed boxes indoors and you will have to prick them out into frames or under mini-greenhouses (see p. 111) as they get overcrowded. As you prick out sow more seed in the seed boxes, for harvesting later in the summer. The cauliflower is always thought of as a difficult crop, but really it must just be sown indoors at the right time, and must be allowed to develop fast at all stages of its growth.

The great English horticulturalist Alan Chadwick, who runs a training center in California, talks about the "breakfast, lunch, dinner" principle. What he means is that you first give your seedlings a good breakfast in the seed box — plenty of nourishing compost. Then you give them lunch when you put them out in frame or holding-bed and put them into even richer soil. And when you finally plant them out in their permanent home — in Chadwick's case always a deep bed — you give them dinner, which is the best meal of all. If you stick to this principle with cauliflowers, and never let them dry out, you should have absolutely no trouble and produce an excellent crop.

Sow summer cabbages now too, in flats or cold frames. Winter cabbages you will be eating, or giving to your neighbors, and the same applies to Brussels sprouts, broccoli, leeks, celery and kale. Rutabagas and parsnips can be left out in the ground until after Christmas, unless you live in a very cold climate indeed; onions and garlic you will get from the strings hung up in your shed. Don't ever store them in the warmth of the kitchen, or they will rot; you can hang one string at a time in the kitchen for immediate use. Don't leave bunches of herbs hung up near the stove to collect the dust either; as soon as they are dry, shred them and put them in jars. If you are lucky you may still have tomatoes ripening away in a drawer. And, of course, you should have plenty of

The Winter Garden

THE PERENNIAL PLOT

If you have left your asparagus ferns on the plants, now is the time to cut them off with a sharp knife and put them in the middle of the compost heap. Do the same to the globe artichokes, which by now will be dying down. Put a heavy dressing of compost, straw, seaweed, or other mulch on the perennial beds; this will protect the roots against the cold, as well as rotting and improving the soil.

TOOLSHED, TOOLS AND FENCES

The winter is the time of year to attend to all garden hardware. Do all maintenance work now so as to spare yourself when the heavy work begins in spring.

SEED AND HOLDING-BEDS

These should be covered with green manure by now. Leave them alone.

PLOT A

Brassica

In mild climates this is the bed you can depend on most all through the winter. At first there will be cabbages and Brussels sprouts to pick and eat; later in the winter when your other cabbages have been eaten, savoys will come to the rescue, along with broccoli which can stand a lot of cold weather; finally, curly and other kale will weather the storms and come through to feed you in the spring. Spring cabbages will have been planted out, and should now be protected if necessary by cloches or a plastic tunnel.

PLOT D

Potatoes/Peas and beans

Leeks, which will have gone in after the early potatoes last year as a catch crop, have grown well, are earthed up, and can be harvested through the winter.

COMPOST

Protect your heaps of compost from winter rain by putting something on top of them: black plastic, old carpets, or even old sheets of corrugated iron. If you have time to turn your compost, so much the better; it will heat up again and mature all the quicker. Don't leave it in the bins too long once mature — get it on to the land.

THE COLD FRAME

Winter lettuces should be growing here. Take your endives out and blanch them indoors in the dark. Open frames a little during warm days. Protect with mats at night.

FRUIT TREES

Plant new trees in late winter. Do winter pruning and winter washing in the late winter months. Give your trees a heavy mulch or otherwise plenty of manure.

RHUBARB

Simply maintain the mulch over your rhubarb crowns. They will stay dormant, but need to be covered to protect them against very hard frost.

Gardening through the Year

HERB GARDEN
In the winter, if the weather is reasonable, you can transplant deciduous herbs (or indeed any others — but remember that you can transplant evergreens in the summer as well). Otherwise now is the best time for the herb garden to rest.

SOFT FRUIT
Towards the end of winter, you can prune your blackcurrants, and other soft fruit. Winter wash if your bushes are attacked by aphids or borers in the summer.

THE GREENHOUSE
As the winter goes on you will come to sow more and more seeds in seed boxes. As you clear the winter lettuce, dig and manure the soil in preparation for planting next year's crops in spring. It is a good idea to alternate your cucumber and tomato houses or, at least, the soil in which you grow these vegetables. Every winter, it may be necessary to remove all the earth underfoot and replace it with new topsoil to prevent disease. Plastic bags bought ready-filled with peat may be cheating, but they will certainly save you all this trouble.

BEES
Leave your bees severely alone, but ensure that the hives are not blown over in winter gales.

PLOT B
Miscellaneous/Roots
This is another plot you can count on most of the winter, if you can dig up the carrots, beets and celery frozen into the ground. The rest of the plot should be sleeping peacefully under a winter coat of green manure and you can leave it strictly alone until the spring. If you happen to get a series of fine dry days, however, you may take a spade or fork to it, and get some digging done before the big rush begins in spring.

PLOT C
Roots/Potatoes
There may well be some parsnips left in this bed, which last year held the root crops. The parsnips you can leave in the ground until you want them, except in regions where there is snow or a very hard winter frost. So all of this bed will have been dug up, or will be on the point of being dug up: in other words the bed lies fallow through the winter. Wheel manure out on to it whenever the weather allows, in preparation for it to become the new potato plot in the spring.

jars of tomatoes, sauerkraut and chutney in store.

The root cellar, or those old crates in the garden shed, will be yielding up their store of potatoes, turnips, carrots, beets, kohlrabi and so on. There is no point in surviving the winter to find you still have a ton of old roots which you don't really know what to do with. So be generous to yourself. But, at the same time, don't forget that the new potatoes very likely won't be ready as early as you think they will.

Now is the time you will be glad you salted down the pole beans. In the pouring rain, or when there is a heavy frost, or when a blizzard is blowing, think how nice it is not to have to go outside, and down to the garden to pick Brussels sprouts or kale.

In the south you can plant trees or bushes through the winter, as long as the ground is not too wet or frozen. Thin raspberry canes and tie them to the wires, and prune your blackcurrant bushes. Mulch or manure all soft fruit heavily and top fruit too if you have the manure to spare. It is far better to suppress grass and weeds with mulch near soft fruit bushes or fruit trees than to hoe or dig. Digging is particularly bad for the spreading roots of raspberries and not good for currants either. I leave the pruning of fruit trees until February, and after pruning I spray with winter

wash (see p. 104). If your trees are heavily coated with lichen it may be a good idea to spray with a lime-sulfur wash. If you can't get this, one pound (400 g) of caustic soda dissolved in six gallons (23 l) of water will do the job.

By late March you will already feel the approach of spring and begin impatiently to start putting seeds in. Take care not to start too soon. If the ground is dry enough and unfrozen, parsnips and shallots can go in. And you can sow all sorts of seeds: leeks, lettuces, onions, cabbages, cauliflowers and Brussels sprouts. Sow celery seeds in seed boxes in a warm house. It is always best, particularly with plants you wish to start growing early, to plant little and often, rather than to risk the lot at one go and find later that nothing has grown because of a late frost.

SPRING

As winter fades, too slowly, into spring, the sap begins to rise not only in the gardener, but in the garden. And now is the time when you must resist a mounting feeling of panic. You cannot do everything that you have got to do, but the spring is longer than you think: as long as you got things fairly straight last fall and kept them so all winter, you will find that by simply digging your garden quietly, all the spring jobs will get done in good order.

And don't be in too much of a hurry. If you put seed in very early, as early as many people tell you to, all too often cold weather, or wet weather, or dry weather, will set in and your seed will rot in the ground. Sow a little of each kind of seed early (very early if you have previously warmed up the soil with cloches or mini-greenhouses), and then wait until things warm up a little more before sowing the rest. Nature is not in too much of a hurry in the spring, nor should you be.

Anyway if you think about it, you do not want all your early potatoes or whatever very early. If you have just a few plants, or a short row, of very early earlies, these will be enough to give you a treat before the main crop of earlies (if such a thing can be) comes along a couple of weeks later.

As for the true main crop plants — winter

DEEP BED IN WINTER
In winter the deep bed which will grow next year's peas and beans should be limed if the pH is below 6.5. Sprinkle the lime on with a trowel and then rake it in, taking care not to walk on the bed.

brassica for example – these want to go into a dry warm bed. If you put them into a freezing wet one, they won't come up any quicker than if you waited two weeks longer before putting them in, and some of them won't come up at all.

Before spring actually arrives, you should be thinking about those two hardy plants, parsnips and Jerusalem artichokes. In England I always sow some parsnips and plant some Jerusalem artichokes in February if the ground is not frozen solid. The artichokes really don't mind what you do to them; if you put them in the ground they will come up. However, parsnips, which come from seed, need seed-bed conditions. But don't sow seed in soaking wet ground just because the time of year seems right.

And if you are faced with a sullen, sour, thoroughly frozen surface, looking like concrete and nearly as hard, you will have a well-nigh impossible job turning it into a seed-bed. Wait for a spell of sunny dry weather.

The ideal way to sow seed is in irrigation conditions. You sow your seed in ground as dry as dust (and dry ground is warm ground) and then you flood it. In temperate climates you can't do that, so you must just wait for those few warm days when the ground dries out to seed-bed conditions. If you have dug the land up during the winter, the loosened soil gets a better chance to dry out quickly in the first warm wind.

Here also the deep bed scores, as it scores in so many other ways. Because the beds are raised and the soil is very loose, the surface dries out very quickly and warms up at the same time. A quick fork-over should be perfectly possible without treading on the soil, and is enough to let sunshine and air in to sweeten the soil.

There are lots of tasks in the garden in spring, and it is worth listing them chronologically. You can try putting in a few very early potatoes in the first week of April, particularly if you can protect the seedlings from hard frost later on. At the same time sow leek, lettuce, onion, parsnip (if you didn't sow them in March), pea, radish, spinach and turnip seed.

In the herb garden you must lift, divide, and replant many perennial herbs and sow seeds of others. In the greenhouse or hot-bed sow more cauliflower seed in pots or seed boxes, and tomato and celery seed if you didn't sow them in March.

There are two ways of hastening growth in early spring. One is glass or plastic. You will achieve good results simply by spreading a large sheet of transparent plastic over a piece of dug ground and weighting it down with stones. The plastic keeps the rain off and allows what sun there is to warm up the ground. After two weeks or so you remove the plastic, sow your seeds, water well, and replace the plastic again. As soon as the seedlings appear and make some growth, take the plastic right off during the daytime and replace it at night. After hardening off the plants for a week or two take the plastic right away and put it over something else. The mini-greenhouse (see p. 111) is a modification of this and is a very good way of drying and warming the soil. Don't forget that all plants under such protective devices need some water.

The other way of speeding growth is to start things off indoors, in seed boxes, pots, or peat pots. "Indoors" can mean a greenhouse, frames, or just the kitchen window sill. Timing is the important factor. You have complete control over the environment until the seedlings are planted out in the garden. This must therefore occur at the right time – that is, not when a vicious frost is going to descend on you, not when the plants should have been happily growing out in their permanent positions for weeks anyway, and not when they have grown too weak and gangly in the pots indoors. If you can give the tender young plants the temporary protection of a mini-greenhouse or its equivalent the minute they are planted out, so much the better.

You can, of course, grow a lot of good food without any mini-greenhouses, cloches, or any other protection, even in cold climates. Staple vegetables, like brassica, leeks, potatoes and onions will all thrive without protection. But in very cold climates you cannot grow things like melons, tomatoes, eggplants or peppers without starting them off indoors so as to give them warmth for germination. You are, in fact, cheating the climate by extending it forwards when you plant indoors and plant out later. You may well get a really hot summer even in the far north, but it will be a short summer and so you have to try to prolong it.

In April you may wonder what has hit you. This is one of the busiest months of the year. You should now sow the seed-bed with brassica and leeks. This little seed-bed, even if it is no bigger than a table-top, is the most important thing in your garden. It holds what will eventually be your main winter vegetable supply.

Beets, carrots and, if you have the room, second sowings of lettuces, peas, spinach, turnips

The Spring Garden

THE PERENNIAL PLOT
You should have removed the straw mulch from your globe artichokes and they will be shooting up fast. The asparagus is growing well and will soon be ready to cut. You will have dug and raked your seed-bed and sown rows of cabbage, kale, cauliflower, Brussels sprouts, all the broccolis, leeks, onions and lettuces.

PLOT A
Brassica/Miscellaneous
You will find that the cabbage tribe plants still gallantly surviving on this plot are a sorry sight. They have been supplying you with greenstuff all winter, they have suffered gales and frosts, but some of them are still there — the curly kale particularly and perhaps the broccoli. You will probably have picked all your Brussels sprouts, but the tops can still be used for spring greens. The spring is the true "hungry gap": the lenten fast when men and women begin to feel the dearth of fresh greenstuffs. So the remnants of your brassica are useful to you now. Dig over the rest of the bed ready for planting tomatoes, lettuces, cucumbers, spinach, sweet corn, squash, zucchini and melons.

PLOT D
Peas and beans
The leeks that have grown through the winter are your great standby now. As your brassica get fewer, and your stored onions run out, so the leeks come to the rescue. As the leeks are cleared you should sow early peas under plastic or cloches to protect them.

THE COLD FRAME
In the cold frame you can sow early lettuces and early cabbages.

FRUIT TREES
Your fruit trees will be bursting into glorious flower. Try to keep birds away from them. Use nets (though this is laborious), scarecrows, pieces of mirror or shiny tin, loud noises and anything else that works. Put a grease band round each tree to stop insects crawling up.

COMPOST
You will have built up a lot of compost over the winter, after almost emptying your bins in the fall for the great soil feeding that follows the harvest. Some can go into the soil now, especially into the potato plot.

RHUBARB
In early spring cover your rhubarb plants with upturned pots or buckets. This will force the rhubarb's growth, so that you can begin eating it earlier.

Gardening through the Year

SOFT FRUIT
Prune your gooseberries early in spring. Set out strawberry plants in late spring.

THE GREENHOUSE
There is plenty to do in the greenhouse in spring. You must sow seeds of several kinds: celery, tomatoes, peppers, frame cucumbers and melons are the most important. Put them in seed boxes or peat pots. Keep them watered and plant them out as the spring advances. If your greenhouse is heated, you will begin to get a crop from the tomatoes sown in early winter. As the weather gets warmer begin to ventilate your greenhouse.

BEES
Your bees have been dormant throughout the winter. Now you can take the blanket and wire mouse guard out of the hive.

PLOT B
Roots
The green manure crop of vetch, or other winter legumes, is ready to be turned in with a spade or rototiller. Then the first root crops should be planted. Parsnips should be planted first, onions should follow and then a row of early carrots.

HERB GARDEN
In early spring you can set out new herb plants grown from rooted cuttings indoors or in the greenhouse over the winter. This is also the time to lift, divide and replant some of your older herb plants. Mint, thyme, chives and sage benefit from this treatment.

PLOT C
Potatoes
You will have planted early potatoes here, if possible in trenches full of manure or compost. Put one row under cloches or a transparent plastic sheet and you will have these to eat before the others. In late winter you should have brought out manure or compost and left it on the frosty ground ready for digging in with the main crop, which should be planted in the late spring.

and radishes all go into their permanent quarters in April. These vegetables don't like being transplanted and don't need to be; you should sow them in their permanent beds.

April is also the time to plant out all those eager but pampered young semi-hardy creatures that have been growing under glass: cabbages, cauliflowers, early leeks and onions. Their places indoors may be taken by hot-climate seeds such as melons, eggplants and peppers. Sow all these in good potting compost in a warm place.

From now on you will have to keep a constant watch on plants outdoors so that they don't get over-crowded. You will need to thin seedlings carefully, unless you have planted them with a precision drill. The weeds too will by now be feeling the spring. Hoe them out or dig them in. Never let them get too rampant or you will have ten times the work dealing with them.

You may well be planting out new strawberry plants in April. You won't get much fruit off them this year but you will next. You must keep a careful watch this month for insect pests in your tree fruit, and take appropriate action if they get out of hand.

When it comes to planting out plants that have been grown indoors, into frames or under mini-

greenhouses, you should give them plenty of protection and not too much air for the first few days, until they have rooted themselves really well into the new soil. A transplanted plant is an invalid for a few days; be kind to it.

Small plants, put out into a deep bed which has been warmed for a couple of weeks with a mini-greenhouse, do far better than those put out in orthodox frames. Of course a true hot-bed is the very best of all; there is nothing like it for hastening things along.

In early May be on the watch for signs of frost late at night. One of these may nip your early potatoes right down and give Mr. Jones next door the opportunity he has been waiting for — his chance to gloat over you as he lifts some tubers the size of small marbles and you don't. If it looks like frost (a clear sky and no wind) cover those potato shoots with something; it hardly matters what. If you are caught out by frost, get out early in the morning and wash the frost off the potato tops and any other plants that may suffer, with cold water.

As ground becomes available, plant out main crop *brassica* from the seed-bed into permanent quarters; or, if you use the holding-bed method, plant them out into the holding-bed. The plants can live happily in the holding-bed until August, moving into their permanent quarters as land becomes free when you harvest other crops. Plant out a few leeks as well, so that you have early leeks in the fall. Main crop ones will transplant much later.

Prepare your celery trenches in late April. This is one of the most useful plants of all because it can be harvested well into the winter. It makes a big difference to the flavor of winter soups and stews, and crisp white celery eaten raw with cheese is a rare delight in winter.

Keep on sowing successionally in May. All the things you sowed outside last month can be sown again now. Keep thinning young plants as they need it: choose rainy days to thin onions or carrots so as not to attract the wily onion and carrot flies. And keep hoeing. An hour of hoeing or weeding in May will save you days later on when the weeds have got the better of you. Hoe the weeds almost before they appear.

Watch top fruit carefully for pests. Remove dead flowers and thin fruit during early June. If you thin all apples, pears and peaches this month you will have a bigger weight of better fruit in the fall. A fruit every five inches (13 cm) is what to aim for.

DEEP BED IN SPRING

In spring you can sow pea seed in the deep bed soil that was limed in winter. Sow to a triangular pattern so that the plants form clumps and not rows. The overall effect will be of very closely spaced diagonal rows. If you can't reach the middle of the bed, lay a board about five feet by three feet right across and sit on it.

SUMMER

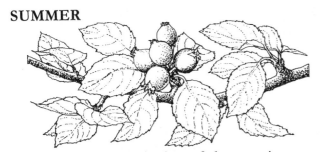

By now the strong rhythm of the growing season should have you in its grip and you will be carried along by the inexorable progress of nature. But the early summer does not immediately bring with it the end of the hungry gap.

It is now that you will be grateful that you sowed lettuce, radishes, spring onions and spinach early. These vegetables will give you fresh vitamins at a time when you sorely need them. It is now that you will be watching those very early potatoes with great impatience although their moment of glory will not quite have come.

As far as planting and sowing goes, don't give up now. Successional sowing should be the slogan for this time of the year just as much as it is in the spring. Continue to sow lettuces, radishes, carrots, corn, bush beans, beets and rutabagas little and often; in this way you will have fresh tender young vegetables all through the summer and the fall. It is from this angle that as a home gardener you are at such an advantage. You don't need vast quantities of anything so you can put in half a row – even just a few seeds – and give yourself a constant supply of fresh young food.

As soon as all fear of frost is past and the ground is warm enough, in should go the tender vegetables that can't stand any frost at all, like seeds of pole and bush beans, and soybeans too if you can grow them. At the same time out go the seedlings that you have been nurturing in the greenhouse.

As June begins, the hungry gap eases up and your garden starts to hint at the abundance to come. It is a beautiful month in the garden. You may even be able to stand back and admire your own work for a moment or two every now and then, although this does not mean that you can relax – what gardening writer would ever suggest that? It is in June that the neighborhood contest to see who lifts the earliest potatoes rages. Spring cabbages will be a great standby and spring onions should be available in plenty. If you haven't sown them specially, there will always be thinnings from your main crop onion bed.

June is a bad month for insect pests, but then it is also the month when strawberries come in to cheer the heart and the taste buds. By the end of June you should have stopped cutting asparagus altogether; don't cut another shoot. Give the plants a chance to grow and store up food for next year.

As summer wears on, you will have to consider the question of whether to water or not. In a few fortunate places you can garden all your life, never put a drop of water on the land and yet always have good crops.

A few summers ago throughout the worst drought I have ever known the vegetable garden on my farm grew marvelously, and I never put a drop of water on anything. But the secret is that my land is full of humus and is constantly manured, so my land holds the water like a sponge. Even at the tail end of the drought I could dig down half a spade's depth and find moist earth; the roots of the vigorous, humus-fed crops all went down deep enough to reach it. If I had splashed water about from time to time I would have caused roots to form on the surface where the water was, at the expense of deep penetrating roots, and I would not have had anything like such good plants.

But where I could water really thoroughly I did. For example, I diverted a stream through big plastic drainpipes and directed the water so that it flowed on to my main crop potatoes, and thus I got a heavy yield of potatoes where gardeners who couldn't irrigate got very few.

So the rule is: water well if you water at all. Let the water sink right down to the lowest roots of the plants. This kind of watering does help; summer cauliflowers and lettuces particularly don't grow well during a drought.

The deep bed method is excellent from a water conservation point of view: you need just half as much water for a deep bed as you need for a conventional garden. This is because the looseness of the soil prevents the water rising too rapidly to the surface by capillary action and evaporating; it also permits the roots of plants to move downwards very freely and reach water.

Rain falling on the deep bed sinks in immediately and does not run away, lie on the surface, or evaporate as it does in a conventional garden.

The deep-bed practitioners in California favor a good sprinkling every day or so, so as to keep a moist mini-climate under the leaves of their close-planted crops. But their climate is totally without rain in the summer time and they have to water. The same does not apply in the British Isles or in

The Summer Garden

THE PERENNIAL PLOT

Remember the rule that no more asparagus must be cut after the last day of June: the beautiful ferns must now be allowed to grow undisturbed. Globe artichokes are growing vigorously and will be ready to eat soon. Try to pick your globes very young, for you can then eat practically the whole flower, wasting nothing.

SEED AND HOLDING-BEDS

The brassica plants you sowed in the seed-bed will all have left it by now. Some are in the holding-bed and others are in their permanent bed, Plot D. The seedling leeks, lettuces and onions in the seed-bed are beginning to get overcrowded and should be planted out as soon as possible.

PLOT A

Miscellaneous

This was last winter's brassica bed, but from now on it will be taking most of the vegetables that don't fit naturally anywhere else. Tomatoes, sweet corn, spinach, lettuces, celery and all the squash tribe fall into this category. If you suffer from eel worm badly, it will pay you to put tomatoes in with the potato patch, so as to give a longer break between solanaceous plants.

PLOT D

Peas and beans/Brassica

The broad beans will be almost finished by now so you should soon be removing the plants, just leaving a few to produce seed for next year. As these crops are cleared, you will be moving brassica plants out of the seed-bed or holding-bed to take their place. Plant bush beans in early summer. Along with peas and pole beans they will begin to bear as the summer wears on.

COMPOST

At this time, when growth is at its most rampant and many plants must be pulled up or cut back, your compost heaps will grow very fast. Through them you feed the soil, through that your crops and through these yourself!

THE COLD FRAME

By now this will be full of cucumbers, peppers, eggplants, melons, and any other vegetables which need extra warmth. Make sure that they are well-ventilated on hot days and give them shade when there is a lot of strong sun.

FRUIT TREES

Thin out young fruit in early summer; otherwise you may find that you suffer from the "June Drop" which is when immature fruit falls to the ground. Later on you will have some summer pruning to do. Watch out for infestations of insects; otherwise leave fruit alone. Late summer will see you harvesting early varieties of top fruit.

RHUBARB

Eat your rhubarb in early summer. Pull out the big stalks and leave the young ones. From late summer onwards give the rhubarb a rest.

Gardening through the Year

SOFT FRUIT
If you are starting a new strawberry bed, high summer is the time to plant out seedlings which will begin to fruit next year. Most of your strawberries will have been picked in early summer. Pick currants and gooseberries as they ripen.

THE GREENHOUSE
In summer the greenhouse can be left dormant, or given over to flowers.

BEES
The summer is the time when your bees need special attention. In the early summer stop them swarming; later on take honey from them as they make it. Always see that they have enough spare combs to build on.

PLOT B
Roots
All you need to do here during the summer is hoe, watch onions for onion fly, carrots for carrot fly, and wait for things to grow. If you have space to spare, sow some more carrots, as well as rutabagas, turnips and beets.

HERB GARDEN
The summer is the time for harvesting herbs, for drying them quickly in the wind and shade, and for storing them in airtight jars when they are quite dry.

PLOT C
Potatoes
Most of this bed will be occupied with main crop potatoes. You must weed them, and spray them with Bordeaux mixture if you fear blight. The earlies will mostly have been pulled by now and their places taken by leeks.

most parts of the United States.

Don't leave any land idle in the summer. As soon as one crop comes out another ought to go in. I even like to replace a single plant when it is harvested. Out comes a cabbage, in goes a lettuce. Out comes a lettuce, in goes another one or else some radish seed. If you think of nothing else you want to grow, grow a green manure crop, preferably a leguminous one like vetch. This is nothing but beneficial, for the land and for you.

If you can't even get round to that, rejoice to see nature do it for you by letting a fine healthy crop of chickweed and other annual weeds establish themselves. Let them grow: they take up nitrates from the soil, hold them safe and prevent them from washing away. But don't let them seed. Dig them in when they are at the flowering stage, or before. They will then rot down quickly, form good humus and release their stored nutrients into the soil again. Grass clippings spread on the soil also help to nourish the soil besides keeping down weeds and holding in moisture. Idle land is not only wasting its time, it is wasting its substance; land, like people, benefits from plenty of hard work.

Now, abundance takes hold in July. Start taking out every other carrot, onion, turnip, beet and so on, so that you have fresh tender young vegetables to eat. This will give more room to the ones you leave in for winter storing. Keep picking

DEEP BED IN SUMMER
By late summer you will have pulled your broad beans. The soil should then be forked over before brassica are planted out. Fork half the deep bed from one side and the other half from the other.

peas and pick all the beans; do not let them get old and rough and stringy. Pick and pick again. To leave beans on the plant unless you want them for winter drying is wrong, because they only sap the strength of the plant and stop others growing. The more beans you pick, the more you will get.

You need to tie your tomatoes to stakes now, pinch out their side-shoots, and feed them with manure or comfrey tea (see p. 103). Celery and leeks can do with liquid manure. Celery in particular must be watered if the weather is dry; it won't grow at all in drought conditions or at best it will just bolt to seed. All *brassica* plants can do with plenty of nitrogen at this time of the year — now is the time for your top dressing of chicken manure or other organic high-nitrogen manure if your land is not naturally sufficiently fertile. Don't put any on later than July: you don't want plants to grow too lanky and sappy before the cold weather sets in.

Now is the time also to lift shallots and dry them well before storing them. Spray main crop potatoes with Bordeaux mixture (see p. 104) if you are afraid of blight. Watch like a hawk for carrot and onion fly.

Don't forget to sow onion seed during the summer so that you will have strong plants to set out next year. If you have a cold frame or a mini-greenhouse, sow a few cauliflower seeds as well. If you keep these growing on quickly you will get excellent heads in the fall. Generally, cauliflower does better in the U.S. as a fall crop rather than a spring crop.

Pinch out cucumber side-shoots. Protect plants growing under glass against the sun by whitewashing the glass or setting up screens.

In August your work will be mostly weeding and harvesting. Cut cauliflower curds as they are ready; to leave them too long is only to waste them. Clear early potatoes and fill their space with leeks or green manure. Earth up celery, and earth up all *brassica* plants as you hoe them; they all benefit from earth heaped around their stems. Plants that have been harmed by cabbage root fly, or even by clubroot, will often save themselves by putting out new roots from their stems.

Complete the summer pruning of your fruit trees in August. You can still undertake the budding of fruit trees in this month if you didn't do it in July. Root strawberry runners in small peat pots for transplanting. August is a good month to establish more strawberry plants for fruiting next year, although early September is not too late.

Cut cucumbers and all the squash tribe as soon

as they are ready, even if you cannot eat them all, to keep the vines fruiting. Don't let anything go hard and bitter on the vine.

Lastly, hoe, hoe and hoe. Your success or failure as a gardener depends more than anything else on how you use, or fail to use, your hoe. Hoe weeds when they are tiny, or even before they emerge. A good hoeing does more good than a good watering. Hoe early and often and you won't have to hoe so hard.

AUTUMN

Autumn is the time of harvest. In comes crop after crop, to be eaten, preserved, or stored; your store cupboards should get filled with jars, your cellar with roots; your crocks and carboys with wines fermenting away.

As you clear bed after bed of its crop, do not neglect to sow green manure if you are not following one food crop with another, which is the best thing to do. Unfortunately leguminous plants, which make far and away the best green manure crops because they fix nitrogen, are mostly summer things and tend to die down in the winter. I find that red clover, sown early in September, makes quite a good growth before the winter kills it; I am also getting good results from winter vetches, but the seed is expensive. An advantage of vetches is that, if you keep rabbits or poultry, the crop can feed these animals before it goes back into the land as manure.

You should consider the whole question of saving your own seed (see p. 91) very carefully, because seed is becoming more and more expensive.

In September you will be harvesting the last bush, pole and lima beans. Salt down the bush and pole beans and possibly dry some, and dry your lima beans. Winter squashes and onions should be harvested when ripe and carefully stored.

Beets, carrots, rutabagas and turnips may still have some growth left in them, so pull a few for eating fresh, but leave your main crop for storing in the ground. Celery and parsnips are not ready to lift yet, even for eating fresh, because both need a frost on them to give them flavor.

September in the fruit garden is the time to pick apples and pears. The soft fruit (apart perhaps from late strawberries and raspberries) will already have been picked.

In your greenhouse, frames, or mini-greenhouses, water less and ventilate less, but don't let things get too tender. Like human beings, plants are healthier kept slightly on the cold side. Plants protected too much will not stand up well to any winter frosts.

October brings the major job of lifting and storing the potatoes. Beets, turnips, rutabagas and carrots should also be lifted and stored now. Hill

DEEP BED IN FALL
In the fall you will have some young brassica growing in place of the peas. You must hoe between these, but the leaves of the more mature brassica in the bed now cover the soil; weeds cannot grow and moisture is conserved.

The Autumn Garden

THE PERENNIAL PLOT

You will still be eating those delicious globe artichokes. Ignore all advice to cut down the asparagus ferns; leave them there to supply sap to the roots.

SEED AND HOLDING-BEDS

These can be sown with a quick-growing crop, such as lettuces, radishes, turnips or spinach. Otherwise sow green manure.

PLOT A
Miscellaneous

Your sweet corn should now be in full yield. Pick it before it gets too tough and rush it to the boiling pot. As you harvest crops from this bed, fork over the soil quickly and sow green manure seed: rye, or vetch, or both. Be patient with your outdoor tomatoes. They can ripen later than you think: I have often picked good ones in early autumn.

PLOT D
Brassica

As summer advanced you will have cleared the pea and bean crops and followed them immediately with the brassica plants from the holding-bed. These will be your winter standby and much depends on them. Do not give them nitrogen or rich manure at this stage or they will grow weak and sappy, and won't be able to stand the winter's frosts and gales.

COMPOST

Compost "makes" very quickly in the heat of the summer and by now you will have quite a lot. Get it out on to your beds and make room for more, because the time of harvest is the time when large quantities of plant wastes are available for the bins. Do not neglect to bring in what you can from outside too. If your neighbor does not want his grass mowings, collect them and compost them.

THE COLD FRAME

As you clear out the squash plants, with the eggplants and the peppers, put winter lettuces in, along with chicory and other Compositae for winter forcing.

FRUIT TREES

Now is the time to harvest the later varieties of tree fruit. Attend to hygiene: burn all fallen branches and those fallen leaves that are diseased; put other dead leaves in the middle of the compost heap.

RHUBARB

Mulch your rhubarb well with compost, manure, leaf-mold or seaweed and leave it alone. It needs a dormant period during the cold weather.

Gardening through the Year

SOFT FRUIT
Don't be in too much of a hurry to prune your blackcurrants. Let the sap go down into the roots first. Mulch the soil heavily with organic manure.

THE GREENHOUSE
On the ground you may well plant lettuces as you harvest other crops. Clean and clear the shelves for propagation of early seedlings later on.

BEES
You should have left the bees some honey, but the shortfall should by now be made up with sugar. Put in a blanket and wire mouse guard for the winter. In very cold climates you can wrap the hives with heavy duty black polyethylene.

PLOT B
Roots
Parsnips, carrots and rutabagas will stand up to cold weather. Beets will, too, if hilled up. All other roots must be harvested and stored in a cellar, shed, or clamp. Get green manure seed into this bed if you possibly can.

PLOT C
Potatoes
In November get the last of your main crop potatoes out of the ground. The leeks that followed the earlies will be well hilled up by now. Follow the main crop with green manure: rye is probably the most practical.

HERB GARDEN
Now is the time to harvest carefully such herb seeds as you require. Let seeds get quite ripe, pull the plants out, and hang them up in an airy place to dry. Cut off any stems that have died.

65

up leeks and celery as required, and bend the leaves over the curds of your cauliflowers so as to protect them from the weather. Keep a vigilant eye out for slugs and snails, which love a warm wet autumn.

Harvest all tree fruit before October is out, and rake up and compost all dropped leaves under the fruit trees. This piece of hygiene helps greatly toward preventing fungous disease. If you put the leaves right into the middle of your compost heap, no harmful organisms will survive.

Seedling cauliflowers, sown in seed boxes in early October, should be pricked out into a frame. Some people sow straight into a frame ignoring the seed box stage; but I prefer to remember the "breakfast, lunch, dinner" principle — that at every transplanting, plants benefit by getting an even better meal from richer soil than they were growing in before. So I sow the seedlings in seed boxes first in ordinary seed compost, then prick them out into frames full of very rich compost with plenty of manure in it, and, come spring, I transplant them outside into a deep bed, very well manured. Be careful not to let the frames get too damp and stuffy. Open them up on all fine days and close them only at night. Remember not to over-water in frames or greenhouses: growth and evaporation both slow down in the fall.

Once you have had a good frost, you can start pulling celery and parsnips for eating fresh. Both can be left in the ground and pulled when required until well into the winter.

November is a month you just have to put up with. The thing is not to feel defeated but to dig when you can dig, and when you can't to get out regardless and tidy up. Pull dead leaves off the *brassica* plants and put them on the compost heaps; left where they are they only harbor slugs. Cover winter crops such as celery with straw or bracken to keep the worst of the frost out, and in the same way protect such tender perennials as asparagus and globe artichokes that have died down and are dormant in the ground. Seaweed makes a marvelous mulch for this purpose.

Ventilate your frames or mini-greenhouses when it is not actually freezing, but cover them with matting, old sacks, or straw when there is hard frost. Winter lettuces in the greenhouse or in frames should be kept warm, but not too humid and stuffy. Like so many plants, they must not be subjected to frost, but at the same time it is not good to baby them.

THE VEGETABLE GARDENER'S CALENDAR

	January	February	March	April	May	June	July	August	September	October	November	December
Beans broad		Sow spring seed				Harvest		Clear		Sow winter seed		
French				Sow under cover	Sow		Harvest					
runner					Sow		Harvest					
Beetroot				Sow			Hoe			Harvest	Clamp	
Broccoli			Sow as you harvest		Plant out							
Brussels sprouts	Harvest		Sow		Plant out						Harvest	
Cabbage spring				Harvest			Sow		Plant out			
summer	Sow under cover		Sow				Harvest					
winter	Harvest			Sow		Hoe						Harvest
Carrots				Sow		Hoe	Sow	Weed		Harvest		
Cauliflower		Sow in heat						Harvest	Sow under cover		Harvest	
Celery		Harvest	Sow under cover			Plant out	Earth up			Earth up	Harvest	
Kale		Harvest			Sow in seed-bed	Plant out				Hoe		Harvest
Leeks		Sow as you harvest					Plant out	Hoe				Harvest
Lettuce		Sow and harvest most of the year							Sow under glass in winter			
Marrows					Sow under cover	Sow	Hoe		Harvest			
Onions		Sow	Thin		Weed			Sow		Harvest		
Parsnips		Sow			Hoe					Harvest		
Peas				Sow			Hoe	Harvest			Sow	
Potatoes			Plant out and hoe			Harvest		Spray	Harvest			
Radishes			Sow				Sow as you harvest					
Spinach					Sow and harvest all the year							
Tomatoes			Sow under cover		Plant out		Hoe	Harvest				
Turnips/swedes				Sow			Hoe		Harvest			

CHAPTER THREE

Planning the Food-Producing Garden

Containing the organization and laying out of the vegetable plot, the herb garden and the orchard, and the principles of rotating crops.

Planning the Food-Producing Garden

Lucky indeed is the man who can plan his garden starting with a piece of bare land. Unfortunately, most of us inherit a muddle of one sort or another – and there's no simple planning formula. You have to take into account several factors, and of course each garden, and each gardener, has different requirements. But whatever you want of your garden, my advice is always to plan now, whenever now is. Don't put off planning. The sooner you do it, the sooner you will be able to harvest your first crops.

The individual's requirements

The first principle of planning is, obviously, to consider what produce you need and want. And don't neglect your personal tastes here: it's pointless to grow a huge crop of pole beans if you don't actually like them. So, before anything else, I suggest you make a list of the crops which you'd like in your ideal garden.

In the countryside when I was a boy, farm workers needed a great bulk of easily grown food to supplement the meager diet that their low weekly wages could buy them. So they grew potatoes on at least half their gardens in the summer, and always a long row of pole beans, than which nothing is more productive. Then they grew as many *brassica* plants as they could in the winter. Many of them did not bother with much else. But if poverty isn't an urgent consideration, I think it's better not to devote all your space to the bulk crops. Instead, grow vegetables like peas and sweet corn which are best when eaten as fresh as possible. (There's a saying among sweet corn lovers that you can walk down the garden to pick the corn but you have to run back with it once it's picked.) Apart from early potatoes, rutabagas and beets, which are so delicious when young and tender, I recommend the gardener with limited space to buy his main root crops from a good market or friendly farmer, and use the space for more delicate vegetables which don't keep so well.

The true self-sufficient gardener, however, will want to be in a position where he has to buy no produce at all, and here we come to the tricky question of just how much you can expect to get from a given piece of land. Unfortunately there's no easy way of estimating this, other than by long experience and an intimate knowledge of your own garden. The best general rule in my view is to grow as much as you possibly can. If you use intensive gardening methods such as the deep bed (see p. 106) you will be amazed how many people you will be able to feed from quite a small plot.

Garden geography

Once you have got a list of the produce you want from your garden, the next thing is to ask yourself whether the general geography of the garden will let you grow it.

Aspect In my opinion, people worry too much about whether their gardens face north, south, east or west. It's true that a south-facing slope warms up quicker and better than a north-facing one. But it's also true that a south-facing slope is hit as hard by a late frost as a north-facing one. In practice, I find that north-facing crops are really not so far behind south-facing ones as many people expect. And don't underestimate the value of a north-facing slope: for example, it is often better not to force early potatoes too quickly in the early season sun on a south-facing slope because they may not have the strength to survive a freak last frost.

On the whole then, you need not be too concerned about the aspect of your garden. Remember that a good gardener will always do better in a north-facing garden than a bad gardener will in a south-facing one.

Shade What is much more important than aspect is shade. When planning your garden you must take into account how much of it will be in the shade, and for how long, during the course of the day, and the year. Certain plants just won't grow where it is too shady – just as others won't grow where there's too much direct sun. I suggest you make a rough sketch of the garden at different times of the year and color in the areas which get the sun the whole day, those which are sunny only half the day, and those which are in the shade all the time. When you have done this, you will have a clear idea of exactly how much space you will be able to devote to sun-loving and shade-loving crops respectively.

On this question of sun and shade, I've heard it said that crop rows should always run north and south rather than east and west so that the rows do not shade each other. But this is bad logic. In the northern hemisphere in the summer the sun always rises and sets to the north of the east and west points on the compass. In other words, the only time it shines directly from the south is at noon, when it is so high that shading between rows is minimal anyway. For most of the day, when it is lower and shading *is* important, the sun is shining from the east or the west. If anything, rows should be planted east and west to avoid too much shading. But personally I've never found it makes the slightest difference which way the rows go.

Planning the Food-Producing Garden

Trees There are certain features of the layout of your garden which may interfere with your planning intentions – for instance, that enormous tree in your neighbor's garden which overhangs your own garden. Not only does it shade a large part of your available growing area, but the roots creep under your land and suck out nutrients.

I'm certainly not against trees – indeed the nourishment which they take from your soil will eventually be returned when the leaves fall and begin to rot. But there are times when they really do inhibit what you can grow, and if your neighbor refuses to cut it down – as he probably will – you'll have to find some way of minimizing the inconvenience. It may be illegal to kill the tree by creosoting the roots, even if they are on your side of the fence, but it is perfectly all right to trim branches which overhang your garden and roots which burrow under it.

Sloping land If your garden slopes steeply, this can not only make gardening highly inconvenient, but can also lead to erosion of your valuable soil. The best solution here is to terrace the slope (see p. 241). Initially it's back-breaking work, but it's well worth it in the end: the garden will be far more productive, much easier to work in, the soil won't wash away, and a terraced garden can look both unusual and pleasing.

Climate

It is likely that your ideal list of the produce you want from your garden will already have been pared down by taking into account the geography of the garden. Now you'll have to pare it further by considering how many of the plants you want will grow well in your climate. While sometimes it can be fun to push your luck with plants which don't generally grow in your climate zone, for the most part it's hopeless trying to compete against the climate – better to use it as an ally.

Frost The trouble is, of course, that it's not easy to predict with any certainty what the weather will be like from season to season – or even, as most of us know from long experience of weather reports, from day to day. The most experienced gardener can be caught out by a sudden hard frost in the middle of spring. Still, I suggest you try to work out roughly how long a growing season you can expect in your area: say from the last frost of the spring to the first frost of the late fall. (For climate maps see p. 248.) It's always a good idea to make friends with a gardener who knows the district really well, and to ask him how long he expects the growing season to be.

Unless you decide to go in for extensive protection of your plants with greenhouses, mini-greenhouses, cloches, and so on, there's not much you can do to extend the growing season. But you may be able to take precautions against other climatic factors.

Wind Something you should include in your shade/sun chart of the garden is the direction of the prevailing wind, and an indication of which parts of the garden are sheltered or exposed. While some plants tolerate wind – though you might need to stake them – there are others such as most fruit crops, Brussels sprouts and the taller *brassica* which won't.

If the garden is particularly exposed to wind, the obvious thing is to build some sort of wind-break. A fence with gaps acts as a much more efficient wind-break than a solid wall since the wall creates swirling eddies in its lee which can do as much damage as unrestrained wind.

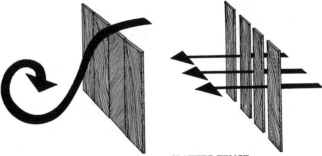

SOLID WOODEN FENCE
Wind swirls over a solid wooden fence, forming potentially harmful eddies.

SLATTED FENCE
Wind passes through a wooden fence with gaps, but with its force drastically reduced.

If a fence is impractical, plant a hedge (see p. 243), bushes or a line of trees – whatever will allow some wind through. Obviously you'll have to give up some growing space for this, but it's quite possible that the increase in crops because of the shelter will make up the loss.

Water In most climates it's necessary to have a water source near your seed-bed to help the seeds establish roots. Once the roots are firm, regular watering is not so vital, except in very dry climates or during a drought. In these cases, I recommend laying water-lines. It's not a difficult job nowadays since plastic pipe is easily available. Just lead the pipe from wherever your water source happens to be. If there's a chance of hard frost, bury the pipes underground – though normally plastic pipes don't burst as readily as metal ones. In fact, I think it's a good idea to bury the pipes anyway to keep them out of the way. And plastic can be affected by strong sunlight.

Soil conditions

One final, but very important matter you need to take into account when planning your garden is the nature of the soil. You may find that many of the plants you're thinking of growing need soil which is, for example, more or less acid, than the soil you have in your plot. Fortunately, it's not difficult to correct the nature of your soil (soil tests and treatments are discussed on pp. 80-90). But I strongly advise you to get your soil balance right before you actually start planting. You can — and should — give your soil regular treatment even when it is occupied, but of course it's much easier to dig in, say, compost or manure when the land is bare than to wait for a time when it's covered by a crop.

Positioning the different elements

After considering the various factors which will influence your first list of the produce you would ideally like in your garden, you should now have a clear idea of what you can and what you can't grow. The next question, of course, is whether you have the space in your plot for the various crops. To estimate this, you'll need to take into account the basic elements which every garden

should include. In my view, the best basic garden site should be worked around the following elements: a seed-bed; a holding-bed; a herb garden; a bed for perennials; a bed for perennial soft fruit; four beds for annual vegetables; and either an orchard or a smaller area to accommodate fruit trees. Garden constructions should include compost bins, a place to house animals, a garden shed, and, if you want one, a greenhouse. These form your basic working areas, but I think you should also allow for both a lawn and a small flower bed. You'll be grateful for a lawn where you can lounge in the sun when you've done the weeding, and it refreshes your senses — and your soul — to have a small plot containing some of those delightful old-fashioned cottage garden flowers.

The shape of your garden will obviously determine where you can put what. But there are a few siting rules which I think are worth noting. It saves both labor and frustration if you don't continually have to walk the length of the garden to perform one simple garden task.

Seed-bed The most important consideration in siting the seed-bed in my opinion is to have it close to a water source. Ideally, put it next to a faucet. If that is just not possible, then lay

GARDEN LAYOUT

The house is at the top end of this garden, closest to the herb garden, greenhouse and garden shed, and furthest away from the livestock and compost. The lawn, screened from the compost by cordons, provides a "pleasaunce" at the end of the garden.

Garden shed
Greenhouse
Plot A
Plot B
Plot C
Plot D
Standard fruit tree
Lawn

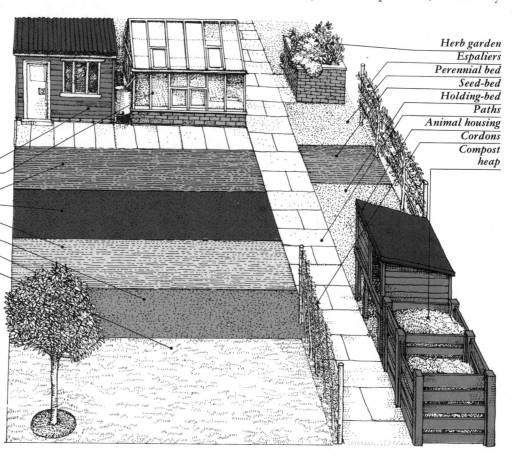

Herb garden
Espaliers
Perennial bed
Seed-bed
Holding-bed
Paths
Animal housing
Cordons
Compost heap

permanent water-lines (preferably buried out of the way) to the seed-bed.

Holding-bed Since you will be transferring seedlings to the holding-bed from the seed-bed, try to have them adjacent — perhaps separated by a narrow path.

Herb garden There's nothing worse when you're in the middle of cooking than to have to run to the end of the garden in a downpour in order to pick a handful of herbs. So put the herb garden as close as you can to the kitchen door.

Compost bins Obviously it's best to have the compost bins near to the growing beds to save you maneuvering barrows of compost up and down the garden. But there's a more important consideration here. If you keep livestock, then it's so much easier to be able to clean out the houses and dump the manure straight on to the compost heap. And since you won't want the animals too near to your own living quarters, I think the compost bins should be next to the livestock at the end of the garden.

Bee hives You'll no doubt want to avoid getting stung by bees if you keep them, so it's not a good idea to put your bee hives with the other animal houses. Besides, bees like the sun, and they don't like being under dripping trees. So I suggest you site them somewhere high up — on a roof or a specially built platform. This will definitely save you getting stung because the flight path of bees living high up is not going to be obstructed by a perspiring gardener.

Greenhouse and garden shed I would advise keeping both the greenhouse and the garden shed near to the house. In fact, the ideal in a small garden is to have a lean-to greenhouse against the house wall since this saves space. If a greenhouse is too far away from the house, you may have a problem with your electricity supply for lighting and heating. If you want to use your garden shed for potting as well as keeping tools, consider putting it adjacent to the greenhouse — perhaps even interconnecting with the greenhouse.

THE SIZE OF THE GARDEN

Since there is no such thing as a standard-size garden, it's probably best to consider a basic garden plan and think of it as coming in three models: small, medium and large. Once you have worked out which vegetables you require, whether you have the conditions in which to grow the crops, and where you are going to site the various garden constructions, you must still accommodate everything in the available space.

The small garden

"Small is beautiful" is Dr Schumacher's famous phrase, and a small garden can be quite as beautiful — and, if it's intensively cultivated, almost as productive — as a large one. In fact, it's often much easier to practice intensive gardening methods in a small garden: for example, a sackful of leaf-mold gathered in a nearby park or forest will make a significant difference to the fertility of a small garden, while you would need a lot more for it to be effective in a large one.

However, in a small garden you must learn to make use of every possible bit of growing space — and there are many more possibilities than you might think. In the first place, consider the third dimension of the garden: in a large garden there's no problem about spreading out horizontally, but in a small one it's an excellent alternative to garden vertically.

Vertical gardening Garden fences, fence posts, walls — even the walls of your house — all provide vertical growing space. Peas, the climbing beans, tomatoes, cucumbers and many of the squash tribe can all be trained upward with a system of ties and wires. Never let vertical space remain idle in the summer. And don't forget you can grow down from a height by using hanging tubs.

USING SPACE IMAGINATIVELY
A hanging basket full of zucchini is making effective use of vertical space. Standing a bay tree in a tub on a plank on castors means it can be wheeled indoors.

Window box gardening Remember that window ledges give you another horizontal plane for gardening, and it's very simple to construct suitable containers. It seems to me a pity always to put geraniums in window boxes: geraniums are nice, but tomatoes and lettuces are nicer to a hungry man, and they'll both grow successfully in window boxes.

Roof and patio gardening A roof or a patio, if you have one, provides useful space for tubs and similar containers, or for grow bags filled with peat or other mixtures. (But remember to allow for the weight of the containers and the soil, if you contemplate using, say, an old outhouse roof which may not be very strong.) Broad beans, pole beans, broccoli, Brussels sprouts, cabbage, lettuce and cucumbers will all grow well on a roof or patio; and if the climate is hot, so will peppers. Bay trees and lemon or orange trees planted in tubs which can be moved indoors in cold weather are also a good idea.

Indoor gardening Nearly all vegetables and small fruits can be grown indoors, and, especially if you have a small garden, you should think of every window sill, except those which face north, as an extension of your garden. Window sills can be used to grow herbs, tomatoes, lettuces, carrots, radishes and spring onions, and almost any kind of container will do. Just punch holes in the bottom for drainage, and place it on a waterproof tray to catch seepage. Put three inches (8 cm) of gravel at the bottom of the container and fill it up with equal volumes of potting compost, garden compost and good garden soil.

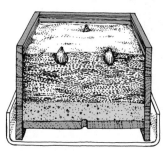

WINDOW SILL GARDENING
This cross-section through a window box shows shallots growing in equal parts of potting compost, garden compost and garden soil. Three inches (8 cm) of gravel help drainage through small holes in the box, which stands on a waterproof tray.

When all your window sills are occupied, consider other parts of the house too. Mushrooms, for example, grow very well under the stairs, in a basement or cellar – even in the bottom of an old wardrobe. For this, it's best to use special mushroom compost (see p. 166), which you can either buy or make yourself.

Recently it's become quite common to garden under artificial lighting, and of course this can be arranged virtually anywhere in the house. Fluorescent tubes are best – a combination of two four foot (1.2 m) tubes of forty watts each, one cool white and the other warm white. (Avoid using standard white or "daylight" tubes.) You can grow a number of plants successfully under lights: beets, carrots, lettuce, celery, cucumber, tomatoes, herbs, and mustard and cress. My only reservation about the system is that, given the current high price of energy, it isn't very cost-effective. But the investment is well worth it if you really haven't got any garden or outdoor growing space at all.

The medium-sized garden

A medium-sized garden – I'm thinking of something like the larger type of city garden or one of the bigger suburban gardens – allows the gardener greater freedom. But don't indulge the freedom too much. My advice is always to start small and intensively, and only gradually take in more and more land as you get the feel of the garden. Don't, for example, dig up the whole plot at the outset because you'll never cope without working it full time.

Even though there's more growing space, it shouldn't be wasted – for instance, by allowing an old, straggling and unproductive apple or pear tree to dominate. Cut such trees down (apple and pear trees make excellent firewood). It's a much better use of space to arrange that a fence or two are covered with cordon or espalier apple and pear trees (see p. 101), which in fact often bear a heavier crop than an old, neglected, standard tree.

The medium-sized garden will probably also accommodate a modest greenhouse, and that can be worth its weight in – well, tomatoes anyway. You'll be able to start plants off early in the season, and may manage to avoid the dreaded hungry gap in the spring. Cold frames will also extend the growing season, and if you have the space you can look on them as fairly permanent. I think it's a good idea to have them adjacent to the greenhouse, so you can harden off the greenhouse seedlings conveniently.

A particular advantage of the medium-sized garden is that you can pay more attention to decorative and non-productive areas – the "pleasaunce" where you can idle away a few hours in the sun. I must say I think the conventional ideas about siting it are mistaken: usually it's put next to the house because people think it nicer to look out on flowers and a lawn rather than on the vegetable beds. But consider the view when you're actually out there – the back of the house, which is often pretty ugly anyway, with all the gutters and drains. I would have a lawn right at the end of the garden, screened from the vegetables by, say, an espalier fence, and with a few flower beds for fragrance, and perhaps some small fruit trees. Keep your tame rabbits here, and with all the birds twittering around you, you'll have a real haven as far as possible from buildings – your own, and those of prying neighbors too. Remember, incidentally that a lawn is not only a leisure area – it is a consistent source of good mulching material. If you don't use your clippings as mulch, put them on the compost heap.

Planning the Food-Producing Garden

The large garden

No matter how much space you have in your garden, remember once again to start small. Master small areas first, and then you'll have the experience to work on a larger scale.

But even if you don't use the whole of your plot at the same time, you can still make it all work for you without expending much effort. Nothing improves the general heart of your land more than to lay it to pasture and graze stock on it for three or four years. At the end of this period, convert the pasture, bit by bit, into beds which can be taken up into your crop rotation. Grass and clover pastures are fine, but I suggest planting the deep-rooting crops like alfalfa or comfrey. These all mine up useful minerals from the depths of the subsoil, and whether you dig them in as green manure, put them on the compost heap, or merely feed them to the poultry, the minerals will eventually be spread about your garden. This method of resting the land will also ensure that any residual disease which remains in the soil from previous crops won't give you trouble when you come to plant vegetables.

With a large garden, you can consider planting standard fruit trees instead of the dwarf varieties or cordon and espalier-trained trees which are space-savers in smaller gardens. The modern dwarfing root stocks probably will give you a higher yield of fruit more quickly than a standard tree will, but at the same time few things look more beautiful than a fine orchard of large standard fruit trees. Standard plum and greengage are particularly delightful when they get really huge, and of course their fruits are so marvelous. It's always a temptation, in fact, to let big plum and greengage trees get out of control because they're so pleasing to look at, but remember that this will end up by limiting cropping. And don't forget walnut trees: posterity will always bless you for planting a walnut.

PLANNING THE VEGETABLE BEDS

When I discussed the various elements of the basic garden, I recommended that you allow four beds for vegetables, and there is a very special reason for this. In my view, a crop rotation cycle is essential in growing vegetables, and since I would advise a minimum of a four year rotation, you'll need four beds. More is better: for instance, if your garden is large enough, then you'll be able to rest some of the beds, as I suggested, by putting them to pasture and grazing livestock. And remember that if you're unfortunate enough to be hit by clubroot disease, the only way to get rid of it is to rest the land for nine years! The four year rotation cycle, however, is the most practical, other things being equal.

Even if your garden is very small, don't look on the four bed system as a luxury you can't afford. The need for a rotation cycle still applies, however small the garden, and it's not much more trouble to make four tiny beds than, say, two larger ones.

Siting the vegetable beds

Once you've decided in which area of the garden you're going to keep the vegetable beds, it is a matter of setting them out. It is not particularly important in my opinion which direction the beds run, unless you intend to use a rotary tiller to dig them. In this case, it's better if they don't run up to a fence or wall, because you will find it difficult to maneuver the machine. And remember to leave paths between the beds to make working easier. If your land is sandy and well drained, you probably won't need to gravel the paths, but if it's muddy you will (see p. 241).

The four year rotation cycle

The two major worries about growing vegetables are clubroot disease in *brassica* and eel worm infestation in potatoes, and these can easily build up in the soil if *brassica* and potatoes are planted year after year in the same bed. This is the primary reason for rotating your beds annually, though other crops will also benefit from being grown in different beds in successive years.

Planning a rotation cycle is a complex business, for you have to bear in mind whether the condition of the soil, after one crop has been lifted, is really suitable for the next crop to go into. There are four rules I recommend here. First, while potatoes need to grow in heavily manured soil, root crops tend to fork in such conditions: so keep potatoes as far as possible from the root crops in the rotation cycle. Second, peas and beans — the legumes generally — like well-limed soil, but potatoes don't: so avoid growing potatoes immediately after the legume break. Third, *brassica* do like lime, but only if it has been in the soil for some time: thus, it's best to plant your *brassica* after the legumes when the lime has had a chance to establish itself in the ground. Fourth, what I call the miscellaneous crops (outdoor tomatoes, melons, the squash tribe, lettuces, radishes and so on) are better for a good mulching with well-rotted compost: since this will assist the root crops – and certainly it will avoid the problems of forking – it's a good idea to put in the root crops after the miscellaneous crops.

To conform to these rules, I suggest the following cycle for each of your four beds. But remember, of course, to start each bed off at a different point in the cycle.

First year Manure the bed heavily in the first year and sow potatoes. (If you like, devote a small area of the potato bed to spring cabbage, leeks and turnips in order to save for the hungry gap in the following spring.) When you have harvested the potatoes, put down a crop of winter rye which you can dig in early in the second year as a green manure.

Second year After you have dug in the green manure crop, lime the soil fairly heavily and sow peas, beans and the other legumes. Since these will be harvested from about midsummer onward, one possibility which should be considered seriously is to replace the legumes immediately with your *brassica*, which have been growing at the same time, first in the seed-bed, then in the holding-bed. This may seem to be cramming plants in a little too optimistically, but it is a technique which I use successfully. Transplanting *brassica* from seed-bed to holding-bed to final bed in such a short period of time actually seems to benefit the plants — and I always think it's wise to get plants accustomed to transplantation. The main advantage of this technique of course is that, in effect, you squeeze what would otherwise be one year of a rotation cycle between two others, and since you'll be harvesting the *brassica* in late winter this simply means that you'll be getting a lot more food from your garden. Many people devote an entire year to *brassica* and have them in their final bed before the legumes are ready for harvesting. You can do this if you have space for five beds.

Third year Assuming you have managed to get the *brassica* in during the later part of the second year, in the third year you can straightaway begin to plant miscellaneous crops. As the *brassica* are ready for lifting, and when the weather begins to warm up, replace them with the miscellaneous crops, leaving the quicker-growing plants like lettuces until the last. Remember that a good mulch of well-rotted compost will help the miscellaneous crops immensely. At the end of the third year, again I recommend putting in a winter rye crop for digging in as green manure.

Fourth year Root crops should be sown in the fourth year, when the manure which was spread for the potatoes is no longer exercising a direct influence in the soil.

FOUR YEAR ROTATION
Rotating your beds annually is an essential part of successful vegetable growing. A four year cycle, using four beds, A, B, C and D, works very well. The brassica follow the legumes—peas and beans — in the same year. Both crops like lime, so this is a good idea.

Potatoes
Roots
Miscellaneous
Legumes and brassica

First year

If your garden is large enough to extend the rotation cycle, then leave the plot lying fallow during the fifth year, or grow yet another green manure crop — preferably one of the deeper-rooting crops such as alfalfa or comfrey, because they will be of longer-lasting benefit to the soil. Otherwise, start the whole cycle all over again by manuring heavily and sowing potatoes once more.

Alternative rotations

The four year rotation cycle is, I should emphasize, just one of several possibilities. I find it suits me very well, despite a couple of objections which the purist might make. The first objection is that I put tomatoes in with the miscellaneous crops, not in the potato patch, as is more common: thus, there are two solanaceous plants growing in the same bed in a space of less than four years. However, I don't grow very many outdoor tomatoes, and since I do like to have a lot of potatoes I'm a bit reluctant to give over some of the potato bed to tomatoes. If you really are a purist, then cut back on the potatoes and plant the tomatoes with them. In this way you will be certain that you are not encouraging disease.

The second objection is that I plant radishes — which are cruciferous — along with the miscellaneous crops, instead of in the *brassica* bed, thus tempting fate to nurture or perpetuate clubroot disease in the soil. In fact I don't think clubroot is a serious possibility here, because the radishes are harvested quickly, before the disease really has a chance to establish itself. But never leave the radishes to get old in the ground, or you might have a problem with clubroot.

Try out my suggested rotation cycle, but of course if it doesn't suit you, consider some alternatives. For example, I know of very successful gardeners who always follow *brassica* with the legumes, not, as I recommend, the other way round. Another possibility is to have a much less strict rotation cycle, where crops are jumbled up. The only rule here is to avoid planting the same crop in one bed in successive years. Personally, since I'm not good at remembering just what I've had in and where, I prefer a clearer system to work to. But if you keep good records, then the casual rotation might well suit you. I would advise making a map of your garden and noting what you have sown and planted, and when, together with details of how you have treated the soil that year.

PLANNING A HERB GARDEN

At the Covelo Garden Project in California, you can find what is probably the most elaborate and sophisticated herb garden in the world. A large amphitheater has been excavated, and the inside slopes have been terraced: the terraces on the north side are facing south and those on the south side face north. At the highest point on the terraces the soil is kept well drained and dry, while the lower parts surround a pond which provides moisture. So the optimum conditions have been created for growing all the culinary and medicinal herbs in the world — whether they like sunny, shady, wet or dry conditions — and it presents the most pleasing and attractive scene.

No doubt when you plan your herb garden you will be content to settle for something less grand than the Covelo garden, although similar principles of siting the individual herbs will apply. Herbs have a great range of climatic and soil preferences — from the hot sun and dry sandy soils favored by the herbs which have a Mediterranean origin like anise, basil and oregano, to the partial shade and rich, damp soil favored by plants like lovage and mint. The individual preferences of the different herbs are described in The Cultivation of Herbs chapter (pp. 191-202). Obviously you will have to do with less than ideal conditions for many of the herbs you grow, but when you plan your herb garden try to select a site which offers at least a modest range between full sun and partial shade.

As I have already suggested, it is best to site your herb garden near to the kitchen door. If sprigs of this or that fresh from the garden are within easy reach when you are cooking, you might resist the temptation to pick out a jar of dried herbs from your store cupboard. Needless to say, fresh herbs are infinitely more fragrant and flavorsome than those which have been drying up over a number of years.

While herbs vary as to whether they prefer sun or shade, most do like a sheltered spot, so if you can manage to put the herb garden against your kitchen wall this will certainly help.

Raised bed for herbs

An excellent idea for a herb garden is to build a raised bed with stone or bricks. There are a number of advantages here. First, the soil will be well drained and dry, and this is important for many herbs. Those which like damper soil and more shade can be planted at the base of the raised bed at the front or side. Secondly, the raised bed

RAISED HERB BED
You can build a raised bed made of brick or stone for your herbs. The soil will stay dry and well drained, which suits most herbs; the height of the bed means less bending; and the extra surface area encourages those herbs which like to straggle across walls.

entails less stooping for planting, tending and picking. And thirdly, it provides more surface area for the straggly plants to trail over the walls.

If you build a raised bed against your kitchen wall, however, don't build it higher than the sills of the house, or you will find yourself eating herbs in a damp house.

Rockery for herbs

Since many of the herbs are delicate and beautiful plants, another idea you can consider is to grow them in a small rockery (a miniature version of the Covelo herb garden, perhaps). If you're in a sandstone area, the pinks, reds, ochres and whites of the stones you use in the rockery will complement the rich greens of the herbs. The rockery, too, will have the advantage of being well drained. It may be that you won't be able to keep the damp-loving plants like mint in a rockery. If so, grow your mint in that damp shady patch which is found at the end of most gardens.

PLANNING THE FRUIT GARDEN

Two hundred years ago in his *Cottage Economy,* William Cobbett advised his cottagers not to grow fruit: in his view it took up too much good land and served only to give children belly-aches. But then Cobbett wasn't as vitamin-conscious as we tend to be nowadays, and personally I think there's nothing to compete with fruit for providing you with gastronomic delight and with what your body needs at the same time. There are few pleasures equal to eating the first juicy strawberries of the year, or a fine, sharp fruit cocktail picked from your own garden. Besides, the sense of spiritual well-being which comes from walking through a glorious orchard, in full bloom or in full fruit, is one of the great luxuries of gardening.

However, planning a fruit garden requires a lot of hard thought. For one thing, you are dealing with three different kinds of plants: fruit trees, soft fruit bushes, and ground plants. For another, you must take into account what else you are growing in the garden, since all fruit will draw a great deal of nourishment from the soil, and fruit trees create large areas of shade. Finally, and this is the important consideration, fruit-growing will take up a great deal of space in the garden.

How much fruit to grow

The size of your garden will have a fundamental influence on how much fruit you can expect to grow. Most gardens can — and should in my view — accommodate some soft fruit. But if your garden is tiny, I doubt that the space-effectiveness of fruit trees — even the dwarf varieties or trained trees — makes them worthwhile. It is a pity, but you ought to think how many apples, say, you will get from a single cordon, and weigh this against the number of beans or potatoes you will get from the same piece of land.

Even if you have a garden with more space, you must think carefully about planting fruit trees. Remember that what seems to take up only a little space now will be a quite different proposition in ten years' time. Unless your garden is really enormous — big enough for a full-scale orchard — I would recommend you to avoid standard (full size) fruit trees altogether. Several dwarf varieties, and, say, a few cordons and espaliers are a better use of space. This of course, limits the kind of fruit you can have: many fruit trees can be dwarfed or trained, but you can't do this with stone fruit trees such as plums, greengages or cherries.

If you have a large area in your garden to devote to fruit, then standard trees can be considered. An area 175 feet (54 m) square, for example, will accommodate 16 huge standard apple or pear trees. When these are mature, they will produce up to eight bushels of fruit each. The initial drawback with standards is that you won't get fruit until three to six years after they have been planted, although you will get fruit for 40 or 50 years after that. Dwarf varieties fruit earlier but have a shorter life. In the same area, you could plant 64 semi-dwarf trees and get about the same total yield (a semi-dwarf gives about a quarter of the yield of a standard), and they will fruit two to five years after planting.

Soil for fruit trees

When choosing a site for a fruit garden, take into account the quality of the soil. Most fruit needs good rich soil, with plenty of manure or compost worked into it, because the trees and bushes quickly exhaust the nutriments in the soil. Figs will grow in poor soil, and peaches prefer a light, sandy soil. All fruit requires well-drained soil, so if your land is wet, you will have to provide drainage (see p. 240). You will also need deep soil for fruit trees: standards and semi-dwarfs, particularly, send roots deep into the ground, although fan-trained fruit trees planted against a wall can put their roots out under unproductive land where a path or patio has been laid. It is worth digging deep when planting any fruit tree.

In a large orchard, you may think you will be able to grow at least some crops underneath the standards. Fundamentally you can't: a few daffodils might grow, but nothing edible. The best plan, if you want to use the space, is to graze sheep (just so long as they can't reach up to the leaves and branches of the trees). The manure makes a beneficial contribution to the soil in the orchard.

Generally, young fruit trees bear more fruit, more quickly, if the ground over the roots is left bare. Commercial fruit growers achieve this by spraying the area with herbicides, but I would suggest simply mulching the area heavily. However, if the ground is left bare, cut down on the amount of manure you put into the soil since this encourages tree-growth at the expense of fruit-formation. Don't clear the ground over the tree roots by mechanical means, because you may damage the roots near the surface.

Shade from fruit trees

Large fruit trees cast a considerable amount of shadow. If you can plant them at the north end of the garden the problem is easily resolved, but if they have to go in at the south end, remember that you will be able to grow only shade-loving plants such as rhubarb or mint immediately to the north of them.

Laying out a fruit garden

In view of the shading problem, I suggest you arrange the fruit garden in a stepped form. For example, to the north of the garden, put in a row of standard fruit trees, then, working progressively south, a row of semi-dwarfs, then bush trees, then some apple or pear fruit espaliers. In front of these, put a few rows of raspberry canes, then a few currant bushes, and finally a strawberry bed. This is an ideal arrangement of course, and obviously you would need an extensive garden to do it. But the principle is quite simple: have the taller plants to the north, and the smaller to the south and you won't have a shading problem.

THE IDEAL FRUIT LAYOUT
To avoid shading problems, grow taller plants to the north and smaller ones to the south of the garden. An ideal order of rows starting from the south would be: strawberries, followed by currants, raspberries, espaliers, semi-dwarfs and finally standards.

Choosing fruit trees

While deciding which fruit trees to plant is largely a matter of taste (and of the conditions in your garden), one important consideration is fertilization. It is no use planting, say, McIntosh apples alone for they must have another variety of apple to act as a pollinator. One way to achieve this is to get what is called a "family" tree – that is, one root stock which has had several varieties grafted on to it. Another solution is to grow several cordons or other small forms of different varieties. If you're lucky enough to have a friendly neighbor who also grows fruit trees, consult with him before selecting your trees. You'll both benefit if your trees pollinate each other. And of course, even if your neighbor isn't a friend, examine his trees anyway – he can't prevent the bees from carrying his pollen to your blossoms, and he shouldn't want to, since he will profit from the arrangement as well.

In general, my advice is to select as wide a variety of fruit trees as possible, bearing in mind the need for fertilization. Grow some very early varieties of fruit, a main crop, and some late ones which store well. If you do this, it won't be difficult to achieve self-sufficiency in fruit. One final piece of advice, though, is that some varieties of fruit are particularly sensitive to locality. So be sure to consult a local expert fruit-grower about which varieties do best in your area.

Protecting the fruit

One of the primary factors to take into account in planning a fruit garden is whether you will be able to protect the fruit from birds. Birds are probably the biggest single hindrance to successful fruit growing. Plan to protect soft fruit completely – a fruit cage (see p. 184) is probably the only really effective answer here. Cherry trees are particularly vulnerable to birds, and unless you net them completely, the birds will have stripped them bare before you have a chance to eat a single cherry. Fruit trees can be ravaged by bullfinches, and I know of no protection against these pests except the gun.

You must also consider the damage which your trees may suffer from other animals. Hens will not attack fruit beds, but they do peck at the fruit, so keep them away from fruiting trees. Both geese and goats need to be kept away from all trees: they will bite the bark off a tree virtually on sight and kill it immediately. Solve the problem either by keeping them right out of the orchard, or by circling the trunks with wire netting, which makes it impossible for the animals to reach the trees.

THE PLANNING REQUIREMENTS OF GARDEN VEGETABLES

	Prefers full sun	Prefers partial shade	Tolerates full shade	Prefers well-drained soil	Prefers damp soil	Tolerates dry soil	Prefers sandy soil	Prefers clay soil	Prefers rich soil	Tolerates poor soil	Prefers high pH (alkaline) soil	Prefers neutral pH	Prefers low pH (acid soil)	Requires long growing season	Requires short growing season	Benefits from frost	Tolerates frost	Tolerates wind
Artichokes globe	●			●					●		●		●					
Jerusalem			●	●			●		●		●		●				●	●
Asparagus	●			●			●		●		●		●				●	
Eggplants				●					●			●		●				
Beans broad		●						●	●		●						●	●
bush	●			●					●		●							
Lima	●			●					●		●							
pole	●			●	●				●		●				●			
soy	●			●					●					●				●
Beets			●		●				●		●							●
Broccoli			●		●				●	●	●		●				●	●
Brussels sprouts			●	●	●				●		●			●		●		●
Cabbage			●	●	●				●		●			●				●
Chinese cabbage		●			●					●			●					●
Peppers	●				●		●				●		●					
Cardoons	●			●		●				●	●		●					
Carrots	●			●	●		●		●		●				●			
Cauliflowers			●		●		●	●	●		●		●				●	●
Celeriac			●		●				●				●			●		●
Celery			●		●				●		●		●			●		●
Chicory			●	●	●					●	●							●
Cresses			●		●										●			●
Cucumbers	●			●	●				●		●				●			
Dandelions			●		●					●							●	●
Endive		●	●	●	●					●	●							●
Florence fennel	●			●	●				●		●							
Hamburg parsley	●			●	●				●		●			●				
Kale			●	●	●				●			●		●		●		●
Kohl-rabi			●	●	●	●			●			●						●
Leeks		●	●	●	●				●			●		●			●	●
Lettuce			●	●	●		●		●		●				●			●
Squash tribe	●				●	●			●		●				●			
Melons	●				●	●			●		●				●			
Okra	●				●	●		●	●		●				●			
Onions	●						●		●			●	●					●
Parsnips			●	●	●				●		●					●		●
Peanuts	●				●		●					●		●				●
Peas		●		●	●				●		●				●			
Potatoes		●		●	●				●				●					●
Radishes			●		●				●			●			●			●
Rhubarb			●		●				●			●		●			●	
Salsify		●			●				●		●		●					●
Seakale			●		●				●		●							●
Spinach			●		●				●		●					●		●
Spinach beet			●	●	●				●				●			●		
Rutabagas & turnips			●		●		●				●		●				●	●
Sweet corn	●			●					●		●		●					
Swiss chard			●	●		●			●		●			●				●
Tomatoes	●			●					●		●		●					

CHAPTER FOUR

The Essentials of Good Gardening

*Containing the methods of digging, composting,
fertilizing, soil testing, propagating, grafting, pruning,
training, mulching, protecting against pests, storing,
and gardening by the Deep Bed technique.*

Treating the Soil

Clearing overgrown land

Land left to itself in a temperate climate will turn first to grass, then to scrub, then to forest. So if you start with badly neglected land, the first thing to do is clear it.

Long grass or tall weeds should be cut down with a scythe or sickle. Scything is faster, but for a small garden it probably is not worth buying a scythe. But don't try to cut bushes with either a scythe or a sickle or you will quickly ruin the blade. A long-handled slasher, or brush-hook, or machete is best for bushes, or, if you haven't got one of these, a short-handled slasher, an axe or even a hatchet. However, if you have to dig out the bushes later on anyway, it's better not to cut them down at all: if there's no top left on the bush you will have nothing to heave against when you come to pull out the roots. After you have got bushes out, you should burn them if local laws permit it, because the ashes will give you potash for your soil.

You will need a wheelbarrow to shift what you clear. In my view, the most useful (and also beautiful) kind was the old fashioned gardener's barrow with a wooden wheel and wooden extension sides which could be fitted for high, light loads and taken off for heavy ones. Nowadays, a good wheelbarrow to get is a builder's barrow

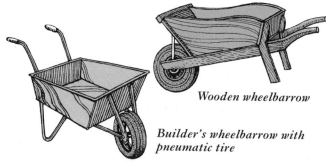

Wooden wheelbarrow

Builder's wheelbarrow with pneumatic tire

with a pneumatic rubber tire. These move a lot more easily, especially on uneven ground, than those that have solid tires.

Establishing a vegetable garden

If you throw some seeds on top of the ground the birds will eat them. If you dib a cabbage plant into a grass field, the grass will smother it and it will die. If you remove the grass, and all other wild plants, and dib a cabbage plant into the bare earth, weeds will grow up unless you stop them, and again the cabbage will be smothered. All our crop plants have been evolved over the centuries to be good to eat, to crop heavily and to be nutritious, at the expense of other qualities, like hardiness and competitiveness among wild plants.

So, if you want to feed yourself from the produce of your soil, you must cultivate it. There is such a thing as the "no-digging technique" and I will discuss this, but if you inherit a normal garden, whether well-maintained or neglected, or if you want to establish a garden in a grass field, you will have to start by digging, or turning the soil.

Now, assuming you have a plot of old grassland which you want to turn into a garden, there are several ways you can go about it. One is with pigs. Run pigs over your plot (keep them in with an electric fence) and they will root up the turf and leave it in a condition which makes it easy to fork over and turn into a garden.

Bastard trenching

The most traditional means of rescuing neglected ground is with a spade. And when you dig old turf for the first time with a spade you must make a very thorough job of it. If you just turn the grass over, it will come up and grow again and you will have endless trouble. You cannot plant garden plants in half-buried turf. It is far better to do it by the time-honored method of "bastard trenching" (see illustration right).

Once you have completed the bastard trenching, your grass plants, roots and all, will be completely buried more than a foot deep. They will not grow

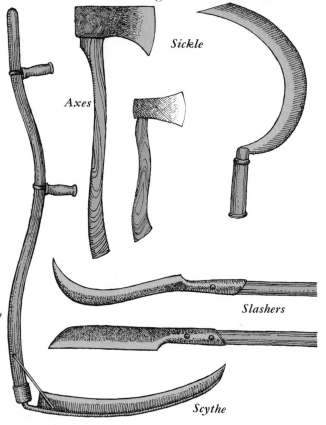

Sickle

Axes

Slashers

Scythe

up again to haunt you. Your soil will be loosened to a depth of about two feet, which is good for aeration, drainage and deep-rooting plants. And your new topsoil will be bare, broken up, and ready for planting with any crop immediately.

Some gardeners will tell you not to bury the scalped-off turf, but to lay all the turves in a pile, upside down, on top of each other. They will rot down over time and make the basis of splendid potting compost. There is nothing wrong with this, as long as you remember that you are severely robbing the bed from which you take the turf.

You can bastard trench any garden that you take over; if it is not grassland you can throw manure or compost into the trenches instead of turf. I would bury manure, compost, or turf once with a new garden, but I would never do it again, because I would rely on the earthworms to do it for me. Let them work their backs, and not me mine. Bastard trenching is especially worthwhile if your land is heavy, because it will break up any pan (hard impervious layer) that there might be down below.

BASTARD TRENCHING

Divide the bed in half lengthways. Mark out, with string if you like, a trench two feet (60 cm) wide across one half of the bed. Shave two inches (5 cm) of turf off it and pile this next to the top end of the other half of the bed. Dig earth out of the trench to a spade's depth, and put it next to the pile of turf. Mark out another trench next to the first. Scalp the turf off this, throw it into the bottom of the first trench and break it up small with the spade. Dig a spade's depth of earth from the second trench, invert it and throw it into the first trench. Carry on like this until you reach the other end of your plot. Cross over to the other side and work your way back (see illustration, right) and fill the last trench with the turf and earth from the first one.

Once you have dug your land over in this way, spread plenty of compost or manure on the surface. The earthworms will drag this deep down into the soil, and dig and aerate the soil for you themselves. Some old-fashioned gardeners will tell you to bury your manure or compost so as to incorporate it into the soil. This may well sound reasonable, but it is now known — and organic gardeners have proved it over and over again — that if you just lay compost or manure on top of the soil the earthworms will dig it in for you. In a very short time it will just disappear. And the more humus you get into your soil in this way the quicker it will disappear, because the more earthworms there will be and the more active, biologically, the soil will be. I bury manure when I plant potatoes, and I would bury manure if I took over an old, chemically-worked and exhausted garden. I would never bury manure if I had dug in old turf, for the simple reason that turf is manure. I would spread manure or compost on the surface, though, for the worms to drag down.

It will pay you for the first few years — until you have put a lot of compost on your land — to dig once a year, and if you want to turn your newly created garden into a deep bed garden (see p. 106), the first year after bastard trenching is a good time. For conventional gardening, use a fork for digging after the first year as long as your earth forms large enough clods. Just dig trenches one spit deep. Put the dug out earth in a pile as you did before, turn the next spadeful over into the empty trench, and keep going until you have been right round the plot; throw the first pile into the last trench (see below).

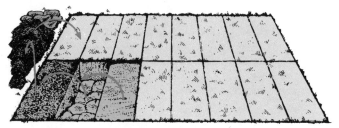

Digging with spades and forks

Even if you take over a well-ordered garden you may still have to dig. But don't dig just for the sake of digging; dig shallowly and in moderation. Your soil will get deeply dug whenever you grow potatoes, or celery or the other vegetables that grow in trenches or on ridges. The soil needs to be loosened to some depth for root crops like parsnips or carrots, but you can do this without inverting the soil — just push a fork in and break it up. For shallow rooted crops a mere shaking up of the top four inches (10 cm) of the soil is enough. Time spent in what old-fashioned gardeners called "thorough digging" is wasted and in fact counter-productive.

The basic tool you need for digging is, obviously, a spade. Stainless steel spades are excellent but extremely expensive, and I doubt if the expense is justified, so long as you look after an ordinary spade properly (see p. 244).

There are two types of spade: the round-pointed spade, with a heart-shaped blade and a long handle; and the square-pointed spade, with a rectangular blade and a shorter handle which is shaped into a "T" or a "D" at the end (the "D" handle is by far the more comfortable for digging.) A round-pointed spade with a long handle is the spade I prefer. Without too much backbending, you can work comfortably and quickly along the line of a furrow for, say, potatoes, or you can dig a trench for, say, celery; and the spade is

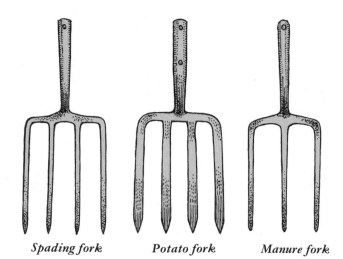

Spading fork   *Potato fork*   *Manure fork*

AERATING THE SOIL
The worms will usually aerate your soil for you, but they tend to be less active in dry weather, and in land which has lain fallow for some time. In these instances it is worth prodding your soil with a fork to aerate it.

"D" handle

"T" handle   Square-pointed spade   Round-pointed spade

incomparably better for excavating holes. However, for precision digging the square-pointed spade is better: it's difficult to dig down vertically with a round-pointed spade since the blade naturally goes in at an angle. For bastard trenching, or for digging a deep bed (see p. 106), I recommend using a square-pointed spade for turning the upper layer, and then a round-pointed spade for loosening the ground below.

For excavating hard earth, it's best to loosen it first with a pick, and then remove it with a spade. If you watch a professional gardener use a spade you'll see how the right knee shoves against the right hand to push the spade into the soil.

The experienced gardener often uses a fork rather than a spade. The advantages are that it's likely to be quicker, breaks up clods better and is easier to push into the ground than a spade. And

if you are cursed with creeping root weeds such as couch grass, ground elder or bindweed, then a fork is marvelous for raking the long roots out of the ground. It goes without saying, of course, that a fork is better than a spade for digging out root crops (a potato fork has flat tines to stop the spuds being speared). A manure fork has thin tines so that the manure will fall easily through on to the ground as soon as the fork is shaken. The only times a spade is really essential are for digging in grassland, turning heavy clay, or digging light sand.

Digging with a machine

There are two basic sorts of garden tractor: the kind which actually pulls a sort of plowshare along and inverts the soil as in a plowed field, and the rotary tiller type. The former has to be a very strong and heavy machine to be of any use and I would suggest it only for people who have large gardens, say half an acre (2000 sq m).

Rotary tillers on the other hand are smaller but nonetheless effective, and they accord more nearly with the ideal of the organic gardener which is not to invert the soil too much but to leave the topsoil on top.

My own feeling about all garden tractors is that they are only really worth buying if you are going to grow and sell vegetables on quite a large scale. I have found, after most of a lifetime of doing it, that I can provide all the vegetables for a large family quite easily with hand tools alone.

Having said that, I freely admit that a rotary tiller will perform the equivalent of digging, the equivalent of forking, and go a long way toward breaking down clods, although a raking with a hand-rake afterward is generally necessary before you can plant seed. A rotary tiller will kill weeds, and is good at incorporating green manure into the soil. It will even reclaim old grassland for you as long as you go over the ground many times, say once a month for several months. This is because you must hit the tough grasses again and again, as they begin to recover, so that eventually you kill them and incorporate them into the soil. If you till old grassland and broadcast a good cover crop, like mustard, or rye in the winter, and till that in when it is at the flowering stage, you will come near to producing a good garden soil. If you take time and dig in two successive cover crops, your soil will be even nearer perfection.

If you do decide to buy a rotary tiller – or hire one for a specific job, which to my mind is more sensible – you must bear in mind that there are two kinds: the kind that drives itself along by the turning of its rotor alone, and the kind that pulls itself along with driving wheels while the rotor just churns up the ground behind. The former probably does more work for less power but it works the gardener as well as the garden. Considerable strength is needed to control it. You have to hold it back to get it to dig deep.

The wheel-driven rotary tillers are generally bigger, more expensive machines, but they are far easier to manage; you just walk along behind them and they do all the work themselves. Some of them even have a reverse gear, so that you can back away from a hedge or path. Both kinds can be used with a range of attachments such as hedge clippers and even a circular saw.

"No-digging"

The basic principle of the "no-digging" technique is always to have at least two inches (5 cm) of well-rotted compost on the surface of your soil and to renew it from year to year, and you simply sow your seeds, or plant your plants, in that. That is all there is to it. Some no-diggers have not put a spade in their ground for thirty years and yet every year they get fine, disease-free crops – crops which are consistently much better than crops grown on chemically-fed land.

But no-diggers do use an awful lot of compost. In fact they put so much on their soil that it is

GARDEN TRACTOR
Garden tractors invert the soil using a plow attachment. They are useful in large gardens, say more than half an acre (2000 sq m).

ROTARY TILLER
The rotary tiller, below, drives itself by the action of its tines. Wheel-driven rotary tillers are easier to use, but more expensive.

almost pure compost. All the no-diggers I know bring in organic material, in large quantities, from outside their garden, because no matter what crops they grow they cannot obtain enough organic material from their own gardens to make the necessary compost. One no-digger I know gets tons of swept-up leaves delivered by the local parks department. Another lives next door to a large flower nursery, whose proprietor is only too pleased to dump tons of what he calls "trash" over the fence.

I am not decrying these practices; I think they are marvelous. All gardeners should be constantly on the lookout for organic material and seize it whenever they can. But obviously every gardener in the world cannot do it; and you can be sure that if one plot of land is using this technique it is robbing another plot of land which is either being flogged with chemicals or left unproductive.

COMPOST

It is generally thought that compost is the invention of Sir Albert Howard, who first experimented with making it at Indore, in India, before World War One. But of course compost has existed ever since green plants invaded the land. Any vegetation that falls to the ground and rots "aerobically", meaning that it uses oxygen as part of the rotting process, turns into compost. (Vegetation that rots "anaerobically", or without oxygen, turns into peat and ultimately, under pressure, into coal.) But why then go to the trouble of making compost? Even when you pull weeds out and lay them on the ground they rot and the earthworms pull them down into the soil, making compost. If you dig them in, the same thing happens but underground, and quicker. So why not just dig any vegetation you can find into the soil and let it rot and turn itself into compost?

The reason is that the bacteria which rot vegetable matter (by eating it) use a lot of nitrogen in the process. So when you dig vegetation into the soil the bacteria seize all the nitrates and nitrites that are in the soil and use them to break down the vegetation. Thus they starve the soil of nitrogen to the detriment of the plants. The starvation is only temporary, for when they have finished their job the bacteria die and release the nitrogen again, plus any nitrogen that was held in the vegetation. So you get it all back in the end. But you have to wait for it.

A far better method is to put all surplus vegetation through a compost heap. Here you supply the nitrogen required yourself (if you have it, or can get it) so that the putrefying bacteria get to work quickly to break down all the organic matter and — this is an important factor — generate a lot of heat. The compost heap should reach a temperature of at least 150°F (66°C). In fact many a compost fanatic will take the temperature of his compost heap as a doctor might take the temperature of his patient. The heat in the compost heap is crucial: first, it kills most weed seeds and disease spores; second, it causes actual changes in organic matter and these are beneficial.

But what happened before Sir Albert Howard's invention? Well, farmers of course have made compost since the year dot. They throw straw into the yard, and then let their cattle or pigs or poultry do the work. The animals produce vast amounts of dung and urine which they tread into the straw. At that point, when the muck becomes consolidated, and therefore anaerobic, it may not rot down completely in the yard, so the farmer hauls it out and makes a "mixen" of it, which is farmers' language for a dung-heap. This process aerates the muck thoroughly and it turns into compost, which is exactly what Sir Albert achieved with his heaps of vegetable matter at Indore. It was this muck which was the basis of good farming before the invention of artificial manures. In fact it enabled farmers of the early nineteenth century to grow more wheat per acre than is grown as a national average even now, despite huge applications of power-derived fixed nitrogen.

But, the gardener hasn't got an animal yard, so if he wants to garden without large amounts of bought nitrogen he must make compost. Plants grown in compost-rich soil grow tough and strong, and very resistant to most diseases and pests. Applied inorganic nitrogen on the other hand, makes rapid and sappy growth which has no resistance to disease. Moreover, compost will keep the soil healthy.

Making compost

There are as many methods of making compost as there are rabid compost enthusiasts. Sir Albert Howard, for example, made a six inch (15 cm) layer of green matter, then a two inch (5 cm) layer of dung or manure, then a layer of earth, ground limestone and phosphate rock, then another layer of green material, and so on to the top. He found that the optimum size of heap — which he didn't enclose in a bin of any sort — was ten feet (3 m) wide and five feet (1.5 m) high.

Another method, invented by Dr Shewell-Cooper, who has also spent many years experimenting with compost, is to use a wooden bin, inside which the first layer of vegetation is laid directly on the earth so the worms can get into it easily. Alternate layers of vegetation and nitrogenous substances—dung, manure and so on—are then added and eventually the whole pile is covered with a piece of old carpet. This method makes magnificent compost. If you use a black plastic sheet instead of carpet, you will get good compost very quickly. You must, however, keep the heap well watered under the plastic, because the bacteria and other organisms need plenty of moisture.

If you don't have a bin, and can afford the time and effort, it's a good idea to turn the compost. After the heap has got to its hottest and then started to cool down, turn it, putting the top and outsides in and the insides out. Sprinkle water on as you do this. The water and the aeration speed up decomposition and raise the temperature again. My own recommendation is that you use compost

The Essentials of Good Gardening

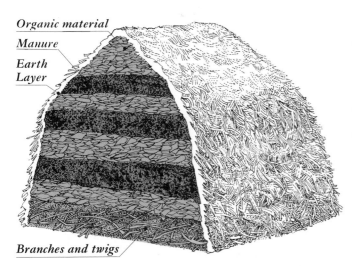

Organic material
Manure
Earth
Layer

Branches and twigs

BUILDING A COMPOST HEAP
So that your heap receives air from underneath, begin with a layer of branches and twigs several inches deep. If you have any unrotted organic matter on another heap, use this to cover your base layer. On top of this lay all your waste vegetation and all your other waste organic material which will rot down easily — such things as newspapers, wood shavings, egg shells, fish heads and so on. When this layer is nine inches to a foot (23-30 cm) high, cover it with a thin layer of manure, or, if you don't have manure, sprinkle on some highly concentrated nitrogenous substance, such as fish meal or blood meal. On top of this build another layer of organic matter; then another layer of manure or high nitrogen, and so on until the heap is about six feet (1.8 m) high. Keep the sides fairly straight to begin with, then let them taper inwards to form a peak at the top. If there is no rain, sprinkle water on each layer to keep the heap moist. Tread the heap or thump it with a spade every evening. When the whole heap is built, cover it with a layer of earth.

COMPOST BINS
Compost bins are both convenient and effective. The very best thing is to have three bins, although for a small or medium-sized garden two will be quite adequate, and one is well worth having. Fill one bin at a time, so that you always have one containing mature compost. Bins should be about five feet (1.5 m) square and five feet deep, made of seasoned wood, brick, stone or concrete, set in bare earth. The fronts should be removable, and there should be gaps in the sides for ventilation. When a bin is full, cover it with earth, carpet or black plastic.

COMPOST IN CONTAINERS
You can make compost in containers such as perforated oil drums or small wire cages. The ratio of surface area to volume is not ideal in small containers, but the compost is certainly worth having nonetheless.

Wire cage

Brick compost bin

Oil drum

bins, three if possible, about five feet (1.5 m) square and five feet (1.5 m) deep. It doesn't really matter whether the bins are made of wood, brick, stone or concrete, provided they are well-ventilated (though not too well-ventilated or they won't retain heat). If you have wooden bins, use wood treated with wood preservative; otherwise they will rot down along with the compost. And it's a good idea to make them so you can take out the front planks for easy access. If you fill one bin at a time, you should always have one that is ready for digging in, or spreading on your vegetable beds. In a very small garden you could use an oil drum punched with ventilation holes.

Fill the bins with a layer of any vegetable matter, say, six inches (15 cm) to a foot (30 cm) deep, then either a sprinkling of high nitrogen matter, or a two inch (5 cm) layer of animal (or even human) manure. Go on building in this way till the heap is complete. Water the material if it is very dry as you put it in. Don't bother to add lime, but throw in a few spadefuls of earth from time to time when you are building since this will introduce worms and bacteria.

If you haven't got manure and have to buy high nitrogen material, then fish meal, blood meal or seaweed meal all do the job. As a last resort, use artificial nitrogenous fertilizer – though I've personally never yet come to that. Finally, when the bin is complete, cover with a layer of earth, a piece of old carpet or a sheet of black plastic and let alone for a while.

If you just can't get round to building a bin, or if your existing bins are full, then make a free-standing heap. Lay any branches and twigs you can find on the ground to a depth of, say, nine inches (23 cm). If you have it, dump any old but unrotted compost material from another heap on this, then lay organic matter on this, day after day, up to about a foot (30 cm) high. At this point, put on a sprinkling of highly concentrated nitrogenous material such as fish meal, or a two inch (5 cm) layer of manure if you have it. Continue building like this as more organic matter becomes available. Keep the sides of the heap quite straight at first and tread it nightly. Water each layer if it is dry. When you've got as much as you want, encase the heap in earth or cover it with old carpets.

GREEN MANURE

The point of green manuring is to increase soil fertility by growing a crop for the express purpose of working or tilling it into the ground. Alternatively, the crop can simply be cut or pulled and left as a mulch, where it will rot and be taken down by the worms. A less direct form of green manuring is to grow a crop which is then left to rot on the compost heap.

In any normal rotation, a good deal of land will be left bare in the winter and nutriments in the soil will constantly be carried away by rain, or nitrogen will be given off into the air in the form of ammonia gas. But if a green manure crop is growing on the soil – even just a crop of weeds – fixed nitrogen is immediately taken up and held in organic form so that it is lost neither through rain nor to the atmosphere. Subsequently, the nitrogen is released for use by the following crop after the green manure crop or weed cover has rotted down. And an added benefit of keeping the land covered with a crop is that the crop will provide resistance to erosion by rain or wind.

It is unfortunate that the best crops for green manuring, the legumes (which fix nitrogen in their root nodules), tend not to grow well through cold winters. It is best to use crops which produce lush green plants which will rot quickly. If possible dig them into the ground when the plants are still young, preferably before they flower.

Of the common green manure crops, the following have specific values.

Mustard

This is much grown by gardeners in cool climates because it grows very quickly and thus does not use the ground too long. Mustard grows a good bulk. It seems likely that it suppresses eel worms which are bad for potatoes.

Tagetes minuta

Although it is a bit too tough for direct green manuring, *Tagetes minuta* makes a fine bulk of composting material. It is particularly effective against eel worm, and it will also suppress couch grass, ground elder, and other perennial weeds. It is best to start the crop off indoors, and then plant out a foot (30 cm) apart in the spring.

Comfrey

Since it is perennial, comfrey is not a true green manure, but it is a compost plant. It sends its roots down deep into the subsoil, bringing up all sorts of nutrients. In good conditions, it will grow an enormous amount of leaf in one year which will dry down to make one tenth of the weight of good compost. It is worth growing a patch of it so that you can cut the leaves every year, and either put them on the compost heap or bury them green under your potatoes. Comfrey can also be used to make "comfrey tea" for feeding tomatoes (see p. 103).

Winter legumes

Winter vetch can be sown in late summer, after you have harvested the summer crops, and will grow until well into the winter and stand, if it is not too cold, until the spring when they can be dug in. Like all legumes, vetch is valuable because it creates fixed nitrogen.

Other legumes which will withstand mild winters are: rough pea, sour clover, Persian clover, fenugreek, crimson clover, bur clover, Austrian winter pea.

Summer legumes

Summer legumes are useful if you have a large garden, some of which you want to leave fallow through the summer. There is a wide variety of summer legumes, including sweet clover and lespedeza, both of which are much used (the latter particularly in the south); red clover, particularly good for a cool temperate climate; crotalaria, which is good for poor sandy soil in southern climates; and cowpea, which grows almost anywhere in the summer. Annual lupines are best sown in a seed bed and planted out in the early summer a foot (30 cm) apart. Alsike clover is a biennial and should be dug in during the first autumn. Alfalfa, or lucerne, is a splendid crop which can put its roots down 40 feet (12 m). This means that it can really break up and aerate the soil, as well as bringing up nutrients from the subsoil to the surface. On a garden scale you should dig it in long before it reaches maturity.

The choice of green manure crops will probably seem bewildering. What I would recommend, if you have enough land to let some lie under green manure during the summer, is red clover. For a winter green manure I would recommend a mixture of rye, which grows well in winter, with vetch. Indeed a mixture of rye and vetch is good anywhere for land left fallow in the winter, since it increases soil fertility.

With the exception of *Tagetes minuta* and annual lupines, whose sowing directions I have already mentioned, green manure crops should be established simply by broadcasting seed sparsely on a prepared bed and then raking it in.

FERTILIZERS

In the nineteenth century, Justus von Liebig, a German chemist, made the discovery that plant growth depends on the presence of three main elements: nitrogen, phosphorus and potassium. The discovery, however, had little immediate effect on crop husbandry at a time when farmers and gardeners had the convenience of easily available horse manure, which contains all three elements. But when motor transport replaced the horse, things changed dramatically – and, from the gardener's point of view, detrimentally. For today, the legacy of von Liebig's discovery is the utterly simplistic view that all you need do is to dose your plants with chemical fertilizers containing nitrogen, phosphorus and potassium. The result of this has been that, although chemically-fertilized crops do grow lush, their quality tends to deteriorate and they begin over the years to lack resistance to pests and diseases. So the chemists cope with this new problem by inventing all sorts of pesticides, fungicides and bacteriacides. But of course they have to go on inventing them, because the pests and diseases quickly develop immunity to the poisons.

The good organic gardener doesn't need chemical fertilizers. I never use them, and my gardens produce extremely high yields of good quality crops and vegetables. As a growing number of gardeners are coming to realize, there are much better organic methods of ensuring your land has the right amount of nitrogen, phosphorus and potassium as well as the minor, or "trace" elements.

Nitrogen

Of the three major elements, nitrogen has a more dramatic effect on crop yields than the others. But before plants can use it, it has to be fixed, not free (as it is in the atmosphere). Nitrogen can be fixed chemically in a nitrate but there are four things wrong with this. First, it is a very expensive process since it requires an enormous expenditure of power, and the price of nitrogen goes up every time there is a rise in the price of oil. Second, chemically-fixed nitrogen causes too lush a growth and greatly weakens the resistance of plants to pests, diseases and winter frosts. Third, it has been conclusively proved that excessive use of chemically-fixed nitrogen lowers the quality of plants as it increases the yield. Finally, and this is the most important point, nitrogen is already being fixed constantly from the air in organic soils by nitrogen-fixing bacteria. If you add chemically fixed nitrogen you do these bacteria out of a job and they fade away. So you destroy the soil's capacity to fix its own nitrogen and, instead of getting it free, have to pay for it.

Thus, I would advise the gardener to apply nitrogen only in bulky organic form: as manure; as compost; as leguminous green manure; or as the residue of leguminous plants (which fix their own nitrogen) from the compost heap (where it is legitimate to use high-nitrogen matter, such as fish meal or blood meal, to activate the heap and so release the plant foods in the composting material).

You can apply nitrogen in concentrated organic form such as fish meal, blood meal, seaweed meal, dried sewage sludge or chicken manure, but do this only as an emergency measure as a tonic for a crop that desperately needs it. I am thinking here principally of *brassica* plants that have been hit by cabbage root fly and need something to get them over the bad period before they put out more roots and get a grip on life again.

The amount of fertilizer needed to correct nitrogen deficiency isn't critical. If you use cow manure, I would suggest about one pound (0.5 kg) per square foot (900 sq cm). Half this amount of poultry manure would be right; and with dried poultry manure, say, a fifth of the amount. These dressings will also improve the phosphorus and potassium content of your soil.

Phosphorus

If your soil is deficient in phosphorus, then, again, you could use a quick-acting chemical additive like superphosphate. But the organic gardener will use simple cow manure, which contains five pounds (2.3 kg) of phosphoric acid per ton. If you cannot get hold of enough cow manure, and a test shows that your garden is deficient in phosphorus, use ground rock phosphate – which may act slowly but goes on acting over many years – bone meal, dried blood, sewage sludge or cottonseed meal. (The firms which supply these phosphate additives have to provide an analysis with them, so you'll be able to compare how much phosphorus you get for your money.) And remember that phosphate-rich organic additives have other organic side benefits. Incidentally, if you live near a steel industry center, basic slag is an excellent phosphatic mixture.

If you need to correct a phosphate deficiency in your soil, don't worry about putting too much phosphate-rich dressing on: it won't harm the plants, and it will go on doing good for many years. I would suggest about three pounds (1.4 kg) per hundred square feet (9.3 sq m).

Potassium

The third element of the trio is potassium or potash, which is specially necessary for root crops, though it improves the quality and stamina of all plants. Potassium is present in most soils, and clay usually has an adequate amount, but if you find you have a potassium deficiency then you can correct this without resorting to expensively-mined potash. Wood ash is specially rich in potassium, but farmyard manure or good compost has it as well as the other vital elements. Greensand, greensand marl and granite dust are excellent sources of potassium and are readily available. As with phosphatic fertilizer, three pounds (1.4 kg) of dressing per hundred square feet (9.3 sq m) is about right.

Trace elements

In addition to nitrogen, phosphorus and potassium, you may find your soil is deficient in what are called "trace elements": that is, elements which are essential in soil, though present only in minute quantities. These include magnesium, zinc, sulfur, manganese, molybdenum and boron.

A well-composted soil is unlikely to be deficient in any of the trace elements, and, in general, a good dose of animal manure, sewage sludge, or seaweed compost should cure any symptoms of deficiency. But there are specific remedies for the lack of one or another of the trace elements. For magnesium deficiency, for instance, use epsom salts: one ounce (28 g) dissolved in 1.2 gallons (4.5 l) of water per square yard (0.8 sq m). For sulfur deficiency, use sulfate of ammonia. For manganese deficiency, spray one ounce (28 g) of manganese sulfate dissolved in five pints (3 l) of water over 30 square yards. For molybdenum deficiency, use a few ounces of sodium molybdate per acre. For boron deficiency, use one ounce (28 g) of borax dissolved in 2.4 gallons (9 l) of water over 20 square yards (17 sq m).

Soil testing

There are a number of soil-testing "kits" on the market which will adequately show up any deficiencies in nitrogen, phosphorus, potassium and the trace elements. But many of them only give you the amount of inorganic fertilizer which the makers consider you should add to correct the deficiency. Otherwise, consult your County Agent, or write to your State Extension Service. But probably the simplest way is to check your plants for symptoms of element deficiencies (see following table).

Symptoms of soil deficiency

Symptom	Element deficiency
Leaves appear chlorotic (pale green or yellow color); older leaves turn yellow at the tips; leaf margins remain green but yellowing occurs down the midribs.	Nitrogen
Plants are stunted and dark green in color; older leaves develop a purple hue.	Phosphorus
Unnatural shortening of plant internodes (areas of stem between the nodes, or swellings in the case of grasses and sweet corn); leaf tips turn yellow and appear scorched.	Potassium
Older leaves turn yellow and then develop whitish stripes between the leaf veins.	Magnesium
New leaves develop whitish areas at the base on each side of the midrib; internodes appear shortened.	Zinc
Plants develop general chlorosis of the leaves	Sulfur
Mottled effect on new leaves; in apples, a spotty chlorosis appears between the lateral leaf veins, and the chlorotic areas die, leaving holes.	Manganese
Brassica plants particularly show cupping, an inward curling of the leaves, and the leaf tips become wrinkled.	Molybdenum
Root crops, especially turnips and rutabagas, turn gray and mushy at their centers.	Boron

Lime

There is one more important element in soil — calcium, or, in gardening terms, lime. Lime is, in a way, the key element, because if the lime content of your soil is not right then this is likely to affect the other elements.

Soil varies considerably in what chemists call its pH value, from extreme acidity to extreme alkalinity (see the table overleaf giving the range of soil pH values). And it is within this range that you may need to add — or withhold — lime in order to get the proper balance for plant growth.

The specific action of lime is to neutralize soil acidity. But as well as this, it has a number of beneficial effects. For instance, lime improves the structure of clay soils by causing the minute soil particles to "flocculate", or stick together in crumbs, so that the soil becomes softer and easier to work. (Clay is generally acid, and this gives rise to deflocculation, where the soil becomes hard and impervious to water and air.)

Lime will also reduce the action of denitrifying bacteria, and thus save loss of nitrogen from the soil. It also releases phosphorus and potassium which get locked up in acid soils. Where there is an excess of some of the trace elements, especially manganese, lime renders them insoluble, so they can't do the plants any harm. Finally, lime reduces the soil's take-up of strontium 90 — which, with the proliferation of nuclear power stations, may well become a serious problem for gardeners.

But you need to be careful in applying lime, because too much of it is as bad as too little. If you overlime, you may cause deficiencies in some of the other soil elements, particularly phosphorus, manganese, zinc and boron.

What you need to do first is to test your soil for its pH value. Simple pH testing kits can be bought at most gardening shops. And I would recommend fairly regular testing in order to check that the pH value is kept constant.

If you find you need to add lime to neutralize acidity (the optimum level is between pH 6.5 and 7), then you can get it in various forms. I prefer ground limestone (dolomitic limestone is best if you can get it), but slaked lime (limestone which has been burnt and then slaked with water) is also commonly used. Chalk, too, is simply a soft limestone, and sea sand from certain coastal areas is rich in lime, which it gets from the shells of molluscs. As a rule, it is just a matter of getting what is easily available, and lime isn't an expensive item. If you are really stuck, you could buy lime used for whitewash from a do-it-yourself store.

TESTING SOIL FOR pH
The simplest soil testing kits consist of two test tubes, a bottle of solution and a colored chart. **1** *Fill one test tube a quarter full of soil.* **2** *Fill the other tube half full of solution.* **3** *Pour the solution into the tube with the soil in it.* **4** *Cork it up and shake it.* **5** *Allow the soil to settle, and compare the color in the tube with the colors on the chart.*

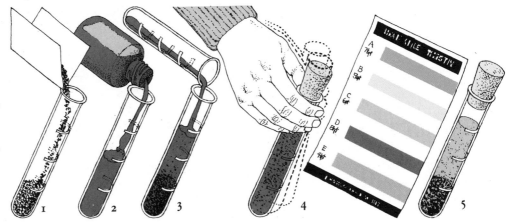

How much lime you need to dress your soil with depends on the soil's pH value, and on what you want to grow. Five pounds (2.3 kg) of lime spread over a hundred square feet (9.3 sq m) will increase the pH value by 75 percent. If your soil is very acid, I would advise using this amount about every five years. Otherwise, if your soil has a pH value of, say, 5, and you want to neutralize it at 7, then dress it with two pounds (0.9 kg) of lime per hundred square feet (9.3 sq m). However much you need, avoid liming the soil at the same time as you add manure. It is best to leave a six-month gap. Generally, I apply lime before planting crops which particularly need it—the legumes, for instance.

Range of soil pH values

pH value	Level of acidity and typical location	Typical plants
3.5-4	Extremely acid. Rare but it occasionally occurs in forest humus areas of the north-eastern states	None
4-4.5	Still extremely acid. In humid forest areas, or sometimes where there is wet, peaty soil	None
4.5-5	Acid. Mainly in cold damp areas	Blueberries, cranberries
5-5.5	Fairly acid. Typical of unlimed soil in very wet climates	Potatoes, tomatoes, raspberries, strawberries, rye
5.5-6	Slightly acid. Moderate climates with high rainfall	Grasses
6-6.5	Neutral. Moderate climates without too much rain	Most garden crops
6.5-7.5	Neutral. Hot, dry climates	Most garden crops, but not potatoes or tomatoes
7.5-8	Extremely alkaline. Semi-desert areas of the western states	None

Routine fertilizing

After you have corrected specific deficiencies in your soil by direct dressing of the ground, I would advise you to add further regular but small amounts of phosphate and potassium fertilizers to your compost heap. Recent research, principally in Russia, has shown that phosphates certainly, and probably potash too, give better results when mixed with compost (or manure) since the acids in the compost help to release the elements. Also, by adding a phosphatic mixture to the compost or manure heap you help to fix nitrogen that would otherwise blow away as nitrogen gas. My suggestion is that you should estimate the area of your garden and add about a quarter of a pound (114 g) each of phosphatic and potassium fertilizers to your compost heap for every hundred square feet (9.3 sq m) of garden. Just buy the appropriate amount of the fertilizers every year, keep them in your garden shed, and sprinkle them into the compost heap as you build it, so that you get an even distribution throughout.

The final point I want to emphasize about fertilizers, though, is that virtually any organic manure will supply all the elements essential to soil (except, perhaps, lime). In fact, animal manures contain a great variety of chemical elements. If you keep livestock of any kind in your garden (animals or birds) you should never have any problem caused by lack of fertilizer. But remember that all organic manures should first go through the compost heap. Even human manure is excellent, so long as it is put into the compost heap and buried under fresh greenstuff or other organic material. The heat of the compost, and the general bacterial activity, will destroy all pathogens, or harmful organisms in the manure long before you dig it into the soil. In my view, it's just a puritan prejudice that you can't use good, honest human manure – and there's no supply problem.

Elements in organic fertilizers (by percentage)

	Nitrogen	Phosphoric Acid	Potash
Bone meal	2-4	22-25	—
Fish meal	7-8	4-8	—
Dried blood	13.0	0.8	—
Hoof and horn	13-14	2.0	—
Fresh seaweed	0.6	0.2	2.0
Bracken (dried)	1.4	0.2	0.1
(green)	2.0	0.2	2.8
Tea leaves	4.2	0.6	0.4
Coffee grounds	2.1	0.3	0.3
Meadow hay	1.5	0.6	2.0
Straw	0.4	0.2	0.8
Compost from old mushroom bed	0.8	0.6	0.7
Wood ash (not rained on)	—	1.5	7.0
Soot	5-11	1.1	0.4
Farmyard manure	0.5	0.1	0.5
Horse manure	0.7	0.3	0.6
Poultry manure	1.5	1.2	0.7
Rabbit manure	2.4	1.4	0.6
Pigeon manure	5.8	2.1	1.8

Propagation

When a gardener is said to have "green fingers", all that's meant is that he has the gift of sympathy for living plants. And where green fingers really show up is in the various propagating processes. Put a tiny seed in concrete-like clay and you'll suffocate it. Try and strike a stem in wet mud and it too will die. Let your seeds and cuttings dry out too much — or keep them too wet and short of air — and you'll undoubtedly kill them. But if you think of your plants as living things, and treat them with the same sympathy you would any living thing, then there is no reason why you should not have a successful garden.

Saving seed

Buying seed is a lot cheaper than buying vegetables of course, but the true self-sufficient gardener will grow most of his own seed himself. If you grow a few more plants than you want for eating, and let the extra ones go to seed, then you'll be able to collect the seed and go on sowing it year after year.

If you are saving your own seed, it's best to "rogue" your plants — in other words, pull out any that aren't true to type (unless of course they're better than type) — and use only the very best ones. It's only because for thousands of years gardeners have planted the best seed that we now have the plants we do instead of the weeds they were originally bred from.

Remember too, that since seed takes a long time to ripen, it's best to give the plants which are growing seed for you a head start by getting them off as early as possible in the year — even if you have to do it under glass. Warm climate plants which are grown in cold climates (pole beans, for instance) have difficulty in ripening their seeds effectively in short summers unless they have help.

Seed of biennials The problem with saving the seeds of biennials is that normally they make growth in their first year and seed in the next. Some of them "bolt" of course — that is, they shoot upwards and seed in their first year — but resist the temptation to gather seed from these. Bolting carrots — like bolting spouses — are no good. Beets, carrots, parsnips, onions, turnips and rutabagas are best lifted in their first autumn, stored where it's cool, and replanted in late winter or early spring, when they will take root again, shoot up and go to seed. Leeks I generally just leave in the ground: they shoot up taller than I am and make gorgeous round flower-heads which then go to seed. You can leave onions out all winter too, but it is safer to store them inside and

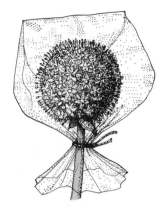

COLLECTING ONION SEED
Onion seed must be collected in the second year of the plant's growth. It is best to lift the onion plants in their first autumn and keep them in pots indoors until spring. When the flowers appear, tie plastic bags round them. The seed will fall into this instead of blowing away in the wind.

plant them out in the spring. Salsify and scorzonera can be allowed to grow on for their second year and then they'll seed.

Brassica seed *Brassica* seed, however, is far better bought; it costs very little anyway. For one thing, all *brassica* plants — together with that noisome weed charlock — can interbreed and so you don't know what the genetic gambler is going to pull out of the bag. For another thing, growing seed from these plants means leaving them in the ground for a very long time where they take up room and are liable to suffer from clubroot.

Tomato seed Tomatoes are easy to save for seed. Label a few fruits on your best (and earliest) greenhouse plants, and let them get fully ripe. Pick them, cut them open and wash the seed out of the pulp. Then lay the washed seed on newspaper in a warm place to dry.

Cucumber seed Cucumbers are more tricky, for you must help them to mate. Take a male flower (the one without a miniature cucumber behind it), cut off its petals so as to expose the stamen, and, with a small paint brush, brush the pollen into the middle of some fully-open female flowers. The female flowers stay fully open and receptive for two or three days, so, to make absolutely sure, brush pollen into them every day that they are like this. When the cucumbers are fully ripened, remove, wash, and dry the seed as with tomatoes.

Squash tribe seed Squashes, pumpkins, melons and other gourds don't always have to be artificially pollinated. I have often just planted the seeds of squash tribe vegetables that I have bought at the supermarket and they have grown satisfactorily. It is safer to buy seeds for these vegetables but if you want to try saving seed, leave the fruits in a warm place and let them get as ripe as possible — even to the point when they begin to rot — before extracting the seed.

Lettuce seed Lettuce is easy, but make sure you select the best specimens to breed from — and that does not mean the earliest ones to form seed-heads. Leave a row of good lettuces for seed, harvesting the smaller ones to eat, then rogue the ones that bolt first. Take your seed from a large and late-flowering plant; watch it pretty carefully, though, to catch the seed before the wind blows it all away. One lettuce plant will very probably keep you in seed for years.

Pelleted seed If you decide to buy seed, it's worth considering pelleted seed. This is simply seed that has been coated with some nutrient substance, so that each individual seed is inside a little pellet of nourishment. This feeds the seed when it is wetted and starts to grow. The pellets make every seed the same size, which means you can sow such seed very easily in a seed drill. But even if you do not use a seed drill, pelleted seed has the advantage that very small seeds can be sprinkled more thinly on the ground (or on sowing compost) than would otherwise be possible. Seed tapes also make it easy to handle seeds and reduce the time spent thinning. However, both are expensive.

Forcing seed indoors

If you want to get out-of-season crops, or grow crops outside their normal climate zones, you'll need to force your seeds indoors. There's nothing wrong with forcing seed in my view: it's fun, you get more to eat and a more interesting diet.

Propagators Seed must be forced in a propagator; the basic idea is to keep the temperature up and constant at about 70°F (21°C) and the humidity at the right level. The simplest form of propagator is just a shallow seed box covered with a sheet of glass with a folded newspaper laid on top. This is quite adequate, but it is better to have a hinged lid (preferably of glass) with some device to keep the temperature up, and a thermometer to check it. You can make one of these yourself, or you can buy propagators of varying degrees of complexity.

To keep your propagator moist, either use a vaporizer for making mist, 'or if you are using an ordinary seed box, lower it into water – about halfway up – for long enough to let the water soak up from below. Using a mist propagator is a good idea anyway, because if you douse tiny seeds you may wash them away.

Tiny seeds must not be buried beneath the seed compost. Sprinkle them sparsely on top and cover them with a layer of finely-sifted sand. Larger seeds should be covered with compost to a depth of about three times their diameter.

As soon as the seedlings begin to show, un-cover the propagator to give the seedlings light,

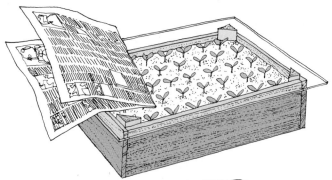

PROPAGATORS
You can make a propagator by filling a seed box with seed compost, covering it over with glass and laying newspaper on top of this. In a warm place this will work well. Alternatively, you can buy ready-made electrically heated propagators, with or without thermostats.

and move it into progressively cooler and drier conditions until they are well grown (this hardens them off for planting outdoors). Don't water the seedlings until they are really well established, and then start sprinkling from above. If you use seed composts that are inert – that is, without nutrients – you should feed the seedlings with manure water (see p. 103).

Pricking out

When the seedlings are established they should be pricked out – that is, replanted with more space between them (use a pointed stick to do this). For vegetables that don't like being transplanted, I would recommend sowing the seed in peat pots rather than directly into the propagator. The peat pots can then be placed in the propagator. Later, when you plant them out, the peat rots down and the expanding roots push through.

Seed and potting composts

Most gardeners buy prepackaged seed and potting composts from the local garden shop, and this is the best thing to do unless you have the time to make your own. When you buy your compost, examine it carefully. It should be light and porous, almost fluffy in texture.

You can make your own composts, starting with the three basic ingredients, loam, peat and sand. You get loam by first cutting sods about four inches (10 cm) thick from a clean, well-drained pasture (try to find one with a medium-clay soil and a pH of 6.5 or less). Water the sods if they are dry, and then, in the early summer, start stacking them grass-side down. Make the stack about five feet (1.5 m) square and five feet high, and, as you build, put in alternate layers of strawy manure, mixed with ground chalk or limestone – you'll need about five pounds (2.5 kg) of one or other of these throughout the stack. When the stack is finished, cover it to keep the rain off, and in about six months the loam will have decomposed. Just cut it up and shred it with a spade. The loam now has to be sterilized, either by steam at a temperature of 212°F (100°C) or in an oven at 170°F (77°C).

The best peat to use is either sphagnum moss peat or sedge peat. (Unless you're near a peat bog, you'll probably have to buy it.) The sand should be coarse and sharp, and it's best to use river sand.

To make seed compost, mix two parts of loam to one part each of peat and sand, and add about two pounds (0.9 kg) of superphosphate per cubic yard (0.7 cu m). To make potting compost, mix seven parts of loam to three parts of peat and two parts of sand. To this you should add either some very well-rotted compost from your compost heap, or alternatively about five pounds (2.3 kg) per cubic yard (0.7 cu m) of a proprietary brand compost additive. A good additive contains two parts by weight of hoof and horn meal to two parts of superphosphate and one part of sulfate of potash.

An excellent potting compost known as the Cornell mix is widely used. To make this you'll need two gallons (9 l) each of vermiculite and shredded peat moss, to which you add two level tablespoons each of superphosphate and ground limestone, and eight heaped tablespoons of steamed bone meal or an equivalent amount of cow manure.

In general, of course, it's quite possible to grow many plants without seed or potting composts at all, although they are definitely a good idea for celery and tomato seeds.

Finally, remember that when you've finished with the seed and potting compost you can put it all into your ground to increase fertility.

Seed-beds and holding-beds

Often you will find that the land in which you want to sow seeds is already occupied by something else, so it may be necessary sometimes to sow first in a seed-bed, and transfer the seedlings later to a larger holding-bed. In fact, provided the plants are eventually planted out with care, most of them actually seem to benefit from transplanting. The idea which has grown up lately that plants should never be moved is, in my view,

nonsense – as anyone who tries it will find out. In an average garden, the seed-bed can be quite small: say about a yard (90 cm) square. A yard row of seedlings is actually a considerable number of plants. Soil for the seed-bed should preferably be light, dry and well drained, with plenty of peat, compost or other organic material worked into it. I would advise raking in finely-rotted compost every year, and liming it lightly every two years to maintain a pH of between 6.5 and 7.

The holding-bed will obviously have to be bigger, since the seedlings you put in should be spaced about six inches (15 cm) apart. In general, treat the soil exactly as for the seed-bed, but here you must watch out for clubroot because your holding-bed will almost certainly contain *brassica*. Regular liming should prevent any build-up of the disease, and I'd also recommend rotating the holding-bed from time to time. There's no need to do this with the seed-bed if you put compost on every year.

Rollers If you're putting *brassica* plants and onions into the seed-bed or holding-bed, then the soil should be firm. A roller is the best solution here, and it saves time. But many gardeners get on perfectly well without one, and your feet are almost as good if you can learn that strange gardeners' dance which might be called the sideways tramping scuffle. Personally I would not put a roller very high on my list of essential gardening tools.

Rakes When you come to sow your seed in the bed, a good rake is indispensable since small seeds

Steel rake

Seed drill

SOWING SEED
Seed sown by hand should be raked in and then the soil should be firmed with the flat of the rake. A seed drill saves a lot of time and effort; it will bury the seed at a pre-set depth.

need to be sown in fine tilth. The best type of rake is a strong steel one which is not too wide. There are cast aluminum rakes on the market which are cheaper, but after an hour of working fairly stony ground they begin to resemble old men's smiles before the invention of false teeth. The rake is in very frequent use in the garden, so don't begrudge investing in a good one.

Sowing seed To sow your seed, first fork over the surface lightly. Deep digging isn't necessary — in fact, keep the topsoil at the top. And only fork the bed over when the soil is dry. Next, rake the soil well, removing any stones, until it is reduced to a fine tilth. And, finally, score lines across the bed with the corner of a hoe before sprinkling seed on sparsely. Remember that small seeds should be sown shallowly: most *brassica* seeds, for example, need only about half an inch (1 cm) of soil or compost over them.

Seed drills You can of course use a seed drill, and in big gardens they do save time and your back. They save you the trouble of making a seed furrow and sprinkling seed from the corner of a packet, or one by one from your fingers; instead a seed drill lets you go along at walking pace simply pushing the drill into the soil where it automatically drops the seed. Don't forget though that you can't actually see the seed going in, so if the drill happens to get bunged up you may find you have embarrassing gaps when the plants come up.

A more sophisticated version of the seed drill is the precision drill, which works on the same principle but drops the seeds one by one at exactly the right distance apart. The advantage here is that you save an awful lot of seed, since otherwise, no matter how carefully you seem to be sowing it, you'll probably sow far too much and end up having to single the plants later. But precision drills are expensive, and many of them only work with pelleted seed anyway, so unless you're working on a market-garden scale I wouldn't advise getting one.

Covering seed When you've got the seeds in the ground, rake the soil again lightly and tamp it down with the back of the rake. You should sow only when the soil is dry enough not to stick to your shoes, but once the seed is in, it should be watered if no rain seems likely. Look out for flea beetles at this stage (see p. 124). A good shower of rain will disperse any which appear, but if they get bad and the weather's dry, dust the bed with derris or pyrethrum. And, above all, suffer no weeds to grow in the bed; any which come up should be pulled out immediately.

Vegetative propagation

It is a good idea to propagate fruit trees and perennial plants, such as soft fruit bushes and many of the herbs, by taking cuttings. In this way you get a mature plant much more quickly than you do from seed.

The principle of striking cuttings is in fact quite simple: cut a piece from an existing plant, put it into the ground, and it will strike new roots into the soil which eventually form a new plant. In fact a cutting from almost any part of a plant will form another plant if it is nurtured in the right environment. The new plant is, of course, produced vegetatively. It will be exactly like its parent plant because there is no sexual crossing — in fact it is the same plant.

Hardwood cuttings Hardwood cuttings are taken from hard sections of the plant or tree's stem or branches. They are generally taken in the fall from the new season's growth, although with some species, such as the fig and the olive, two or three-year-old wood can be used. Some hardwood cuttings should be buried in sand and stored indoors through the winter for planting out in spring. Others can be planted straight out in fall. Broadly this depends on the hardiness of the species. (See the Cultivation of Vegetables, Fruit and Herbs pp. 113-202). The most delicate hardwood cuttings are best planted in a mist propagator (see p. 92) if they are to thrive.

Softwood cuttings Softwood cuttings are cuttings taken from the tips of healthy young branches. Propagating from these is more risky, but it should work well with citrus trees and olives. Take cuttings in the spring and keep in a cold frame until they have rooted.

Both hardwood and softwood cuttings should be struck in moist, sandy ground, or in a special cutting compost made with three parts sand, one part leaf mold and one part loam.

Propagating from clumps To propagate clumping plants such as rhubarb, globe artichokes and shallots you should dig up the clumps and split them into smaller ones which you then plant separately.

Propagating from runners Plants which put out runners — either overground, like strawberries, or underground, like raspberries — can be multiplied by first severing the runner and the new plant that forms at its end from its parent, then digging it up and transplanting it.

Propagating from layers Gooseberries are good examples of the type of plant which can be multiplied by layers. You simply bend a branch over and peg it down to the ground. The branch then sends

The Essentials of Good Gardening

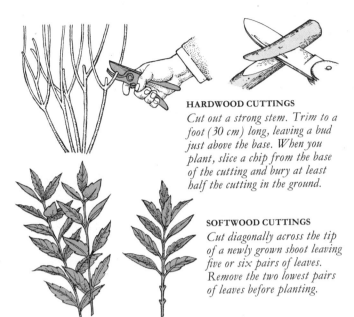

HARDWOOD CUTTINGS
Cut out a strong stem. Trim to a foot (30 cm) long, leaving a bud just above the base. When you plant, slice a chip from the base of the cutting and bury at least half the cutting in the ground.

SOFTWOOD CUTTINGS
Cut diagonally across the tip of a newly grown shoot leaving five or six pairs of leaves. Remove the two lowest pairs of leaves before planting.

DIVIDING A CLUMP
Dig up the clump. Push in two forks back to back, and lever the clump apart between growing points before planting.

PEGGING LAYERS
Bend a branch and peg it to the ground. When it has rooted, cut through the original branch. Lift the new plant and move it to a new site.

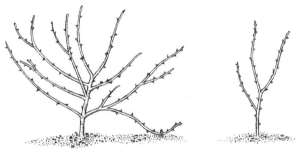

SEVERING RUNNERS
It is easiest to bury a flowerpot under a runner before it roots.

Once it has rooted, cut through the runner, pull up the pot and replant in a new site.

down roots and, when they are well established, the new plant can be separated, lifted and finally transplanted to its permanent position.

Protecting plants

Seedlings and young plants should be protected in the early spring until the weather is warm enough for planting out. There are a number of types of frames, cloches and mini-greenhouses used for this purpose, all made from glass or transparent plastic. But don't forget the humble window sill: a huge number of plants can be brought on in seed boxes placed on the window sill of the average house. Or, of course, you get the same effect by putting the seed boxes on the shelves of a heated greenhouse. However, with both these methods of protecting the plants, you must remember to give the plants a chance to harden off before planting them out. I recommend a period of about two weeks in which you progressively give the plants more air and less heat. It can be fatal to take plants from a warm place and immediately transplant them outside into a cold one.

Cold frames A cold frame is simply a wooden frame with a removable glass lid. It is particularly useful for hardening off your plants. Simply take the seed boxes from where they've been in the warmth and put them into the cold frame. Open the top of your cold frame on warm days and close it up at night.

Hot frames A hot frame is commonly used for forcing garden crops out of season. It is similar to a cold frame except that it contains manure or compost (or both) to raise the temperature. As a

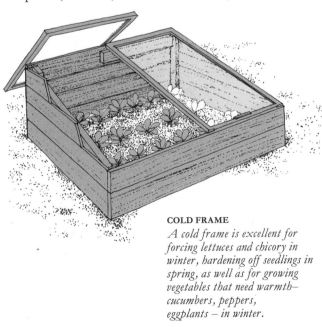

COLD FRAME
A cold frame is excellent for forcing lettuces and chicory in winter, hardening off seedlings in spring, as well as for growing vegetables that need warmth—cucumbers, peppers, eggplants – in winter.

base, I think it's best to use the same compost as for mushrooms (see p. 166). Put this in the frame, and cover it with a layer of six inches (15 cm) of good loam. Make the compost up in the frame rather than outside on a heap so that you get the full benefit of the heat it generates. And after one crop has been taken out, put the spent compost on the garden and mix up another lot for the hot frame.

Hot-beds Nowadays there are plenty of under-soil electrical heating systems designed for forcing on early plants in frames or greenhouses. These of course all cost money and energy, both to install and to maintain. The true self-sufficient gardener will be more interested in practicing the good old-fashioned hot-bed system of the old gardeners. It may seem a lot of work – and a lot of manure – but it is pleasant work and it gives you an appetite to eat what you grow by it. It is basically a more elaborate and more effective version of a hot frame.

HOT-BED

A hot-bed is a pit filled with manure covered by a frame.

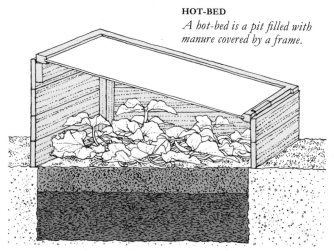

Dig a pit 18 inches (45 cm) deep, either in your greenhouse or where you intend to build a frame outside. Seven days before you want to plant in it, fill the pit with a mixture of one part by volume of loam to two parts of fresh horse manure. Moisten this and tread it down. After three days turn it and, if it's dry, moisten it again. After four days "case" it: that is, add six inches (15 cm) of good rich soil. Meanwhile, if your pit is outdoors, erect a frame over it. If it is in your greenhouse, of course you don't need to bother.

When you plant or sow in the bed in spring it will provide a moderate and steady heat for as long as it takes to force your plants to maturity a month early. During the summer, you can get a good crop of tomatoes as a second crop, and after that winter lettuces, before you dig out the manure mixture and put it on the garden to increase fertility.

Cloches Cloches are used to bring on plants up to three weeks early in the spring, and I suggest you also use them all the year round on delicate or out-of-season plants, because in this way you will derive the most benefit from them.

A good sequence in my view is to have lettuces under your cloches in the winter, early potatoes in the early spring, tomatoes, eggplants and melons in the late spring, eggplants and cucumbers in the summer, and tomatoes again in the fall (take the tomatoes off their stakes and lay them flat on beds of straw under the cloches).

Cloches are made either from glass or transparent plastic. Personally I prefer plastic ones since I constantly break the glass ones, and of course they are much cheaper. You can get them made from either hard or soft plastic. In my view the soft plastic tunnels are the best. They are available at garden suppliers, together with wire supports,

GLASS OR PLASTIC CLOCHES?
Glass cloches last a good deal longer than soft plastic ones and are a lot more stable. They also retain more heat at night. But plastic cloches are much cheaper and lighter than glass, and they are also unbreakable.

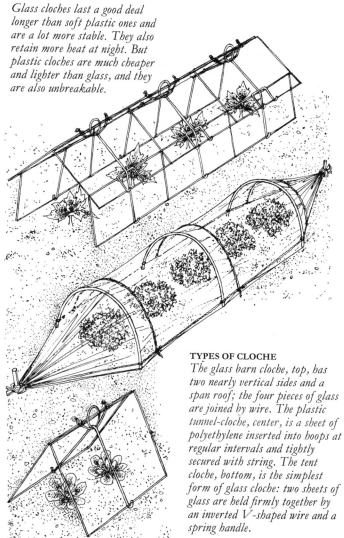

TYPES OF CLOCHE
The glass barn cloche, top, has two nearly vertical sides and a span roof; the four pieces of glass are joined by wire. The plastic tunnel-cloche, center, is a sheet of polyethylene inserted into hoops at regular intervals and tightly secured with string. The tent cloche, bottom, is the simplest form of glass cloche: two sheets of glass are held firmly together by an inverted V-shaped wire and a spring handle.

though you can use willow wands pushed into the ground at one end and then bent over. Plastic tunnels are simple to erect and fold away easily for storage.

Mini-greenhouses The trouble with cloches is the difficulty of moving them for weeding, watering (although you can lay a trickle-pipe under them), keeping pests at bay and harvesting, so I'm very much in favor of a simple new idea, the mini-greenhouse. This can easily be tilted and propped up with sticks, or removed altogether. Instructions for building a mini-greenhouse are on p. 111.

Other forms of protection You can use inverted jam jars as mini mini-greenhouses until your seedlings get too big (but remember to allow a period for the seedlings to harden off). Transparent plastic bags inverted over bent wire coat-hangers or twigs can also serve the purpose. I've managed to get new potatoes earlier than anyone else

amber-colored and give each plant about a pint (0.6 l) of the solution immediately after transplanting; the result can only be beneficial.

Intercropping

To get the heaviest cropping from your garden, it is a good idea to practice intercropping when sowing and planting. As a rule, a small garden should be cropped as heavily as possible, though of course you must avoid crowding plants — a vegetable slum is very unhealthy. While there are several different possibilities for intercropping, I would particularly suggest the following.

Broad beans can be sown with cabbages. Space the cabbages a little further apart than normal — say, 18 inches (45 cm) apart with about two feet (60 cm) between rows — and dib broad bean seeds into the row between the cabbages. The tall beans don't seem to interfere with the squat cabbages.

JAM JARS

Use inverted jam jars to give your seedlings some protection during the period when you are hardening them off.

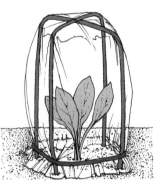

PLASTIC BAGS

A plastic bag inverted over a bent wire coat-hanger will do the same job as a jam jar, even if it does not look as neat.

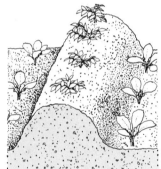

INTERCROPPING BETWEEN EARTHED-UP ROWS

After planting celery, you will have time to sow, grow and harvest lettuces along the ridges on each side of the celery trench before it is time to hill up the celery, left. In the same way, plant baby cabbages between rows of hilled-up main crop potatoes, right.

simply by laying a transparent plastic sheet over part of the potato bed. When the plants begin to grow, take off the sheet during the day and replace it at night. Keep putting the sheet on at night until all danger of frost is over. When the plants reach a height of six inches (15 cm), support the sheet on boxes or flowerpots.

Starter solutions

Plants may well suffer "shock" during transplanting. So it's a good idea to give them a tonic, called a "starter solution", each time you transplant.

A good starter solution can be made by quarter-filling a barrel or drum with farmyard manure (halve the quantity if you're using chicken manure), and filling it up with water. Stir it well and let it soak for two or three days. When you're ready to use it, dilute it with water until it's

Winter *brassica* such as Brussels sprouts, broccoli or kale can be planted between the rows of main crop potatoes. Space the potato rows six inches (15 cm) further apart than you usually would. When the potatoes are ready, be sure to lift them with special care so as not to loosen the soil under the *brassica* plants, and then ridge up the soil against the *brassica*. Don't plant the *brassica* until the potatoes have already been ridged up.

Lettuces can be sown or planted along the ridges thrown up on each side of the celery trench after the celery has been planted. The lettuces will have been removed and eaten before you have to earth up the celery.

Pumpkin and melon seeds can be sown in with sweet corn. The crops seem to suit each other very well, and I've always got heavy yields by intercropping them.

Planting a tree

As with all transplanting, putting a tree in demands your sympathy for the young sapling's needs. It is quite a complicated process, and awkward if you try to do it alone, so it is a good idea to get a friend to help.

First, dig a hole at least twice as big as the root ball of the tree you want to plant. It's often suggested that you do this a few days before the tree is to go in, but I think this is a mistake: the surface soil in the hole is liable to harden into a pan. And remember when you dig, to put the topsoil in one pile and the subsoil in another. Put a layer of stones in the bottom of the hole to help with drainage. It is also a good idea to bury dead animals under newly planted trees. They provide the sapling with calcium and other useful elements released as it decomposes. Shovel some manure into the middle of the hole and cover it with a mound of topsoil. Now spread the roots of the tree over the mound, cutting off any damaged ones. (In fact, a little root pruning is a good idea since it encourages the tree to put out new fibrous roots.) At this point you should drive a stout stake into the hole to support the tree. Get your friend to hold the tree upright as you do this.

Check that the tree is in at the proper depth: that is, the union between the scion and the root stock – the bulge or deformation at the bottom of the trunk – should be about six inches (15 cm) above the soil. In very dry climates, plant your tree six inches (15 cm) deeper. If the tree is too high, you'll have to make the hole deeper; if it's too low, increase the size of your mound of topsoil in the hole.

With your friend still holding the tree upright, replace the topsoil around the roots. (I recommend mixing the soil with compost in a ratio of three parts soil to one part compost.) Press the soil down firmly – but not so firmly that you tear

PLANTING A TREE

1 *Dig a hole twice as big as the root ball of the tree to be planted. Put the topsoil in one pile, the subsoil in another.*

2 *Put a layer of stones in the bottom of the hole to help with drainage.*

3 *Spread the roots over a mound of manure and topsoil. Drive a stake in between the roots to support the tree, left. Check that the tree is at the proper depth by laying a plank across the hole and seeing where it touches the trunk.*

4 *Replace the topsoil, pressing it down gently but firmly. Then give the whole area a really good soaking.*

5 *Mulch the tree with eight inches (20 cm) of organic matter, but don't let the mulch quite touch the trunk.*

6 *Tie the tree to the stake with a stocking, or else you can use an adjustable strap.*

the delicate root hairs – and make sure you leave no gaps. Try to arrange it so that the roots lie as they naturally want to. As you go on filling the hole, gently tread on the top of the soil to firm it around the roots.

Don't quite fill the hole; leave a depression in which water can stand, and then give it a really thorough soaking. Next, mulch the tree with about eight inches (20 cm) of organic matter such as old hay or straw, leaf-mold, manure or compost, without letting the mulch touch the trunk.

Once you've planted the tree, tie it to the stake, but be careful about this. Don't ever use thin hard string which will cut into the bark as the tree waves about. The best thing I've found for tying is an old stocking, but you can use webbing or leather collars, or wide ribbons plaited from sisal bailer twine. And watch the tree as it grows to make sure that it is not strangled.

Grafting

The purpose of grafting is to get a fruiting spur, or scion, of one tree to grow on to the root stock of another by bringing the cambium layers of each into contact with one another. (The cambium layer, which is the growing part of a tree, is the whitish area just under the bark.)

Most trees that are grown for their fruit are grafted, because the varieties that bear the best fruit are rarely the most hardy or vigorous varieties. Scions are therefore chosen principally for their fruit-bearing qualities, while root stocks are chosen for their strength and their tendency to produce a tree of a given size – dwarf, semi-dwarf, half-standard, standard and so on.

Since grafting is a non-sexual way of propagating plants, you must make sure that the scion is compatible with the root stock. Compatible pairings for different fruit trees are discussed in the Cultivation of Fruit chapter (pp. 167-190).

Grafting is an extremely old art, and several methods are now practiced. In my view the three most important are whip grafting, budding and cleft grafting. Whip grafting and budding are both methods of joining one-year-old scions to root stocks which have been planted out the previous year. In my experience both methods work very well and there is little or nothing to choose between them.

Cleft grafting is a way of resuscitating an old or sick tree. All the main branches should be sawn off to within a foot (30 cm) of where they join the trunk. A cleft graft should then be made in the end of each sawn-off branch.

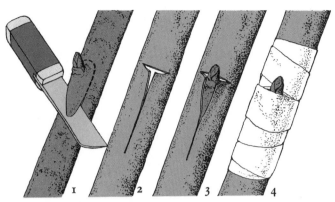

BUDDING

1 Take the scion from the current season's growth, and cut out a shield-shaped chip containing one bud. 2 Cut the root stock off a foot (30 cm) above where the bud is to go. Make a T-shaped slit an eighth of an inch (0.5 cm) deep. 3 Peel back the flaps of the slit and insert the chip. 4 Bind the joint tightly with plastic tape, leaving the bud itself exposed.

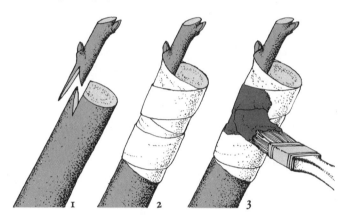

WHIP GRAFTING

Do this in early spring, using a length of dormant one-year-old scion with four buds on it. Cut the root stock, planted the previous year, to within four inches (10 cm) of the ground. 1 Cut a notch in the top and a matching one at the base of the scion; fit the scion on to the root stock. 2 Bind the joint with either raffia or plastic tape. 3 Cover this and any other cut surfaces with grafting wax.

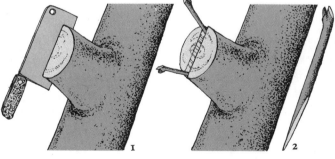

CLEFT GRAFTING

Saw through all the main branches a foot (30 cm) from where they join the trunk. 1 Take a sharp cleaver and use it on one of the sawn-off stumps. Cut two scions to a chisel shape at one end. 2 Force open the cleft and insert the two scions into this, lining up the cambium layer of scion and old wood. Let the cleft close up, thus clenching the scions into place. Pour hot wax all over to protect cut surfaces.

Care while Growing

Pruning trees

There are three basic reasons for pruning trees: first, to remove damaged, diseased and awkwardly placed branches; second, to shape the tree, for convenience of cultivation; and third to increase the crop and improve its quality.

Pruning unwanted wood In the first case, the general principles are to cut out any dead or unhealthy branches, and any which are overcrowded. You should also cut out any branches which point in toward the middle of the tree, and all suckers – the long, straight, vigorous shoots which will never bear any fruit. This heavy pruning should be done in late winter – though never when the temperature is lower than 20°F (−7°C). Make sure you cut out branches flush at the joints, and paint the wounds with one of the proprietary tree paints, or with any oil-based paint.

Pruning for shape Pruning and training for shape should for the most part also be done in the late winter, and it is important to establish the general shape, or "scaffold", when the tree is still young. The scaffold is formed by the leaders, or main branches which spring from the trunk (sub-branches which grow from the leaders are called the laterals). It's best to keep the number of leaders which form the scaffold to a minimum.

How you prune will depend on the general shape you want. For example, if you want a branch to spread from the middle of the tree, cut it down to an outward-pointing bud. If you want to prevent the tree from spreading, cut it down to an upward-pointing bud and try to gather the tree together. In each case, it's important to cut to a quarter of an inch (1 cm) above the bud.

Until recently, experts have advocated the open-centered cup or goblet scaffold, where the spreading branches allow light to get to the middle of the tree. But, along with an increasing number of growers, I favor the basic "Christmas tree" shaped scaffold, called a pyramid or spindle. The reason for this is that the short branches of the pyramid shape are less likely to break if they have to carry a great weight of fruit, or of snow and ice, than the spreading branches of the goblet shape.

There are, however, several specific shapes which have advantages in certain circumstances. In small gardens where space is at a premium, I recommend shapes such as the dwarf pyramid, half-standard and bush, or, if you can grow against a wall or fence, the espalier, fan and cordon. Dwarf trees fruit earlier, but don't live as long as full-size ones, and they should be pruned very carefully. A dwarf pyramid must be cut back each spring so that it is no higher than you can reach. In late summer each year, shorten all branch leaders to six inches (15 cm), cutting to outward-pointing buds, and shorten laterals arising from the leaders to three inches (8 cm). Any shoots emerging from what is left of the laterals should be shortened to one inch (2½ cm). Do this pruning in the first week of August. In large gardens and orchards, full-size stock is better and less complicated to cultivate.

PRUNING TOOLS
A pruning saw cuts through thick branches and tapers to a narrow end that will reach awkward places. For small branches use a pruner instead.

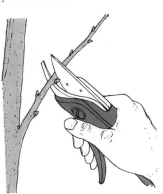

PRUNING TO A BUD
When you are pruning to a bud, for whatever reason, always cut to a quarter of an inch (1 cm) above the bud.

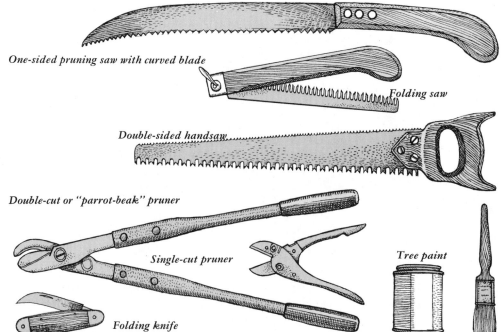

One-sided pruning saw with curved blade

Folding saw

Double-sided handsaw

Double-cut or "parrot-beak" pruner

Single-cut pruner

Tree paint

Folding knife

In general, winter pruning has the effect of encouraging tree growth. If a tree is growing weakly, then heavy pruning is advisable — as much as half the tree may well be pruned away. But cut very little off if a tree is growing vigorously, because you are liable to make it get straggly.

Pruning to encourage fruiting Summer pruning has the opposite effect from winter pruning: that is, it inhibits tree growth by encouraging the fruit spurs to develop rather than the lateral branches. Trimming back the new season's growth helps the tree to fruit more heavily and earlier. If the fruit spurs are overcrowded, you should thin them out to allow the fruits to flourish. With summer pruning, never cut into old wood, and remember if you're cutting back to a bud to cut to a quarter of an inch (1 cm) above the bud.

Pruning tip-bearers Certain varieties of apple and pear trees bear fruit at the tips of their branches. Prune these very little; just cut out surplus branches. If you tip the leaders and the laterals, the tree will cease to bear fruit altogether.

TREE SHAPES

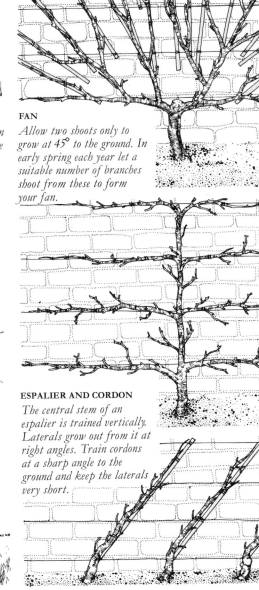

PYRAMID
This is the basic "Christmas tree" shape. It is increasingly favored over the goblet, because the side-shoots are kept very short and are less likely to break under a heavy weight of fruit or snow.

GOBLET
The shape of the tree resembles an open-centered cup or goblet; prune so that the arms are outward-spreading and the light is let into the middle of the tree.

FAN
Allow two shoots only to grow at 45° to the ground. In early spring each year let a suitable number of branches shoot from these to form your fan.

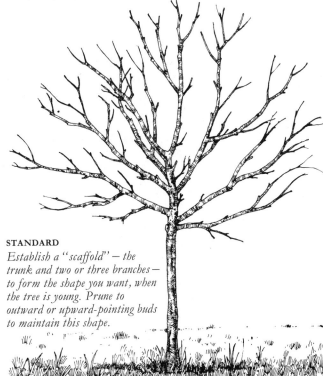

STANDARD
Establish a "scaffold" — the trunk and two or three branches — to form the shape you want, when the tree is young. Prune to outward or upward-pointing buds to maintain this shape.

ESPALIER AND CORDON
The central stem of an espalier is trained vertically. Laterals grow out from it at right angles. Train cordons at a sharp angle to the ground and keep the laterals very short.

Watering

Watering is necessary where rainfall is not sufficient to maintain good plant growth. In some areas, if you are very lucky, you need hardly water at all. In desert climates, however, you can grow practically nothing without frequent watering. But, even in wet climates it is often desirable to water young plants that are struggling to survive in dry periods. And there are few crops that do not show an increased yield when they are watered even in rainy climates. The metabolic process in a plant stops without water, for it is water that carries every useful element, all the way through the plant's body.

Seedlings and tiny plants should be watered little and often. Larger plants should be heavily watered but not so frequently. If there is enough water to sink deeply into the ground, it draws the roots of the plants deep too, to where there is more nourishment. An advantage of the deep bed method (see p. 106) is that it enables water to percolate deeper and quicker, thus encouraging strong root development.

Weeding

Weeds are in a strong ecological position: they were evolved by nature to occupy just the places where they are found. Crops, on the other hand, were evolved partly by mankind to provide good food and as a result their capacity for survival has been somewhat neglected. Don't believe people who tell you to tolerate weeds among your crops. No crop plants ever do their very best with competition from weeds.

On the other hand, if you leave your ground fallow and don't plant a green manure crop to dig in and improve fertility, the weeds will actually do this for you. Let them grow under such circumstances – but *never* let them seed. "One year's seeding is seven years' weeding." Always dig weeds in before they seed.

Hoeing is the usual method of destroying weeds. The secret is to hoe the weeds before they declare themselves, or very soon afterwards. Keep using your hoe regularly. It takes little time to whip over a pretty bare piece of ground with a hoe, but a long time to hack through ground heavily infested with weeds.

Hoes There are several kinds of hoe; the two most common are the draw hoe and the push, or Dutch hoe. Personally, I've always preferred the draw hoe since I learned how to hoe from professional farmworkers – and you never see them tackling a field of turnips with push hoes. The

PUSH HOES
You can walk backward as you use a push hoe, thereby leaving the soil untrampled.

DRAW HOES
A small draw hoe is ideal for weeding. Use a large one to break up heavy clods.

WHEEL HOE
You can hoe between rows very quickly with a wheel hoe, but you can't get really close to the plants.

MATTOCK
A mattock will break up rough ground, or clear weeds from an overgrown vegetable bed.

advantage claimed for the push hoe is that you can walk backward as you use it and so do not trample on ground you've just hoed, but I've never found this very significant. Recently, however, I've discovered that a push hoe is quite useful for working deep beds (see p. 106).

I recommend having two draw hoes: a good heavy one for chopping up unoccupied land and loosening the surface; and a light, sharp-cornered one for whipping out weeds which grow up between plants, or for singling out individual plants from a bunch.

There are also wheel hoes — some of them beautifully crafted tools with wooden shafts. The tool bars in fact take several kinds of attachment, such as plow blades (which I think are useless since they only scratch the surface), ridgers, raking spikes and harrows, as well as hoe blades. It's true that the wheel hoe can save time and effort, and it works quite well. I don't use a wheel hoe myself, however: for one thing, I find I can't get as close to plants with a wheel hoe as with a hand hoe.

Mattocks It's worth mentioning the mattock along with the hoe. As a sort of cross between a spade and a heavy hoe, it's good for breaking up the surface of rough ground. You can use it to make a seed-bed in a hurry, by going over the ground first with a mattock and then raking it. And if you return from a vacation to find your garden in a horrible mess, a light mattock is often a better tool to use than a hoe.

If weeds get too tall to hoe easily, you will just have to pull them. Either put them on the compost heap or leave them to rot on the ground as a mulch. If the weather is wet, the compost heap is better, because weeds left as a mulch may start rooting again.

Mulching

Mulching is the technique, much favoured by organic gardeners and farmers, of covering the soil with some organic material. The benefits of mulching are that it prevents the evaporation of soil moisture by stopping the wind from blowing directly on the soil and the sun from shining on it; it prevents weed growth; and ultimately the mulch rots down and adds to the humus content of the soil. Mulches are particularly useful under fruit trees, canes and bushes since they suppress weeds without damaging surface roots.

Many different organic materials can be used as a mulch. Weeds which have been hoed or pulled out of the ground and left between the crop plants (or just on bare ground) make a good mulch, and so does bracken, which has been dumped from elsewhere.

Wood chips, chopped bark or sawdust form a mulch which is excellent for suppressing weeds, but there is one danger: when wood products rot down, they draw nitrogen from the soil in order to feed the bacteria which break down the cellulose of the material. This results in a temporary but serious loss, and you have to add extra nitrogen to do the job. Wood products also take a long time to break down and add their nutrients to the soil.

Recently, I've come across the technique of using black polyethylene or other inorganic substances as a mulch. I am very much against this: it seems to me quite wrong to deprive the soil life of all sun and air. Ultimately, all soil life is killed by such practices and the soil turns to sterile dust.

Mulches are unfortunately fine homes for slugs and snails. So, if you are mulching, you must remember to take special precautions by trapping and killing them (see p. 104).

Top dressing

The practice of putting fertilizer on land once the crop has already started is known as top dressing. It is favored mainly by inorganic gardeners, who use highly soluble substances such as sulfate of ammonia. However, these substances are quickly leached out of the soil, so, if you do use them, it is best to apply them to the crop little and often.

In my view, really fertile soil doesn't need top dressing. The bacteria in the soil constantly break down organic substances and convert them into nitrogen which is made available to the plants. But certain very nitrogen-hungry crops, like *brassica*, do benefit from a top dressing of organic nitrogen (poultry manure, blood meal, fish meal), particularly if they have been checked by drought or root maggots for example. If phosphates, potash or trace elements are needed by the soil, they are better applied before the land is occupied by a crop than added to it at a later stage.

Manure water When you apply organic manure, compost, or green manure, to the land it gets moved about by worms and rots down, so it eventually becomes available to the crop. But if you want to give a quick boost to a particular crop, you may well consider the technique of soaking organic material in water, thus dissolving out some of its useful constituents, and then pouring the water on the crop. Do this by putting some manure or compost in a container such as an old oil drum. Fill this up with two to three times the quantity of water, and leave for a week or so. Manure watering is excellent when the fruit is forming on crops, such as tomatoes, cucumbers and the members of the squash tribe. But you can grow very good crops, consistently, outdoors, without resorting to such means, if you have built up a good organic fertility in your soil.

Comfrey tea When made into a tea in the same way as you make manure water (see above), comfrey leaves will provide a rich, crash dose of potash for those crops which particularly need this element.

Controlling Pests and Diseases

INSECT PESTS

I would never recommend using chemical insecticides. All life is one, and as a rule anything which destroys one form of life will damage another — perhaps even your own. There are, however, certain vegetable substances which will kill or deter harmful insects without damaging your crops or, most important, your insect predators. Remember: to kill a pest *and* its predator is very stupid. The pest will return and rage in an even more uncontrolled way.

Nicotine mixture If used with great discretion, a form of insecticide which is worthwhile is a solution made by boiling up four ounces (114 g) of cigarette ends in 1.2 gallons (4.5 l) of water. Strain and bottle this, and, when diluted in two parts of water, it's a good standby for getting rid of leaf miners, weevils and caterpillars. But it is a strong poison and may destroy some useful insects too. Don't leave the solution lying about, and always wash after using it.

Aphid deterrents Aphids do not need the same drastic treatment as most other insect pests. A squirt of water – especially soapy water – is usually enough to knock them to the ground and they won't be able to get back on to the plant again. If aphids are a particular nuisance, then I recommend you to spray with either derris or pyrethrum, both of which are obtainable at garden shops. Quassia, if you can get it, will kill aphids but not the helpful ladybird. As an aphid repellent rather than poison, a good idea is to boil up the leaves and stems of certain plants which aphids don't attack, such as marigolds, asters, chrysanthemums, anise, coriander and rhubarb. Make fairly strong solutions of these and experiment to see which is the most effective. Rotenone is the ground-up roots of the derris plant; it will discourage and control most chewing and sucking insects.

Fruit tree sprays For fruit trees, winter wash sprays of various kinds can be bought from garden suppliers, but it's easy to make your own. They are effective against aphids, red spider, mealybugs, scale insects and other pests which lay eggs on the tree bark. Mix 1.2 gallons (4.5 l) of light oil with two pounds (0.9 kg) of soft soap. Boil this up and pour it back and forth until it is very well mixed. Dilute this with 24 gallons (90 l) of water and spray the trees immediately.

Grease banding Grease bands prevent ants and other pests from crawling up tree trunks. How to make one is explained on p. 170. In general ants are useful in the garden, but they can be harmful when they "herd" aphids on to bushes and trees.

Wasp jars Wasps are harmful to certain ripe fruits, such as plums, and, if left unchecked, can ruin a crop of grapes. There are several wasp destroyers available which you put into the nest holes, but I find that to fill jars with sweet stuff like syrup, and hang them in the trees the wasps are attacking, is just as good. I admit, though, that you will need a lot of jars.

Millipede traps An effective device against millipedes – not centipedes, which are "goodies" – is a number of old cans punched full of holes and filled with potato peelings. Bury them in the soil; every few days, lift them out and put them under the tap to drown the millipedes.

Slug and snail control You can trap slugs by sinking some old plates or bowls in the ground and filling them with a little sugar or beer. But you'll need a lot of traps to keep the slugs down. Otherwise, try going out at night and sprinkling salt on every slug you find. The most effective way of killing snails is simply to step on them, but that always seems to me a pity — if you eat them, what was a curse becomes yet another harvest to add to all the rest.

ANIMAL PESTS

Mole deterrents I used to trap scores of moles, but I gave it up long ago. They lift up a row of seedlings now and again and mice sometimes travel along their burrows, but otherwise they don't do any real harm. So for most of the time I just let them burrow away.

During droughts, however, moles can be a pest when they tunnel along potato ridges where the soil is softer and full of worms. Row after row of potatoes can get lifted. A plant called caperspurge is supposed to repel moles, though the only time I ever tried it the moles just heaved it up. Alternatively, bury some empty bottles in the ground so that the wind can blow across the tops of the necks. The vibrations of the sound spread through the ground and scare away the moles, who have very sensitive hearing.

Mouse control Cats are best for keeping mice down; otherwise mice can be deterred from eating pea and bean seed by soaking the seed in kerosene. If you suffer from them very badly, warfarin poison is safe for all animals except rodents.

Gopher control Gophers can be a real enemy to the gardener. Tiny windmills which make a clicking noise are said to deter them, although I have seen gopher damage quite close to such windmills. A more effective remedy is simply to put a gopher snake down the gopher's burrow.

Harvesting and Storing

Bird control For the most part, birds are useful since they eat insects, but they can do serious damage to vegetables, especially to a stand of corn, and of course small fruit, such as currants and raspberries, must be protected.

Birds can be prevented from attacking most crops with fine black thread stretched over the garden: the birds fly into the thread and frighten themselves. Nets are also effective. The traditional fruit cage (see p. 184) is effective but expensive. A good idea, I think, is to use a mini-greenhouse (see p. 111) with plastic or wire netting instead of the transparent plastic sheeting. Put this over the bed which is being attacked. It's easy to remove, or you can just prop it up while you're working. And of course you won't be duplicating equipment because you'll use the mini-greenhouse at other times of the year for its main purpose.

FUNGUS DISEASES

It's possible to garden all your life without resorting to a single fungicide spray and still get good crops. But there are times when even the best organic approach won't be enough to protect your potatoes, tomatoes or even your fruit trees.

Bordeaux mixture In blight years, potato blight can reduce your crop by as much as a half. To confine it, use Bordeaux mixture made by dissolving about half a pound (225 g) of copper sulfate in about six gallons (23 l) of water. Next, make a "cream" of five ounces (150 g) of quicklime mixed with a little water and pour the cream into the copper sulfate solution through a fine sieve. Test the mixture with a clean knife: if the blade comes out coated with a thin film of copper, add more cream to get the copper fully dissolved. If you make Bordeaux mixture yourself, use it within a day or two. Alternatively, you can buy it already made up at a garden shop.

Burgundy mixture For potatoes which are already suffering from potato blight, use a Burgundy mixture. This is made like Bordeaux mixture except you should use about two pounds (0.9 kg) of washing soda instead of the slaked lime.

HARVESTING

To get the fullest flavor from your vegetables and fruits, harvest them just before they reach maturity. As a rule, with most plants, the sugars which provide so much of the flavor begin to turn to starch at full maturity. New potatoes, for example, taste much sweeter than old ones – and sweet corn is so dull when it gets old that I generally give it to the chickens. However, you can't put everything into the cooking pot just when it's right for eating, and vegetables and fruits for storing should be harvested when they are well and truly ripe.

STORING

Seeds and pods It's essential that all seeds and pods are bone dry before they are stored, whether they are eventually to be eaten or used for seed. Hang them upside down by their stalks in a well-ventilated place under a roof. When seeds are dry thresh them out by hand – knocking the plants over the rim of a barrel is a good way – and hang them up in bags made of calico or other loose-woven fabric.

Stems and leaves In all but the coldest climates those vegetables of which you eat the stems and leaves, such as the *brassica*, celery, leeks, spinach and lettuces, can be left in the ground until required. In the coldest climates the *brassica*, celery and leeks can be stored in a cool cellar or basement.

Vegetable fruits The squash tribe are best hung in nets indoors at a temperature around 45°F (7°C). Green tomatoes should be stored at 60°F (16°C) in a drawer or some other dark place. Peppers can be dried indoors or out. Dry them on their vines and hang them up until you want them.

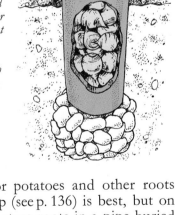

STORING ROOTS AND TUBERS
Bury a large diameter section of drainpipe, say 18 inches (45 cm) long, in well-drained soil. Leave a few inches exposed at the top and put small stones in the bottom for drainage. Fill it up with any root crop and cover it with a wooden lid. In frosty weather lay straw on the lid and weigh it down with a stone.

Roots and tubers For potatoes and other roots and tubers a root clamp (see p. 136) is best, but on a smaller scale you can store roots in a pipe buried in the ground. Carrots and beets can be stored indoors in containers filled with sand. Potatoes can be stored indoors at 45°F (7°C). Keep them in the dark, otherwise they will turn green. Other roots and tubers can be stored indoors at about 37°F (3°C); they must be well ventilated.

The Deep Bed Method

It would be unthinkable to publish a book on gardening for self-sufficiency at this time without fully describing the new method of gardening – or rather the very old method now revived – called variously the Chinese Method, the French Intensive Method, the Biodynamic/French Intensive Method or, by some of its practitioners, just the Method. The word "biodynamic" applied to gardening, is of course tautologous, because all growing things operate bio-dynamically: that is, they live and they move. I call this method, quite simply, the Deep Bed Method, because this describes it exactly.

In the nineteenth century the French "maraichers", or market gardeners, were working as near to Paris as they could get on small patches of expensive and scarce land. However, they had unlimited supplies of horse manure – for at that time Paris moved on horses – and they developed a system of gardening of a productiveness that has never been surpassed. It is not surprising that Chinese gardeners, also working near cities and therefore compelled to produce as much as they could off a limited amount of land, arrived at the same solutions as the French did.

Alan Chadwick, an English actor who studied gardening first under Rudolph Steiner and then at Kew, started experimenting with deep bed cultivation in South Africa. He moved to California in the 1960s and established a four acre (1.6 hectare) organic garden using this method at the University of California at Santa Cruz. Having established this he moved to the Round Valley in Northern California, where he now runs a seven acre (2.8 hectare) garden and has 60 students working with him. It was Chadwick who coined the name Biodynamic/French Intensive Method, using the word biodynamic after Rudolph Steiner.

Meanwhile several Chinese immigrants to the US had also been practicing the Deep Bed Method and one of them, Peter Chan, wrote a book about it: *Better Vegetables the Chinese Way*. Give or take a few inessentials the two methods are the same.

Digging a deep bed

The method is this. Drive four posts in at the four corners of your proposed bed and put a string right round them. The bed should be five feet (1.5 m) wide and as long as convenient, but remember that to make it too long is to give yourself a long walk to get round it because you never tread on it. Twenty feet (6.1 m) long is about right; this gives you a hundred square foot

SPREADING MANURE
Before you start to dig, lay a good covering of manure all over the top of the bed.

DIGGING THE FIRST TRENCH
Starting at one end of the bed, dig a trench a spade-length deep. Put the earth in a wheelbarrow.

LOOSENING THE SUBSOIL
Dig your fork deep into the trench and waggle it about to loosen the subsoil.

bed, which is convenient for making calculations about yields and so on. (The people who have been researching the method so far have been using the hundred square foot bed as a standard for calculations and comparisons.)

Lay a covering of manure on top of the proposed bed. The digging is basically bastard trenching, but you must be sure to loosen the subsoil. Take out a trench a spade wide and a spade deep at the top of the bed. Dig your spade or fork into the bottom of the trench and work it about so as to loosen the subsoil as deep as you can. Dig out a second trench next to the first one and throw the topsoil, and the manure that lies on it, into the first trench. Work the subsoil in the bottom of that too. Move on to the third trench and throw the topsoil into the second trench. Continue in this way until you reach the end of the bed. Then throw the soil you took out at the starting end of the bed into the empty trench that will be left at the completion end of the bed. The bed is then well and truly dug.

You can of course split the bed into two down the middle (see p. 81) and then you don't have to wheel the earth from end to end.

Thereafter — and I must repeat even to the point of tedium because it is the key to the whole matter — never tread on the bed nor let anybody else tread on it until you come to fork it over the next year again.

John Jeavons, another California deep bed practitioner, has written a very good little book about the method (*How to Grow More Vegetables than you ever thought possible on less land than you can imagine*) and has carried out very careful controlled experiments for four years at Palo Alto. He estimates that it takes from six to ten hours to dig a hundred square foot bed for the first time. He believes in bastard trenching his deep beds every year, and finds that after the first year this does not take more than six hours, because the texture of the soil has been so improved since it has not been trodden on.

Peter Chan does not recommend digging again after you have done it once, and my own experience tends to make me agree with him: provided you put on plenty of manure or compost every year, and fork the land over once, the roots and earthworms will ensure that the subsoil does not get compacted again, and it is the compaction of the soil that inhibits plant growth. I find I can fork over a hundred square foot well-established deep bed, one spade deep, in ten minutes and it is light work.

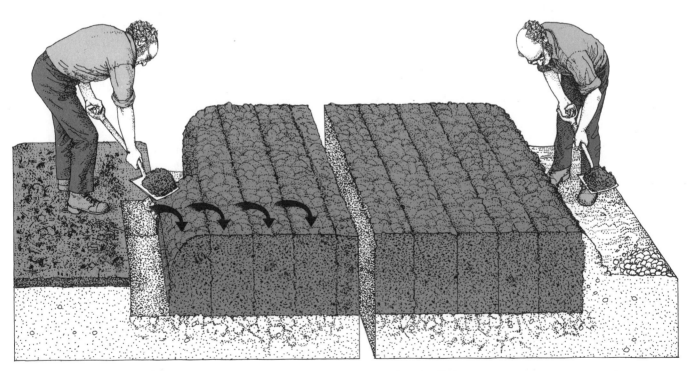

BASTARD TRENCHING THE DEEP BED
Dig a second trench next to the first one, throwing the topsoil and manure into the first trench. Work the subsoil in the bottom of the second trench. Dig a third trench and repeat the process.

MAKING THE PATH
As you dig, throw all pebbles and stones to the side of the bed. When you finish, throw the topsoil from the path-to-be back on top of the bed. Spread the stones evenly over the surface of the path.

If you have several beds side by side, leave narrow paths between them. These paths are never dug, simply walked on. Some people leave their paths very narrow, but I find this makes it difficult to maneuver a wheelbarrow between the beds. So I make them 18 inches (45 cm) wide. You may feel you lose land by having all these paths, but the much closer spacing of the deep bed makes up for this loss of land and in fact you lose a strip of land almost as wide as this between every row in conventional gardening. Also, as the years go by your deep beds will get more and more convex until they stand perhaps 18 inches (45 cm) above the paths.

As you dig your deep beds throw any stones you find in a pile on one side. Then, when you make the paths, throw the topsoil from the path on the bed and scatter the stones in their place.

Some deep bed gardeners build small walls of brick, stone, or timber around their beds to hold the sides up. In my view such arrangements only harbor slugs and are not necessary, because the beds do not, in practice, erode. Ordinary good organic practice dictates that the earth should be covered for most of the time by a crop, even if it is just a green manure crop, and this will hold it together. In any case well manured soil will not erode even if it is left bare in high beds.

DEEP BEDS IN DRY AREAS

In very dry areas it is worth shaping the beds with a draw hoe, so that they rise steeply at the sides and form a basin shape at the top. The moisture is then conserved when the beds are watered. In wetter regions the looseness of the soil in the deep bed is enough to ensure that rain or spray percolate into the earth at once.

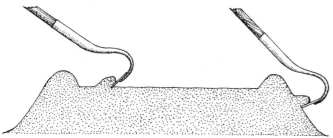

Sowing and planting in a deep bed

Now, in your newly dug bed, either plant out plants from a seed-bed or seed boxes, or simply sow the seed direct into the ground, just as you would with a normal bed. The difference is that you sow or plant four times as densely, or thereabouts, as you do when gardening in the traditional way. The reasons for this are explained in detail further on, but are to do with the fact that you never walk on the earth between the rows so that the soil remains loose and uncompacted.

You do not sow or plant in rows with wide spaces in between. Instead you work to a triangular pattern so that your crops grow in clumps. The overall effect is of very closely spaced diagonal rows. And in almost all cases you should allow much less space between the plants in all directions than you would between plants in traditional rows. The basic objective is to space the plants so that their leaves are just touching when they are mature.

You do not need the normal spaces between rows, because you never walk between the rows. The soil is loose and untrodden, so the roots of the plants can go down straight and deep – when you pull a plant grown in this way, you will be amazed by the size and length of its roots – and therefore the plants do not need nearly so much space at the surface.

The fact that the plants' leaves just touch when they are mature means that they create a mini-climate in dry weather which conserves moisture. You should find that you use from a quarter to a half of the water you use in conventional gardening. Weeds are of course suppressed by this close planting; you can hoe gently from the sides of the bed before the plants meet each other or, even better, just hand-weed. Out of this soft deep soil weeds come out so easily, roots and all, that there is no trouble getting rid of them. Weeds are really no problem with deep bed gardening.

An obvious question is – what about crops like *brassica* and onions which gardeners have always believed need firm soil? What about all those exhortations to stamp and dance about on beds before planting them? Well, in husbandry only one argument is of the slightest weight and that is experience: what actually happens. I have grown crops of *brassica* by this method; the vegetables have been magnificent and the yields have been extremely impressive.

All that you do when you plant out *brassica* or onions is plant considerably deeper than you would normally and then press the ground fairly firmly down around the plant with your hands. Only the top few inches of the soil are thus compressed but in practice it seems to be enough. This does not, in this very loose soil, make onions "bull-neck" – in any case you can gently remove the earth from around the onions later on.

The deep bed practitioners favor frequent transplanting of plants before they are put out in the beds, but they always plant into, if possible, better and looser soil than the plants were in before. Thus, if you prick plants out from a seed

The Essentials of Good Gardening

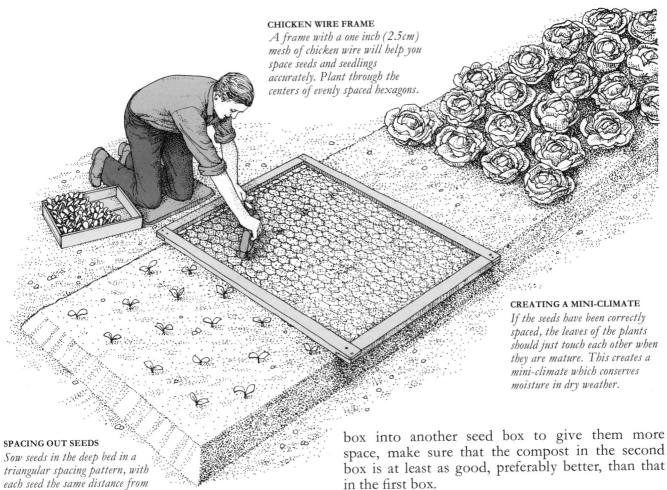

CHICKEN WIRE FRAME
A frame with a one inch (2.5cm) mesh of chicken wire will help you space seeds and seedlings accurately. Plant through the centers of evenly spaced hexagons.

CREATING A MINI-CLIMATE
If the seeds have been correctly spaced, the leaves of the plants should just touch each other when they are mature. This creates a mini-climate which conserves moisture in dry weather.

SPACING OUT SEEDS
Sow seeds in the deep bed in a triangular spacing pattern, with each seed the same distance from those surrounding it.

USING A BOARD
If you dislike stretching to the center of the bed, squat on a piece of board five feet by three feet (1.5 x 0.9 m). Your weight, evenly distributed, will not compact the soil.

box into another seed box to give them more space, make sure that the compost in the second box is at least as good, preferably better, than that in the first box.

The spacings for sowing and planting different crops are given in the chapters on the Cultivation of Vegetables and Fruit (pp. 113—190). These should be used as a guide only; every person should experiment for himself and use his common sense. After all — how big is an onion — how big is a carrot? Everybody knows, and provided the tops of the plants are given sufficient room their roots will be all right because there is plenty of room below a deep bed.

With conventional gardening the roots cannot penetrate the compacted earth below, and must spread out laterally where they compete mercilessly with each other, and get cut and damaged every time you tread near them. With deep bed gardening the roots go way down into the loose soil, with nothing to stop them, and there is nothing to damage them when they are there.

Deep bed yields

Careful records have been kept, at Santa Cruz and other places, and the deep beds have been found to yield, quite consistently, four times the crop produced by conventional gardening.

I, like many other vegetable gardeners had read these figures but did not fully believe them. So I went to California to see for myself, and spent some time there searching out every example of deep bed gardening that I could find. Seeing is believing and in this case I am completely convinced of the superiority of this method. Four times the crop is about right and I never saw a case of this gardening being practiced correctly that did not, more or less, bear out this figure. On the strength of this I returned home and tried it for myself, and I have now proved, through personal experience that it certainly does work.

Deep beds for perennial vegetables and herbs

Obviously you cannot dig perennial beds every year, but it is well worth creating a deep bed by digging the land very deeply once – perhaps three spade lengths deep – but leaving the subsoil underneath. After that never tread on the bed.

Deep beds for fruit

All soft fruit bushes, and also top fruit trees on dwarfing root stocks trained as goblets or dwarf pyramids, can be grown successfully in deep beds. Alan Chadwick is experimenting with dwarfed top fruit trees with other crops growing under and around them. This is a new technique (the French deep bed gardeners never bothered to grow top fruit on their deep beds), but it seems successful.

If you like big fruit trees, you can plant them in circular deep beds – one tree to a bed. Simply mark out a circle round the likely drip-line – the area to be over-hung by the tree. Double-dig this circle around the edges and dig very deeply – four spade lengths would be ideal – at the spot where you are actually going to plant the tree. Plant the tree in the normal way (see p. 98).

It is known that the roots of trees advance much more quickly in unconsolidated soil. It is also easy to observe that roots tend to come upward toward the surface. If you can keep the earth within range of a tree's roots soft and open, you can give the roots the conditions they need for rapid growth without constantly digging into them with a spade or cultivator. The only way you can achieve this is by not treading on the soil ever, at all, after you have done the initial deep digging.

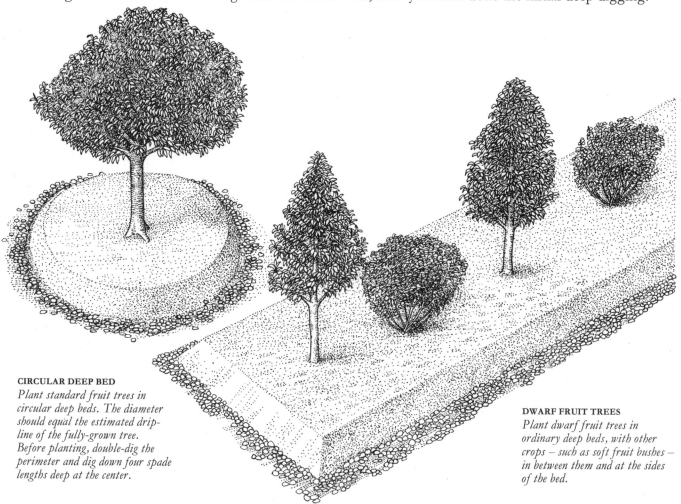

CIRCULAR DEEP BED
Plant standard fruit trees in circular deep beds. The diameter should equal the estimated drip-line of the fully-grown tree. Before planting, double-dig the perimeter and dig down four spade lengths deep at the center.

DWARF FRUIT TREES
Plant dwarf fruit trees in ordinary deep beds, with other crops – such as soft fruit bushes – in between them and at the sides of the bed.

Mini-greenhouses

The idea of the mini-greenhouse, which has been growing in popularity, is to bring lightness, mobility, flexibility, and economy into the business of protecting plants from the weather. The trend in the last twenty years has been toward cheap plastic structures, principally plastic-covered tunnels. These work, but are troublesome. You cannot hoe under them without removing them and this is always awkward and time-consuming.

The mini-greenhouse, on the other hand, is very light and can be moved easily by two people from one bed to another. A proper rotation of crops that are usually grown indoors can be practiced without the laborious soil changes, or expensive soil sterilizations, that have to be carried out in fixed greenhouses. In other words you never have to grow either tomatoes or cucumbers two years running on the same bed.

Building a mini-greenhouse

A convenient size for a mini-greenhouse is 20 feet by five feet (6 x 1.5 m), because this will fit over a standard-sized deep bed, and besides it is fairly

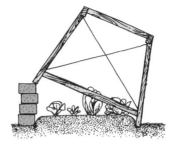

OPENING MINI-GREENHOUSES
When you want to work on a deep bed under a mini-greenhouse — for hoeing, thinning, harvesting and so on — all you need to do is to prop up one side of the mini-greenhouse on a pile of bricks or on a piece of wood.

easy to handle. Use two inch by one inch (5 x 2.5 cm) wood, and for permanence make proper mortise and tenon joints. Brace the structure with ordinary thin wire; this hardly adds to the weight and does not cost much, but it increases rigidity enormously.

The wires should be pulled quite tight. Tie one end of a wire to a top corner of the mini-greenhouse, drill a hole in the strut at the opposite corner and thread the free end of the wire through the hole. Haul the end of the wire as tight as you can with a pair of pliers. I always grip the wire tight with the pliers just where it emerges from the hole and twist the pliers round the strut so that they act as a lever to pull the wire even

MINI-GREENHOUSE COMPONENTS
Use two inch by one inch wood for the basic structure. Make proper joints, join the pieces with long nails hammered right through both pieces of wood and clenched. Strengthen the structure with wires. Use nails and wooden battens to fix a large sheet of transparent plastic right over the top and sides. Fit smaller pieces of plastic to the ends. Make pinholes in the top to let the rain in.

STRAINING THE WIRES
When you have fitted a double length of wire (below right), push a stick between the two wires and twist until the wires are taut. Then tie the stick to the wires.

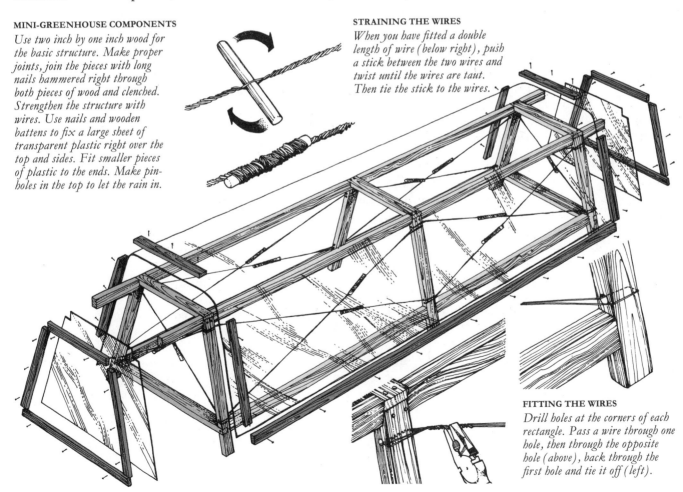

FITTING THE WIRES
Drill holes at the corners of each rectangle. Pass a wire through one hole, then through the opposite hole (above), back through the first hole and tie it off (left).

tighter. You can then just wind the end of the wire round its own standing part.

Alternatively, you can use a much longer wire, double it back and poke its end through a hole near the top corner where the wire came from; strain it there and tie it off. In this way you have strained wires side by side and you can strain them further by pushing a stick through them and winding it round and round. When the two stretches of wire have been twisted round each other, fix one end of the stick to the wires with another short piece of wire so that the bracing wire does not unravel. Beware any loose ends of wire that will puncture your plastic sheeting. Use a single large sheet of plastic to cover the top and sides of the structure, and small piece at either end. Attach all the edges of the plastic to the structure with wooden battens. Don't leave any ends unattached: if you do, the plastic will rip in the wind. Make a row of tiny holes in the top sheet of the plastic to allow rain water to sprinkle down on to the plants below, instead of forming a lake.

Using a mini-greenhouse

Use the mini-greenhouse as much as possible. Use it in winter to cover winter lettuce. Move it on to newly planted cauliflowers after that. When they have got a hold move it to protect early potatoes and then on to bush beans perhaps. In the warmer weather use it on tender vegetables like eggplants, melons and peppers. And you can cover your mini-greenhouses with bird netting instead of plastic to protect your seed-beds.

PLANNING A DEEP BED GARDEN

If I were to take over a new garden I would have no hesitation about turning it into a deep bed garden as soon as possible. I am, in fact, turning my existing garden into a deep bed garden at the moment. There is some capital labor – work that only has to be done once – involved in doing this, and maybe this should be done little by little, one bed at a time when the time and energy are there. However, the aim should be a whole garden of deep beds. Once your garden is completely given over to deep beds, you will need to do much less work on it than you used to do in your conventional garden, but the results should be considerably more impressive.

Except that you will be more or less tied to beds five feet (1.5 m) wide or less, and that it is a good idea not to have beds so long that it becomes a bore to walk round them, there is no difference between the general planning of a deep bed

CONVERTING YOUR GARDEN TO DEEP BEDS
This is the garden shown on page 70, replanned so that the same crops can be grown in deep beds. There is room for six deep beds, each 20 x 5 feet (6 x 1.5 m): four for the vegetable rotation, one for perennial vegetables and one for soft fruit. The old perennial bed in front of the espaliers which now stand in a deep bed, now contains alternate dwarf fruit trees and soft fruit bushes. The herbs are now also in a deep bed, and a standard fruit tree has been planted in a circular deep bed. The seed and holding-beds remain the same.

garden and that of an orthodox one. The rotations will be just the same. The general layout will be similar, although in larger gardens each division of the rotation may take up two or more separate deep beds, because of the width limitation.

Your perennials and herbs will be planted in deep beds not more than five feet (1.5 m) wide. If your herb bed – or any other bed – is up against a wall it will need to be about three feet (90 cm) wide, because you will only be able to reach into it from one side. Your soft fruit bushes can share a deep bed with some dwarf fruit trees, and you can plant standard fruit trees in circular beds.

You will very likely find yourself doing far more in the way of interplanting. You might even try the sort of mixed tree fruit, soft fruit, vegetable and flower beds that Alan Chadwick is trying in California. In your deep beds you are exploiting another direction in gardening: downward. You are making it possible for the roots to go deep, and saving them the necessity of spreading out laterally and thereby competing with one another for space. You can cram plants closer together.

Remember that this form of husbandry is in its infancy in the West (no matter how long it may have been practiced in China and Japan) and there is plenty of scope for learning and experimenting.

CHAPTER FIVE

The Cultivation of Vegetables

*Containing the sowing, growing and harvesting
instructions for members of the families Leguminosae,
Cruciferae, Solanaceae, Umbelliferae, Liliaceae,
Chenopodiaceae, Cucurbitaceae, Compositae,
Gramineae, Malvaceae and Polygonaceae.*

Leguminosae

Peas, broad beans, pole beans, bush beans, lima beans, soybeans and peanuts are all members of the *Leguminosae*. For those who wish to grow as much of their own food as they can in a garden, this family is surely the most useful of the lot. In the first place – it provides more protein than any other. It is hard to see how a vegetarian, or for that matter any person who aims to be completely self-sufficient without much meat, can subsist in a healthy state, without the *Leguminosae*.

The other useful thing about the *Leguminosae* is their nitrogen-fixing ability. Organic gardeners who don't like spending their money on expensive nitrogenous fertilisers (which make the soil lazy about fixing its own nitrogen) find that peas, beans and the clovers are the answer. For the *Leguminosae* are the plants which are able to fix nitrogen in the nodules on their roots. Pull out any healthy leguminous plant and examine its roots. You should find small pimples or nodules. If you were to cut these open and examine them with a powerful microscope you would see bacteria. These live symbiotically with the plant. The plant feeds them with everything they need except nitrogen: they fix nitrogen from the air (combin-ing it with oxygen to form nitrates), and this they use themselves and also feed to the host plant.

If you grow any leguminous plant, and dig it into the soil when it is lush and green (at the flowering stage) it will rot down very quickly, providing its own nitrogen to feed the putrefactive bacteria, and this nitrogen will then be released into the soil. It is worth growing clover for this very purpose. If you put leguminous plants on the compost heap they will have the same beneficial effect. If you have a lawn, remember that if you put nitrates on it, you will encourage the grasses but suppress the clover. If you put on phosphate you will encourage the clovers at the expense of the grasses.

Leguminous plants should account for at least a quarter of your garden each year and there is nothing wrong with having far more than that. They are not acid-loving plants, so if your soil is acid give it lime. They also like phosphate and potash. But in good garden soil that has been well manured or composted over the years, and in which any serious lack of lime, phosphate or potash has been corrected, you can grow peas and beans without putting anything on at all.

Peas

GARDEN PEAS

The first fresh peas of the summer eaten raw are one of the great rewards of growing your own vegetables. And later in the season, of course you can cook them and dry them. Whatever you do they are a great source of nourishment. Dwarf peas are a good idea for a small garden.

Soil and climate

Peas are not too fussy as regards soil; light soil will give you an early crop, heavy a late one. A rich loam is best, and any soil can be turned into this by constant composting. As for climate, peas are not a tropical crop and will grow well in cool climates, with plenty of moisture, but too much rain when they are ripening will give them mildew. In hot latitudes they generally have to be grown in the spring or fall, to avoid the very hot part of the summer. As small plants they are frost-hardy, therefore in climates where frosts are not too intense they can be sown in the fall for a quick start in the spring. They will not grow fast and produce flowers and pods, however, until the arrival of spring and warmer weather.

Soil treatment

Peas need deeply cultivated ground. If you are trying to grow them in land that has previously been gardened inorganically you should try to spread 700 to 1000 lbs (350 to 500 kg) of manure or compost on every 100 square yards (84 sq m). Put this on the land the previous fall, and possibly

DRILLS FOR PEA SEED
Use the flat of a draw hoe to make broad drills about two inches (5 cm) deep and four inches (10 cm) wide.

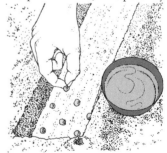

SOWING PEA SEED
Sow evenly, leaving an inch or two between seeds. If necessary you can keep mice away by dipping the seed in kerosene before planting.

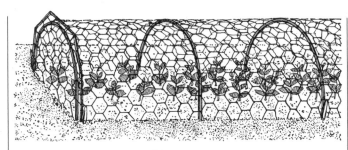

PROTECTING PEAS FROM BIRDS
Wire-netting pea-guards, which you can easily make yourself, will protect seeds and seedlings from attack by birds. So will mini-greenhouses (see p. 111) such as you use for deep beds; but you should cover them with wire rather than with plastic.

25 lbs (11 kg) of slag or ground rock phosphate per 100 square yards (84 sq m) and 10 or 12 lbs (4.5 to 5.4 kg) of wood ash. Peas don't like acid soil; if the pH is about 6.5 that is all right. If it is below this, lime it; a quarter of a pound (100 g) per square yard is about right.

If your soil is not yet sufficiently fertile and you cannot bring in enough compost or manure from outside, you can still grow excellent peas over trenches taken out the previous year and filled during the winter with kitchen garbage and other material which will readily decompose, such as old newspaper. The organic gardener's aim, though, should be to raise the whole of his garden to a high level of fertility, so that such piecemeal treatments as this are unnecessary.

Propagation

I make broad drills with the flat of the hoe, about two inches (5 cm) deep, and four inches (10 cm) wide. I then sprinkle the seed in evenly, so there is an inch or two between each side. I then rake the earth back into the trench from each seed and bang down firmly with the back of the

rake – or, if the land is puffy and dry, I tread it with my feet. A good soaking of the drill, if the soil is dry, will then start them growing. If you use the deep bed method (see p. 106), allow three inches (8 cm) between plants all ways. You leave this distance in the deep bed because you are not sowing in rows, of course, but in clumps.

Many people speed up germination by soaking the seed, for as long as forty-eight hours, before they plant it. It should be remembered that all these seeds that are large and edible, like peas and beans, are an open invitation to rodents and birds, and so the sooner they start to grow the less time there is for them to be eaten by something. Birds may have to be kept away by thin black threads, or, better still, inverted wire-netting pea-guards. And if you are troubled by mice, dip the seed into kerosene just before planting. The mice don't like the smell.

Now peas take about three months to grow to maturity: perhaps two and a half if you plant early varieties or if you like your peas very young like I do. Sow them successionally, every two weeks from late winter to mid spring and you will get fresh peas most of the summer.

Care while growing

All but the smallest dwarf peas are better if they have sticks to grow up. Any fine branches with some twigs left on them will do for this. Hazel trimmings make ideal pea sticks. If you need a hedge between your garden and the next one use hazel. It will give you nuts as well as pea sticks. If you just can't get pea sticks then use wire netting. Get the coarsest mesh you can (it is cheaper), say three feet (90 cm) wide, and make an inverted "V" of it so that a row of peas climbs up each side. This method has the advantage that many of the peas hang down inside the wire where the birds can't get at them. If the wire is wide gauge, you will be able to get your hand in to pick the peas; otherwise you can put your hand down through the gap in the top. There are plenty of dwarf

BUILDING WIRE PEA FRAMES
You can build a "fence" of wire netting for peas to climb up, or you can build an inverted "V" shape and train a row of peas up each side. The peas will dangle into the middle where the birds can't get them. Use wide gauge netting because it is cheaper and you can get your hands through the mesh quite easily.

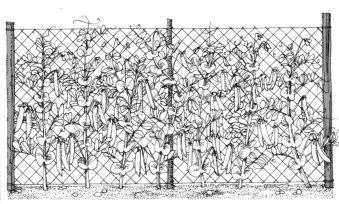

TRAINING WITH PEA STICKS
Any branch with a few twigs left on it will make a pea stick. Hazel branches are especially good, as they will provide you with nuts as well as sticks. Cut them to a length of about four feet (1.2 m), sharpen the thick end and drive well into the ground beside each plant.

pea varieties available, and these generally need no support at all. They are worth growing in a small garden, but the yield is low and unless you take precautions (see p. 104) slugs are likely to attack the peas near the ground.

Peas don't like drought, and watering in dry weather always pays in more peas, but remember that soil rich in humus retains water more efficiently.

Pests and diseases

Pea and bean weevil This creature is the color of soil, falls off the plant and plays dead when you disturb it, and is nocturnal; it hides under clods of earth during the day. No-digging gardeners suffer from it badly because the compost with which they have to cover their ground gives it splendid cover. It nibbles round the edges of young pea leaves and often eats out the growing centers. Dusting the plants with lime, while the dew is on them, is usually an effective deterrent. Alternatively you can spray the young plants and the surrounding ground with quassia spray, or nicotine mixture (see p. 104).

Pea moth This is a small brown moth that lays eggs on young pea pods. The larvae bore in and eat the peas. If you dig, or cultivate, the soil frequently, but very shallowly, during the winter you can get rid of these pests, for the birds (chiefly robins and starlings) will come along and eat the pupae – thereby breaking the moth's life cycle.

Pea thrips These are tiny browny-black insects which make minute holes in the leaves of pea plants. The plants become yellow and shrivel up. A thorough drenching with soapy water will get rid of them.

Mildew In very damp weather pea leaves and pods may go white with mildew, and then rot. Using tall pea sticks, so the peas can climb high, helps prevent this. Don't water the foliage of peas in hot muggy weather. Spraying with Bordeaux mixture sometimes works. Otherwise there's not much you can do about it, but it is not disastrous.

Harvesting

Always use both hands to pick peas! Put the basket on the ground, and hold the vine with one hand and the pod with the other.

Very young peas taste quite exquisite raw and contain high doses of vitamins A, B and C. They are very sweet because they contain sugar. A few hours after the peas are picked this sugar turns to starch, which is why bought peas taste dull and dried peas completely different. If you pick peas and freeze them immediately you can preserve this sugar, which is why frozen peas don't taste too bad.

I like to eat fresh peas all summer and then enjoy dried peas, rather than frozen peas, during the winter, so that I come to the first fresh peas in early summer with a fresh palate and enjoy what is then an exquisite gastronomic experience. The palate jaded by "fresh" peas all the year round never has this great sensation.

As fresh peas grow older and tougher on the vine you have to boil them. When your peas get too tough to be good boiled, leave them on the vines and just let them go on getting tougher. Wait until they are completely ripe, as hard as bullets; then pull the vines out and hang them up in the wind but out of the rain. When they are thoroughly dry thresh the peas out of them; either rub the vines hard between your hands, or pound them over the back of a chair. Put the peas away, quite dry, in covered containers. When you want some in the winter soak them in water for a day or two. Then boil them with salt until they are soft, and eat with boiled bacon. A plate full of that, in December, and you are fit to go out and dig for a few hours.

Pea pods make the basis of a good soup. Boil them well and pass them through a sieve.

SUGAR PEAS

These are also called edible podded peas. Cultivate them like ordinary peas. The difference is that you harvest and eat the pods with the young peas inside them, because they lack the hard membrane that lines the ordinary pea pod. Start picking and eating the pods as soon as they are about two inches (5 cm) long and when the peas inside are tiny flat bumps. You then have a long picking season because you can go on picking until the peas inside are quite big. These are widely used in Oriental dishes and are noted for their sweet flavor and crisp texture.

ASPARAGUS PEAS

These are not true peas, but you can treat them the same way, although you must plant them later, say in mid-spring, and if you live in a cold place, protect them with cloches. Support them just like peas. Cook the complete pods when they are about an inch long. They are quite delicious.

LENTILS

Lentils are closely related to peas and are excellent for drying. However, they are low yielding and are really only worth growing if you have space to spare after allowing for your staples. They like the same climatic conditions as peas, and do best on a sandy loam. Propagate them and care for them exactly as though they were garden peas. When the plants are well ripened, pull them out and hang them up in a shed. Thresh when required.

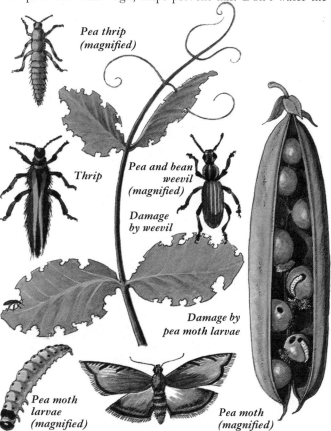

Pea thrip
(magnified)

Thrip

Pea and bean
weevil
(magnified)

Damage
by weevil

Damage by
pea moth larvae

Pea moth
larvae
(magnified)

Pea moth
(magnified)

Broad Beans

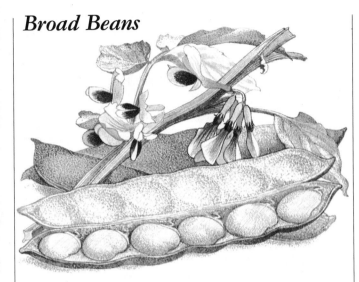

For the self-supporting gardener broad beans are one of the most important crops. They really will feed you and your family right through the year, and if you have dried broad beans and potatoes you will not starve. The old English broad bean was the "longpod", and this is still the bean to grow if you really want food which will keep you in high protein vegetable nourishment right through the winter as well as the summer — (unless your climate and conditions enable you to get a good yield with soybeans). All the other beans, like pole beans, bush beans and dwarf beans are native to the American continent, especially the hot parts of South America. They are all very frost tender. The longpod broad bean however, can stand up to a fierce winter and get away early in the spring. It stands up straight and tall, needs no support, and produces a heavy crop of fine big kidney-shaped seeds, which can be either cooked and eaten fresh, or dried and kept for the winter.

Tic beans, horse beans and cattle beans, which are all grown by farmers to provide high protein grain for feeding animals in the winter, are varieties of the same plant. Their seeds are smaller and white, but they are heavy cropping. They are more liable to get chocolate spot disease than broad beans and they are said not to be edible before Christmas. But then they are said not to be fit for human consumption yet I eat them freely every winter.

The ordinary longpod broad bean, however, is the best thing for the gardener; but if you can get a handful of tic beans from a farmer, why not experiment with them and see what happens?

Soil and climate

Broad beans like strong soil, even heavy clay, but compost rich soil suits them no matter what the original soil was — clay or sand. Their behavior in different climates is very similar to that of peas (see Peas). If you can plant out your peas in the autumn, then you can do the same with your broad beans, for they are rather more hardy than peas.

Soil treatment

Beans don't like too much acid; like peas they find a pH of 6.5 ideal. Potash does them a lot of good, so if you have a limited supply of wood ashes put it on your broad bean patch at a rate of about four oz (100g) to two yards of row. Comfrey too, dug in as a green manure, is good, both for the potash that it contains and for its capacity to hold water.

Dig the soil deep and well, digging in ashes and comfrey leaves if you have them, and as much manure or compost as you can spare. I like to plant broad beans after main crop potatoes, so the soil is already full of manure which was put in for the spuds, and it has been well worked. Lime, then, is only necessary if the pH is much below 6.5

Propagation

It is far and away better, if you live south of the heavy snow line to sow your broad beans in the fall, in say October or November. If the birds get them, or it is too cold where you are, sow them as early as you can in the spring — as soon as the soil can be worked with ease. It is best to soak the seeds in cold water for twenty-four hours before planting them; this softens them up and gives them a head start over the birds.

Take out drills about three inches (8 cm) deep with the hoe, drills about two feet (60 cm) apart, and put the seeds in six inches (15 cm) apart. Or — and here I think is a very good tip — sow them in rows six feet (1.8 m) apart and, later, sow bush or dwarf beans in between the rows. Broad beans make a fine nurse-crop for these more tender plants, keeping the wind off them. Instead of digging drills you can put out a garden line and make a hole with a trowel for each seed. If you use the deep bed method (see p. 106) leave four inches (10 cm) between plants in all directions.

INTERCROPPING WITH BROAD BEANS
Tough, tall broad beans make an excellent nurse-crop for smaller plants like bush beans. Plant the broad beans in rows six feet (1.8 m) apart in fall or early spring. When the weather warms up in early summer fill the spaces between the rows with low growing bush beans.

Care while growing

As the young beans grow it is a good idea to hill them up a little with the hoe. Keep them clear of weeds of course. In windy and exposed positions, it is worth driving in a stake at the corners of the rows, and running a string from stake to stake right around each row, to prevent the beans being blown over. In most gardens though this is not necessary. Any sort of mulching between the plants is valuable.

Pests and diseases

Chocolate spot This looks exactly like its name, and if you get it there is nothing you can do. If you get it early, it will lower your yield considerably, but a late attack is not so bad. To guard against it you need plenty of potash in your soil. If you keep getting it in autumn-sown beans, you must give up autumn sowing and sow your beans in the spring instead, because these are less liable to attack.

Bean rust You are not likely to get this. The symptoms are small white spots on leaves and stems in the spring. Spray with diluted Bordeaux mixture (see p. 105), and burn all your bean straw after harvesting to destroy the spores.

Black fly or aphid If you sow spring beans you are very likely to get this, and in fact unlikely not to get it. It does not trouble autumn-sown beans very often. The aphids can only pierce the skin of tender young growing points and the winter beans are generally grown enough by the time the aphids are around. If aphids do attack you will find them clustered on the tips. If the beans have already grown high enough pick these tips off; this will deny the fly its food. You can cook and eat the tips; they are tender and juicy. If you get a really bad attack spray the plants hard with soft soap and kerosene solution. Bees love bean flowers, so it is important not to spray with anything that will harm bees. Pyrethrum sprayed at night will kill the aphids and not harm the bees in the morning.

Pea and bean weevil (See Peas).

Bean mildew Spray with Bordeaux mixture.

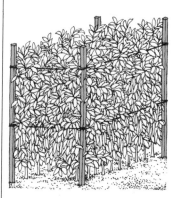

SUPPORTING BROAD BEANS
If your broad bean patch is exposed to wind, support the plants with strings run between stakes, which are driven in at the ends of the rows.

BANISHING BLACK FLY
If you get black fly or aphids on your broad beans they will almost certainly cluster on the tips. If the beans have grown high enough, simply pick the tips off.

Harvesting and storing

The tips of growing broad beans, nipped off in the spring to thwart black fly, are one of the first and most tasty fresh greens of the spring. Soon after eating these, you can start pulling the very small pods and cook them as they are. Later the pods get too tough for this so you split them open, remove the beans from their silky beds and cook the seeds. When the seeds get too tough for this let them dry on the plant, and harvest by pulling out the whole plant. Then hang it in an airy but dry place. Shuck the seeds out when they are quite dry and store them for the winter. Soak them for at least twenty-four hours (twice that long is not too much) before cooking and then boil them well. Eaten either with butter, or with bacon, they will give you strength to face the winter.

Pole Beans

Pole beans, as the name implies, are climbers. They take up little space and can be trained easily up walls, fences or wires. They are both attractive and nutritious, and are therefore ideal for the small-scale vegetable garden.

Soil and climate

The pole bean is not frost-hardy and it prefers a warm sunny climate, although this is not essential. In warmish climates, it will survive the winter, underground, and grow up again in the spring as a perennial. In very cold climates you can get a crop by sowing in peat pots indoors and planting out after the last frost. The pole bean needs plenty of moisture at its roots, and its flowers will not set without an occasional shower of rain, or spray from a hose. It will grow in most soils but likes rich ones; it benefits from plenty of humus and plenty of moisture. And it does not like acid soils. 6.5 pH is ideal, so lime if necessary.

Soil treatment

The classic method is to take out a deep trench in the fall or winter and fill it with manure or compost, or else spend the winter filling it with kitchen garbage and anything else organic you can find. In the spring cover the trench with soil and plant on that. The compost, or whatever it was, will have subsided as it rotted and so there will be a shallow depression for the water to collect and sink into, and beans like plenty of water. If you don't dig a trench, you must still dig deeply and put in plenty of compost.

SOWING POLE BEANS
To get as many plants as possible into the space available, sow seeds three inches (8 cm) deep, ten inches (25 cm) apart in two rows one foot (30 cm) apart. Stagger the seeds in the rows. You can speed germination by soaking the seed in water before planting, although you should not do this if you suspect halo blight.

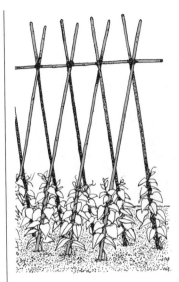

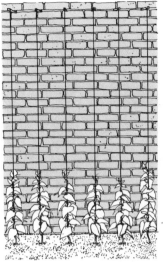

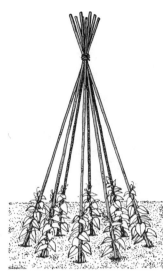

STAKING POLE BEANS
Each pole bean plant must have its own stake, anywhere between seven feet (2 m) and 12 feet (3.5 m) high. With two rows, you can use the crossed pole method, where pairs of poles are tied together to form forks near their tops and the whole row is made secure with a pole laid through the forks and tied down. If you want your beans against a wall fix wires close to the wall by attaching them to long nails top and bottom. The wigwam method is excellent, even in a tub or large barrel. Sow eight to twelve seeds in a circle; when the plants come up give them each a pole and tie them all together near their tops.

Propagation

If you want early pole beans sow in peat pots in the greenhouse, or in a sunny window, during late spring. A temperature of about 55°F (13°C) is fine. Most people just sow them out of doors after the last frost. I draw two drills a foot (30 cm) apart and sow the seeds three inches (8 cm) deep, ten inches (25 cm) apart in the rows and staggered. If you use the deep bed method (see p. 106), you must still plant in a row so that all your plants receive plenty of light. Therefore plant no closer.

Care while growing

Weed them of course, water them in dry weather, and before they are many inches high stake them with stakes at least seven feet (2 m) high. They will climb as high as 12 feet (3.5 m) if you give them long enough stakes, and personally I like them tall. The more beans the better, and you can always stand on a box to pick them. Put in stakes when two true leaves are well opened. There are several methods of training pole beans. As long as you have plenty of space – enough for two rows of plants – you can use bamboo or bean sticks (like pea sticks, only longer) to build a row of crossed poles, with their apexes in between the rows. Tie them together where they meet and strengthen by tying canes along the top. If you are short of space you can plant your beans in a circle and build a wigwam of poles around the circle. (This is better in my opinion than using dwarf varieties in a small space.) Another method is to plant the seeds along the bottom of a wall and train the plants up wires against the wall. I love to see a really high screen of beautiful pole beans, sited so as not to shade anything that must have sun (plenty of plants, like lettuces, grow well in shade) and screening some ugly feature in the garden.

If the flowers are out in a dry period spray them lightly with water – preferably water which is not too cold. This helps the flowers to set.

Pests and diseases

With good organic soil you are unlikely to get trouble, but you might just have one of the four varieties below.

Bean disease This is a fungal disease which causes black spots to appear on the pods of pole and bush beans; later on the spots develop reddish outlines. At the first sign of this disease spray with Bordeaux mixture, but if the disease gets a strong hold, root out the affected plants and burn them. Never save seed if you have had an attack of bean disease.

Halo blight Caused by bacteria, this results in semi-transparent spots surrounded by a yellow halo on leaves. Spray with Bordeaux mixture. Do not save seed for next year, and if you have any doubt about your seed do not soak it before planting.

Mosaic disease This shows itself as yellow blotches on the leaves. It lives in clover, so do not plant pole or bush beans in soil where old clover has been dug in. If you do get it, pull up the plant and burn it.

Mexican bean beetle This is a brown spotted beetle a little bigger than a ladybug. If your beans are prone to attack, you will find they will attack your main crop more than your early crop. So put in your main crop as early as you can. Pick off and kill any beetles you see, and rub out the yellow larvae on the undersides of leaves. Dusting with rotenone is effective.

Harvesting and storing

Pick pole beans, like peas, with both hands. Hold the vine in one hand and pull the pod with the other. Harvest on the "pick and pick again" principle. Keep on picking them when they are young and tender, and don't allow them to get old and haggard on the vine. If you keep picking they will keep coming – they are the most generous of crops.

If you can't eat them all salt them (see p. 215). But remember, salt them only when they are young and tender.

PICKING POLE BEANS
Pick beans and peas with two hands. If you pick with one hand you can do lasting damage to the vine. Pick them while they are young, and you will be encouraging more to grow. Don't ever leave them to get old on the vine: if there are too many for you to eat all at once, salt them. Frozen pole beans don't taste as good as salted ones.

Bush Beans

Bush beans are nothing like so hardy as broad beans. When fully ripened and dried, they form a rich source of winter protein.

Soil and climate

Plant when the soil has warmed up in the summer. They prefer a lightish soil or a soil well-improved by compost, and a pH of about 6.5

Soil treatment

Don't lime for them if your soil is not too acid. The more humus you can incorporate when digging the soil the better.

Propagation

When sowing in drills have the rows two feet (60 cm) apart and sow two inches (5 cm) apart in the drills – deep bed method four to six inches (10-15 cm) apart (see p. 106). Modern bush beans mature so rapidly that you can plant repeat crops throughout the summer.

Care while growing

Keep the bed well weeded and the soil loose.

Pests and diseases

Cut worm   Cut worms are rarely troublesome, but can be kept away by placing a three inch (8 cm) cardboard collar around the stem of the plants (see p. 124). Bend the cardboard so that it is half an inch (1 cm) from the stem all round. Allow one inch (2.5 cm) below ground and two inches (5 cm) above. Alternatively place a ring of wood ash around each plant.
Wireworm   If you are troubled by wireworms try to trap them during the winter by burying cut pieces of potato six inches (15 cm) deep at intervals of about a yard. Mark them with sticks, carefully dig them up each evening and destroy the wireworms which you will find there.
Mexican bean beetle   See Pole beans.

Harvesting and storing

Like all beans, bush beans are grown for two purposes: for the green pods with immature beans inside and for the ripened beans which can be dried. To dry beans you just let them ripen, hang the vines upside-down in a shed, and thresh them when you want them. To harvest pick the beans by hand. They can be stored green in salt.

Lima Beans

These are beans from tropical America which have been bred for growth in warmish temperate climates. They can be cooked and eaten when green, or dried for winter storage. There are bush and climbing varieties.

Soil and climate

Unless they are started off under glass, they need three months of fairly warm days and nights. The seed needs warm soil to germinate, so don't plant until two or three weeks after the last frost. And bear in mind that the first autumn frost will cut them down. If you have this sort of climate, they are worth growing because they are very heavy cropping. Limas like lightish soil but will grow in any soil except heavy clay. Untypically for beans they prefer a slightly acid soil; a pH of 6 is about right.

Soil treatment

Limas should follow a well manured crop such as potatoes or celery. Simply dig the soil fairly deeply and, if you can spare it, mulch with compost.

Propagation

Sow the seed about six to eight inches (15-20 cm) apart for bush varieties and eight inches (20 cm) apart for climbers. The former should be in rows 24 inches (75 cm) apart; the latter should be in one row. For the deep bed method (see p. 106) allow one foot (30 cm) between bushes, six inches (15 cm) between climbers which should still be planted in one row. In colder regions plant indoors in peat or paper pots and plant out in warm weather.

Care while growing

Mulching is very valuable, and the beans must also be kept well watered.

Pests and diseases

Downy mildew   This is often a serious problem in damp weather. To control it destroy diseased plants after harvest and rotate plantings at wide intervals.

Harvesting and storing

For eating green, harvest on the "pick and pick again" principle, once the beans are swelling in the pod. Don't pick them too late because, like pole beans, they get tough. If you want to dry them, leave the pods on the plant until the plants are dry. Pick the beans by hand, or thresh by walking on the plants.

Soybeans

You can eat soybeans green in the pods, shell them or dry them. They are very high in protein. The beans can be crushed for their oil and the flour which is left can be added to the flour of cereals to make a high protein bread.

Soil and climate

Soybeans grow well only where it is warm. They don't mind slightly acid soils, like high organic matter, and will grow in quite moist conditions.

Soil treatment

Soil with plenty of humus in it just needs a light forking. Otherwise dig thoroughly and lime for a pH of 6.5.

Propagation

Sow them outdoors in early summer; a good rule is to sow when the apple trees are in full bloom. Sow an inch (2.5 cm) deep and three inches (8 cm) apart in the rows – deep bed method (see p. 106) four inches (10 cm) apart. Where the beans have not been grown before, the seed should be inoculated with nitrogen-fixing bacteria, because it is likely that the right bacteria do not exist in the soil.

INOCULATING SOYBEAN SEED
Where soybeans have not been grown before, the soil may not contain the right nitrogen-fixing bacteria. Prepare seeds by stirring them up with water in a bowl. Add nitrogen-fixing bacteria to the water-coated seeds, making sure each seed is thoroughly covered with the bacteria. Careful inoculation will increase your yield by up to a third – and improve your soil into the bargain.

Care while growing

Hand weed rigorously, and mulch with compost if you can.

Pests and diseases

Soybeans are very hardy but they can suffer from various fungus diseases (see Pole beans). These can be prevented by proper crop rotation.

Harvesting and storing

Pick soybeans green and eat them whole, or wait for them to ripen, in which case steam or boil the pods for a few minutes before shelling them. Otherwise pull the plants and hang them up to dry.

Peanuts

Peanuts, or ground nuts or monkey nuts, are very rich in the vitamins A, B and E. They grow extensively in the southern states but can only be grown in the colder northern states with glass protection at each end of their season. As they are quite cheap to buy and as there are so many other things we really need our glass for they are hardly worth growing in cool climates.

Soil and climate

Peanuts need a warm growing season of over four months; five is ideal. They like sandy soil and, unlike most legumes, they like an acid soil: pH of 5 is about right.

Soil treatment

Dig deeply and incorporate plenty of compost. Never lime for peanuts.

Propagation

You can plant peanuts, shells and all, or shell them and plant the nuts. Plant shells eight inches (20 cm) apart, nuts four inches (10 cm) apart. For the deep bed method (see p. 106) allow four inches (10 cm) and three inches (8 cm) respectively. In warm climates plant four inches (10 cm) deep, but in cool climates make it only one and a half inches (4 cm). To give them the longest possible growing season in cool climates they should be planted at about the time of the last probable frost. You may need to start them off under glass, if you live in a very cold place. Sow them in rows 30 inches (75 cm) apart.

Care while growing

The yellow flowers are the staminate ones; the productive pistillate flowers are inconspicuous, and after being fertilized they bury themselves in the ground and develop into peanuts. Raise the soil in a circle around the plant so that the fruits forming at the ends of their stems can easily bury themselves. Peanuts will only ripen below ground.

Pests and diseases

Peanuts are hardy and rarely suffer from pests or diseases.

Harvesting and storing

In a warm climate pull the vines when the leaves go yellow and hang them in a dry airy place. In more temperate climates leave them until after the first frosts – the nuts will continue to ripen underground even after the leaves have frosted away. Before eating them roast your peanuts in their shells for 20 minutes in a 300°F (150°C) oven and leave them to cool – a vital part of the peanut roasting process.

Cruciferae

Cabbages, Brussels sprouts, cauliflowers, broccoli, kale, kohl-rabi, rutabagas, turnips, seakale, cresses and radishes all belong to the *Cruciferae*, which is one of the most important families, for it includes the genus *brassica*, the cabbage tribe. This contains a great variety of plants which have been bred by mankind to a profusion of different forms most of which are very good to eat. The reason for the peculiar succulence of the *brassica* is that nearly all the cultivated members of it are descended from the sea cabbage, and this gives them certain important characteristics. One is that they share with desert plants the ability to make do on very little fresh water, and another is that they are adapted to store what water they can get. It is this last fact that makes them so succulent. They guard the water they get under a waxy, waterproof cuticle.

Another characteristic of the *brassica* is that they are biennials: that means they store food in themselves during their first year of life and then flower and go to seed in their second. The stored food and energy of the first year's growth is available to us and our animals all winter.

Seed-bed for brassica

There are spring cabbages, summer cabbages and summer cauliflowers, but you can take it that most of your *brassica* will be for winter use. So you will find yourself, around early spring in temperate areas, establishing a seed-bed (see p. 92). This might be an area – depending on the size of your garden – as big as a table top. Work it to a very fine tilth, score parallel lines six inches (15 cm) apart with the corner of the hoe, lightly sprinkle seed along the rows, then cover the seeds with fine compost or earth, firming with the side of the rake. Plant a row each of cabbage, red cabbage, Brussels sprouts, fall cauliflower, sprouting broccoli (including calabrese) and, for good measure, leeks. I know the latter are not cruciferous but they go in there just the same. You must keep this seed-bed well watered, and when the plants are about five inches (13 cm) high, plant them out in their permanent beds, or if you are trying to get two crops, their holding-beds. In cold climates you must sow these seeds in seed boxes (flats) indoors, and plant them out later.

Cabbages

COMMON CABBAGES

You can grow cabbages all the year round in temperate climates and in climates with freezing winters you can easily store them the winter through in a shed or cellar. They are delicious raw and, if organically grown and cooked for a very short time, they are equally good served hot. They come with round or conical hearts, but this makes no difference to the way you grow them. Winter main crop cabbages are very high yielding: it is not unusual to get, on a field scale, forty tons per acre (100 tonnes per hectare). On a garden scale you can reckon on getting from a pound to a pound and a half (500–700 g) of cabbages per foot (30 cm) of row. So they are a good crop to grow, even if you only have a small garden.

Soil and climate

Cabbages will grow almost anywhere, but in hot dry areas they can only be grown in the fall and winter. They will stand winter frosts down to 20°F (−7°C): below that it is better to store them. They are greedy plants and like good soil, with plenty of organic matter in it and plenty of nitrogen and lime.

Soil treatment

Unlike the other *brassica,* cabbages like deeply dug ground with plenty of humus worked into it. If they follow the *Leguminosae* (pea and bean family) they will not need lime. If they don't they may well fare better if you do add a generous helping of lime.

Propagation

If you want cabbages all the year round, you have to divide them in three groups: winter, early and mid-season.
Early cabbage Early varieties may form their small heads in under 70 days from seed and require only a square foot each in which to develop. For a spring to summer harvest sow the seeds in greenhouse or hot-bed or cold frame about six to ten weeks before the last expected killing frost. As they prefer cool moist conditions plant outdoors as soon as danger of hard frost has passed.
Midseason (summer) cabbage These will probably form

the greater bulk of your cabbage plantings. They can be planted in greenhouse or hot-bed or cold frame at the same time as the early crop, but they take longer to mature. Although they stand the hot weather better than the early types, they should still be given an early start so they can really get growing before the heat hits them. You can grow them quite easily as long as your summers are not too hot and dry. Plant out when they are tiny, about two inches (5 cm) high, in very good soil and keep them well-watered. Plant them in staggered rows 18 inches (45 cm) apart with 18 inches (45 cm) between rows. If you use a deep bed (see p. 106) allow 15 inches (38 cm) between plants.

Late fall or winter cabbage Late cabbages are usually started in early summer and harvested in late fall. They are less susceptible to heat than the earlier kinds and make their heads during the fall weather.

You can double-crop – that is take two crops of different vegetables from the same bed in quick succession. To do this you must plant them out firmly in a holding-bed (see p. 93), a piece of the garden set aside for them, with each plant about six inches (15 cm) from its neighbors. Then, when ground becomes available as you harvest your early potatoes or peas and beans during the summer, you can plant out your cabbages and any other *brassica* which are in the holding-bed. They don't seem to suffer from this double transplanting.

Planting out

Plant out cabbages and all *brassica* firmly. Make a hole with a dibber, put the plant in at the same depth as it was in the holding-bed, and firm the soil around it with either the dibber, your hand or your shoe. Dipping *brassica* roots in a bucket of thin mud with a handful of lime in it before planting out helps them a lot. This brings the roots into instant contact with the awaiting earth. I knew an old gardener who dipped his plants in a paste of half earth and half cow dung with a handful of soot in it; he grew magnificent cabbages.

Care while growing

Cabbages must suffer no set backs. They must have plenty of water and nitrogen and no weed competition. If you are going to the extravagance of using some organic high-in-nitrogen manure like blood meal, bone meal, cotton seed meal, chicken or rabbit manure, then the *brassica* crops are good ones to put it on. Use it as a top dressing when they begin to grow. If the plants are checked, say by cabbage root fly, help them on with a dressing of this kind. You may save them. Don't put nitrogen on just before the winter; it drives them on too fast, makes them sappy and susceptible to frost damage. Hill up the stems as the plants grow.

Pests and diseases

If you are a good organic gardener and lucky, you may avoid these pests and diseases.

Clubroot One of the most troublesome things in the garden, but many people live all their lives and never see it. Your garden either has it or it hasn't. Beware, though, if it hasn't got it, because it can get it: by your buying infected plants; your bringing in manure from a contaminated source; you can even bring it in on your shoes, after visiting a neighbor's garden which has it. Don't put the stems of bought cabbages on your compost heap unless you have inspected them first and made absolutely sure they have not got clubroot.

When you have got clubroot you will find lumps or malformations on the roots of your wilting cabbages. You can get this with all the *brassica*. Cut a few of your root swellings open. If there is a maggot inside one, what you have probably got is cabbage gall weevil, not clubroot. Rejoice. At least that is preventable. But you can, of course, be favored by both.

Clubroot is caused by microscopic spores of a fungus which can lie dormant in the soil for up to seven years. The disease can be eradicated if the land is rested completely from cruciferous plants for seven years, and that means no cruciferous weeds either – so no shepherd's purse or charlock. The disease thrives in acid soil so lime helps to reduce it. If you can get the pH up to 7 you may get rid of it. But many gardeners have to live with clubroot (I have done so for several decades) and just grow *brassica* crops in spite of it. Non-organic gardeners dip the roots of their plants in calomine at the planting out stage. Calomine is a highly poisonous mercuric compound. The mercury is persistent in the soil and over the years inevitably builds up to serious proportions. Furthermore, the treatment is only occasionally effective. I fear that the plants are often infected invisibly at the seed-bed stage in which case nothing will cure them.

Preventive measures are: strict rotation so that cruciferous plants don't recur more often than once in four years; liming; burning of all affected roots; putting half a moth ball (camphor) down each hole before planting; putting a half inch (1 cm) length of rhubarb stem down each hole before planting; putting an equal mixture of wood ashes and crushed eggshells, down each hole. I have not had complete success with any of these, but they may help depending on your particular circumstances.

A new line of attack, which is being researched by the Henry Doubleday Association in Essex, England, is to douse the land that is not being planted with *brassica* with water in which *brassica* plants have been boiled. The effect of this is to wake the sleeping spores by fooling them into thinking that *brassica* have been planted. But there are no *brassica* and

DIPPING, DIBBING AND FIRMING
Prepare cabbages for planting by dipping the roots in a bucket of thin mud mixed with a handful of lime. Remember cabbages should be planted firmly. Use a dibber to make a hole to the same depth as the plant was growing in the holding-bed. Then pack the soil around the plant and heel in firmly with your shoe.

the awakened spores, being unable to go dormant again, die.

Yet another approach, which is worth trying, is to sprinkle affected ground with 65lbs (30kg) of quicklime per 100 square yards (84 sq m) and then leave the ground *brassica*-free for at least five years.

Cabbage root fly This attacks cabbages and cauliflowers but is less likely to go for Brussels sprouts or broccoli. If your plants wilt and you pull them out and cut into the roots and stems and find maggots, those are cabbage root fly maggots. When plants are badly affected their leaves appear bluish, with yellow edges. The fly, which looks like a house fly, lays its eggs on the top of the ground near the plants. The larvae hatch out, dig down through the soil, and then burrow up into the stem. Once there, nothing will shift them completely and they can kill the plant. Poisons don't help because they kill predators but on the whole tend to miss the maggots.

Small squares of tarpaper put like collars around each plant can obstruct the maggots. Either slit a five inch (13 cm) square piece of tarred paper from one side to the middle and slip each plant into the slit, or else fold the paper in half, snip a "V" out of the middle and thread the plant through the resulting hole. The flies lay their eggs on the paper and the maggots can't get down into the earth. A smear of kerosene on the paper is a good idea.

If plants do become infected, I hate to say it but a teaspoonful of nitrate of soda, or some other high inorganic nitrogen substance works wonders. It not only helps the plant to start growing quickly and make new roots, but it also seems to disperse the maggots. Banking the soil up around the stems of affected plants also seems to help them; the plants can put out new and healthier roots. Kerosene just sprinkled on the ground around each plant, once a week until they are large and healthy, also acts as a deterrent.

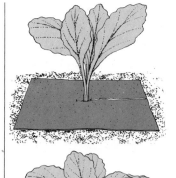

A TARRED COLLAR
Slit a five inch (13 cm) square of tarred paper from one side to the middle and slip it around the plant. A smear of kerosene or grease on the paper is also a good idea. The cabbage root fly will lay its eggs on the paper, but the maggots will not be able to get down into the earth to burrow up inside the plant stem.

A SEED PACKET COLLAR
An old seed packet, torn at both ends and placed over your cabbage plant, is effective protection against the destructive cut worm. Alternatively surround each plant with a ring of wood ash.

Burn all infected roots after the plants are lifted and fork the soil over frequently in winter to allow the birds to help themselves to the pupae which are lying dormant in the soil.

Cabbage gall weevil These sometimes attack plants in the seed-bed, and you will see small galls on the roots when you come to transplant. If there's only one gall, cut it open and kill the maggot. If there are more, burn the plant.

Cut worm These minute worms frequently nip small plants off at ground level. Keep them away with a ring of wood ash or by placing a cardboard collar around each plant. A simple collar can be made by tearing both ends from an old seed packet.

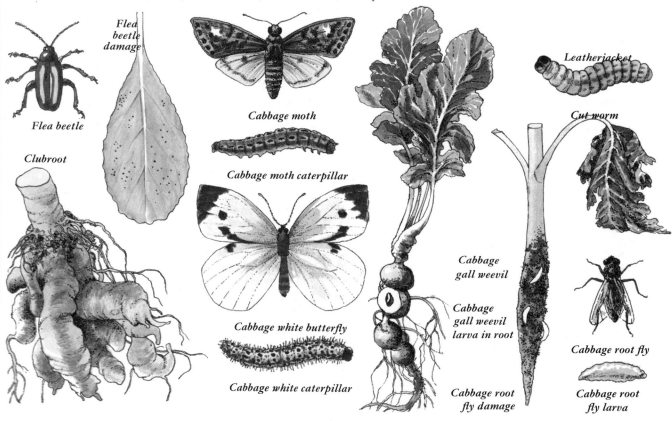

Flea beetle

Flea beetle damage

Clubroot

Cabbage moth

Cabbage moth caterpillar

Cabbage white butterfly

Cabbage white caterpillar

Cabbage gall weevil

Cabbage gall weevil larva in root

Cabbage root fly damage

Leatherjacket

Cut worm

Cabbage root fly

Cabbage root fly larva

Cabbage white butterfly The caterpillars of these can completely ruin a stand of cabbages if allowed to go unchecked. The best way to get rid of them on a small scale is to pick them off. Other remedies are to soak with soapy water, or sprinkle with a mixture of soot and lime.

Cabbage moth Pyrethrum or derris spraying will kill these larvae which eat the hearts of cabbages and whose droppings can cause mold.

Leatherjackets These are the gray-brown legless larvae of the crane fly. They sometimes eat the roots of *brassica* seedlings in late spring, causing the plants to wilt and die. All you can do is dig the ground very thoroughly and frequently in early spring so that the birds can eat the larvae.

Harvesting and storing

When you have cut a cabbage pull the root out immediately; if you leave it in, it will encourage disease. If the plants are healthy, you can hammer the stems with a heavy mallet or sledge hammer, or else run the garden roller over them. The object is to crush them, so that they can be put on the compost heap or buried in a trench over which you will plant next year's pole beans.

Cabbages can be stored by putting them on straw in a frostproof shed or cellar and covering them with more straw. In temperate climates just leave them growing until you want them: 20°F (—7°C) won't hurt them.

HARVESTING CABBAGES
Cut your cabbages at the top of the stem with a sharp knife. Remember to pull the stem and root from the ground.

HAMMERING CABBAGE STEMS
Hammer the uprooted cabbage stems with a mallet. The crushed stems can be left to rot for compost or buried in a trench.

SAVOYS

These are the hardiest cabbages, and for late winter and early spring use the most valuable. Treat them like winter cabbages, but don't eat them until the winter is well advanced and most other vegetables have gone. They fill a gap in the early spring.

RED CABBAGES

Start seed of fast-maturing varieties indoors in late winter for a spring crop. Sow slower maturing varieties outdoors in a seed bed and plant out in permanent positions in the summer. Make sure the soil is firm, otherwise the cabbages will not develop large and compact heads. Remember that although you can eat red cabbages raw, if you cook them they need far longer than ordinary cabbages – up to two hours.

Chinese Cabbages

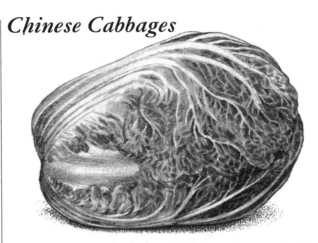

There are different varieties of Chinese cabbage – the Wong Bok produce rounded heads, the Michihli forms a tall cylindrical head and the Pac-Choy are loose-leaved.

Soil and climate

Chinese cabbage is not so winter-hardy as cabbage, but nevertheless it does not do well in heat. It does not like acid soil.

Soil treatment

They like plenty of humus. A four inch (10 cm) covering of compost on the soil forked in before planting is ideal.

Propagation

Sow the seed *in situ* in late summer or even later if you have no winter frost. Either broadcast and single out later or sow thinly in rows.

Care while growing

Chinese cabbages need plenty of water. Mulching when the plants have grown to six inches (15 cm) helps to conserve moisture. Tying with raffia at top and bottom also helps to conserve water. Thin to about nine inches (25 cm) apart. If the plants grow big and crowded, uproot half and eat them. They suffer very little from pests or diseases; what they do have will be something that afflicts cabbages (see Cabbages).

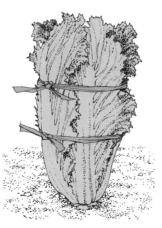

TYING A CHINESE CABBAGE
You must never allow a Chinese cabbage to go without water. When it has grown to about six inches (15 cm), a good mulching will help to conserve moisture. But as soon as the heart begins to form, it is an excellent idea to tie the leaves together top and bottom with strips of raffia. This will keep the plant sufficiently moist and at the same time blanch the inner leaves. Later on thin the plants to about nine inches (25 cm) apart; if they still grow crowded, uproot half and eat them.

Harvesting

Uproot them and eat them, either in salads or as cooked greens, as soon as they have a good heart. This can be as soon as ten weeks after planting.

Brussels Sprouts

Don't be put off Brussels sprouts by the store-bought ones. They have usually been picked at top-size and have a strong flavor. Home grown sprouts, picked small, are quite different.

Soil and climate

Sprouts grown in regions which have no frost are tasteless, but where there is frost they make a noble standby for late winter and spring. Sprouts grow well in any good soil.

Soil treatment

Deep cultivation and plenty of manure or compost are the rule. They need lime if the soil is acid. The traditional way to grow them is in very firm soil. Deep bed gardeners can transplant them into soft deep beds (see p. 106) by planting them deeper than usual and pressing down the soil around them with one hand before and during planting.

Propagation

Traditionally seeds are sown in an outdoor seed-bed in early spring. But you can get better results by sowing indoors in seed boxes (flats) from midwinter onward. Prick them out into frames if you sowed them early, then when they are about five inches (13 cm) tall plant them in a holding-bed (see p. 93) and then again into their permanent quarters where they should be three feet (90 cm) apart in rows three feet (90 cm) apart. Like other *brassica* they seem to benefit from transplanting. Deep bed gardeners should allow 20 inches (50 cm) between plants.

Care while growing

Brussels sprouts gain a lot from being earthed up while they are growing, and mulching is also good for them. Like all other *brassica* they don't like weed competition. Brussels sprouts grow very tall, so in very windy positions in exposed gardens, it may be necessary to stake them, but in most places a good earthing up will provide sufficient support. It is important to strip the lower leaves off when they begin to turn yellow.

Pests and diseases

Brussels sprouts are prone to all the diseases that afflict cabbages (see Cabbages).

Harvesting and storing

Seed sown in midwinter, indoors, will give sprouts as early as September, but these will not have the flavor of the later ones which have the benefit of a touch of frost. Like all vegetables, other than roots, they can be picked just as soon as they are ready. Pick the bottom ones first, then pick upward along the stems as more ripen, and finally eat the tops of the plants. If you have chickens, hang the denuded plants upside down in the chicken run. You can go on eating fresh sprouts in temperate climates right into the spring. If you grow sprouts, your garden in late winter may well be just a bare and untidy mud patch, with a sprinkling of snow on it and a few dozen tattered Brussels sprouts, naked as to their lower parts, bravely leaning against the freezing wind, sleet or hail.

In regions of intense cold or deep snow you can harvest the sprouts by pulling the plants out of the ground before the worst weather comes, and store them by heeling them into the earth or sand in a cellar or store room. If it is cold enough they will keep for months like this.

ROLLING THE BED
Sprouts need firm soil or they'll grow loose-leaved. Prepare the bed for planting by stamping on it or rolling with a heavy garden roller.

EARTHING UP
Deep cultivation is essential for sprouts. At regular intervals earth up around the base of each plant with a hoe.

STAKE SUPPORTS
Sprouts can grow very tall, so it's a good idea to stake the stem of each plant – especially if it is growing in a windy position.

PICKING SPROUTS
When the sprouts have grown to the right size, pick first from the bottom of the stem, then work upward to the top of the plant.

Cauliflowers

EARLY AND MAIN CROP CAULIFLOWERS

To develop cauliflowers, and also broccoli, man has taken the basic biennial cabbage plant, which naturally flowers in its second year of growth, and bred it to flower in its first. Cauliflowers have heads made up of tightly bunched white or purple flowers; the purple ones, sometimes called purple hearting broccoli, turn green when cooked. When you grow cauliflowers remember that you are asking biennial plants to get through the whole of their life-cycle — growth, storage of nourishment, and flowering — all in one short season.

Soil and climate

Cauliflowers do best in temperate climates. They prefer heavy, moist soil with plenty of humus. They simply won't grow on poor soil, or in bad conditions.

Soil treatment

They need very firm soil, so don't pull out the pea or bean plants which may precede the cauliflowers in the bed, because this will loosen the soil. Hoe them off instead, leaving the roots in the ground. Then roll or tramp. Like all *brassica*, cauliflowers don't like acid, so you must lime as necessary. Fork on a good dressing of fish manure (see p. 90) two weeks before planting. They also need some potash.

PLANTING OUT CAULIFLOWERS
Young cauliflower plants can be removed from the seed box as soon as they have grown three true leaves in addition to the original two seed leaves. But check that the plant isn't "blind" — meaning that it has failed to develop a bud in the center. If it is blind, then it won't be of any use to you — without the bud, your cauli just won't flower.

Propagation

You can get very early cauliflowers by sowing seed in mid-winter indoors and planting out as soon as the ground has warmed up after the winter — probably in the middle of spring. With luck you will be eating them by midsummer.

For your main crop sow seed in your brassica seed-bed (see p. 122) after the last frost. Sow a quick-maturing variety so that you can begin to harvest in late summer, alongside a slower variety which can be harvested in the fall and early winter. Plant out as soon as the plants have three true leaves as well as the two original seed leaves. If you are double-cropping, plant out in your holding-bed (see p. 93) and move them to their final position after peas or beans in mid-summer. Examine the plants when you take them out of the seed-bed. If they are "blind", meaning they have no tiny bud in the middle, throw them away. They won't make curds as the flowers are called. For the final planting out allow two feet (60 cm) between rows with 20 inches (50 cm) between plants. Allow 15 inches (40 cm) between plants if you use the deep bed method (see p. 106).

Care while growing

Do plenty of hoeing. Top-dress the growing plants with high nitrogen if you have it, but if your ground is really organic, with plenty of humus in it, a mulch of compost will do very well. Don't let your cauliflowers dry out because they must keep moving.

BLANCHING THE CURDS
Sunlight striking cauliflower curds can cause not only discoloration, but sometimes even a bad taste, so you need to protect them from the sun. Cover them by bending or breaking some of the outer leaves of the plant, and tying these in position over the plant with string.

If you don't want the trouble of blanching your cauliflowers, try growing purple ones. They last longer in the ground than the white headed variety and need no blanching. The heads are deep purple on top and turn green when cooked; the flavor is like a mild broccoli.

Pests and diseases

Cauliflowers share their pests and diseases with cabbages.

Harvesting

Harvest your cauliflowers as soon as they develop solid curds. The first should appear in late summer. If you wait the curds will loosen and deteriorate. Cut well below the head if you want to eat the cauliflower immediately. If you pull them up by the roots you can store them in a cold cellar for up to a month.

WINTER CAULIFLOWERS

Winter cauliflower is also known as self-protecting broccoli, but it looks and behaves like cauliflower, except that it is hardy in mild climates and comes to harvest from midwinter. Sow in late spring and treat like main crop cauliflower.

Broccoli

Kale

The broccoli most commonly grown in the U.S. forms a green head, and is known as calabrese in other countries. It is very easy to grow and has more flavor than other varieties, but the plants are less hardy. The purple and white sprouting varieties are winter-hardy and can be harvested from late winter on.

Soil and climate

Good soil is not essential and they will grow in any but the very coldest climates.

Soil treatment

Give them very firm ground; even grassland from which you have just stripped the turf will do. Sprinkle with lime if your soil is at all acid.

Propagation

For an early crop sow broccoli indoors in early spring and plant it out after last frost. For a slightly later crop sow seed outdoors just before last frost. White and purple varieties are sown in the brassica seed bed in spring and planted out when there is room for them. Allow 18 inches (45 cm) between plants and 30 inches (75 cm) between rows. For the deep bed method (see p. 106) allow 18 inches (45 cm) all ways.

Care while growing

Mulch between the rows in summer. Mulch with straw in winter and stake the plants if they grow tall.

Pests and diseases

Broccoli gets clubroot mildly. It does not suffer badly from pests.

Harvesting

Pick, and pick again, from the little flowering shoots as these become available. Keep picking right through summer. White and purple varieties can be picked through fall and even winter.

Kale is very winter-hardy and is often the last of the winter *brassica* left standing. It will withstand temperatures below freezing and may be used nearly all winter as far north as Philadelphia. There are many varieties, both crinkly and smooth leaved, including collards. Kale is a non-hearting cabbage plant. All you get is the green leaves and these are much better after a frost. Although they don't have the same delicacy of flavor as other brassica, they are very nutritious and rich in vitamins. Cooked kale, provided it is only lightly cooked, has twice as much vitamin C as the equivalent weight of orange juice.

Soil and climate

Grow it wherever there are frosts. Any soil will do, but it crops best on rich soil.

Soil treatment

Kale likes fertile soil which need not be especially firm.

Propagation

Grow kale for eating in your *brassica* seed-bed (see p. 122) and plant it out, when you have room, 20 inches (50 cm) apart in rows 30 inches (75 cm) apart. If you use the deep bed method (see p. 106) allow 15 inches (40 cm) between plants in all directions.

Pests and diseases

Kale has a strong built-in resistance to clubroot. You can protect it from cabbage root fly and cabbage white butterfly by spraying with nicotine in the autumn. Kale is very tough but all the same it can suffer from any of the cabbage pests and diseases (see Cabbages).

Harvesting

Harvest from midwinter onward. Pick leaves and side shoots, but always leave some on the plant. Your crop will last you till late spring if you are very lucky. Young leaves can be eaten in salads; other ones are good boiling greens.

Rutabagas & Turnips

Rutabagas and turnips are both *brassica* in which the first year's nourishment is stored in the root instead of, like the other *brassica*, in the stem or the leaves. Rutabagas are orange whereas turnips are white, and rutabagas have their leaves coming out of a neck on top of the root whereas turnip leaves grow directly from the root. Turnips will not stand severe frost, but rutabagas are a lot more hardy.

Turnips will come to harvest between 60 and 80 days after sowing. Rutabagas take about a month longer. Both can be sown late in the summer. They therefore make a good "catch crop"– a crop put in late after you have cleared the ground of something else. This is another way of getting two crops from the same plot in one year. When you are choosing what variety of turnip to plant, don't overlook the fact that some varieties can do double duty by producing both edible leaves and roots. In some varieties the foliage can be used for greens a month after seeding.

Soil and climate

They do best in a cool and damp climate. In hot weather they become hard and fibrous and are likely to go to seed. If you live in a hot climate you must sow either very early in the spring so that they can be harvested when very young and tender, before the hot weather of the summer, or late in the fall when they will grow happily into the winter and come to full maturity. A light fertile loam is ideal, but they will grow in most soils. They like a neutral or slightly alkaline soil like all *brassica*, so lime if your soil is acid.

Soil treatment

Cultivate deeply. Like all root crops, turnips and rutabagas like a very fine tilth. If you get a lot of rain in your area, grow your turnips and rutabagas on ridges. You can encourage their capacity for fast growing by manuring a year in advance.

Propagation

In cool temperate climates turnips for picking and eating young should be sown in late spring and then, if you are a turnip lover, twice more at monthly intervals. Sow main crop turnips for storing in late summer. Even early fall is not too late to get a good crop of "turnip tops", which are even tastier than spinach and contain lots of iron. Sow

rutabagas in early summer. The same sowing will provide young sweet rutabagas for eating in late summer and main crop for storage. Sow both turnips and rutabagas thinly in shallow drills where they are to grow. An ounce (28 g) of turnip or rutabaga seed will sow 250 feet (75 m) of row.

THINNING THE SEEDLINGS
Turnips or rutabagas shouldn't be crowded together. Start thinning them out, using a hoe, when they are still quite small. Leave about nine inches (23 cm) between plants. If you're using the deep bed method, a distance of about six inches (15 cm) between plants will be enough.

Care while growing

When the plants are still tiny thin them out with the hoe so as to leave one plant about every nine inches (23 cm) – deep bed method, one plant every six inches (15 cm). Leave a shorter distance for successional summer sowings which are to be eaten very young, and a greater distance for the winter main crop which is intended for storing.

Pests and diseases

Turnips and rutabagas are subject to most of the pests and diseases which afflict cabbages and the same remedies can be taken (see Cabbages).
Flea beetle When they are very young turnips and rutabagas may get flea beetle (see p. 124). This shows as tiny holes on the leaves. A good shower of rain should cure it, or a good hosing with water if there is no rain. If this doesn't work, either derris or pyrethrum dust will kill them.
Boron deficiency Turnips and rutabagas are usually the first vegetables to suffer from boron deficiency. The core of your turnip or rutabaga will develop grayish-brown areas which will eventually rot and stink. A minimal amount of boron dissolved in water and added to the soil is sufficient to correct this deficiency.

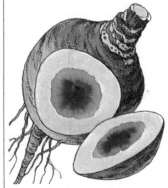

BORON DEFICIENCY
Turnips and rutabagas are good indicators of boron deficiency in your soil, since they are generally the first vegetables to suffer. The core of the turnip or swede will turn a grayish-brown color and begin to rot and stink – sometimes becoming completely hollow in the center. An ounce (28 g) of boron is sufficient to restore a quarter of an acre (1000 sq m) of land. Dissolve it in enough water to cover this area.

Harvesting and storing

The early successionally-sown crop should be pulled during the summer when they are not more than three inches (8 cm) in diameter and are then at their sweetest. Main crop turnips should be harvested before the first very hard frosts and put in either a root store or a clamp (see p. 136). Rutabagas in all but the severest climates can be left out in the ground until they are wanted. So, eat your turnips before your rutabagas.

Kohlrabi

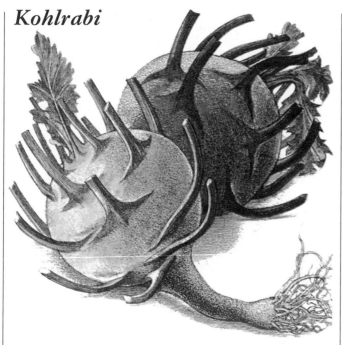

This strange looking plant is merely a cabbage in which all the nutrients are stored in a swollen stem instead of in tight-packed leaves.

Soil and climate
Kohlrabi likes the same conditions as other *brassica* but is even more dependent on moist soil; drought makes them hard and woody.

Propagation
It is better not to transplant kohlrabi, but to sow the seed out where the plants will grow. Sow thinly in two or three successional sowings between late spring and midsummer.

Care while growing
Thin the plants you want to eat in the summer to six inches (15 cm) apart — deep bed method four inches (10 cm). Those you want to store through the winter thin to ten inches (25 cm).

Pests and diseases
Kohlrabi can suffer from everything that afflicts cabbages.

Harvesting and storing
Pick the plants very young and tender — about two and a half inches (6 cm) across — and eat them raw or cooked. Store them, as shown below.

STORING KOHLRABI
Pack kohlrabi in an unheated shed or cellar between layers of straw.

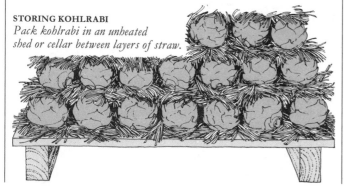

Radishes

SUMMER RADISHES
Radishes grow in three to four weeks, are rich in iron and vitamin C and are excellent for adding bite and crispness to salads. They are good for growing in odd vacant corners, and they do well in window boxes as well. Winter radishes are larger and can be black, white, red, or red and white.

Soil and climate
Radishes like good rich damp soil and a cool moist climate. Since they grow fast and are eaten quickly it does not matter if they are grown in beds not reserved for *Cruciferae* for they don't have time to develop diseases. In hot regions they can be grown only as a winter crop. In temperate climates they can be grown in spring, summer, and fall.

Soil treatment
Like most *Cruciferae* they don't like acid soil, so you should lime if it seems necessary.

Propagation
Just sprinkle the large black seeds thinly in shallow drills and cover them, or else broadcast and rake in. Sow very few at a time, but sow often — even every two weeks — so you have fresh tender radishes whenever you want them. The seeds will keep for five years, so don't throw them away. If you want early radishes, you can sprinkle them among other crops that you are forcing in a hot-bed, or in a deep bed covered with transparent plastic or glass. In the deep bed (see p. 106) sow one inch (2.5 cm) apart in each direction.

Pests and diseases
Flea beetle (see Rutabagas and Turnips).
Root maggot Keep these away by scattering small pieces of tarpaper among your seedlings.

Harvesting
Just pull, wash and eat. If you have too many, pull them out anyway. Don't let them grow up hard and woody, or go to seed. If you can't eat them, feed them to the rabbits.

WINTER RADISHES
White radishes should be sown between late spring and midsummer; others toward the end of the summer. They will all be ready for harvest at the end of the autumn. White ones must be dug and stored in peat. The others can be left in the ground until required during the winter.

Seakale

Seakale is a perennial whose young shoots should preferably be harvested in spring, but if you so wish it can be forced for eating fresh in winter.

Soil and climate
Seakale likes a rich deep well-manured loamy soil and a cool damp climate. Don't try to grow it anywhere hot and arid.

Soil treatment
Dig deeply – at least two spade lengths – and incorporate plenty of rich manure.

Propagation
Seakale can be started from root cuttings, called thongs, or from seed. The former method is preferable, because plants started from root cuttings begin to yield the second year, a year earlier than seedlings. However it is said that a new race should be raised from seed from time to time. Get your thongs from a seed dealer or a fellow gardener. They are just bits of root about four inches (10 cm) long. Plant them six inches (15 cm) deep and 30 inches (75 cm) from each other in late winter – deep bed 15 inches (38 cm) apart. If you plant from seed, sow in shallow drills in early spring.

Care while growing
If you sow seed, thin to four inches (10 cm) apart and transplant to 30 inches (75 cm) apart the following spring.

Keep well weeded. You cannot eat green seakale because it is bitter. Therefore the plants must be blanched – that is deprived of light completely so that they go quite white. You blanch them by covering them with buckets, boxes, or upturned flowerpots with the drainage holes blocked up. If you want fresh seakale during the winter you can force its growth. Either spread hot manure over the blanching covers so as to provide heat, or take the roots from their outdoor bed in the fall and plant them in loam in a hot-bed, or warmed frame, or even in a warmed cellar. Keep your seakale warm – the soil should be 55 to 60°F (13-16°C) – and dark, and you will get a good winter crop.

Pests and diseases
Small seedlings are occasionally attacked by flea beetle (see Turnips); otherwise they are not prone to attack.

Harvesting
Cut shoots when they are about a foot (30 cm) high in spring, unless you have forced the plants for a winter harvest. Like all perennials that are harvested for food, seakale must be treated with respect. After you have taken what you need let it grow up into the sunshine, green and strong, and build itself up for next year.

Cresses

WATER CRESS
If your garden has a corner which is persistently damp, water cress is the ideal crop. It has the distinctive hot flavor of the *Cruciferae*.

Soil and climate
It does best in cool climates, but will grow perfectly well in a warm one especially if it is standing in cold flowing water.

Propagation
It is possible to create a bed, next to a flowing stream. Flood the bed by admitting water from the stream after sowing the water cress. You can grow it from seed, either planting the seed in the wet mud just above the water or sowing it indoors, in potting compost, in earthenware pots which should be kept in a tray into which water flows constantly. You can bring it to maturity like this or else plant it out in a stream or damp bed. Another method is to buy really fresh commercial water cress from the farmer's market, put it in a plastic bag with some water, take it home and plant it.

Care while growing
Pinch out the top shoots to make the plants bushy. If a plant flowers, cut it right back.

Pests and diseases
Never grow water cress in water to which sheep or cattle have access. If you do, you might just get liver fluke.

Harvesting
Pick out side shoots. The more you pick, the more grow.

GARDEN CRESS
Like mustard (see p. 199), cress is eaten in the seedling stage, although if you are growing them together remember that cress takes a few days longer than mustard to germinate. Grow it on damp sacking or a damp peat bed. Sow it thickly throughout spring and summer.

UPLAND CRESS
Also known as American cress, this is a relatively hardy salad plant, which should be pulled after about seven weeks of growth. Sow successively through the summer for several months' salad supply. Sow half an inch (1.5 cm) apart and later thin to about six inches (15 cm) between plants. Find a fairly shady site which will not dry out, and protect the crop under glass as the weather becomes colder.

Solanaceae

Potatoes, tomatoes, peppers and eggplants are all members of the *Solanaceae*. There is something a little exotic about this family, for it includes such dark and midnight subjects as deadly nightshade and tobacco, as well as such luscious tropical annuals as green peppers and chilis.

But there is nothing exotic about the potato. Even that great English farmer and writer of the early nineteenth century, William Cobbett, termed it "the lazy root", for he thought it would supplant wheat, the cultivation of which he considered to be the nursery of English virtues.

The other important member of the family is the tomato. Early European explorers in America found the plant growing wild and it was regarded as highly poisonous by the Indians. It is so closely related to the potato that a hybrid has been created which has inferior potatoes on its roots and inferior tomatoes on its stems.

Most of the edible *Solanaceae* come from tropical south and central America and they require very rich, damp and fertile soil, as similar to the rich leaf-mold of the tropical jungle as possible. Furthermore, none of the food-bearing *Solanaceae* are frost-hardy, which means, if you live in a cool climate, you must either start them off indoors, or not plant them until all danger of frost is past.

The *Solanaceae* have several pests and diseases in common and it is therefore advisable to grow them all in the same bed, or in the same part of the rotation. In this way your land is given a rest from solanaceous plants for the full cycle of four years, and there is no chance for disease to build up or for pests to accumulate. Certain eel worms, for example, can multiply to frightening proportions if tomatoes and potatoes are grown too often on the same land. Never touch any solanaceous plants when your fingers have been in contact with tobacco, because tobacco is a member of the *Solanaceae* and frequently contains virus disease.

One of the great values of most plants of this family is that they are rich in vitamin C. Potatoes are the richest source of this for most inhabitants of temperate regions, and chilis are the richest source in many parts of the tropics. The reason why Asians eat hot curry is not to cool them down, but to provide themselves with vitamin C.

All in all life would be much poorer were it not for this tribe of strange, soft-stemmed, potash-hungry, tropical-looking plants.

Potatoes

The potato is one of the few plants on which a person could live if he could get nothing else; and, unlike the others, it requires very simple preparation: no threshing, winnowing, grinding, or any of the jobs that make grain consumption a difficult technical operation.

Self-sufficiency from the garden in temperate climates is unthinkable without the spud, and I would recommend anybody, except those with the tiniest of plots, to devote at least a quarter of his land to it, and preferably as much as a third. Being a member of the family, *Solanaceae*, it provides the soil with a rest from those families which are more commonly represented in our gardens. Without the potato break we would find ourselves growing *brassica,* for example, far too frequently on the same ground.

Soil and climate

Never lime for potatoes. They thrive in an acid soil: anything over a pH of 4.6. Scab, which makes them unsightly but doesn't really do them much harm, thrives in alkaline conditions but is killed by acidity. Potash is essential for good potatoes (but if you put on plenty of manure or compost you will have enough of that) and so is phosphate. Nitrogen is not so important, although a nitrogen shortage (unlikely in a good organic garden) will lower your yield.

Unfortunately the potato did not originally evolve for the climates of the northern hemisphere. It evolved in the Andes, and the wild potato is a mountain plant, although tropical. Its provenance makes it very frost tender; the least touch of frost will damage its foliage and halt its growth.

Soil treatment

It is well worth digging the soil deeply the previous fall, and incorporating a heavy ration of manure or compost while you're at it; 8 cwt (400 kg) per 100 sq yds (84 sq m) is about right. Another excellent thing to do is to broadcast some green manure crop, such as rye, the previous autumn after your root break. If you do this you should leave the crop undisturbed until a month or two before you want to plant your potatoes – unless, that is, your green manure is clover in which case you should dig it in in the autumn. In any case dig the green manure crop well into the ground and at the same time dig in compost or manure. Or, and this works perfectly well, you can, if you have been short of time in the winter or if the weather has not enabled you to dig, actually dig the green manure crop in at the time of planting the potatoes. Throwing any available compost or muck into the bottom of the furrow, plant the potatoes on top of this and fill in with the green manure.

Plant your potatoes where a green manure crop like winter rye has been growing. A month before planting, dig the green manure crop into the ground along with compost or manure.

SOWING EARLY POTATOES
Make a trench five inches (13 cm) deep with a hoe, put in manure or compost if you have it and put the seed potatoes in, rose-end up, about a foot (30 cm) apart.

COVERING EARLY POTATOES
Three to four inches (8 to 10 cm) of soil is enough covering for newly-planted early seed potatoes. You'll be hilling them up later on anyway.

Propagation

I know of nobody who grows potatoes from actual seed, although potatoes set seed in little green fruit that look just like small tomatoes. It is better to use sets which are, in fact, just potatoes, although they are called "seed". If you plant a potato it will grow into a potato plant which produces between six and a dozen more potatoes. (The actual potatoes, by the way, are not *roots* — they are swollen underground *stems*.)

Potatoes grown in temperate areas toward sea level are heir to certain diseases which are the price they pay for growing in the wrong place. Among these are certain virus diseases which are transmitted by aphids. If you plant potato "seed" you will probably get a good crop of potatoes. But if you plant them where aphids abound, and you plant the new generation of sets from them the next year, the crop is likely to be slightly less. If you go on for a third year, and a fourth year, the crop will diminish even further. This is because there is a build-up, with every generation, of the virus diseases introduced by aphids. The remedy is to get your "seed" from people who grow potatoes in places where there are no aphids. In practice "seed" potatoes must be grown above a certain altitude, or else on some wind-swept sea island where aphids wouldn't have a chance. The specialist seed growers carefully "rogue" the potato plants as they grow (that is pull out any weak or diseased potatoes) and protect them from infection. The tubers that they lift for sale to their customers are therefore disease-free seed.

All this does not mean that you cannot keep and plant your own tubers. Most people do, and you can even buy "once-grown" or "twice-grown" seed from your neighbors. And if you have land at over 800 feet (240 m) in the northeastern US, or on a sea-girt island, you can probably grow "seed" for ever, both for yourself and to trade for other goods with your neighbors. Seed potatoes should, ideally, be about 1½ ounces (42 g) in weight. You can cut larger tubers in half, provided you leave some "eyes" (small shoots) on each half but I don't like doing this as it can let in disease. Ideally seed should be "chitted" before being planted. That is, it should be spread out, one spud thick, in a cool place, and in diffused light. Don't allow frost to get to it (frost will immediately rot potatoes) and keep it out of hot sunlight. If the place is too hot and dark, long gangly shoots will grow off the potatoes and tend to break off before you plant them. (If you *can* plant them without breaking these shoots off though, the potatoes will grow very well.)

So the best thing to do with your seed potatoes is to lay them in chitting boxes in midwinter. These will stack one on top of the other and admit light and air to the potatoes, and can be carried conveniently out to the garden for planting.

New potatoes New potatoes grow very quickly and can be eaten straight from the ground. They are not for storing. Plant them as early as you can, but remember that frost will kill them once they appear above the ground, unless they are protected with cloches or a thick covering of straw or compost. If they get frosted you may be able to save them by hosing the frost off with warm water.

Main crop Your store of "main crop" potatoes will go a long way toward keeping you alive during the winter. Plant them in late spring.

Chitting is almost essential for new potatoes, but if you don't get round to chitting for your main crop, never mind, plant them just the same. You will still get a crop – it will be later, that's all. And never plant any diseased tuber, or one that looks defective in any way. You will simply be spreading disease among your own crops, as well as those of your neighbors.

Don't put new potatoes in too deep: if they have four inches (10 cm) of soil over them when you have finished, that is enough. If the land has been dug before, that is, if you are not digging it for the first time since the previous fall, just make a furrow with the corner of a hoe, about five inches (13 cm) deep, put the potatoes in, and cover with about

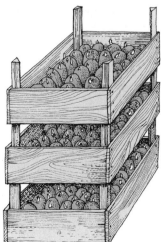

CHITTING SEED POTATOES
Place seed potatoes in single layers in chitting boxes. Put the seeds in "rose-end" up — the end with the most eyes. Protect from frost and direct sunlight. Before planting rub off all but three sprouts at the "rose-end".

USING A POTATO PLANTER
If your soil is light, loamy or sandy, you can save yourself some toil by using a potato planter. Ram it down into well-dug ground with your foot, drop a potato into the cup, then close the cup by pushing the handles of the planter together. Withdraw the planter, and the potato will be left buried in the ground. The method isn't quite as good for the potato as simple trenching, but it is easier and quicker. The potato planter is useless for sowing in heavy soil or clay, but it is ideal for the deep bed method.

four inches (10 cm) of soil. You will hill them up well later, and do not want the crop to grow inconveniently deep in the ground. If you have light, loamy or sandy land you would do well to get a potato planter, which is also the ideal thing for the deep bed method (see p. 106).

For new potatoes have the drills about two feet (60 cm) apart, but have them 30 inches (75 cm) for main crop. Put earlies in a foot (30 cm) apart in the rows: main crop about 15 inches (38 cm). Remember main crop have much longer to grow and produce much bigger and heavier crops.

Now there are other methods of planting potatoes. One excellent one is to plant the potatoes on compost, cover them with more compost and then a thick mulch of straw or spoiled hay. Or you can use leaves or leaf-mold in this way with good results. If you grow new potatoes with this method you can gently remove some of the mulch, take a few potatoes, and let the plant go on growing to produce some more. All these mulch-cover methods do great good in that they enrich the soil for other crops after the potatoes are finished. As you rotate your potato crop around your garden the whole holding becomes enriched.

A very effective method, which has the advantage that it can be done in a small space — even on a patio — is to grow potatoes in a barrel. Fill the bottom of a barrel with a thin layer of earth and plant a single "seed" potato in it. Keep adding more soil as the plant grows upward and you will find that more and more tubers will form in the new soil.

PLANTING ON COMPOST
Put a good layer of compost in the furrow, and plant the potatoes on top. Cover them with compost, then mulch with straw.

HARVESTING FROM COMPOST
Lift some of the mulch, pull a few potatoes and replace the mulch. The plant will go on to produce the main crop.

Finally the green plant will be sprouting out of the top of the barrel. Wait for the plant to flower and then simply empty the barrel out. You will find a huge number of potatoes in it.

You can work the same principle to even better effect by laying an old car, truck or tractor tire on its side, filling it with earth and planting one or more potato sets in it. When the plants have grown, but before they flower, add another tire and fill it with earth. Allow the plants to continue growing. Keep adding tires until the plants reach about four feet (1.2m). Then harvest by dismantling the whole structure. This is better than the barrel method because the plants

GROWING POTATOES IN TRASH CANS
Growing potatoes in trash cans is particularly useful is your space is limited — even a patio will do. Take an old can, and fill about a sixth of it with earth. Plant one or more potato sets. When the plants have grown, but before they flower, put another layer of earth on top. Continue building up layers of earth as the plants appear until they reach about four feet (1.2 m). When the potatoes are ready for harvesting, simply empty out the bin and you'll find you have a surprisingly heavy crop.

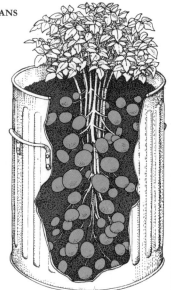

have plenty of light throughout their growth. Painting the tires white makes them more attractive.

If you plant in a deep bed you should get an enormous crop. You can plant 18 inches (45 cm) deep. And in the very soft earth of the deep bed you can plant with a potato planter. Leave a foot (30 cm) between potatoes.

Care while growing
Potatoes need a lot of room under the ground, and they will turn green if exposed for more than a day or two to the light, in which case they become bitter and poisonous. This is because they produce a toxin called solanin. It is usual therefore to hill them up, that is to draw or throw earth up around the plants so as to protect the growing tubers from the light and give them plenty of room for growth and expansion. Of course people who grow beneath a mulch don't have to do this, but they do have to make sure that there is plenty of mulch to cover the potatoes completely. Potatoes do not like weed competition, and in the very rich, deeply cultivated soil that they grow best in, weeds grow at an amazing rate. When you ridge up you must be sure to kill the weeds. When weeds sprout up on the ridges between the potatoes you must either hoe them out or pull them by hand. Throw them down in the furrows to rot and they will help by forming a mulch.

One tip about hilling up potatoes: for some reason the plants stand upright at night and in the early morning, but sprawl helplessly during the heat of the day. Potatoes are far easier to hill up early in the morning when they are standing up like soldiers on parade. Like real soldiers, when the sun

HILLING UP POTATO PLANTS
Draw up soil around the plants with a hoe, covering any exposed tubers and giving them room for further growth. It's best to do this at night or in the early morning when the plants are standing upright.

gets hot they are inclined to faint. You may have to hill up several times; the final one should be thorough, the ridges patted down with the back of the spade and made steep and even, for in this way they defy the spores of potato blight should this disease strike (as it very likely will).

When the tops of the main crop meet over the rows they will suppress weeds and, after the final hilling up, you can relax for a while.

Pests and diseases

Potato blight The degree of blight trouble depends largely on the section of the country and weather conditions. Wet seasons favor the disease, which shows first as water-soaked areas on the leaves with a mold on the underside. The spores are dropped from the leaves and washed down into the soil where they infect the tubers which go soft and rot. Late blight which is caused by *Phytophthora infestans* is probably the most generally destructive potato disease. In 1845 it swept right across Ireland causing the deaths of nearly a million people.

No cure was found for blight until toward the end of the last century somebody noticed that potatoes growing downwind from copper smelting plants did not get blight. So could copper prevent this dreaded disease? A mixture of copper sulfate and lime was tried – similar to the mixture already being used by the vignerons of Bordeaux against mildew on their grapes. It was found that if the foliage was sprayed with this at "blight times" – when the temperature and humidity of the air were above a certain point – the foliage was protected from the drifting spores of the blight. So now, to avoid blight I spray, very thoroughly above and below the leaves, with Bordeaux mixture, and I do it about once every two weeks throughout the hot and humid weather of the summer. If you are in a dry windy area you may not get blight. Ask your neighbors. You can buy a proprietary spray or else mix up your own Bordeaux mixture (see p. 105).

And what if you do get blight? You will know by black patches which appear on the leaves, and thereafter develop borders of white powdery stuff which is, in fact, the spores of the fungus which causes the disease. You cannot cure it by spraying then, although you may protect healthy plants from its spread. But do not despair. Unless the attack is a very early one the spores will not spread down to your tubers, and if you have earthed up well, spores that are washed down by the rain will not sink into the earth and come into direct contact with the tubers. You must cut the haulms (foliage) off with a very sharp blade (sharp so as not to drag the potatoes out of the ground) and burn them. It is sad for an organic gardener to have to say burn anything, but – yes – burn them. Then leave your tubers undisturbed in the ground for at least three weeks after you have removed the haulms. If you lift them immediately they will come into contact with billions of spores on the surface of the soil. If you leave them be the spores will be washed down the steep sides of the ridges into the furrows where they will sink harmlessly into the soil below. Leave the potatoes for as long as possible. In the moderate climate where I live I often don't lift them until I need them to cook – even after Christmas sometimes. They are safer there in the ground than they are if I lift them.

Wart disease The disease manifests itself by wartish growths which look like dirt on the surface of the potato. The cooking quality is not affected but if such potatoes are used for seed the seedlings may be girdled and die. The disease manifests itself by wartish growths that can cover the surface of the potato. Burn all such potatoes. I have grown wart-free potatoes for a lifetime, but when it does infest your ground you should plant only immune varieties. Otherwise don't grow potatoes for six years on that land and just hope the disease will die out. 65 pounds (30 kg) of quicklime per 100 sq yds (84 sq m) of infected land are said to kill it.

Scab You will probably get this if you grow potatoes in very alkaline soil or in soil that has been recently limed. It is not serious. If you want to sell potatoes it matters, for they don't look nice. If you just want to eat them don't worry about it; simply peel the scab off. But plenty of manure or compost will prevent scab, so organic gardens simply shouldn't have it.

Potato root eel worm This attacks chiefly the monoculturalists who grow potatoes on the same soil year after year – or at any rate too frequently. Don't grow potatoes too often on the same soil. If you get it really badly you will have to give up growing potatoes there for at least ten years, although it is said that if you grow several crops of *Tagetes minuta* on the land, and compost it, or dig it in as green manure, it will suppress eel worm. And, if you grow a crop of *Tagetes minuta* the year before planting potatoes, it will fool the eel worm cysts, by its secretions, into remaining dormant during the tenure of the potato crop.

Colorado beetle This is yellow with four black stripes on its back. It hibernates deep in the soil and emerges in early summer to lay its eggs on potato foliage. The grubs then eat the leaves and can easily destroy a whole crop. Potatoes grown on a very large scale are the most susceptible. If you

SPRAYING FOR BLIGHT
During hot and humid weather you can protect your potato crop against blight by spraying over and under the leaves every two weeks or so with Bordeaux mixture. If some of your crop is affected in spite of this, continue spraying the healthy plants, so that the disease is prevented from spreading.

Leaf blight *Eel worm damage*

Scab

Tuber blight *Colorado beetle* *Wart disease*

do see a beetle on the leaves squash it, and immediately notify the nearest Agricultural Agent, and take his advice. The grubs can be sprayed with derris, pyrethrum or, best of all, nicotine. Deep dig in the winter to expose the beetles to attack by birds.

The other diseases of the potato (and there are over a hundred) should not be a problem provided you use only clean, healthy seed and grow on heavily manured or composted ground, preferably not more than once every four years. Don't suffer "volunteers" to exist; that is plants which have grown up from potatoes which you have inadvertently left in the ground. They will only cause a build-up of disease.

Harvesting and storing

You can harvest any time after the plants have flowered. Dig potatoes carefully with a fork, taking great pains not to spear any, and if you do spear any, eat those first, for if you store them with the others they may cause rot. You can scrape and eat new potatoes immediately: just dig them as

you want them half an hour before a meal. New potatoes have a lot of their carbohydrates in the form of sugar, because they are still busy growing and must have their energy in a still soluble form.

Main crop potatoes, however, have ceased to grow, and the sugar has all turned into starch, which is really what potatoes are. So lift your main crop potatoes as late as you like but before the very hard frost sets in, and preferably in dry weather. By then the tops will have wilted and dried. Leave the potatoes lying on top of the ground for a day or two for the skins to "set", or harden, and the potatoes to dry. Don't leave for longer, because potatoes left too long in the light will grow green and become bitter and poisonous, but two days won't hurt. If you have a lot of potatoes – say a ton (1000 kg) or more — you can clamp them. That is pile them in a steep-sided heap, cover with straw or dry bracken, and then cover with earth. The colder your winters the thicker the covering of straw you will require. In places with very cold winters you cannot clamp at all because the potatoes will become frosted. Leave small chimneys of straw sticking out on top of the ridge of the clamp every two yards or so, and build straw-filled tunnels at similar intervals around the base. Beware, a thousand times beware, of rats. If they make their homes in your potato clamp, it's good-bye to your potatoes.

If you have less than a ton (1000 kg), or live in a very cold climate, store your potatoes indoors. The requirements are: they should be in complete darkness; they should be ventilated; they should be as cold as possible but not subjected to frost, which rots them. So, a plastic or metal garbage can with a few ventilation holes knocked in the top and bottom will do, or else wooden tea chests, or barrels, but again, with ventilation. And in fact your potatoes will come to no harm if you just leave them in a heap in a completely dark corner of a frost-proof cellar or shed. Sacks are no good, except for certain open-weave man-made fiber sacks; "gunny", jute or canvas will rot, and so will paper.

The root cellars which are found in the northern states are ideal for very hard winters. In most parts of the USA the clamp is the best way of storing potatoes in large quantities, and on the whole it is the method of storing I prefer.

DIGGING AND CLAMPING
Harvest your early potatoes at any time after the plants have flowered. Late potatoes can be left in until the plants have died down. Dig potatoes out carefully with a fork, making sure you don't spear any. If you do, don't store them because they will very likely cause rot. If your crop is large — say over a ton (1000 kg) — it can be stored in a clamp, (right). Pile your potatoes steeply on a bed of straw, cover with more straw and mound over with earth. Ventilation is important, so make small chimneys of straw every two yards along the top of the clamp, and insert straw tunnels at the same intervals at ground level.

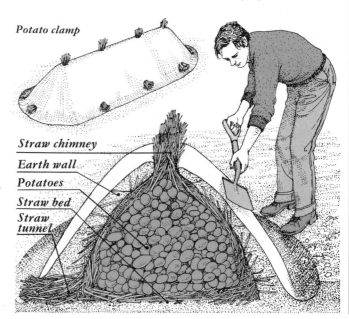

Potato clamp

Straw chimney
Earth wall
Potatoes
Straw bed
Straw tunnel

Tomatoes

Like the potato, the tomato is a native of tropical America. It is a perennial, but in temperate climates, where it is only half-hardy, it is grown as an annual. The tomato has enormous value for the self-sufficient gardener, for not only does it improve any dish to which it is added, it is also a very rich source of a whole range of vitamins and, most important, these do not seem to be damaged a great deal by cooking or canning. If you grow enough tomatoes in the summer to have them canned all winter you will not suffer from vitamin deficiency.

Soil and climate

To grow tomatoes out of doors you must have at least two and a half months of warm weather with plenty of sunshine. If you don't live in this sort of climate, you must start them off indoors and plant out in the late spring. If the summer turns out too cold or cloudy to bring them to ripeness, they can be ripened indoors or else made into green tomato chutney. In cold or temperate climates they grow well in greenhouses, and are far and away the most valuable greenhouse crop. But remember that, unlike cucumbers, they do not like a lot of humidity.

Tomatoes do well in any rich soil. In light soil they will give an earlier crop than in heavy soil. On the other hand they grow well in heavy clay that has had several years of compost application.

Soil treatment

For each seedling I like to dig a hole about a foot (30 cm) deep and as wide across, and fill it nearly to the top with compost, as though I were planting an apple tree. Then I fill the hole up with earth and when the time comes plant out in that. It is best to do this about six weeks before planting out. In fact it is a good idea to prepare the holes at the same time as you sow the seed indoors. However you manage it, tomatoes need rich soil, with plenty of good rich manure or well rotted compost. As the compost rots and settles, the ground sinks a little around the roots, which helps the tomatoes retain water.

Propagation

Except in very hot climates sow the seed indoors in seed boxes during spring. In all but the coldest climates an unheated greenhouse will do; a temperature of 70°F (21°C) is ideal. Sow thinly in either a proprietary compost, or a mixture which you can make yourself (see p. 92). Cover the seed boxes with newspaper during the night, but in the day make sure they are in full sunlight. Two or three weeks after sowing prick the tiny plants out three inches (8 cm) apart in larger seed boxes or, better still, peat pots. Again use proprietary compost or your own mixture. Don't water too much; keep the compost slightly on the dry side – just dry-to-moist. And always give them all the sun there is.

After a month start gently hardening the plants off. Put them outside in the sun in the day but indoors at night, or else move them to cold frames and keep the covers on at night but off in the day. At the beginning of summer they should be sufficiently hardened off for planting out in their prepared holes. If you have cloches plant your tomatoes out two weeks earlier and keep them covered for that period.

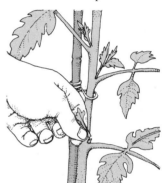

PLANTING OUT SEEDLINGS
Avoid disturbing the soil around your tomato seedlings. Two weeks before planting out, cut squares around each plant in the seed box, so as to keep the soil intact when it comes to planting.

PINCHING OUT SIDE-SHOOTS
With your fingers, pinch out the little shoots which emerge at the point where the leaf stalks meet the main stem.

Planting out

You should provide tomatoes with adequate vertical support, because by nature they are trailing plants. The best way is to use stakes, at least five feet (1.5 m) tall. Sink them about a foot (30 cm) into the earth. Position the stakes when you plant out the tomatoes, but don't damage the root clusters. Plant the tomatoes quite deeply so that the lowest leaves are just above the ground. Tomatoes are liable to put out adventitious roots from their stems and this should be encouraged. If you have any long straggly plants, you can make them stronger by laying a length of the stem horizontally in the ground; the stem will send out new roots.

Spacing depends on what sort of plants you intend to grow. In cooler climates plants should be kept small, and two feet (60 cm) apart in rows three feet (90 cm) apart is about right. In warmer climates they can grow larger, so more space should be allowed. In hot climates you can let them sprawl and then plants should be four feet (1.2 m) apart. If you use the deep bed method (see p.106) allow two feet (60 cm) between plants.

A method which is worth trying in a small garden is to plant out leaving only a foot (30 cm) between rows. Then stop the plants when they have set one truss only and allow no side-shoots to develop. This sounds ruthless but you should get more ripe tomatoes than with usual methods.

When planting out take great care to disturb the soil around the roots as little as possible. If you are using peat pots, just soak the plants and plant the peat pots as they are. If you use seed boxes, cut the soil in squares around each plant down to the bottom of the tray with a knife. Do this two weeks before you plant out, and try to retain that soil intact when you plant.

Ring culture Ring culture is another way of growing tomato plants from seedlings. It is best practiced in the greenhouse, though it can be done outdoors. The method is worthwhile if you are short of soil or short of space, or if your soil is disease-ridden.

Two weeks before you want to plant your seedlings stand rings of plastic or linoleum nine inches (23 cm) in diameter and nine inches (23 cm) high on a bed of clean gravel. Fill with proprietary compost or your own mixture (see p. 92). Two days before planting, water the gravel and the rings with water in which a complete organic compost or manure has been steeped – a thick soup in fact, and lace it if you can with a little fish meal.

When you plant the seedlings water the rings with ordinary water, and continue watering through the rings only for the next ten days. After that, when the roots have reached the gravel, water the gravel only, and ensure that it is permanently moist. Once a week give the gravel a good soaking with your organic soup. Otherwise treat like ordinary tomatoes.

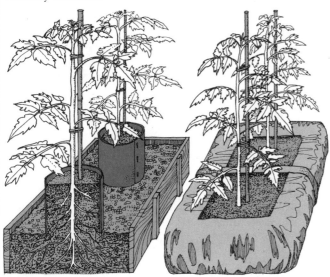

THE RING CULTURE METHOD
Stand rings of plastic or linoleum on a bed of clean gravel, fill with potting compost, and plant seedlings. Feed the plants with organic compost or manure steeped in water. After ten days water the gravel only.

PLANTING IN PEAT BAGS
Plant four seedlings in a commercially-prepared peat bag or in an old fertilizer bag filled with peat. Take care with watering since the bags won't drain and the plants may become waterlogged.

Peat bags This is a space-saving method which works indoors and outdoors, and is especially good for people who have just a patio or a balcony. Buy a specially prepared bag or simply fill an old fertilizer bag with peat. Plant four seedlings in each bag and water carefully; there is no facility for drainage so the plants can easily get waterlogged.

Care while growing

Tie the plants loosely to their stakes with soft string and keep tying as they climb. Don't tie too tightly or you will cut the stems. An excellent alternative is to drop a tube of wire netting, about 15 inches (38 cm) in diameter over each plant. The plants will climb inside the tubes.

Pinch out the little shoots which spring up at the base of each leaf stalk; otherwise you will get an untidy straggling plant which probably won't set any fruit. And don't let your plants get too high.

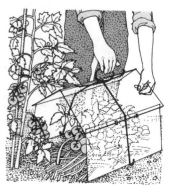

KEEPING TOMATO PLANTS LOW
Four trusses on each staked plant are enough. To stop them growing higher, simply break off the tops above the fourth truss.

AUTUMN RIPENING
When the nights draw in, take the plants off their stakes and lay them on straw under cloches. Tomatoes must be warm to ripen.

Tomatoes do not want too much water but they want some; if the ground dries right out, the fruit will crack. The very best thing to water the plants with is liquid manure. (Make it by half filling a barrel or tank with farmyard manure and topping up with water.) Remember that tomatoes need warm roots, so nip the bottom leaves off and train the plants as upright as possible so that the sun can get to the soil round the roots. In the fall when the nights begin to draw in, it is a good idea to take the plants off their stakes, lay them down horizontally on straw and cover them with cloches. This certainly helps to ripen the fruit.

Pests and diseases

Blight Outdoor tomatoes are just as susceptible to potato blight as potatoes are, so spray your tomatoes with Bordeaux mixture (see p. 105). Spray once every two weeks during the warm summer weather, and if it pours with rain just after you have sprayed, spray again.

Cut worm (see p. 124).

Horn worm Green worms devour leaves. Squash them.

Blossom end rot Large watery spots turn black at the blossom end of the fruit. This can be prevented by cultivating and watering well.

Harvesting and storing

Pick the fruit gently with the stalks on and take great care not to damage the skin. Red tomatoes must be eaten fresh, or must be canned immediately.

Green tomatoes, or tomatoes which are not quite ripe, can be covered with cloth or paper and kept in a cool place until they ripen. They must be in the dark: never lay them in the sun. A time-honored method is to lay a sheet of soft felt in the bottom of a drawer in a cool room, lay a layer of tomatoes on top of it making sure none of them are touching each other, lay another piece of felt on the tomatoes, then more tomatoes, and so on. Lay the greenest at the bottom and the ripest on top. Be sure the tomatoes are all healthy or you may end up with a drawer full of mold. Green and ripe tomatoes can be stored as chutney (see p.218).

Peppers

Peppers are divided into two groups: sweet and hot. They are among the most ornamental plants in the garden and come in many shapes, colors and sizes.

Soil and climate
They are slightly hardier than tomatoes. You can grow them out of doors in warmish climates, but they are better started off under glass, and can do all their growing under glass. They need at least 65°F (19°C) when they are flowering or they won't set fruit.

Soil treatment
They prefer a light soil and benefit from compost.

Propagation
You can buy seed, but I think it is much better to buy some ripe red peppers of the kind you like best, break them open and take the seed out. Sow the seed indoors at least six weeks before the last expected frost. Sow a few seeds in each pot and when they are about five inches (13 cm) tall thin to the strongest one. Plant outside about three weeks after the last expected frost (two weeks earlier if you have warmed the ground with cloches) in beds prepared as if for tomatoes (see Tomatoes). Like tomatoes plant them deeply.

Care while growing
Treat just like tomatoes but give them more water while they are young. Always water the roots, never the peppers; if they get too wet, they are liable to rot. Mulch heavily.

Pests and diseases
Anthracnose As long as you plant your peppers well away from your beans, they will not suffer from anthracnose. If they do get it, they will go bad. Burn them.
Cut worm Protect your seedlings with cardboard collars (see p. 124) when planting out.

Harvesting and storing
Cut them off (don't break them) with an inch (2.5 cm) of stem on each fruit. If you have more than you can eat fresh, hang the vines up in a dry windy place to dry. You may have to finish the drying process by hanging them over mild heat indoors. You can then just hang them, decoratively, in your kitchen or store room until you want them in winter.

Eggplants

Even the most dedicated flower gardener has to appreciate the eggplant. As well as their luscious fruit they have luxuriant purple flowers and large velvety leaves. They are not high in nutrition, but they make up for this with their unique flavor.

Soil and climate
In warm frost-free areas the eggplant will grow as a perennial bush, but where there is the slightest touch of frost it must be grown as a tender annual. It needs a hot summer and deep rich soil with plenty of moisture, but it does not thrive in wet weather.

Soil treatment
Dig plenty of manure or compost into your soil. Eggplants like a pH of about 6.

Propagation
Sow the seed indoors about ten weeks before you plant out. Soak the seed overnight and then plant each seed in a peat pot filled with good potting compost. If you have no peat pots, sow an inch (2.5 cm) apart in seed boxes filled with potting compost. When the seedlings are two inches (5 cm) high, plant out into even richer compost four inches (10 cm) apart in seed boxes or in a cold frame.
When your plants are about ten weeks old, and the ground outdoors is warm to the hand, plant the peat pots out three feet (90 cm) apart — 18 inches (45 cm) apart if you have a deep bed (see p. 106). Take great care not to damage the roots.

Care while growing
Until the warm weather comes keep cloches over them if you can spare them, and if you have a deep bed use mini-greenhouses. Keep them well watered — with manure water (see p. 90) if possible — but don't over-water.

Pests and diseases
Flea beetle These pests may attack when the plants are young. The leaves are quickly eaten away if they are not checked. Use derris dust to get rid of them.
Mildew The plants may get a mildew in damp climates. The answer is to reduce the humidity in the air, so that the mildew dries up. If your plants suffer much, try in future to use fungus resistant strains.

Harvesting
Cut them off — don't pull them — as soon as they have that lovely high gloss and before they are fully grown. The plants will then continue to fruit.

Umbelliferae

Carrots, parsnips, celery, celeriac, Hamburg parsley and Florence fennel are all members of the *Umbelliferae*. The family also includes several herbs including caraway, angelica and parsley.

Umbelliferous plants have numerous tiny flowers borne on radiating stems like umbrella ribs. They are a decorative family: the foliage of carrots is very attractive and will look good among your ornamental shrubs. Many members of the family are good to eat, although hemlock is poisonous, and very many are eaten by animals. Cow parsley, for example, is well worth gathering for feeding to rabbits.

Carrots

Like so many valuable food plants the carrot is a biennial, and stores in its first year what it is going to spend in its second in the form of seed. We thwart its aims by gobbling it up in the first year before it has time to grow to maturity. Carrots have been bred to be either long and slow maturing but heavy cropping, or short, stubby and quick maturing but lighter cropping.

The most important constituent of carrots is carotene, which the human body converts to vitamin A. No other vegetable or fruit contains comparable quantities of this vitamin, which, among its other virtues, improves your eyesight; hence the parental exhortation to generations of children: "Finish up your carrots and you will be able to see in the dark."

Soil and climate

Carrots are a cold climate crop. They can be sown very early in the spring in temperate climates, or in the fall or winter in sub-tropical ones. Carrots prefer to follow a crop that has been manured the previous year. A sandy loam is ideal for them. Heavy clay is not good for them, but if that is the soil you are blessed with you can improve it enormously by copious and constant manuring or composting.

A feature that all members of the *Umbelliferae* share is that their seed is very slow to germinate. So do not despair if you sow some *Umbelliferae* seed and the plants take ages to show their heads. Just sow a few radish seeds along with the others; the radishes will be up in no time and will show you where the rows of your *Umbelliferae* are.

The members of the *Umbelliferae* family are closely related to all sorts of interesting plants, wild and cultivated, including such exotic things as ginseng, whose ground-up roots are said to "relieve mental exhaustion", and sarsaparilla, which is used to make a soft drink.

Two buckets of compost and two of leaf-mold applied to every square yard will convert even a heavy clay into suitable soil for carrot-growing. They like a deep soil, particularly the heavy cropping long-rooted main crop varieties.

Soil treatment

Do not apply fresh manure just before sowing carrots because it makes them tough, watery, and inclined to fork. If the land is acid it should be limed although they will flourish in a pH as low as 6. Like all root crops they like both phosphate and potash; plenty of manure or compost should supply this, but be sure to apply manure at least six months before the carrots are planted. Rock phosphate and wood ashes are also worthwhile. The land should be dug deeply and raked down to a fine tilth.

Propagation

Draw little furrows about half an inch (1 cm) deep if you live in a moist climate but an inch (2.5 cm) deep in a drier one. Sprinkle the tiny seeds fairly thickly – four or five to an inch (2.5 cm) as some of them don't germinate. With the deep bed method (see p. 106) sow two inches (5 cm) apart each way. Pelleted seed (seed which has been coated with fertilizer so that each seed forms a little pellet) can be used

DREDGING CARROT SEEDS
Since carrot seeds are hardly visible, it is difficult to scatter them sparsely. Coat the seeds by shaking them up in their packet with a spoonful of slaked lime or ground limestone.

GERMINATING CARROT SEEDS
Carrot seeds need moisture if they are to germinate properly. Two days before planting, encourage them by placing between two sheets of wet blotting paper. But watch for mold.

to good effect with carrots. Sow it with a precision drill, far more thickly than you think you need to, as germination is even poorer than in conventional sowing. Cover the seed lightly with fine earth or, better still, with fine dry compost. In dry weather soak the furrows well. Don't worry if nothing happens for a bit. Carrots take a long time to come up.

Try interplanting carrots with onions row by row. This is said to deter both carrot and onion fly for the scent of the one conceals the scent of the other.

Care while growing

You can just leave early carrots as they are in the ground, which will be very overcrowded, and pull them for what gardeners call "bunching". They are tiny like this but they taste very sweet.

Main crop carrots, which you want for the winter, you will have to thin and here your problems start. For as soon as you bruise a few carrots, and disturb the soil around their roots, you attract the carrot fly which is said to be able to smell a bruised carrot for up to six miles. In areas where carrot fly is very bad it is often best to do your thinning only on a wet day, preferably in light rain. Then, after pulling the thinnings, carefully tread the ground down around the remaining carrots. Thin to an inch and a half (4 cm) between plants first; later on thin to three inches (8 cm) apart. For a deep bed (see p. 106) thin once to two inches (5 cm). You can eat the thinnings.

Don't hoe near carrots. It is not good to loosen the soil and even worse to cut the carrots. You can hoe between the rows but hand weed only in the rows. Try not to let the carrot bed dry out. If you have to water the soil, give it a very thorough soaking; you want the water to go deep down and pull the carrots downward with it. Just watering the surface is no good at all.

Pests and diseases

Carrot fly Carrot flies lay eggs on carrots; the larvae burrow into the root and spoil the crop. The carrot fly looks much like a small housefly; still it is not the fly itself you are likely to notice, but the leaves of your carrots turning dark

red as a result of the damage to the roots. They can be kept away by mixing an ounce (30 cc) of kerosene in a gallon (4.5 l) of water and sprinkling that on, shaking it up well as you do so. Alternatively mix a pint (0.6 l) of kerosene with a bushel of sand and sprinkle that on at the base of the plants. If the carrot flies are bad you may have to repeat the dressing every two weeks, especially if there is a lot of rain. If you have suffered from a very bad attack, dig the bed thoroughly in the late fall, so that birds have a chance of getting at pupae in the soil. In an organic garden you will have lots of beetles, and these may well eat up to half the carrot fly eggs before they hatch.

Carrot disease This can be bad in inorganic gardens but is unlikely to worry the good organic gardener. Brown spots appear on the roots and ultimately tiny red spores come to the surface of the soil; these are the spores of the mycelium which causes the disease. Burn all diseased roots and sprinkle the diseased soil with two parts of sulfur mixed with one part of lime and don't plant carrots there again for at least five years.

Harvesting and storing

If you pull carrots out of the rows at random you will attract carrot fly. So when you pick early carrots for eating fresh in summer start at one end of the row. Main crop carrots for winter storing can be left in the ground until well into the winter. Where there are very severe frosts lift them before the ground gets too hard and store them, not letting them touch each other, and twisting off the leaves first. Pull your carrots as early as possible if you have had a bad attack of carrot fly. The emerging larvae are then unable to pupate and produce a new generation of flies. If you do leave the carrots in the ground too long in wet weather, the roots are inclined to split; make sure that when you lift the carrots you take care of the roots. Eat any damaged in lifting; don't store them with the others. And remember that if you wash carrots before storing they will inevitably go totally rotten.

Store in a well-ventilated, cool place; just above freezing suits them best. Do not store year after year in the same root cellar because disease will gradually build up. It is best to store them in sand or peat. You can use a variety of containers: a garbage can with plenty of holes knocked in it to let in the air; a wooden crate; a barrel; a dark corner of a cold shed (but beware of rats and mice); or even a box sunk in the ground out of doors, covered with a lid, some straw on top of that and then some earth. If you have a very large number – you can clamp them (see Potatoes).

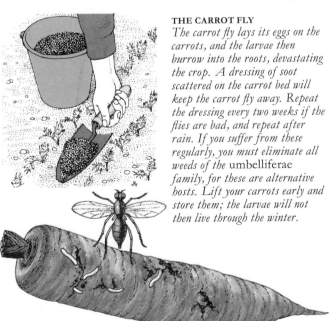

THE CARROT FLY
The carrot fly lays its eggs on the carrots, and the larvae then burrow into the roots, devastating the crop. A dressing of soot scattered on the carrot bed will keep the carrot fly away. Repeat the dressing every two weeks if the flies are bad, and repeat after rain. If you suffer from these regularly, you must eliminate all weeds of the umbelliferae *family, for these are alternative hosts. Lift your carrots early and store them; the larvae will not then live through the winter.*

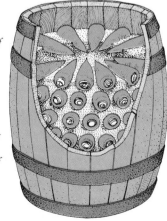

STORING THE CARROT CROP
When harvesting your carrots, be careful not to damage the roots. If you do, then don't store with undamaged carrots. It is best to store in a cool but well-ventilated place. An old barrel makes a good container. Place the carrots so that they don't touch each other, and build them up in layers of sand or peat. Make sure the barrel is ventilated – drill holes if necessary. Don't store carrots year after year in the same place because you may get a gradual accumulation of disease.

Parsnips

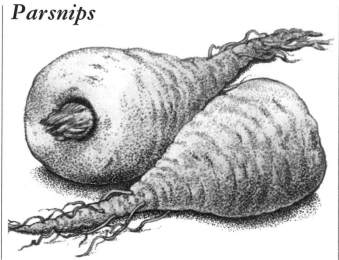

Parsnips are biennials like all good root crops and are even slower growing than carrots. They are a good crop to grow in dry soil, because they are capable of forcing their food-storing tap-roots two feet (60 cm) down into the soil in their search for water.

Soil and climate

Parsnips will grow in fairly poor soil; they are so slow growing that they do not need very rich conditions. On the other hand in good soil they will grow better, more quickly and produce more tender roots. And, of course, like every plant they flourish best in soil in which there is a high content of organic matter. They like soil about neutral: pH about 6.5. Very heavy soil is not good for them because it makes them fork. Stones and too much fresh manure also make them fork. A cold climate suits them best: without frost they don't develop their full flavor.

Soil treatment

The deeper you dig the better; for a really heavy crop dig in very well rotted manure or compost at least 18 inches (45 cm) deep – any less and your parsnips will fork.

Propagation

Traditionally parsnip seed is the first of the year to be planted outdoors (not counting shallots, which are not a seed anyway). They were, and often still are, sown in late winter – February in New England. However, in common with many other gardeners, I find it better to sow them later – well into the spring. Parsnips sown late are smaller, sweeter and less woody, and they keep better. But, unless your garden really is an old-established organic garden in which the soil is largely humus, you should give late-sown parsnips a dressing of fish meal, bone meal, or some other organic fertilizer high in phosphate (see p. 90).

Again breaking with tradition, I like to sow parsnip seeds sparsely, but continuously, in drills, and thin the plants to about ten inches (25 cm) apart when they grow up. With the parsnip seed I sow radish seed. The radishes grow much more quickly than the parsnips and show you where the rows are so that you can side-hoe (the radishes "declare themselves" as gardeners used to say). The radishes also keep the crust of the soil broken thereby giving the parsnips a better chance, and the leaves of the radishes shelter the young parsnip shoots from the sun.

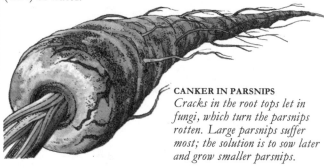

The drills should be about an inch and a half (4 cm) deep. After sowing the seed push the earth back with your foot and walk along the row to firm it. Better still, cover the seed with fine compost and then firm it.

Care while growing

Young parsnips need plenty of moisture. Hoe from time to time, and mulch with compost if you have it.

Pests and diseases

Celery leaf miner If you see tunnels mined in the leaves of your parsnips, look for the maggots, which will be living in blisters on the leaves, and squash them. To guard against this pest spray with an ounce (30 cc) of kerosene to a gallon (4.5 l) of water.

CANKER IN PARSNIPS
Cracks in the root tops let in fungi, which turn the parsnips rotten. Large parsnips suffer most; the solution is to sow later and grow smaller parsnips.

Canker This is very common. The tops of the parsnip roots go rotten and brown. The worst attacks of canker occur in acid soil and in soil which contains too much fresh manure. So, if your parsnips suffer badly, lime before sowing and refrain from adding fresh manure. A late crop is less likely to get canker than an early one.

Rust fungus This appears as a rusty mold on the crown of parsnip plants. Mix two parts of lime with one part of sulfur and sprinkle this on the soil around the plants. Don't grow parsnips on that bed for at least five years.

Harvesting and storing

Parsnips are completely frost-hardy but they don't like alternate freezing and thawing, so don't just leave them in the ground until you want them. Dig them up carefully and store in earth, sand or peat in a very cold place. The very best thing is to make a heap outdoors. Do this with alternate layers of earth and parsnips – cover the whole heap with straw as an insulator, and cover this with patted earth to stop the straw blowing away.

Celery

Celery, like parsnips, benefits from frost. In my view it should be eaten only in winter, when it is the most delicious vegetable available. During the rest of the year it is tasteless and insipid, because it has not had the benefit of frost.

Soil and climate

An organic soil, such as peat or soil rich in humus, is best for celery, and above all it needs constant moisture. It was originally a marsh or streamside plant and it suffers badly if it dries out. A high water table is desirable, but if you don't have that, you need plenty of humus in the soil and you must water frequently if the weather is dry. Celery stands fairly acid soil and does not need lime. Grow it in any climate where there is frost.

Soil treatment

I like to take out trenches about a foot (30 cm) deep and 15 inches (40 cm) wide, and dig plenty of compost or peat into the bottom. I do this in spring.

Propagation

Prepare a seed box by filling it with either a compost of three parts sifted loam, one part of leaf-mold and one part of sharp sand, or a proprietary compost. I prefer to do this in late winter but early spring is not too late. After the compost has been well soaked, sow the seeds sparsely and give them a light covering of compost. Place indoors at a temperature of about 60°F (16°C) with either glass or old newspaper over the seed box. If you use glass, wipe off the underside twice a day to prevent moisture dripping on to the seedlings. Keep the plants near the panes of the greenhouse or window so they don't get drawn sideways. Keep the soil just damp at all times; it is best to water with a fine spray, or you can stand the seed box in an inch (2.5 cm) of water and let the seedlings soak it up.

The plants will produce seed leaves before forming true leaves. As soon as the first pair of true leaves has appeared, prick out the plants into another box, which should contain three parts of loam, one part of leaf-mold, and half a part of rotted manure. Alternatively, use store-bought potting compost. Put the plants in carefully, two inches (5 cm) apart, and continue to spray them with water. Gradually harden them off by admitting more air, until late spring when they can be put outside. Never let young celery plants dry out or your sin will be brought home to you months later when they suddenly run to seed before they are ready.

Although mature celery benefits from frost, the young plants will be damaged by it. So don't plant out until you are sure there won't be another frost. Plant out a foot (30 cm) apart, – deep bed method (see p. 106) six inches

TRENCHING FOR CELERY
Dig trenches for celery, a foot (30 cm) deep and 15 inches (38 cm) wide. Tread in three inches (8 cm) of manure, and cover it with three inches (8 cm) of topsoil.

PLANTING OUT SEEDLINGS
Plant out the seedlings a foot (30 cm) apart in the prepared trenches. Water them regularly until they are established, and continue if there is no rain.

EARTHING UP AND TYING
In late summer, gather up the celery leaves and stems in a bunch. Tie the tops together; pack soil tightly around the plants, and remove the ties.

EARTHING UP AGAIN
Two or three weeks after the first earthing up, repeat the process; bank up the soil around the plants until only the leaves are still left showing.

(15 cm) apart – in the bottom of the trench you have already prepared for them. If you have two or more rows of celery, plant them three feet six inches (105 cm) apart, because when you come to hill them up you will need the space. Sow lettuces, radishes, and other quick-growing catch-crops between the rows. Harvest these before you need the soil to hill up the celery. Keep them well watered, especially for the first two weeks, if there is no rain.

Care while growing

There are several ways to hill up celery. If you have no help, tie the tops of the plants together, and pack the earth around the plants as tightly as you can, but without getting too much earth inside them. Fill the trench level in this way, then remove the ties on the tops of the plants. This should be done in late summer. Two or three weeks later hill up again, using more lime to thwart slugs, and bank the soil well up around the plants. A further hilling up may be necessary in another few weeks. If you have enough peat, use it in the later hillings up but lay slates or planks on the slopes of the bank to stop it washing or blowing away.

The purpose of all this hilling up is to keep the stalks away from the light. Like potatoes they become bitter as they turn green from exposure to light, so the higher you keep them hilled up the more crisp white celery you will have to eat. You can wrap the celery in collars of paper or plastic sheet before it is hilled up to prevent soil getting inside the plants, but this method attracts earthworms and slugs.

Pests and diseases

Leaf miner This is very common. It occurs when the maggots of the celery fly begin to mine tunnels into the leaves of the celery plant. Pick off any affected leaves and burn them. To control the disease, spray liquid manure over the plants once a week. The smell deters the flies from laying their eggs.

Leaf spot Also known as "celery blight", leaf spot can destroy your celery if it is not quickly checked. The disease, which is spread through the seeds, will cause small yellowish brown spots to appear on the leaves. Spray immediately with fungicide or the whole plant will become affected. Next year dip your seeds in formalin before sowing them.

Damping-off disease Young celery plants will suffer damping-off if they get too much water or too little air. The main symptom is a watery soft rot. Wipe off condensation if you're growing seedlings under glass, and make sure the seedlings are properly aired.

Harvesting and storing

Pull celery whenever you want to eat it, and if you are interested in flavor do not start eating it until there has been a frost. Thereafter try to make it last until well into the winter. It is a very good idea to protect part of a row with cloches as soon as the really heavy frosts set in. This will keep the celery good until late in the winter. (So as not to waste cloche space, plant a double row of celery in the same trench.) If you haven't got cloches you can use straw or bracken at night, but take it off on warmer days.

SELF-BLANCHING CELERY

To my taste, self-blanching celery is not as good as celery, but it is easier to grow. You raise it from seed in the same way as celery, plant it on the flat in late spring or early summer, and it is ready to eat in late summer. It won't stand frost at all.

Celeriac

The most delicious part of a stick of celery, in my opinion, is the crunchy base – the heart, as it were, of the celery. With celeriac you grow all "heart" and no stem. It tastes like a combination of celery and parsley. It can be eaten raw, but is usually boiled and added to soups or stews. Grow it exactly as you grow celery.

Soil and climate

Celeriac needs rich and mellow soil which has been well-manured. It grows best in a cool, moist climate.

Soil treatment

The deep bed method (see p. 106) is ideal for celeriac, but, whether you use it or not, dig deeply and incorporate plenty of manure or compost.

Propagation

Sow indoors in late winter or outdoors in a nursery bed at the beginning of spring. Plant out in early summer.

Care while growing

Celeriac should be watered frequently and kept free from weeds. When you hoe draw soil away from the plants. Don't hill up as you would for celery.

Pests and diseases

Celery leaf miner Like celery, celeriac can be attacked by leaf miner though usually to a lesser degree. Simply pick off affected leaves or spray the plants with liquid manure.

Harvesting and storing

You can begin to harvest in the late fall. In a very cold climate store celeriac in a root cellar, but if your winters are temperate leave them in the ground and harvest them as you want them.

Hamburg Parsley

Hamburg parsley or "parsnip-rooted" parsley grows as a root vegetable and can therefore be stored. It is not just an herb for flavoring things, although the leaves taste very like ordinary parsley and can be used as such; the roots can be eaten raw or cooked like parsnips, which they resemble.

Soil and climate
You can get a good crop wherever ordinary parsley will grow, namely in temperate climates. The more sun the plants get, the better.

Soil treatment
Hamburg parsley tolerates poorer soil than most root crops, but dig deeply and work in plenty of well-rotted manure.

Propagation
Like all the *Umbelliferae* the seed takes a long time to germinate. Soak the seed before planting and sow sparsely in drills either in the fall or early spring. A dressing of a high phosphate fertilizer such as fish meal or bone meal is useful.

Care while growing
When the plants come up, you should thin them out to about four inches (10 cm) apart, either in the rows or the deep bed (see p. 106). Hoe the plants. They don't need to be watered much unless it is a particularly dry summer.

Pests and diseases
Canker It is possible that the canker which can attack ordinary parsley may also attack Hamburg parsley. It gives a rusty appearance to the stems and causes the roots to decay. To prevent it, do not water too much. If you do get it, burn all your diseased plants.

Harvesting and storing
The leaves can be picked off and used as an herb, but the roots should be pulled as late as possible, because – and this is unusual – the largest roots taste the best. But don't leave the plant in the ground after the first frost. Store it in peat or sand, in crates or garbage cans in a root cellar, basement or other similar cold storeroom.

Florence Fennel

Unlike ordinary fennel, which is used only as an herb (see p. 196), Florence fennel can be eaten on its own because the leaf-stalks swell at the base of the leaves to form large bulbs. Sliced raw, these can be added to salads. The stems can be eaten raw like celery, and leaves and seeds can be used for flavoring. It is well worth growing for its unique taste which combines the flavors of aniseed and licorice.

Soil and climate
Florence fennel will grow as a perennial only in hot climates, but it can be grown as an annual nearly anywhere. If you want really tender and delicious stems grow it in the richest ground you have.

Soil treatment
Prepare the ground as for celery, digging deeply and incorporating a lot of manure.

Propagation
Sow seeds thinly in shallow drills either in the late fall, or early spring.

Care while growing
Florence fennel needs very little attention. Thin to six inches (15 cm) apart in the rows or deep beds (see p. 106) and water when required. It is worth hilling up the bulbs to blanch them and to help the plants retain moisture.

Pests and diseases
Florence fennel is happily disease-free, as well as also being highly resistant to pests.

Harvesting
Cut the heads when they are about two inches (5 cm) across. The stems above them should be harvested before they get too old and stringy and stripped of their outer skin.

Liliaceae

Onions, leeks and asparagus are all members of the *Liliaceae*, or lily family.

As I have discussed elsewhere (see p. 19) the main subdivisions of the plants which provide us with nearly all our food are the two great classes: the monocotyledons (monocots for short) and the dicotyledons (dicots for short). Most of our vegetables are dicots. That is, they have two seed leaves — the first leaves they make — while the monocots have one. But the important difference between the two classes is nothing so trivial: it is that they have entirely different ways of growing. The dicots grow outward from the edges of their leaves. The monocots grow from the bases of their leaves — thus pushing their leaves up and out from the bottom.

The members of the lily family are monocots, as you can easily see by looking at their leaves. These don't have the network of veins that dicots have, but instead have parallel veins — each vein starting at the base of the leaf. Onions and leeks make use of this particular form of leaf growth to store nourishment in hard swollen bulbs, which are nothing more than many leaf bases compressed together to form a bulb. Asparagus is not so instantly recognizable as a monocot, but it is one nonetheless. The shoots, which are the edible part, grow from a "rhizome"– a horizontal stem which remains underground. The attractive fern-like branches which sprout as the shoots grow taller are like leaves and these grow up from their bases like the leaves of the other monocots. The rhizome takes nourishment from the leaves in one year and uses it to produce the next year's shoots.

Humans and many other animals have always made use of plants that form bulbs in their first year as a convenient way of storing the energy they will use to produce flowers and fruit in their second year. Although we don't eat lily bulbs we do eat onions, leeks and asparagus.

Onions

COMMON ONIONS

With careful growing, harvesting and storing, there should be no part of the year in which your kitchen lacks that most indispensable ingredient, the onion. But you may well feel confused by the amount of conflicting advice that is available. Onions have been grown for centuries, and it sometimes seems as if each grower has his own special technique. In fact the right timing and method depend largely on where you live.

Soil and climate

Onions need good rich soil. Sandy loam, peat and silt are all fine, but onions don't like clay, sand or gravel. They grow successfully in widely different climates, although they prefer cool weather while their leaves are growing and developing followed by very much hotter weather while they make their bulbs.

Soil treatment

Onions have very shallow roots and grow quickly so they need plenty of nourishment in the top four inches (10 cm) of soil. Prepare the bed well the previous fall with well-rotted manure or, even better, with a large amount of thoroughly rotted compost. They like plenty of potash and phosphate but not too much nitrogen. It is useful to add any of the following to your soil: wood ash, ground rock phosphate, soot, seaweed meal, a sprinkling of salt. The soil should have a pH of 6. If it is lower, add lime.

Before planting out, firm the ground by treading or rolling — preferably both. And the soil must be dry, whether you are sowing seed or transplanting.

Propagation

If your neighbor is a successful onion-grower, it's a good idea to ask him for advice. There are four possibilities.
Late summer sowing The idea of this is to get the onions to form bulbs by the early spring, before hotter weather causes them to bolt, and then allow them to mature through the summer. Sow the seed thinly in shallow drills, cover with half an inch (1.5 cm) of compost and firm the ground. If the winter is particularly hard, put cloches out during the worst of it. In the spring, thin out the onions to about six inches (15 cm) apart. The thinnings can be used in salad.
Winter sowing In very frosty areas, it is best to sow onion seeds indoors in midwinter, for planting out in the spring as soon as the ground is dry enough. Sow seed thinly in seed boxes filled with either a proprietary compost or a mixture of three parts sifted loam, one part leaf-mold, one part fine compost and a sprinkling sand. Keep moist but not wet, and cover with glass or paper. When the seedlings show, remove the covering and keep the seed box at about 65°F (19°C) near a window. When the second leaf is about half an inch (1.5 cm) long prick the seedlings out into another box so that each plant is two inches (5 cm) away from the next. Use the same mixture of compost for the pricking-out box, but add one part of well-rotted manure. Harden the plants off gradually until they are in the open air, in a sheltered place by the last frost. Plant the seedlings

out in the spring. It is best to leave their permanent bed rough until the last moment so the soil can dry out. Before planting, rake it down as fine as powder and tread firmly.

Spring sowing This is only good where there are cool damp summers, and you won't be able to store the bulbs. Sow out of doors as you would onions sown in late summer and thin them out to four inches (10 cm) apart when they are big enough for the thinnings to be used as salad onions.

PLANTING ONION SETS
To grow onions from sets it is essential to press the soil very firmly around each set. Make holes six inches (15 cm) apart; press the sets into the holes. Contrary to the usual advice (which is to leave the tops just showing), I suggest that you bury the sets completely, so that they are out of the reach of birds.

Onion sets If you prefer them to seed, onion sets grow best in temperate climates where they should be planted in the spring. Make dibber holes every six inches (15 cm) — deep bed method four inches (10 cm) — along a line and push the sets into them, pressing down the soil around each set to hold it firm. I bury the sets completely—so that the top-knot is just below the surface where the birds can't pull it out.

Care while growing

The most important thing is to keep your onions well weeded. In their later stages they benefit from a mulch and this can be done with uprooted weeds. If your onions flower, pinch out the stems while they are still small.

PICKING OUT FLOWER STEMS
If necessary pinch out the flower stems while they are still quite small. If you don't do this, the plants will "bolt", that is to say, they will produce flower heads. These in turn prevent the bulbs forming properly. When you are picking out the flower stems, take care not to loosen the bulbs.

Pests and diseases

Onion fly The maggots of the onion fly are one of the nastiest pests we have to suffer as they can stop onions growing altogether. The maggots eat into the bulbs of seedlings. Spring-sown onions are the worst hit, but onions grown from sets aren't likely to be affected. To deter onion flies and their maggots dust your rows of onions with flowers of sulfur, or sprinkle with an ounce of kerosene to a gallon of water. Dust fairly regularly, particularly when you thin the plants.

Downy mildew This occurs particularly during wet seasons, and causes grayish or purple streaks on leaves. If you find it, dust with Bordeaux powder (see p. 100).

Eel worm These microscopic worms will cause the tops of your onions to wilt. Burn all affected plants and don't grow onions or allow chickweed, which also harbors them, to grow on that land for six years.

Neck rot This disease attacks onions in storage. A gray mold forms on the onion skins and later the centers turn brown. Prevent it by drying your onions off well after harvesting and storing in a cool airy place.

Onion smut Onion smut shows as black blisters on stems and bulbs. If you get it in your garden, water the rows with a solution made from a pint (0.5 l) of formalin and four gallons (18 l) of water when you sow. But you are unlikely to get this.

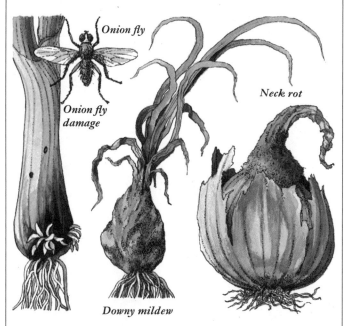

Onion fly

Onion fly damage

Neck rot

Downy mildew

Harvesting and storing

It is well worth bending over the tops of your onions when they will grow no more. This will start them ripening. In a hot dry autumn, ease the onions out of the ground and leave them a week or two in the sun to dry. But don't damage the skin or you'll let in neck rot. In wet places, lay the onions on wire netting after harvesting — an old spring bed would do — in order to keep them off the ground. But put them under cover if it's rainy.

BENDING THE TOPS
When the tips of the leaves start going yellow, it is time to bend over and break the necks of the onions. This starts the ripening process. At the same time loosen the onions with a fork to start them drying, but take care not to damage the skins. A few days later ease them out of the ground and leave them in the sun to finish drying out.

It is vital to dry onions well. When they have dried, the best thing to do is string them. Otherwise, put them in layers in some cool, airy place. They must not suffer severe frost, but it is better for them to be cool than hot. If you hang a string by your stove use them fast before they rot.

STRINGING ONIONS

1 Knot together the ends of a three foot (90 cm) length of string and hang the loop from a hook. Weave the first onion through the loop.

2 Use the leaves of the second onion to weave in and out of the string. The weaving must be tight and the second onion should finally rest on the first.

3 One by one add onions to the original two, weaving first from the left then from the right. As the bunch grows, check to make sure it is well balanced. When you finish, hang up the string in a cool, dry airy place and the onions should keep until early summer. Remember that all onions for stringing need long, dry leaves.

SPRING ONIONS

To fill the gap after the last of your stored onions have gone rotten — if you haven't planted spring onions specially — buy bunches of spring onions and plant them out three inches (8 cm) apart. They will quickly produce small bulbs. Alternatively, sow any onion seed, or the special spring onion varieties in late summer, and pull them in the spring. But, of course, if you have sown onions out of doors in late summer, you will have spring onions anyway as a result of thinning them.

SCALLIONS

Any onion can be harvested young and used as scallions or green bunching onions, but there are special bulbless bunching varieties that are bred for this purpose. These produce clusters of long, slender white stalks but do not form bulbs.

SHALLOTS

The mild but distinctive flavor of shallots is essential to French cooking. Shallots are expensive, so it is worth growing your own. Plant them any time before early spring. Prepare the ground in the same way as for onions, and plant the shallots as you would onion sets, about six inches (15 cm) apart. When you harvest, store them in a string bag.

Leeks

The leek is sometimes rightly called "the gourmet's onion". The Welsh, recognising its fine qualities, have made it their national emblem, and have created a superb leek soup named "cawl". If you wish to grow only one vegetable of the *Liliaceae* family, begin with the leek. It will not let you down.

During the dreary hungry gap when all else fails, which stretches from late winter through to the middle of spring, the stalwart leek is there to relieve you from a diet of salted this and frozen that.

Soil and climate

Leeks like a rich loam, but they can, and often do, put up with practically anything. Still, for leeks that you can be proud of, give them plenty of manure and plenty of compost. They need a moist but well-drained soil, and they like a high pH – between 6 and 8. They are temperate climate plants but will grow in any climate except a tropical one. In my view, though, leeks grown in dry weather don't seem to have the flavor of those grown under cloudy skies.

Soil treatment

For really fine leeks, treat your soil as you would for onions (see Onions). It is common to follow early potatoes with leeks – forming a part of the legume plot in our recommended rotation (although they are not of course legumes). In this case the heavy manuring the potatoes have had will be perfect, though the leeks will probably want some lime.

However, I generally plant leeks with the brassica because they are then sharing the only bed that does not need digging up until late the following spring. While leeks are very closely related to onions they do not fit easily into the onion bed, for the onions are strung and hung up in a cool shed before we even start to eat the leeks.

In hard ground trench for leeks, digging one spade depth deep and mixing in plenty of compost or well-rotted manure.

Propagation

In very cold climates, sow seed indoors in late winter and keep them at about 60°F (16°C). For summer leeks you should do this anyway, but I think it a pity to eat leeks in the summer – "the fruits of the earth in their season" is what suited Adam and Eve before they tasted of the wrong fruit – and it is nice to come to leeks around Christmas with an unjaded palate. For winter leeks, in all but the coldest climates sow fairly thickly along the drills in the *brassica* seed-bed in early spring. Do not throw the left-over seeds away after sowing; each quarter ounce (7 g) holds about a thousand seeds, and they keep for around four years. Plant out in the garden when they are four inches (10 cm) high.

It is common advice to snip an inch off the tops of the plants and at the same time snip the roots to about half their length. Then simply drop each plant into a hole made with a dibber and pour a little water in. This works perfectly well but, since I prefer not to mutilate plants more than I have to, I plant them as I do cabbages. Simply make a hole with your dibber, pour a little water in, and push the unmutilated leek down into the mud. I suggest you try half a row each way and see which grows better. Plant them six inches (15 cm) apart – deep bed method four inches (10 cm) (see p. 106) – in rows wide enough to work between – say 16 inches (40 cm).

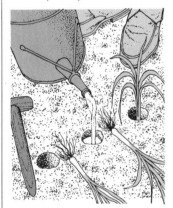

PLANTING LEEKS
Using a long dibber, make holes eight inches (20 cm) deep and six inches (15 cm) apart, in rows wide enough apart to allow space for maneuvering – say 16 inches (40 cm). Pour a little water into each hole, push the leeks down into the mud, roots first. To snip an inch off the top and the longer roots beforehand is a matter of personal preference.

Care while growing

Never let leeks go short of water. Hoe them and mulch if you can. Earth them up every now and then as they grow, in order to blanch them.

Pests and diseases

Leeks are said to suffer from all the same pests and diseases as onions, but I have never known a leek to suffer from anything – except somebody digging it out of the ground and eating it.

Harvesting and storing

When digging up leeks, avoid cutting off too much of the foliage; the leeks' prime food value consists of the vitamin A to be found in the leaves. So, as well as eating the stems, try and make use of the leaves, in soups and so on: they taste very savory.

In freezing climates leeks can be dug up before the first severe frost and heeled into earth in a cellar. In less severe climates they should be hilled up nearly to the tops of the plants. In temperate climates, leave them in the ground if possible until at least Christmas, and spare them even after that until late winter when the Brussels sprouts begin to look a sorry sight and you are tired of broccoli and kale. Then dig them up as you need them. However, if you wish to clear the bed for something else, it is perfectly all right to dig all your leeks up and heel them into the ground in a short row out of the way and near the kitchen.

Asparagus

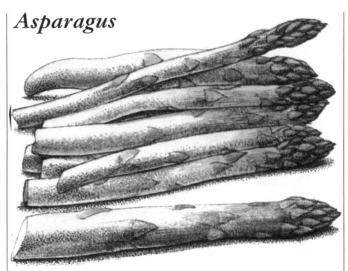

Asparagus is an excellent vegetable to grow, for it gives you a fresh bite of green-stuff in the spring. It can be cut and cut again for a period of six to eight weeks, and it is impossible to conceive of anyone ever getting tired of so exquisite a taste. If you care for your asparagus bed properly, it will go on producing for anything between ten and forty years. On the other hand, an asparagus bed takes up a lot of space, especially since you have to wait for three years from the time of sowing for your first taste.

Soil and climate

Asparagus came from the seaside and can put up with salt. It likes a mild, moist summer and a cold enough winter to make it go to sleep for half the year. Only a very severe frost will harm it after it has died down for the winter, but it is a good idea to cover the bed with straw if the winter is frosty. The plant flourishes in a light, well-drained loam and it will grow well in sandy land if it has been well-manured and composted and is not allowed to dry out. The soil should have a pH of 6.5, which may mean you have to add lime. It is possible to create soil suited to asparagus artificially – heavy clay, for instance, can be properly modified by adding plenty of compost and sand – and it is well worth doing this, as asparagus is a perennial and will go on feeding you for years.

Soil treatment

The bed must be entirely free from perennial weeds, because once the roots of these are thoroughly intertwined with the roots of the asparagus, which spread out as far as five feet (1.5 m) you will never get them free. So the fall before you intend to plant, fork the planned bed over and over again and remove every last inch of couch grass root, ground elder, or convolvulus.

Then, if your land needs it, fork in lime and also if necessary rock phosphate or wood ash or some other form of potash, but if you have enough compost you needn't bother with this. Half a pound (200 g) of fish meal and half a pound (200 g) of ash per square yard is a good insurance.

The old-fashioned method of preparing the bed, and one which I think can't be beaten, was to take out a trench five feet (1.5 m) wide and one foot (30 cm) deep, placing the top soil to one side separately. Put six inches (15 cm) of good stable manure in the trench, six inches (15 cm) of rotted turf on top of this, and another few inches of well-rotted manure or compost. Replace the topsoil on this and you will have a bed for three rows of plants. An alternative is just to dig plenty of manure or compost into the soil in the fall and plant in that, in either single rows or rows about four and a half feet (1.4 m) apart.

Propagation

Asparagus can be grown from seed. Collect your own seed by hanging some of the female ferns up when they are quite ripe, letting them dry, and then rubbing the seed out with your fingers. But if you grow them from seed you won't get any asparagus to eat for three years. If you can't wait that long, buy two or three-year-old crowns from a nursery. Even one-year-old crowns save you some waiting time, they are cheaper than older plants and transplant more easily.

If you are sowing seed, either do it indoors in seed boxes or outdoors in a seed-bed, sowing in early spring and later thinning to three inches (8 cm) apart.

Whichever method you choose, when the plants are ready for their final bedding out, take out a trench or trenches nine inches (25 cm) deep and a foot (30 cm) wide, make a cushion of fine soil in the bottom, slightly convex in section, and lay the plants on that, two feet (60 cm) apart in the rows – deep bed method 12 inches (30 cm) apart (see p. 106). Never let asparagus crowns dry out. If you buy the crowns from a nursery, keep them moist right up to the time you put them in the ground and then give them a good soaking. Cover immediately with fine earth and compost.

Care while growing

Asparagus benefits enormously from heavy mulching. I like to mulch with seaweed, but otherwise mulch with any organic material which is non-acid – don't for instance use pine needles or oak leaf-mold unless you mix thoroughly with lime first. If you use sawdust or anything very hard to break down, put some high nitrogen material on, like blood meal. Don't hoe too deeply or you'll damage the asparagus roots. Your mulch is the best weed suppressor.

Many people cut the ferns down in the fall as soon as they turn yellow, but I prefer to leave them to die down naturally and return their goodness to the plants.

Pests and diseases

Asparagus beetle Use your fingers to pick off any beetles which appear on the asparagus shoots and kill them. Do it early in the morning when the beetles can't fly. Otherwise dust with derris powder when the dew is on them.

Asparagus rust If you live in a very humid area your asparagus may be affected by this fungus, so plant a rust-free variety. If you still get it, spray with Bordeaux mixture.

Harvesting and storing

Don't touch the plants for three years if you grew them from seed, or for two years if they grew from roots. Then cut the shoots before they begin to open as you want them. Cut for six weeks after they begin to shoot the first year, and thereafter for two months. The middle of June is the latest you should let yourself cut asparagus. From a five-year-old bed sporting two healthy plants, you will probably find that you can cut enough asparagus for one person to have one helping a week throughout the cutting season.

To avoid a dearth of asparagus reckon on ten years as the lifetime of a bed, and then plant a new one. A good tip, when you scrap an old bed, is to take the plants out carefully at the end of the fall and plant them in a hot-bed. You'll benefit by getting asparagus a month earlier than usual.

Asparagus can be canned or frozen (see p. 220 and 227). My personal prejudice is against doing either because the great pleasure of eating fresh asparagus in the spring – surely one of the heights of gastronomic experience – is lost if the palate is jaded by having munched away at canned or frozen stuff the rest of the year

TRENCHING FOR ASPARAGUS
Dig a trench nine inches (25 cm) deep and a foot (30 cm) wide. Leave the bottom slightly convex, so that it will hold water, and cover it with a layer of fine soil.

PLANTING THE CROWNS
Set out the plants on the layer of fine soil, two feet (60 cm) apart. Lay them with the roots spread out carefully to absorb all available moisture.

MULCHING THE PLANTS
Seaweed or fish meal is ideal for heavy mulching; otherwise use any non-acid organic material. When the ferns turn yellow in fall, let them die naturally.

HARVESTING THE CROP
Three years from sowing or two from planting is the time to harvest. Cut the shoots for not more than six weeks the first year, and two months subsequently.

Chenopodiaceae

Beet, spinach, Swiss chard or seakale beet and spinach beet are the edible members of the *Chenopodiaceae*. This very distinctive family originally came from the seashore, and the members of it share with the cabbage tribe the characteristic that their leaves have a tough, cutinous surface which is designed to limit transpiration (the escape of water from the plant) and thus preserve the moisture which the plants win so precariously from their salty surroundings. Seashore plants share with desert plants the need to conserve moisture, for their salty environment tends to draw it out of them by osmosis. The beet family also has the peculiarity of producing its seed in little fruits that remain intact until they germinate in the ground. What we plant as the "seed" of beet and spinach is in fact a small fruit containing four or five seeds, each of which grows into a plant. Thus you find that when you plant these fruits you get plants coming up in clusters. The clusters should be thinned to leave one plant from each for the best beet or spinach.

The family includes sugar beet, which is grown for sugar of course (the roots can be up to 21 per cent sugar), and mangels, or "cattle-beet", which are grown specifically for feeding to cattle and making into sugar. The beet family are characterized by the fact that the swollen roots that we grow them for display rings when you cut them across. These rings are alternately storage tissue and conveying tissue. It is the storage tissue that contains the nutrients which the beet stores up in its first summer, so that it can leap ahead quickly in its second summer and produce seed before it dies. The conveying tissue transfers the nutrients from the roots to the rest of the plant.

Beet and spinach can send their roots down ten feet (3 m) or more into the soil. They also occupy the soil very fully, filling it with a mass of fibrous rootlets. This has a good effect, breaking up the soil and loosening it, so when the roots rot they leave passages for water and air far down into the subsoil.

It is possible now to get fragmented seed of the *Chenopodiaceae* – where the fruitlets have been broken – or to get pelleted seed. Each of these makes it possible to sow singly, either by hand or with a precision drill, which saves thinning later. But the expense is really only justified if you are growing on a large scale.

Beet

The western culinary imagination never seems to get much beyond boiling beet for many hours and then soaking it in vinegar. But we have only to look to Russia and to the delicious borsch to see just what can be done with this sadly under-used vegetable.

Soil and climate
Beet is really a cold climate plant; in hot countries it must be grown in the winter, early spring or fall. It likes well-drained soil, with plenty of humus, but not fresh manure. It won't grow at all if the ground is too acid, and needs a pH of about 6.5.

Soil treatment
In my suggested four-course rotation, beet should be grown in the root plot. The land should by then have been heavily manured three years before for the potatoes, limed two years before for the *Leguminosae*, and probably well-mulched with compost one year before for the *brassica*. The soil should be well dug and without too many stones.

Propagation
The main crop of beet for storing should be sown about three weeks before the date of your usual last frost. But you can go on sowing successively until midsummer. It's worthwhile soaking the seed a day or two before sowing. Sow the seed thinly three-quarters of an inch (2 cm) deep in drills a foot (30 cm) apart. When the plants appear, first single each cluster, then thin out to three inches (8 cm) apart for small beet and nine inches (25 cm) apart for large beet for winter storing – deep bed method (see p. 106) four inches apart (10 cm). You can eat the baby thinnings.

Care while growing
Hoe several times to suppress weeds until the shiny leaves of the beet start doing the work themselves. Beet grown in dry conditions become hard and woody and they can often bolt. Mulching and watering should prevent this.

Pests and diseases
Leaf miner The larvae of the beet fly will bore through the leaves. Pull off the affected leaves and burn them.
Beet beetle Beet may become infested with tiny black beetles. Water the plants with nicotine water.

Harvesting and storing
The tops of beet can be eaten as well as the roots but, if you're going to store beet, wring the tops off – don't cut them since it makes them bleed. And avoid bruising.

By far the best way to store beet is to lay them gently in peat – or moist sand – without allowing them to touch each other. If you lay them in the open they will shrivel up.

Spinach

Of all the popular vegetables spinach contains the most vitamin C, iron and calcium. You can have it all year round with careful planning. It is a cool weather crop and will even grow in Alaska's colder zones. In hot climates or even in more temperate ones, New Zealand spinach, (which belongs to the *Tetragoniaceae* family) is a good substitute and can be grown in the summer.

Soil and climate

High temperatures during the first couple of months of its growth will cause spinach to bolt to seed, so it is really a winter crop in hot climates. It likes good rich loam, and should be kept damp, but it will grow in most soils if there is enough organic matter present. It isn't a good idea to plant in soil where fresh manure has recently been applied.

Soil treatment

Spinach will go in odd corners as a catch crop, but it doesn't like an acid soil, so lime if necessary to bring the pH to between 6 and 6.5. If the soil is over 6.7 then spinach will be one of the first plants to show manganese deficiency, since manganese gets locked up by too much lime. The ground should be well dug; alternatively, use a good layer of compost.

Propagation

In cool climates, the prickly-seeded variety of spinach is best in the winter and the smooth-seeded variety in summer. In hot climates the smooth-seeded variety should be planted in winter. Even in pretty cold climates you can sow smooth-seeded spinach in winter (though not of course where the

ground is frozen) and successively thereafter — say once a month — until late summer. In wet winters it is a good idea to sow spinach on raised ridges for better drainage. In spring and summer, sow on the flat. Sow three-quarters of an inch (2 cm) deep and, when the plants declare themselves, thin to four inches (10 cm) in rows a foot (30 cm) apart. Allow three inches (8 cm) in both directions between thinned plants in the deep bed (see p. 106), and take care not to step on the bed when thinning.

Care while growing

Hoe and mulch if you can to keep down weeds. Water only if the weather is very dry; if the soil is allowed to dry out the plants will bolt.

Pests and diseases

Mold Spinach is virtually free from pests and diseases in good organic gardens, but in muggy, damp weather it can get moldy. This mold manifests itself as yellow patches on the leaves and grey mold on their undersides. If it appears, the best thing to do is scrap it and plant some more. If you plant some every month (a short row of course), you won't have to go long without it. If it bolts, then the only place for it is the compost heap.

Harvesting

Simply pluck the leaves from your spinach as you need them. In fact, if you want the plant to go on bearing you should pluck the outer leaves fairly often. Spinach tastes best if you simply rinse it quickly and put it, still wet, straight into a pan with a close-fitting lid. Don't add any more water; just leave it to simmer for five minutes or so.

HARVESTING SPINACH
You need a lot of spinach before you have enough for one helping. The secret is to have sown enough plants: as long as you spread the plucking over several plants, the more often you pluck the leaves the better. Pick young leaves from the outside, taking care not to denude any one plant.

NEW ZEALAND SPINACH

New Zealand spinach is not in fact a member of the *Chenopodiaceae* family but it is similar enough to warrant talking about here. New Zealand spinach doesn't have the high oxalic content of true spinach, so its nutritional value is more available. It is less frost-hardy than true spinach and it should be grown in the summer. In very hot climates it will stand up to heat far better than ordinary spinach, but it does need protection from the sun.

Don't sow until all danger of frost is past. Grow New Zealand spinach in rows four feet (1.2 m) apart in good soil, or closer together in poor soils. When sown directly into a deep bed, it will grow particularly well. Soak the seeds in water for twenty-four hours before sowing; otherwise their hard cases make them slow to germinate. Plant three seeds in each position and later pull out the two weaker plants. Otherwise treat New Zealand spinach just as you would treat true spinach.

Swiss Chard

Swiss chard or seakale beet is just a beetless beet, as it were: it's a beet which puts down deep narrow roots instead of making one swollen root. It is an excellent crop for your garden since it sends its tough roots three feet (90 cm) down into the subsoil and draws up what is good down there. Both the leaves and the midribs of the leaves can be eaten; you should cut the midribs up before cooking them, and they need cooking longer than the leaves.

Soil and climate
Swiss chard will grow in most climates except the very hottest and in any soil which is not waterlogged.

Soil treatment
Swiss chard, like the other beet crops, needs a pH of about 6.5, so lime if necessary. A small amount of well-rotted compost or manure is a good idea.

Propagation
Soak the seed well, just as you would beet seed (see Beet). Sow seeds an inch (2.5 cm) deep and three inches (8 cm) apart – deep bed method (see p. 106) also three inches (8 cm) apart. The plants need room, so make the rows 18 inches (45 cm) apart. The seed should be sown two or three weeks before the last expected frost, though in mild climates you can sow in late summer for harvesting and eating in winter and spring.

Care while growing
Swiss chard needs little attention, though mulching is worthwhile.

Pests and diseases
Swiss chard is hardy and resistant to pests and diseases.

Harvesting
When the leaves are seven inches (18 cm) long start breaking the outer ones off and eating them. As the leaves get bigger, tear the thin leaf off the midribs.

RHUBARD CHARD
Rhubard chard is exactly like Swiss chard except that its leaves and stems are deep red in color. It is said to thrive in heavy soils better than its rivals.

Spinach Beet

Spinach beet is a beetless beet, meaning that it does not make a swollen root, like common beet. It is also known as "perpetual spinach", because you can get a year's supply of leaves from only two sowings, instead of having to sow successively through the year, as with spinach. You can eat the leaves and the plant will go on to produce more. Spinach beet is hardier than spinach; it is unlikely to bolt in summer yet can withstand frosts in winter. It tastes similar to spinach, but contains less oxalic acid.

Soil and climate
A cool moist climate is best for spinach beet, and it likes good deep soil. It grows very well, like the rest of the deep-rooting beet family, in deep beds (see p. 106).

Soil treatment
Dig deeply and add as much compost or manure as you can spare. You don't have to worry about forking roots with spinach beet, so there is no danger of adding too much fresh manure as there is with many root crops.

Propagation
If you sow in spring and again in midsummer, you can have leaves to eat throughout the year. Sow seeds an inch (2.5 cm) apart in rows 18 inches (45 cm) apart. When the seedlings are well established, thin to leave six inches (15 cm) between plants. If you have a deep bed (see p. 106) allow six inches (15 cm) between plants in all directions.

Care while growing
Keep the ground clear of weeds and pick off any flower stems that appear. Your crop will benefit from mulching.

Pests and diseases
Spinach beet is not greatly affected by pests or diseases, but watch out for slugs (see p. 104) in the fall.

Harvesting
Pull the leaves off the plants carefully by twisting them downward. Pick from the outside leaving newer younger leaves to go on growing. Never denude a plant altogether. Don't allow any leaves to become large and old, for this will stop the plant producing more. If they grow too old for eating, pull them off and put them on the compost heap.

Cucurbitaceae

Cucumbers, squashes, zucchini, pumpkins and melons belong to the *Cucurbitacea*, a family which has evolved to live in extreme climatic conditions.

Nothing is more fascinating in working with nature than observing how plants have evolved to fill nooks and crannies left in the complex ecosystem of the larger and grander species. Thus in the huge tropical rain forests, where mighty trees strive against each other to reach the light, you will find soft, apparently defenseless fast-growing creepers using their mighty rivals to support themselves, making use of speed in growing and flexibility of habit to carry on a kind of guerilla existence down below.

Other members of the *Cucurbitaceae* are adapted to deserts, and these again make use of speed of growth, sacrificing strength and rigidity and all sorts of other virtues to this end. They shoot away quickly from a seed that has been lying dormant perhaps for years and store away the water of a flash rainstorm in quick-growing fruit. The Tsava melons of the Kalahari and Namib deserts of Africa are prime examples of this. As soon as it rains these spring up all over the formerly waterless and barren deserts and Bushmen, and other desert dwellers, are able to leave the water holes to which they have been confined and roam where they will — secure in the knowledge that they will find water wherever they go, in the Tsava that lie all about. Meanwhile the Tsava benefit from their depredations, for as animals and men eat their fruit and suck in their water the seeds get dispersed, to lie dormant perhaps for years again until the next rain.

Melons and cucumbers seem to be made to comfort men in hot dry climates — in Persia a dish of sliced cucumber in vinegar is often offered to the thirsty guest.

Cucumbers

In temperate climates nearly all the cucumbers that have smooth edible skins can only be grown in greenhouses (see p. 204). There is one smooth-skinned strain, optimistically called "Burpless", that is hardy and can be grown out of doors, but otherwise the methods described on this page and the next apply only to common cucumbers. The common varieties of cucumber are not fully hardy, but can be grown with success in temperate regions as long as all risk of frost is avoided. They are much easier to grow than greenhouse cucumbers, and very prolific in favorable conditions.

Soil and climate

Cucumbers like soil that is nearly all compost or well-rotted manure. They will not stand wet feet, although they like plenty of moisture all through their growing period. Outdoor cucumbers can be grown successfully in most parts of the United States: they are fast growing and complete their life during the heat of the summer. Although they are easily injured by frost, they mature fast enough to be unaffected by winter weather.

Soil treatment

The soil needs deep digging to ensure adequate drainage, and a large quantity of ripe manure or compost. Half manure and half earth is ideal. Dig it in a foot (30 cm) down in each position. Like tomatoes, cucumbers must have full exposure to the sun. The two crops like much the same soil, so it is a good idea to alternate cucumbers with tomatoes in a sunny bed up against a south wall or fence. Remember that cucumbers are good climbers, and take up far less room and do better if they are allowed to climb. If you can train them up a fence or a trellis on a wall so much the better.

Propagation

You can sow cucumber seeds out of doors after all danger of frost is past. If there is an unexpected cold spell, cover them with glass jars. Remove the jars when the plants get too big for them. Cloches are even more useful, because they can be left on longer and can be improvised with transparent plastic and wire.

SOWING SEED INDOORS
To get early cucumbers, start them off indoors in peat pots or soil blocks. Sow two seeds on edge in each pot or block. Do not press the compost down; cucumbers are that rare thing, a vegetable which dislikes firm soil. Water them and keep them warm, but out of direct sunlight. You can then transplant them, at about the time of the last expected hard frost, without disturbing the roots. Sow more seed outdoors at the same time.

The alternative is to start your cucumbers indoors in peat pots or soil blocks. Then plant them out, long after the last possible frost, in their prepared positions. If your land is heavy and wet it is best to plant them on ridges; because if you plant them on the flat in badly drained land, they are likely to die from damping off.

If you are not letting them climb they can do with six feet (1.8 m) of space all round them; four feet (1.2 m) is the absolute minimum. If you are planting them in a deep bed (see p. 106), allow two feet (60 cm) each way, or else stagger them among other crops. I sometimes plant mine right on top of an old compost heap. They love it. When you plant them out sow some more seed outdoors as well – this will give you a second crop just when your first is running out.

Care while growing

Cucumbers must have water all the time: many people sink a flowerpot into the ground near each plant and pour water straight into this so that the water quickly reaches the roots. Keep them well weeded.

TRAINING CUCUMBERS
Cucumbers thrive if they are encouraged to climb. Train them up a fence or trellis (left); when they reach the top, pinch out each growing point (below).

When they have six or seven true leaves – not seed leaves – it is best to pinch out the growing points to make them branch and straggle. Do not remove the male flowers from outdoor cucumbers. Do this only with smooth-skinned cucumbers – the ones that you can only grow in the green house. Keep the fruit off the ground by placing a piece of plastic sheet, tile or glass under each one.

Pests and diseases

Mildew or blight This can develop in very hot and muggy conditions. It produces white powdery patches on leaves and stems. Avoid by planting resistant varieties.
Cucumber beetle These are spotted or striped beetles. The adults attack the leaves, and the larvae the stems and roots. Repel them with nicotine spray (see p. 104).
Cucumber mosaic virus Leaves become mottled and shrivelled. Pull and burn immediately. Plant resistant varieties.

Harvesting

Pick and eat your cucumbers as soon as they are ready. Above all don't leave any to grow old on the vines.

GHERKINS

The gherkin is the favorite for small pickles and relish. Gherkins don't need quite as much space between plants as cucumbers do; two feet (60 cm) is about right. Pick them when they are only two inches (5 cm) long.

Pumpkins

Pumpkins are a must for Halloween carving and Thanksgiving pumpkin pie. They also make delicious custards and casseroles, and hull-less seeds make a good snack.

Soil and climate

Pumpkins like humus if they can get it, but they will grow on unmanured ground as long as it is well drained. They need plenty of water.

Propagation

You can sow pumpkin seed out of doors, under polyethylthene cloches or inverted jam jars in spring, or else without protection in early summer. You can also sow seed indoors in peat pots or seed boxes shortly before the last frost, and plant the seedlings out at the start of the hot weather. Allow four feet (1.2 m) between plants, or 30 inches (75 cm) if you use a deep bed (see p. 106).

Care while growing

Let each side-shoot grow a male flower – a flower without a pumpkin attached to it. Then, when the next female flower – a flower with a tiny green pumpkin – appears, cut the shoot short just above the female flower. This will encourage the growth of several smallish pumpkins instead of one enormous one. Place upturned saucers under your pumpkins to prevent them suffering from rot (see Squashes).

Harvesting

Color is no indication of ripeness. It is best to wait until the first frost before cutting off the pumpkins. Leave about two inches (5 cm) of stalk on each one.

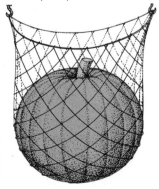

STORING PUMPKINS
Pumpkins need to be stored at a warmer temperature than any other vegetable. 50-60°F (10-16°C) is ideal. Never hang them up by their stalks, as eventually these will shrivel up, and the pumpkins will drop and bruise. By far the best way of storing them is to hang them in nets in an airy place.

Squashes

There is a bewildering variety of squashes. The best thing to do is to try several different ones, see which you like, and then plant one good one for eating fresh and another that is good for storing. Summer squash is one of the most prolific vegetables you can grow, so don't overplant. Size is unimportant; very large squashes tend to be tasteless. They are delicious, especially when stuffed with sausage and baked.

Soil and climate

The best place to grow squashes is on a compost heap. They will not grow very well on unmanured ground and like as much humus as they can get. They don't like poorly drained land, but they do need plenty of moisture during their short, quick growing season. Work in plenty of compost or manure, and lime if the pH is below 6.

Propagation

In warm climates sow the seed straight outside in the bed at the beginning of summer. In areas with very short summers

POLLINATING THE FLOWERS
Dust a little pollen from the male flower into the open female flower. To tell them apart, look for a tubular swelling, directly behind the female flower; this is absent in the male.

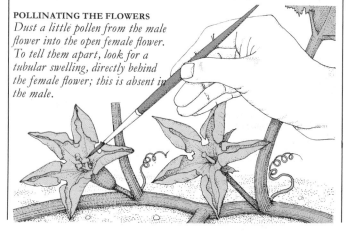

you can sow them inside in peat pots or seed boxes two weeks before the last frost and plant them out toward the beginning of summer. Otherwise sow the seed out of doors *in situ*, under cloches or upturned jam jars, and remove the cloches when the warm weather begins. Allow four feet (1.2 m) between plants – 30 inches (75 cm) for a deep bed (see p. 106). Sow two, or even three, seeds two inches (5 cm) deep in each position, and when they declare themselves remove the weakest plants, leaving only one. It is said to be best to sow the seeds on edge and not lying flat. I find they grow whatever I do.

Care while growing

Never let them go short of water. Mulching is very good for them. Though insects pollinate some flowers, it is important to pollinate by hand as well. Trailing varieties must be trained up fences or a wigwam of sticks.

TRAINING UP TRIPODS
If trailing varieties of squash are allowed to grow along the ground, they take up a great deal of room; the shoots can be several yards long. To save space, train them to run vertically. Grow them up trellises or chicke wire; alternatively train them up tripods. Tie three poles, seven feet (2 m) long, together at the top, and train one squash plant up each pole. When the shoots reach about five feet (1.5 m) high, pinch out the growing points.

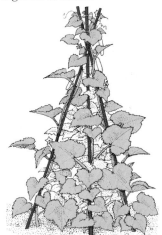

Pests and diseases

Mildew White patches caused by lack of moisture in the soil, and a high degree of humidity in the air, appear on leaves. The solution is to water them more.
Vine borer This pest hollows out the squash stems; the leaves go limp and die. Burn affected stems and prevent the pest spreading by earthing up the remaining ones.

SUPPORTING SQUASHES
As the winter squashes appear and grow to their full size, there is a danger of rot coming up from the earth and affecting them. So keep the squashes just off the soil, by laying a piece of plastic sheet, tile, wood or glass under each one.

Harvesting and storing

Pick summer squash and zucchini when small. If you leave them to mature, they will lose flavor. Keep picking to make more grow. Don't harvest winter squash until they are hard, or until the frost is really threatening. Cut the stems off several inches from the vegetables; don't break them off, as the wound lets in rot, and be certain not to bruise them. Store like pumpkins (see Pumpkins).

Melons

There are three main types: the true cantaloupe, which comes from Europe, the muskmelon, and a group which includes honeydews and casabas. My own preference is perhaps for the cantaloupe, but I have never tasted a melon – as long as it was ripe and freshly picked – that was not a memorable experience.

Soil and climate

Wherever you get three months of summer which culminates at melon-ripening time with days of 80°F (27°C) and nights of not less than 50°F (10°C) you can grow melons if the soil is right. Honeydews and casabas take another month or more.

They like lightish soil with plenty of humus, not heavy clay, and they like it alkaline: a pH over 7 is best. You will probably have to lime for them.

Soil treatment

Unless your soil is already half manure or compost dig in plenty, enough to give you a covering of at least four inches (10 cm) before you work it in. Or else dig out "hills" or stations, spaced about four feet (1.2m) apart, digging to one spade's depth and several spade widths square. Dump in a big forkful of manure at each hill, and then cover this with earth again so that each station forms a shallow mound.

Propagation

In hot and temperate climates just sow the seeds two weeks after the last frost, edge-upward, six to a hill, and an inch and a half (4 cm) deep; keep them well watered. If you have a deep bed (see p. 106), you should sow melons 18 inches (45 cm) apart; they will do better if you intercrop them with other plants. Thin to two or three plants in a station when the seedlings are established.

In cold climates you must sow indoors in early spring or else outdoors under cloches, mini greenhouses (see p. 111) or upturned glass jars. If you sow them indoors don't transfer them out of doors until all frosts are past and summer has definitely begun.

A method of getting them off to a flying start is to sprout the seeds first, by putting them between wet blotting paper, in a warm place until they begin to sprout. Do this about a week before you would normally sow the seeds, indoors or out. Don't let them dry out but don't drown them. Be careful not to break the sprouts when planting out.

Growing melons in a cool climate is a race against time. Fruit which sets after the middle of summer should ripen before the frost kills it off.

Care while growing

Treat just like outdoor cucumbers. As soon as the little melons are as big as your fist, balance them on a glass jar or an old can to keep them off the ground. They are more likely to ripen and less likely to rot like this.

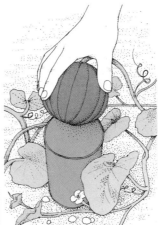

PROTECTING MELONS
You should care for your melons in the same way as for outdoor cucumbers. They need plenty of water and must be kept weed-free. When the little melons have grown to about the size of your fist, balance them on an old can to keep them off the ground. This will keep out rot and also makes them more likely to ripen.

Pests and diseases

Cut worm These pests eat through the stalks of young seedlings. If you get them in your garden, put paper or cardboard collars around the small plants when you plant them out.
Anthracnose This is a fungus disease which causes brown spots on the leaves and ultimately causes the melons to go moldy. You can avoid it – along with some other fungus diseases – if you don't grow cucurbitaceous plants more than once on the same ground in four years.
Botrytis, or gray mold Very wet conditions may bring this on. Although the plants need constant moisture there is no need to soak the ground. If botrytis strikes, all you can do is to destroy all affected fruits and herbage.

Harvesting

Melons generally begin to crack around the stems when ripe, and the fruit will break easily from the stem. Tapping helps when you have had experience: a ripe melon makes a unique hollow sound. Some experts get on their hands and knees and sniff the melons to see if they are ripe. You don't store melons; you just pick them and eat them.

WATERMELONS

These need really warm weather for at least four months and a terrific lot of space because the vines straggle over large areas. Unless you have both of these, and a sandy or very light soil, don't consider them. But if you have these conditions, go ahead and grow them – there is nothing so refreshing on a hot day. When you think a watermelon is ripe knock it with your knuckles and heed Mark Twain's advice: a ripe melon says "punk", an unripe one says "pink" or "pank".

Compositae

Lettuce, chicory, endive, salsify, scorzonera, dandelions, globe artichokes, cardoons, and Jerusalem artichokes are all members of the *Compositae*.

The *Compositae* derive their name from the fact that their flowers, which look just like single flowers, are in fact clusters of many small flowers packed together and cunningly disguised as single flowers. The family contains two important groups, which are best described as the salad group and the thistle group. The salad group — lettuce, chicory, endive, salsify, scorzonera and dandelions — are fast-growing, soft-stemmed plants, which gardeners should usually treat as annuals. They have white milky sap in their stems and a slightly bitter taste. This is the family from which most of the ingredients that make up the basis of good salads come.

The thistle group embraces a lot of the world's thistles, of which globe artichokes and cardoons are of especial interest to gardeners. Closely related to these are a number of other plants that look very different, but to a botanist are quite similar; these include Jerusalem artichokes, Chinese artichokes and sunflowers. The vegetables in this group generally have to be cooked, but it is surprising what you can eat if you are hungry. Not long ago I was cutting down spear thistles in my meadows when somebody came along and told me that I could eat them. She proceeded, somewhat painfully, to peel the stalk of one of them (a young one) and yes, you could indeed eat them. You would have to be very hungry to make a meal of them though — unless you found a better way of getting the prickles off.

Lettuces

Lettuces have been cultivated for such a long time that several distinct and firmly-fixed varieties have developed. The three common types are cabbage lettuce, cos lettuce and butterhead lettuce. The cabbage variety is green on the outside with crisp, white leaves which form a closed heart; the cos has tall green leaves and forms a loose, elongated head; and the butterhead has tender, green leaves in a flattened, soft head.

With careful planting and selection of varieties you should be able to grow lettuce for a large part of the year, at least in temperate climates. For the purposes of cultivation, lettuce falls into three categories: winter lettuce, spring lettuce and summer lettuce. Winter varieties are bred to grow through mild winters. They do especially well if they are covered with cloches. Spring varieties are very fast growing so that they can come to harvest in early summer. Summer lettuces grow big and lush and form the vast bulk of the lettuce crop. Lettuces are excellent for small gardens and window-boxes, and grow well indoors too.

Soil and climate

Lettuces like cool moist conditions. They will grow well in shade, and are inclined to "bolt", or run too quickly to seed, in hot sun. Thus they do best in cooler and moister climates, and should only be grown in winter in hot ones. To grow lettuces well you need good rich soil. The ground should be well-drained but humus-rich to retain water. Lettuces will not grow well in heavy ground, so if you have, say, a clay soil, you must temper this for some years with plenty of manure or compost. The deep bed method (see p. 106) is ideal for lettuces.

Soil treatment

The best plan is to give the lettuce bed a heavy dressing of really well-rotted manure or compost: a pound (500 g) to the square foot (900 sq cm) is not too much. The soil should be pH 6 or 7, so lime if necessary.

Propagation

You can sow lettuce seed direct in the bed, or in a seed-bed or seed boxes for transplanting. Seed will only germinate in fairly cool moist conditions, so in very hot countries it is a good idea to put the seed between two sheets of wet blotting paper and keep it in a refrigerator for five days before planting. Allow ten inches (25 cm) between plants and one foot (30 cm) between rows — deep bed (see p. 106) eight inches (20 cm) all round.

Winter lettuce should be sown out of doors in the early fall. Spring lettuce can be started indoors in seed boxes (or peat pots) in late winter, or else sown out of doors in fall and allowed to stay more or less dormant during the winter protected by cloches or even some straw or leaves. Summer lettuce is best sown direct out of doors, and sown successionally right through the summer. Lettuces are also a good crop for window-boxes or indoor culture.

Care while growing

Lettuces should be hoed, and watered if necessary. Mulching is also beneficial. Shade the plants if there is a very hot sun, and in winter protect them from heavy frost.

Pests and diseases

Cut worm Cut worms sometimes gnaw into the stems of seedlings near the ground. If your lettuces suffer badly from this, you should place collars around the seedlings when you plant them out. This will also discourage slugs, who love to eat lettuces.

Lettuce rot In some gardens there is a rot which comes from the soil and may attack the lettuces spreading through the plants. This can be prevented by a layer of sand on top of the ground around each lettuce. With proper rotation, however, this should not be a problem.

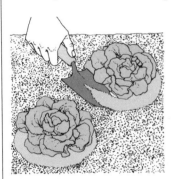

PREVENTING LETTUCE ROT
Lettuce rot comes from the soil and spreads through the plant, via the lowest leaves that are touching the soil. Avoid it by spreading a layer of clean sand over the soil around each lettuce. Also, never plant lettuces in the same place two years running.

Harvesting

Lettuces will not store and lettuces that have been stuffed inside a refrigerator for days are worthless. So pull them when you want them—making sure that the roots come out with the lettuces. Don't let them grow to seed (unless you want seed), but pull them before they have a chance to bolt, and give them to your poultry or put them on your compost heap when they become over-ripe.

CELTUCE

Celtuce or stem lettuce, is grown for its thick stems as well as its leaves. It needs a soil with lots of manure or compost added to it. Sow successively in shallow drills from spring to midsummer, and thin the seedlings to about twelve inches (30 cm) apart. Water the plants well, as they tend to get tough if allowed to dry out. Otherwise treat them as you would lettuce. The stems will be ready for cutting three months after sowing. You can eat the leaves as well, and these should be harvested as they form.

CORN SALAD OR LAMB'S LETTUCE

In my view corn salad, or lamb's lettuce, which is a member of the family *Valerianaceae,* is rather tasteless, but its virtue is that it provides salads during the winter. It grows wild in corn-fields, and this gives it an extra hardiness when it is cultivated in gardens. Sow it in early autumn and treat exactly as you would lettuce. When the seedlings have three leaves, thin them to six inches (15 cm) apart. If the winter gets very hard, cover the plants with a mulch of leaves until early spring when you can begin picking again. Harvest a few leaves from each plant as you need them.

Chicory

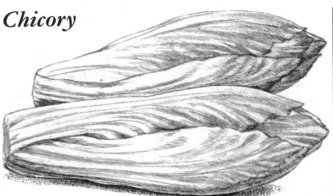

Chicory, which is also called French or Belgian endive, produce green leaves which are eaten as salad in summer, and, more importantly, shoots which are forced indoors to provide winter salads. Witloof is the best variety for winter forcing.

Soil and climate

Chicory prefers a coolish climate, but will grow virtually anywhere. A rich soil with a neutral pH – 6 to 7– is best.

Soil treatment

Dig the bed at least two spade-depths deep, so that the long straight roots will come out easily when you need to dig them up in the autumn. Chicory grows well without mature compost or manure, but if you have some to spare it is worth digging it in well, especially in deep beds.

Propagation

Grow chicory from seed sown half an inch (1 cm) deep and three inches (8 cm) apart in rows two feet (60 cm) apart, or, if you have a deep bed (see p. 106) in positions six inches (15 cm) apart in both directions. Sow successively through spring and summer for salad; in June for winter forcing.

Care while growing

Weed your chicory bed and keep the soil loose. If you sowed chicory for forcing, thin to six inches (15 cm) apart and eat the thinnings as salad. Chicory suffers very little from pests and diseases.

Harvesting and storing

Pick leaves for summer salad as you want them. Dig your roots for forcing after the first bad frost, and force them as described below.

FORCING CHICORY
After the first bad frost dig up a few chicory roots for forcing. Cut off the tops to within an inch (2.5 cm) of the crown. Plant them in a pot, or box of soil in a dark cellar, with the temperature not less than 50°F (10°C). Shortly new sprouts, or chicons, will grow; if you break them off carefully a second crop will follow. Never pick them until you need them — even an hour in the light will make them droop.

Endives

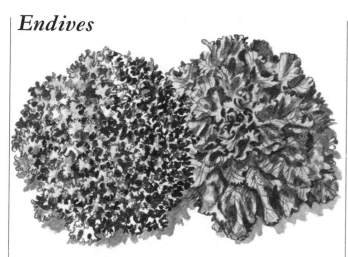

Endive is one of the many minor salad plants, which can be eaten either raw or cooked. It has more flavor, but lacks the delicious crispness of lettuce. Curly endive comes to harvest in late summer; broad-leaved, or Batavian, endive is picked in autumn or winter.

Soil and climate
Endive will grow in practically any soil. A neutral pH between 6 and 7 is best, and the more humus in the soil the better. Endives prefer a cool moist climate to a hot dry one.

Propagation
Sow curly endive seeds thinly in shallow drills at the beginning of summer. Make two more sowings at three week intervals. Sow broad-leaved endive in late summer. Single the seedlings when they appear, to nine inches (23 cm) apart or six inches (15 cm) in deep beds (see p. 106).

Care while growing
Endives don't like too much sun, so shade them if necessary and keep them moist. In cooler climates this shouldn't be necessary. Three or four months after sowing start blanching by covering the plants with something that will keep out the light. Whitewashed cloches are ideal. Alternatively, you can pull them up and plant them in earth in seed boxes and put them in a dark place.

BLANCHING ENDIVES
Blanch endives by putting white-washed cloches over them in late summer, or cover with opaque plastic.

Harvesting
Simply eat endives once they are blanched; this will be about three weeks after you covered them.

Salsify

Salsify or "oyster plant" is grown mainly for its long roots, though the leaves may also be eaten. The root has a delicate oyster flavor and is delicious both cooked and raw. Parboil, then brown in butter for a real treat.

Soil and climate
Salsify likes a deep, rich loam. If you have to grow it in heavy clay take out a trench a foot (30 cm) wide and 18 inches (45 cm) deep and fill it with well-rotted manure.

Soil treatment
A bed dug deeply with well-rotted manure or compost is best. Fresh manure will cause the salsify root to fork. The soil should have a neutral pH, between 6 and 7.

Propagation
Sow seed in early spring an inch (2.5 cm) deep and two inches (5 cm) apart in rows about a foot (30 cm) apart. In a cold climate you can sow it anything up to a month before the last frost, but you must cover it with glass. Thin to four inches (10 cm) when the plants appear. Sow closer and thin to three inches (8 cm) in a deep bed (see p. 106).

Care while growing
Keep the salsify weeded, and mulch in the fall before hard weather sets in. It rarely suffers from pests or diseases.

Harvesting and storing
The roots should be allowed to grow to an inch and a half (4 cm) in diameter and eight inches (20 cm) long before you harvest them. They are improved by frost — even quite a hard frost — so you can leave them in the ground quite late. But in very cold climates, harvest them in the autumn and store them in damp sand in a cool cellar. Since salsify is a biennial, it will go to flower and seed in the spring of its second year. If you still have some in the ground at this stage, cut the flower stalks before they get too hard; you will find they taste very good if you eat them like asparagus.

SCORZONERA
Scorzonera, known also as black or Spanish, salsify is grown in the same way. One minor difference is that you can, if you want, treat it as a biennial, digging up and eating the roots in their second year of growth.

Dandelions

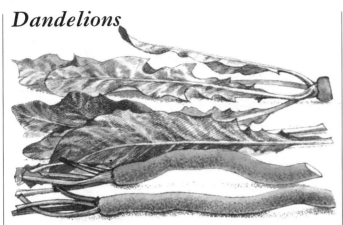

The wild dandelion has been tamed and improved to make a very useful vegetable. The leaves can be used, sparingly, in salads and are especially useful for salads early in the year before the first lettuces are ready; mulched over, the plants will survive the winter and grow away fast in the spring. Cooked dandelion leaves make an excellent vegetable, better tasting and far more vitamin-rich than spinach. The roots may be dried, ground, and used as a substitute for coffee. The coffee tastes quite good, but doesn't give you the lift that caffeine does. We might all be a lot healthier if we went over to it. The flowers make fine wine, but it is sensible to eat the leaves of your cultivated dandelions and gather flowers from wild dandelions.

Dandelions are perennials; if you look after them they will last for years.

Soil and climate
Dandelions thrive in any soil and any climate except very hot ones.

Soil treatment
Dig well and incorporate compost or manure.

Propagation
Dandelions grow easily from seed which can be bought from seed merchants. Sow successively from the middle of spring until midsummer. Sow thinly in rows 18 inches (45 cm) apart and thin to a foot (30 cm) apart in the rows when the leaves are two inches (5 cm) long. On the deep bed (see p. 106) broadcast and subsequently thin to about a foot (30 cm) apart each way.

Care while growing
Water if the bed dries out and keep it well weeded. Cover the plants with a light mulch in cold winters. Pick off any flowering shoots (use wild dandelion flowers for wine).

Pests and diseases
Cultivated dandelions are closely related to their wild ancestors and are therefore very resistant to disease. Keep the slugs away though (see p. 104).

Harvesting
Dandelions are perennials so you must not cut too many leaves off during the first summer of their lives, because the roots gain strength from the leaves. Cut them hard the second year. You can dig dandelion roots up in the autumn and force them to grow shoots in the same way you can force chicory (see p. 159).

Globe Artichokes

Eaten as it should be – that is, when still young and tender – the globe artichoke is, in·my view, supreme among vegetables. But more than that, it is as beautiful a plant as you are likely to have in your garden. A thistle *par excellence*, I've actually seen a globe artichoke grow to a height of ten feet (3 m). You will, however, need a fair amount of space to grow globe artichokes, so they are better left out of the very small garden. On the other hand, they are decorative enough with their fern-like, greyish leaves not to be grown only in the vegetable garden. They are very different from Jerusalem and Chinese artichokes.

Soil and climate
Low-lying black alluvial soil is ideal for globe artichokes. It should be moist but not waterlogged. If you have not got this – and there is a good chance you won't have – any rich, moist soil will do. They are not really winter-hardy in cool temperate climates since hard frosts cut the leaves right down. Even so the roots will survive and the plants will shoot up in the following spring. Some protection, such as straw or leaves, helps them to survive the winter.

Soil treatment
The bed for your globe artichokes should be dug deeply. Work in large amounts of organic material. The pH should be around 6.5, so test for lime.

Propagation
Globe artichokes can be grown from seed and it doesn't take as long to get heads from them this way as many people seem to think. Sow the seed in a hot-bed in late winter, plant out in spring, and you should be eating artichokes in early autumn. You can also sow seeds in their permanent position in the spring, but you will have to wait to harvest blooms until the next year.

A popular alternative to sowing seed is to grow the artichokes from suckers or offsets. If you uncover the old plants at the roots in the spring or autumn, according to your climate, you will find a number of small shoots getting ready to grow. Cut some of these out carefully, taking with each shoot a "heel" which is a bit of the mother plant. But don't take so much as to harm the mother plant. Plant these suckers straight into the ground at about the same depth they were before. Do this in early spring in cold climates or in autumn in hot ones. They should give you heads by the following summer.

Spacings vary according to variety and the kind of soil the plants are to grow in — in very rich soil plant them further away from each other because they are likely to grow much bigger. Generally, four feet (1.2 m) between plants is about right. Make it five feet (1.5 m) in a deep bed (see p. 106), because the soil will be rich.

You can have good heads to eat for six months of the year in cooler climates if you protect some old plants very well in the winter. These will give you blooms in late spring and early summer. If you planted good suckers in early spring these will give you a crop in late summer. And you'll get heads in the fall from suckers planted say six weeks after the first planting. In very hot climates you should get most of your crop in the winter and spring.

Since globe artichoke plants tend to lose vigor after a few years (though I have had good crops from an eight-year-old plant), try replacing a quarter of your total crop every year with new plants. That is, each autumn dig out the oldest quarter of the crop, and replace them in the spring with new plants. But take the suckers from the old plants before scrapping them and plant them in sand or soil indoors. In the spring these can be used for replanting.

Care while growing

Heavy mulching with compost or manure is always a good idea with globe artichokes. And where the winters are cold, it is best to cut the plants down to the ground in the fall and to pile hay, straw or leaves over them. But if you do this, uncover the plants on mild days to let them dry out. In summer droughts, soak the ground around the plants regularly and thoroughly.

Pests and diseases

Botrytis This causes a gray mold on leaves and stalks and may attack plants in very warm wet seasons. If it does, remove and burn all affected plants.
Artichoke leaf spot In hot muggy weather, leaves may go brown and die. Use a weak solution of Bordeaux mixture.

Harvesting

Ignorance of the following rule makes artichokes less popular than they should be: harvest them when they are very young! Don't wait until they are huge great prickly things, as hard as wood and as sharp as needles. If you cut them when they are still tight, green and small you can eat practically the whole thing. If they are too old only the bottom tips of the leaves and the heart will be edible. Simply cut through the stalk about an inch below the globe.

HARVESTING GLOBES
If you harvest your globe artichokes while they are still very young, you can eat the whole head, instead of just the heart and the base of the inner leaves. Harvest the globes by cutting through the stalk about one inch (2.5 cm) below the globe.

Cardoons

Cardoons are thistles which are very closely related to globe artichokes. They have been specifically bred for their stems, which should be eaten blanched. They take up a lot of space but are delicious deep-fried, sautéed or in soups and stews.

Soil and climate

Although strictly speaking perennials, cardoons are always grown as annuals, so they are not so fussy about soil as globe artichokes. Cardoons grow primarily in warm climates and they don't like it too wet.

Soil treatment

Dig holes about one foot (30 cm) across and three feet (90 cm) apart, and fill these with compost. Or you can dig out trenches as for celery (see Celery).

Propagation

Sow three or four cardoon seeds in each hole or at three foot (90 cm) intervals along the trench in the spring. Alternatively, sow in peat pots a little earlier and plant out toward the end of spring. Pull out all but the strongest plants when they appear.

Care while growing

Cardoons should be kept watered and weeded, and, since they need blanching, they should be hilled up like celery (see Celery). But before hilling up you should wrap the plants in straw, or put a length of drain pipe over them to protect them. They are rarely affected by pests or diseases.

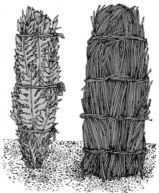

BLANCHING CARDOONS
About three weeks before harvesting, bunch up the cardoon plants and tie them together. Then wrap them round completely with straw, or anything else that will keep out the light. Leave the tips of the leaves showing. When the blanching process is complete, you will have cardoons all through the autumn and winter.

Harvesting

You can begin to harvest your cardoons in autumn and continue well into the winter. Three weeks before you intend to harvest a batch, blanch the plants, which may be three feet (90 cm) tall. Gather them up and tie them together, then wrap each one round with straw.

Jerusalem Artichokes

It is most unfortunate that the Jerusalem artichoke was so named, since people constantly mix it up with the globe artichoke. Strangely, they are members of the same family, but only a botanist could see any resemblance between them. The Jerusalem is in fact more closely related to the sunflower; the plant looks very similar except that it has small flowers and tubers on its roots. The tubers are pleasant to eat and are especially good for diabetics because they contain a special form of sugar and no starch.

Soil and climate
Jerusalem artichokes grow best in light or sandy soil. They do very poorly in clay. In light land they will grow like weeds if you let them – as high as seven feet (2 m) – and they will smother any plant that tries to compete with them. They grow in practically any climate.

Soil treatment
If you have to grow them in heavy soil dig it well, make sure it is free of perennial weeds and add as much manure or compost as you can. Sandy soil is little trouble, although the more manure the bigger the crop.

Propagation
Simply dig a hole with a trowel and plant the tubers six inches (15 cm) deep. I put them in in late winter. Even a tiny scrap of a tuber will produce a plant. Plant 18 inches (45 cm) apart each way – deep bed method (see p. 106) 15 inches (38 cm). They make a smother crop.

Once you have had a crop of Jerusalem artichokes it is very difficult to get rid of them. They will come up again year after year unless you hoe them out constantly.

Care while growing
In light land you don't need to do anything. In heavy land hoe between them because Jerusalem artichokes are not vigorous enough to beat weeds. Alternatively, mulch heavily. Pests and diseases rarely affect them.

Harvesting and storing
Dig them up in the late fall, or else leave them in the ground until you want them. In climates with hard frost dig them up after the tops have died back and store them. The tops are fine for mulch, and can be woven as a windbreak.

CHINESE ARTICHOKES
Strictly speaking a member of the *Labiatae* family, the Chinese artichoke is also grown for its tubers, in exactly the same way as the Jerusalem artichoke. Regular watering and feeds of soluble manure will add extra flesh to the tubers, which should be lifted in autumn when the leaves die.

Sweet Corn

Sweet corn, which is basically field corn picked very young, is a member of the *Gramineae,* or grass family: this includes popcorn and all the world's cereal crops and a lot of other species.

The plants, which I have seen as tall as 12 feet (3.6 m), send a mass of fibrous roots deep into the soil. This takes a lot out of the soil, but when in due course the plants are returned in the form of compost they put most of the goodness back again. There are small varieties bred for gardeners which grow to only four feet (1.2 m). These are useful in a small garden because they don't cast so much shade.

Soil and climate
Sweet corn likes a deep, well-drained, humus-enriched loam. Clay is too cold for it in northern climates; it must have an early start, as it needs ten to twelve weeks to come to maturity. It will grow in light sandy soil, but only if there is plenty of humus in it. Hungry old gravels and sands just won't grow it at all. It needs good soil.

Depending on the variety, sweet corn prefers about three months of hot sun and warm nights. However you can grow it in fairly cloudy places, if you start it early enough.

Soil treatment
Sweet corn needs plenty of humus thoroughly mixed into the soil (not just dumped on top at the last minute) because the roots go deep as well as spreading wide. A couple of inches (5 cm) of well-rotted manure dug well in a spade's depth deep is ideal. Alternatively plant sweet corn after a heavily manured main potato crop. Soil must be neutral: pH 6.5 to 7.

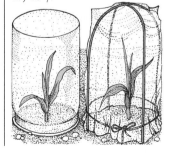

Propagation

It is better to sow sweet corn in wide blocks instead of in long thin lines. This is because it is wind-pollinated and in a thin line some plants may get missed. If this is difficult, plant two close rows which will form tassels at the same time. To give it a flying start sow it outside two weeks before the last probable frost. Sweet corn doesn't take to being transplanted but this doesn't mean it can't be done.

Sow the seed about a foot (30 cm) apart each way, in blocks or in the deep bed (see p. 106).

Care while growing

Sweet corn doesn't like to got short of water. Mulching does it nothing but good. Hilling up is beneficial too, because the plant will put out more roots higher up its stem. These and

HILLING UP SWEET CORN
If you intend to hill up your sweet corn stalks while they are growing, sow the seed 18 inches (45 cm) apart instead of 12 inches (30 cm) apart. Pulling up the soil around the plants in this way gives them support while they mature and causes them to put out more roots higher up.

the soil help protect it against storms. If stems get broken, pull them upright and bank soil around them.

Pests and diseases

Earworm These bore into the tips of the ears of corn. If you see them when you are picking the ears, destroy them.
Smut Smut is a fungus which causes large gray boils to appear on the kernels. Burn the affected plants and don't leave rotting sweet corn about on the ground; bury it or compost it. Otherwise it may develop smut.
Corn borer This flesh-coloured, black-spotted worm breaks the tassels. If it is troublesome, destroy the plants after harvest.

HARVESTING SWEET CORN
Pick the corn by jerking the cobs sharply downward and breaking them off; if you cut them off you risk damaging the plant.

Harvesting

The ears are ready to pick as soon as the white, silky tassels go brown; otherwise test for ripeness by opening the husk and pressing your fingernail into a grain. If it is firm but still milky it is ready. Rush the corn to a pot of boiling water! The moment you pick it the sugar starts turning to starch and the flavor is lost.

Okra

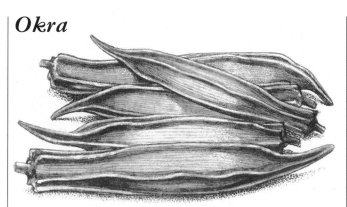

Okra, sometimes known as "gumbo", is a tropical vegetable, of the *Malvaceae,* or mallow family, whose most renowned member is the cotton plant. The pods of the okra plant make the most delicious vegetable with a very subtle and distinctive taste. They are much used in curries. When the seeds are well developed they can be shelled and cooked like peas. The whole plant is extremely attractive with large yellow and red flowers. Three or four plants will keep a family well supplied with okra.

Soil and climate

Okra can be grown in greenhouses in cold climates. Outdoors it needs a lot of summer sun, and it is not much good trying to grow it in places with cool cloudy summers. But where outdoor tomatoes really thrive and crop reliably, okra can be grown. It likes a light soil with plenty of humus but not too much fresh manure, since this will produce too much leaf and not enough fruit.

Soil treatment

Okra grows especially well by the deep bed method (see p. 106) and in cooler climates can be grown under portable deep bed mini-greenhouses (see p. 108). Otherwise cultivate deeply and work in some well-rotted compost. The soil should have a pH between 6 and 7.

Propagation

Okra can be started indoors, but only in peat pots because it doesn't like being transplanted. If you sow the seed outdoors, wait until the soil is thoroughly warm. You can help here by warming the soil yourself under a mini-greenhouse or under cloches (see p. 96). Dwarf varieties should be sown 30 inches (75 cm) apart; larger varieties three and a half feet (1 m) apart.

Care while growing

Okra should be watered occasionally, but not swamped.

Pests and diseases

Caterpillars Pick caterpillars off and tread on them.

Harvesting and storing

You can harvest about two months after sowing. Harvest when the okra is still quite young, a few days after the flowers have fallen. Pick pods every other day whether you need them or not, so that the plants keep producing more. Pods can be frozen or canned, and in Italy I have seen them laid out on a rack in the sun and dried. They keep well like this, but I prefer them fresh. Keep picking them as long as they grow, which can be right up to the first frost.

Rhubarb

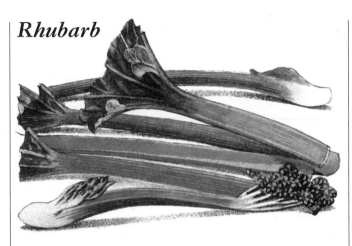

Rhubarb is a vegetable because we eat its stems, not its fruit. It is thought of as fruit merely because our whim is to eat it as a dessert, like most other fruit. These days there is so much fruit available, fresh or frozen, through the year, that there is no longer an endless gap between the last of the stored apples and the ripening of the raspberries. In the old days that gap was filled with rhubarb. But rhubarb is still well worth growing, for it is a good fruit substitute. Its stems contain oxalic acid, which scours pans clean and sets your teeth on edge

Soil and climate

Rhubarb likes a cold climate (it comes from Mongolia) and is no good at all in a hot one. Unless it enjoys frost in the winter it does not have the dormant period which it needs, and its stalks, instead of being red and edible, are green and inedible. It likes quite acid soil so don't give it lime, but otherwise it will grow in any well-drained soil, and it seems to thrive in that milieu of nettles, old rusty cans, and broken bottles that is found at the bottom of many gardens.

Soil treatment

Put rhubarb in a part of the garden devoted to perennials because, properly treated, it will continue to grow and yield for years. Clear its bed of perennial weeds, dig it deeply, and put plenty of manure on it. It pays to dig a deep pit, discard the subsoil, and fill in with manure and topsoil.

PLANTING RHUBARB CROWNS
It is possible to raise rhubarb from seed, but this is not the most reliable method of growing it. It is best to get hold of some rooted crowns. Dig a deep hole, fill it with compost, put back the topsoil and plant the roots, right way up and three feet (90 cm) apart. They are sure to grow.

Propagation

Rhubarb seldom breeds true with seed, and so the usual method is to use divided roots. Commercial growers generally dig up their beds every four years, divide the roots, and replant on fresh ground. You can either buy root cuttings or get them from a neighbor who is in the process of dividing his rhubarb. Just plant the bits of root the right way up three feet (90 cm) apart, and up the plants will come. Nothing can stop them.

Care while growing

Plentiful mulching is good for rhubarb. In the winter, when it dies down, you can bury it deeply in a mulch of manure, leaf-mold, compost or what you will. As long as it is provided with ample organic matter in this way you need not dig it up every four years: it will last almost indefinitely.

CUTTING OFF FLOWERS
Flowering rhubarb will not produce succulent juicy stems. The flower stalks divert all the nourishment away from the plant; cut them off when they appear.

In the spring draw the mulch away from around the plants to let the sun warm the soil. Then, when the plants begin to grow well, you can cover them with old buckets and in the winter, cover the buckets with fresh long-strawed manure, so that the heat from the manure will force the rhubarb on, and you will get stems to eat early in the spring. You can cover the crowns with oil drums, painted black to absorb the heat of the sun, open at the bottom end, and with a six inch (15 cm) diameter hole cut in the top. The oil drums should then be pressed firmly into the ground around the plants; they should be adequately weighed down to prevent them from blowing over.

Pests and diseases

Rhubarb curculio This is a colored beetle about an inch (2.5 cm) long. It bores into every part of the plant, especially the edible stalks, but can easily be picked off. The beetle lives in dock plants, so do not permit docks to exist near rhubarb.

FORCING RHUBARB
Cover each plant with an old bucket, and when winter comes insulate the bucket with long-strawed manure. If you lift two-year-old roots in late autumn and force them indoors, you can have rhubarb to eat through the winter. Otherwise start forcing the plants in the same way outdoors in very late winter, and you will reap the benefits in early summer.

Harvesting

Spare the plants altogether for their first year, and thereafter only harvest the big thick stalks: let the thinner ones grow on to nourish the plants. Never take more than half the stems of a plant in one year. Don't cut the stems, as this lets in rot; break them by pulling them back from the plant, then forcing them downward and inch or two. This does not hurt the crown. Stop harvesting altogether in July.

You can make jam with rhubarb (see p. 222) but the best thing you can do with it is to make wine (see p. 224).

Mushrooms

Mushrooms, which are fungi and not vegetables at all, are an obvious choice for the self-sufficient gardener who has space to spare indoors. Mushrooms have a higher mineral content than meat (twice as high as any other vegetable), and contain more protein than any other vegetable except for certain types of bean. Another good thing about growing mushrooms is that the compost you need for growing them can all end up in your garden outside.

Climate

In warm weather you can grow mushrooms outdoors or indoors without artificial heating, using the method I shall describe. In the winter keep the temperature over 60°F (16°C). Never leave mushrooms in direct sunlight.

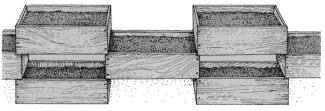

STACKING MUSHROOMS IN BOXES
Allow at least six inches (15 cm) between the top of one box and the bottom of another. There should also be perhaps a dozen half inch (1.5 cm) holes in the bottom of each box. I like cedarwood boxes best, but you can use fiberglass trays.

Soil treatment

To grow mushrooms you need boxes which ideally should be two and a half feet (75 cm) long, nine inches (25 cm) wide and nine inches (25 cm) deep.

You can buy suitable compost and this is really the best thing to do for small quantities. However, to make enough compost for 60 square feet (6 sq m) is not difficult. Get four bales of wheat straw (no other straw will do) and shake it out into layers, soaking it thoroughly with water. Leave it for a day or two, but throw on more water from time to time, because it must be saturated. You should also have: seven pounds (3 kg) of gypsum (from a builder), 28 lbs (12.7 kg) of poultry manure, 14 lbs (6.3 kg) of mushroom compost activator.

When the straw is thoroughly wet, spread some out 12 inches (30 cm) deep over an area five feet (1.5 m) square. Shake over this layer a trowelful each of the poultry manure, gypsum and activator. Add another foot (30 cm) of straw and on this another sprinkling of the other goodies, until all the materials have been used up. The heap should be about six feet (1.8 m) high. If it is out of doors cover it with an old carpet, paper, or plastic.

By the fourth day the temperature of the heap should be 160°F (71°C). Leave it another two days and then turn it so that the outsides are in the middle. If any part of the heap appears dry at this turning sprinkle water on it, just enough to moisten it but not enough to wash away the special ingredients. When you turn the heap, shake out the straw thoroughly and rebuild very carefully. The success of your crop depends on this care.

After another six days turn again. Be even more sparing with water, but if there are any dry patches or gray patches, sprinkle them lightly. Then, after four more days, turn yet again. If the compost appears too damp apply more gypsum. Six days later the compost will be ready for the boxes.

Propagation

When it is ready for use, the compost should be fairly dry and springy; it should consist of short pieces of rotted straw but should not be sticky. Fill each box, tamping the compost down well with a brick, until the final topping up is level with the top of the box.

By now you will have bought some spawn. There is "manure" spawn which comes in lumps which you break into small pieces, and "grain" spawn which you simply scatter on the compost. I suggest that beginners use manure spawn, because it is easy to use and reliable.

MUSHROOM SPAWN
Plant each piece of manure spawn about an inch (2.5 cm) deep, with five inches (13 cm) between the pieces. Then cover with a layer of wet newspaper.

Care while growing

During the next week or two, do not let the temperature fall below 60°F (16°C); 70°F (21°C) is even better. On the other hand beware of overheating; 90°F (32°C) may kill the spawn. After three weeks you should see the white threads of the mycelium growing in the compost. At this point you must apply "casing". Mix some well moistened horticultural peat with the same bulk of freshly sterilized loam (the loam should be from permanent grassland). Put an inch and a half (4 cm) layer of mixed peat and loam on top of the compost and press it down gently. Mushrooms should appear about three weeks later. Give them a little water. Keep the temperature between 60°F (16°C) and 64°F (18°C).

Harvesting

When you harvest mushrooms twist them out. When the crop seems over, try and persuade it to go on cropping a little longer by watering it with a dilute salt solution. Eventually dump the spent compost on your compost heap, wash the boxes with formaldehyde solution, and put the boxes out to weather for several weeks before you use them again.

CHAPTER SIX

The Cultivation of Fruits

*Containing the planting, growing and
harvesting instructions for members of the families
Rosaceae, Rutaceae, Grossulariaceae, Moraceae,
Ericaceae, Oleaceae and Vitaceae.*

Rosaceae

Apples, pears, quinces, cherries, peaches, nectarines, apricots, plums, damsons, raspberries, blackberries and strawberries, all belong to the useful and beautiful family of the *Rosaceae*. It is a huge family which includes agrimony, burnet, mountain ash, 500 species of hawthorn and, of course, the mighty rose.

Most of the fruits grown in temperate climates belong to this family, which splits into several subdivisions: among them are plants which have stone fruit like cherries and plums, those which have berries like strawberries and raspberries, and these which have what botanists call pomes like apples and pears.

All the species are insect-pollinated, which is why they have such enticing flowers. They also depend on birds and animals to scatter their seed — suitably manured — which is why they have attractive and edible fruits. And so, with the help of other living things, the cycle renews itself, and the *Rosaceae* continue to enhance our lives.

Apples

Apples are far and away the most important tree fruit crop of temperate climates. If you grow early and late varieties and a variety bred for keeping, you should have apples to eat throughout the year. The gap will come in the summer when you should have plenty of soft fruit. How many trees you should have and whether they should be standard, semi-dwarf, dwarf, espalier or cordon is discussed on page 76. A single apple tree will not fruit by itself; you must plant two or more different varieties to ensure fruit production.

Soil and climate

Apples prefer a good, deep, well-drained loam, though they will do well on a heavy loam. They do not thrive on gravels, very sandy soils, heavy stubborn clays or on shallow soils above chalk or limestone. But, if you have unsuitable soil you can always dig a big pit where you want to plant a tree and bring in some good topsoil from outside. And of course any soil can be improved — be it too light or too heavy — with plenty of compost or manure.

In places where figs, citrus fruit, dates and such warm-climate things grow well and freely out of doors it is better not to grow apples. The apple is a cold climate tree and does better for a period of winter dormancy. It doesn't mind very cold winters (certain varieties will even grow in Alaska) but it doesn't like late frosts once it is in blossom. Late frosts are generally the sort that creep over the land on a still, clear night. Therefore take care not to plant apples in frost pockets — those places where cold frosty air gets trapped after it has flowed down from high ground. The floors of valleys and dips in the sides of hills — especially if they

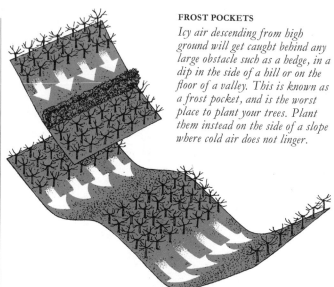

FROST POCKETS
Icy air descending from high ground will get caught behind any large obstacle such as a hedge, in a dip in the side of a hill or on the floor of a valley. This is known as a frost pocket, and is the worst place to plant your trees. Plant them instead on the side of a slope where cold air does not linger.

contain some obstruction, such as a thick hedge — are likely to be frost pockets. If your land is not flat, plant your apple trees fairly high on the side of a hill, or on a gentle rise, where cold air will not linger. But don't plant them where it is too windy.

Soil treatment

It is a good thing to clear-cultivate land — thoroughly dig it over — before you plant fruit trees on it. Ideally after clear-cultivating you should grow a crop or two of green manure (see p. 86) and dig, plow, or till this into the soil. But you may be in too much of a hurry to do this — I always am — in which case simply clear-cultivating is perfectly adequate. It improves drainage and kills perennial weeds. Firm the soil well after digging by rolling or treading it. Then leave it for two weeks to settle. Make absolutely sure the land is well drained.

If you have heavy land, be very careful. You might easily dig a hole for a fruit tree, fill it with magnificent free-draining loam and compost, and find that you have done nothing more than dig a pond. Water sinks freely into the loam, fills the hole, then cannot get away because of the surrounding clay, and the tree dies for lack of air to its roots. You can get round this problem by filling the bottom foot (30 cm) of your hole with loose stones and then laying a line of drain pipes to connect each hole to a ditch or a low-lying piece of ground. Such an arrangement will enable the water to run away.

Soil should be around neutral for apples, about pH 7. So if your soil is acid, lime it. But take care not to make it too alkaline, for although stone fruit trees need plenty of lime, apples don't like too much.

Propagation

Most varieties of fruit tree will not breed true from seed. Seeds are the product of sexual reproduction and therefore each seed will have characteristics of both father and mother in it. To establish new varieties you have to grow trees from seed (indeed there is no other way), but once you have found a good variety the only way to reproduce it faithfully is by vegetative, rather than sexual reproduction. In other words you use hard wood cuttings instead of seed.

Unless you are interested in the propagation of fruit trees for its own sake, it is best to buy them from a nursery. Most of the fruit trees that you buy will consist of two different cultivars, or varieties, of the same species of tree grafted together. Nurserymen select root stocks for such qualities as hardiness and degree of vigor, (vigor to a nurseryman means the size of the tree when it is fully grown) and then select other varieties for good fruiting qualities, and graft the latter on top of the former. Planting a tree is described on page 98.

If you were to plant a Cox's orange pippin seed straight into the ground it would give you Cox's apples (that is if it survived at all), but the tree would not have anything like the hardiness and vigor that would result if you grafted a Cox on to the root stock of a crab apple tree. It is the root stock which decides the growth habit of the tree. So by employing dwarfing varieties as root stocks you can grow dwarf, or smaller, fruit trees than would grow from seed.

There is one organization that is eminent throughout the world for the breeding of new root stocks and that is the East Malling Research Station, in Kent, England. There thousands of new varieties of apples and pears are grown, and watched and evaluated, and successful ones are selected for widespread vegetative reproduction. All over the world apples and pears are grown on Malling root stocks.

You can plant pips to grow your own root stocks and cut your own "scions", which are healthy fruiting twigs of the current season's growth, usually about 18 inches (45 cm) long. You can then join the two together by grafting or budding. This is interesting to do if you have orchard space to spare, and it can be a profitable sideline. The techniques of grafting are described in detail on p. 99.

For many reasons dwarf apples trees are ideally suited to the home garden. First, one tree is not likely to produce more fruit than can be used during its season; second, an orchard of 15-20 dwarf trees can be grown in the space that one standard tree requires; third, dwarf apple trees that are well cared for, bear within two or three years of planting.

Plant standard apple trees 16 feet (5 m) apart. You can grow large trees in a circular deep bed (see p. 110): goblet or dwarf varieties thrive in an ordinary deep bed, six feet (1.8 m) apart, with other plants growing in between the trees and all along the side of the bed.

Care while growing

Maintain a mulch around the tree at all times. Bear in mind that mulches quickly disappear; the earthworms pull the organic material down into the soil where it rots and does a lot of good. So replace the mulch as often as necessary.

For the first four years of the tree's life keep the ground around it free of grass; in an orchard this means all the ground between the trees. You may well grow strawberries on this ground for these will not interfere with the nourish-

ment of the apple trees. But the very best thing you can do for the young trees is to keep the ground clear-cultivated all summer, and then sow a winter green manure crop in the fall. A mixture of half winter rye and half winter vetch is ideal. Till, or dig this in shallowly in the spring.

Pruning Pruning fruit trees is a science in itself, and the best way to learn about it is to watch an experienced pruner. The basic techniques are described on p. 100.

The idea of pruning is to shape the tree, and control the number of fruiting spurs so that you get plenty of good fruit and not too much inferior fruit. There are two main forms of pruning: winter pruning and summer pruning. They are quite different and have different purposes.

Winter pruning, which is principally to shape the tree, encourages growth but may delay fruiting: the more you prune a tree in winter the faster it will grow. But a tree putting all its energy into growing can't produce fruit. So once a tree has reached its adult size (usually after about four years for standards) restrict winter pruning to a minimum. Summer pruning, which consists of shortening the current year's growth, helps to stop the tree growing too fast or too big, and encourages earlier fruiting.

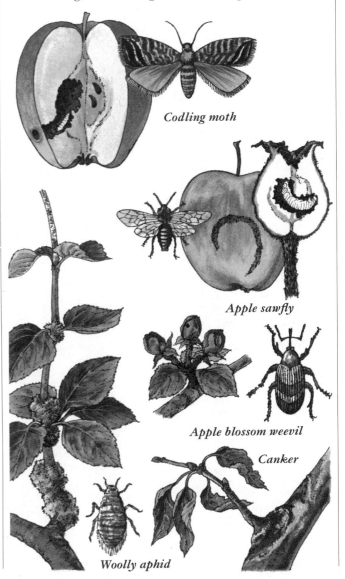

Codling moth

Apple sawfly

Apple blossom weevil

Canker

Woolly aphid

Pests and diseases

Most commercial fruit-growers combat pests and diseases by constantly spraying with deadlier and deadlier fungicides and insecticides. The pests are poisoned, but so are their natural predators. As the pests build up a resistance to various pesticides, the pesticides have to be applied in larger and larger quantities: to spray twelve times in a season is not unusual.

My own belief is that a thorough spraying with a proprietary winter wash (see p. 104) in late winter, well before the buds even think of opening, is all the spraying you should need to do. But apart from spraying there are several other things you ought to do.

First and foremost, be hygienic. Do not leave prunings, dead dropped fruit or other rubbish lying on the ground. If you can't eat dropped fruit, put it on the compost heap. Burn all prunings. When the leaves fall leave them to be dragged down by the worms unless they have mildew on them, in which case you should burn them. Don't just leave diseased or cankered trees; pull them out and burn them.

If you have a lot of trouble with pests, wrap a band of paper, or cloth, covered in grease around the trunk of each tree. Any pests that walk up the trunks will get stuck.

GREASE BANDING
There are various organic ways and means of keeping down pests, but if you find that you are still having a lot of trouble, you can cover a band of paper or cloth with grease and wrap it around each tree. All the pests walking up and down the trunks will get stuck and die.

If you have hens, keep them under your fruit trees, because they eat a lot of harmful grubs. In midsummer carefully examine all your trees, remove any deformed or diseased fruit and put it on your compost heap.

Mildew If your trees suffer from either downy or powdery mildew, which causes a whitish down on the leaves, then you should burn all the leaves when they fall in the autumn or put them right in the middle of a compost heap.

Codling moths Codling moths lay their eggs on the blossom and eventually the caterpillars burrow into the fruit. The solution is to wrap corrugated paper or old sacking around the trunks and major branches in midsummer. The caterpillars will take refuge in these to pupate, and when they do so you can burn them in the autumn. In the old days people used to build bonfires in their orchards in midsummer simply so that the codling moths would fly into the flames.

Scab Scab is a fungus which makes brown patches on fruit. As long as the scabs are small they are not important. Winter washing and careful hygiene are the only cures.

Apple sawfly Yellowish maggots tunnel into the fruit, sometimes leaving them completely inedible. This happens in late summer, and the apples are covered in ribbon-like scars. Trap the maggots at this time in glass jars, covered with screenwire with holes too small to admit bees. Fill the jars with water mixed with sugar, honey, treacle, or else molasses, and then hang them from the branches on the sunny sides of your trees.

Woolly apple aphid Woolly apple aphid is an irritating pest which attacks apples and leaves, causing growths that look like cotton wool on the leaves. Painting such patches with methylated spirits will kill the grubs. You can also grow buckwheat near your fruit trees. This will attract hoverflies, which lay their eggs near the woolly aphid. When hatched the hoverfly will crawl under the "wool" and eat the aphid.

Apple blossom weevil Apple blossom weevils lay their eggs in the blossom. This often causes the blossom to turn brown and die. The adult weevils eat the leaves. If you get these, put on the sacking or paper trap for codling moths a month early. It will then trap both pests.

Canker Fruit trees are mainly attacked by canker in wet climates. Rot develops on branches or trunks. Prune off the affected branches and the affected parts of trunks down to the clean wood and paint the wounds.

PICKING APPLES
Don't bump or bruise apples in the process of picking them. The time to pick them is when they come off at once as you twist their stalks sharply upwards. Pick over the same tree several times if necessary, so that each apple is picked when it is just ripe.

Harvesting and storing

Summer, or early, apples should be picked and either eaten or preserved pretty fast. Late apples are the ones for storing.

Don't try to store any damaged, unripe, or overripe fruit, or fruit from which the stalks have come out. A temperature of 40°F (4°C) is ideal for storage. Frost is fatal and so are excessively high temperatures. Ventilation must be good but not too vigorous; you don't want them in a draft. Too dry a place is also to be avoided; it is a good idea to throw water on the floor if the air seems too dry. Places with thick walls and stone, earth, or tiled floors are better than attics. Either lay the fruit out in a single layer so they are not touching each other, or better still wrap each fruit in newspaper or even oiled wraps. Don't store any fruit together with strong-smelling substances.

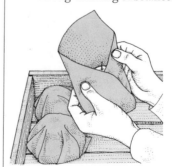

STORING APPLES
Late apples are the ones to store. They should be kept in a well-ventilated room, free from drafts and very dry air. A temperature of 40°F (4°C) is ideal. The very best way of storing is to wrap each fruit in oiled paper, and place them in boxes or crates, in a single layer, not touching each other.

A new way of storing both apples and pears is in thin polyethylene bags, and the apples need not be individually wrapped. Seal the bags and store them at an even temperature; 40°F (4°C) is ideal. Make pinholes in the bags, one for each pound of fruit stored inside.

Pears

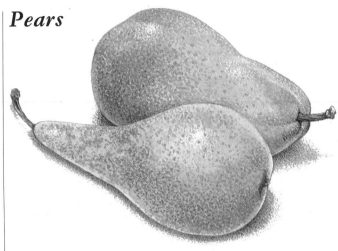

If you have space to spare after putting in three apple trees, a pear tree is a good fourth choice, but remember that most varieties need a partner nearby for pollination. The culture of pear trees is very similar to that of apple trees (see Apples), although pears are rather more fussy and they need extra care and attention.

Soil and climate

Pears suffer more from frosts than apples do, because they blossom earlier and the frost can kill or severely injure the blossom. They also need a dormant period in order to fruit. They prefer heavy soil, but it must be well drained.

Soil treatment

Before planting any fruit tree you should clear-cultivate the soil (dig it over thoroughly), and pears are no exception to this rule. Soil should be around neutral, pH 6.5 to 7.5.

Propagation

Pears will not breed true from seed. To produce trees which will fruit well and are also hardy and vigorous requires grafting (see p. 99). The difference between apples and pears is that pears sometimes have to be "double worked".

"DOUBLE WORKING" PEARS
Pears are generally planted on quince root stocks (the quince is closely related to the pear, but hardier and smaller). However, some varieties of pear will not take on quince root stock and must first be grafted on to a compatible pear variety, which is itself grafted on to the quince.

East Malling Research Station (see p. 169) is a worldwide source of pear root stock. Malling Quince A is most commonly used. Malling Quince C is the best root stock if you want dwarf trees. Pears are often self-sterile and have to be planted with mutually fertilizing varieties. Plant pear trees in the way described on page 98. They can also be grown in a circular deep bed (see p. 110), or six feet (1.8 m) apart in an ordinary deep bed as long as they are kept small.

Care while growing

Except that pears can bear heavier pruning than apples without being stimulated into rampant growth, the pruning procedure for apples and pears is identical (see Apples and p. 100). And tip-bearing pears should be treated like tip-bearing apples.

If a pear tree ceases to produce new growth — and this can happen in a tree that is still very much alive — cut back into two or even three-year-old wood in order to stimulate new growth.

Fire blight

Leaf blister mite

Pests and diseases

Pears can get all the apple diseases and the same steps should be taken (see Apples). There are also some pests and diseases which are peculiar to pears:

Fire blight This attacks at blossom time, causing the blooms to blacken and shrivel, and subsequently every part of the tree blackens as though it has been on fire. Cut out all affected parts at least six inches (15 cm) back from the site of infection with a sterilized knife and burn them immediately. It is important to disinfect the knife after making each cut. Several varieties of pear are resistant to fire blight.

Leaf blister mite These tiny mites attack leaves in spring, causing green or red blisters to appear. Pick off and burn the leaves immediately.

Phytophthora rot This is a disease caused by a fungus. Brown patches appear on the skin and the flesh rots. Burn all rotten fruit and spray with Burgundy mixture.

Harvesting and storing

Pick pears a little before they are completely ripe, as soon as they come off the tree easily when you lift them away. Take exaggerated precautions not to bruise them. Store them like apples as near 30°F (−1°C) as possible, but before you eat them bring them into room temperature and wait for them to ripen. Eat them when they are slightly soft. There is one day in the life of every pear when it is perfect, and with pears, perfect is perfect.

Cherries

It is only really worth planting a cherry tree if your garden or orchard fulfils two conditions. First, there must be ample space to spare after allowing for your vegetables, your soft fruit and your staple tree fruit — apples, pears and plums; a cherry tree can cover an enormous area of ground, often about 500 square feet (45 sq m). Secondly, your garden must be relatively free of birds. If it isn't, the birds will eat the lot in which case the best thing to do is grow your cherries against a wall and hang a net over them.

There are two kinds of cherries: sweet and sour. Generally speaking, sweet cherries are for eating fresh, and sour cherries are for cooking, canning and jam-making. Sour cherries have the advantages that they are less attractive to birds and can be grown anywhere in the garden, while sweet cherries need a sunny position or a south-facing wall. The "montmorency", which is a sour variety, is the best cherry to grow, because it is hardy and self-fertile.

Soil and climate

Sweet cherries thrive on lightish well-drained loam. They even do quite well on gravelly soil, although they send their roots deep and need a good depth of soil beneath them. Sour cherries will do better on clay than sweet cherries will, but they also prefer light deep soil. Both sorts prefer a pH of 6 or 7, but will tolerate more lime than apples, so a pH of 8 will do. They will grow in temperate climates and there are even varieties which will fruit in very severe climates. The blossoms of most varieties, however, are frost tender and should not be grown in frost pockets (see p. 168).

Soil treatment

Clear-cultivate the soil (that is, dig it thoroughly).

Propagation

Cherry scions are mostly grafted on wild cherry root stock. The simplest thing is to buy the cherry tree you want, already grafted, but if you want to do your own grafting, the appropriate methods are described on p. 99. As nearly all cherries are not self-fertile, it is a good idea to have two varieties grafted on one tree. Choose varieties which flower at the same time. Sweet and sour will cross-pollinate. Plant the trees just like apple trees (see p. 98). In an orchard they should be 45 ft (13 m.) apart. If cherries grow in a border up against a wall, it can be dug as a deep bed (see p. 106).

Care while growing

Prune cherry trees as illustrated below. It is an advantage to apply material high in nitrogen — about an ounce (28 g) for each year of the tree's growth until it is five years old. Simply sprinkle it on the ground near the base of the tree. Thereafter apply five ounces (140 g) per year. One ounce (28 g) is found in one pound (500 g) of cottonseed meal or a half pound (225 g) of blood meal.

Keep the soil bare under cherry trees for the first five years, but don't dig deeply. Hoeing or mulching is sufficient. After the fifth year clear all weeds away, plant some daffodils, tulips and crocuses around the tree, grass the land down, and leave it. The other alternative is to run chickens under your cherry tree. If you do this make sure you have enough chickens to produce about 25 pounds (11 kg) of manure in a year.

Pests and diseases

Black cherry aphid These aphids cause severe leaf curl, which is sometimes accompanied by black patches on the leaves. If your cherry trees are badly affected spray with tar wash or Burgundy mixture (see p. 104).
Silver leaf disease If left unchecked silver leaf disease may kill the tree. It is caused by a fungus which lives on dead wood, so you won't get it as long as you prune well in early summer and cover all wounds with paint.
Brown rot See Peaches and Apricots.

Harvesting

Harvest sweet cherries when they are quite ripe and eat them immediately. With sour cherries pull the fruit off, leaving the stalks; otherwise you will tear the tree.

PRUNING A CHERRY TREE
Start with a "maiden" tree. In the spring shorten all its branches by six inches (15 cm). The next spring cut out all main branches but five. A year later prune all but two secondary branches on each main branch. Every spring thereafter cut out all dead or inward-pointing branches.

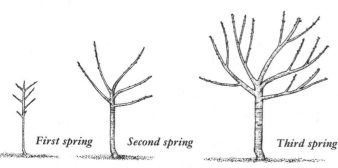

First spring *Second spring* *Third spring* *Fourth spring*

Peaches & Apricots

Peach and apricot trees are very similar and should be grown in the same way; they share the same pests and diseases. Nectarines differ from peaches only because they have smooth skins; botanically they are identical.

Soil and climate

Peaches and apricots will grow in sand, or a very sandy or gravelly soil, provided there is plenty of humus in it. They like a hot summer and a fairly cold winter. Ideally the winter temperature should go below 40°F (4°C) for some weeks to give them a dormant period, but it should not get too cold. However, peaches are grown as far north as Maine and as far south as northern Florida. Apricots can be grown even farther north but not as far south. Peach and apricot trees must have a sunny position and must not be grown in frost pockets (see p. 168). Land sloping down to a lake, river, or estuary is fine.

Soil treatment

Dig the soil well and dig in plenty of humus, but not humus too rich in nitrogen. Too much nitrogen makes peach trees rampant, sappy and more susceptible to frost damage. Peat and leaf-mold are very good. A pH of 6 or over is ideal.

Propagation

Plant peach trees in the early spring, except in very mild climates, because cold weather could injure them in their first year. Choose a variety that is known to be suitable for your area (ask your local nurseryman), and plant the trees as you would apple trees (see p. 98). Peaches can be grown in a circular deep bed (see p. 110). You can buy peach trees ready grafted, or you can do your own grafting (see p. 99). Choose those recommended as of highest dessert quality; avoid those described as long keepers. Special hardy varieties of peach are now bred which do not need grafting.

Care while growing

The fruit only grows on the previous year's wood and it is as well to remember this when pruning. When you plant a sapling, cut the tree back to about two feet (60 cm) above the ground, cutting just above a branch. Prune it hard again in the early summer; cut back all branches to within an inch

(2.5 cm) of the trunk (not flush with it). New branches will sprout that first summer beside the stubs of the old ones. Rub off all of them except three, which will form the framework, or "scaffold", of the tree. Do this as soon as the tiny branches show themselves.

The aim now is either to let the most upright of the new branches go upward and make a trunk, or, better still, to let all three grow up and away from each other and form an upside-down tripod. All your subsequent pruning, which must be done each year in early summer, should maintain this shape. Cut out all inward-pointing shoots and cut back all shoots which have died at the tip, until you reach clean white wood with no brown in the middle. Protect all wounds meticulously with tree paint.

In cold climates give all peach trees nitrogen in the very early spring, about an ounce (28 g) for every year of the tree's growth. This controlled amount of nitrogen enables the tree to grow and fruit vigorously in the summer but to stop growing long before the freezing winter sets in when new sappy wood would suffer from frost. Give dressings of compost or manure, in late fall.

Fruit should be thinned so as to give one fruit every six to eight inches (25 cm) of wood. This is best done in two stages: in early summer thin to four inches (10 cm) apart and then, about four weeks later when the fruit is the size of a walnut, thin to nine inches (25 cm).

Pests and diseases

Peach leaf curl   This is more common in northern states. Leaves curl and crinkle. Spray with Bordeaux mixture (see p. 105) in midwinter and again a month later. Spray once more in the autumn just before leaf fall.

Leaf spot   This is a bacterial disease which causes brown spots on the leaves, and it can be serious. If a tree gets it, give it plenty of manure and it should get over it.

Brown rot   This is a serious fungus disease that affects all the store fruits. Leaves turn brown and often fruits become

Peach leaf curl

covered with soft brown spots which produce white spores. Branches may develop sticky conkers. Cut out and burn all infected branches.

Harvesting and storing

When peaches have turned yellow and are slightly soft to gentle pressure, it is time to pick. Turn the fruit slightly and it will come off. It can be stored for up to two weeks in a cool cellar or it can be frozen (see p. 227) or canned (see p. 220). Apricots should be picked and eaten when soft and ripe, or they can be picked a little earlier when still firm, and then dried. To dry them split the fruit in two and remove the stones. Leave them in trays in the sun, split side up, for up to three days.

Plums

Plums of three types are commonly grown: European, Japanese and native American plums. They are all fairly hardy, don't get many diseases and yield very heavily in some years.

Soil and climate

European plums like deep soil, and will flourish in deep loams or clays as long as they are well drained, but they do not thrive in dry, shallow soils. Japanese and American kinds are more tolerant of shallow soils. Plums flower early and are therefore susceptible to spring frosts, so don't plant them in a frost pocket (see p. 168). Like other temperate climate fruits, plums need to lie dormant through a cold winter.

Soil treatment

A neutral soil is best, around pH 7, so lime if your soil is acid. Clear-cultivate (thoroughly dig) the land before planting plums, and then, ideally, grow a crop, or even two crops, of green manure. Dig, or till these into the soil. The land must be well drained. If it is not, fill the bottom foot (30 cm) of the hole you dig for each tree with stones, and bury a line of drain pipes to lead the water away to a ditch or lower piece of ground.

Propagation

Plums should always be grafted (see p. 99), and nearly always will be if you buy from a nursery. Plant plum trees as you would apple trees (see p. 98). Most plums are not self-pollinating, so you must plant at least two, and preferably several, compatible varieties. Japanese plums cannot pollinate European plums, or *vice versa*. Native American varieties are pollinated by other native varieties, or by certain hybrids. American-Japanese hybrids can be pollinated by Japanese varieties. You must get advice from your nurseryman on this. Allow 24 feet (7 m) between standard trees and 15 feet (4.5 m), between trees planted on semi-dwarfing stock. Plums can be planted in the circular deep bed (see p. 110). Plant plum trees in early winter; but in areas with exceptionally cold winters plant in early spring.

Care while growing

Plums benefit from quite rich feeding. It is an advantage to have hens or other poultry running under them. Otherwise apply heavy dressings of compost, stable or cow manure.
Pruning Plums can be pruned to form all the tree shapes described on p. 100. Prune when you first plant the tree, and thereafter confine pruning to early summer only, because silver leaf disease may develop if you prune in winter.

In some years plum trees bear a considerable weight of fruit, and because their branches tend to be quite slender, those which carry a lot of fruit may need support. There are two ways of doing this. You can build a T-shaped wooden scaffold which should be firmly rooted in the ground next to the trunk and secured to it with a plastic strap. Ropes from the top of the "T" can be tied round the drooping branches. The other solution is to use a forked branch as a support. Protect the branch with sacking to save it from chafing.

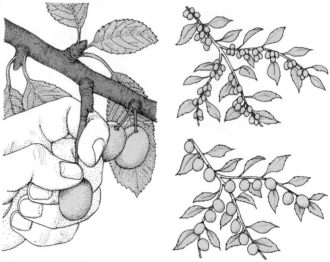

THINNING PLUMS
If your crop is allowed to become too heavy the plums may be small and tasteless. Therefore you should thin, when the plums reach about half their final size. Don't pick off the stalk when you pinch off the fruit. Leave at least two or three inches (5-8 cm) between remaining plums.

Pests and diseases

Plums suffer from the same pests and diseases as apples (see Apples), as well as a few of their own.
Silver leaf disease The symptom of this is silvering of the leaves, but the disease attacks and can kill the whole tree. It is caused by a fungus which grows in dead wood. As long as you rigorously prune out all dead wood in early summer, burn the prunings and cover the wounds with paint, your trees won't suffer from silver leaf.
Bacterial blight This shows first as black streaks on the young shoots. Later on black spots appear on leaves and fruit which become inedible. There is no cure for this, beyond the pruning and burning of all diseased wood. Some varieties are more resistant to this than others.
Heart rot Leaving sawn-off stumps of branches on a tree can cause heart rot; the stumps heal slowly, so bacteria can get in and kill the wood under the bark. You won't get it if you cut all branches flush with the trunk.
Brown rot See Peaches and Apricots.

Harvesting and storing

For jam or jelly, or for canning (which suits plums admirably) pick the fruit as soon as the bloom appears on their skins, but before they get soft. For eating fresh pick them when quite ripe, which is when they give a little and come easily off the tree. In hot dry climates plums to be turned into prunes can be left on the tree until they are quite dry and ready to be shaken off. They should then be dried in the sun on trays. In damp climates they can be dried artificially (see p. 216).

Quinces

Quinces are so closely related to apples and pears that the latter are often grafted on to quince stock, because quince stock is hardy and produces small trees. Quinces are not grown as much as they should be; they have a very special and delicate flavor and quince jelly is one of the world's great gastronomic experiences. They are self-fruitful.

Soil and climate
Quinces will grow in any soil or climate that apples will (see Apples), although they are a little more tender. They prefer a warm summer and a fairly cold winter. Heavy soil suits them best, but it must be well drained.

Soil treatment
Dig the land thoroughly, and if you are not in a hurry, grow and dig in one or two crops of green manure. The soil should be neutral, pH 7. Quinces don't like too much nitrogen but need phosphate and potash.

Propagation
If you don't buy a seedling from a nursery, the best way to propagate is from cuttings made from the suckers which quinces throw out every year. In the autumn cut lengths about nine inches (23 cm) long, and bury two thirds of their length in sandy soil. After a year move these to their permanent positions.

Care while growing
You can prune quinces to all the tree shapes (see p. 100) or you can leave them strictly alone, in which case you will get a spreading bush shape. Quinces are not prone to being attacked by pests and diseases.

Harvesting and storing
You can leave the fruit on the tree until after the first hard frost. Then make jelly (see p. 223) right away, or if you don't have time to make jelly immediately you can store the quinces in cool moist conditions for up to three months.

MEDLARS
Medlars are hardier than quinces and can therefore cope with colder conditions. They do best if they are grafted (see p. 99) on to thorn, pear or quince root stock. Otherwise treat them like quinces. The fruit is unusual in that its five seeds are visible and it is only edible – and it is actually very good to eat – when it is half rotten.

Raspberries

Raspberries are one of the best soft fruit crops the self-sufficient gardener can grow. They are hardy, and will stand neglect, although they shouldn't have to. They are easy to grow, self-fruitful and heavy yielding.

Soil and climate
They prefer the soil to be slightly acid, so do not lime under any circumstances. Lime can cause chlorosis (yellowing of the leaves). They do need good soil though, so if your soil is light and sandy, put in plenty of manure. Raspberries prefer sun, but if you have a garden where sun is at a premium, grow your raspberries in a shady area. They will stand colder climates than most other fruits.

Soil treatment
In the fall dig a trench two spade-depths deep and fill it with soil mixed with compost or manure. They need a lot of potash, so incorporate wood ashes with the soil if you have any; otherwise mix in some other potash fertilizer. They have both shallow and deep roots, and need a lot of humus.

If you want only one row you have no problem: but the roots spread far and wide so if you want more than one row then have them quite far apart: six feet (1.8 m) is usual in commercial gardens but four feet (1.2 m) will do if you are trying to save space.

PROPAGATING RASPBERRIES
Like strawberries, raspberries propagate by "walking". Raspberries "walk" by pushing out roots which send up suckers to form new plants. Just let your plants send up suckers, cut off the roots connecting them to the parent plant with your spade, then lift the suckers and re-plant them.

Propagation
Different varieties will give you fruit from midsummer till hard frost. I strongly advise you to buy stock certified to be virus-free. Such plants will give higher yields and last far longer than the plants your neighbor offers you when he has to get rid of his suckers in the fall. The certified plants you get will consist of one cane, or whip, with a heel of root attached to it. Plant roots a foot (30 cm) apart in rows four feet (1.2 m) apart. Put the root down about three inches (8 cm), cover with soil, and firm well. Immediately cut the cane down to nine inches (23 cm) above the ground.

There is no reason why you should not then multiply your own raspberry plants in subsequent years. Like strawberries, raspberries "walk", but they do it in a totally different way. In the deep bed (see p. 106) raspberries should be planted in three rows with 18 inches (45 cm) between the rows. Their shallow roots make intercropping inadvisable. Don't plant raspberries where raspberries have been before. Don't plant them immediately after potatoes or tomatoes either, for these plants get some of the same diseases.

Care while growing

Don't let them fruit the first summer: remove the blossoms, otherwise the plant will be weakened by fruiting. By the second summer they should bear well. Keep weeds down near the plants by heavy mulching – say within a foot (30 cm) of them. Grass cuttings, leaves or compost are all good. Hoe between the rows. Don't allow grass or weeds to establish themselves; raspberries will not flourish in grass. So be sure that the mulch is thick enough every spring. The raspberry rows are a good repository for wood ashes.

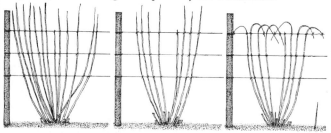

PRUNING RASPBERRY CANES
After cutting out all the old wood thin the new canes, leaving only the best six or eight to fruit the next summer. When these grow over the top of the top wire, shorten them to six inches (15 cm) above it; or else bend them over in an inverted "U" shape and tie them to the wire.

Training is simple but necessary. You must have a fence, with three wires, the top one five feet (1.5 m) from the ground, the others at regular intervals below it. Tie the canes to these. Some people have three pairs of wires and simply shove the canes in between each pair. This works, but individual tying is better.
Pruning In the fall, after the leaves have died off, cut off all the canes which have fruited close to the ground and prune as shown above.

Remember that raspberries act like biennials, although actually of course they are perennials. The wood made in one year fruits the next and then dies down. So cut out the wood that has fruited every year and keep the wood that grew that year, because that will fruit the next.

Pests and diseases

There are several virus and fungoid diseases that raspberries get. If you see any discoloration or other sign of disease cut out and burn the affected part.
Mosaic disease This is the worst of various virus diseases and makes the leaves curl and show red and yellow mottling. Dig the bushes that have got this right out and burn them. If you don't, aphids will spread the virus to other plants.
Iron deficiency If you see yellowing between the veins of the leaves suspect iron deficiency. This is especially likely if you have very alkaline soil.

Harvesting and storing

Eat as many as you can ripe and raw with cream. Store the rest; they freeze well (see p. 227) and can well (see p. 220). When rain falls on ripe fruit, pick the fruit immediately the rain stops and can or freeze it; if you don't the raspberries will go moldy. Don't leave moldy fruit on canes, because the mold will spread to the others.

Blackberries

In most temperate parts of the world wild blackberries grow nearly everywhere and it is fun hunting for them. Nevertheless, for a regular supply it is worth keeping a few bushes.

Soil and climate

There are several species of blackberry, and cultivated varieties have been developed from them that will grow happily in every climate from the very coldest temperate region to the sub-tropics. They prefer rich, well-drained soil (pH 7), and a sheltered site.

Propagation

You can propagate blackberries from cuttings, suckers, by layering (see p. 95), or by division of roots – digging up a piece of plant with roots on it, and replanting. The simplest method of all is to propagate from tip cuttings – cut the tip off a cane, push it into the ground and it will root. Wrap all planting material in moss or wet newspaper and store it in a plastic bag until you need it.

If you want to grow blackberries from seeds you must "stratify" them; this means that over the winter you must keep the seed in a box full of sand at a warm room temperature for three months, then store them at 40°F (4°C) for another three months.

Plant cuttings, layers, roots or seedlings in late fall or early spring. Plant seeds in early spring. Allow six feet (1.8 m) between bushes. It is a good idea to plant along a fence, and dig the bed to form a deep bed (see p. 106).

Care while growing

Blackberries fruit on last year's wood, so prune in winter by cutting out all wood that has just fruited unless you have varieties which fruit for several years on the same wood. If you have these varieties, wood which has fruited should not be cut out so ruthlessly. As a general rule, leave about ten strong newly grown canes to fruit the following year. They are very greedy plants and need rich mulching.

Pests and diseases

Orange rust This shows up as bright orange spores under the leaves. Look for these if your plants give out spindly shoots with narrow leaves. Root out and burn infested bushes.

Harvesting and storing

Blackberries are ready for picking when they almost fall off the bush into your hand. Put them in shallow boxes and store in a refrigerator, or freeze (see p. 227) for eating in winter.

LOGANBERRIES

Grow loganberry bushes in a sheltered place; although they flower later than blackberries, severe spring frosts will damage the canes. Plant the bushes ten feet (3 m) apart. Unlike blackberries, loganberries only fruit in late summer for a two to three week period.

Strawberries

Strawberries are fun to grow, and a good cash crop. Most gardeners would agree with the remark "Doubtless God could have made a better berry but doubtless God didn't".

Strawberries are a "walking" plant, because they are perennials which don't have an elaborate root system. Therefore they exhaust the ground on which they grow within a year or two. To escape from it and find fresh ground they send out runners which meander over the ground until they find somewhere to send down roots.

STRAWBERRIES IN BARRELS
Strawberries grow well in pots and tubs of all kinds. A barrel makes an ideal container. Drill several staggered rows of holes three inches (8 cm) wide and 15 inches (38 cm) apart. Drill the rows at eight inch (20 cm) intervals. Drill several holes in the base and put a layer of gravel in the bottom. Then insert into the center a vertical wire mesh tube four inches (10 cm) in diameter. Fill it with gravel. Then fill the barrel with potting compost up to the first row of holes. Set one plant next to each hole, with the crown emerging. Repeat all the way up the barrel, watering each layer as you go. Finally set four or five plants in a circle at the very top.

There are several varieties of what are called "everbearing" or "perpetual" strawberries. These fruit later than ordinary strawberries and continue fruiting into late fall. It is a very good idea to plant a few, so as to give yourself a treat in the cold weather. If you force ordinary strawberries in the spring under cloches, plastic tunnels or mini-greenhouses (see p. 111) and have "everbearing" as well, you can have strawberries from early summer to late fall.

Soil and climate

Strawberries are a woodland plant, and you should bear this in mind when choosing a site for them and looking after them. It means that they tolerate shade, although they fruit far better in sun; they like plenty of humus (they will grow in almost pure leaf-mold as they do in the wild); and they don't object to fairly acid conditions. They do better on light soil than clay, but granted plenty of humus they will thrive in any well-drained place. They are a temperate climate crop and develop a far better flavor in a cold climate than a hot one. It is best to move on to totally fresh ground every three years with new plants.

Soil treatment

Dig the land one spit deep, incorporating plenty of compost or any well-rotted organic manure. Strawberries do well on the no-digging system (see p. 83) as long as the bed has had enough compost put on it. They are also potash-hungry so, if you have wood ashes to spare, use them on your strawberry patch. Farmyard manure can be rich in potash.

ENCOURAGING RUNNERS
Start with disease-free strawberries from a reputable source. From then on you can propagate from runners. Every year you should remove the blossom from a proportion of your healthy plants, so that they are encouraged to send out plenty of strong runners.

Propagation

The first time you plant strawberries, get virus-free stock, from a reputable source, certified healthy. Unless you want to grow new varieties of strawberry, in which case you should grow them from seed, the best thing to do is to multiply them from runners. There are a few varieties that do not make runners, and these are multiplied by dividing up the crowns themselves.

Most varieties of strawberry will make runners that will root themselves whatever you do, but you can encourage them by removing the blossom from a few of your plants. You have merely to sever the runners from the main plant, dig out the little mini-plant on the end of it, and transplant it. But an even surer way of doing it is to bury small pots of soil in the ground near the parent plants and peg the ends of runners down on these pots. When the runners have rooted properly, sever them from the parent, dig up the pots, and transplant to their new positions. In this way you can establish a new strawberry bed every year and scrap one every year, after it has fruited for three seasons. Every fall you will have a newly-planted bed, a year-old bed, a two-year-old bed, and a three-year-old bed, the last of which will be ready for digging up. Always plant your new beds as far from the old ones as you can, to hinder the spread of disease.

You can plant or transplant strawberries at any time of the year (if the winters are mild enough) but it is traditional to plant in spring up to July, as you can then harvest a crop the next year. Plant 15 inches (38 cm) apart with 30 inches (75 cm) between rows. Plant so that the crown is at ground level but the roots are spread out widely and downward. Water the new plants well.

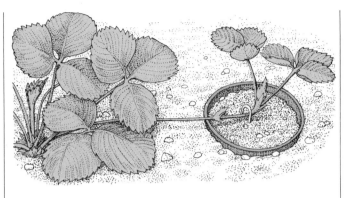

NEW STRAWBERRY PLANTS FROM OLD
Bury pots of soil in the ground near the parent plants, and peg down the ends of runners on top of the pots. Eventually you will be able to sever the old plants from the new, dig up the pots, and transplant them to their permanent positions.

Strawberries do very well on the deep bed (see p. 106). Plant and space them as for a conventional bed.

Care while growing

It is very easy for a strawberry bed to become infested with weeds. The plants straggle relentlessly and make most methods of weeding very difficult. Hoe for as long as you can hoe and then weed by hand. If you have planted between the end of one summer and the beginning of the next let the crop fruit in the year after that but not before: during the plants' first summer, pick off the flowers.

Prick over the ground with a fork in the spring and, as the crop begins to spread, put plenty of straw under the straggling stems. This suppresses weeds and keeps the fruit clean and healthy. But keep a weather eye out for slugs.

PROTECTING THE PLANTS
When the fruit begins to form put a good mulch of straw under the plants. This keeps weeds down and keeps the fruit clean and disease-free. If birds are a nuisance, make a net. Set up posts and invert a glass jar over each one, before putting the netting over the framework; the jars stop the netting catching.

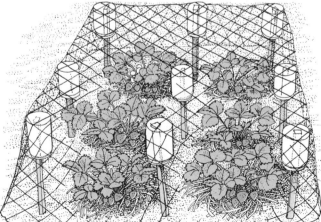

If you suffer much from birds you will *have* to use a net. You can either have a net low over the strawberries, in which case you will have to remove it every time you want to pick a strawberry, or else a fruit cage (see p. 184), which is expensive unless you make it yourself.

Pests and diseases

Don't try to force your strawberries with nitrogen, because it makes them soft and open to disease.
Powdery mildew This white powder will make strawberries turn a dull brown color. Spray with sulfur at regular intervals.
Aphids These are a menace because they spread virus diseases, principally strawberry crinkle and strawberry yellow edge, both of which show in the leaves and weaken the plant. To prevent it, spray the plant centers hard in April with a nicotine spray or with derris. Don't use the nicotine when the berries are nearly ripe. Remove any stunted or discolored plants and burn them; these diseases are incurable.

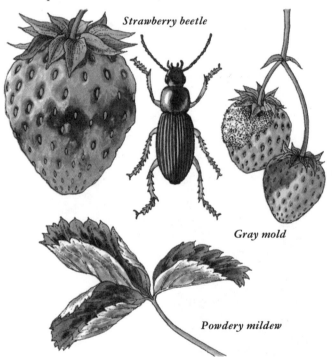

Strawberry beetle

Gray mold

Powdery mildew

Strawberry beetle This little pest feeds on strawberry flesh. Keep the bed well weeded, and it will be discouraged from settling near your strawberries.
Gray mold This is also called botrytis. It appears first as a gray spot on the flowers and then on the strawberries themselves where it grows to form a gray fur which rots the fruit. Dust with flowers of sulfur at the very first sign.
Rot If berries rot after rain, remove them to the compost heap. Pick all ripe berries immediately after rain.

Harvesting

Pull the fruit off the plant with their stems intact. Leave the stems on until just before eating; when the stems are removed vitamins and other nutrients are lost. Store them in the shade for a few hours, or in a refrigerator for a day or two. Strawberries can be frozen, but go soft when thawed.

After you have harvested your crop remove the straw from under the stems and clear the bed of dead leaves, surplus runners and weeds.

Rutaceae

Oranges, tangerines, kumquats, lemons, limes and grapefruit are all members of the *Rutaceae*. Because it includes the genus *Citrus* the *Rutaceae* family is as important to people who live in the sub-tropics as the *Rosaceae* family is to people who live in temperate climates. Citrus plants are very aromatic, broad-leaved evergreens.

Citrus fruits grown in the tropics do not taste as good as those grown in what is known as a Mediterranean climate. At the other extreme they can't stand frost, although oranges can bear marginally lower temperatures than lemons, which are damaged and sometimes killed at temperatures below 26°F (−3°C). This means that citrus fruits growing out of doors tend to be limited to Florida, southern California, Louisiana, Texas and parts of Arizona in North America; and to the Mediterranean seaboard in Europe, South Africa, sub-tropical South America and Australia. But this does not prevent citrus from being a viable greenhouse crop: in the 18th century indoor orangeries were common among the wealthy in England.

My own feeling is that if I only had the space under glass to grow one citrus tree I would grow a lemon. One orange tree provides only a small proportion of the fruit needed by a family through the year, whereas one lemon tree would fill a family's requirements.

Oranges

What the apple is to temperate regions the orange is to the sub-tropics. It is heavy-yielding, delicious, will keep well, and has the enormous advantage that it can just be allowed to hang on the tree, for as long as six months. It is a rich and reliable source of vitamin C. In temperate climates oranges must be grown under glass. This is described on p. 212. They can be grown in tubs, which must be brought indoors in the winter, but the yield from trees grown like this is fairly low.

Soil and climate

Orange trees can stand winter frosts as low as 20°F (−7°C) but fruit and young growth are injured at temperatures below 25°F (−4°C). Oranges like lightish land: sandy loam is ideal; heavy clay is unsuitable. Deeply drained soil is necessary, for they will not thrive on a high water table. Slightly acid soil is best for them: they will tolerate a pH anywhere between 5 and 7, although they prefer it to be around pH 6.

Soil treatment

Make sure the site is well drained. Dig deeply, and incorporate phosphatic material and potash into the soil. Rock phosphate, granite dust, wood ashes, compost or farmyard manure, all make a reserve for the roots to draw on in time to come.

Propagation

Nearly all orange trees are grafted on root stocks, because the best fruiting varieties are not the most hardy and vigorous. It really is best to buy them ready-grafted, because grafting oranges is a delicate process, but if you want to graft your own, the techniques are described on p. 99. When you buy your trees you should take note of the root stocks, as these will affect the type of fruit which your trees produce. The most common root stocks are listed below:

Trifoliate This is best for most gardens. It is disease-resistant, very hardy, can put up with cold better than most other varieties and is a dwarfing stock.

Cleopatra This is the best root stock for tangerines and small oranges.

Rough lemon This root stock thrives on sandy soil. It produces fruit early, but the trees are rather short-lived.

Sweet orange Good on well-drained sand, this root stock is useless on clay, where it gets foot-rot. It produces juicy, smallish fruit.

Sour orange Strange as it may seem, the sour orange root stock is good for sweet orange fruiting stock, because it is hardy and disease-resistant.

There is a huge selection of fruiting stocks available. They are all either sweet for eating, or sour for making marmalade. The most common sweet varieties are "Hamlin", which are small and sweet, "Valencia", which are good to eat and have a long fruiting season, and "Washington Navel", which is the best one for growing in hot dry climates like the desert states of the Southwest.

You can plant orange trees at any time of the year as you would apple trees (see p. 98). All varieties are self-fruitful. Good nurseries send the trees out with their roots balled and burlapped or in large cans. Plant orange trees with extreme care so as not to disturb the earth around the roots.

Place the roots, burlap and all, in the hole; pour some topsoil around the ball, then carefully withdraw the wrapping. A big tree should be 25 feet (7.6 m) from its neighbors: one on a dwarfing stock such as Trifoliate, 20 feet (6 m). Water well after planting and make sure the tree is well watered for two weeks. After that, continue to water regularly – about once a week, depending on the soil.

PLANTING ORANGE TREES
Your orange tree should arrive from the nursery with its roots already "balled"; that is to say, with a ball of soil wrapped around the roots with burlap. Place the tree in the hole prepared for it with the wrapping still around the roots. Pour some topsoil into the hole before gently removing the sacking.

A modification of the deep bed method may be used for oranges and all other citrus fruits. Deep dig a circle for each tree. The diameter of the circle should correspond to the drip-line – that is, where the branch extremities of the adult tree are expected to be. Keep the circle of earth raised, heavily mulched, and don't tread on it.

Care while growing

In regions with high rainfall some watering in dry periods may be necessary for the first three years; after this none is needed except in cases of real drought. In dry areas, where there is little rainfall, trees need a good soaking every two or three weeks; this means 20 to 30 gallons (90-140 l) per tree. More water than this may wash the nutrients down out of reach of the roots. Watering "little and often" encourages foot-rot but watering too sporadically causes fruit-splitting.

You should also feed the soil by mulching heavily with organic material once a year. If low-nitrogen material is used, such as hay or straw, some source of more concentrated nitrogen – bloodmeal or cottonseed meal – should be added to help rot the material down. If rotted compost is used nothing need be added.

Pruning is minimal with orange trees. Trees should come from the nursery already pruned so as to leave a suitable "scaffold" of four or five branches. Small sprouts that come from the trunk under this scaffold should be rubbed out by hand when they are tiny. Old weary trees can be stimulated into new life by pruning some of the old wood away; choose wood in the center of the tree, which does not get

RUBBING OUT SHOOTS
You will usually receive your tree with a good scaffold of four or five branches already established; it is therefore unlikely to need much pruning. If you notice any new shoots emerging from the trunk, rub them out by hand while they are still very small.

much sun. Cut out any frost-damaged branches, but not until the summer after the frost. It is important not to stimulate trees into excessively rank growth by cutting out too much wood. Sometimes upper branches grow so long that the lower growth is shaded. You cannot remedy this by pruning. But in a group of several trees, the solution is to take out one or two, so that more light reaches the rest.

Pests and diseases

The many pests that trouble orange trees in inorganic orchards are seldom present in organically managed ones. Eel worm, for example, never becomes a serious problem in an orchard planted on organically rich soil, because predators thrive on unsprayed trees.

Foot-rot In long periods of wet weather orange trees are susceptible to foot-rot, which rots the bark near the soil line and in extreme cases can kill the tree. You can prevent this by observing a few simple rules: keep the mulch at least a foot (30 cm) away from the trunk of the tree; keep that circle free of fallen leaves and debris; don't water right up against the trunk, and don't water too *often*; always keep the junction of trunk and roots clear of soil.

Harvesting and storing

The delightful thing about oranges is that you can leave them on the tree and just pick them when you want them. Pull tight-skinned oranges off with a twist: loose-skinned ones should be snipped off with a little stalk left on them. They can be stored under refrigeration – at 30°F (−1°C) with a humidity of 80 or 90 per cent – but you are unlikely to need to do this, because oranges have a very long harvesting season. And remember that a green orange is not necessarily unripe. Orange-colored oranges will sometimes turn green again when the weather gets warmer. They still taste the same.

TANGERINES, MANDARINS AND SATSUMAS

Tangerines, mandarins and satsumas are all classified as *citrus nobilis*. Tangerines have a deeper-colored skin than mandarins and the name satsuma was originally applied to a particular variety of tangerine. The terminology has now become confused and the names mandarin and satsuma are often used to apply to the whole group. The fruits are in general smaller than ordinary oranges, the skins are looser and the sections separate more easily. The advantage is that the trees are smaller and more hardy than orange trees and are therefore suitable for small gardens, roofs, and patios. Cultivate the trees as you would orange trees, bearing in mind that most varieties are not as productive as sweet orange trees.

KUMQUATS

A kumquat tree is an attractive proposition, particularly in a small garden, and they can be grown on roofs and patios in tubs. Kumquats belong to the *Fortunella* genus, but this is so closely related to *Citrus* that crosses between kumquats and oranges can be made. Certainly the orange-colored kumquats look exactly like tiny oranges. The fruits are rarely bigger than one and a half inches (4 cm) in diameter, but are very juicy and good to eat; also the peel is spicy and makes splendid marmalade or candied peel. Kumquat trees are very decorative and rarely grow taller than ten or twelve feet (3 m to 3.5 m), and their other advantage is that they are hardier than virtually any other citrus fruit (especially if grafted on to Trifoliate root stock). You grow them in exactly the same way as oranges.

Lemons & Limes

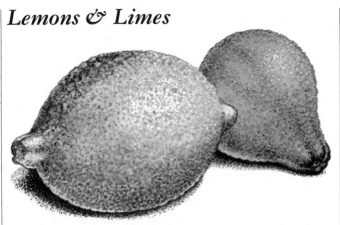

Apart from ordinary lemons, you can also grow the Meyer lemon, which is a hybrid particularly suitable for small gardens. It is hardy — sufficiently so to survive temperatures of 15°F (−9°C) — and quite small. Out of doors it makes a bush about six feet (1.8 m) tall. It grows well in tubs, on roofs and on patios. Growing lemons in a greenhouse is described on page 212. Limes are used in much the same way as lemons, but contain more acid and more sugar.

MEYER LEMON BUSHES
This hardy little lemon hybrid will flourish, given a sheltered spot, full sunshine and plenty of compost. Flowers, immature fruit and ripe fruit are all to be found on a thriving bush at one and the same time.

Soil and climate
Lemon trees are slightly more tender than orange trees and prefer a heavy soil. As they fruit all year round the crop can be badly damaged by winter frosts. This also applies to limes, which are less hardy still. Lemons and limes are very much a sub-tropical fruit. They will tolerate most soils, provided that the water table is below the depth of their roots which go down no more than four feet (1.2 m). You should incorporate plenty of phosphatic material (see p. 90) into the soil.

Propagation
Buy lemons and limes already grafted. All are self-fruitful. Plant them as you would any other tree (see p. 98). The most usual root stocks are the same as for oranges. You can plant lemons in a circular deep bed (see p. 110).

Care while growing
Lemons need a little more pruning than oranges, enough to stop them from straggling and becoming vulnerable to bad weather. Shorten any outward-straggling branches to inward-pointing buds so as to keep the tree compact. You can do this at any time of the year. Limes do not need any pruning. If your trees are thriving but not bearing, protect them from the wind and feed them a lot of extra compost; this extra attention should make all the difference.

Harvesting
Both lemons and limes bear all the year round in suitable climates, so just pick them when you want them.

Grapefruit

Grapefruit evolved in the West Indies as a mutation of the shaddock which is a coarse and rather unattractive fruit, but the grapefruit, as we all know, is delicious. It is also a rich source of vitamin C, and is self-fruitful.

Soil and climate
Grapefruit must have deep, well-drained soil and like it to be slightly acid: a pH of 6 is best. As for climate they can stand as much cold as oranges, 20°F (−7°C), but they need more heat to ripen perfect fruit. In temperate climates grapefruit must be grown under glass.

Soil treatment
Well-drained soil is most essential. Deep digging – four spade lengths deep if possible – is important, and you should incorporate some phosphate and potash into the soil. Compost or manure buried below the roots can only do good.

Propagation
Grapefruit are generally grafted on to sour orange root stock, although on poor sandy soil it is better to use lemon. Plant the young trees (see p. 98) at any time of the year; because they are evergreens, one time is as good as another. You must plant them very carefully, as you must other evergreens (see Oranges). Plant trees 25 feet (8 m) from their neighbors. You can plant them in a circular deep bed (see p. 110).

Care while growing
Grapefruit need plenty of water. In high rainfall areas they need watering for the first three years and then probably not at all. In dry areas they need a good soaking – say 25 gallons (110 l) a tree every three weeks. Don't put water actually on the trunk. Heavy mulching can only do good, provided you keep the mulch two feet (60 cm) away from the tree. Prune them in exactly the same way as oranges; they suffer from the same pests and diseases (see Oranges).

Harvesting and storing
They will stay happily on the tree for months, but when the fruit begin to turn yellow test an occasional one so that you know when to pick them. When they are just right pick them, wipe them with a clean damp rag, let them sit in a cool place in a breeze for a few days, then put them in the refrigerator. If you haven't got a refrigerator put them in a water-cooled safe.

Grossulariaceae

Blackcurrants, red currants, white currants and gooseberries are members of the family *Grossulariaceae.* They belong to the important genus, *Ribes,* all of whose members are shrubs which display familiar small round berries. Currants and gooseberries are exceptionally hardy and are cultivated almost as far north as the Arctic circle. They are less popular in north America than in Europe, because they can be alternative hosts to white pine blister rust and are for this reason prohibited in some areas. Personally I would rather have blackcurrants and gooseberries and prohibit white pines, because I think they are both magnificent fruits, and blackcurrants are probably the best source of winter vitamin C available to mankind. White currants, which are actually nearer yellow than white, have a fine, distinctive flavor when eaten raw. Red currants are grown primarily for making into red currant jelly, though they are good eaten raw or cooked.

Gooseberries

Gooseberry bushes are good plants to grow in smallish gardens because they yield a lot of fruit from a small area. They can be trained as cordons (see p. 101), in which case they take up hardly any space at all. They are self-fruitful.

Soil and climate

Gooseberries will thrive in almost any soil but have a slight preference for heavy soils. They like a cool climate, and are very tolerant of shade. They can therefore be planted in places where there is too much shade for most plants.

Soil treatment

Dig deeply and incorporate manure or compost in the top spit, over quite a wide area, because the roots are shallow but spread a long way laterally. A pH of 6 to 8 is suitable for them. Incorporate some lime if the pH is less than 6.

Propagation

Plant new bushes in early spring. Bush plants should be five feet (1.5 m) apart and cordons a foot (30 cm) apart in the row. In a deep bed (see p.106) gooseberries should be planted four feet (1.2 m) apart in a line down the middle of the bed.

Care while growing

When the bushes are two or three years old cut half the length off each leader to a suitable bud. If the plant is droopy cut to an upward-pointing bud: if it is upright cut to an outward-pointing bud. Cut all lateral growths back to within three inches (8 cm) of the stem. In each subsequent year cut out a good proportion of the old wood.

Every summer shorten all laterals, keeping about five leaves on each. At that time you can examine the bushes for mildew, and cut out any shoots that are infected. Goose-

"MOUNDING" GOOSEBERRIES
Cut an old bush back in early spring to within twelve inches (30 cm) of the soil. This encourages new shoots to grow. Then in midsummer build up a mound of earth and compost around the bush, so that only the tips of the canes are visible. By fall the canes will have put out roots. You then gently remove the earth, cut out the canes with the strongest roots and transplant them.

berry bushes should be grown on a "leg", a short main stem. You must keep the ground under and between the bushes clear of weeds. Don't dig, for fear of injuring the shallow roots, but hoe, scuffle or till very shallowly.

Pests and diseases

Powdery mildew The first symptoms of this is a white felt which covers the young leaves and shoots. The berries themselves acquire a brownish covering. The best prevention is not to give the bushes too much nitrogen. If you do get it pick off and burn all affected shoots, and spray, in midsummer, with a mixture of half a pound (225 g) of soft soap, one pound (450 g) of washing soda, and six gallons (23 l) of water. You can spray with this again in the spring when the bushes flower and once again when the fruit is set.
Gooseberry sawfly These are small caterpillars with green and black spotted bodies and a yellow tail. They produce three generations in a season and can strip your bushes of leaves. Spray hard with derris or pyrethrum.
Red spider mite The tiny red mites cluster on gooseberry leaves causing them to turn bronze with a white area underneath. Ultimately the leaves will dry up and die. The answer is to knock them off the bush with a jet of water.

Harvesting

Strip the fruit off by pulling the branches through a hand protected by a thick leather glove. The fruit falls off and can be caught in a sheet. It can then be separated from the leaves and other flotsam that get stripped off by rolling the whole lot down a board. The fruit rolls, the rest does not. If you don't eat them fresh, can them or make jam.

Currants

BLACKCURRANTS

Blackcurrants are one of the best and most reliable sources of vitamin C in cold, moist climates. Alaska is not too far north to find them growing and they thrive on a cool north slope. They are hardy and easy to grow, store well and make all sorts of delicious preserves and wines. They are heavy yielding, self-fruitful and take up little room. You do not have to wait too long to start picking either. In my view, of all fruits either "hard" or "soft", blackcurrants are the most rewarding to grow.

Soil and climate

A fertile heavy clay-loam with plenty of organic matter in it is perfect for blackcurrants, but you can grow them on practically any soil if you add enough compost or farmyard manure. I have grown them with great success on heavy boulder clay and on sand, but with both I had to mulch heavily every year with organic material. A great advantage of blackcurrants is that they are hardy enough to be planted in frost pockets. They like a cool and moist climate, because hot winds dry up their leaves. But they can be grown in hot dry states as long as they have some shade, such as the north-facing wall of a house. You can also intercrop with apple trees in an orchard, although in this case make sure that the bushes are not starved of moisture as well as being protected from heat.

Soil treatment

Blackcurrants are shallow-rooted. Nevertheless prepare the ground by digging deeply, because they benefit from soil that is well drained and aerated. Also incorporate plenty of organic material before planting. Dig in ground rock phosphate if you can get some cheaply, bone meal or anything else that is going to last a long time and release nutrients slowly. I always give blackcurrants plenty of manure, but I don't use well-rotted compost, because I reserve this for the things that really cannot do without it. For all my soft fruit, including blackcurrants, I use long-strawed stable or cow-shed manure.

Make sure the ground is free of perennial weeds: once the bushes are in the soil it will be hard to destroy any weeds that are left.

TRIMMING BACK ROOTS
When you are planting your blackcurrant bushes, the roots should be wet. Spread them out well over the shallow holes you have dug in readiness, and cut back first any roots which are broken or torn. Then trim back any very thick roots, but leave all the fine, fibrous ones intact.

Propagation

To start off it is best to buy bushes from a reliable nursery so that you are sure they are healthy. After that you can multiply your own stock for the rest of your life, because blackcurrants grow very easily from cuttings. Because currant buds start growing very early in spring, plant the bushes in late winter; if your winters are not harsh, plant in the fall, so the roots can get established before the ground freezes.

When you plant your new bushes dig wide shallow holes four feet (1.2 m) apart. If the roots of the bushes are dry when you get them, soak them in water for several hours before planting. Spread the roots carefully, first snipping off any very long or broken ones. If you use the deep bed method (see p. 106) plant a row of bushes along the middle of the deep bed at intervals of four feet (1.2 m), preferably alternating currants with gooseberries. Use the space at the edges of the bed to grow annual vegetables. As soon as you have planted the bushes snip off all the branches to outward-pointing buds, leaving at least three or four buds on every shoot.

When you come to propagate from cuttings you must use the current year's wood. Blackcurrants fruit on the previous year's wood, so it is not expedient to cut too much new wood off the bushes. But when you are pruning older bushes you will inevitably cut out a certain amount of old wood on which some new wood has sprouted.

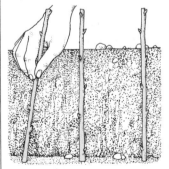

PROPAGATING FROM CUTTINGS
Prune off cuttings of new wood from eight to twelve inches (20-30 cm) long, and in the fall plant them deeply in good light soil with two buds above ground. Keep them from drying out, and protect them with a straw mulch; plant out the following spring.

Care while growing

Prune the bushes annually in early winter. The thing to remember is that they fruit only on the previous year's wood, so you cannot expect any fruit the first year. Therefore, preserve all new wood (which is yellow or light brown) every year, if you possibly can, so that it can fruit the following year, but cut out all the wood that has already fruited. You can tell which is the older wood because it will still have the little stalks of the berries on it.

Mulch with plenty of manure, and wood ash when you have it, and keep the ground clear of weeds.

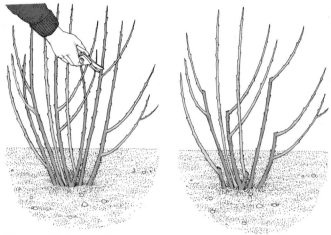

PRUNING BLACKCURRANTS
Every year in early winter cut out as much old wood that has already fruited as possible, while preserving the new wood. Cut off the old wood just above a good new low-growing shoot.

Pests and diseases

Leaf spot fungus   This distressing disease can cause all the leaves to turn brown and drop off in midsummer. Rake up all the affected leaves and burn them or put them in a hot compost heap.

Currant maggot   The blackcurrants themselves are sometimes attacked by maggots. This can ruin your crop, so keep an eye out for it. Currants that ripen before their time should be examined and any with maggots destroyed.

Big bud   This very common disease causes the new buds of the plants to swell unduly in midsummer. Simply pick off all such swollen buds and burn them.

Reversion   The big bud mite carries the reversion virus. The leaves of the bushes change shape and look rather like nettle leaves. The bushes flower earlier and the flowers are brighter than usual, but the crop is poor and dies fast. There is no cure for reversion, so the moment you notice it you should root up the bush and burn it.

Currant shoot borer/Currant core borer   Apply a winter wash in January with a tar-oil spray to prevent these pests;

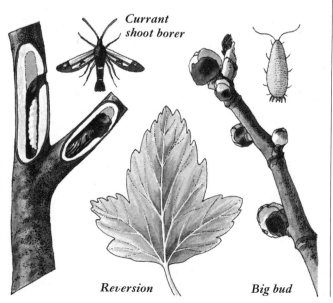

Currant shoot borer

Reversion   *Big bud*

the spray will also keep off aphids. If you do see a cane's leaves wilting at the tip, cut the branch back until you find the tunnel, and kill the borer.

Coral spot/Dieback   These two fungus diseases are caused by too much nitrogen. Cut back any wood that seems to be dying, or which shows the distinctive red spots of coral spot on the branches. Cut right back to sound white wood, and burn the affected branches. Then stop feeding the bushes with high nitrogen manure such as stable manure; mulch instead with waste vegetable matter, spoiled hay or straw, and a little well-rotted compost.

PROTECTING BLACKCURRANTS
If birds are likely to strip you of your entire blackcurrant crop, you must protect the bushes. An excellent way of doing this is with a fruit cage of wire mesh supported on a frame.

Harvesting and storing

You can just leave currants on the bushes if there are no birds; likewise if you grow them in a fruit cage there is no hurry to pick. But don't leave them too long, or they will fall off the bush. Currants freeze well, can well, and make fine wine, jelly or jam. They are one of gardening's greatest rewards eaten raw with cream.

RED AND WHITE CURRANTS

You should treat red and white currants in exactly the same way as blackcurrants, but there is one important difference. The fruit on red and white currant bushes is borne on two or three-year-old wood. This means that you prune for the first time when the bush is two years old, by cutting out all the wood except seven or eight good shoots. Each year after that cut out all new shoots, except for three or four which suit your plan for the shape of the bush. In the third year and every year after that cut the oldest shoots right back to the ground.

The aim is to have a few one-year-old, a few two-year-old and a few three-year-old branches on every bush, with plenty of short fruiting spurs on each branch. The other important thing is a good shape — open in the middle, not too spread-eagled and yet not too bunched up.

Prune the fruiting spurs as you would on an apple tree (see p. 170), because the fruit is borne on spurs like apple spurs. The principle is to snip back side-shoots to one or two buds to encourage spur-making.

Bush trees should be trained on "short legs" (main stems a few inches high), but red and white currants are also excellent for cordon training or espaliers (see p. 101).

Moraceae

Figs and mulberries belong to the family *Moraceae*, whose other members include: hemp; hops; the rubber trees of south-east Asia and their diminutive, the popular household rubber plant; and a number of tropical and semi-tropical trees with exotic-sounding names like the breadfruit tree, the snakewood tree and the trumpet tree. Figs and mulberries are unusual members of the family in that they thrive in temperate climates. All they ask is plenty of sun. And figs do better on poor soil than on rich soil, where in order to make them fruit their roots must be confined artificially. Figs and mulberries are both delicate fruits which do not travel or store well. They should therefore be eaten fresh from the trees; otherwise figs must be dried or canned, and mulberries must be made into jam or wine. Both trees are attractive and long-lived and grow to about 30ft (9 m) high.

Figs

In ancient Greece figs were said to be the food of the philosophers. Whether this is so or not they are quite an experience to eat. They will also grow in much colder climates than is generally thought, as long as they get all the sun going and plenty of water. The common types are self-fruitful.

Soil and climate

In temperate climates, figs will flourish on the worst soil you have, provided that it is well drained and in full sun. They grow very well against a south-facing wall and will tolerate clay, lime-rich soil, sandy soil or rubble.

Soil treatment

Figs like plenty of humus so you can mix compost with their earth. Give them a little lime as well. In heavy clay, poor gravel or sandy soil you will have no problems; this is the sort of soil found in the warm countries where the fig is native. But in all other soils it is best to confine the roots. This can be done by growing the trees in a concrete box, or in any other sturdy receptacle, buried in the ground. They will also grow in barrels or huge pots, indoors or on a patio. Allow for drainage from the box or container.

Propagation

Figs will grow from suckers, cuttings or layers (see p. 95). To grow them from cuttings, cut lengths of ripe wood about a foot (30cm) long from an existing tree in late fall. Plant these cuttings in a shallow trench of good light loam, so that they come out of the earth at an angle of 45 degrees. Leave one growing point only above the surface. Plant the cuttings at nine inch (22 cm) intervals. Cover them with loose earth during the winter, so that they are completely buried. In spring scrape away the surface soil and expose the cuttings, cover them with cloches, and water them whenever the soil is dry. They must not dry out. When the weather has really warmed up, remove the cloches, mulch well, and keep them well watered until the fall. Then plant out the cuttings in their final position, taking great care not to damage the roots.

If an old tree throws up suckers from its roots you can dig these out in late autumn, keeping the roots intact, and plant them in their permanent position. You can also layer a low branch by pegging it down to the soil. Once it has rooted, transplant it.

Care while growing

Cut out a branch from time to time to keep the tree open, if it seems to be overcrowded. And in early summer each year nip off the first half inch (1 cm) of all the leading branches to make them bush out instead of allowing them to grow long and straggly.

When the fruit begins to swell, water copiously. Two and a half to three and a half gallons (9-14 l) a day in dry weather.

Pests and diseases

Cotton root rot Figs get this disease if they are planted after cotton. It is incurable; trees wilt and die.
Souring If disease-carrying insects get into the open end of the fruit, the fruit will shrivel and taste sour. Pull off any diseased or shriveled fruit and put on the compost heap.

Harvesting and storing

Eat your figs straight from the tree when they are ripe. Any that you can't manage to eat should be dried. This can be done in hot sun, on racks, or in a drying box (see p. 216)

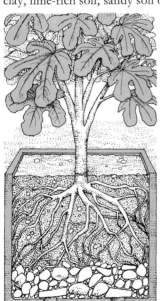

CONFINING FIG TREE ROOTS
If you plant a fig tree in good soil, it will grow well and get very large, but it may not set any fruit for as much half a century. This is because the roots spread so much further than the top of the tree that a severe imbalance is caused: nourishment at the root tips never reaches the leaves, so branches straggle and growth is weak. The solution is to confine the roots. Grow the tree in a concrete box buried in the ground. Allow for drainage from the box by making one or more drainage holes in the bottom. Shield the holes well with tiles or broken crockery, so that water can get out but the roots stay in.

Mulberries

The name mulberry in fact refers to a multitude of fruits, from a white or red mulberry tree 50 or 60 feet (15-18m) tall, right through to a white mulberry shrub grown to feed silk-worms. The white mulberry grown so freely in the mountains of Persia is an insipid fruit, but the wine-red mulberry grown in America and Europe is a splendid fruit and deserves to be cultivated a lot more. It is self-fruitful.

Soil and climate
Mulberries will grow in any garden soil with a neutral pH. Most varieties are very hardy in temperate climates, apart from the black mulberry which grows only in hot regions.

Soil treatment
Dig deeply and incorporate compost or manure.

Propagation
If you can get a tree from a nursery, just plant it as you would an apple tree (see p. 98). Allow it plenty of room to grow; trees should be about 30 feet (9 m) apart. They can be planted in circular deep beds (see p. 110). After you have planted one or two, the trees will proliferate, because birds drop seeds far and wide; otherwise you can propagate from cuttings (see p. 95).

Care while growing
There is nothing difficult about growing mulberries. Just give the trees a good mulching now and again. They are rarely attacked by pests or diseases. When the trees are established, sow grass around them, because this will facilitate harvesting.

Harvesting and storing
Mulberries are highly perishable, so eat them when they are ripe. From a commercial point of view this is a disadvantage; the fruit does not keep for any time at all and must be eaten very quickly. Wait for the fruit to fall to the grass below the tree and gather it immediately. If the tree is situated so grass cannot be grown beneath it, spread hay or straw on the ground during the fruiting season. A word of warning: mulberry juice stains very badly, so wear old clothes when harvesting.

Mulberries and cream are delicious; mulberry wine (see p. 224) can be superb. Birds adore mulberries; if you grow them near cherries they will eat the mulberries and leave the cherries; if you grow them in or near a chicken run, the great weight of fruit that a mature tree produces every summer will fall to the ground and feed the hens, and you will get all you want too.

Blueberries

Blueberries are the fruit for those who have sandy, acid, waterlogged soils in cold climates. Blueberry is often mis-used as a collective name for several species of the *Ericaceae* or heath family, which includes such fruits as bilberries and cranberries. All these edible fruits grow wild, in cold mountain climates where no other fruit will grow. Only the blueberry proper can be cultivated with success, however, and there are several improved cultivars. It can grow as high as 15 feet (4.5 m). The bushes are slow to mature; after three years they will probably provide you with at least some fruit, but it may take as long as eight years before they bear a full crop. Mature bushes bear very heavily, especially if you plant two or more varieties together.

Soil and climate
Wild blueberries grow on very acid soils with a high water-table. They do not possess root hairs, so they cannot suck moisture from damp soil particles as other plants can. They therefore need water within reach of their roots. Also they cannot absorb nitrates and must therefore have their nitrogen in the form of ammonia. This means they must have an acid soil because ammonia-forming bacteria cannot live in anything else.

Ideally they should be planted in light loamy soil with plenty of humus and some sand, and the pH should not be above 5; 4.5 is ideal. They must have a cold climate with at least 100 nights at a temperature as low as 40°F (4°C), but they should be planted in full sunlight.

Soil treatment
Blueberries must have plenty of organic material. They will not grow in purely mineral soils, no matter how much artificial fertilizer is put into it. If the pH is above 5 you should lower it by digging in plenty of leaf-mold, sawdust, or peat some months before you intend to plant.

Propagation
Blueberries do not root easily and it is better to buy plants from a nursery. Plant them in spring six feet (1.8 m) apart in rows eight feet (2.5 m) apart, in shallow holes which have been filled with an equal mixture of topsoil and organic matter. After planting, mulch heavily with sawdust, and cut half the length off each branch. Blueberries will grow from layers (see p. 95) as well. Nick the underside of each branch before pegging it down for layering.

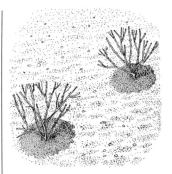

PLANTING BLUEBERRY BUSHES
*Immediately the bushes are planted, give a four to six inch
(10-15 cm) mulch of sawdust (above left). At the same time, cut all
the branches back by half (above right); this gives the roots a chance to
catch up with the top growth.*

Care while growing

Keep the soil constantly moist under the mulch during the
first year. For the first four years don't allow the bushes to
fruit at all. Strip off all flower-clusters. From the fifth year
on remove all fruiting buds except one for every three
inches (7 cm) of branch. Cut out some of the main branches,
aiming to leave one for every year of the tree's age. Cut out
all small weak laterals every summer. The bushes do not
reach full maturity until they are ten to fifteen years old.
From then on they will yield as much as 30 pints (17l) per
year. When strong new shoots grow up above the top of the
bush cut them down to the level of the bush to encourage
the growth of laterals. Every year the trees must be heavily
mulched with organic material. Don't let any lime or sea-
sand come near them.

Pests and diseases

Tent caterpillars These pests are the most harmful insects
to attack blueberries. They spin tents of silk over the leaves;
either pick off the eggs during the winter or remove caterpillars and eggs in the spring.
Canker This causes reddish-brown wounds on the stem
which kill the buds nearby, and in severe cases can girdle the
trunk and kill the whole cane. Canker can be prevented by
growing the blueberries in an airy place, by keeping the
bush open by pruning, and by immediately removing any
cankered material.

HARVESTING BLUEBERRIES
*Leave the fruit on the bushes
until it has become really soft.
Then test each one by rolling it
gently between thumb and finger:
the ripe berries will come off
easily and the unripe ones will
stay on.*

Harvesting and storing

Let the fruit stay on the bushes until it really begins to
soften, which will be about ten days after it turns blue. This is
when the sugar content is at its highest, and consequently when
the flavor is strongest and sweetest. If you pick the fruit
any earlier, they will be rather tasteless. Then roll the berries
gently so that the ripe berries come off and the unripe ones
stay on. Store in a refrigerator, or freeze (see p. 227).

Olives

Not only can a man live on olives, bread and wine alone
(and many a man has), but from this fruit is expressed the
best edible oil in the world. Olive trees are not reliably self-
fruitful. It is best to plant two or more varieties.

Soil and climate

The olive will thrive in practically any soil; it grows in
Mediterranean countries where there is no true topsoil at all.
But as to climate it is very specific. It needs a cold winter –
around 45 to 50°F (7-10°C) – but never below 10°F (−12°C),
because this will kill it; even 18°C (−8°C) will do it some
damage. Although they don't suffer from late frost, they
need a hot summer; it can scarcely be too hot. If you are
not between latitudes 30° and 45°, either north or south of
the equator, it is not much good trying to grow olives; nor
can they grow above 2500 feet (800 m).

Propagation

The easiest thing to do is to buy a sapling, and plant it like
any other tree (see p. 98). Otherwise olives are best propagated from cuttings in a mist propagator (see p. 97). It is best
to use softwood cuttings of the current season's growth.
Take the cuttings in early autumn. Small cuttings should be
planted vertically, larger ones horizontally below the soil.

Care while growing

In the first three years after planting the tree should be
shaped to make four or five good strong branches for the
scaffold. Cut out all other branches, crossing branches, and
branches which grow inward. Let the new laterals on the
main scaffold branches grow. By the fifth or sixth year the
tree should begin to fruit. If in any one year the tree bears a
huge amount of fruit, thin it; otherwise it will strain itself
and not give any fruit next year. In countries with very dry
summers irrigate plentifully during fruiting.

Pests and diseases

Olive knot This causes swellings on any part of the tree.
Cut out such swellings and paint the wounds with tree paint.
Split pit Heavy watering after a drought when the fruit is
swelling causes the stones inside the fruit to crack, ruining
the fruit. Keep watering regularly while the tree is fruiting
and you won't get it.

Harvesting and storing

Pick the biggest olives by hand from the tree in the fall and
use them for pickling (see p. 218). Fruit from which you
wish to press oil should be left on the tree until late in the
winter, when it will be quite shriveled. You then beat the
branches with poles and catch the olives on tarpaulins spread
on the ground.

Grapes

"Without wine all joyless goes the feast" sang the poet and certainly since ancient times the vine has had a notable effect on the development of civilization and culture.

Like the olive, the vine, which belongs to the family, *Vitaceae*, grows out of the subsoil. There is a theory that the early Mediterranean mercantile civilizations came about because the overcropping of wheat, and the grazing of goats, caused the topsoil to waste away in those countries. The inhabitants were forced to farm their subsoil, which they did with such crops as vines and olives. They were then forced to trade wine and oil for wheat. This meant they had to become potters (because they had to make *amphorae* to carry wine and oil), shipbuilders, sailors and merchants. This in turn sped up their industrial and mercantile development.

Some variety of grape is native to nearly every temperate region of the world, and to several subtropical ones as well. Grapes of the Mediterranean species, *Vitis vinifera,* and their hybrids will grow and ripen to wine status in virtually all mild parts of the U.S. Americans are also lucky in having two native species: *V. labrusca,* also known as the fox grape or Concord, and *V. rotundifolia,* the Muscadine or southern fox grape.

Soil and climate

Vines grow well on poor, dry, stony soil. They will grow on limestone soil, and certain varieties will even flourish on chalk, although this is not ideal.

Stony soils on slopes make good vineyards. Many of the best French vintages come from alluvial gravel terraces. I have grown grapes successfully on soil composed largely of decayed fossil seashells. Rich clay soil is bad for grapes, causing them to lose their fruit or ripen it too late. It is fortunate for mankind that the vine thrives on soil that is little good for anything else.

The climate most suitable for grapes is the Mediterranean type. The winter must be cold enough to give them a dormant period, but not so far below freezing as to harm their dormant vines. Most varieties can take temperatures as low as 27°F (−3°C) or even 17°F (−8°C). In cases where the temperatures are lower than this the plant vines can be bent down and covered with earth to protect them from the elements. Alternatively you should plant exceptionally hardy varieties. Most varieties are self-fruitful.

But more important than winter temperatures are the warmth and sunshine which grape vines must have in the summer, both for the fertilization of the flowers in late spring, and for the ripening of the fruit in late summer. Dessert grapes do not need as long a ripening period as wine varieties; grapes that are pleasant to eat may still not contain enough sugar to make good wine. Late spring frosts are not a problem, because the vines start growing late enough to miss them.

Soil treatment

Clear the soil completely of perennial weeds; incorporate rock phosphate and potash, and dig deeply. If the pH is much below 6, lime to bring it to about 7. Good drainage is absolutely essential.

Propagation

You can, of course, buy year old plants from a nursery. But most vines are grown from cuttings, although it's often hard to stop them growing from pips, which rarely produce strong heavy-yielding vines. If you have existing vines, make cuttings by separating your winter prunings into two bundles: the ripe, reddish-brown wood and the tender new wood. Tie the ripe wood in bundles, marking the top end with a tiny scratch, label the bundles with the variety, and bury them in moist sand. Feed the new wood to rabbits or goats, or put it on the compost heap. Take the bundles out in March and select the pieces which are about as thick as pencils; make cuttings by chopping them into foot-long (30 cm) lengths, with a bud near the bottom of each. The best cuttings are made from canes with about three or four buds to the foot. Make a long deep nick with a spade in the sandiest soil you have and plant the cuttings the right way up. The top bud should be just above soil level. Stamp the cuttings in hard.

During the summer most of these cuttings will root, and by the following spring, they will be ready to re-plant. Now, most experts tell you to dig a wide hole for each cutting and spread the roots carefully over a mound of earth. I suggest that you simply snip off all the roots of each new plant to about two inches (5 cm) so that it looks like a shaving brush, then make a hole with a crowbar, about six inches (15 cm) deep, drop the plant in, and stamp the soil down firmly. I know this works because I have done it successfully and seen it done in Italy. You will get excellent results this way because the new vine is forced to put out plenty of new fine roots.

Grafting Grafting grapes is quite simple and should be done in winter. Wood of the root stock should be cut to one foot (30 cm) lengths with three or four buds on each. The scions should be cut to two or three inch (5-8 cm) lengths with one bud. Cut the scion and the stock as you would for any other grafting (see p.99), and tie them together with raffia or sticky tape. Cover the joint with wax.

When this process is complete bury them shallowly in layers in moist clean sand. Put the box containing them in some place where the temperature does not fall much below 70°F (21°C): a heated greenhouse is ideal. As soon as warm weather comes, plant them out at a slant in a holding-bed, with one bud of the scion just above the soil. Soon after midsummer scrape the soil away and cut off any roots that have grown from the scion with a sharp knife. Do this again at the same time the next year. Do not allow the scion to put down roots.

Plant out stocks and scions in the vineyard in the second or third year. Plant them with the joint just above the ground, but then heap some soil over the joint to cover it. After a year hoe the soil away, since the joint will now be

TAKING GRAPE CUTTINGS
In winter, tie ripe prunings in bundles and bury them in damp sand. Take them out in the spring and chop the best into sections a foot (30 cm) long, leaving a bud on each. The best cuttings have about three or four per foot.

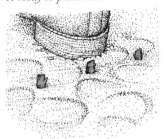

PROPAGATING FROM CUTTINGS
Take a spade and make a long deep nick in sandy soil. Plant the cuttings, leaving the top bud just above soil level. Stamp them in hard. Most of the cuttings will root and by the next spring will be ready to plant out.

strong enough not to need this protection.

If you wish to change the scion of an unsatisfactory vine you can try approach grafting. This is a very simple method. Plant a cutting of the desired scion in a pot. When it has taken, place the pot near the growing vine and slice off a short piece of bark with a little wood from the stems of both vine and scion. Put the two cut faces together, bind and wax them. When the graft has taken, cut off the scion plant below the graft and the root stock plant above it.

Most European vines are grafted on to American root stocks, because *Vitis vinifera* cultivars, which Europeans prefer, cannot be grown on their own roots; they are attacked by an aphid called *phylloxera*. American root stocks have a high degree of immunity to this insect.

APPROACH GRAFTING
You can improve the quality of a vine by changing the scion. Plant the new scion in a pot near the vine; chop off a little slice of wood from both vine and scion (above left). Put the two cut faces together, bind and wax as usual (above right).

Care while growing

For the first three or four years it is most important to keep the ground beneath and between vines free of weeds. At first you can do this by deep digging or plowing. Then, as the roots spread, shallower cultivation is better, because this will not damage them. A rotary tiller is useful for this job, but shallow scuffling with a hoe will do as well. Heavy green mulching is also effective: comfrey or lucerne (alfalfa) are good for this. Moderate feeding with manure or compost from time to time is beneficial.

Pruning Training and pruning are subjects of labyrinthine complexity and endless argument: only the benign fermented juice of the grape itself serves to prevent such arguments from becoming vitriolic. The best thing to do, I suggest, is to copy your grape-growing neighbors. But as a general rule the colder your climate is the smaller you should keep your vines. In Italy you may find great straggling vines growing up elm trees. In the U.S. the native grapes are often grown that way too, but it is generally advisable to cut them back rather hard.

The thing to remember when pruning vines is that grapes only grow on this year's shoots, sprouting from last year's wood. Old wood will not fruit, nor will new shoots springing from two or three-year-old wood. Therefore there must be just enough of the last year's wood to produce the current year's fruiting spurs. And it is these fruiting spurs which will send out new fruiting spurs next year. You can keep some of the present year's canes free of fruit, by stripping young fruit off them, and use them as the next year's base for new fruiting canes. But this method is expedient only in climates where grapes grow freely.

Guyot method In practice, in cold climates, you will probably need to use the Guyot method, which works as follows. Plant the vines four feet (1.2 m) apart in rows six feet (1.8 m) apart. Erect a two-wire fence along each row with the bottom wire 15 inches (38 cm) from the ground and the top wire a foot (30 cm) higher. Set a light stake four and a half feet (1.3 m) long and tie it to both horizontal wires. In the third winter after planting cut all the canes except two down close to the ground. Tie the two remaining canes to the upright stake and pinch them off when they get a few inches taller than the stake. Do not allow them to fruit, and pinch the laterals off when they are a few inches long.

The following winter cut one of the two vertical canes right off (it was only spare), bend the other one over and tie it along the bottom wire. Come summer it will send out fruiting branches. When they are long enough, tie these to the top wire. Prune any that are not going to bear and snip off the ends of the fruiting branches, leaving four to five leaves above the flowering bunches. Now new shoots will come from the stool (stem) of the plant. Keep two of them and cut off all the others. Cut the tips off when they are taller than the stake, say five feet (1.5 m) high. The next

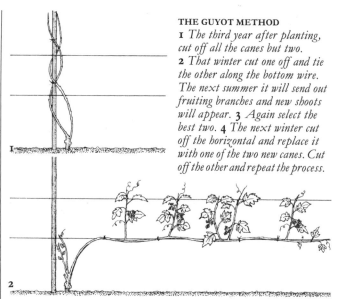

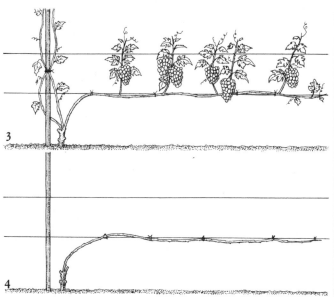

THE GUYOT METHOD
1 The third year after planting, cut off all the canes but two.
2 That winter cut one off and tie the other along the bottom wire. The next summer it will send out fruiting branches and new shoots will appear. 3 Again select the best two. 4 The next winter cut off the horizontal and replace it with one of the two new canes. Cut off the other and repeat the process.

winter cut right off the horizontal that bore the fruiting branches, bend down the better of the two vertical canes to take its place, and cut the other cane right off. Next year repeat the process. In this way every summer you always have one horizontal cane bearing fruiting wood, and two of the current year's canes being kept in reserve to fruit the following year.

If you are training vines up walls – one of the best ways of growing them – you can practice exactly the same method in a modified but more extensive form (see below).

It is a good idea to grow vines on south-facing walls: they are more decorative than any ornamental creeper and far more useful.

Pests and diseases

Powdery mildew or oidium This is a very common complaint. A fine dusty film forms over the vine. To prevent it dust with sulfur every three weeks from the flowering stage until the grapes start to ripen.

Downy mildew This causes a much thicker layer of white down than powdery mildew. To prevent it spray with Bordeaux mixture (see p. 104) every three weeks. You will not get the disease under cloches or in greenhouses, because it is spread by droplets of rain.

TRAINING UP WALLS
A modification of the Guyot method works well. Instead of cutting the vine right back each year, let it establish a framework of old wood and then allow horizontal branches to develop as if the top of the old wood were at ground level. If the wall is high, plant two vines or more; let the permanent wood grow tall on some and keep it short on others. Vines fruit at their extremities, so if you try to make one vine cover the whole wall, you will only get fruit at the top.

Black spot or anthracnose This can appear after periods of wet weather. It causes well-defined black spots on the leaves. Routine spraying for downy mildew should prevent it. If it does not, increase the strength of the mixture to one pound (450 g) of copper sulfate, 14 ounces (400 g) of lime, and seven gallons (27 l) of water.
Vine mite This produced blisters on the tops of the leaves. Sulfur dusting for powdery mildew will also control this.
Birds It is quite possible to lose your entire grape crop to the birds. If you suffer from them badly you must enclose your vines with netting.
Wasps Wasps can decimate a crop of grapes. Prepare a bait made of some sweet stuff, include a few squashed grapes and mix some poison in with it. Track down and destroy nests.

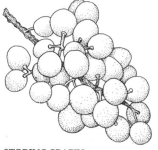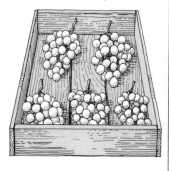

STORING GRAPES
Spread out the bunches in single layers as far as possible, and leave them after picking until the stems begin to shrivel (above left). Then store them in trays in a cool place (right).

Harvesting

Leave the fruit on the vines until they are fully ripe, because the riper they get, the sweeter they taste and the better wine they make. They are ripe when the stem of the bunch begins to turn brown.

Snip the bunches from the vines with shears. Spread out the bunches in single layers and leave at 50°F (10°C) until the stems begin to shrivel. Then store in shallow trays in a cool, slightly humid cellar or storeroom at 40°F (4°C). Grapes will keep fresh for several months stored in this way. For instructions on making wine see p. 224.

CHAPTER SEVEN

The Cultivation of Herbs

*Containing the sowing, growing
and harvesting instructions for the many
useful herbs that can be nurtured
in the kitchen garden.*

Angelica
Biennial

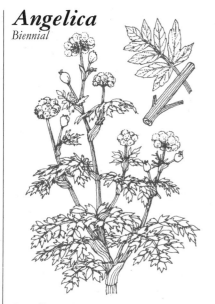

Angelica takes up a lot of space; the plants can reach six feet (1.8 m) high and are quite imposing. If your space for herbs is in any way limited, this is one you can think of doing without. The leaf stalks can be candied or crystallised, and the roots and stems can be cooked with stewed fruit to provide natural sweetness.

Soil
Angelica is best grown at the back of the herb garden, in deep rich soil and partial shade.

Propagation and after-care
The seed does not keep very long; to make sure of good results I pick the seed fresh and ripe in the autumn, seal it up in an airtight container and sow it early in the spring an inch (2.5 cm) deep in moist soil. The seeds will take a long time to come up. Seedlings should be given six inches (15 cm) of space toward the end of the first year, two feet (60 cm) in the second and anything up to five feet (1.5 m) after that. Angelica usually flowers in its second year, so strictly speaking it is biennial. However, sometimes it does not flower until its fourth or fifth year. After it has flowered the plant will die.

Harvesting
If you want to harvest the leaves, cut them in early summer when the oils are strongest. As well as eating the leaves as a vegetable, you can dry them very successfully. Leaf stalks for candying should be picked at the same time as the leaves. As for roots, dig them up in the second autumn, because they become too woody after that.

Anise
Annual

Anise seed can be baked into cookies and cake, and used to flavor cheeses, desserts, candies and cordials with its delicate licorice scent. An ounce (28g) of seed in a half a pint (300 ml) of brandy, allowed to stand in the sun for two weeks, makes a fortifying drink.

Soil
Anise likes warm, well-drained soil, and a sunny position.

Propagation and after-care
Sow seeds in spring *in situ,* thinning when the plants are established to eight inches (20 cm) apart. Take care when thinning, because the herb is easily damaged. The more sun the seeds get, the more quickly they will mature.

Harvesting
You should be able to harvest in midsummer, when the seed heads have turned gray-brown. Cut the stalks, tie them in bunches and hang them up to dry them out. Thresh them when they are thoroughly dried. Save some of the seed to sow the following spring.

Balm
Perennial

Balm, or lemon balm, as it is sometimes called, adds a subtle flavor to fruit salads or cooked fruit and is good when added to poultry stuffing. Its pleasant smell recommends it to makers of *pot-pourri* and the scent lasts for a very long time. If you have it in your garden it will attract bees, which is a good thing because they will pollinate your vegetables.

Soil
Balm likes shady places and rich moist soil, but it needs a little sun to prevent it getting stringy and blanched.

Propagation and after-care
Sow seed in spring or early summer indoors or in a cold frame. It will take three or four weeks to germinate. Plant out when the seedlings are four inches (10 cm) high. Alternatively, sow seed outdoors in midsummer, then lift and replace the seedlings early the following summer.

If you have an existing clump or can buy or beg one, divide it up and plant the portions in the autumn or spring. Balm divides easily into clumps. There is no difficulty in looking after it.

Harvesting
Harvest some leaves just before the buds flower, and then cut the plants right down in the autumn and cover them with compost or leaf-mold.

Balm bruises easily so be careful when picking and don't expect too much during the first year's growth. Dry it in a dark airy room and store in sealed jars in the dark.

Basil
Annual

In cool climates basil must be sown every year, because frost will kill it. In warm climates you may be able to turn it into a perennial by cutting it right back in the autumn, so that it shoots up in the spring. Basil grows very well in containers indoors.

Basil leaves have a strong flavor and used in large enough quantities will dominate even garlic. In France many cooks steep basil leaves in olive oil and keep this for dressing salads.

Soil
Basil needs dry, light, well-drained soil. A sunny but sheltered position is what it likes best.

Propagation and after-care
Sow seed indoors in early summer. Wait until the soil is warm before planting out the seedlings, eight inches (20 cm) apart in rows a foot (30 cm) apart. Water the plants well, to keep the leaves succulent

Harvesting
Pick off leaves as soon as they unfurl and use them fresh. Cut the plants down for drying in late summer or early fall; basil takes longer to dry than most herbs.

Bay
Perennial

Bay has a hundred uses in the kitchen and because it is evergreen there is no problem about storing. Freshly dried leaves to put with pickled herrings, with stews, casseroles and soups, should always be available.

Soil and climate
Bay will do well on any average soil. It likes some sun, but needs sheltering from harsh winds. Bay is susceptible to frost, so in cold climates you should grow it in tubs which can be moved indoors in winter. Add compost occasionally, and some bone meal or other material which contains phosphate.

Propagation and after-care
You can buy a young tree and plant it in the winter, or you can propagate it easily from hardwood cuttings or half-ripened shoots.

Harvesting
Pick leaves fresh all year round. You must dry them before you can eat them. Dry them in layers (see p. 216) in a warm shady place. Never dry them in full sun. If the leaves begin to curl, press them gently under a board. After two weeks drying put them into airtight containers, preferably glass jars, because the leaves exude oil.

Borage
Annual

Both the flowers and the leaves of borage are used in many different cool drinks, as they contain viscous juices which actually make the drinks cooler. You can sprinkle the blue flowers over salads, or use them for a tisane. The plant is very decorative.

Soil
Borage will grow on any piece of spare ground, but it likes sun, and prefers a well-drained loamy soil.

Propagation and after-care
Borage can only be propagated from seed. Sow the seed in spring, in drills one inch (2.5 cm) deep and three feet (90 cm) apart. Cover the seed well with soil. The plant will self-sow.

Harvesting
Eight weeks after sowing begin cutting the young leaves and keep cutting from then on. Pick the flowers when they appear. You may get two flowerings in one season. Dry quickly at a low temperature.

Burnet
Perennial

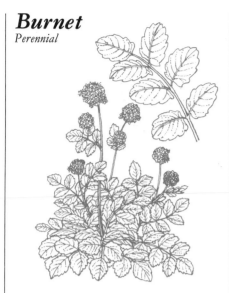

Use fresh young burnet leaves chopped up in salads or as a flavoring in sauces. Add the leaves to cream cheese, where they enhance the cool taste. Dried leaves are well worth adding to vinegar, and they can also be used to make a fragrant tea.

Soil and climate
A dry light well-limed soil suits burnet best. The plants need full sun in order to flourish. But burnet is hardy and will do well in most climates.

Propagation and after-care
Sow the seed in early spring, and later on thin the seedlings to a foot (30 cm) apart. It is a good thing to sow seed each year for a continual supply of fresh young leaves. If you want leaves specifically for drying rather than just fresh, you can propagate burnet plants by division.

Harvesting
Pick the young leaves frequently, use them fresh or dry them carefully.

Caper
Perennial

The flower buds of this herb are pickled in vinegar a few hours after being picked, and then become what we know as capers. These are used to much effect in rice dishes, salads, stuffings, and sauces for meat and sea food. Caper grows wild in warm climates where it flourishes, but it is a difficult herb to grow in temperate climates (where nasturtium may be considered an acceptable substitute).

Soil
Caper does best on poor dry soils; it needs full sun and grows well on slopes.

Propagation and after-care
In sub-tropical areas grow capers from cuttings or division, planting out the established bush into a well-drained mixture of gravel and sand. When you plant the bush, sprinkle enough water to set it, and thereafter hardly water it at all. You can grow caper successfully in rock gardens, if you simply drop the seeds with a little sand into crevices between rocks. In temperate climates try growing caper under glass, in a well-drained sandy loam, planting out the cuttings in early spring. It also makes an attractive pot plant on a sunny window-sill, but in these circumstances it is unlikely to produce enough buds for culinary use.

Harvesting
Pick off the flower buds as soon as they are fully developed. Leave them in the dark for a few hours before pickling them.

Caraway
Biennial

Caraway seeds have long been used in cakes, breads, cheeses, candies and sauces. Ground seeds can also be added to rich meats such as roast pork or to spicy stews like goulash. You can use the leaves of the plant in salads, and the roots can be cooked and served as a vegetable.

Soil and climate
Caraway is adaptable and will accept most soils, as long as they are not too wet, but it prefers a clay loam and a sheltered location. It is winter-hardy and is best suited to a cool climate.

Propagation and after-care
Sow seed as soon as it ripens on an existing plant; alternatively sow bought seed in late spring. Thin seedlings to a foot (30 cm) apart and keep them weed-free. Then leave them until the following year, when they will flower and seed. Caraway plants need protecting from wind, so that the seed heads don't shatter before the seed is ripe.

Harvesting
When the seed turns brown snip off the flowerheads, and dry the seed in an airy place (see p. 216) before threshing.

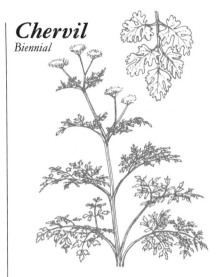

Chervil
Biennial

Chervil is a most important herb, a top priority if you are choosing to grow only a few. It is a substitute for parsley but its leaves have a far finer flavor; it is the basis of French cookery with *fines herbes,* the fundamental ingredient of a magnificent soup; it is a fine constituent of salads, one of the very best flavorings in the world for omelets, and it takes its place proudly in many a noble sauce. The habit of boiling chervil is an unfortunate one; it must be added to cooked dishes at the last moment so that its delicate flavor can emerge unimpaired.

Soil
Chervil will grow in any soil except heavy clay or wet ground. It needs some shade in summer but full daylight in winter, so ideally grow it in the partial shade of a deciduous tree.

Propagation and after-care
You should sow some seed in the spring for summer use, and then some more in high summer for cutting in winter. Many chervil-lovers sow successionally all through the summer. Chervil does not take to being transplanted, so sow it where you mean it to stay, in drills ten inches (25 cm) apart, thinning later to about eight inches (20 cm) between plants. From then on it will self-sow quite rapidly. I often cloche a summer sowing; alternatively chervil grows well indoors in containers.

Harvesting
You can eat chervil from six to eight weeks after sowing. Cut the leaves off with scissors before the plant flowers. Chervil is tricky to dry, because it needs a constant low temperature, but luckily you can get it fresh all year.

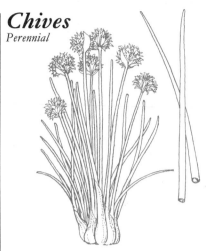

Chives
Perennial

Chives are mini-onions and like onions are members of the *Liliaceae,* but you eat the leaves of chives and not the bulbs. They are perennial, easy to grow, and you can go on snipping the grass-like tops and flavoring all sorts of food with them.

Soil
Chives will grow in most conditions, but they will do best on good soil with plenty of humus and they prefer a warm, shady position. They will grow well in containers indoors. They like a pH of 6 or 7.

Propagation and after-care
You can sow seed in the spring but you will get quicker, and better results if you plant seedlings or mature plants. You can buy clumps or get them from a neighbor. Simply divide the clumps up and plant them. The spring or summer is the best time for this. You must keep them moist so it is best to plant them near a pond or water tank, or even a fawcet. The plants die down in the winter but you can keep some going for winter use by planting them in a container indoors and putting it on the kitchen window-sill. Every three years or so dig up your chives and replant in fresh soil.

Harvesting
Chives are ready for cutting about five weeks after the seeds were sown. Just clip the "grass" off as you need it to within two inches (5 cm) of the ground. You can clip the tips of the leaves as much as you like without damaging the plants because like all the *Liliaceae,* chives are monocotyledons (see p. 18). Thus clipping the tips off has no effect whatever on the growing point down below. The more you cut them the better they will be.

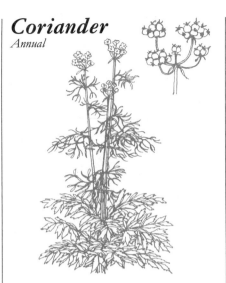

Coriander
Annual

Don't be put off by coriander's unpleasant smell, because the seed is a most important cooking ingredient. It is essential to Asian cooking: you can use the seeds crushed or whole in curries and mixtures for stuffing vegetables like zucchini, tomatoes and peppers. If you coat coriander seeds with sugar you can add them to your homemade marmalade, or your children can eat them as sweets.

Soil
Rich soil suits coriander best. It also needs a sunny, well-drained site.

Propagation and after-care
Sow the seed in late spring in drills 12 inches (30 cm) apart; later thin to six inches (15 cm). The plants will very probably reach a height of two feet (60 cm) or more.

Harvesting
When the seeds begin to turn brown, cut the plants near the ground and hang them up to dry. Thresh the seeds when they are thoroughly dried and store them in jars. Never use partially dried coriander seeds; they have a very bitter taste.

Dill
Annual

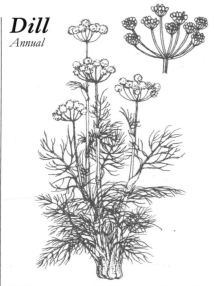

Dill seeds are mildly soporific and are much stronger than the herb derived from the leaves. They are traditionally put in with dill pickles. The slightly bitter taste of the seeds is absent from the leaves, which bring out the taste of fish or chicken.

Soil

Dill accepts almost any soil as long as it is well-drained. It must have sun but should not be allowed to dry out.

Propagation and after-care

Sow seeds in the bed in the spring, pressing them slightly into the earth. Sow successionally all through spring and summer for a continuous supply of dill leaves. Thin the plants to nine inches (23 cm) in rows a foot (30 cm) apart. As long as you keep them well watered, the plants will grow fast, producing great numbers of leaves before flowering. Very dry weather and inadequate watering will cause them to flower before the leaves are fully grown. Fennel is a bad neighbor for dill as cross-pollination can take place.

Harvesting

You can start cutting the leaves when the plant is about eight inches (20 cm) tall and keep on cutting right through to late autumn. The best time to cut for drying is just before the plant flowers. If you want to use the seeds for pickling cut them when both flowers and seeds are on the head. Seeds you want to use for flavoring or for sowing the following spring should be left on the plant rather longer, until they go brown. Dry the seed heads before threshing them. The drying temperature must not rise above blood heat.

Fennel
Perennial

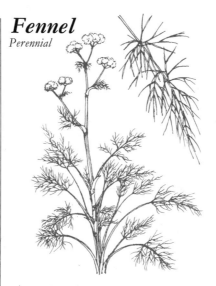

Fennel looks very like dill, but has a quite different, stronger flavor. The leaves are much used for flavoring oily fish such as mackerel or herring, and should make part of the stuffing for "a pike with a pudding in its belly". You can use them raw in salads as well. The seeds are nice to chew and can be added to liqueurs.

Soil

Fennel grows well in any garden soil provided it is not acid, too heavy or too wet. It prefers a rich chalk soil and a sunny location.

Propagation and after-care

Sow the seed in the fall for a crop the following year. Sow three seeds in a station and leave 18 inches (45 cm) between stations. If you want seeds and not leaves sow in early spring under glass. Another approach is to treat fennel as a biennial by digging up roots in the fall and storing them through the winter indoors in sand. The following spring divide the roots (see p. 95) and plant 12 inches (30 cm) apart in rows 15 inches (38 cm) apart.

Harvesting

Cut leaves through the summer; harvest the seeds when they are still green and dry them out of the sun in thin layers, moving them as they sweat. Drying fennel leaves can be done if you use great care and a low temperature; it is best to use them fresh.

Garlic
Perennial

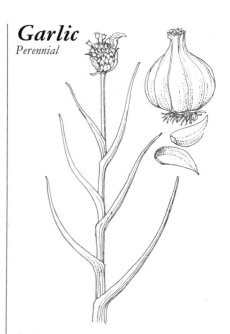

Garlic can be added to almost any dish. It can be eaten cooked or raw, and it can even be chewed by itself. So grow plenty and use it with abandon.

Soil and climate

Garlic is native to southern Europe, but it will grow in cooler temperate regions. It needs the same sort of good rich soil as onions need with plenty of manure or compost incorporated. Plant it where it will get plenty of sun.

Propagation and after-care

Buy garlic bulbs, from the supermarket if they are cheaper there than at the seed merchant. Pick off the individual cloves and plant them. You can plant them in the autumn, or in the early spring. The sharp end is the top end of the clove – plant each one in a hole deep enough to leave the top just covered with soil. Plant four inches (10 cm) apart in rows as close together as you can manage, or four inches (10 cm) in all directions in a deep bed (see p. 106). Keep the cloves weeded. They don't want too much water.

Harvesting

Fork the garlic out of the ground when the stems dry up and dry them out for a few days in the sun if possible, or under cover in some place where the rain won't reach them. Drying is essential if you want to store garlic. Tie the heads into bunches and hang them up in an airy, cool, dry place; use them as you need them, but keep some to plant the next year.

Horseradish
Perennial

The roots of horseradish make a hot tasting herb. Either grate the roots and use them as they are, moistened a little with vinegar, or make a sauce by mixing them with oil and vinegar or grated apples and cream. Horseradish goes well with roast beef, cold meats and smoked fish.

Soil and climate
Horseradish likes a deep rich soil and will grow in any climate that is not too hot. In hot climates it must be grown in shade.

Propagation and after-care
Just plant three inch (8 cm) pieces of root, about as thick as your finger. Contrary to normal practice I prefer to put them in nearly horizontal and only two inches (5 cm) below the surface. You can plant horseradish any time of the year and once you have got it you have got it for ever. The problem is how to stop it spreading across the garden. You can confine it inside slates or tiles dug deeply and vertically into the soil. Another method is to set a twelve inch (30 cm) land drain pipe into the soil on its end, fill it with loam and compost and plant a piece of root in it. The plant will grow very well, produce clean, tender roots, and be very easy to harvest. And it won't spread. If you don't confine the roots you must dig it out of the ground where it is not wanted.

Harvesting
All parts of the root are edible. Just dig them up and grate them. In cold climates you can store the roots like carrots, in a container of moist sand.

Hyssop
Perennial

Hyssop is a member of the *Labiatae* family and has a pungent and rather bitter taste. The leaves and the ends of the stalks contain the flavor and will go with a variety of dishes. Hyssop is a good plant for encouraging bees into the garden, where they do a lot of good by pollinating vegetables, especially beans.

Soil and climate
Hyssop prefers chalky soil, well-drained and containing plenty of lime. It thrives in warm weather, but will manage to withstand winter in cool temperate climates.

Propagation and after-care
You can sow seed in drills a quarter inch (0.5 cm) deep and transplant the seedlings in midsummer to the open bed when they are about six inches (15 cm) high. Plant them in rows two feet (60 cm) apart.

Harvesting
Once the plants are mature, about 18 inches (45 cm) high, cut back the tops frequently so that the leaves are always young and tender. Cut leaves and stalks for drying shortly before the plants flower.

Lovage
Perennial

All parts of lovage except for the roots can be used in cooking. The bottoms of the stems can be blanched and eaten like celery. The leaves have a strong yeasty celery-like flavor as well, which means they can be used to flavor soups and casseroles when celery is not available. The seeds taste the same as the rest of the plant but the flavor is more concentrated.

Soil
Lovage is a hardy herb and likes a rich, damp soil and a shady site.

Propagation and after-care
Plant seeds in midsummer, in drills an inch (2.5 cm) deep. Transplant the seedlings in autumn or spring to positions two feet (60 cm) apart. By the time the seedlings are four years old they will have reached their full size and should be spaced about four feet (1.2 m) apart. Lovage grows immensely tall; one large plant will be enough to keep a family adequately supplied through the year.

Harvesting
If you want the very large, aromatic leaves for flavoring, water the plants especially well. If they have enough water you will be able to take plentiful cuttings at least three times a year. If you want only leaves, don't allow plants to flower and seed. Lovage can be dried successfully in a cool oven, at a temperature of less than 200°F (94°C), with the door left a little ajar.

Marjoram (Pot)
Perennial

Pot marjoram is the only type of marjoram that is truly winter-hardy in cool temperate climates. It is a plant which tends to sprawl, throwing out long flowering stems.

Soil

Pot marjoram prefers a dry, light soil, with a modicum of sun.

Propagation and after-care

You can grow it from cuttings established under glass and planted out in the spring, or by putting in bits of root in spring or autumn. Keep it moist until it is well established. The alternative is to sow seed in spring, in drills half an inch (1 cm) deep and eight inches (20 cm) apart. Thin to 12 inches (30 cm) apart when the seedlings are big enough to handle.

Harvesting

Harvest leaves and stems in late summer. Pot marjoram dies down in winter, but it is a good idea to pot it and bring it indoors each winter. If you do this the plant will grow through the winter and may well last years longer than it would if you left it outside. Seeds for sowing next year ripen in late summer or early autumn.

Marjoram (Sweet)
Annual

Sweet marjoram is the only annual of the three marjorams; it has a delicate aromatic flavor, and goes well with game and poultry stuffings.

Soil

Sweet marjoram needs a medium rich soil, with a neutral pH; it wants a good helping of compost and a warm, sheltered spot.

Propagation and after-care

Sow seeds in pots under glass in early spring. Plant out in early summer 12 inches (30 cm) apart. A combination of warmth and humidity is vital to the good growth of the seedlings while they are still young.

Harvesting

Pick leaves and stems toward the end of summer, before the buds open. Use them fresh or dry in thin layers in the dark (see p. 216) and you will get a strong-smelling green herb.

Mint
Perennial

As well as common mint (also known as spearmint), you can grow apple mint, which combines in one plant the flavors of apple and mint; orange mint, whose leaves have a delicate orange flavor; or peppermint, used to best advantage in peppermint tea. All these mints are slightly and subtly different, but you grow them all in the same way.

Soil

Mint likes a moist soil – next to a stream is ideal. It needs sunlight to make it grow with full flavor, although it will stand partial shade.

Propagation and after-care

The best way of establishing mint is to get some roots from somebody who is being overrun by it. In the spring lay them horizontally in shallow drills three inches (8 cm) deep. Don't harvest much mint that first summer. In the autumn cut the plant right down and cover the roots with compost. If you are overrun by it, simply hoe it out.

If you want to force some mint for using in winter, dig up some roots in the autumn, plant them in a seed box in good compost, and keep them indoors or in a greenhouse under slight heat, say 60°F (16°C). Mint grows well in containers indoors.

Harvesting

Cut fresh leaves whenever you want them. If you want mint for drying, harvest it in midsummer just before it flowers, but don't cut it after a shower of rain; wet leaves will just turn black and go moldy. Peppermint leaves for tea should be dried and stored whole.

Mustard
Annual

Mustard is grown extensively by gardeners for digging in as a green manure crop, just before it flowers. It grows quickly, makes a bulky crop, and deters the potato-loving eel worm. Mustard can be grown in the herb garden for seed, however, and it is this that makes the mustard that goes in mustard pots. The seeds are ground very finely and the resulting powder kept dry until it is needed, for mixing with water or vinegar. Seeds can be used whole for pickling or for adding to casseroles. Young mustard shoots cut two or three weeks after sowing form the mustard ingredient of the traditional salading, mustard and cress.

Soil
The seed needs good rich soil, with a pH no less than 6.

Propagation and after-care
The culture of mustard for seed is very easy. Sow in early spring. Broadcasting very thinly will do, but it is better to sow thinly in rows two feet (60 cm) apart and thin to nine inches (23 cm) when the seedlings are established.

Harvesting
Pull the plants out of the ground before the pods are fully ripened, when they are a yellow brown color. Hang them up in bunches to dry, and thresh the seeds out when the pods are well dried. Grind with a pestle and mortar.

Nasturtium
Annual

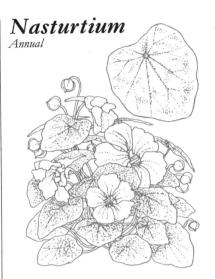

Nasturtium is a great asset in the organic garden, because it seems to keep pests away from other plants, especially peas, beans and soft fruit. People who love pepper but who find it upsets them should turn joyously to nasturtium for it is an excellent substitute. The leaves spice up salads and add taste to a bland cream cheese spread. You can use the flowers and seeds in salads, and you can pickle the seeds while they are still young and green to use them like capers.

Soil
Nasturtium is an easy-going plant and will grow anywhere, given plenty of sun and a light, sandy soil. Poor soil is best if you want a good crop of flowers; but if leaves are your priority, add plenty of compost to the soil.

Propagation and after-care
Sow the seeds *in situ* in late spring. Water them sparingly. The seedlings need little attention. Nasturtium will adjust quite admirably to being grown in containers.

Harvesting
Cut the leaves in midsummer, just before the plants flower. Chop and dry them, before shredding and storing. The flowers do not dry well and are best eaten fresh.

Oregano
Perennial

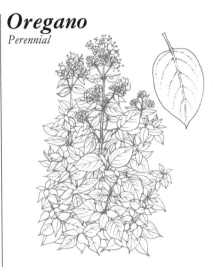

Oregano, or wild marjoram, is a favorite ingredient in Italian cooking. Known as the "pizza herb" its strong spicy flavor suits strong-tasting, oily dishes; if you use it in more delicate dishes you should use it in moderation.

Soil
Oregano prefers a chalky or gravelly soil, and a warm, dry location. Hillsides are ideal.

Propagation and after-care
Sow seed in early spring, thinning later to between eight and twelve inches (20-30 cm). The final distance between mature plants should be 20 inches (50 cm). Hoe the seedlings well. Like pot marjoram, you can grow oregano from cuttings. It is slow to grow, and needs a hot spell to bring it on really strongly.

Harvesting
Pick leaves and stems in late summer. Seeds for sowing ripen in early autumn. Use fresh or else dry in thin layers in the dark.

Parsley
Biennial

Parsley will enhance almost any dish you care to mention, from the blandest poultry to the spiciest sausage. Its great virtue is that it never overpowers the natural taste of food, just brings it out more fully. Broad-leaved, or French parsley, which is grown in the same way, is more substantial and can be used as an ingredient in salads.

Soil

Many people think that parsley is difficult to grow, but I find that as long as it is given rich enough soil, with plenty of humus, this is not the case. The earth needs to be well worked so that the roots can penetrate deeply. Parsley thrives in containers, but again the soil must be rich and well drained.

Propagation and after-care

You can grow parsley from seed, but the seed is extremely slow to germinate. (A good tip to speed germination is to put the seed between two layers of wet blotting paper in your refrigerator for about two weeks.) Sow seed in spring, and exercise patience. Put the seeds in drills half an inch (1 cm) deep; later thin to three inches (8 cm) and eventually, when the plants are mature, to eight inches (20 cm). You can sow in late summer, for winter forcing. In the winter put a cloche or two over some of your parsley patch. Parsley usually runs to seed in the second year, so you should sow it fresh every year to ensure succession.

Harvesting

Pick a few leaves at a time from each plant. If you want bunches, you can pick off whole plants close to the soil, once the stem is eight inches (20 cm) high. For drying you should pick leaves during the summer and dry them quickly. Parsley is the only herb to need a very high drying temperature — between 100 and 200°F (39-93°C). Dry it in an oven with the door open.

Rosemary
Perennial

This woody shrub originates from the dry chalky hills of southern France. It is very ornamental and can grow to more than five feet (1.5 m) so it is useful grown in rows to divide vegetable beds. It goes best with rich meats, such as lamb, mutton or pork. Its piney flavor is pleasant but pervasive, so exercise some restraint.

Soil

A light, sandy, rather dry soil suits rosemary best. It needs plenty of lime, shelter and a southerly aspect.

Propagation and after-care

Sow seeds six inches (15 cm) apart in shallow drills in spring. When the seedlings are a few inches high, transplant them to a holding-bed, leaving six inches (15 cm) between plants. When they are well established, plant out three feet (90 cm) apart. Seeds do not always germinate, so taking cuttings — before or after flowering — is more efficient. Cuttings should be six inches (15 cm) long. Remove the lower leaves and bury two thirds of their length in sandy soil in a shady position. By autumn they will be ready for planting out. Protect them during their first winter by cutting them back to half their length in late summer; this enables the new shoots to harden off before the onset of cold weather. Then mulch with leaf-mold and cover securely with burlap.

Harvesting

Pick sprigs in small quantities from the second year onward. You can do this at any time of the year, but late summer is best for drying. You can use rosemary flowers for flavoring as well as stalks and leaves. Pick the flowers just before they reach full bloom.

Sage
Perennial

Sage is strong-tasting stuff — too strong to mingle well with other herbs, but it goes well with spicy sausages, fresh garden peas or as a flavoring for cream cheese. For cooking use narrow-leaved sage, for drying, broad-leaved. A mature bush is about two feet (60 cm) high and is both a useful and an attractive plant to grow in a small garden.

Soil

Sage likes well-drained chalky soil, so lime well if the ground is at all acid. It does not like damp ground or too much water.

Propagation and after-care

Narrow-leaved sage can be grown from seed sown in late spring. Transplant seedlings 15 to 20 inches (38-50 cm) apart in early summer.

Broad-leaved sage is always grown from cuttings. Take cuttings with a heel of stem on them, plant out in spring and water well at first. Sage will last for several years but it is just as well to establish a new bush from time to time.

Harvesting

If you want leaves rich in oils it is best to wait until the second year. Cut narrow-leaved sage in early autumn. Broad-leaved sage will not flower in temperate climates; it should be cut in midsummer and again a month later to stop it going woody. The leaves are tough and take longer to dry than most herbs.

Savory (Summer)
Annual

Summer savory is an annual and tender in cold climates. It can be used fresh or dried. In spite of its strong aromatic smell it has a more delicate flavor than winter savory. You don't need to grow large quantities, as it grows fast and you only need a little at a time.

Soil and climate
Summer savory will accept poor chalky soil, but thrives on a rich humid soil as long as it has not been freshly manured or composted. It will grow in all but the coldest climates.

Propagation and after-care
Sow in late spring in rows a foot (30 cm) apart, and thin seedlings to six inches (15 cm). It is said that the seed should lie just on top of the soil to germinate, but I find it germinates quite well just below the surface where it is less likely to be eaten by birds. Work the soil well before sowing and keep it damp afterward. Summer savory will often seed itself and shoot up again in the fall.

Harvesting
You should be able to cut summer savory twice from the one sowing; once in summer and again in the autumn. Cut shoots just before the flowers open. Harvest the seeds for sowing next year when they go brown. To dry summer savory lay it on frames (see p. 216), cover with a fine-meshed net and put it in a dark cupboard with a low temperature.

Savory (Winter)
Perennial

Winter savory is more hardy than summer savory. It grows a foot (30 cm) high and is bushy, making it an ideal plant for filling the low gaps in garden hedges. Winter savory's strong flavor makes it a good accompaniment for baked fish or lamb.

Soil
Winter savory grows well on poor soil and likes well-drained chalky land. It needs plenty of sun.

Propagation and after-care
Sow seed 12 to 15 inches apart in drills in late spring. Don't cover the seeds because they need light to germinate. You can also propagate by planting out cuttings two feet (60 cm) apart in the spring.

Harvesting
You can cut shoots in the second year from early summer onward. As with most herbs, harvest before flowering so that you get the maximum content of volatile oil; this also stops the stalks going woody. Winter savory leaves become very hard when dried, so you should grow the herb indoors during the winter and pick it fresh.

Sorrel
Perennial

Sorrel has a refreshingly acid taste. It is a close relative of the dock and looks rather like it. It can go raw into salad, and is very good cooked with spinach, omelets, veal or fish. Sorrel and lettuce soup can be quite exquisite.

Soil
Sorrel likes a light, rich soil in a sheltered place, with plenty of sun, but it will grow very adequately in the shade.

Propagation and after-care
You can sow seed in spring and thin the seedlings out later to six inches (15 cm) apart. Alternatively you can propagate by dividing roots (see p. 95) in the spring or fall. When the plant flowers in early summer, cut it back before it goes to seed.

Harvesting
You can start harvesting four months after thinning, or whenever a plant has formed five strong leaves. Cut the leaves with a knife or pull them straight off the plants; cook with them in an enameled pot because an iron one will turn them black. You can dry leaves in the dark and store them in airtight jars.

Tarragon
Perennial

Tarragon is traditional with chicken, good with fish, and excellent in soups; and tarragon vinegar is an excellent salad dressing. There are in fact two varieties which are often confused: Russian tarragon and French tarragon. Russian tarragon is the tougher and the taller of the two plants; French tarragon is stronger flavored and needs to be checked in its summer growth to stop it becoming too bushy in the winter.

Soil
Tarragon does not like "wet feet" so good drainage is vital. Try to plant it on a slope so that the roots never get waterlogged. Tarragon likes being exposed to the elements, and puts up with fairly poor soil; it does not even mind stony ground.

Propagation and after-care
It is best to buy young plants or divide mature ones, planting them out to two feet (60 cm) apart, after the last hard frost. Every four years transplant cuttings so that you have plants with a full flavor. Do this in spring or autumn. You can grow tarragon in pots which you bring indoors in the winter, or cut the outdoor plants right down every autumn and cover them well with compost or other litter.

Harvesting
Pick fresh leaves all through the growing period; this will encourage new ones to grow. If you want to dry them, cut the plants down to just above the ground before they flower. You may manage to cut three times during the growing season of an established plant. Dry in the dark at a fairly low temperature.

Thyme
Perennial

This hardy perennial is native to southern Europe. Common thyme has a sharp bitter-sweet taste. Shoots, leaves and flowers can all be used – fresh or dried – in soups, stews and meat dishes of all kinds. Less hardy than common thyme, lemon thyme has a beautiful scent and taste. The leaves are delicious, chopped fine and sprinkled sparingly, on salads or meat. Otherwise lemon thyme is mainly used for flavoring. It is a good plant to grow if you have bees; it gives honey a delicious fragrance, but bees will collect the nectar only in hot weather.

Soil
Thyme likes a light, well-drained soil which has been well limed. It does best in a sunny position, and is excellent in rock gardens.

Propagation and after-care
If you grow thyme from seed, sow it in late spring in drills a quarter inch (0.5 cm) deep and two feet (60 cm) apart. It is more usual to propagate by division from an established plant, or by cuttings taken in early summer. Keep the beds well watered and weed-free. Cut back a little before the winter and in subsequent springs cut the shrubs well back to encourage new growth. Lemon thyme trails and in exposed positions should be protected during the winter with straw or leaf-mold.

Harvesting
Cut once in the first year, but from the second year onward you can cut twice. Cut early if you want to, but flowers can be used with leaves, so you can cut during the flowering period. Cut off shoots about six inches (15 cm) long, rather than stems from the base of the plant.

Tree Onions
Perennial

Tree onions are delightfully pungent, and can be used for pickling as well as in stews, or chopped up raw in salads. Also known as Egyptian onions, they differ from other onions in that the onions grow at the top of the stems. The parent bulb stays in the ground to produce another crop the next year, although if you want you can eat the underground bulbs as well as the ones that form on the flower stems.

Soil
Tree onions like a sunny and well-drained spot. They should be started off with a heavy mulch either of compost or well-rotted manure.

Propagation and after-care
Plant bulbs in the spring. Plant them in clumps, six inches (15 cm) apart in rows 18 inches (45 cm) apart. Mulch from time to time with compost. The stems may grow as tall as five feet (1.5 m), so when the little onions begin to form, use sticks to support the weight of the plants.

Harvesting
Pick the bulblets from the top of the plants as and when you need them.

CHAPTER EIGHT

Growing in the Greenhouse

*Containing advice on the choosing and
equipping of a greenhouse, and instructions
on the sowing, growing and
harvesting of greenhouse crops.*

Growing in the Greenhouse

The primary function of a greenhouse is for propagating seeds and growing a few winter vegetables. It is therefore well worth having some form of greenhouse in all but the smallest garden. For very small gardens, seeds can be propagated on a convenient window sill.

Now, there is a huge variety of greenhouses and you should think very hard about what best suits your needs and your pocket. I suggest you should start by getting hold of as many suppliers' catalogues as possible, and by having a look at the greenhouses of as many of your neighbors as you can and asking their opinions.

TYPES OF GREENHOUSE

Starting with the smallest form of greenhouse, I suggest that you consider the window-greenhouse. You can buy one of these and fix it over a convenient south-facing window. Alternatively, consider taking a window out of its frame, building a wooden platform out from the house at the base of the window, and erecting a glass casing above it so as to form a protrusion from the house. This greatly increases the size of the platform that the original window sill provides, and also pushes the seed boxes or pots right out into the light where the seedlings and plants do better. And you have the advantage that, if the room behind is heated, the window-greenhouse is heated too. A small window-greenhouse will grow enough tomatoes to keep the average family well supplied.

A lean-to greenhouse is a very common and sensible arrangement. It is best if there is a door leading from the house straight into the greenhouse, and it is even better if there is also a window connecting the two. Either door or window can be left open, in winter for warmth to get from the house to the greenhouse, and in the summer for the delicious aroma of plants to enter the house.

One advantage of a lean-to greenhouse is that you save half the cost of a free-standing greenhouse. Disadvantages are that it is often difficult to effect the join between walls and roof of the greenhouse, and the wall of the house itself. Also you often end up with too shallow a pitch in the roof of the lean-to, which can cause leaves, rubbish and water to collect. The best things about a lean-to are that it acts as a sun-trap, is nice to work or sit in, and helps considerably to warm the house in winter. You do not get as much light from the sky as you do with a free-standing greenhouse, but the increased warmth from proximity to the house more than compensates for this. A

PLASTIC GREENHOUSE
You can build this kind of greenhouse yourself, using plywood and plastic sheeting. Flexible sheeting is cheaper than rigid plastic and easier to cut up, but it must be renewed every three years or so.

LEAN-TO GREENHOUSE
A lean-to greenhouse attached to a south-facing house wall is ideal in a small garden. A door or window connecting house and greenhouse allows heat to pass both ways.

DUTCH STYLE GREENHOUSE
The sloping sides enable the greenhouse to attract more light, and the whole construction is very stable. You cannot grow very tall plants close to the walls.

CURVED-EAVES GREENHOUSE
Greenhouses with curved eaves are very popular, because the transparent fiber glass walls are erected in fewer pieces than conventional greenhouses.

free-standing greenhouse can be a very ambitious affair, as large as you have space and money for. It gets more light than a lean-to, but has much worse heat insulation. If I built one I would build an insulated wall of stone or brick to the north side and paint that black to absorb sunlight during the day, and I would build it with a steeply sloping roof.

Lean-to and free-standing greenhouses can be built in all shapes and sizes and can be made from many materials. You can buy a greenhouse ready-made from a specialist firm, you can build one yourself, or you can build a basic structure yourself and buy components — panes of glass in wooden or aluminum frames — and fit them in to it. Nowadays, it is probably cheaper as well as quicker, to buy your greenhouse ready-made. The most common shapes are described above.

Basic materials for greenhouses

As far as the framework of your greenhouse is concerned your choice is really between wood and

Use the dark area underneath the staging to grow mushrooms.

Rainwater collected in the water barrel is warmed by greenhouse air.

FREE-STANDING GREENHOUSE
Most free-standing greenhouses are all glass. They allow in maximum light, and are ideal for growing fruit trees or large plants directly in soil, on the greenhouse floor. An alternative is to have low brick or wooden walls; this cuts down heat loss drastically, but means that you must have raised staging. Many greenhouses have a low wall on the north side, and glass all the way down on the south side.

WINDOW-GREENHOUSE
These are designed to replace ordinary house windows. They are extremely efficient, because they get heat from the sun and from the house.

STAGING
If you want to grow plants in pots or seed boxes you will need staging. This is best made of wooden slats supported on frames made of or seasoned wood.

CREATING HUMIDITY
In hot weather spray the gravel path occasionally with water, to create humidity. For the same reason, rest your seed boxes on large trays full of moist gravel.

GROWING IN SOIL
Tomato and pepper plants are very suitable for growing directly in greenhouse soil, or in peat bags.

aluminum, although a third choice – plastic piping – is currently being developed and may prove cheaper than the others.

Aluminum will not rust or rot, but it is generally agreed that it reacts more strongly to hot and cold than wood and therefore cools the greenhouse in winter; my own belief is that this is not a significant factor. Aluminum looks ugly, is hard to work yourself and is fairly expensive. If you decide on aluminum you have really got to buy your greenhouse ready-built.

Wooden greenhouses must be made from a decay-resistant wood like cedar, redwood, or cypress. It is pointless using soft wood or any wood that requires constant painting to stop it from rotting. Wood has a tiny disadvantage in that it obscures more light than aluminum, but it looks nicer and you can work it yourself. And a cedar greenhouse should last as long as you will.

The choice of transparent sheeting for greenhouses lies between glass, and three kinds of plastic: fiber reinforced, which is a transparent form of fiber glass; PVC or acrylic modified plastic, which is a fairly stiff plastic; and polyethylene which is flimsy.

Glass lets in a lot of light, looks good, lasts a very long time, is seldom broken by wind and can easily be mended, but it costs a lot and requires a strong framework to carry its weight.

Fiber reinforced plastic comes in large sheets; it is easy to fit and does not need extensive framing. It also takes some of the heat out of a hot sun, which is a very good thing. However, it does not admit as much light as glass and this is a serious disadvantage in winter. It is also inflammable, and will only last twenty years.

PVC and acrylic modified plastic are cheaper and transmit light well, but they will last only five years and can be ripped by a gale.

Polyethylene is very cheap – about a tenth the cost of glass – and transmits light very efficiently. But it will only last one or two years, and is very easily ripped by gales.

Transparent plastics are becoming very popular all over the country, and as long as plastics remain cheap, relative to glass, they are well worth using. Glass is, of course, better in the long term, but it represents a substantial capital investment nowadays.

Heated or unheated?

The other great decision to make about your greenhouse is whether to heat it or not. My own feeling is that for the person genuinely gardening for self-sufficiency a heated greenhouse is a luxury that defeats its own object. It is very easy to put more calories of energy into a heated greenhouse than you get out as food produced. A heated greenhouse is fine for the specialist who wants to grow flowers out of season, or the commercial grower who wishes to supply a luxury winter market, but for the person who is genuinely trying to be self supporting at low expense, it is not really worthwhile unless he can provide himself with cheap energy such as water or wind power, or has a good source of wood for burning.

There are useful crops that can be grown in an unheated greenhouse all the year round anyway, and there are excellent ways of storing summer crops so they don't have to be forced in the winter. In the summer time, even in quite a cold climate, you can use an unheated greenhouse to grow, or start growing, most of the crops that grow their whole lives outdoors in warmer more humid climates – tomatoes, cucumbers, melons, peppers, eggplants and so on. And in winter your unheated greenhouse will enable you to grow lettuces, radishes, spinach and a few other cold climate crops. Surely it is better to eat canned tomatoes and eggplants in the winter than to try forcing such things unnaturally and at great expense. A little heat occasionally, when the temperature is very low in the winter, just to prevent the cold climate crops you are growing at the time from dying, is quite justifiable, but this is a very different matter from running a heated greenhouse all through the year.

Interior fittings

Inside your greenhouse you will need some staging. You can, of course, grow plants in the soil on the floor of the greenhouse and not have staging at all; for the big plants like tomatoes and cucumbers, and for all fruit trees, this is the best way. But, for your seed boxes, and for the other vegetables which you will grow in pots, you need staging. Using benches in tiers is undoubtedly the best way to get the greatest possible number of crops into your greenhouse.

Your benches should be between two and a half and three feet (75-90 cm) wide: not wider than three feet because that makes them awkward to work on. In a greenhouse ten feet (3 m) wide two rows of benches – one on each side – are enough; against the north wall have a three-tiered bench, on the south a single tier so that it does not obstruct too much light. If the greenhouse is much wider than ten feet (3 m), you can consider having another bench down the middle; this should be a double tier. If your greenhouse is as narrow as seven feet (2 m), have just one bench of three tiers against the north wall. If you take it that your path or paths should be 20 inches (50 cm) wide, you can easily work out the best arrangement for a given width of greenhouse.

To support your benches consider using old galvanized water or gas pipes. These are strong, easily cleaned, and very permanent. Plate glass is best for the actual benches, if you can afford it. It is easily cleaned, lets light down below, and does not allow water to drip. If you use wooden slats for the benches you should place glass, plastic or slate underneath the lowest tier to stop water dripping on the plants below.

If you use wood for anything in a greenhouse be careful about using creosote. The fumes can kill plants. Old creosote is probably safe.

Paths should be gravel, crushed rock, or concrete. I prefer the two former. If you sprinkle gravel or crushed rock with water and rake it occasionally, it creates a cool moist atmosphere in hot weather.

If you have dark spaces under your benches you can grow mushrooms there. They provide a great deal of good protein in a very little space and don't mind the dark.

Greenhouse soil

Ideally, the soil of a permanent greenhouse should be "artificial". That is, it should not be the original soil of the site but a soil made up and brought in from outside. A good mixture is as follows: one part sphagnum-moss peat; one part coarse sharp sand; two parts good garden topsoil. If you mix a bucketful of vermiculite or perlite to a wheelbarrow of this mixture so much the better. Vermiculite and perlite are fragmented rock products that keep the soil open and loose; they have no nutrient value in themselves.

Many growers pasteurize all their soil before bringing it into the greenhouse and then pasteurize it every year. If you grow the same crop year after year in the same soil you have to do this in order to avoid a build-up of disease. I prefer to dig out the soil my tomatoes have grown in, put it outside and bring in fresh soil.

Soil for seed boxes

You really should pasteurize – and I mean pasteurize, rather than sterilize, because sterilization kills all life in the soil and this is not the organic gardener's aim – all soil for seed boxes, unless you buy professionally-made seed compost which is in fact a very sensible thing to do; you use so little that the expense is minimal. A three cubic foot (0.08 cu m) bag will fill 18 seed boxes, 20 by 14 inches (50 x 35 cm) to a depth of one and a half inches (4 cm).

If you do want to pasteurize your own soil, put it in an oven pan, cover with tinfoil, and bring it to 180°F (83°C) – no more than that or you will kill useful bacteria as well as harmful ones. Alternatively, you can drench the soil in boiling water and then let it drain quickly, or you can cook the soil in a pressure cooker for twenty minutes at five pounds (2.3 kg) pressure.

Before filling seed boxes soak the seed compost in water: one gallon (3.8 l) of water to five pounds (2.7 kg) of compost. Leave it for a day before putting it in the boxes or pots. If you are short of seed compost, put two inches (5 cm) of sand and peat mixed in the bottom of each container and then add just half an inch (1.5 cm) of seed compost on top.

It is best to cover your benches with something which will absorb water – cinders are ideal – before you put seed boxes or pots on them. This keeps the plants from drying out and cinders discourage slugs and snails.

Greenhouse temperature

Even in a heated greenhouse the temperature should vary between night and day. In a general greenhouse, with many different things in it, 65°F (19°C) by day and about 45°F (7°C) at night is ideal. If the temperature outdoors does not go much below 25°F (−5°C) you may be able to maintain these temperatures without any artificial heat, especially if you have a lean-to or a free-standing greenhouse with a black-painted north wall. If you can keep the air stirring in the greenhouse, with an electric fan for example, this will help a lot. Heat rises, so the hot air tends to go up into the ridge, and its heat is lost. Stirring the air forces the heat down again and in this way the temperature remains even. It would be worth experimenting with a very small windmill fitted

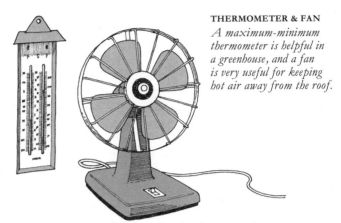

THERMOMETER & FAN
A maximum-minimum thermometer is helpful in a greenhouse, and a fan is very useful for keeping hot air away from the roof.

with a direct drive to a fan in the greenhouse.

A good way to keep heat in is to double-glaze. This can be done temporarily for the winter, by attaching plastic sheeting to the inside of the greenhouse. You can also keep the temperature up in winter by keeping the wind off your greenhouse. A screen of evergreens planted on the side

DOUBLE-GLAZING
The surest means of keeping your greenhouse temperature up in winter is to double-glaze. It is cheap as long as you use plastic sheeting and attach it with pins to the inside of the greenhouse. You will want to remove it when the weather warms up anyway.

which faces the prevailing wind can be very effective protection for a free-standing greenhouse.

If you need some artificial heat in winter an electric heater with a thermostat is ideal, but it is expensive to run. The alternative is a special greenhouse kerosene heater. These give off fewer fumes than household kerosene heaters, and fumes are bad for plants. The disadvantage of these is

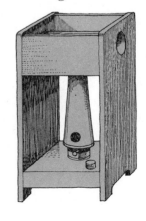

ELECTRIC & KEROSENE HEATERS
Electric heaters can be controlled thermostatically, but they are expensive to run. Kerosene is cheap, but the burner must be adjusted regularly.

that you must constantly check the temperature in your greenhouse and turn the heater on and off, because the greenhouse must not get too hot.

Keeping cool in summer may be as hard as keeping warm in winter. Plain honest whitewash on the glass panes is a very useful device. It

WHITEWASHING GLASS
Whitewash painted on to a glass greenhouse keeps out the sun's hottest rays in summer. You can whitewash the whole greenhouse, or just the side which receives most sun; how much whitewashing you do will depend on what you are growing and the climate in your part of the world.

GREENHOUSE BLINDS
Bamboo blinds are a convenient and attractive means of keeping greenhouses cool. Roll them down whenever the temperature threatens to get too high.

washes off naturally when the fall rains come on and you don't need it any more. (Don't use whitewash on plastic. You may have to wash it off artificially, and this may scratch the surface.) Screens of bamboo or other sticks, or screens of plastic can be used either inside or outside the greenhouse, but they are expensive and don't last long. A good idea, especially in sunny climates, is to plant a screen of deciduous trees between the greenhouse and the sun. The leaves shade the house in the summer and die away in winter when you don't want shade.

TREES FOR SHADING
Deciduous trees planted on the sunny side of your greenhouse will keep it cool in summer. The leaves will fall in autumn, when the greenhouse needs sun again. Don't plant the trees too close to the greenhouse, because their roots will take nourishment from the greenhouse soil.

Ventilation

Ventilation is very important. Never let the air become "dead" as greenhouse growers call it, meaning stagnant; you must keep it "buoyant". This is difficult, given that you have to maintain a temperature as well, but constant attention to opening and shutting ventilators achieves a lot. Thermostats are fairly cheap and can be fitted to ridge ventilators.

WATERING GREENHOUSE PLANTS

Watering plants in the greenhouse is difficult and requires great judgment. To water too much is counter-productive; at worst it kills plants. But to leave plants until they droop from drought is obviously disastrous as well. Watering little-and-often is bad policy. Plants need a good soaking every now and then, and dry periods in between.

You can check whether a plant needs watering by sticking a skewer into the soil. If it comes out clean and dry, the plant needs watering. If particles of earth cling to the skewer, the plant is all right as it is. Tapping the sides of a clay flowerpot is another indication. If it rings hollow, water. If it doesn't don't.

Don't, as a rule, water foliage in your greenhouse. Put the water on the soil only. Water in the morning — never in the evening; plants don't want to go to bed sodden and cold. Don't use freezing cold water; if you can manage it, 70°F (21°C) is best for most greenhouse plants. It is an excellent idea to have a water barrel in a greenhouse; the water then reaches the temperature of the air.

GREENHOUSE CROPS

If I had a criticism of the divine plan it would be that tomatoes flourish in very different temperature and humidity conditions from cucumbers, and these two crops are far and away the most valuable things that a gardener can grow under glass. There are three things you can do: set yourself up with two greenhouses; divide your greenhouse up with a partition; use your greenhouse to grow cucumbers, eggplants, melons and other vegetables which like humidity, and grow tomatoes under mini-greenhouses (see p. 111) out of doors. (You have no problem, of course, if you are blessed with a climate in which it is possible to grow tomatoes reliably without any protection at all.)

If you divide your greenhouse up, I would suggest that you partition off a small area of the greenhouse where you will grow a few very early tomatoes in the winter and cucumbers in the summer. The main part of your greenhouse will then be for that most important of all crops, tomatoes, in the summer. In winter it will be devoted to lettuces. The information about growing individual crops, which follows, is intended to supplement the information provided in the Cultivation of Vegetables and the Cultivation of Fruit sections (pp. 113-190).

Tomatoes

Soil treatment Prepare the greenhouse soil by forking in at least half a wheelbarrow load of well-rotted compost per square yard. Some wood ashes, fish manure, or other high potash fertilizer are worth adding if you have them.

Propagation Sow seed in the last week of January. Sow it in the greenhouse if you have some heat, otherwise sow it indoors. Plant seeds carefully in a seed box in a good proprietary seed compost. It pays to buy this from a reputable merchant as you need such a tiny amount and the subsequent crop is so important to your family economy. However, you can make your own (see p. 92). If you have no propagator (see p. 92), keep the seed box at about 70°F (21°C) by day and 65°F (19°C) by night, by covering the tray with glass and putting newspaper over the glass. It is important to wipe the underside of the glass every day to prevent water dripping on to the seedlings below.

PLANTING TOMATO SEEDLINGS
Tap the pot gently all round. Scissor the plant between your fingers and upend the pot into your hand. Pull the pot away leaving the root ball intact. Plant gently and water straightaway.

After eight or ten days – as soon as the little seed leaves are fully out – prick out into three inch (8 cm) peat or clay pots. After about three weeks when the plants in the pots are well grown, plant them out in the bed, leaving 15 inches (40 cm) between plants. Give each plant a stick or string to climb up. In the case of peat pots, just plant the pots; with flowerpots tap the plants gently out of the pots, keeping the ball of soil as intact as you can and plant carefully. Water the plant at once.

You can, of course, grow the tomatoes in pots, or other containers, without even planting them in a bed. In this case, you should use good growing compost in ten inch (25 cm) pots.

Care while growing Keep the temperature in the greenhouse between 65 and 73°F (19-23°C) by day and don't let it drop below 50°F (10°C) at night. In some states you should be able to achieve this without any artificial heat. For early winter-sown tomatoes, you may need some form of heating. Keep the greenhouse well ventilated; tomatoes don't want a stale and humid atmosphere. Water very well – on the soil not the plant – whenever the leaves begin to wilt, but don't water too much. A good soak about once a week is perfectly adequate.

Pinch out side-shoots. When the fruit begins to ripen remove some leaves to let the sun get in if this seems necessary, but don't keep hacking the leaves out for they are what make the plants grow. Don't overfeed tomatoes. Once every two or three weeks, it's a good idea to give them a bucket of compost or manure soup, or comfrey tea (see p. 103).

A very good method of growing tomatoes in greenhouses is in peat bags (see p. 138). These are plastic bags which you fill with peat or specially prepared compost. Apart from the fact that you get far more from them than you pay out for the bags, the peat or compost ultimately adds to the fertility of your garden. Ring culture (see p. 138) also works well in a greenhouse.

Harvesting Pick tomatoes as they come ripe. You should be picking from midsummer until well into the beginning of the fall. In early fall pick the remaining green tomatoes and put them in a drawer to ripen.

Cucumbers

Soil treatment The bed of the greenhouse should be dug well and plenty of compost or manure – strawy manure is best – should be incorporated. For each plant make a mound of compost mixed with loam and sand. Mounds should be about six inches (15 cm) deep and a foot (30 cm) wide. Allow two feet (60 cm) between mounds.

Propagation Sow the seed from midwinter onward in small peat pots or flowerpots – one seed to each pot. Use a proprietary seed compost or its equivalent (see p. 92). Stand the pots where the temperature will never go below 70°F (21°C). If your greenhouse is unheated, keep them in your house. If they are in flowerpots, it is a good thing after two weeks to pot them on into bigger, say six inch (15 cm) pots, using a good growing compost. Don't jam the compost around them too hard, soak well after repotting, but thereafter water only when the soil inside is dry.

When the plants are six inches (15 cm) high, plant them carefully in the middle of the prepared mounds in the greenhouse. The temperature when you do this must be at least 70°F (21°C).

Arrangements must be made for the vines to climb, so give each plant a vertical wire or push in a substantial cane. Take these up the sides of the greenhouse to the roof, and put in horizontal wires at 18 inch (45 cm) intervals. Now the temperature must never fall below 70°F (21°C) and it is best if it rises to about 90°F (32°C) in the day. When the plants are young they need hardly any ventilation. If you do open the ventilators a little during the morning, close them early in the afternoon. This is why cucumbers don't co-exist happily with tomatoes which need much drier air.

Care while growing By about midsummer you may have to whitewash the glass above the cucumbers so that they don't receive much direct sun. At this time of year you need high humidity but you must not keep the roots constantly wet. A good watering twice a week is enough. But syringe the plants with warmish water once a day, and keep the floor and walls of the greenhouse moist.

PICKING OUT MALE FLOWERS
You must pick out the male flowers of greenhouse cucumbers. They are the ones that grow on stalks and not on tiny cucumbers like the female flower in the foreground.

As the plants grow you must train them. Tie the vines loosely to the wires or canes. Stop the main stem by pinching out the growing point when it gets to the roof or when it is six feet (1.8 m) high. Nip out all male flowers (the ones that grow on little stems and not on the mini-cucumbers) so that they will not pollinate the fruiting females and produce bitter fruit with large pips. Nip out any female flower that grows on the main stem. Stop all laterals (branches from the main stem) at two joints and each sub-lateral (branches from a lateral) at one joint.

A good dose of compost, manure, or comfrey tea from time to time will be all to the good.

Harvesting Cut your cucumbers when they reach an appropriate size, and eat them as soon as you possibly can. Never leave them to grow old and shrivelled on the vine.

Melons

Soil treatment Melons will grow very happily in any greenhouse, or part of a greenhouse, where cucumbers are growing. They need the same temperature and humidity conditions as greenhouse cucumbers, and the soil should be treated in the same way. It is well worth preparing mounds for melons, as you would for greenhouse cucumbers.

Propagation Propagate melons as you would cucumbers, by sowing one seed to a flowerpot or peat pot in midwinter, and make sure that the temperature does not drop below 70°F (21°C). Plant the seedlings out when they are six inches (15 cm) high. You will need to give them vertical and horizontal wires or canes to climb up.

Care while growing Protect your melons from direct sun in the middle of the summer. Water them fully about twice a week, but don't water round the stem of the plant at soil level, because

WATERING MELONS
You must not wet the stems of melons because they are liable to rot. Sink a porous flowerpot into the soil six inches (15 cm) from the stem, and water into that.

this is likely to cause collar rot — a disease which rots the base of the stem. Instead, sink a flowerpot into the ground six inches (15 cm) away from the plant and water into that, taking care not to splash the stem of the plant. Give the whole plant a light syringeing with water once a day.

As your melons climb, attach the plants loosely to the wires or canes. Large melons may need to be supported in nets or cloths. Fix these to the sides of the greenhouse or to your supports.

Harvesting Melons are ripe when the skin around their stems begins to crack and they come away easily from the vine. Pick them when they are ripe and eat them as soon as you can.

Eggplants

Soil treatment Eggplants like rich soil, so dig in plenty of compost.

Propagation Eggplants are best grown in summer, unless you have a heated greenhouse. Sow seeds in peat pots, because eggplants do not like being transplanted. The seeds need plenty of heat: 75 to 85°F (24 to 30°C). If the temperature falls below 70°F (21°C), they very likely won't germinate. Keep them, therefore, in the part of the greenhouse where you grow your cucumbers. When the seedlings are four inches (10 cm) high, transplant them into their permanent bed.

Care while growing Keep your eggplants well watered, preferably with manure water (see p. 103).

Harvesting Cut eggplants as soon as the skins are shiny and deep purple. The plants will then produce more.

Peppers

Soil treatment Dig well and incorporate compost.

Propagation If you have an unheated greenhouse, you must grow peppers in the summer if you live in a cool climate. In a warm climate they will thrive in an unheated greenhouse even in winter.

It is best to start the seed off in a propagator or in a seed box with a pane of glass over it. The temperature should be about 80°F (27°C). When the seedlings are two inches (5 cm) high, transplant them into peat pots. When the plants are four inches (10 cm) high plant the pots in their permanent positions. This should be in the part of the greenhouse set aside for cucumbers, because peppers need plenty of warmth and moisture.

Care while growing Keep well watered; be sure to water the roots and not the peppers. Water on the peppers will cause them to rot.

Harvesting When they reach the right size, cut them from the vine leaving a stalk an inch (2.5 cm) long on each pepper.

Okra

Soil treatment Dig deeply and work in plenty of compost. Manure is not good for okra; it causes the plant to put its energy into making leaves rather than fruit.

Propagation Unless you have a heated greenhouse, sow your okra seed in early summer. Okra seed is stubborn, so soak it in water for twenty-four hours to get it started, and then sow it in peat pots in a propagator (see p. 97). If you don't use a propagator, still use peat pots, because okra seedlings prefer not to be transplanted. Plant out when the plants are two inches (5 cm) tall.

Care while growing Like cucumbers, okra plants thrive on heat and moisture; hot dry air is bad for them and can cause the buds to drop off. Give them a good watering twice a week, and syringe them with water daily.

Harvesting Pick the pods when they are young – about two inches (5 cm) long. The plants will then go on bearing.

Lettuces

Soil treatment Rake a good measure of compost into your soil or, if you grow lettuces in containers, make sure the soil contains peat or compost.

Propagation Sow the seed in a seed box in late summer if you want lettuces for eating in winter. Keep the seed box moist, at about 60°F (16°C), and covered with glass and newspaper. Remove the newspaper when the seedlings first appear. When they are half an inch (2 cm) high prick them out, using extra seed boxes, to give them more room. Remove the glass and keep them at about 55°F (13°C).

Water occasionally, but take care not to over-water. When the lettuces are three inches (8 cm) high plant them out into the greenhouse bed or into suitable containers. This final planting out should occur in mid-autumn when you will still be eating your outdoor lettuces.

If you want early spring lettuces sow some seed in mid-autumn for planting out in midwinter. You may well find yourself planting next year's tomato crop among these spring lettuces. This does not matter: you will clear away the lettuce long before the tomatoes need the room.

Care while growing Keep the lettuces watered, but do not wet the plants – only the soil. If you let the soil dry right out the poor lettuces will flop on the ground and will very likely suffer from gray mold (see p. 157). The ideal temperature for the winter lettuce house is 65°F (19°C) by day and 55°F (13°C) by night. They are, after all, a cool climate plant, and will survive out of doors all winter in a temperate climate if they are protected with cloches.

Harvesting Pick lettuces young or old, when you want them, but remember that, if they are left too long, they will bolt.

Radishes

Radishes are easy to grow in an unheated greenhouse. Simply broadcast the seed in the greenhouse soil and rake it in, or sow it in seed boxes. They can be harvested within a month and present no problem at all.

Peaches

Soil treatment Before planting, incorporate plenty of humus into the soil, but avoid an excess of nitrogenous material because this encourages unnecessary growth. Keep the soil moist but not sodden — spraying it on sunny days will maintain humidity. When the fruits are ripening, apply liquid manure.

Propagation Plant the tree in potting compost in a ten gallon (38 l) tub; keep it in the greenhouse until all danger of frost is past and then put it out for the summer, in a sunny but very sheltered place. Alternatively, if you have a fairly large greenhouse, you can grow a fan-trained peach tree: train it along wires parallel to the wall and eight inches (20 cm) away from it.

Care while growing Hand-pollinate the flowers on the tree with a small brush. Later, when the fruits are about half their final size, thin them so that there are nine inches (25 cm) between fruits. You must prune fan-trained trees by cutting back old fruiting shoots after the fruit has been harvested to a point where a new shoot is emerging. You then train the new shoot along the wire. In early summer prune off unwanted wood.

Harvesting Pick the peaches as and when they are ripe; this is when they turn yellow and give very slightly under pressure.

Oranges, lemons and mandarins

Soil treatment Citrus trees need well-drained soil which should be a mixture of sand, compost, loam and peat — ideally in roughly equal proportions.

Propagation It is best to buy orange or lemon saplings from a nursery rather than try to grow your own from seed. Mandarins are especially good indoors, because they are small. Plant the trees just as you would outdoors (see p. 98) directly in greenhouse soil.

Care while growing Keep indoor citrus pruned small. Hose the foliage down on hot days. If you grow them in tubs put them outdoors in the summer, but don't ever leave them out in a frost. In winter allow the temperature of the house to go down to 45°F (7°C).

One important point: you will have to fertilize the flowers of indoor citrus trees. You can easily see which are the male organs, the stamens, because they have pollen on them. Take some off with a small paint brush and put it on the female stigma which sticks out beyond the petals.

Harvesting Ripe fruit can be left on the tree for weeks, even months. Just pick it when you want it and don't worry about storing it.

Figs

Soil treatment It is best to grow figs in tubs which can be moved outside in summer. Fill the tubs with earth which contains plenty of compost, and mix in a little lime. Be sure the tubs have drainage holes.

Propagation *Ficus carica* is the ideal variety for growing indoors in a tub, and the best thing is to buy a young one from a nursery. But, of course, like all figs, they can be propagated from cuttings (see p. 185). Plant them in their tubs as you would any other tree (see p. 98).

Care while growing Water enough to keep the soil damp, but not saturated, and spray the leaves from time to time. Move the tubs outside at the beginning of summer, and bring them in when the leaves have fallen or when the first mild frost comes in the fall, whichever occurs first.

Harvesting Eat figs fresh as soon as they are ripe. Otherwise dry them (see p. 216).

Grapes

Soil treatment The soil for grape vines must be well drained. Dig it deeply and apply rock phosphate and potash. Add lime if the pH is below 7.

Propagation Buy year old vines from a nursery or propagate from cuttings as you would if you were growing vines outdoors (see p. 188). Greenhouse vines can be planted inside or outside the greenhouse. If your greenhouse is heated it is best to plant the vines in the soil on the floor of the greenhouse. However, if you want to train vines inside an unheated greenhouse, it is a good idea to plant them in a well-prepared bed just outside the greenhouse, and train them through openings in the greenhouse wall. If you have more than one vine, plant them 10 feet (3 m) apart—indoors or outdoors.

Care while growing Vines should be trained up the south-facing wall of a greenhouse. Let each vine fan out to form six strong vertical branches, and tie these permanently in place against the wall.

Now, pretend these verticals are the ground and do your Guyot method pruning (see p. 190) using pairs of strong laterals that spring from them. In this way you will be able to cover your wall with fruiting spurs.

Harvesting Cut bunches with shears when the stems of the bunches begin to turn brown.

Strawberries

Strawberries are very easy to grow in the greenhouse. Treat them exactly as you would outside. You can plant them in good rich compost either on the ground, on a bench, or in pots.

CHAPTER NINE

Preserving Garden Produce

*Containing instructions on the salting,
drying, pickling, bottling and freezing of
crops, and on the making of jams,
jellies, chutneys, wines and cider.*

Preserving Garden Produce

Your aim as a self-sufficient gardener is to provide yourself and your family with a rich, varied, and high quality diet throughout the year. This means that you must store a lot of your produce, and much of it will not store for long unless it is processed, or "preserved", in some way.

Grains, root vegetables and potatoes are easy to store. Green vegetables are more difficult. However, if you live in a warm or temperate climate, or even in a colder than temperate climate you do not need to store them. I eat fresh green vegetables picked straight from the garden all year round. I have no desire to eat frozen peas in the winter or frozen Brussels sprouts in the summer, when, with much less trouble, I can eat them both fresh in their seasons. However, although I prefer to eat as much fresh food as I can, I still have to store and preserve a good deal.

Of course, in very cold climates, where snow covers the ground for months at a time, or where frost penetrates deep into the earth, you cannot go out into the garden and pick fresh vegetables in midwinter. Therefore all your winter food must come from your stores. And, even in warm climates, there is a strong case for storing certain crops. Tomatoes are a good example. There is no fresh equivalent of tomatoes at times of the year when you cannot pick them fresh. Nothing takes their place, and your cookery will be severely restricted if you do not have them in some form.

Food rotting agents

There are four main causes of food going bad:
Enzymes These are natural chemicals within most plants. Over a period of time they can cause changes which will spoil food. They cannot function in freezing conditions and are destroyed by temperatures above 140°F (60°C).
Molds Molds can actually be seen – the white fluff on jellies or jams, the grayish dust on the rind of bacon and so on. Some molds are not harmful, but many are, and in any case all molds – except those of blue cheeses – are best avoided, because they can weaken the food's resistance to more harmful organisms, especially bacteria. Molds won't spread at any temperature below freezing point, or above 120°F (50°C). They begin to die above 140°F (60°C). To be sure of killing them, you must heat food to 185°F (85°C).
Yeasts These function at about the same temperatures as molds. They cause fermentation which turns sugars into alcohol. This has its uses in the making of wine, beer and sauerkraut, but you don't want it to happen all the time.

Bacteria Some bacteria are your worst enemy although others actually assist in preserving processes. Harmful bacteria not only rot food, making it unpalatable, but some of them can even kill you. Bacteria vary as to the temperature that is needed to kill them. Two of the worst – the *Staphylococci* and, the most dangerous of all, *Clostridium botulinum*, which causes the deadly botulism – need 240°F (115°C) to kill them, their spores, and the poisons they leave. 240°F cannot be achieved by boiling water, which will only go to 212°F (100°C). So boiling – except for a very prolonged period, or in a pressure cooker – is not sufficient to rid food of these bacteria.

However, bacteria are not active in acid food. All food that tends toward acidity – a pH of less than 4.5 – is safe for canning without the use of a pressure cooker. These foods comprise all the fruits, including tomatoes, and rhubarb. Other vegetables must be pressure cooked for safety. This is extremely important.

Methods of preserving

There are six main ways of preserving food:
Salting Salt draws some of the moisture out of vegetables, thereby inhibiting the activity of the rotting agents. It also keeps bacteria away, for the simple reason that they do not like salt.
Drying This process removes the moisture which is necessary to the functioning of the various spoilage organisms. Vegetables should be dried so that they contain no more than ten percent water; fruits can contain up to 20 percent.
Pickling and chutneying With these methods you increase the acidity of whatever you are preserving by adding vinegar. Thus you do not need the prolonged boiling, or the superheating in a pressure cooker, or the very careful hermetic sealing, that you need with plain bottling.
Canning This method works because all the living organisms and enzymes in the food are first destroyed by heat. Then the sterilized food is put into clean containers, which are sealed to stop the entry of any new organisms. The containers are then heated again to make quite sure of killing any organisms that might have got in by mistake.
Jam and jelly-making You make use of both heat and sugar to preserve fruits which have a fairly high acid content.
Freezing This works simply because spoilage organisms cannot operate at low temperatures. They are not necessarily killed, but they are prevented from multiplying and are unable to spread their beastly poisons.

SALTING

The art of salting is of great relevance to the gardener. Pole beans in particular are best preserved in this way: salted beans taste far nicer than frozen ones and in fact are almost indistinguishable from fresh beans. And salting them means that they are not taking up unnecessary room in the freezer. Salted pole beans are a great winter standby: a big crock or two, or a barrel, will give you good green food all winter, whatever happens to the garden outside; so it is well worth growing more than you can eat fresh and salting the remainder.

SALTING POLE BEANS

1 *Take tender young beans and shred them. Put a layer of salt into a container, and then a layer of beans on top of that. Add more salt.*

2 *Using a wooden pestle or a bottle, ram the beans down carefully but firmly. Continue to add salt and beans in alternate layers.*

Beans

Only salt tender young beans, never old stringy ones. Put some dry salt in the bottom of a clean crock or barrel. If you can get "dairy" salt or block salt this is best, but you can make do with ordinary household salt. Absolute cleanliness is essential. Put a layer of shredded beans in the container – it is useless to put them in unshredded – and ram them down gently but firmly with a wooden pestle or a bottle. Add more salt and more beans in alternate layers, as the bean-picking days go on, until the barrel is full. Then cover it with an airtight lid and leave it in a cool place until winter. A pickle will form which will drown the beans. Do not drain off the pickle, because it acts as the preserving agent, but every now and then skim off any scum that forms. When winter comes, pull out a handful of beans when you want them, rinse them well in cold water for five minutes, soak them for no more than two hours, boil them and eat them. I suggest you use a pound (500 g) of salt to three pounds (1.4 kg) of beans, but if you just use common sense you should not go far wrong.

Other vegetables

You can salt other vegetables as well as pole beans – any vegetable in fact that is crisp and hard. Salting changes other vegetables more than it does beans, but they are still good to eat. The change occurs because of the formation of lactic acid, which is what turns milk sour. The lactic acid, created by bacterial action, is beneficial because it inhibits growth of harmful organisms, but it affects the taste of most vegetables slightly.

Take clean, fresh, undamaged vegetables. Wash them carefully, put them down in a crock and cover with a ten percent brine solution. The brine is made of salt dissolved in water, which you boil as you stir in the salt. You then allow the brine to cool, keeping it covered. Generally speaking your brine is strong enough if a potato will float on the surface. (Incidentally, this same brine can be used for preserving all kinds of meat.)

From time to time add more vegetables, more brine, and every now and then add more dry salt on top. This last is important, because the water in the vegetables will dilute your brine and you must keep its strength up. Cover the crock with a plate weighted down with a stone (never with metal) and keep it at ordinary room temperature for three weeks. Skim the surface of scum if necessary. Then move the crock to a cold larder and pour half an inch (1 cm) of vegetable oil on top to seal the brine. Cover it again. When you want to use the vegetables pull them out and rinse them for half an hour to get the salt out.

Sauerkraut

Sauerkraut is a fine substitute for clamping the cabbages that you harvest in late autumn. You

MAKING SAUERKRAUT

1 *Shred white cabbage hearts very finely, before packing them into a barrel or crock in a series of layers.*

2 *Sprinkle salt between the layers. Cover the crock with a cabbage leaf and a cloth, before weighing the lid down.*

shred white cabbage hearts pretty finely, and pack them tightly into a barrel or crock, sprinkling dry salt between the layers of cabbage, at the rate of half an ounce (14 g) of salt to a pound (500 g) of cabbage. Cover the top of the crock with a big cabbage leaf and put a cloth over it. Then cover with a lid, weighted down with a stone. Store the barrel in a warmish place – about 70°F (21°C) is fine. Skim off scum from time to time. After two or three weeks transfer the barrel to the coolest place you have got (but not to a deep freeze), and keep it until you want it. Rinse the sauerkraut under a faucet before eating it. At all stages the salt must cover the sauerkraut. If it doesn't, add more salt. Additions of dill, ground celery seed or ground caraway seed all help the flavor.

Dill pickles

The dill pickle is a great American institution. Pack a large number of cucumbers, along with a few onions, green peppers, cauliflower florets, green tomatoes, carrots and chopped parsnips into a crock with plenty of dill, and cover them with brine as described above. When you come to wash the salt out, the sharp taste of the dill remains.

DRYING

Drying is one of the simplest methods of storing vegetables, fruit and herbs. Nothing is added: instead just water is taken away. You could dry almost all your garden produce, but the process works best with all the herbs, many of the fruit and just a few vegetables. If you live in a warm climate, consider drying as a method of storage very seriously. Your produce will dry much more readily in a warm climate than in a cool one.

Fruit

Almost any fruit can be dried successfully, but apples, apricots, peaches, grapes, currants, plums and figs dry most easily. To dry fruit, start by slicing it up. If you are using large fruit like apples, slice them into thin slices; smaller fruit, like peaches and apricots, should be halved; plums and anything smaller are best left intact. Fruit that is being dried whole benefits from being blanched before it is dried. To do this either steam the fruit or plunge it into boiling water for a minute, and then put it into cold water to cool. Dry your fruit using one of the drying devices described below.

To preserve color, commercial driers burn sulfur under fruit. You can achieve this by dissolving two grams of ascorbic acid in two and a half pints (1 l) of water and dipping the fruit into it.

BLANCHING PEPPERS

1 Before drying whole peppers blanch them by soaking them in boiling water for a minute.

2 Cool the peppers by soaking them in cold water. Drain immediately.

Vegetables and herbs

All herbs, but only some vegetables – peas and beans, peppers, asparagus and sweet corn – are easily dried. If you are going on a long Antarctic voyage, it might be sensible to dry all sorts of other vegetables too, like cabbages and squashes. Blanch and dry vegetables just as you would fruit. Herbs do not need to be blanched; dry them in any of the devices opposite.

Sweet corn Sweet corn, especially off the cob, is an excellent thing to dry. It stores well in a small

DRYING SWEET CORN
Blanch the cobs in boiling water for ten minutes. Impale the cob on a nail sticking up at an angle from a piece of wood. Slice the kernels off the cob with a sharp knife. Dry in a slow oven and store in jars. To reconstitute the sweet corn, pour boiling water over it; then leave it until it has absorbed as much water as possible.

space and can be reconstituted easily. Begin by blanching the cobs in boiling water for ten minutes. If you just want to dry the kernels, impale the cob on a nail sticking up at an angle from a piece of wood. Then slice the corn off with a knife. Dry the kernels in a slow oven, and put them in jars. If you want to dry corn on the cob, strip off the husk and dry in a slow oven. When the cobs are dry you can either store them as they are, or you can get the corn off the cob by grabbing with both hands and twisting in opposite directions.

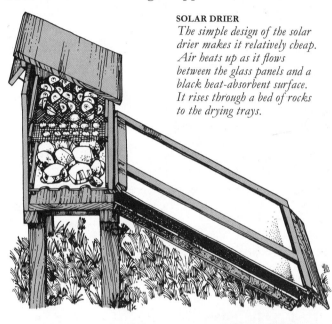

SOLAR DRIER
The simple design of the solar drier makes it relatively cheap. Air heats up as it flows between the glass panels and a black heat-absorbent surface. It rises through a bed of rocks to the drying trays.

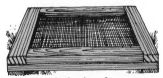

Wire mesh drying frame

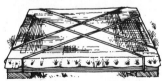

Cheesecloth drying frame

Cheesecloth protection for fruit

DRYING FRAMES
Frames can be made from wood and cheesecloth or wire mesh. Cover wire mesh with brown paper to protect the food.

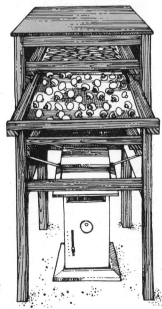

DRYING CABINET
A series of trays and a kerosene heater make up this cabinet.

Drying devices

Trays Any kind of tray that is perforated to let the air circulate can be used to dry fruit and vegetables. Put them either outdoors or in a warm place indoors.

Cabinets A drying cabinet can be simply a home-made structure which has slots to hold trays. An electric or kerosene heater can be placed underneath, if required. Alternatively, you can buy a drying cabinet, either metal or wood, which has an electric heater built in.

Ovens As long as you take great care, you can use your kitchen oven to dry most vegetables, fruit and herbs. As a rule use a low heat, especially for herbs. You may find it best to leave the oven door open. Use solid metal trays, instead of metal racks, to be sure that nothing catches fire.

Solar driers These are catching on more and more, because they are an easy and effective way of using solar heat. Air is admitted through an adjustable flap and crosses over a blackened surface underneath glass panels heating up as it goes. The hot air rises through a bed of rocks and then through a series of perforated trays, which hold the produce to be dried. The rock bed heats up slowly through the day, and retains some heat throughout the night, which prevents condensation forming on the glass.

DRYING IN BUNCHES
Dry herbs in bunches upside down, so that the volatile oils flow into the leaves.

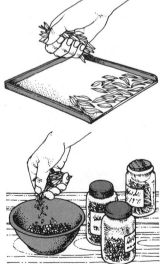

DRYING ON TRAYS
Alternatively, you can dry herbs on trays in your oven. Shred the leaves before storing them in jars.

Hanging bunches You can dry herbs, apple slices and mushrooms by stringing them and hanging them up. A temperature between 70 and 80°F (21-27°C), and a strong draft are ideal for herbs.

Reconstituting dried food

To reconstitute dried food, pour boiling water over it. Allow the food to absorb as much moisture as it can. Many fruits cannot be reconstituted: currants and raisins are a case in point.

MAKING PICKLES AND CHUTNEYS

Pickles and chutneys are both means of preserving produce and enhancing its flavor at the same time. Both processes involve flavoring fruit and vegetables with spices and then storing them in vinegar. To pickle something you store it in cold, spiced vinegar, whereas to chutney something you cook it in vinegar until its consistency becomes thick and syrupy.

If you buy – rather than make – your vinegar, remember that there is a wide range of strengths and flavors. Distilled, or fortified vinegar is the very strongest; of the natural vinegars wine vinegar is the strongest, and this also has a purer flavor than either cider or malt vinegar. These factors are worth bearing in mind: you will pay according to the quality of your vinegar. You may find it economical to use cider vinegar in chutney – where the liquid is all boiled away – whereas in pickles you may well want to use a purer vinegar, since the flavor of the vinegar is more likely to affect the taste of the pickle.

Pickles

I believe in spicing the vinegar I use for pickling. You can add any spices you like, although I recommend that you use whole ones for an attractive end-product; ground spices will turn the vinegar cloudy. The very best way of making spiced vinegar is to steep all the spices in cold vinegar for two months; it will then be ready to use. For a quicker method study the pictures below.

MAKING SPICED VINEGAR

1 *Take a stick of cinnamon, some cloves, peppercorns, mustard seed, mace, allspice, garlic and, if you like them, a chili or two.*

2 *Tie the spices in a muslin bag, and pour two pints of vinegar over them. Bring to the boil, and boil for a few minutes at most.*

You can pickle virtually any vegetable or fruit, and you can use them whole or sliced up. Even okra, eggplants and Jerusalem artichokes make good pickles. The principle of pickling is the same whatever the vegetable or fruit: draw out some of the excess water from moist vegetables by soaking them in brine or coating them with dry salt, and then put them in vinegar. Crisp vegetables can be put straight into the vinegar. Cold vinegar is usually perfectly adequate, but boiling your vinegar and sterilizing your jars is safer if you want to keep the pickle for a long time. As for spices and herbs – every person to his own recipe. Let imagination and experimentation reign supreme.

Remember when you store away your jars of pickles, seal them tightly to prevent evaporation. Six months is probably the longest they will keep and still retain all their flavor. Take care that the vinegar is not in contact with the metal lid.

Pickled onions Soak small pickling onions in a brine of salt and water, using four ounces (114 g) of salt for two and a half pints (1 l) of water. Leave them overnight and then skin them. Put them in fresh brine for three days; submerge them using a plate and a stone. Then drain them, pack them in jars and fill the jars with cold spiced vinegar. Add a little sugar for a mellower flavor, and store for two months before eating.

Pickled green tomatoes Slice the tomatoes and mix them with a few sliced onions. Sprinkle thickly with salt, and let the mixture stand overnight. Then rinse it well in water. Put it into hot sterilized jars and pour boiling spiced vinegar over it. You can pickle peppers in exactly the same way.

Pickled gherkins or small cucumbers Use a gallon (3.7 l) of spiced vinegar to one and a half gallons (5.5 l) of cucumbers. The latter should have been salted (see p. 215), removed from the brine and desalted ready for pickling by being soaked in cold water for 12 hours. Boil the vinegar and then add the cucumbers. Boil for two minutes, and then leave them covered for three weeks. If you don't want to eat them immediately drain the vinegar off and pack the cucumbers in sterilized jars. Pour fresh boiling vinegar over them, seal the jars and immerse in boiling water for ten minutes. Treated in this way pickled gherkins should last indefinitely. To make a sweeter pickle mix honey or sugar with the last lot of vinegar.

Chutneys

Most fruits and vegetables can be turned into chutney but the best are tomatoes (green or red), eggplants, peppers, apples, squashes, pumpkins, rutabagas, plums, pears, oranges, grapefruit, lemons and any other citrus.

Preserving Garden Produce

MAKING TOMATO CHUTNEY

1 Take two pounds (900 g) of tomatoes, two onions, a cooking apple, some raisins, garlic, brown sugar, salt, spice and two ounces (300 ml) of vinegar.

2 Skin and peel the onions, peel and core the apple. Then chop them up finely together.

3 Simmer the onion in a small pan with a little water. Add the apple and raisins, and cook gently until they soften.

4 Skin the tomatoes (see p. 221), and then chop them up roughly into large chunks.

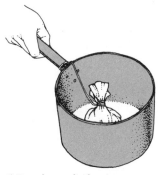

5 Crush the garlic and ginger with some salt in a pestle and mortar. Tie up a mixture of spices – say, some chilies, bay leaves and cloves – in a little muslin bag.

6 Put the muslin bag in a saucepan and tie it to the handle so as not to lose it in the chutney.

7 Pour in all the ingredients and cook on a low heat for an hour, until the mixture thickens so that you can see the bottom of the pan when you draw a spoon through.

8 Pour the mixture into hot clean jars. Seal the jars to make them airtight, label and store them.

All good chutneys are heavily spiced. You can use any herb or spice that you like or can get hold of. The following are commonly used: garlic, bay leaves, cayenne, chili, paprika, cumin, horseradish, coriander, mustard seed, cinnamon, peppercorns, cloves, ginger and allspice. Salt and sugar also play an important part; most chutneys go dark as they cook, but if you want a really dark one use brown sugar or even black molasses.

Never use copper, brass or iron pans for boiling your chutneys. Unchipped enamel, stainless steel, or, at a pinch, aluminum will do. You can make chutneys in earthenware crocks placed in the oven; I personally find this method is the best. If you are mixing hard produce like apples or onions with soft things like tomatoes or squashes, simmer the hard ingredients first in water until they are soft. Soak any dried fruit you use. Put whole herbs and spices into a muslin bag, which I suggest you tie to the handle of the pan; otherwise

powder them first and then put them straight into the mixture. Before adding garlic or fresh ginger crush them with a mortar and pestle.

Put all the ingredients into the container. Just cover them with vinegar, and boil very slowly until there is no free liquid left. Be very careful not to let the chutney burn on the bottom of the pan. Stir frequently during the final stage of boiling. Pack into sterilized jars, cover and put them away. Make sure that the jars are tightly sealed; I recommend using twist-on metal caps from old jam or pickle jars. Then cover the lids with a cloth that has been dipped in melted wax.

CANNING

The principle of canning is very simple. You heat food in sterilized jars, close these hermetically, and then heat them again so as to kill any stray living organism that may have got in. Finally the jars are allowed to cool. Provided that there was no living

219

thing inside the jar when it was sealed, and provided that the heating process was sufficient to kill all bacteria, mold and viruses, there is no reason why the food should ever rot. Food canned 75 years ago has been opened and found edible.

Canning most fruit – including plums and some soft fruit – is entirely satisfactory, completely safe and well worth doing. Tomatoes, which are technically a fruit and not a vegetable, are easy to can and the results taste delicious. Tomatoes alone make canning a worthwhile process. However, I have reservations about the canning of vegetables, as opposed to fruit. Heating by boiling is not sufficient to sterilize them, so you need to use a pressure cooker, which affects the taste. And remember that vegetables can be stored easily and safely in many other ways.

COLD WATER BATH

1 *Put the fruit into jars, along with a weak syrup of sugar and water.*

2 *Put the jars into a container with water. Place on the stove and heat very slowly (see chart). Use a thermometer to measure the temperature.*

SLOW OVEN METHOD
Can the fruit without liquid. Cover with a loose lid and put into a low oven. Fill with boiling syrup after taking them out.

HOT WATER BATH
Pack your jars with fruit and pour in boiling syrup. Put lids on loosely and lower into warm water; boil and simmer.

Jars for canning

There are many kinds of proprietary jars with tops that can be hermetically sealed, made especially for canning food. Most people use the very expensive but extremely good "Mason" jars. These are easy to use and certainly very safe. The jars can be re-used and so can the metal bands, but the lids with the rubber rings must be used once only and then be discarded. It is worth considering ordinary screw-topped jam jars too. Some jams and jellies are also sold in suitable screw-top jars. Tops which have rubber rings stuck to the inside of the lid are best and will keep food for several years. Never let metal lids come into contact with the contents of your jars. Buy jars of a size you or your family can empty in a day, or at the most two days, because once you have opened a jar you must eat the contents before the bugs have time to get to work on it.

Heating jars You can heat the jars in any large pot filled with water on a stove. Unless your pot has a false bottom, lay a towel, piece of wood, or piece of tin inside it – anything to put the jars on to stop them touching the bottom. Otherwise they may crack.

Canning methods

There are three well-tried methods of canning fruit (including tomatoes).

Cold water bath method Put the fruit into jars. If you are canning tomatoes, fill the jars with brine. If you are canning other fruit fill with a weak solution of sugar and water. Put the jars into a container of water on a stove; raise the temperature very slowly so that it takes an hour to reach 130°F (54°C), and then another half hour to reach the temperature given in the chart below. Use a thermometer to measure the temperature.

Slow oven method Put the fruit into jars, without adding any liquid. Cover each jar with a loose lid or saucer and put the jars into a low oven – about 250°F (121°C). Leave them in the oven for the time given in the chart on the facing page. Take them out and top up each jar with fruit from one of the jars (if there is any fruit left in that jar when all the other jars have been topped up, eat it for supper). Fill the jars with boiling brine (for tomatoes) or syrup (for fruit), screw on the tops and leave them to cool. Do not delay for more than a few minutes between taking the jars out of the oven and filling them with boiling liquor.

Hot water bath method This method is for people who have neither oven nor thermometer. Again use brine for tomatoes and other vegetables, and syrup – sugar and water – for fruit. Pack your jars with fruit and pour in boiling syrup or boiling brine – the jars must be hot first or they may crack. Put the lids on loosely – if

Preserving Garden Produce

SKINNING TOMATOES

1 *Remove the stalks from your tomatoes, and use a knife to score the skins.*

2 *Put the tomatoes into a bowl and pour boiling water over them. Leave for a few minutes until the skins have loosened.*

3 *Drain the tomatoes; cover them with cold water, but don't leave them for very long or they will go soggy.*

4 *Using a sharp knife, peel off the skins carefully, so that the tomatoes keep their shape and don't lose any juices.*

CANNING TOMATOES

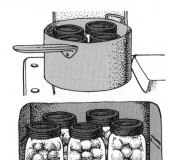

1 *Pack skinned tomatoes tightly into jars, using a wooden spoon to push large ones into position.*

2 *Pour brine into the jars beforehand if you are sterilizing in water, afterward if you are using the oven. Fit airtight lids.*

3 *Put the jars into a pan of water or stand them on newspaper in the oven. Heat slowly in both cases (see chart, below).*

4 *When the jars are cool, check that they are vacuum-sealed by lifting them up by the lids alone.*

TIMES AND TEMPERATURES FOR CANNING

	Cold water bath		Hot water bath		Slow oven	
Basic method	Take 90 minutes to bring water from cold to required temperature. Then follow instructions given below.		Start at 100°F (39°C) taking 25-30 minutes to reach required temperature of 190°F (88°C). Follow instructions.		Preheat to 250°F (121°C). Leave jars according to times given below.	
Liquid in jars	Put cold syrup or water in before processing.		Put hot liquid at 140°F (60°C) in before processing. For tomatoes, liquid is optional.		Add boiling liquid at end of processing.	
	Temperature	Time	Temperature	Time	Temperature	Time
Soft fruit Including apple slices.	165°F (74°C)	10 mins	190°F (88°C)	2 mins	250°F (121°C)	45-55 mins
Stone fruit and citrus fruit	180°F (83°C)	15 mins	190°F (88°C)	10 mins	Heat oven to 300°F (149°C) and put hot syrup in before processing them.	40-50 mins
Tomatoes	190°F (88°C)	30 mins	190°F (88°C)	40 mins	250°F (121°C)	80-100 mins
Purées and tight packs	Allow 5-10 mins longer than times shown above and raise temperature a little.					

they are tight the jars may explode — and lower them into warm water with the lids just above the surface. Bring to the boil and simmer for the length of time shown in the table below.

Skinning tomatoes

It is best to skin tomatoes before canning them. Do this by scalding them in boiling water and then plunging them into cold water. Score half round each tomato first and the skins will then come off easily.

Tomato juice

If you have plenty of tomatoes, a good way to store them is in the form of tomato juice. Cut tomatoes in halves and put them into a saucepan. Put the pan on a very moderate heat until juice begins to flow. Keep pressing down with a pestle, and, as the juice flows, move the pan to a hotter source of heat and boil for half an hour. Then strain the juice through a fine sieve or colander, and return it to the stove. Add salt and pepper to taste (I like a crushed chili as well), and boil for another half hour. Then pour the juice into hot sterilized jars and seal at once. The end result is infinitely better than the bought tomato juice which is packed with chemical preservative.

Canning rhubarb

Although rhubarb is not of course a fruit, it can be canned like one. Treat it as advised for "soft fruit" in the table on page 221. It is very good with elderberry juice added to it; this imparts a certain subtlety to the taste.

Opening jars

If you have trouble opening a jar, invert it in boiling water for half a minute and then unscrew. Jabbing a hole in the top renders the jar useless for further service, and the cost of special jars for canning is very high.

MAKING JAMS AND JELLIES

The secret substance that makes jam and jelly-making possible is pectin. This is released when the fruit is first cooked, and is what causes the jam or jelly to set.

There is plenty of pectin in apples, black-currants, red currants and gooseberries; there is less in plums (including greengages), apricots, peaches and raspberries; and there is hardly any in blackberries, strawberries, cherries, pears and rhubarb. When you make jam with fruit from the last category, you will need to add some pectin.

To add lemon juice is one answer and it does sharpen the flavor; a more common method is to combine high pectin fruits, like apples, with low pectin fruits like blackberries. The third alternative is to go about making a form of fairly concentrated pectin yourself.

MAKING PECTIN

1 *Peel and core some apples and cut them up into chunks. Put them into a pan and simmer them gently until they are thoroughly softened.*

2 *Strain them through a jelly bag and pour the juice that comes through into sterilized hot jars. This is pectin.*

Pectin To make pectin, cut up apples and boil them until they are really soft; strain them through a jelly bag, pour the juice that comes through into sterilized hot jars, and cover the jars. For jam or jelly of any sort, use this pectin in the proportion of a pound (450 g) of fruit, 12 ounces (300 g) of sugar and ten ounces (300 ml) of the pectin or apple juice. The jam or jelly will then set whatever fruit is used.

Jams

Jam-making simply involves cooking fruit with sugar. After you have softened the fruit by slow cooking so that the pectin is released, you add sugar and boil the fruit rapidly. Weigh the fruit first, so that you know how much sugar to add. Boil the fruit until setting point is reached. The setting point is critical. You can be sure when it has been reached by doing a simple test. After the mixture has boiled merrily for a while, take a little out in a wooden spoon and put it on a cold plate. If it is at setting point, a skin will form over the jam that will crinkle if you push it with your finger. The jam is now ready. If a skin does not form, allow the mixture to boil some more and try again.

Strawberry jam Take ten pounds (4.5 kg) of strawberries, eight pounds (3.5 kg) of sugar, and the juice of four lemons. Put the fruit and the lemon juice in the preserving pan and heat slowly, stirring gently. Add the sugar and boil until

TESTING FOR SET

1 Boil the fruit for some time in a large container on the stove, until setting point has been reached. You can tell when this is by doing a simple test.

2 Put a little of the mixture into a wooden spoon and place it on a cold plate. If the jam has reached setting point, a skin will form over it; it will crinkle when you push it with your finger.

setting point is reached. Then immediately take the pot off the fire, skim off the scum, stir the jam once, and pour it into hot sterilized jars. Cover the jars and store them.

Rhubarb jam This is much better than it sounds, particularly if you mix ginger with it. Take two pounds (900 g) of rhubarb, two pounds (900 g) of sugar, two lemons, and one ounce (28 g) of bruised ginger. Cut the rhubarb up small, put it in a bowl with sugar and lemon juice, stir it well and allow the juices to be drawn out. Then pour it into a saucepan, together with the ginger tied up in a muslin bag; boil until setting point is reached, and store the jam in sterilized jars.

Gooseberry jam Use slightly under-ripe gooseberries and boil them alone in a little water until they are soft; then add an equal weight of sugar and boil until setting point is reached.

Jellies

Jellies are made in the same way as jams, except that they are passed through muslin or a fine strainer, so that the solids are left behind. It is necessary to boil hard fruit for quite a long time to make jelly; soft fruit like raspberries or strawberries do not need quite so long. Use plenty of water for hard fruit and just enough to prevent burning for soft. Begin by boiling slowly to release the pectin. Add lemon juice if you are using low pectin fruit. Next comes the part that makes it jelly: you strain the juice out of the fruit through a muslin jelly bag or a fine-meshed strainer. It is the juice which makes the jelly.

With gooseberries, currants, blackberries and raspberries, you can often get two extractions of jelly-juice. After the first straining put the pulp

back in the saucepan with just enough water to make it a sloppy mess, boil it and strain it again. In this way you will get more jelly. Your chickens will enjoy the residual pulp.

Now you have your fruit juice. Measure its volume and weigh out a pound (450 g) of sugar for every 20 ounces (600 ml) of juice. Bring the juice to the boil, tip in the sugar and stir the mixture. Boil until setting point is reached, exactly as for jam. Then skim the brew, pour the hot jelly into hot sterilized jars, and cover.

Blackcurrant jelly Add ten ounces (300 ml) of water to every pound (450 g) of blackcurrants. Boil and strain the fruit, then add a pound (450 g) of sugar to every 20 ounces (600 ml) of juice. Boil the mixture until setting point is reached.

Blackberry jelly Add the juice of a lemon to every pound (450 g) of blackberries, and follow the recipe for blackcurrant jelly.

MAKING WINE

Making and consuming wine are two of the great joys of the self-sufficient way of life. And they are also extremely efficient methods of storing and ingesting goodness. I strongly urge you to try wine-making if you haven't already, for wine can be made from almost any vegetable or fruit that you have in surplus. However, there is no denying that grapes make the very best wine, and that certain vegetables and fruit — parsnips and rhubarb in particular — make a much more wholesome brew than others that I won't bother to mention.

Wine is made with sugar, in the form of fructose which comes from fruit, or sucrose which comes from sugar cane or sugar beet. This sugar is turned by yeast into carbon dioxide and alcohol. The carbon dioxide either escapes into the air or is trapped in the bottle where it gives the fizz to champagne and other sparkling wines.

Really ripe grapes will make wine by themselves without the addition of extra sugar or yeast. In fact pure grape juice, with nothing added to it at all, will of its own accord turn into wine. There is enough suitable yeast in the bloom and fructose in the flesh of ripe grapes. The yeast simply turns the sugar into alcohol.

But most of our "garden", or "country", wines are made from vegetables or fruits which do not contain sufficient sugar or suitable yeast. Thus sugar and yeast must be added.

Country wine

Many country wines are nothing more than cane or beet sugar dissolved in water, flavored with

MAKING PARSNIP WINE

1 To make five gallons (18 l) of wine, you need 20 pounds (9 kg) of parsnips. Scrub them well, but do not peel them.

2 Chop the parsnips into cubes about two inches (5 cm) across, and put them into five gallons (18 l) of boiling water.

3 Boil the parsnips until a fork will penetrate them easily. Use a jug to scoop out ten ounces (300 ml) of boiling liquor. Keep this to one side. Later you will add yeast to it, and it will be your "starter".

4 While the bulk of the liquor is still warm, strain it into another vessel through muslin or a fine strainer.

5 Stir in 12 pounds (5.5 kg) of sugar and two teaspoonfuls of lemon juice or citric acid.

6 Stir two tablespoons of sugar into your ten ounce jug. Cool this mixture to blood heat by standing the jug in cold water. Add yeast and cover with a cloth.

7 When the bulk of your liquor has cooled to blood heat, add the starter which should be frothing well. Stir the mixture and cover it with a cloth.

8 The next day move the vessel to a warm place and skim off the scum. Syphon the liquor into narrow necked containers through a plastic tube.

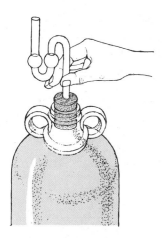

9 Seal the containers with fermentation locks, or cotton balls. When the bubbles cease to rise, rack the liquor into bottles leaving the sediment behind.

CORKING WINE BOTTLES

1 Cork wine bottles as soon as you have filled them. Put your corks in boiling water and take them out as you need them.

2 You can drive a cork in with a wooden mallet, but it is easier to use a corking tool. Open it up and fit a cork.

3 Rest the loaded tool on the neck of a bottle. Push down firmly on the lever to drive the cork right in.

the fruit or vegetable in question, and fermented with yeast. But the best country wines, and in my view the only ones that are worthwhile, are those in which the garden produce itself makes the wine, apart from the addition of a relatively small amount of sugar to assist the sugar contained in the vegetables or fruit. The good country wines, in order, as I see it, of quality and usefulness, are the following: parsnip, rhubarb, blackcurrant, raspberry, blackberry, strawberry, gooseberry, apple, pear, cherry, plum, and carrot.

Once you have learned to make one fruit wine you can make the lot, and once you have learned to make one root wine you can make all of them too. It is all common sense once you have learned the principles. To explain the principles I have written detailed directions for making two country wines: parsnip and blackcurrant. As long as you adjust the amounts of water, you can substitute another root vegetable for parsnips, or another fruit for blackcurrants.

Parsnip wine Of root wines parsnip is by far the best. Why it should be that this rather earthy root should make such fine wine I cannot say: I just know that it does. You need: 20 pounds (9 kg) of parsnips; 12 pounds (5.5 kg) of white sugar, five gallons (18 l) of water; two teaspoons of citric acid or lemon juice; some yeast, ideally white wine yeast.

Scrub, but do not peel, the parsnips. Slice them into cubes two inches (5 cm) across, and boil them in the water until a fork will penetrate easily. If you boil them for too long, you will end up with a mush that will never clear. Strain off the liquor while it is still warm and stir the sugar into it. Pour in the lemon juice or citric acid. Wait until the mixture cools to blood heat and then add your yeast to it.

The best way to add the yeast is as follows. While the liquor is still boiling, scoop out ten ounces (300 ml), stir two tablespoons of sugar into it, and cool it quickly by standing the jug in cold water. As soon as it reaches blood heat add the yeast and cover with a cloth. By the time the bulk of your liquor is cool, your "starter", as this lesser amount is called, will be frothing merrily and can be added to the bulk. Stir it in with a wooden spoon, cover the container with a clean cloth, and leave. The reason for using this starter method is that it gets the yeast working more quickly in the bulk of the wine and there is less chance of alien organisms getting a hold.

The following day, after the first rapid fermentation is over, put the vessel in a warmish place –

room temperature. Skim off the scum, pour the wine into narrow necked containers. This is most easily done by syphoning through a rubber tube. Close the containers either with fermentation locks or pieces of cotton wool. This is to allow the carbon dioxide gas to escape, but to stop harmful organisms from getting in. When all fermentation has ceased "rack" the wine, which means pour it gently into bottles without disturbing the sediment. Cork the bottles and store.

If you want sparkling wine, put a teaspoonful of sugar and a couple of raisins into each bottle before corking. A secondary fermentation will then start in the bottles and form more gas to make the wine sparkle.

Blackcurrant wine This is the best of the fruit wines, except of course grape wine. You need: twelve pounds (5.5 kg) of blackcurrants; ten pounds (4.5 kg) of sugar; five gallons (18 l) of water; and yeast.

Crush the currants; don't bother to top and tail them and, if some have short stalks attached, leave them on as well. Boil the water and pour it on, cover well and leave to soak. Stir once or twice daily. After three days strain into another bowl, and add the sugar and the yeast. Pour the mixture into fermentation jars and leave it in a warm place until the fermentation has stopped. Then move them to a cool cellar or store room for three weeks, rack into another container, and store this in the cold for six months. Then rack into bottles and leave to mature for a year – if you can.

Grape wine

Red wine 12 pounds (5.5 kg) of grapes should yield a gallon (3.7 l) of wine. Crush the fruit – an easy way is to pass it through an old-fashioned mangle set on its side – but don't crush the pips. Put this, which is called the "must", in a big tub and rake most of the stalks and pips out – a few don't matter.

Unless your grapes are really ripe, in which case the sugar content will be sufficiently high, measure the specific gravity (S.G.) at this point. It is best to measure it with a hydrometer. If the S.G. is less than 1.075, which is called 75°, add sugar to bring it up to at least 1.075, or even more – 1.100 is sensible. To raise the S.G. by 5° you have to add three ounces (85 g) of sugar to a gallon of must.

Raise the temperature to 65°F (19°C) by taking a bucket or two out, heating the contents, and returning it to the bulk. It is a good idea at this stage to add a yeast starter. Stir the whole mass occasionally and constantly break the "cap" of skins and floating debris on the surface and submerge it. Do this several times a day. Keep the vat covered with a blanket or sheet at all times when you are not actually working on it. When the S.G. has dropped to 1.010 draw the wine off from the bottom of the vat. If you want some really fine wine, leaving the rest inferior, keep this wine separate from that which you get from subsequent pressings. Next press the "marc" as the mass of grape tissue left in the vat is called. Wrap it in muslin and press it in a press. If you don't have a press, you can improvise with a car jack. Get every drop of juice you can out of it.

Now put all the wine into a cask or casks for the second stage of fermentation, and make sure that from now on the wine is protected by a fermentation lock; otherwise it will turn to vinegar. Here is a difficulty — you have to keep topping up all vessels so as to keep them absolutely full. Air spells danger. You may find it best to keep some wine in small containers and top up the big ones when necessary.

When the S.G. has fallen to 1.000 (that of water) you can replace the fermentation lock with a solid bung. You will still have to top up at intervals. After a few weeks rack the wine off its "lees" or sediment and bung it up again. Still top it up occasionally. After three months rack the wine again. You can now store it as long as you like — six months or a year — before you rack it into bottles.

White wine Follow the instructions for red wine, but press the grapes as quickly as possible and skim off the grape skins as soon as you can. Do not allow the must to ferment with the grape skins in it. Black grapes make white wine, just as white ones do: it is fermenting with the skins which gives the color to red wine.

Hygiene

Only with perfect hygiene can you make fine wine. To sterilize your vessels, wash them to remove any solid matter, scald with boiling water or heat in a hot oven, and turn upside down to drain and store. Wooden casks are especially difficult to keep clean. Steam them thoroughly by inverting them and allowing a pipe from the spout of a kettle to blow steam upward through the open bung. The condensed water will run out of the bung. Then fill them with a solution of half a pound (225 g) of washing soda in 24 gallons (90 l) of boiling water and let them stand for 24 hours. Empty them and rinse them out thoroughly in cold water.

MAKING CIDER

If you crush apples, put the juice into a vessel and leave the vessel covered against unwanted organisms, the juice will eventually turn into cider. But the cider will be terribly sharp, "rough" enough to make your hair stand on end and only a hardened drinker will be able to tolerate it. To make cider that will be more palatable to your neighbors, you will need to add sugar. If they are impatient and you want to speed up the fermentation process, you will need to add yeast. Wine yeast works faster than wild yeasts.

It is not always possible to estimate how much cider you will get from a given number of apples because apples vary considerably in their juice content. But as a rough guide you should get a gallon (4.5 l) of cider from 10 to 12 lbs (4.5-5.5 kg) of apples. The best cider is made from a combination of very sweet and very sour apples. This means that the mixture is rich in sugar and acid. If crab apples are added, the mixture will also be rich in tannin, and this improves it.

Don't hurry to pick your apples. Wait until they are really ripe — ideally, pick them ripe and then leave them to soften in heaps for two or three days. You can add windfalls and bruised or damaged apples to your heap as well — they don't seem to affect the quality of the cider at all. Then crush them. For this, a cider mill is ideal, but it is an expensive item to buy. Alternatively you can use any hard object, such as a mallet, as long as it is not metal. Crushing by hand is very arduous, however; you might try using an old-fashioned horizontal mangle, which I have seen prove just as effective. When the apples have been reduced to pulp, put the juice into a fermenting vat — a wooden barrel or an earthenware crock will do — and wrap the pulp in coarse cloth to form "cheeses". Then pile the "cheeses" on top of each other in a press, press two or three times to extract the juice, and pour the juice into your fermenting vat. Add a culture of yeast if you wish.

If you want a sweet cider, rack the fermenting cider off its lees (syphon it off without disturbing the sediment), and for every 12 gallons (45 l) add approximately six pounds (2.7 kg) of sugar. Allow the cider to ferment another week, then rack it again.

If you don't have the space or the means — or the apples — to make cider on this scale, there is a simpler method of making it on a small scale. Cut up your soft ripe apples very small, pulp them if you can, put the pulp in a crock and cover it with boiling water. Leave the crock covered for ten days, then strain off the liquid, add 12 ounces

(400 g) of sugar to each gallon (3.7 l), bottle and fit airlocks or cotton swabs to the bottles. Cork after two weeks. The cider will improve with keeping.

If you want a sparkling cider, start by bottling a small quantity. Half-fill a screw-topped flagon, screw it up and leave it in a warm place. Six hours later open the flagon. If the cider has thrown a heavy deposit and if the flagon is filled with gas, the cider is not ready for bottling. Wait until there is no heavy sediment and the cider just gives off a little fizz of gas.

You can make an apple wine from crab apples that is sharper and sweeter than cider. Add about eight pounds (3.6 kg) of sliced crab apples to a gallon (3.7 l) of water, cover and leave to soak for a week. Then strain and add two and a half pounds (1.2 kg) of sugar to every gallon (3.7 l) of liquor. Leave to ferment for three days, skim off the scum, and rack into another vessel. After about two weeks, when the fermentation has ceased, rack into bottles and cork.

MAKING MEAD

To make mead you need two and a half pounds (1.2 kg) of honey to a gallon (4.5 l) of water. If you cannot spare this much pure honey, you can make up part of the required amount with comb cappings, bits of broken comb and other honey oddments. Melt the honey in the water – don't boil it – and ferment. But as honey is deficient in acid and tannin – both necessary for proper fermentation – you will need to add these. The juice of three or four lemons will provide the acid; half a pound (225 g) of crushed crab apples will supply the tannin. You could add tea – I have heard of this but never tasted the result.

When the honey has dissolved, add your yeast starter. Leave it to ferment, then rack and bottle. But be prepared to wait a long time for your mead to be ready. It will take at least six months to ferment: if you can wait longer – two or three years – the mead will be even better.

FREEZING

If you have a food freezer, allow plenty of space for your meat and fish because these cannot easily be stored in any other way. Vegetables can be stored in other ways and should therefore take second place. However, as long as you have ample freezer space – six cubic feet (0.22 cu m) per member of the household is pretty adequate – you may like to freeze the following vegetables, which freeze easily and do not suffer from the process unduly: globe artichokes; asparagus; all kinds of beans; Brussels sprouts; cauliflower; sweet corn; peas; sweet peppers. Pumpkins and tomatoes freeze well if you puree them, and you can freeze tomato juice, if you don't can it (see p. 221).

Unless you have meat to freeze, or intend to buy cheap meat wholesale and store it by freezing, think hard before you buy a freezer. The money you spend on it initially, and on maintaining it, replacing it, and running it, would buy an awful lot of food. I personally do not think it's worth buying a freezer for vegetables alone. If you do buy one I would strongly recommend you to get a chest freezer, rather than an upright one. Upright freezers lose all their cold air every time you open the door; because cold air is heavier than warm air, it just flops out.

Freezing vegetables

All fruit and vegetables should go to the freezer as soon as they are harvested. To leave them sitting about allows the sugars to start turning into starches and thereby the flavor is lost. If you

FREEZING AND THAWING VEGETABLES

1 *Before you freeze vegetables you must blanch them. Use a wire basket to immerse them in boiling water for a short time – between two and four minutes.*

2 *Remove the vegetables from the water and immediately plunge them into cold water for the same number of minutes.*

3 *Let the vegetables drain. Then, put them in a plastic bag, and suck the air out through a straw. Put the bag in your freezer.*

4 *To thaw frozen vegetables quickly, bend the bag about with both hands. This will break up the ice and separate the vegetables.*

FREEZING SOUP

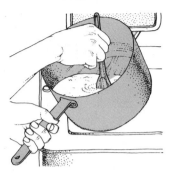

1 *To freeze soup, first prepare the soup and allow it to grow cold in a cool place; don't put it in the refrigerator.*

2 *Put a plastic bag inside the saucepan which you will use to reheat the soup. Pour the soup into this bag, which should be a special "freezer weight" bag.*

3 *Put the saucepan containing the plastic bag and the soup inside the freezer. When the soup has frozen solid, remove the saucepan.*

4 *When you want to reheat the soup, remove the plastic bag and drop the frozen lump of soup into the saucepan. It will heat up very quickly.*

haven't time to prepare the food for freezing immediately, put it in the freezer as it is for a few minutes to chill it, but don't let it get frozen solid.

You should blanch most vegetables before you freeze them to inactivate the enzymes in them. This means plunging them into boiling water. Two or three minutes in the water is adequate for most vegetables, but a big solid thing, like a globe artichoke, should have four minutes. Blanching is easy if you use the wire basket you fry French fries in. When you remove the vegetables from the boiling water, plunge them straight into cold water with ice floating about in it. If you can, chill some water in your refrigerator the night before, preferably in large containers like cake tins. Dip the blanched vegetables, in the wire container, straight into the cold water, and pull them out after the same number of minutes that they were in the boiling water. Let them drain thoroughly and pack them in containers. They must be quite dry by this time.

If you pack them in a plastic bag, expel all the air by sucking it through a straw before you put the twist-tie on to stop it getting in again. It is a good idea to stuff the filled plastic bag into a carton. This gives it a square shape which stows more easily and makes better use of freezer space.

Freezing soup

When you freeze soups, put the plastic bag containing the soup inside the cooking pot that you intend eventually to reheat it in. The top of the pot must be wider than its diameter lower down. Put the pot into the freezer and, when the soup has frozen, pull it out. Knock the plastic bag with its block of frozen soup out of the pot, and pack the block in the freezer. When you come to heat the soup, just remove the plastic bag, and drop the frozen soup into the pot.

Sweet corn responds very well to freezing, and when it is unfrozen it is still fresh and sweet. It is best to freeze the kernels only; it is a waste of space to freeze whole cobs. Cook the corn on the cob first for ten minutes. Let it cool, and strip the corn off the cob with a knife. Let it drain, then pack it in containers and freeze. When you want to eat it, just simmer in water or milk for two to three minutes.

Freezing soft fruit

Soft fruit can be frozen in syrup, or in dry sugar, or just by itself. I always freeze it by itself because I can add what I want when it is unfrozen. You can just put soft fruit into containers and pack them in the freezer without more ado. Some people like to wash soft fruit in ice water before freezing it. If you do this you must dry it thoroughly before putting it in the freezer.

Containers for freezing

Everything you put in your freezer must be wrapped up in an airtight container; otherwise it just dries up. You can just use plastic bags, but there are more sophisticated containers made from waxed cardboard, plastic, glass and aluminum foil. Coffee tins with plastic tops are good for storing things in freezers, and so are glass jars. Beware of freezing food in any container which curves in toward the top, so that you can't get the food out before it thaws. Food will thaw much more quickly once it is out of its container. If you use plastic bags, make sure they are "freezer weight" bags: thin ones are not really suitable, although you can use them at a pinch. Once filled, the container must be sealed firmly.

CHAPTER TEN

Miscellany

*Containing the keeping of poultry, rabbits and
bees, the laying of paths and drains, the mending of
fences, the maintenance of tools, the life of seeds,
the variations of climate and other topics.*

Miscellany

CHICKENS

Chickens provide you with a constant supply of good fresh eggs, with chicken manure to activate your compost heap and with occasional table poultry. So chickens may well make the difference between just growing a few vegetables and true self-sufficient gardening. There is a great deal to learn about keeping chickens, and before starting the beginner will be wise to seek advice from an experienced neighbor.

Anyone who understands organic gardening will appreciate that chickens must be allowed to scratch about outdoors as nature intended; to keep them otherwise is cruel and breaks the cycle of nature which is so beneficial to the garden. I know people who happily let hens run in their gardens most of the time. They do some damage, but also do good because they eat insects. But I personally haven't got the nerve to do this; a hen can scratch up a new seed-bed in half an hour flat.

The Balfour method

If you have only a small garden and do not want to let chickens run loose on it, you can still keep chickens, using the Balfour method — so named after Lady Eve Balfour who invented it. With this method you will not need a separate compost heap, because the hen run is the compost heap. You take an ordinary hen house — that is a good, solid, waterproof, draft-proof, well-ventilated wooden house with perches and nest boxes inside it. In front of it or around it you have a

THE BALFOUR METHOD
Build your hen house solidly out of wood, so that it is waterproof and draft-proof, yet well-ventilated. Next to it put a scratching pen, sheltered from wind. Throw in all the vegetable matter you can spare; the hens will turn the pen into a compost heap.

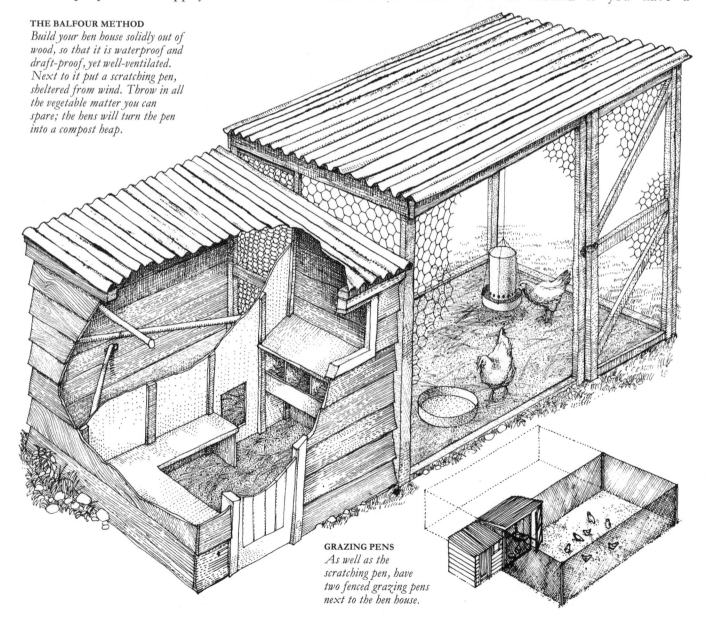

GRAZING PENS
As well as the scratching pen, have two fenced grazing pens next to the hen house.

scratching pen which ideally should be sheltered from wind. This becomes your "compost heap". You throw into this area all the vegetable matter you can get; the more the better. All the kitchen scraps, all the waste material from the garden, plenty of straw, bracken, spoiled hay, grass clippings, everything you can lay your hands on goes into it. Your hens spend hours scrapping about in this material, because worms, earwigs and other insects abound in it.

Apart from the scratching pen you should have two grazing pens — or three if you can afford the space. These are just fenced pens, with gates arranged in such a way that the hens can be admitted into one of the pens while being denied access to the other. The two pens should sown with a grass, clover and herb mixture. You allow the hens to run in one pen for two or three weeks, until the grass is eaten right down; then you admit them to the other. Because the hens are doing most of their scratching in the scratching pen they should not tear up the grazing pens too severely. If you find that they do, you can limit their access to only a few hours a day.

The Balfour method has several advantages. Even though your property may be very small, your birds have access to herbage; at the same time the herbage is not lethally damaged by the hens' scratchings; the main thing is that the scratching pen provides a quantity of magnificent compost. Every few weeks you empty the scratching pen completely and build it into a proper compost heap. You need add no extra nitrogen to activate it.

A refinement of the Balfour method is to arrange things so that after a year or two you can pull the fences down from the scratching pen and the two grazing pens, and re-erect them on the other side of the hen house. Open the pop-hole on that side so that the hens can make use of the fresh ground, while you dig up their former pens and bring them into cultivation as part of your garden. You will thus regain the very considerable fertility built up by the hens.

Another possibility is to give your hens access to your soft fruit patch, and to your tree fruit orchard, during the winter. Hens can roam among fruit trees all summer as well, and they do a lot of good by killing many of the insects that would otherwise harm the trees, and by fertilizing the soil around the trees. They do a good job among soft fruit bushes too, except that obviously you cannot leave them there when the fruit is ripe or they will eat it. There is also a danger that they will eat the buds in spring. But certainly in winter it can do nothing but good to let them run among your bushes and trees. You will be sparing your Balfour grazing pens, so that they are more productive when spring comes and the hens have to be moved away from your soft fruit. If hens are run temporarily over any bit of land they will do it good: and the more changes they get the better.

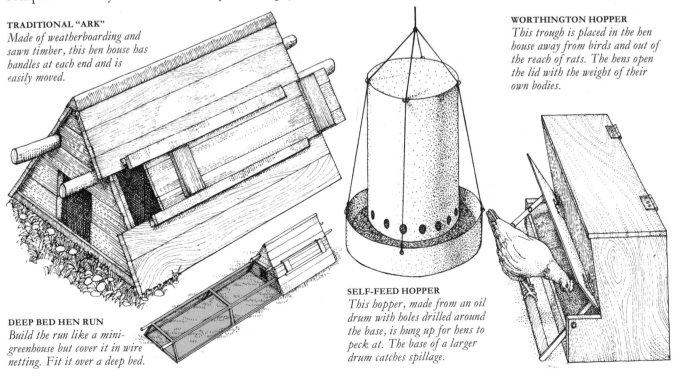

TRADITIONAL "ARK"
Made of weatherboarding and sawn timber, this hen house has handles at each end and is easily moved.

DEEP BED HEN RUN
Build the run like a mini-greenhouse but cover it in wire netting. Fit it over a deep bed.

SELF-FEED HOPPER
This hopper, made from an oil drum with holes drilled around the base, is hung up for hens to peck at. The base of a larger drum catches spillage.

WORTHINGTON HOPPER
This trough is placed in the hen house away from birds and out of the reach of rats. The hens open the lid with the weight of their own bodies.

Chicken-tractor

Another way of keeping hens in a small garden is the amusingly-named "chicken-tractor", which is being developed at the Santa Barbara Urban Farm Project in California. This is still at an experimental stage and the exact effects it will have on your soil are not known. But used in the right way, it should considerably improve the fertility of your garden.

The tractor is simply a hen run, with a sleeping shelter attached to one end of it. The shelter should contain nesting boxes and have a floor made of spaced wooden dowels. The run itself can be built to fit exactly over the standard 20 foot by 5 foot (6 m x 1.5 m) deep bed (see p. 106). If you don't use deep beds, then build the run to the dimensions of your vegetable beds. Construct it in exactly the same way as the "mini-greenhouse" described on p. 111; the only difference is that you cover it with wire netting instead of plastic. It need have no floor.

The run can be separated from the night shelter so that it can be moved easily by two people, and then re-attached. The night shelter can be carried, even with the birds in it.

Eight hens is the ideal number for a chicken-tractor. You place the run over one deep bed, which should have had rye or some other quick-growing grazing crop sown in it a month or two beforehand, to provide the hens with something to eat. The hens manure the bed, scratch it over deeply and eat all the insects they can find. They also destroy all the weeds. When another bed is ready to receive them, you just move the "tractor" on to it. The old bed will be well-manured and weed-free; dig it up and plant vegetables or fruit.

Feeding chickens

There are several views about feeding chickens: most orthodox methods recommend feeding a dry mash prepared in controlled quantities. I favor what is known as the Worthington Method (named after its inventor). This is simply that you allow hens ample greenstuff – this means a lot of greenstuff, not just cabbage. You also let them have access to whole grain – wheat is best – and some high protein food such as fish meal.

Let them feed as much as they want of whatever they want, and you will find that they eat a balanced diet, do not overeat and lay plenty of eggs. What they eat will, in practice, average out at about four and a half ounces (128 g) of wheat per day each, and well under half an ounce (14 g) of fish meal. For fish meal you can substitute any other high protein food: soy meal; chick peas;

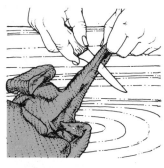

KILLING A CHICKEN
Take the legs in your left hand; hold the neck in your right hand so that it protrudes through your two middle fingers, with the head cupped in your palm. Push your right hand down and turn it so that the head bends back. Stop when you feel the backbone break. If you can, pluck the bird while it is still warm; the skin is far less likely to tear.

PREPARING THE CHICKEN

1 *After you have plucked the bird, cut around its legs with a sharp knife and proceed to draw out the tendons.*

2 *Cut the head off, and slide the knife down the neck to leave a flap of skin.*

3 *Break the neck off further down than the flap, using a pair of kitchen scissors. You can then use it along with the giblets.*

4 *Put your finger into the hole left by the neck, and twist it round to break the ligaments which hold the innards.*

5 *Cut all the way around the anus, taking care not to make a mess of the guts.*

6 *Put your hand in and pull out all the innards, including the lungs. Then wash the bird well inside and out.*

cracked beans; meat meal or flakes. I knew a man who used to get fish heads and guts from a fisherman, boil them up, and offer them to his hens. They laid superb eggs. As for the whole grain, use good oats or barley if these are more plentiful than wheat in your area.

Other garden produce which contains protein and is good for hens includes: sunflower seed, especially if you husk and grind them; lupin seed, ground or whole; peanut seed; alfalfa meal; crushed or ground peas and beans. If you grow too many potatoes it is a kindness on cold winter evenings to boil some up with a little skimmed milk, or milk gone sour, or water the fish was boiled in, and feed them to the hens before it gets too dark.

If you feed your hens according to the Worthington scheme you must feed them on this diet from an early age and you must feed them from hoppers. These should be in the hen house away from sparrows, and hung up or set up in such a way that the rats can't get at them. The Worthington hopper is a most excellent device and will save pounds of food over the years. The hens open the lid to the trough by the weight of their own bodies.

All poultry must at all times have access to dust baths, fresh water and sharp grit — they use grit instead of teeth. Also lime-rich material, such as crushed sea shells, is very good for them.

If you are kind to your birds they will be kind to you. But kindness should not go so far as keeping on non-laying birds for months. Cull the too fat, the too thin, the sick, lame and lazy, and they will do you the final favor of making you some excellent soup.

Breeding chickens

You won't get any more eggs if you keep a cockerel among your hens, but your eggs will be fertile. Then, if a hen goes broody, you can let her sit on her eggs and soon you will have some young chickens to increase your flock, to eat, or to sell. Nine times out of ten if you leave a broody hen alone and at peace to sit on her eggs, she will bring them off and care for the chicks, with no trouble at all.

Feed the chicks the diet recommended for ducks for a few days. If you wish to eat the chicks, feed them freely. It is better to feed them mash (a mixture of grain meal and protein), and a proprietary mash is quite adequate. Either kill them at ten weeks as "broilers" weighing two or three pounds, or keep them until they are 14 or 15 weeks old and kill them as "fryers".

DUCKS

If you have a pond, or a stream running through your land, consider keeping ducks. They will provide you with eggs and meat. Duck eggs are delicious as long as they have not been lying in dirty water or mud; and some breeds such as Khakis and Campbells lay more eggs than chickens do. It is cruel and unnatural to keep ducks away from water on which they can swim. Pond water must be clean and changed from time to time.

Breeding ducks

If you keep a friendly drake and up to six ducks at the bottom of your garden, the ducks will lay eggs and hatch them. If you manage things well, you can have a constant supply of eggs and meat. However, ducks make very bad mothers. Always confine a mother duck, even if you leave her ducklings free to wander away and come back to her, otherwise she will drag her brood through

NESTING BOXES
Make partitions along a wooden plank. Allow one box for every three ducks.

mud and wet grass, weakening them and even possibly killing them.

Chickens are much better at hatching out duck eggs than ducks are, so it is best to put fertile duck eggs under a broody hen if you have one. Otherwise treat ducklings in just the same way as you would treat young chicks.

You can also hatch duck eggs in an incubator. In this case, brood the ducklings at 94°F (34°C) for the first week, lower the temperature gradually to 50°F (10°C) the second week and never let the ducklings get chilled. After two weeks let them run out, but provide warm shelter, as well as giving them access to shelter from the sun.

Duck eggs take 28 days to hatch. When the ducklings are first hatched, feed them four or five times a day on a rich mash made of grain meal, preferably barley, with milk and a mashed hard-boiled egg in it. After three or four days you can reduce the number of times you feed them, but not the total amount of food. Leave out the egg, and, if you want to, you can give them bought pellets, and a little grain instead of, or as well as, the mash. They will do well on boiled-up kitchen scraps, or boiled potatoes and greens. Ducks are omnivorous, so you can give them meat or fish scraps.

Older birds should be fed exactly the same diet as chickens (see p. 231). But don't let them get too fat or they won't breed. Ducks need plenty of clean drinking water at all times.

You should kill table ducks when they are eight and a half to ten weeks old — no sooner and no later. A duck should have eaten about 20 pounds (9 kg) of feed by this time and should weigh about three and a quarter pounds (1.5 kg).

GEESE

You should only keep geese if you have surplus grass, because they are essentially grazing birds. So if you have a big garden or orchard, it will pay you to buy some young geese in the early summer and fatten them for eating in winter and, of course, at Christmas. As well as grass, feed them any surplus lettuces or other greens you happen to have, and about a fortnight before you kill them feed them heavily on barley meal or boiled potatoes.

Breeding geese

If you wish to breed geese, rather than just fatten young geese, you must of course have a gander, although you can get started by buying some goose eggs and putting them under a broody hen. She will hatch the eggs and look after the young goslings. People commonly keep two or three geese per gander. After 20 years of keeping geese, I have come to the conclusion that it is better to have just a pair. Geese are naturally monogamous. If you allow a goose to sit on her eggs in her own good time, helped and guarded by the gander, you will end up by rearing more live geese over the years than if you have one or more importunate auntie geese flapping around trying to sit on the eggs, or laying fresh eggs in a clutch already started.

Another factor to consider is that geese do not take to each other as readily as ducks and chickens do. A pair will probably have to be kept together for a minimum of six weeks before they will mate at all, and it may take two or three years before a goose is really breeding well. But once a pair is successfully established, you can expect a long productive life from them. There are records — dubious admittedly — of geese breeding for more than 70 years, but if you estimate an average of about ten years for a goose and five for a gander you will be about right. On the whole, geese make good sitters and good mothers, and ganders are usually attentive to the young as well. Eggs take about 28 days to hatch.

Make sure that a sitting goose gets enough to eat, as she will frequently be unwilling to leave the eggs even to feed. When the goslings are ready to leave the nest they may be allowed to run out with their mother. If they are given the chance they will start grazing before they are a day old, and will thrive on good grass. For the first three weeks of their lives feed them well on bread soaked in milk. Goslings grow very fast in the first 12 weeks of life, by which time they may already weigh as much as two thirds of their eventual adult weight.

PIGEONS

If you have a family of four and you want to eat "squab", young pigeon, once a week, you should keep five pairs of breeding pigeons, because a couple can be expected to hatch out ten a year. When the undersides of the wings are fully feathered they are ready for eating. This should be when they weigh about a pound (500 g) and are four and a half weeks old. Do not let them get much older than this, as they lose weight and also inhibit their parents from breeding. Kill, pluck and truss them just like chickens.

Housing for pigeons

Pigeons are strictly monogamous; you should allow four square feet (0.37 sq m) of house-space per pair. Thus a pigeon house five feet (1.5 m) by four feet (1.2 m) is ideal for 5 pairs. You need more nesting boxes than you have pairs of pigeons: seven is about right for five pairs. Orange crates make fine nesting boxes. It is important that the pigeon house is rat-proof. If you build one specially, raise it on legs with inverted dishes under them to stop rats climbing up. The house must also be draft-proof.

Feeding pigeons

Pigeons on free range need a little grain thrown to them every day, as well as some chick peas or other high protein seed. Give them as much as they can clear up in twenty minutes. They will forage for food, but they will probably do very little harm to your vegetables and fruit.

RABBITS

If you aim to be self-sufficient in food and you have a small garden, few things will contribute so much to your ideal as rabbits. In the first place, just one rabbit will provide three cubic feet (0.84 cu m) of droppings a year, which is enough to activate a big compost heap. Together with the soiled litter cleaned from your rabbit run, this equals a fertile garden. Plants and animals evolved to co-exist and to support each other's life systems. Rabbits play their part especially well.

The other thing about rabbits is that they will give you excellent meat. Rabbit meat is very nutritious, free of fat, comes in convenient-sized parcels (one rabbit makes a splendid meal for a small family), and rabbits are easy to kill and to process. Any family can have one rabbit a week to eat, simply by keeping two does and rearing their litters for food.

A doe should have from four to five litters a year, each of about six babies. A doe should live

RAISED HUTCHES
This is a space-saving method of keeping rabbits. The hutches are one on top of the other, and raised a few inches off the ground. Keep them outside, up against a wall, with a lean-to roof positioned carefully above them to keep the rain off. The floor of each hutch is made of galvanized wire mesh, and a metal tray slides in between each hutch to catch droppings.

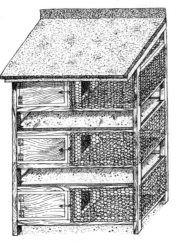

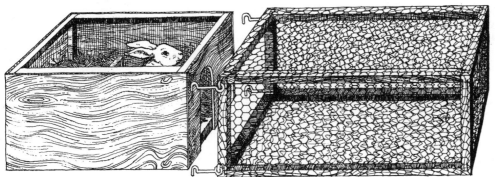

for about two years, but it is the easiest thing to rear up replacements. An important consideration is getting your does "in kindle", or pregnant. If you have a neighbor who keeps a buck, and if he is satisfied that your does are completely healthy and you are satisfied his buck is, you can take your does to be mated. If not, you can, if you want, keep a buck to two does – or even to one. But ten does to a buck is the optimum. With a ten-doe rabbitry you really are in business though. Consider: about 300 rabbits to kill a year. But, if you think about it, that number of rabbits will completely pay your meat bill, for, after you have eaten all the rabbit meat you can stomach, you will have enough to sell to pay for all the meat you want for your family and a lot more besides.

Another thing to remember is that, if you do have to buy food for your rabbits – and you likely will if you have ten does – this food not only feeds the rabbits, it feeds your garden too and in the end feeds you. The same applies to straw or bracken that you bring in for litter. Even if you have to buy the straw, you are not just buying rabbit's bedding, you are buying fertility for your garden. Therefore there is every reason for keeping rabbits.

Caring for rabbits

There is work involved in keeping rabbits of course – particularly when you are getting started, but the thing to do is start small – say with two does and a buck – and build up gradually as you gain experience. Once your rabbitry is established there is not so much work to do: minutes a day rather than hours.

You must consider the various needs and the instincts of rabbits and try to allow them to satisfy them. To keep a rabbit in a wire cage and feed it on nothing but pellets and dry hay is cruel. To allow it access to the ground in summer, so that it can nibble fresh grass and scratch the earth, is kind. And to keep it in a warm dry place in

MOVABLE HUTCH
This hutch, or ark, consists of an enclosed area three feet by two feet (90 x 60 cm) and 18 inches (45 cm) high; if it contains a doe, it should have a nesting box inside it. Attached to the hutch should be a wire netting pen at least four feet by two feet (1.2 m x 60 cm).

winter and feed it on a variety of fresh green things is kind too. You can keep rabbits out of doors in movable hutches all winter as well, but this may not be ideal in cold climates.

Another requirement for rabbits is privacy. Their wild ancestors lived in holes so you must give them the equivalent of holes to retire into. It is cruel to keep them out in the light all the time, or under the gaze of other animals.

Housing for rabbits

There are two basic forms of housing for rabbits. One, the kindest if it is done properly, is to have movable hutches, or arks, out of doors on grass. These can consist of an enclosed hutch three feet (90 cm) by two feet (60 cm) by 18 inches (45 cm) high and, if it contains a doe, put a nesting box inside it. Attached to this should be a wire netting pen at least four feet (1.2 m) long and two feet (60 cm) wide.

The other form of housing is raised hutches, either against a wall outside or, better still, in a shed. If you have them outside I strongly recommend you have a simple lean-to roof over the hutches just to keep the rain off both you and the rabbits. Few things can be more unpleasant than cleaning out stinking wet rabbit litter from under stinking wet rabbits. If rabbits are kept dry, and warm, they will be healthy and will not stink at all. And remember that rain can come horizontally as well as straight down, so be sure to arrange things so that, whatever the weather, neither litter nor rabbits get wet.

If your hutches are indoors, the alley for you to walk in front of them should be at least three feet six inches (105 cm) wide. The ceiling of an indoor rabbit house should be between eight and ten feet (2.4-3 m) high. If it is too low, it will be stuffy; if it is too high, it will be too cold.

If a raised hutch has wire floors, the galvanized mesh should be 14 to 16 gauge $\frac{3}{4}$ inch by $\frac{3}{4}$ inch (2 x 2 cm) mesh. You should have a wire mesh floor only under the outer eating and dunging pen. The sleeping quarters, which should be private and dark, should have a solid floor. Wood is the best material for building hutches, because it is warm. If you do not use tongue-and-groove boarding, coat the hutches with asphalt.

Interior fittings should be kept simple. A rack for hay is very important — you will waste far less hay this way. A bottle drinker — or else piped water laid on to automatic drinkers — will save endless time and be better for the rabbits. Rabbits must always have plenty of clean water. This is essential for their health and don't believe any wiseacre who tells you anything else. If you feed them pellets, a hopper is very useful, or, failing that, some sort of dish which prevents the rabbits from scraping the pellets out and wasting them.

Mating and breeding

Don't buy old or supposedly "in-kindle" does to start off with: buy young does, let them get used to their new homes, and put them to the buck when they are twenty weeks old. At twelve weeks a doe should have her own home. Handle your breeding stock gently — you wouldn't like to be carried about by the ears — and as often as you can. Get them and yourself used to it. If you are rough they may become rough too, and scratch and bite you. Be gentle with them and they will be gentle.

Take the doe to the buck. If he mounts her within five minutes, well and good; if he doesn't, remove her and bring her back to him six hours later. After she has mated carry her back to her own hutch, give her some food and let her be quiet. When she gives birth leave her alone in a nice warm nest box with plenty of hay for bedding, but inspect the litter next day and remove any dead, mis-shapen, or undersized infants — they will not do any good. After about four weeks you can wean the litter — place them in a pen of their own. Mate the doe again immediately. Never allow a buck access to his young children: he may well eat them.

With intensive feeding, meat rabbits are ready for killing when they are ten weeks old. I prefer to feed rabbits less intensively and keep them longer than ten weeks, say for as long as four months. I let them grow slowly mostly on greenstuff and hay with a little oats and boiled potatoes. This way they are bigger and better flavored when you come to kill them. The skins are then good for curing; at ten weeks they are almost useless because all the hair comes out. Starve a rabbit, but give it plenty of water for 12 hours before killing it.

Feeding rabbits

You can feed rabbits entirely on proprietary pellets and hay, but this does not come very close to meeting their natural requirements. You can feed them on nothing but greenstuff and hay, but if you do this you must provide a great deal of greenstuff of a wide variety and very good hay, and you take the risk of having small litters and small rabbits.

KILLING A RABBIT

To kill a rabbit, catch the hind legs in your left hand, put your right hand over the back of its neck and pull suddenly, bending the head up and back as you do so. Death is absolutely painless and instantaneous.

SKINNING A RABBIT

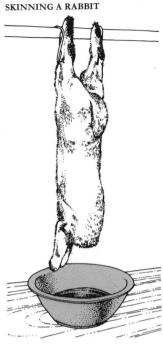

1 *Hang the rabbit on two hooks passed through its hamstrings. Cut off its head and drain the blood into a bowl.*

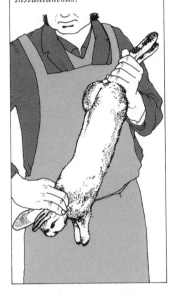

2 *Slit the skin around the hocks and down the inside of the thighs to the "vent".*

3 *Hold the rabbit by its legs and "skin-a-rabbit" in the same way as you would pull a jumper off a child.*

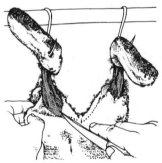

4 *Cut off the rabbit's paws and slit it down the belly, taking great care not to puncture the innards.*

5 *Take out the guts, cutting off the gall bladder, the heart and the kidneys. Keep the liver, and bury the rest deep in a compost heap. Wash the rabbit thoroughly.*

The best approach is to strike a happy medium and feed some grain – oats are best – mixed with hay and greenstuff, and, if you can get them, with bran whole or fragmented. Rabbits also like potato peelings, boiled potatoes, and all the root crops: turnips, mangels, parsnips, carrots, kohlrabi, radishes. Sugar beet is fine for fattening young rabbits, but not for breeding stock; it makes them too fat.

Four ounces (114 g) of pellets, or six ounces (170 g) of oats, per day with as much hay and greenstuff as they want is a good ration for adult rabbits, but this amount must be increased for a doe in kindle to eight ounces (230 g) until the young are weaned, so that she has enough milk.

These rations are all ideal quantities for ideal rabbits. I have kept rabbits on and off for many years, and never weighed anything. I give them as much concentrate – grain or pellets – as they will eat up quickly, and then I give them as much hay and greenstuff as they want. Any food they leave should be cleared up before you give them more. They don't want rotting vegetation.

As for greenstuffs: grass is very good for rabbits, but not lawn-mowings because these ferment too quickly. Greenstuff must always be fresh or else made into hay. Dried nettles are marvelous – high in protein and very good for rabbits. Nearly all garden waste is good for them: the outer leaves of cabbages and the other *brassica*; all root tops except those of potatoes which are poisonous; edible herbs; raspberry and blackberry leaves (particularly good if they get scours – diarrhea); shepherd's purse; sow thistle; dandelion, but not too much; sheep's parsley; coltsfoot; bind-weed; sorrel; daisies; clover; and vetches. Grow kale for feeding to your rabbits in late winter and spring, and they will really thrive.

Silage is good for fattening rabbits for eating, and for feeding to milking does as well. The best way to make it is to cram lawn-clippings into plastic fertilizer bags and seal these so as to exclude all air. Stack the bags upside down on top of each other so the air cannot get in. Leave them until the grass clippings have fermented. This will add to the fertility of your soil once it has been through the rabbits. Don't feed them silage alone though; give dry hay as well.

Never underestimate the appetites of your rabbits. They really need huge amounts of greenstuff, as much as they can eat. It keeps them fit and happy. Give them twigs to chew on: ash, thorn, apple and rose prunings are all good for them and keep them amused.

BEES

The wonderful thing about bees is that they make use of food that does not cost anything — food which cannot, without their aid, be used at all.

Bees in small gardens

Many people are afraid to keep bees in small gardens in urban or suburban situations because of the one thing that all worker bees have in common: their sting. However, you and your neighbors will be quite safe as long as you keep them high up. An older solution is to keep them behind a hedge, which forces them to rise before flying away from the hive so that their flight path is above the human head. This works too, but you need room in your garden not just for the hives, but for a hedge. Keeping bees in urban situations actually has an advantage: you do not risk the appalling massacres which are caused by the spraying of crops in the countryside.

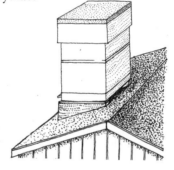

HIVES BEHIND A HEDGE
If you keep your hives behind a hedge, the bees are forced to rise before flying away, so that their flight path is higher than the human head.

HIVES HIGH UP
Another safe place for hives is high up — on a platform or a roof. This uses up much less space than keeping them behind a hedge.

Equipment for keeping bees

Hives The modern method of keeping bees, which is quite rightly the only legal method in many countries, is to use wooden hives, which contain removable frames on which the honey is made. The frames contain wax sheets which are printed with the beautiful hexagonal pattern of bee cells. The worker bees draw out the wax to form cells in which they hope their queen will come and lay her eggs. Sadly, the beekeeper fools the worker bees. He interposes a "queen excluder" between the queen, who is down in her royal apartment called the "brood chamber", and the frames above. The workers fill the cells above the queen excluder with honey, but the queen never lays eggs in them. Therefore the beekeeper does not kill unborn bees, when he takes the honey.

Your beehives should contain the following parts, working from the bottom upward: a base which is a flat piece of wood supported on legs, or struts; a brood chamber, which is a deep box, with no top or bottom, filled with deep frames; a queen excluder — a flat board that fits over the brood chamber with a hole in it big enough to allow worker bees through but not the queen; some supers, which are like the brood chamber only shallower, and containing shallower frames; a lid, which is a box with a top but no bottom.

Clothing As well as your hives you will need various pieces of equipment for your apiary as a whole. Most important of all is protective clothing, and every time you put it on take great care that you leave no openings through which a bee might be able to crawl.

Clearing board A clearing board is very useful. It is a flat board containing a "bee-valve", a device which will allow bees to go down but not up.

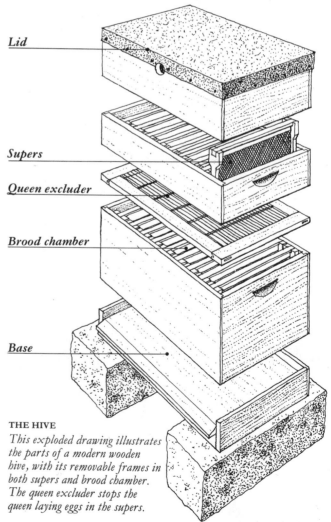

Lid

Supers

Queen excluder

Brood chamber

Base

THE HIVE
This exploded drawing illustrates the parts of a modern wooden hive, with its removable frames in both supers and brood chamber. The queen excluder stops the queen laying eggs in the supers.

You place it between the brood chamber and the supers so as to clear the bees out of the latter, when you want to take the frames out to extract the honey. You can do without a clearing board, in which case you will have to clear the bees out of the supers either by brushing them off with a soft brush, or by banging the supers on the ground. Both these techniques annoy the bees, but if you wear protective clothing you will be safe.

Smoker A smoker is a container in which you burn corrugated paper, or cloth, to stupefy your bees so that you can work them without getting them too angry. This works because when bees smell smoke they think there is a forest fire; they therefore fill themselves up with honey ready to move house. When bees are full of honey they cannot sting, but be careful not to give them too much smoke.

Extractor Once a frame is filled with honey, you can use a honey extractor to get it out. This is a centrifuge which spins the honey out, leaving the combs more or less intact so that they can be replaced in the hive, and used by the bees again. This saves the bees a lot of work and allows them to concentrate on making honey. Before you use an extractor you must decap the combs with a hot knife. Keep the knife hot in boiling water.

Feeder If you are going to feed your bees in winter – and this will keep your bees healthy and give you more honey – you will need a feeder. This is a simple container made of plastic, wood or metal, which you can fill with sugar-water, and place above the top super just underneath the lid of the hive. The sugar-water should be two parts by weight of sugar to one part of water. Boil the mixture and let it cool. Make sure that every colony has at least 35 pounds (16 kg) of honey or sugar-water to last it the winter. Nothing less than this will keep the bees happy, strong and ready to make the best of the nectar flow next spring.

Establishing a bee colony

To start keeping bees you must either buy a colony in an existing hive, buy a nucleus, or hive a swarm. A nucleus is a queen and a few hundred workers in a box. These you must carefully feed with sugar-water until they have established themselves sufficiently to survive unaided. Do not add a super to the nucleus brood chamber until all the frames in the latter are filled with honey.

To hive a swarm you must first find one. Swarms are the children of bee colonies. They consist of a queen and several thousand workers. Their habit is to hang on a tree branch, like a huge football of bees, and stay there while they send out scouts to find a suitable home. When the scouts return the whole swarm flies away and enters the new home. If you are lucky enough to find a swarm, hive it by shaking the branch hard, or cutting it off, so that the whole mass of bees falls into a box. Turn the box upside down and leave it until evening, with a stick under it to leave a gap through which the scouts can return to the swarm. Then carry the box to your empty hive. Lay a white sheet on the ground in front of the door to the hive, and shake the swarm out on to the sheet. As bees always tend to crawl upward, they will crawl into the new hive.

A final few words of advice: before you embark on beekeeping join your local beekeeping society or group, or at least make friends with an experienced beekeeper. Buy, or borrow, a good book on the subject; there is much more to know about bees than I have managed to fit in here.

APPROACHING THE HIVE
Protective clothing is a vital part of beekeeping. Protect your hands and wrists with gloves and your face with a special bee-veil. Wear light-colored clothing, with your trousers tucked into your socks. Use a hive tool or a screwdriver to lever open the hive, from the side or rear if possible. Have a smoker ready-lit, filled with corrugated paper, rags, or any material that will make smoke. The smoke will stupefy the bees; they will fill themselves up with honey, and be unable to sting.

BEEKEEPING TOOLS
You can use a special hive tool to lever open the different parts of the hive, left. Before using an extractor to obtain the honey, you must decap the combs with a hot knife, right.

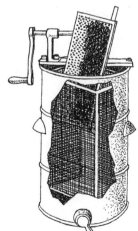

HONEY EXTRACTOR
This device acts as a centrifuge for spinning out honey, leaving the combs intact and re-usable.

DRAINAGE

Wet land is, for nearly all land plants, bad land. The plants grow up late in the spring, grow slowly and badly, and fungus diseases flourish. And wet land is sour and acid. You just have to drain it.

The water table

When water falls on to pervious ground it sinks in and goes on sinking until it hits an impervious layer. If this layer is sloping, the water may continue downhill underground until it outcrops — that is, comes to the surface somewhere. If it outcrops in your garden you will have a spring, and a very wet garden indeed. If the country is low-lying anyway the water will not outcrop, but just stay where it is. The level to which water rises underground is called the water table. If it is only a few inches or even feet below the surface of the soil you have a drainage problem. If it coincides with the surface you have a swamp. If it is above it you have a lake.

You also have a drainage problem if the surface of your soil is heavy clay because no water will percolate through it, either up or down. If your soil is sand or gravel, water will percolate easily, but if there is clay underneath, water can accumulate in the sand or gravel and you still have a drainage problem.

Ditches and land drains

You can lower your water table a certain amount by digging ditches around the edges of your land. If the problem is more acute, you can dig land drains, and these can go across the middle of your land — a herring bone pattern is ideal. Dig trenches and lay perforated pipes or open jointed drains in the bottom. Cover over with gravel or other coarse material, and cover this with soil. Dig the trenches so that they lead the water to a stream or other watercourse that will take it away to the sea.

Drywells

Your garden may be wet because you have a heavy clay topsoil above a pervious subsoil. If so you may well be able to cure the problem by digging a drywell. Dig a pit in the lowest part of your garden; dig through the topsoil and well into the pervious subsoil. Fill the pit with big stones and dig land drains leading to the pit.

A drywell can also be used to deal with damp soil caused by an impervious layer below the topsoil. Simply dig through the impervious layer when digging your drywell. Lay land drains through the pervious topsoil, so that they catch water before it reaches the impervious layer.

If you can't dig through the impervious layer, or you can't lower the water table by any of the

LAND DRAINS AND DRYWELL
If your garden has a heavy clay topsoil on top of a pervious subsoil, you should be able to drain it by installing a drywell. This is a hole dug deep enough — say four feet (1.2 m) — to carry the water down to the subsoil. Fill the pit with porous material such as gravel or broken bricks. Dig land drains running down to the drywell at a gentle slope. Because the ground is porous at the bottom of the drywell, the water will drain away. In a large garden dig land drains in a herring bone pattern — that is to say with branch drains running

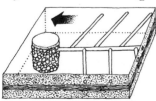

into the main drain leading to the drywell.

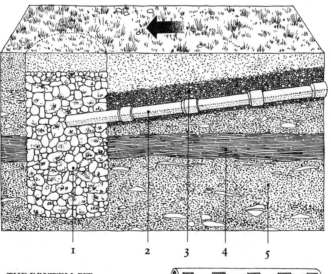

DRAIN CROSS-SECTION
When you lay a drain, cover it with small stones or gravel before you replace the soil.

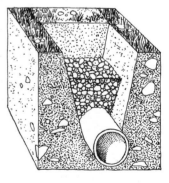

THE DRYWELL PIT
The cross-section above shows the drywell 1, with land drains 2 running down to it. The drains are packed with small stones 3. The layer of impervious material 4 is bypassed by the drywell, so the water can reach the porous layer 5.

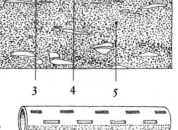

PERFORATED PIPES
This type of pipe is plastic and comes in long lengths; the perforations allow water to enter the drain all along the line.

OPEN JOINTED PIPES
These are short pipes laid end to end; they are not cemented together, so water can seep through the joints and flow down to the drywell.

methods outlined above, you may find that you need a drain not just across your own garden, but across one, or even several, of your neighbors' gardens. Such a ditch will benefit everyone, so it is worth getting together with your neighbors and digging it as a joint effort.

TERRACES

The terracing of steep hillsides has gone on since antiquity, and in many parts of the world it is the only way of farming or gardening on a permanent basis. Cultivation of unterraced hillsides inevitably leads to soil erosion and eventually a complete loss of soil cover. A properly terraced hillside will last for ever.

If you have a steep unproductive slope, it is well worth terracing it. If you acquire land with terraces on it, it is likely to be very productive land. This may be to do with the fact that the initial labor involved in terracing is very high, the cost of terraced land is therefore correspondingly high, and so terraced land is cherished and lovingly cared for.

Constructing a terrace

Your retaining walls can be of stone, brick, concrete blocks or, on not too steep a slope, turf. Masonry retaining walls — and remember they have to be very high — are too expensive nowadays for most people to contemplate. However, you can build turf terrace walls at minimum expense, but at a high cost of labor.

Mark out the width of the proposed terrace and dig a level foundation for the retaining wall at the base of it right along that contour. Peel the turf off the side of the hill to the width of the intended bed. Use the strips of turf to build a wall on your level foundation and give the wall a slight batter in toward the terrace. The wall needs to be half as high as the vertical height of the stretch of slope you are terracing. Level the terrace by throwing the soil from the uphill half of the proposed terrace down to the downhill half which stretches to your wall. The turf which forms the wall will put out fresh grass on its exposed vertical side and take on a new lease of life. It will stand up as well as a stone wall.

Whatever material you use for your walls you must arrange some drainage. Water building up behind a wall can burst it. Below the topsoil, close to the terrace wall, you should build up some permeable material — stones or pebbles. Insert short drain pipes through the wall and into this permeable fill at intervals of about ten yards.

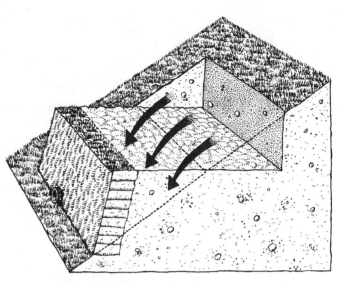

BUILDING A TERRACE
Mark out the width of the proposed terrace, and peel off the turf from the side of the hill to this width. Dig a level foundation at the base of the terrace, and build a retaining wall on top of it with the turf. Give the wall a slight batter in towards the terrace. Build in some porous material close to the wall; then insert short drain pipes through the wall and into this porous fill. Finish by moving the soil from the top half of the terrace to the bottom half. The turf in the wall will put out fresh grass on its exposed side.

GARDEN PATHS

A good paved path running down the backbone of your garden is a great boon. The main highway of a vegetable garden gets too much traffic for a grass path to cope with. An earth path becomes mud, except on very light sandy soil, and pushing a wheelbarrow is much easier on a paved surface. Now that I am going over to deep bed gardening (see p. 106), I am making stone paths between each five foot (1.5 m) wide deep bed by simply throwing all the stones and pebbles that I dig up on to the narrow strips between the beds. I strongly recommend this practice: with a paved path running down the middle of a small garden and deep beds running off at right angles with stone paths between them, it is never necessary to get your shoes dirty at all! This makes quite a difference to the state of your carpets.

Types of path

There are various ways of making a paved path. Concrete is permanent, but is very ugly. And after all you garden for pleasure as well as for food, and therefore aesthetics should be given a fairly high priority. A brick path, possibly with a zig-zag pattern of bricks, is very attractive, and if well made, will last a lifetime. But if it is made badly it will fall to pieces in no time. Crazy paving is fine

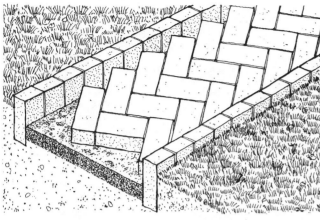

MAKING PATHS

Bricks are laid in a herring bone pattern in the path, above, and held in place by a vertical line of bricks on each side. For a concrete path, below, the edge of a plank should be used to level the mixture to the correct height.

if you like it: personally I think the end result is not worth all the trouble of intricately fitting it together. But flat stone slabs laid properly can be excellent, or a mixture of flagstones and bricks is serviceable and attractive. You can use old bricks and you don't even have to clean them. Gravel, granite chips, or other small loose pebbles are fairly good: perfectly all right if you have a wheel-barrow with a pneumatic tire, but laborious if your wheelbarrow has a bare steel rim; the good old wide wooden wheel, with an iron tire on it, goes quite sweetly over gravel.

Laying a path

Gravel Dig a trench about four inches (10 cm) deep, and to the width you want the path. Fill with plenty of gravel. Never skimp the gravel: use a lot or it will get trodden away to nothing.

Bricks and slabs Dig a trench six inches (15 cm) deep and put four inches (10 cm) of sand in it. Flatten the sand with a plank to make it level and firm. Lay your bricks to a herring bone pattern on the sand. Hit them with a mallet to make the surface level, being careful not to chip off corners. Sprinkle sand over the bricks and sweep over the

surface so the sand falls into the cracks. Hose the path down so that the sand binds together.

The edges are a problem for they can break away. One method of preventing this is to lay a line of bricks along each edge sloping down away from the path and embedded quite deeply in the soil at the side. Bricks set vertically in the soil will fulfill the same purpose.

A flagstone path can be set in place using the same method. The edges will not be a problem because the slabs are so large.

Concrete If your soil is soft and muddy, you will have to dig quite a deep trench – say a foot (30 cm) deep – and fill this to within four inches (10 cm) of the surface with gravel. If your soil is hard and well drained, you need only dig a trench about four inches (10 cm) deep. Now lay planks on their edges for forms along each side of the path. Keep the planks securely in position by driving pegs into the soil beside your trench.

Your concrete should be a mixture of one part of cement, two parts of sand, and four parts of small aggregate. If you can borrow or hire a cement mixer to do the mixing, do so for it will save you an awful lot of sweat. If you can't do this mix your concrete this way: make a pyramidal pile of your aggregate on a hard surface such as concrete. Throw your sand over this pile so that it covers the pile evenly. Then throw on your cement in the same way. Now start shoveling from one side, sliding your shovel in along the floor, and build, shovelful by shovelful, another conical heap nearby. When you have completed this heap repeat the process putting the material back where it was before.

Move it a third time, and then make a hole in the top of your cone like the crater in the top of a volcano. Throw water with a dash of emulsifier in it – if you can't get emulsifier, use detergent – into the hole. Now work your shovel about in the hole so as to blend the dry mix with the water. Beware a break in the circular wall at the bottom of the pile, or you will lose water, cement, and all. When you have mixed as much as you can, quickly shovel the outside of the heap into the middle. Slice it repeatedly with your shovel and sprinkle on more water as you need it. You don't want the mixture too sloppy: just make it all thoroughly wet.

Shovel the mixture into your trench. Level to the height of the retaining planks, and firm the top by pressing down with the edge of a plank. This should leave a pattern of small furrows and ridges which makes for a non-slip surface. If you can give the surface a slight camber this is an advantage for the path will shed water.

You may well find it easier to make a long path in sections, say ten feet (3 m) long. If your path is more than 40 feet (12 m) long, unbroken, put in expansion joints roughly every 30 feet (9 m). These can be thin planks standing up on edge. Just leave the planks there after the concrete has set. They allow for expansion of the concrete; otherwise it might crack in hot weather. After you have made your path keep the concrete wet for three days. Hose it occasionally or cover it with wet sacks. Do not let the frost get at it.

HEDGES AND FENCES

Good fences make good neighbors and bad fences make the other kind. Certainly no-one should put up a boundary fence, or wall or hedge, without consulting his neighbor, and it is far better to compromise if there is a disagreement. You will be far happier with the wrong sort of fence and a friend on the other side of it, than with the fence you wanted and a mortal enemy.

Hedges and fences each have advantages over the other. Hedges look nice, and they are alive and therefore foster other living things, like small animals, birds, moths and butterflies. They add to the biological richness of your garden, and they can be productive. Consider the merits of a crab apple, or a hazel, hedge for example.

However, hedges sterilize a lot of ground: that is to say they shade a wide stretch, but more drastically their roots spread out and draw all the moisture and nourishment out of a wide area. In a big garden this may not matter, but in a small one it does. Hedges can also harbor weeds and harmful insects. Personally I would not grumble about this, because they harbor useful insects — predators — as well, and to an organic gardener anything that increases the richness of life in his garden is to be encouraged. And it is easy enough to stop weeds from seeding in the soil below a hedge. Creeping perennial weeds like couch grass are a problem though, and in a small garden they represent a very strong argument against planting a hedge at all.

Fences and walls take up far less ground than hedges and do not send out roots to deprive the garden soil. Nor do they harbor insects and weeds. A major advantage is that they are quickly established: an instant solution. Most important of all though, is that they can be used for training cordon, espalier or fan-trained fruit trees or any food-bearing climbers, such as pole beans, toma-toes, cucumbers, squashes or melons. This to my mind gives them a very big advantage over hedges. There are not many plants that make a good hedge and at the same time provide food, while a fence or wall will support a great deal of food-bearing life, and you can therefore increase the effective area of your garden by the area of the side of the fence. You cannot do this with a hedge.

However, bear in mind that fences can look ugly, though of course they needn't. Choose one which appeals to you visually — as long as it is strong — use it to support fruit and vegetables, and you will have a beautiful fence. Also remember that fences are generally more expensive than hedges, especially if you gather the material for planting a hedge yourself. And fences don't last as long as hedges. Indeed there are many hedges which are known to be hundreds of years old. Walls are, of course, more expensive than hedges, but they do last.

Building a hedge

For my hedges I always plump for some simple indigenous plant like hawthorn or beech, which is attractive and keeps its brown leaves all winter. I lay, or plash, my hedges every three or four years so as to keep them dense and prevent them from opening out at the bottom. Plashing is the art of cutting almost through the upper stems of the hedge, laying them over at a slight angle to the horizontal without breaking them off, and weaving them together.

The many varieties of trees and bushes normally used for garden hedges, like privet and box, can be trained by clipping with shears. Personally, I could live quite happily without ever seeing another privet hedge, and would only grow box for proper trees; they produce marvelous hard timber which is suitable for making carvings, and for "priests", the small clubs which are so useful for administering the last rites to unlawfully caught fish.

Building a fence

Most gardeners have the fencing they inherited with their gardens. When you have to put up your own fences there are many considerations. The first is probably cheapness. In most parts of America wood is fairly cheap and is probably the best material. In much of Europe the price of wood is prohibitive. It is as cheap, and certainly more permanent, to use brick. Plain brick walls, such as surround many a city garden, can mellow and look attractive, and will last for centuries.

They can be claustrophobic, but they have the advantages of halting the progress of rabbits and storing the heat of the sun. Whatever you use, consider the fence as part of the garden, for growing things on, rather than merely a boundary marker.

If you want wire fences, the sunny side of your garden is an ideal place to have them. You can train sun-loving plants up them and get the benefit of your neighbor's sunshine as well as your own. A fence intended to break the force of the wind should not be solid. A solid fence causes strong and damaging wind eddies in its lee. A fence through which a little of the wind can percolate — what engineers call spoiling eddies — is a much better wind-break.

MAKING A WATTLE FENCE
To build a wattle fence, take split hazel or willow withes. Weave them into the uprights.

A wattle fence which you can build yourself is ideal for this purpose. A solid wall, particularly if it is painted black, on the north side of a garden, will warm in the sun and force on any tender trees which you train up it.

GARDEN SHEDS

A tiny garden shed that will just hold your tools is better than nothing, but if you can afford the money and space, or the labor and space, a good big shed that you can use as a potting shed, and which has room for a workbench for mending tools is very much better. And, if the shed is big enough to store potatoes, roots, seed, dried beans and even strings of onions, better still. I know a man who keeps two sixty gallon cider casks in his tool shed: one for parsnip wine and one for rhubarb wine. He is a wise and happy man.

Interior layout

My own belief about the insides of sheds is that anything that can be hung up should be hung up. That way you can find it when you want it, and it

doesn't get forgotten in some damp corner where it will go rusty or rot. Personally, I like to paint the outline of every tool on the wall where it is hung. Then I know if the tool is out of place and I go and look for it.

Inside and to one side of the door, out of any rain that may drive in, you should keep your sandbox (see p. 246). It takes only a second to jab your spade, fork, hoe or whatever into this as you bring it in, and if you always do this, you will always have clean, shiny, well-oiled tools. A "man" (see p. 246) should be hung on a string, also near the door. You can use this to scrape the worst mud off your tools before you bring them in. I think it is also a good idea to have a boot-jack on the floor for pulling off your boots. You then leave them in their appointed place in the shed and put on your indoor shoes before going into the house. Calico bags of beans and other large seeds should be hung up overhead. Paper seed packets should be put in a drawer. Herbs and vegetables can be hung up to dry. A small book-shelf for books like this one and for seed catalogs is a good idea.

Building a shed

Before you decide to buy an expensive factory-built shed consider making one yourself out of scrap material. A well-built shed, of second-hand wooden framing and weatherboarding, creosoted inside and well tarred outside, looks extremely good. The roof can be of planking with asphalt roll roofing over it. A roll of such material costs a lot less than new corrugated iron. It is extremely durable and simple to lay.

Another method of roofing which I find works very well is to begin by laying on a covering of corrugated scrap iron with holes drilled in it. Above this lay on plastic fertilizer bags overlapping like tiles so that they shed any water that comes from above. Cover this with another layer of corrugated scrap iron and nail right through. Paint the top layer with asphalt. This form of roof is well insulated, quite weatherproof, and very long lasting, though I cannot claim that it is a delight to the eye.

The most important thing with all wooden buildings is that they should have dry feet. No lumber should be set in the ground. It is a good idea to build the shed on piers of brick or concrete, and put in some form of damp coursing between the masonry and the wood. The very best thing to do is to lay a concrete floor below the shed and build on this.

Insulating a shed

It is a good idea to have your shed insulated. If you wish to store potatoes or other crops in the shed in very cold climates this is essential. Glass fiber insulation, like that used in attics and around hot water tanks is ideal. A method that should cost nothing is to use plastic fertilizer bags to build a false ceiling and false walls inside the shed. This creates a cavity of air between the outer walls and the plastic layer; as long as there are no gaps in the plastic, insulation of this kind can be very effective.

CARING FOR GARDEN TOOLS

Tools, like shoes, are paradoxically expensive if they are cheap. A cheap pair of shoes will last a hard working gardener a year; I have an expensive pair which is just wearing out after fifteen years. The very same principle applies to tools, and my

EQUIPPING A GARDEN SHED

This shed is made of framing and weatherboarding; it is creosoted inside and tarred outside, with a roof made of asphalt roofing. The floor is concrete, so that the wood has no chance of getting damp. Inside the shed all the items are arranged for greatest convenience. The tools are hung up on the wall, each one with its outline in whitewash, to make its absence conspicuous. A sandbox and a "man", along with a bootjack, are placed near the door, so that tools can be cleaned and muddy boots removed first thing upon entering the shed. Books, netting, animal feed and fruit canes are among the many and various things that can be kept in the shed.

advice is that, as long as you can afford them, you buy good quality, well made tools. Examine the joint between the handle and the metal working part. Are the two held together with one or two rivets, or is there a well-crafted snugly fitting join?

Replacing handles

The handles on good tools wear out faster than the tools themselves. But you can increase the life of wooden handles enormously by doing two things: oiling them with boiled linseed oil once a year, and keeping them indoors out of the rain.

Handles are notoriously expensive nowadays, but remember that every time a farmer lays a hedge he cuts out and burns scores of good potential handles. It pays, on visits to the country, to keep a look-out for lengths of clean, straight-grained, ash (or curved ash for particular jobs). Bring them home, hang them up in the tool shed to season, and then shape them to fit into your tools as handles.

Sharpening tools

Tools that are meant to be sharp should be kept sharp. Hoes particularly should have an edge: not a razor-sharp one that will crumple on hitting the first stone, of course, but a slightly rounded obtuse-angled edge. Spades, too, although the best ones are made to be pretty well self-sharpening, should be kept fairly sharp.

This does not mean that you should grind away at your hoes and spades until they are all worn to stumps, but that, when you find an edge badly worn away, you should use a file. A file is better for such tools than a grindstone.

All cutting tools like axes, hatchets, and pruning knives, should be kept keen at all costs. It is a complete waste of time to work with blunt tools. Cutting tools can be sharpened on a grindstone, with a hand stone, also known as a "whetstone", whether of carborundum or millstone grit, or with a file. If you use a circular grindstone be sure to keep it wet, otherwise the heat generated may take the temper out of the steel at the very edge of your blade. Be very wary of using a carborundum wheel too much on any one tool at one time. They can easily take the temper out of an edge.

Before sharpening any blade examine the shape of the edge carefully so that you know how to sharpen it. Always keep very strictly to the original angle of the edge of the blade. The blade must always be ground right down again to bring its cutting edge to the original angle.

Some blades, like those of axes and some knives are ground away on both sides so as to leave a symmetrical section. Sharpen both sides of these. Other blades like those of chisels, draw-knives, planes, and some pruning knives, are ground only on one side, so as to leave an asymmetrical section. With these do all your grinding and whetting on one side, and then simply pass the other side, laid quite flat, a few times over the grinding device, just to take off the burr.

You can use a man to clean the worst of the mud off your garden tools. You can make a man yourself by sawing a piece of hard wood so that it has a handle and a wedge-shaped blade. Keep it on a string by the door of your tool shed.

Looking after tools

Man A man is a wedge-shaped piece of hard wood with a sharpened edge. Hang it on a piece of string by the door of your tool shed and use it to scrape the mud off your spades, forks, shovels, hoes and everything else before you take them into your shed and plunge them into the sandbox.

USING A SANDBOX
The best way to keep the blades of garden tools clean is to keep a sandbox – a box filled with old automobile oil and sand – just inside the door of your tool shed. Whenever you bring a tool into the shed, submerge the blade in the sandbox before putting the tool away.

Sandbox There is one terribly simple method of doubling the life, and effectiveness, of steel tools and that is to have a sandbox. Find a box deep enough to hold the blade of your biggest spade. Fill it with a mixture of sand and used oil, which you can get free when you, or someone else, drains your car. Every time you come in from working with any steel tool just plunge the blade into the sandbox. This both cleans and oils the blade. If you keep your sandbox out of the rain, it will last for many years without needing a change of contents.

SEED LIVES AND VEGETABLE YIELDS

	Percentage germination in years			Average yield per 10 ft. row
	Up to 100%	75%+	50%+	
Asparagus	2	3-4	4-5	10 lbs (4.5 kg)
Beans broad	2	4	6	8 lbs (3.6 kg)
bush	2	3	—	8 lbs (3.6 kg)
lima	1	3	—	2.5 lbs (1.2 kg)
pole	2	3	5	17-30 lbs (8-14 kg)
soybean	1	2	6	1.5 lbs (0.7 kg)
Beets	3	6	10	15 lbs (6.8 kg)
Broccoli	3	4	6	12 lbs (5.4 kg)
Brussels sprouts	2	4	5-6	11 lbs (5 kg)
Cabbage spring	3	5	10	5-8 heads
summer	3	5	10	5-8 heads
winter	3	5	10	5-8 heads
Chinese	3	5	7	10 heads
Carrots	2	3	5	8 lbs (3.6 kg)
Cauliflowers	3	4	5	5-8 heads
Celeriac	3	4	5-6	12-20 lbs (5.4-9 kg)
Celery	3	4	5-6	12-14 lbs (5.4-6.4 kg)
Chicory	3	4	5-6	20 heads or 40 roots
Cress and upland cress	3	5	9	Lots
Cucumbers	1	4	6	50 cucumbers
Dandelions	1	2	5	Lots
Eggplants	4	5	—	20 lbs (9 kg)
Endive	5-6	7-8	10	10-12 plants
Florence fennel	3	4	7	20 bulbs
Hamburg parsley	1	2	4	10-15 lbs (4.5-6.8 kg)
Kale	3-4	4-5	6-7	12 lbs (5.4 kg)
Kohlrabi	3	4-5	6-7	12 lbs (5.4 kg)
Leeks	1	2	3-4	20-30 leeks
Lettuce	3	4	6	15 lettuces
Melons	1	2	4	12-16 melons
Okra	4	5	—	16-20 pods
Onions	2	2	4	8-10 lbs (3.6-4.5 kg)
Parsnips	1	1-2	4	15-20 lbs (6.8-9 kg)
Peanuts	1	—	—	2-5 lbs unshelled (0.9-2.3 kg)
Peas	3	4	9	20 lbs (9 kg) pods
Peppers	2	2-4	7-8	7.5-10 lbs (3.4-4.5 kg)
Potatoes	Plant seed potatoes			25 lbs (11.3 kg)
Radishes	4	5	—	Lots
Rhubarb	Plant crowns			30-60 stalks
Rutabagas and turnips	2	2-3	5-6	8-14 lbs (3.6-6.4 kg)
Salsify	1	1-2	3	6 lbs (2.7 kg)
Seakale	1	1-2	3	8-12 lbs (3.6-5.4 kg)
Spinach	2	3-4	5-6	8-10 lbs (3.6-4.5 kg)
Spinach beet	1	2-4	5-6	10-15 lbs (4.5-6.8 kg)
Squashes	4	6	—	8-15 marrows
Sweet corn	1	2	3	30-50 cobs
Swiss chard	2	6	10	8 lbs (3.6 kg)
Tomatoes	3	6	10	20 lbs (9 kg)
Watercress	2	5	9	Lots
Watermelons	3	6	10	5-10 melons

FOR MORE HELP

Information about Organic Gardening

International Federation of Organic Agriculture Movements (IFOAM), Box 900, Emmaus, Pa. 18049

Information about Vegetables and Fruits

For specific information about growing vegetables and fruits, as well as advice about soils and pest problems in your local area, consult your County Extension Agent. You can find the address of your nearest agent in the phone directory under the county-government heading.

The U.S. Department of Agriculture also offers excellent publications on a variety of gardening subjects. For a list of their available publications ($.45) write: U.S. Department of Agriculture, Superintendent of Documents, U.S. Government Printing Office, Washington, D.C. 20402.

Information about Deep Bed Gardening

Covelo Garden Project, Covelo, Round Valley, Ca. 95428

Information about Poultry

Willow Hill Hatchery, Department B, Richland, Pa. 19355 (for chicks, goslings and ducklings)
Stromberg Chicks, Pine River 4, Minnesota 56474

Information about Beekeeping Equipment

Midwestern Hive Co., 1527 East 26th Street, Minneapolis, Minn. 55404
Sunstream Bee Supply, Box 225, Eighty Four, Pa. 15330 (for bees, as well as all types of equipment)

Information about Winemaking Equipment

Continental Products, 5319 West 86th St., Indianapolis, Indiana 47268
Wine Hobby USA, Box 1866-E, Allentown, Pa. 18105
Valport Industries, 1438 North West 23rd St., Portland, Ore. 97210.

CLIMATE ZONES

If you grow only the crops that grow indigenously in your climate zone, you will not suffer many losses due to climate, nor will you have to protect your plants from the weather. But of course gardeners don't do this. Quite rightly they like a varied diet so they push their luck, and try to grow the more succulent and tasty crops farther north or south than the plants really want to grow. This is why an understanding of climate is important to the gardener. It tells him when to plant, when to harvest and, perhaps most important, when to protect his plants artificially.

Cities are always warmer than the open countryside. The waste heat from houses and all those people contribute toward this. So, if you live in a city or its suburbs, you can plant a little earlier, and enjoy a longer growing season than the gardeners in the countryside nearby.

Frost

The period which elapses between the last freeze of the spring and the first freeze of the fall is a crucial time for vegetable gardeners. If you want to grow outdoors those plants which are tender –

and they include all the crops which are indigenous to warm climates: tomatoes, cucumbers, peppers, squashes – you can grow them outside only during this period. Except for root crops and *brassica*, all your vegetables should be harvested before the first fall frost.

The growing period of food plants can be measured against the growing period of grass. When the grass in your lawn starts to grow, after the dormant winter period, you can start putting in seed. Grass begins to grow when the soil temperature reaches 43°F (6°C) in the spring. When the soil temperature falls below that temperature in the fall, grass stops growing.

There are certain factors that affect the dates of the first and last freezes. Proximity to the sea, or any deep water, tends to warm air and prevent frost, while altitude generally increases the cold.

Rainfall

Lucky is the gardener whose land gets just the right amount of water naturally from rainfall. Too much winter rain washes the nutrients out of the soil, erodes the soil itself and prevents the gardener from getting out on to the land as early as he would like. Planting green manure crops on

Last expected frost date

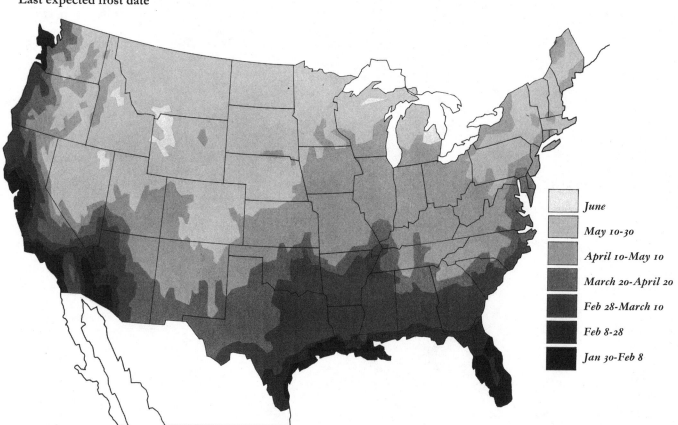

June
May 10-30
April 10-May 10
March 20-April 20
Feb 28-March 10
Feb 8-28
Jan 30-Feb 8

vacant vegetable beds in winter prevents erosion and keeps the nutrients in the soil.

The garden needs rain in the spring and early summer and not too much rain in midsummer. Most of us have to give nature a hand and either dig irrigation furrows or get out the hose or watering can.

Sunshine

Some sunshine is important for all food-producing plants except mushrooms. Crops like sweet corn, eggplants, peppers, melons, tomatoes, cucumbers, peaches and grapes will not ripen without plenty of sun. In areas which get little sun you can, of course, grow these crops under glass or plastic and, if necessary, provide artificial heat. On the other hand some crops cannot take too much sun, lettuce plants go to seed and die when summer heat sets in.

Wind

Many plants suffer badly in windy positions. As well as the strength of the wind itself there is the problem that wind exaggerates the effect of frost. In an area of high winds, try to utilize sheltered spots, or build windbreaks.

The USDA Regions

CLIMATE REGIONS

Region 1 Cool, dry summers with frequent fogs. Heavy winter rainfall.

Region 2 Summers drier and warmer than Region 1. Average low temperatures 10° to 20° F.

Region 3 Hot, dry summers. Mild winters with 8 to 10 inches of rain. Low temperatures: 22° to 24° F.

Region 4 A very mountainous region. Conditions vary greatly according to elevation.

Region 5 Summers on the coast dry and cool, but warmer inland. 10 inches of rainfall in the valleys, 30 inches in mountains.

Region 6 Summers warm. Winter temperatures average 10° to 15° F. Most rain in winter and spring.

Region 7 Summers warm. Winter temperatures range from 0° to 15° F. Rainfall: 10 to 20 inches.

Region 8 Semi-arid – hot summers and cold winters with temperatures between 0° and –10° F.

Region 9 Cold winters. Hot summer days with frosty nights.

Region 10 Scorching hot with a rainfall of 3 to 10 inches.

Region 11 Same as Region 9, but hotter.

Region 12 Elevation and exposure variations mean big differences in rainfall and temperature.

Region 13 Similar to Region 12, but temperatures at same elevations 7° F hotter on average.

Region 14 Similar to Regions 12 and 13 but warmer.

Region 15 Moderately warm summers, but extremely cold winters.

Region 16 Dry farming area, warmer than Region 15. Rainfall 12 to 22 inches.

Region 17 Dry and hot with 12 to 22 inches of rainfall but excessive evaporation.

Region 18 Fairly humid with cold, dry winters.

Region 19 Sudden variations in winter temperature. Hot winds in summer.

Region 20 Transition between dry farming regions to the west and humid climate of eastern Texas.

Region 21 Cold winters with drying winds. The 20 to 30 inches of rain comes mostly in summer.

Region 22 Prairie country with cold drying winter winds. Rainfall: 30 to 40 inches.

Region 23 East warmer and more humid than west, which is similar to Region 21.

Region 24 Moisture-laden atmosphere, 30 to 40 inches of rainfall spread over the year.

Region 25 Warm summer with risk of drought. Moderate winter. Rainfall: 40 to 50 inches.

Region 26 Long days and cool nights in summer. Heavy snowfalls in winter.

Region 27 Abundant rain – 35 to 50 inches – throughout the year. Heavy snow in colder areas.

Region 28 Warmer than Region 27 with possibility of drought at end of summer. Moderate winters.

Region 29 Warm summers and abundant rainfall – 45 to 60 inches.

Region 30 Hot in summer. Short winter with much rain.

Region 31 Warm summers, but killing annual frosts. Rainfall: about 50 inches.

Region 32 No killing frosts and only slight temperature variations. Rainfall: 50 to 60 inches.

Index

Figures in **bold** indicate a major reference.
Figures in *italics* indicate illustrations or
illustrated text.

Index

Index

sweet violet
curry
peppermint
parsley
English thyme
Yarrow
Bea Balm
Chamomile

Acknowledgments

Author's Acknowledgments

I would like to express my gratitude to the many people who have helped in the making of this book, particularly the staff of Dorling Kindersley, who have worked with great devotion and good will for many months — far beyond the call of ordinary duty. I would also like to thank the artists, for doing such excellent illustrations, and the people who live and work at my farm, for their help in carrying out the many experiments and trials that have provided information for the book. Lastly I would like to thank everyone who helped with advice, demonstrations and information, with special thanks to Lawrence D. Hills, Dr. Shewell-Cooper, the East Malling Research Station, the Covelo Garden Trust California, Ecology Action California, and many private gardeners in the United States, Britain, Italy and France.

JOHN SEYMOUR

Repels Aphids
yellow Nasturtiums
Spearmint
stinging nettle
southernwood
garlic

Dorling Kindersley Limited
would like to thank the
following for their special
contributions to the book:

Michael Carlo
Georgina D'Angelo
East Malling
   Research Station
Katherine Fenlaugh
Fred Ford
Ramona Ann Gale
Lesley Gilbert
K. Holmes of Cramers Ltd.
Sally Seymour
Dr W. E. Shewell-Cooper
Martin Solomons,
   Mick Leahy, John Rudzitis
   and the staff of Vantage
Alan Lynch, Geoff Smith
   and the staff of Cowells

ARTISTS
David Ashby
David Bryant
Brian Craker
Julian Holland
Peter Kesteven
Robert Micklewright
Peter Morter
Nigel Osborne
Jim Robins
Malcolm Smythe
Eric Thomas

We the People

THE CITIZEN & THE CONSTITUTION

LEVEL 2

Center for Civic Education

21600 Oxnard St., Suite 500

Woodland Hills, CA 91367

www.civiced.org

818.591.9321

Directed by the

CENTER FOR CIVIC EDUCATION

and funded by the

U.S. DEPARTMENT OF EDUCATION

under the Education for Democracy Act approved by the

UNITED STATES CONGRESS

Cover: Frank Blackwell Mayer, *The Continentals*,

Prints and Photographs Division, Library of Congress,

PGA-Mayer-Continentals (C size) [P&P]

Cover and interior design: Mark Stritzel

ISBN-13:   **978-0-89818-173-9**

ISBN-10:   **0-89818-173-9**

ACKNOWLEDGMENTS

The following staff and consultants have contributed to the development of this text.

PRINCIPAL WRITERS
Charles N. Quigley
Ken Rodriguez

CONTRIBUTING WRITER
Charles F. Bahmueller

EDITORIAL DIRECTOR
Theresa M. Richard

EDITOR
David Hargrove

PRODUCTION EDITORS
Mark Gage
Catherine Saum

CREATIVE DIRECTOR
Mark Stritzel

ILLUSTRATOR
Richard Stein

PRODUCTION DESIGNERS
Erin Breese
Sean Fay

PHOTO RESEARCHER
Natalie Kean

REVIEWERS
Charles F. Bahmuller
Margaret Stimmann Branson
Sally J. Broughton
Terri DuMont
Maria Gallo
Jackie Johnson
Dick Kean
Robert Leming
Clayton Lucas
Lori Mable
Robert McCoy
Donna Paoletti Phillips
Susan Roe
Darnell Tabron
Lynette Wallace

SPECIAL THANKS

We wish to express our thanks to the following
individuals who also contributed to the text:

Kevin Fox, Suzanne Soule, and Sharareh Frouzesh Bennett
for writing the student test; Rose Freeland for illustration retouching;
Robert Meyers for prepress; Sally Mills, our print consultant; and
Robert Sinclair at Sinclair Printing.

CHIEF JUSTICE OF THE UNITED STATES 1969–1986
CHAIR, COMMISSION ON THE BICENTENNIAL
OF THE UNITED STATES CONSTITUTION

The years 1987 to 1991 marked the 200th anniversary of the writing, ratification, and implementation of the basic documents of American democracy, the Constitution and the Bill of Rights. Our Constitution has stood the tests and stresses of time, wars, and change. Although it is not perfect, as Benjamin Franklin and many others recognized, it has lasted because it was carefully crafted by men who understood the importance of a system of government sufficiently strong to meet the challenges of the day, yet sufficiently flexible to accommodate and adapt to new political, economic, and social conditions.

Many Americans have but a slight understanding of the Constitution, the Bill of Rights, and the later amendments to which we pledge our allegiance. The lessons in this book are designed to give you, the next generation of American citizens, an understanding of the background, creation, and subsequent history of the unique system of government brought into being by our Constitution. At the same time, it will help you understand the principles and ideals that underlie and give meaning to the Constitution, a system of government by those governed.

CONTENTS

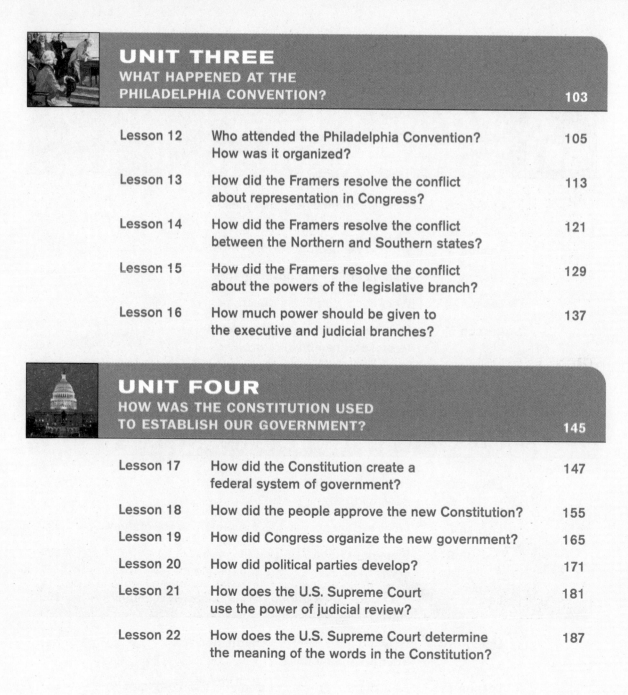

UNIT THREE
WHAT HAPPENED AT THE PHILADELPHIA CONVENTION?

103

UNIT FOUR
HOW WAS THE CONSTITUTION USED TO ESTABLISH OUR GOVERNMENT?

145

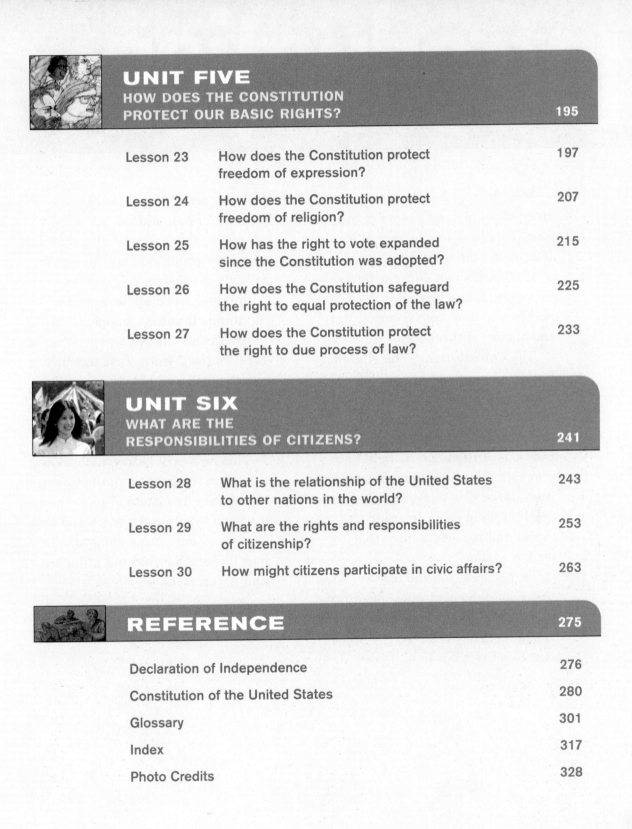

introduction

Most history books tell the story of people and events of the past. This book is a history of ideas. It explains the most important ideas of our Constitution and how they were developed. It also highlights the people and events that were important in the history of these ideas.

The Constitution of the United States was created as a plan for the new government of our country. It was written in Philadelphia in 1787, more than 215 years ago. We study the Constitution and its history to understand our government and how it is supposed to work. Knowing our past will help us understand the rights and responsibilities that we have today.

In this book, you will discover what the people who wrote our Constitution thought the purposes of government should be. They believed government should protect our lives, liberty, and property. They also believed government should promote the common good. You will also learn why they thought it was necessary to limit the powers of government.

You will learn about some of the things that have happened to the Constitution since it was written in 1787. You will study ways in which it has changed and how these changes came about. You will also learn about ways the Constitution has stayed the same.

This book will help you develop a good understanding of the Constitution and our system of government. It will also help you understand more about how our government affects your life, and how you can influence your government.

What were the Founders' basic ideas about government?

unit ONE

In the spring and summer of 1787, fifty-five men met in Philadelphia. These men knew a great deal about government. They wrote our Constitution. They and many other Americans gained their knowledge by reading and discussing books about history and political philosophy. Political philosophy is the study of basic ideas of government.

Americans also knew about government from their own experience. Many of the men who met in Philadelphia had been leaders in the American colonies when they were ruled by Great Britain. Many were leaders in the new state governments formed after the American Revolution.

The men who wrote the Constitution used their knowledge and experience to create the best kind of government they could. An understanding of their knowledge and experience will give you some insight into why they created the kind of government we have today. It will also help you discover and appreciate the most important ideas in our Constitution.

What were the British colonies in America like in the 1770s?

1

LESSON PURPOSE

People living in the American colonies in the 1770s were in many ways quite different from the people living in Europe. The colonists brought British laws and customs to America—but they were developing their own way of life as well.

When you finish this lesson, you should be able to explain how the average person in the American colonies lived in the 1770s. You should also be able to explain how life in the colonies influenced people's ideas about good government.

Founders
government
indentured servants
self-sufficient
subject

Why study the British colonies in North America?

We begin our study of the U.S. Constitution by looking back in history. The period is the 1770s. By that time, there had been European colonies established in North America for more than 150 years. Nations that had set up colonies in America included France, Great Britain, the Netherlands, and Spain.

Our study will focus on the British colonies. It was these thirteen colonies that became the United States of America.

By the 1770s, the British colonies along the eastern coast of North America were well established. The British colonists were subjects of Great Britain. Being a **subject** in this case means being under the rule of a monarch. In 1770, King George III was the ruler of Great Britain. Our nation did not yet exist.

Learning about how the people lived in the British colonies can help us to understand why they developed their ideas about government. When we talk about **government** we mean the people and institutions with authority to make and enforce the laws and manage

What did it mean to the colonists to be subjects of King George III?

disputes about laws. People living in the 1770s in the British colonies held certain beliefs about good government that still affect our lives today.

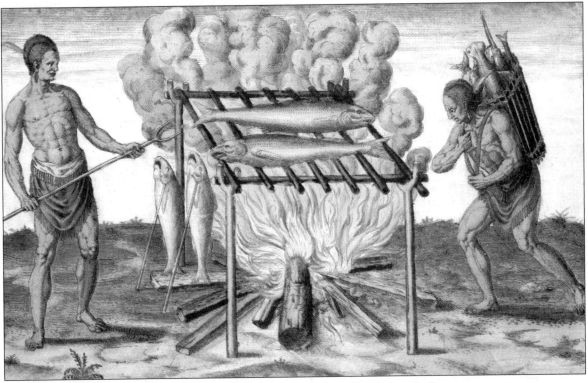

What was life like for American Indians along the eastern coast of North America?

How did American Indians live before the Europeans came?

The Europeans were newcomers to North America. Hundreds of different groups of Native American people had inhabited the continent for thousands of years. Along the eastern seacoast, where the British colonists settled, the native Indian people lived in well-organized tribes. They are known as the Eastern Woodland tribes. They lived by fishing, hunting, gathering wild plants, and tending small crops of corn.

The eastern tribes maintained loose political ties among themselves. In some cases, entire tribes formed leagues so that they could come together to discuss common problems. The best known league was the Iroquois League.

The Iroquois League was made up of five tribes that lived in what today is the state of New York.

Where did the British colonists settle?

The British colonies in America occupied a large area of land. The colonies stretched twelve hundred miles along the coast of the Atlantic Ocean and ran two hundred miles inland. Between the settled area and the Mississippi River lay a vast, forested country. Few Europeans had explored beyond the area of settlement. The nations of Europe were small in area compared to America. Great Britain was only slightly larger than the colony of New York.

Although the land was expansive, there were few people living on it. In 1790, the population of the colonies was almost 4 million, compared with more than 300 million people living in the United States today.

How did people in the colonies earn a living?

Boston, New York, and Philadelphia were the largest cities in the colonies. Each had a population of more than 25,000 people. Most people in cities or towns earned their living by working in professions, trades, crafts, or small factories.

Most colonists did not live in cities. They lived in small communities or villages or on farms. Ninety percent of the colonists were farmers. A typical farm was between 90 and 160 acres. Farm size varied from the small 30-acre plot of the poorest New England farmers to giant Southern plantations with thousands of acres. Not all colonists were independent farmers. Some were hired laborers or craftspeople working on the larger farms.

Outside the cities and small communities, people in the colonies might live as far as ten miles from their nearest neighbor. As a result, they had to develop the knowledge and skills to provide for themselves in order to survive.

The people became self-sufficient. **Self-sufficient** means that people had to provide for their own needs. Not only did the colonists grow their own food,

How was life on a small, Northern farm different from life on a large, Southern plantation?

they also wove cloth to make their own clothing. They made their own medicines, built their own homes and barns, and made their furniture and tools. Colonists took the surplus produce from their farms and traded it for goods they could not make.

Although families worked independently, they traded among their neighbors and helped each other. Neighbors got together to build houses and barns. People rarely traveled more than fifty miles from their homes.

A farm family frequently included a hired laborer or an indentured servant. **Indentured servants** were men and women who sold their labor in exchange for the cost of the trip from Europe to the colonies. Farm families often relied on the labor of slaves, especially in the South.

The typical colonial family in the 1770s worked hard and had the highest standard of living in the world. The land was fertile and crops grew well. As a result, the colonists had diets rich in protein and tended to be healthier than people in Europe.

The colonists were also better educated than most Europeans. In fact, a greater percentage of people in the colonies were able to read and write than in any European nation. The most popular publications, other than the Bible, were newspapers. Four times as many newspapers were published in the colonies than in France.

While most colonists lived fairly well, this was not true of everyone. One-fifth of the population was held in slavery. The slaves were people who were brought as laborers to the colonies from different regions of Africa. Slavery was permitted in all the colonies, North and South. Slavery continued to be practiced until 1865.

How were the people living in the colonies different from one another?

Most colonists were descended from British or Irish settlers. Therefore, most people in the colonies spoke English. Some colonists did not come from English-speaking countries, however. Settlers came from France, Germany, the Netherlands, Spain, Sweden and other countries. All brought with them their own customs and ideas about government and rights.

The colonists also held different religious beliefs. There were many different groups of Protestants; there also were Catholics and Jews. Compared to most European nations of the time, the population of the colonies was diverse.

What contributions have people from other nations brought to the United States?

How did this colonial farmer compare life in America with life in Great Britain?

In the 1700s a French colonist who settled in New York wrote a book that contained a series of letters from a fictional Pennsylvania farmer to his friend in Great Britain. J. Hector St. John was the pen name that Jean de Crèvecoeur used for his book. The letters describe Crèvecoeur's views about life in America. Some sections of these letters follow. Read them and discuss the questions at the end.

*Behold, Sir, a humble American Planter...
addressing you from the farther side
of the Atlantic....*

[The English traveler to America] *is
arrived on a new continent; a modern
society... different from what he had
hitherto seen. It is not composed, as in
Europe, of great lords who possess everything and of a herd of people who have
nothing. Here are no aristocratical families,
no courts, no kings.... The rich and the poor
are not so far removed from each other as
they are in Europe. Some few towns
excepted, we are all tillers of the earth....*
[Here we are] *united by the silken bands
of mild government, all respecting the
laws, without dreading their power,
because they are equitable [fair].*

[Here the traveler] *views not the
hostile castle, and the haughty mansion,
contrasted with the clay-built hut and
miserable cabin, where cattle and men*

help to keep each other warm, and dwell in meanness [humility], smoke, and indigence [poverty].... The meanest [most humble] of our log-houses is a dry and comfortable habitation.

Lawyer or merchant are the fairest titles our towns afford.... We have no princes, for whom we toil, starve, and bleed: we are the most perfect society now existing in the world. Here man is free; as he ought to be....

Can a wretch...call England or any other kingdom his country? A country that had no bread for him, whose fields procured him no harvest, who met with nothing but the frowns of the rich, the severity of the laws, with jails and punishments; who owned not a single foot of the extensive surface of the planet? No! urged by a variety of motives here they came. Everything has tended to regenerate them; new laws, a new mode of living, a new social system....

Formerly they were not numbered in any civil lists of their country, except in those of the poor; here they rank as citizens.

① What was it that Crèvecoeur liked about life in the colonies?

② What rights did he enjoy?

③ Given what you know of Crèvecoeur's experiences, explain why he would or would not favor laws that

- guarantee each individual the right to own property

- limit an individual's right to buy and sell goods to anyone he or she chooses

- give people certain rights because they are wealthy or from a certain family background or group

④ How might people in Great Britain react to Crèvecoeur's comparisons of life in America and life in Europe? Explain.

Why were class differences not important in the colonies?

The colonies were not divided into a few rich people and a large mass of poor people as in most of Europe. In the colonies, there was no royalty and no titled nobility.

The difference between wealthy and poor people was less important in colonial society. A poor person could become wealthy by using knowledge, skills, and opportunities. In many cases, a man who was not part of the wealthy class could be elected to a government position.

Whose opportunities were limited?

Not all people shared the same opportunities to gain wealth or to become leaders. Usually, only adult white males who owned property could vote. In most colonies, a person had to own fifty acres of land to be qualified to vote. But land was easily available. Therefore, more people in the colonies had the right to vote than in any other country of that time.

Native Americans, blacks, white men without property, and women were typically not allowed to vote or hold office. Women usually were not allowed to own property. Under the law, married couples were considered one person and the husband controlled the property.

What does this picture tell you about the right to vote in colonial America?

What rights did the colonists value?

Since most colonists were self-sufficient, they valued their freedom highly. The people in the colonies thought that their society was superior to the corrupt societies of Europe. Colonists considered themselves to be virtuous, hardworking, simple people.

As subjects of Great Britain, the colonists enjoyed the rights included in the British constitution. You will learn about these rights in Lesson 6. Many colonial governments also protected the rights of the colonists. For example, the Massachusetts Body of Liberties of 1641 included the right to trial by jury, free elections, and the right of free men to own property. The state of Pennsylvania guaranteed freedom of belief or conscience.

In the years before the American Revolution, the colonists were very sensitive to any attempts by the British government to limit their rights. After the Revolution, Americans were concerned with protecting the rights they had just fought for.

Who were the Founders?

Throughout this text, we refer to a group of people as the Founders. The **Founders** were the political leaders of the colonies. They had developed their own ideas about what might be the best kind of government. These ideas were formed from their own experiences and their studies of governments of the past. The Founders led the fight to free the American colonies from British rule. The Founders helped to create the state governments, and their ideas influenced the writing of the Constitution. Some of the Founders' names that you might recognize include John and Abigail Adams, Benjamin Franklin, Patrick Henry, Thomas Jefferson, Mercy Otis Warren, and George Washington.

John Adams, one of our nation's Founders, once said that "revolution was in the minds and hearts of the people before Lexington and Concord." What does this statement mean?

1. In what ways were people's lives in the British colonies of the 1770s different from those of people living in Europe?

2. What diversity of people and ideas existed in the British colonies in the 1770s?

3. What difference did gender, race, and wealth make to people in colonial society?

4. What rights did the colonists value?

5. Who were the Founders?

ACTIVITIES

1. Go to your library or search the Internet. Find information about what life in the colonies was like for one of the following groups:

   - children and adolescents
   - indentured servants
   - Native Americans
   - people held in slavery
   - women

2. The British colonies in America are generally divided into three regions: the New England Colonies, the Middle Colonies, and the Southern Colonies. Learn more about what life was like in each region. Write a brief summary for your class.

3. On an outline map of the United States, mark the British, French, and Spanish colonies with different colors. What states are these colonies now?

Why do we need government?

LESSON PURPOSE

Our form of government is based on a set of ideas. These ideas establish what the purpose of government should be and what kind of government is best. This lesson introduces you to some of the basic ideas that were of great importance to the Founders. In this lesson you will learn about the idea of natural rights.

When you finish this lesson, you should be able to explain what the Founders believed to be the natural rights of human beings. You should also be able to explain why the Founders believed that the people need a government, and how people create governments.

2

consent
natural rights
purpose of government
social contract
state of nature

How did the ideas of John Locke influence the Founders?

The Founders were students of history and philosophy. They studied books, read newspapers, and listened to sermons in church. The Founders discussed and exchanged ideas with each other and with other people.

One philosopher whose writings influenced the thinking of the Founders was John Locke. John Locke was a well-known English philosopher. He lived from 1632 to 1704. Locke published a book called *Two Treatises of Government* in 1689. In that book Locke explained his ideas about natural rights. Locke's book was widely read and discussed in the American colonies. Many of the Founders' ideas about government were based on Locke's philosophy.

John Locke arrived at his ideas by imagining what life might be like if people were living in a **state of nature**. By this, Locke did not mean necessarily that people lived in the wilderness. Locke simply saw a state of nature as a condition in which no governments or laws existed at all.

What did John Locke mean by a state of nature?

What might life be like in a state of nature?

It is now your turn to be a philosopher like John Locke. First, imagine that you and all the students in your school are living in a state of nature. You have plenty of food and other resources to maintain life and to live well. But there is no government and there are no laws or rules that you have to follow. There is no one to tell you what to do and no one to protect you.

With your partner or group discuss the following questions about your rights in a state of nature. Be prepared to share your ideas with your class. Finally, compare your ideas with those of John Locke—after you read the section "What were Locke's ideas about natural rights?"

1 What might be some advantages and disadvantages of living in a state of nature?

2 What rights, if any, might you expect to have in a state of nature?

3 What might people who are stronger or smarter than others try to do? Why?

4 What might people who are weaker or less skilled than others try to do? Why?

5 What might life be like for everyone living in a state of nature?

6 Would anyone have the right to govern you? Would you have a right to govern anyone else? Why?

7 What are some things the people could do to protect their lives, liberty, or property?

By imagining life in a state of nature, Locke was able to answer some important questions like these:

- What is human nature? For example, are all people mainly interested in their own welfare, or do they tend to care for the good of others?

- What should be the main purpose of government?

- How do people who run government get the right to govern?

- What kinds of government should people support and obey?

- What kinds of government should people resist?

The Founders discussed and debated John Locke's answers to these questions. The ideas of Locke were used in the Declaration of Independence to explain why Americans were opposed to British rule in the colonies. After winning the Revolutionary War, the Founders used most of the same ideas to write their state constitutions. The ideas of the natural rights philosophy also are important to the kind of government that we have today.

What were Locke's ideas about natural rights?

John Locke believed that through reasoning we can determine what rights people would have in a state of nature.

Locke reasoned that in a state of nature all people seek to have the following rights:

- **Life** People want to survive. People want to be as safe as possible from threats to their lives.

- **Liberty** People want to be as free as possible. People want to be able to make their own decisions and to live as they please.

- **Property** People want to own the things that are necessary to survive, such as food, houses, tools, or land. People want the freedom to work and to gain economic benefits.

Locke said that the rights to life, liberty, and property are **natural rights**. These rights are a part of the law of nature. This means that all people have the rights to life, liberty, and property just because they are human beings.

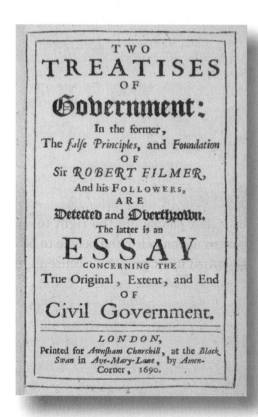

What were Locke's ideas about natural rights?

How does this illustration demonstrate what might happen in a state of nature?

The Founders believed that such rights as those to life, liberty, and property are not man-made. Instead, our rights are based on the laws of nature, which were made by God. The Declaration of Independence, for example, speaks of "the Laws of Nature and of Nature's God." It says that people are "endowed by their Creator" with certain basic rights and that no one may take away these rights.

What did John Locke say might happen in a state of nature?

1. Locke believed that most people are reasonable and good. Most people respect the rights of others because their conscience tells them that they have a duty to do so. But people are also driven by their self-interest. A few humans are not so reasonable and good. Sometimes people who are stronger or more skilled abuse those who are weaker or less skilled.

2. Locke believed that in a state of nature, people protect their natural rights by using their own strength and skill. People who are weaker or less skilled would find it very hard to protect their rights. Instead, weaker people would try to protect their rights by joining together against the strong.

3. Locke believed that in a state of nature, no one's life, liberty, or property would be safe. People would feel insecure. In a state of nature, there are no governments or laws to protect life, liberty, or property. This is why people agreed to form governments. According to Locke, governments do not exist until people create them.

4. Locke believed that in a state of nature, no one would have the right to govern you, and you would not have the right to govern anyone else. According to Locke, there is only one way that people get the right to govern anyone else: the people to be governed must give their consent. **Consent** means to approve of something or allow something to take place. If the people have not given their consent to create a government, there is no legitimate government. In other words, the power of legitimate government comes from the consent of the people.

Why do people agree to form a social contract?

Although people agreed that certain natural rights existed, they worried about how those rights could be protected. In a state of nature, people might feel free to do anything they want to do. Their rights would not be protected, however, and that would make them feel insecure.

For John Locke and other natural rights philosophers, the great problem was to find a way to protect each person's natural rights so that everyone could enjoy them and live at peace with one another. Locke said that the best way to solve this problem is for each individual to agree with others to create and live under a government and give that government the power to make and enforce laws. Locke called this kind of agreement a **social contract**.

As in all contracts, to get something you must give up something. In a social contract everyone promises to give up the absolute right to do anything she or he wants to do. Absolute means without any limits. In return, everyone receives the security that can be provided by a government. Each person consents to obey the limits placed upon her or him by the laws created by the government. Everyone gains the security of knowing that their rights to life, liberty, and property are protected.

Government, then, is the better alternative to a state of nature, which would be imperfect because some people might not respect the rights of others. According to Locke, the main **purpose of government** is to protect those natural rights that the individual cannot effectively protect in a state of nature.

In a later lesson, you will study the Declaration of Independence. You will see how the Founders included all the ideas that you have studied in this lesson. You will also learn to examine questions about what kind of government the people should support and obey and what kind they should resist.

How might individuals protect their natural rights in a state of nature?

What rights do you think all people should have?

Most people would agree that there are certain rights all people should have. For example, you probably agree that everyone has the right to be protected from robbers and murderers. You probably also agree that a person's right to vote should be protected. Most people in the United States share the belief that everyone should have these rights.

Work with a partner or in a group of three students. Together answer the questions that follow. Be prepared to share your ideas with the class.

❶ List five rights that you think all people in our nation should have. Why do you think that it is important that all people should have these rights?

❷ Which of the rights on your list seem to be the most important? Arrange the rights you listed in the order of their importance. Explain why you ranked the rights on your list in this order.

❸ What might you do in order to ensure that these rights are protected?

In a state of nature, how might one's life, liberty, or property be protected?

1. What are natural rights? How do people get their natural rights?

2. What might life be like for people living in a state of nature? Explain.

3. Where does government get its right to govern, according to the natural rights philosophy?

4. What is a social contract?

5. What is the main purpose of government according to John Locke?

ACTIVITIES

1. In this lesson you learned about the social contract. Most passengers aboard the *Mayflower* signed the Mayflower Compact in 1620, before the ship landed in Plymouth. Read the Mayflower Compact below. Write a brief essay explaining how the Mayflower Compact is an example of a social contract.

   Having undertaken, for the glory of God, and advancement of the Christian Faith and Honour of our King and Country, a Voyage to plant the First Colony in the Northern Parts of Virginia, do by these presents solemnly and mutually in the presence of God and of one another, Covenant and Combine ourselves together into a Civil Body Politic, for our better ordering and preservation and further-ance of the ends aforesaid; and by virtue hereof, to enact, constitute, and frame such just and equal Laws, Ordinances, Acts, Constitutions, and Offices, from time to time, as shall be thought most meet and convenient for the general good of the Colony, unto which we promise all due submission and obedience.

2. Draw a cartoon that illustrates what life might be like in a state of nature. Use your cartoon to illustrate why we need government.

3. Read *Lord of the Flies* by William Golding. It is a novel about what happened when a group of young boys found themselves in a situation where there were no laws and no government. Share the story with your class. Does this story support Locke's ideas? If so, which ones?

4. Write a short story that tells how the rights to life, liberty, and property apply to you and your family. Share your story with the class.

What is republican government?

LESSON PURPOSE

This lesson introduces the ideas of republican government, the common good, and civic virtue. These were ideas the Founders learned from studying the government of the ancient Roman Republic. You will learn how these ideas shaped the Founders' thinking about the kind of government they believed to be best.

When you finish this lesson you should be able to explain the ideas of republican government, the common good, and civic virtue.

aristocrats

civic virtue

common good

delegate

direct democracy

factions

representative

representative democracy

republic

republican government

What did the Founders learn about government from the Romans?

Two thousand years before our own nation began, there was a republic that greatly influenced the ideas of the Founders. A **republic** is a country that has a government in which power is held by the people who elect representatives. Those representatives manage the government for the people, for the sake of the common good.

The government that fascinated the Founders was the Roman Republic, which lasted nearly 500 years, from 509 BC to 27 BC. The capital of the Roman Republic was Rome, located in what today is Italy.

The Founders read what historians and the Romans themselves wrote about the people and government of the Roman Republic. The Founders learned that during the Republic, the Roman people governed themselves without a king. In the Roman Republic, both the common people and the **aristocrats**, or wealthy upper class, shared the power to govern.

The Founders called the government of Rome a republican government. **Republican government** is a type of government in which the

What did the Founders learn about government from the Roman Republic?

- citizens have the power to govern

- citizens **delegate** or entrust their power to leaders they elect to represent them and to serve their interests

- citizens and their representatives work cooperatively to promote the common good rather than their

What are the advantages of a republican government in a large and diverse society?

own interests. The term **common good**, or common welfare, means that which is good for the community as a whole.

What advantages did the Founders see in republican government?

The Founders thought a republican form of government was the best form of government they could create for themselves. They thought that they would have some of the same benefits that the ancient Romans had enjoyed. These are some of the benefits the Founders saw in republican government:

- **Representatives are elected to serve the common good**. A **representative** is a person elected to act and speak for others. The main purpose of republican government is to serve the common good. Representatives should not make laws to serve the interests of one person or one group. The representatives make laws that serve the entire community.

- **Having representatives make the laws is more efficient**. To make good and fair laws, you have to understand every problem well. But most people do not have the time to learn about every problem. Representatives can make laws faster and better because it becomes their responsibility to do so.

- **The people have a say in their government**. By delegating power to their representatives, the people do not give up their voice in government. The people still have to decide who will represent them. The people have to communicate their ideas and the actions they want taken to their representatives.

- **The representatives are responsible to the people**. The people hold their representatives responsible for making making good and fair laws. If the representatives do not make good and fair laws, the people can vote them out of office and select new leaders to represent them.

What were the disadvantages of republican government?

The Founders worried about whether republican government would work in the colonies. The Founders saw that republican government as practiced in the Roman Republic had a few disadvantages. These are some of the possible disadvantages:

- Republican government works best in small communities. In small communities, the people know and care for each other and the common good. The colonies, on the other hand, occupied a large territory.

- The people in a republic have to be very much alike. There cannot be a high degree of diversity. The people cannot be very different in their wealth, moral beliefs, or ways of life. In the colonies, however, the people had many different religious beliefs and ways of life.

- People in a large and diverse republic would naturally divide into **factions**, or interest groups. Such interest groups might work against other groups or the people as a whole, rather than work for the common good.

How can the common good be determined in a large and diverse society?

How did the Founders adapt the idea of republican government?

James Madison was one of the most important Founders. We often call him "the Father of the Constitution" because he played such an important role in creating our Constitution. Madison adapted the idea of republican government to the reality of American life.

Madison defined the difference between a direct democracy and republican government in the following ways:

- In a **direct democracy**, the people themselves control government. The people create the laws they need. Direct democracy works best in small communities. As communities grow larger, it becomes difficult for people to make the decisions that are needed for the good of all.

- In a republican government, the people's representatives make the laws and run government. This makes it possible for those in government to administer a much larger area.

Madison believed that America could and should have a republican form of government. Laws would be made and administered by representatives elected by the people. Madison said that members of government should be elected by a large number of the people rather than by a small number or a favored group. Such a government was a democracy in the sense that it received its right to govern from the people as a whole. This kind of government is now called

How did Madison adapt the ideas of republican government to the colonies?

a representative democracy. In a **representative democracy** the people choose leaders to make and administer laws for their country.

Madison also believed that you could organize government in a way that might help to avoid the abuse of power by any one person or faction. You will study these ideas in the next lesson.

Why should citizens promote the common good?

Examine the ideas of "common good" and "self-interest" in the story about Cincinnatus. Then respond to the questions that follow it.

You might want to work with a partner or in groups of three. A spokesperson for each group should explain its answers to the rest of the class.

CINCINNATUS: A MODEL OF CIVIC VIRTUE

In the year 460 BC, Rome was in great danger. An army from the east was burning and plundering the countryside. The enemy surrounded the defending Roman army on all sides. The leaders of the government of Rome decided to ask Cincinnatus, a skilled military leader, to help them during this crisis. The government leaders sent messengers asking Cincinnatus to serve as dictator of the country for as long as the crisis might last.

Cincinnatus was a hard-working farmer with only four acres of land. When the messengers found him, he was quietly plowing the fields. Because he loved his country, he left his plow to go to Rome to lead the army. In a battle that lasted two days, his army defeated the enemy and saved the country. In gratitude,

the people of Rome honored and praised Cincinnatus. But when the crisis was over, Cincinnatus did not try to remain as dictator of his country. He did not want continued power. Instead, he returned to his home and his life as a farmer and a citizen.

By returning to his home, Cincinnatus showed that he valued being a good citizen of Rome more than he valued fame and personal power. He respected the government of Rome. He did not want to use his popularity to take power away from the representatives elected by the citizens.

1 What is the common good as represented in this story? What are the self-interests represented in the story? Do you agree with the actions taken by Cincinnatus? Why or why not?

2 Describe a person you know or a leader in our nation who you think has civic virtue. Give reasons for your opinion based on the person's life.

3 Explain some situations where you think you should put the common good above your own interests.

4 Explain some situations in which you might not want to put the common good above your own interests.

5 Explain some situations in which people might disagree about what is best for the common good. What should be done when there are such disagreements? Why?

Why is civic virtue necessary for republican government to work well?

The Founders thought that republican government was possible in Rome only because of the high degree of civic virtue of the Roman citizens. **Civic virtue** meant that both citizens and their leaders were willing to set aside their private interests and personal concerns for the common good.

The Founders thought that civic virtue was important to make a government work well. Citizens need to participate in their government to promote the common good.

Do you think that a statesman's desire for fame and admiration can lead him or her to pursue the public or common good? Why or why not?

Madison understood the importance of civic virtue to good government. In this way, he was like the other Founders. Madison also accepted Locke's view of human nature. He believed that people are prompted to act by their self-interest. He thought that the pursuit of self-interest could in its own way further the common good. For example, a statesman's desire for fame and the admiration of others could lead him or her to practice civic virtue. The common good could be served by individuals pursuing their economic self-interest. Each would contribute to the general prosperity.

Madison also realized that as people pursue their own interests they sometimes act against the interests of the common good. He knew that civic virtue alone could not be relied upon. Madison wanted a government that would fit human nature as it is, not as one might wish it to be.

How did the colonists teach the values of republican government?

People living in the American colonies were taught the value of civic virtue and other values of republican government in many ways. Parents taught these values to their children. Teachers taught them in school. Clergy taught them in sermons and writings. Leading citizens of the country were expected to set good examples. The values of republican government were a part of the customs and traditions of the people.

The ideas and values of the Roman Republic were promoted throughout the

What ideals of republican government do you think our leaders should promote? Why?

American colonies in the stories that people read. Public buildings designed to resemble the buildings of ancient Rome also reminded people of the ideas and values of the Roman Republic.

The Founders thought it was important to teach and promote civic virtue among citizens. They believed that the Roman Republic had failed in the end because its citizens lost their civic virtue. They had promoted their own interests at the expense of the common good.

By the time of the American Revolution, the Founders had come to believe strongly in the ideals of republican government. They thought that Great Britain was violating these ideals. They claimed the British government was guilty of serving selfish interests at the expense of the common good. It had violated those rights that good government was supposed to protect.

After the Revolution, the Founders were able to establish their own government. They tried to make sure this government would not violate their rights. An essential step, they thought, was to create a constitutional government. You will learn what a constitution and constitutional government are in the next lesson.

1. What is republican government? What are the advantages and disadvantages of republican government?

2. What is the meaning of the term "common good"?

3. What is the difference between direct democracy and representative democracy?

4. What is civic virtue? Why is it important that citizens and their representatives have civic virtue?

5. How were the values of republican government promoted in the colonies? Why were these values promoted?

1. His fellow Americans often referred to George Washington as "our Cincinnatus." Find stories and works of art that illustrate the life of George Washington as a model of civic virtue. Share what you learned with your class.

2. Many government buildings in Washington, D.C., and many state capitols across the country look like Greek or Roman buildings. Find photographs of government buildings. Compare them with drawings or photographs of ancient Greek or Roman buildings. Explain how this architectural style in our country symbolizes the influences of ancient Greece and Rome on the Founders.

3. In this lesson you learned about the values taught in colonial communities. The excerpts on the right are from the *Blue-Back Speller*, a popular school text of the late 1700s. What values do the lessons stress? Draw a poster or cartoon illustrating one of the lessons.

Lesson 6

I will not walk with bad men; that
I may not be cast off with them.
I will love the law, and keep it.
I will walk with the just, and do good.

Lesson 12

Be a good child; mind your book;
love your school and strive to learn.
Tell no tales; call no ill names;
you must not lie, nor swear,
nor cheat, nor steal.

Play not with bad boys; use no ill
words at play, spend your time well,
live in peace, and shun all strife.

This is the way to make good men of you,
and save your soul from pain and woe.

Lesson 15

As for those boys and girls that mind not
their books, and love not church and school,
but play with such as tell tales, tell lies,
curse, swear, and steal, they will come to
some bad end, and must be whipped till
they mend their ways.

4. Look through different issues of your local newspaper. Find articles that concern the common good in your community. Share the articles with your class.

What is constitutional government?

LESSON PURPOSE

This lesson introduces the ideas of a constitution and constitutional government. It also introduces the idea that a constitution is a higher law.

When you finish this lesson, you should be able to explain the ideas of a constitution, constitutional government, and higher law. You should also be able to explain some of the important differences between constitutional governments and autocratic or dictatorial governments.

autocratic or dictatorial government

constitution

constitutional government

higher law

limits

monarchy

private domain

What is a constitution?

A **constitution** is a legal framework for government. A constitution tells how a government is organized and run. Every nation has a constitution. Both good and bad governments have constitutions.

Most constitutions are in writing. The United States and Russia are two examples of countries with written constitutions. Some constitutions contain both written and unwritten parts. The British constitution is the best-known example of this kind of constitution because it is based on both written laws and unwritten customs. It also is possible to have a constitution that is not in writing at all. Many societies in history had constitutions based on unwritten customs and traditions.

You can learn about a government and its citizens by studying a nation's constitution. Here are some of the questions a constitution usually answers:

QUESTIONS ABOUT GOVERNMENT

- What are the purposes of government?

- What is the organization of government? What parts does it have? What does each part do?

What purpose of constitutional government does this painting illustrate?

- How is government supposed to go about doing its business? For example, how does the government make its laws?

- How are people selected to serve in government?

- Who is a citizen?

- Are citizens supposed to have control over their government? If so, how is this control supposed to work?

- What rights and responsibilities, if any, are the citizens supposed to have?

What is a constitutional government?

Having a constitution does not mean that a nation has a **constitutional government**. A constitutional government means that there are **limits** on the powers of the person or group running the government. The word "limits," as used here, means things that government may not do or actions that it may not take.

Our Constitution limits the power of government. The limits are written into the Constitution. For example, the courts cannot force a person to be a witness against himself. The courts cannot deny the accused the right to an attorney.

In some nations, the power of government is not limited. It is possible for the constitution of a nation to provide for the unlimited use of power. In other cases, the constitution of a nation might say that the power of government should be limited. But it might neglect to say how those limits are to be enforced.

Suppose the constitution of a nation does not limit the powers of its government. On the other hand, suppose it limits the power, but those limits are not enforced. In either case, the government is not a constitutional government. We call a government of unlimited power an **autocratic** or **dictatorial government**.

What are the advantages of constitutional government?

What is a higher law?

In a constitutional government, the constitution must effectively limit the use of power. The constitution is a higher law. A **higher law** is a set of laws that establish and limit the power of government. All the people, including government leaders, must obey the higher law of the land. The people running the government must do what the constitution says. The constitution describes ways to ensure that people in government obey the limits on their power.

What role does a constitution play in a constitutional government?

In a constitutional government, the constitution has the following five important characteristics:

1. It lists the basic rights of citizens to life, liberty, and property.

2. It establishes the responsibility of government to protect those rights.

3. It places limits on how the people in government may use their powers. Some examples of how our Constitution limits the powers of government are

   - **Citizens' rights**. People in government cannot unfairly deprive a person of the right to freedom of speech.

   - **How resources are distributed**. People in government cannot take a person's property without paying the person a fair price for it.

   - **How conflicts are handled**. People in government must give all persons accused of a crime a fair trial.

4. It establishes the principle of a **private domain**. A private domain is that part of a person's life that is not the business of government.

5. It can only be changed with the widespread consent of citizens and according to certain set procedures.

How would you solve this issue of power?

Read "The Tragedy of Antigone." The story has been summarized and adapted from a Greek play written in 442 BC by Sophocles.

In the drama, Antigone disobeys her uncle, Creon, the ruler of Thebes. The government of Thebes was a monarchy. A **monarchy** is a form of government in which political power is held by a single ruler such as a king or queen. The king ruled the city; he made and enforced the laws, and he decided on punishments for people who violated his laws. The story raises questions about limits on the power of government.

THE TRAGEDY OF ANTIGONE

Thebes was an important city in ancient Greece. Antigone lived there with her sister, Ismene, her two brothers, Polyneices and Eteocles, and their uncle Creon.

The citizens of Thebes had chosen Eteocles, the younger brother, to be their king. Polyneices believed that since he was older it was his right to rule the land. The two brothers quarreled and Eteocles banished Polyneices from the city.

Polyneices left Thebes and gathered a large army to fight his brother for the throne. It was a long and bitter civil war; many people died and much property was destroyed. Finally, Polyneices and Eteocles killed each other.

The people of Thebes immediately elected Creon to be their next king. Creon decreed that Eteocles was to receive a

hero's funeral for defending the city. But Polyneices was to rot on the battlefield. Any person who tried to bury Polyneices would be put to death. "These are my laws!" Creon declared. "Only by these laws can our city be safe and prosper. Only by obedience to these laws can we avoid civil war and ruin."

The citizens of Thebes debated the wisdom of Creon's law. On one side, many people were opposed to it. These people believed it was the duty of the living to bury the dead. According to this belief, unburied souls were doomed to wander alone throughout eternity. This group of people complained that Creon's law violated their rights without a good reason for doing so.

Other citizens supported Creon. They believed that Creon's law was justified because the city had suffered from rebels and lawbreakers. It was the king's duty to decide what to do with people who violated the law. They felt that the fate of Polyneices could serve as an example to those who did not respect the laws of the king.

Antigone believed that the laws of the gods were more important than the laws of any ruler. So Antigone decided to bury the body of her brother. "I will never be false to my brother," she said. Antigone attempted to convince Ismene to help her.

"Are you not going too far, exceeding the limits, when you do what the king has forbidden?" Ismene asked Antigone. "I do not wish to dishonor our brother, but I have no strength to defy the king. If we defy Creon's law, we will find ourselves alone against the powers of the king and we will perish! Since we

must obey Creon's law, we can ask the gods for forgiveness," Ismene said.

"Obey the law if you must, Ismene. I will not urge you further to join me," Antigone replied.

Later that day, a guard suddenly burst into the garden where Creon was resting. The guard brought the news that Polyneices had been buried. Creon angrily gave orders to find the guilty person. The guard returned with Antigone in custody.

"Tell me, did you not know that there is a law forbidding what you did? Why did you disobey it?" Creon asked. "You are my niece, how can this be?"

"I knew the law," Antigone answered. "If I had allowed my brother to lie unburied, that would have disturbed me deeply. Your law is not part of eternal justice. I disobeyed your law. I am not sorry for what I did," Antigone said to Creon.

"This brother of yours was attacking his own country," Creon replied. "The gods require no such loyalty to evildoers. It is my duty to produce order and peace in this land. If I do not act, the citizens of Thebes will think me weak. The public order, the state itself will be in jeopardy. It is the laws of the state that hold this city together. If those who break the law go unpunished, we will be a lawless city. Even the innocent will suffer. You have thrown away your future happiness, Antigone," Creon said. "You make it impossible for me to avoid putting you to death. Guards, take this woman and lock her away!"

As the guards escorted Antigone from the garden, she turned to Creon and said, "You further violate the rights of the people by passing sentence upon me without a fair and public hearing."

PREPARING

As you were able to observe in the story, there were no laws that set reasonable limits on the power of the king. But the king had a council of advisers, as in some other cities of ancient Greece. The role of the council was to investigate problems and to advise the king on what he might do to solve them.

Let us imagine that Antigone has asked the Council of Advisers to investigate the unlimited power of the king. Further, imagine that Creon agreed to permit the council to study the issue and to make recommendations. The Council of Advisers will conduct a hearing and then decide what recommendations, if any, to give the king.

Your class will work in six groups. Five of the groups should prepare to make a presentation that explains its ideas about limiting the power of the king. The sixth group is the Council of Advisers, who will listen to the presentations.

In preparing your presentations, use what you learned in the lesson as well as the ideas in the story. Each group also should prepare to answer questions from the council.

❶ Creon
Prepare arguments against any limits on the power of the king. Base your arguments on what you read about Creon in the story. During your presentation, be sure to explain the reasons why you believe the power of the king should remain as is.

❷ Citizens Who Support the King
Prepare arguments against limiting the power of the king. Present specific reasons why you support the actions of the king.

❸ Antigone
Prepare arguments in favor of limiting the power of the king. Base your arguments on what you read about Antigone in the story. During your presentation, propose specific limits on the king's power that you would like the council to recommend to Creon.

❹ Citizens Who Support Antigone
Prepare arguments that favor limiting the power of the king. Present specific reasons why you support Antigone's point of view.

❺ Ismene
Prepare arguments that represent Ismene's point of view. Present specific reasons why you hold this opinion.

❻ Council of Advisers
Reread the story and study the role of each group. Then prepare questions to ask each group during the hearing. Select a member of your group to be the president of the council.

38

PRESENTING

The president of the Council of Advisers will call the session to order and explain the purpose of the meeting.

Each group has four minutes to make a formal presentation to explain its position to the council.

After each presentation, council members may ask questions of the group. Every member of the group should help answer the council's questions.

After the hearing, the Council of Advisers will meet to decide what recommendations, if any, to make to the king. The council will then share its decision with the class.

EVALUATING

After the council has made its decision the class as a whole should evaluate the decision. Each student should answer the evaluation questions below and share their conclusions with the class.

* What were the strongest arguments made against limiting the power of the king? Which arguments were the weakest?

* What were the strongest arguments made in favor of limiting the power of the king? Which arguments were the weakest?

* What did you learn about the importance of constitutional government as a result of this activity?

1 What is a constitution? What can you learn about a nation's government by studying its constitution?

2 Explain the differences between a constitutional government and an autocratic or dictatorial government.

3 What are the characteristics that define a constitution as a "higher law"?

4 Identify two areas of private life in which you think government should not interfere. Explain why you think government should not intrude in these areas.

ACTIVITIES

1 In the history of the world, there have been governments that ignored the limits on their power. Conduct research on one of these governments and give examples of how it violated the natural rights of the people.

2 Read the play *Antigone*. Research how the play was rewritten during World War II to inspire resistance to Nazi rule. Write a short report on your findings and share it with your class.

3 Draw a cartoon for your class bulletin board that illustrates the difference between a constitutional government and a dictatorial government.

How can we organize government to prevent the abuse of power?

LESSON PURPOSE

Constitutional governments are designed to protect the people from abuses of government power. In this lesson you learn how people might organize government to make the abuse of power less likely.

When you finish this lesson, you should be able to explain the ideas of separation of powers and checks and balances, know the Founders' reasons for creating a system that limits governmental power, and list some powers of the three branches of government.

bill
checks and balances
executive branch
judicial branch
legislative branch
separation of powers

How might people organize a government to prevent the abuse of power?

Constitutional governments are organized in such a way that one person or group cannot get enough power to dominate the government. Two common ways to do this are

- **Separate the powers of government.**

    Divide the powers of government among different branches, or parts. Doing so prevents any one person or group from having all the power.

- **Balance the powers among the branches of government.**

    Divide the powers of government in such a way that no one branch controls the other branches. Give each branch methods to check the use of power by the other branches.

Why did the Founders believe that all governments need limits on their power?

Why did the Founders fear the abuse of power?

The Founders knew that throughout history many governments had used their power unfairly. This is why they created the system of limits on power described in this lesson. To understand their thinking, read the quotations below. Then, with a partner, discuss the questions that follow.

1. What does each quotation mean?

2. What view of human nature did Alexander Hamilton, Benjamin Franklin, and George Mason share?

3. Do you agree or disagree with these views of human nature? Why or why not?

4. If you do agree with these views of human nature, how would you organize our government to protect your rights?

ALEXANDER HAMILTON

"Give all power to the many, they will oppress the few. Give all power to the few, they will oppress the many."

BENJAMIN FRANKLIN

"There are two passions which have a Powerful influence on the affairs of men. These are ambition and avarice [greed]; the love of power and the love of money."

GEORGE MASON

"From the nature of man, we may be sure that those who have power in their hands…will always, when they can…increase it."

How does separation of powers work?

A study of constitutional governments shows that they are often divided into three different groups or branches. The power of government is not given to any one branch. Instead, some of the power is given to each branch. This is called **separation of powers**. For example, we divide our government into the following three branches:

- the **legislative branch** has the power to make laws
- the **executive branch** has the power to carry out and enforce laws

- the **judicial branch** has the power to manage conflicts about the meaning, application, and enforcement of laws.

How does a system of checks and balances work?

The phrase **checks and balances** means that the powers of the different branches of government are balanced. No one branch has so much power that it can completely dominate the others. Although each branch of government has its own special powers, the powers are checked because some powers are shared with the other branches.

Why are the powers of government separated and balanced?

Which branch of government has the final say about whether a law is constitutional?

According to our Constitution, Congress is the legislative branch. It has the power to make laws. The power of Congress is divided between two houses, the House of Representatives and the Senate. Each house can check the power of the other by refusing to pass a law proposed by the other house.

In addition, our Constitution gives the executive and judicial branches ways to check and control the power of Congress to make laws. For example:

- A **bill** is a proposed law. When Congress passes a bill, the president must sign it before it can become law. The president has the right to refuse to sign a bill. If this happens, the bill cannot become a law unless Congress votes again and passes the bill by a two-thirds majority of both houses.

- The U.S. Supreme Court can check the power of Congress. The Court can declare a law to be in violation of the Constitution and, therefore, invalid.

There are similar ways to check the powers of the president and U.S. Supreme Court. You will learn more about the system of checks and balances in a later lesson.

This system of separation of powers and checks and balances helps ensure that government power is limited. Because constitutional governments are organized in complicated ways, getting things done may take time. Although it might seem strange, this is often considered an advantage. Many people think that these complications make it more likely that when government does finally make a decision, it will be a well thought out one.

1 How does a system of separation of powers work?

2 What are the three branches of our government and what power does each hold?

3 How does a system of checks and balances work? Give some examples.

4 The separation and sharing of powers means that government cannot reach decisions quickly. Why might this be an advantage? Why might it be a disadvantage?

ACTIVITIES

1 Read Articles I, II, and III of the U.S. Constitution. Then, examine the constitution of your state.

Create two charts that illustrate the process of checks and balances, one for your state government and one for the U.S. government. Share your charts with the class.

2 Find newspaper or newsmagazine articles that illustrate our system of separation of powers and checks and balances. Use the articles to create a bulletin board for your classroom.

unit two

What shaped the Founders' thinking about government?

unit two

Articles of Confederation

inalienable rights

popular sovereignty

rule of law

In the last unit, you learned some important ideas and questions concerning government. You studied natural rights philosophy, republicanism, and constitutionalism. These were the ideas that influenced the Founders of our nation and helped shape their views about government.

In this unit, you will learn more about the Founders. You will read about the experiences that shaped their thinking about government. You will study their values and the things they believed were important. You will also learn why they thought a new constitution was necessary.

How did constitutional government develop in Great Britain?

LESSON PURPOSE

Constitutional government developed in Great Britain over a period of many centuries. In this lesson you learn how the monarchy came to share power with the nobles. You will study some documents that limited the power of the British government. This study will help you to better understand our ideas about limited government.

When you finish this lesson, you should be able to describe the struggles for power between the English monarch and Parliament. You should be able to explain how these struggles led to a system of separated powers and representative government. You should also be able to describe some of the important constitutional documents in British history that influenced the writing of our constitution.

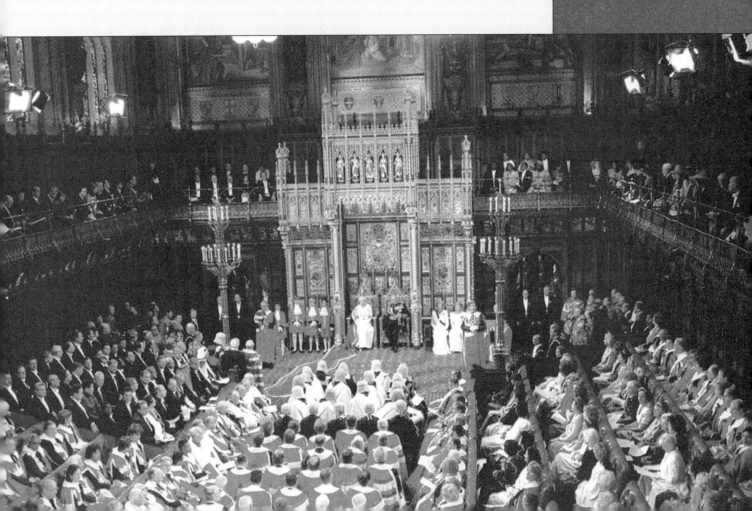

common law

English Bill of Rights

feudalism

Magna Carta

Parliament

Petition of Right

rights of Englishmen

rule of law

Why did the American colonists have the rights of Englishmen?

The **rights of Englishmen** were established during centuries of British history. These were certain basic rights that all subjects of the English king or queen were believed to have. They included

- the right to a trial by jury

- security from unlawful entry into one's home

- no taxation without consent

Before the American colonies became independent, the colonists were subjects of the British monarchy. As subjects of the king or queen, the colonists enjoyed the rights of Englishmen. All subjects of the king or queen had these rights. The colonists knew and understood their rights as Englishmen.

The colonists' experiences with British government greatly influenced what they thought about limited government. For our study, it is important to understand these rights and how they developed over time. It is also important to remember

What were some important rights of Englishmen?

that the constitution of Great Britain is not a single written document. Instead, it is made up of long-established practices known as common law and laws passed by Parliament. **Common law** is based on custom and the decisions of law courts. **Parliament** is the legislative body of British government.

What problems, if any, might arise from dividing society into social groups?

What was the feudal system?

Until 1066, each region of England had its own ruler. William the Conqueror from France invaded England in that year and became king of all the regions.

William the Conqueror brought a system for governing called feudalism. **Feudalism** was a system of social, economic, and political organization. The system was based on the control of land.

Under feudalism, the people in England belonged to one of three social groups.

1. **Royalty.** This was the king and queen and their families. Government by a king or queen is a monarchy.

2. **Nobility.** This group included the "lords" and "ladies" who held titles such as earl, duke, duchess, and baron. The noblemen worked for the monarchy and made it possible for the king or queen to control England.

3. **Common people.** These were the rest of the people. This group included the knights, or soldiers of the king, merchants, and peasants. The peasants were also known as serfs. They farmed the land and were not free to leave the area in which they worked.

All public land in England belonged to the monarch, but it was too much land for one person to rule. So, the monarch gave some responsibility for governing the kingdom to the nobility. Under the feudal system, the nobles controlled parts of the land as well as the people who lived there. In exchange, the nobles pledged to be loyal to the king and to go to war for him.

The nobles further divided the land into smaller areas. A nobleman assigned control of the land and people living on it to men called vassals. The vassals in

How did the Magna Carta limit the power of the king?

turn owed the nobleman loyalty and military service.

For the system to work, it depended on a series of agreements or contracts. There had to be contracts between the monarch and the nobles. There also had to be contracts between the nobles and vassals. Each contract included rights and responsibilities that the parties owed to one another. Thus, feudalism introduced the idea of government based on a contract. Those in power pledged to respect the rights of the people who gave them loyalty.

The feudal system was important to the development of constitutional government. It was during this period that the monarchs started to share power with the nobles.

Why is the Magna Carta an important document?

Under the feudal system, it became a custom or tradition for the royalty to share some of its power with the nobility. As a result, the nobles became used to having certain rights and powers. When King John tried to take back some of these rights, the nobles rebelled.

The nobles were powerful enough to force King John to sign an agreement with them in the year 1215. This agreement is the **Magna Carta**, or Great Charter. The Magna Carta was a major step in the growth of English constitutional government. The Magna Carta was perhaps the most important early example of a written statement of law limiting the power of a ruler. The Magna Carta contains two important ideas that influenced the Founders.

1. Government is based on a contract between the ruler and people to be ruled. Government by contract also includes the idea that if either side breaks the contract, that contract is no longer valid.

2. Both government and the governed must obey the law. This is called the **rule of law**. The law limits the powers of government. The king could not take away the property of a noble without following agreed-upon procedures and rules. The Magna Carta expresses the idea of limited government by requiring the king to govern according to established rules of law.

How do these rights limit the power of government?

Each of the rights listed below was a right of Englishmen listed in the Magna Carta. Work with a partner or in a group of three students. Read the statements below and respond to the four questions that follow them.

- *For a trivial* [minor] *offence, a free man shall be fined only in proportion to the degree of his offence, and for a serious offence correspondingly.*

- *No free man shall be taken, or imprisoned...exiled, or in any way harmed...save by the lawful judgment of his peers* [equals] *or by the law of the land.*

- *No constable* [officer] *or other bailiff* [sheriff] *of ours shall take the corn* [grain] *or other chattels* [personal property] *of any one except...he gives money for them.*

- *To none will we sell, to none deny or delay, right of justice.*

1. What is the meaning of each statement?

2. What right does the statement guarantee?

3. Why is this right important?

4. Explain how this right limits the power of government.

53

What is the relationship between the Magna Carta and constitutional government?

The Magna Carta was a contract between the king and the nobility. Most of the people in England were not a part of this agreement. But the Magna Carta is an early step leading to the idea that government should be based on a contract that includes all the people.

Government by contract means that both sides of the agreement are responsible for fulfilling its terms. The Magna Carta states that the king cannot deprive the nobility of their rights. The nobility, in return, must support and obey the king and the laws.

Why was the creation of Parliament important?

Important changes in the English government caused the establishment of other basic principles of government. These principles are the separation of powers and representative government.

In 1258, the nobles forced the king to create an advisory council. This council was called Parliament. Parliament is the legislative branch of the English government. It was made up of two houses that represented the most powerful groups in the kingdom: the House of Lords and the House of Commons. The House of Lords represented the nobles. The House of Commons represented people who owned large amounts of land but were not nobles.

Gradually during the next centuries the role of Parliament grew. Its members were no longer simply advising the monarch, they were representing the interests of their regions. For hundreds of years after the creation of Parliament, the royalty, nobility, and commons had struggled for power. No one group was able to be completely in control for long.

Then in 1628, the king tried to pressure the people for money without the consent of Parliament. He also required the people to house soldiers in their homes. As a result, Parliament forced him to agree to the **Petition of Right** of 1628. The Petition stated that the king could only raise taxes with the consent of Parliament. It also no longer allowed the king to house soldiers in the homes of the people. The Petition of Right strengthened the idea that

English subjects had certain rights that government could not violate.

The struggle between the monarch and Parliament became so intense during the seventeenth century that a series of civil wars broke out. The nobles finally won and in 1649 Parliament ordered the execution of the king. By 1688 the balance of power had shifted in favor of Parliament.

What is the relationship of free speech in a legislative body to constitutional government?

What was the English Bill of Rights?

In 1689 Parliament passed the **English Bill of Rights**. This law gave certain rights to Parliament that further limited the powers of the monarch. It said among other things that elections to Parliament must be free and that the people have the right to petition the king. It also said that the monarchy was no longer allowed to

- collect taxes without the consent of Parliament

- interfere with the right to free speech and debate in Parliament

- maintain an army in peacetime

- prevent Protestants from having arms for their defense

- require excessive bail or administer cruel punishment for those accused or convicted of crimes

- declare that laws made by Parliament should not be obeyed

By the end of the 1600s, the British government was much more limited in what it could do. This was at the same time that the British were establishing colonies in North America. So, the colonists brought these ideas about good government with them to the new world.

1. Explain how the feudal system promoted the idea that government is a contract between government and the governed.

2. Explain the importance of each of these documents:

   * Magna Carta
   * Petition of Right
   * English Bill of Rights

3. Explain how the struggles between the monarchy and the nobility led to limited government in Great Britain.

1. Learn more about the social, economic, and political aspects of feudalism. Find information in your library or on the Internet. Create a diagram that illustrates how the system worked.

2. Create a script for a talk show for an imaginary television station. The host of the program can interview some of the historical figures who lived during the time mentioned in this lesson such as William the Conqueror, King John, noblemen, vassals, and commoners.

3. Imagine that you are a member of the nobility living in England in the 1200s. Write a letter to the editor or draw an editorial cartoon illustrating the importance of the rights listed in the Magna Carta.

What experiences led to the American Revolution?

LESSON PURPOSE

This lesson explains how British ideas about government were put to use in the colonies. The lesson also describes why the colonists came to feel that the British government threatened their rights.

When you finish the lesson, you should be able to explain how constitutional government developed in the colonies. You should also be able to explain why the colonists decided to fight for their independence.

7

charter

committees of correspondence

Daughters of Liberty

First Continental Congress

Second Continental Congress

Sons of Liberty

writs of assistance

Which ideas did the colonists in America use to create their governments?

To establish a British colony, one generally needed to have a charter from the king. A **charter** is a legal document. In colonial times, a charter granted land to a person or a company along with the right to start a colony on that land.

Most colonial charters said little about what kind of government a colony should have. As a result, the settlers had to develop their own form of government. Each of the thirteen colonies had a government of its own.

In creating their own governments, the colonists tried to do two things. They tried to protect themselves from abuse of power by the British government. They also tried to protect themselves from abuse of power by their colonial governments. To achieve these goals, the colonists used the basic ideas of constitutional government. All colonial governments were based on the following ideas:

1. **Natural rights.** Colonial governments were based on the idea that the purpose of government is to protect

This is the royal charter for the state of Delaware. What is a charter? Why did the colonists need one?

the people's natural rights to life, liberty, and property.

2. **Representative government.** The colonists elected representatives to their colonial legislatures. The first elected legislature was in Virginia in 1619.

This painting shows the founding of the colony of Maryland.
What basic ideas did colonists use when they created their governments?

3 **Rule of law**. The colonists created a government of laws. The people who made and enforced the laws did not have unlimited power and they, too, had to obey the laws. The colonial governments recognized the idea of higher law. This meant that colonial governments could not pass laws that violated the British constitution.

4 **Separation of powers**. The powers of the colonial governments were divided among three branches:

- A governor headed the executive branch. The governor carried out and enforced the law. In most colonies, the king or the owner of the colony appointed the governor.

- The legislative branch made the laws. Most colonies had legislatures with two houses.

- The judicial branch was made up of judges or magistrates. The governor usually appointed the judges. The judges were responsible for handling conflicts about the laws. The judges presided at the trials of people accused of a crime. The judges also made sure that colonial laws did not violate the British constitution.

5 **Checks and balances**. In many colonies the branches of government shared power, but one branch could check the use of power by another branch. For example, the governors could not collect taxes without the consent of the legislature.

Why did the British government tighten control over the colonies?

For much of the colonial period, Great Britain paid little attention to the colonies. Britain had become a world power and was often busy fighting wars in Europe. The government in Britain did not have much time to devote to the colonies. In addition, the colonies were a long distance away. Communication between the colonies and Britain was slow because news had to travel by ship. News of events in the colonies reached Britain months later. Orders from the government to the colonies took months to arrive.

During the years of British neglect, the colonists became used to ruling themselves. Further, the colonists had been able to ignore many of the laws made by Parliament.

By the mid-1700s, however, the British began to show a new interest in the colonies. In 1763, Britain won a long and costly war against France. The cost of the conflict left the British with a large national debt. Parliament saw the colonies as a source of much-needed money. They felt that the colonies should pay their portion of the cost of the war. To reduce the national debt, Parliament raised taxes in both Britain and the colonies. The British government also began to tighten trade regulations between the colonies and other nations.

These are some examples of British laws that affected the colonies.

- **Proclamation of 1763**. The law banned settlement in certain western lands. Its purpose was to reduce tensions between the colonists and Native Americans. The British army could then withdraw from the frontier and, thus, save the government money.

What does this picture illustrate about British control over the American colonies for most of the colonial period?

- **Sugar Act of 1764**. The purpose of the law was to stop the smuggling of goods into and out of the colonies. It gave the British navy greater power to search colonial ships. Naval officers used **writs of assistance**, or search warrants, that allowed them to board colonial ships. The law also required products such as tobacco, sugar, and timber to be shipped directly from the colonies to Britain. The law set taxes on cloth, sugar, coffee, and wine coming into the colonies.

- **Stamp Act, 1765**. The law imposed a tax on every legal document, newspaper, pamphlet, and deck of cards coming into the colonies.

- **Quartering Act, 1765**. The British government moved the army from the western lands into the cities. The law required colonists who were innkeepers or public officials to house and feed the British soldiers.

- **Declaratory Act, 1766**. The law stated that Parliament had the right to pass laws for the colonies in "all cases whatsoever." Its purpose was to remind the colonists that the authority of the king and Parliament was superior to colonial governments.

- **Tea Act, 1773**. The law gave the East India Company the sole right to sell tea to the colonies. The East India Company was a large and important corporation in Britain. The purpose of the law was to keep the company from going broke.

The colonists viewed the new laws differently than did the government in Great Britain. Many colonists came to believe that Parliament was threatening their rights. They believed that Britain was becoming oppressive.

The tax and trade laws meant that some colonists would lose money. More important, the laws went against the

What events led the British government to tighten its control over the colonies? Were the British justified? Why or why not?

colonists' belief in representative government. The colonies had no right to elect representatives to Parliament. Therefore, the colonists claimed, Parliament had no right to tax the colonies. The colonists felt that tax laws should be passed only by their colonial legislatures. "No taxation without representation" became a rallying cry of the colonists.

To the British, the laws seemed reasonable. King George felt that the colonists were acting like ungrateful children. The well-being and safety of the colonies were due to the help they got from the British government. It was only fair that the colonists pay their share of the cost of government. The issue of representation made little sense to most British people. Parliament did not represent individuals. Nor did it represent areas of the country. Instead, Parliament represented the interests of the whole nation, no matter where British subjects lived.

How did the colonists resist British control?

Between 1763 and 1775, tension was growing between the colonies and the British government. To protest against British actions the colonists organized town meetings and wrote angry letters to the newspapers. They also put together independent voluntary groups that organized other ways to resist the British.

The most significant of these groups were the **committees of correspondence**. Their mission was to make sure that each colony knew about events and opinions in the other colonies. Although the committees began as voluntary associations, their success led to their establishment by most of the colonial governments. The committees raised the spirits of the people and united them against the British. Eventually all the colonies were linked by committees of correspondence.

What was the result of colonial resistance?

Why are these rights important?

Each of the following illustrates an event resulting from the enforcement of British laws in the colonies. Examine each situation. If you had been the colonist named in each case, what right or rights would you claim the British government had violated? Explain why you think having each right is important. Share your ideas with the class.

1. Your name is Elsbeth Merrill. While you were baking bread and awaiting the return of your husband, an agent of the king arrived at your inn. The agent informed you that you must house and feed four British soldiers.

2. Your name is Lemuel Adams and you have a warehouse full of goods near Boston Harbor. The king's magistrate issues a writ of assistance allowing British officials to search all homes, stores, and warehouses in Boston. The officials used the writ to search your business for evidence of smuggling.

3. Your name is James Otis. You represent people who are in prison. The judge has denied the prisoners a trial by a jury in their own community. You argue that this is illegal because it violates the British constitution. The judge denies your request and sends the prisoners to England for trial.

4. Your name is William Bradford. You printed an article in your newspaper criticizing the deputy governor of the colony. The king appointed the deputy governor. You wrote that the deputy governor was like a "large cocker spaniel about five foot five." You are under arrest. Your printing press in Philadelphia has been destroyed.

JAMES OTIS

WILLIAM BRADFORD

How did the Boston Massacre change the way some colonists thought about British rule?

Two other important groups were the **Sons of Liberty** and the **Daughters of Liberty**. The Sons began in 1765 and quickly spread throughout the country. The Sons of Liberty organized resistance to the Stamp Act. Mobs of people attacked the homes of tax collectors. The Sons of Liberty burned effigies, or straw dummies, made to look like royal officials. They marched in the streets and sometimes committed violent acts.

Women soon got together and formed the Daughters of Liberty. They helped to make the boycott of British trade effective. Instead of buying British goods, they began spinning their own yarn and making their own linen. After the British Parliament passed the Tea Act of 1773, many women gave up drinking tea.

Both the Sons and Daughters of Liberty continued with acts of resistance until the start of the Revolutionary War. There were two well-known events that resulted in violence.

- **The Boston Massacre, 1770** British troops opened fire on a crowd of protestors outside the customs house in Boston. Five people died as a result. The tragedy convinced many colonists that the British government would use military force to make them obey the laws.

- **The Boston Tea Party, 1773** The colonists attempted to prevent the unloading of a cargo of tea that had arrived in Boston Harbor. The protestors ripped open 342 chests and dumped the tea into the harbor. The British responded by closing the harbor to all trade.

By the fall of 1774, these events had led many colonists to decide that it was time to take united action. The committees of correspondence called for representatives from all the colonies to meet in a general congress once a year. They were to deliberate on the general interests of all the colonies.

This call laid the foundation for the Continental Congress. The **First Continental Congress** met in Philadelphia. Twelve of the thirteen colonies sent representatives. It was the start of a unified American government. The purpose of the Congress was to decide on the best response to the actions of the British government. The members of Congress agreed to impose their own ban on trade with Great Britain. Congress hoped that this move would force the British government to change its policies toward the colonies.

On April 19, 1775, fighting broke out between Great Britain and the American colonies. On that day, British troops marched to the towns of Lexington and Concord in Massachusetts. The army was supposed to capture hidden guns and supplies by surprise, but a system of signals warned the Americans. The Americans fired on the British and forced them back to Boston. That was the beginning of the Revolutionary War.

A few weeks later, representatives of the colonies met in Philadelphia for the **Second Continental Congress**. The delegates to the Congress decided to resist the British. Congress organized the Continental Army and called upon the colonies to send troops. The delegates selected George Washington to lead the army. A year later, Congress asked a committee to draft a document explaining why the colonists felt it was necessary to free themselves from British rule. This document is known as the Declaration of Independence.

What happened at the First Continental Congress?

1. Why was it necessary for the colonists to create their own colonial governments?

2. What ideas of constitutional government did the colonists use in creating their governments?

3. Why did the British begin to tighten control over the colonies after 1763?

4. What tax and trade laws did Parliament pass? What was the purpose of these laws? What effects did the laws have on the colonists?

5. Why did the colonists feel that the laws passed by Parliament violated their rights?

6. Why did the British believe that the tax and trade laws were fair?

ACTIVITIES

1. Many people and groups played important roles in the Revolutionary War. Choose one of the organizations listed below to research. Share what you learn with your class.

   - Committees of Correspondence
   - Daughters of Liberty
   - Sons of Liberty

2. Research the life of Thomas Paine using the school library or the Internet. Write a review of his pamphlet, *Common Sense*. Explain the importance of Thomas Paine's writing to the Revolutionary War.

3. Imagine that you were living in the colonies in the 1770s. Write a speech arguing why the laws passed by Parliament violated your rights.

Then, imagine that you were a Member of Parliament. Write a speech arguing why these laws were necessary. Present your speeches to the class.

4. Create a timeline of the important events discussed in this lesson. Illustrate your timeline with drawings.

5. Draw two cartoons, one showing how the colonists felt about the Boston Tea Party and the other showing the same event from a British point of view.

What basic ideas about government are in the Declaration of Independence?

LESSON PURPOSE

One of the most important documents in American history is the Declaration of Independence. It summarizes the colonists' basic ideas about government. The Declaration lists the colonies' complaints against the British government. The Declaration also explains the reasons why the colonies decided to declare their independence from Great Britain.

When you finish this lesson, you should be able to explain the main ideas that are in the Declaration of Independence.

abolish
Loyalists
natural law
Patriots
self-evident
Tories
unalienable rights

Why was the Declaration of Independence written?

On June 7, 1776, the Continental Congress called for the colonies to declare independence from Great Britain. The Congress had to inform the British and the world that the colonies were now free and independent states. The Congress wanted to be sure that the reasons for its actions were clear.

A committee to draft the Declaration of Independence was quickly appointed. Members of the committee were Benjamin Franklin, John Adams, Roger Sherman, Robert Livingston, and a young Virginian named Thomas Jefferson. Jefferson was a man of many talents. He was a statesman, diplomat, author, architect, and scientist. He was a member of the Continental Congress during the Revolutionary War. Jefferson was a quiet, shy man, not known as a great speaker. He worked well in small groups and was an excellent writer. The committee chose Jefferson to write the first draft of the Declaration of Independence.

Jefferson spent many days writing. He discussed the draft with other members of the committee. They suggested changes

Why do you think Congress appointed a committee to draft the Declaration of Independence?

and Jefferson made the revisions. When the committee finished its work, they sent the document to Congress.

On July 4, 1776, the members of Congress passed the Declaration of Independence.

How is the Declaration of Independence organized?

The Declaration is not a very long document. It is easy to understand when you see how it is organized. The Declaration has four important parts.

- **Ideals**. The Declaration sets forth the Founders' beliefs about the purposes of government. It explains how government is created. It is one of the best statements of the ideals of our nation.

- **Arguments**. The Declaration gives the reasons why the colonies thought they were justified in breaking away from Great Britain.

- **Complaints**. The Declaration includes a list of complaints against the British king. The items on the list are there to show how the British government violated the rights of the colonists.

According to natural rights philosophy, what do the people have a right to do when the government breaks its contract with them?

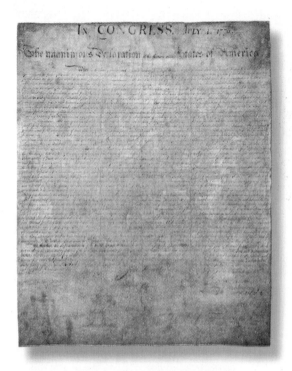

Why do you think the Founders wanted a written Declaration of Independence?

- **Conclusion**. In the end, the Declaration states that the bond between Great Britain and the colonies is dissolved. It states "that these United Colonies are, and of Right ought to be, Free and Independent States."

What principles of government does the Declaration include?

The Declaration of Independence sets forth some of the most important ideals of our nation. The Declaration states that "all men are created equal" and that they all have certain basic rights. These are the rights to life, liberty, and the pursuit of happiness.

What ideas from John Locke did Jefferson include in the Declaration of Independence?

Part of the Declaration is printed below.

We hold these Truths to be **self-evident** *[easy for anyone to see], that all Men are created equal, that they are endowed [given] by their Creator [God] with certain* **unalienable Rights** *[rights that cannot be taken away], that among these are Life, Liberty, and the Pursuit of Happiness—That to secure these Rights, Governments are instituted [established] among Men, deriving [receiving] their just Powers from the Consent [agreement] of the Governed, that whenever any Form of Government becomes destructive of these Ends [purposes], it is the Right of the People to alter or to abolish [overthrow or put an end to] it, and to institute new Government.*

What reasons does the Declaration give for independence?

The Declaration was a justification for the American Revolution. Jefferson used the ideas of the natural rights philosophy in this argument. The main points of the argument are listed below. See if you can identify its relationship to the natural rights philosophy.

1 The rights of the people are based on **natural law**. This means that there is an unchanging set of laws that govern human relations. Natural law is a higher law than law made by man. The Founders believed that natural law came from God. No constitution or government may violate the natural law. The only purpose of government is to protect the people's natural rights.

2 If a government violates the natural law, the people have the right to change or **abolish**—put an end to—that government and form a new one.

3 An agreement existed between the colonists and the king. The colonists consented to be governed by the king so long as he protected their rights to life, liberty, and property.

4 No agreement existed between the colonists and Parliament. Therefore, Parliament had no right to govern the colonies or to tax them. This was especially true, argued the colonists, since they did not have the right to send representatives to Parliament.

⑤ The king violated his agreement with the colonists. The king acted, along with Parliament, to deprive the colonists of their rights. Therefore, the colonists had the right to withdraw their consent to be governed by the king. The colonists were free to establish their own government.

What complaints against the king does the Declaration include?

The Declaration contains a long list of complaints against the British king. For example, the Declaration accuses the king of

- refusing to approve laws necessary for the public good

- seeking to destroy the colonial legislatures

- obstructing justice by refusing to give certain powers to the colonial courts

- keeping standing armies in time of peace

- requiring the quartering or housing of British soldiers

- imposing taxes without the consent of the people to be taxed

- cutting off trade between the colonies and all parts of the world

- in some cases, denying the colonists the right to trial by jury

What ideas about government are in the Declaration of Independence?

Work with a partner or in groups of three. Each group should examine the text of the Declaration of Independence and select three complaints against the king. Groups should then complete the following steps and report their findings to the class.

- Rewrite the complaint in your own words.

- Explain the basis of the colonists' complaint.

- Explain what ideas about government are implied by each complaint.

Why did some colonists want to remain British subjects?

To rebel against the British government was a serious matter. After all, generations of colonists had been loyal to Great Britain. It is understandable, then, that some people did not support the Revolution.

The colonists were almost evenly divided into those who supported the Revolution, those who did not, and the undecided. The people who remained loyal to the king were called **Loyalists** or **Tories**. They held deep feelings of loyalty to the home country.

Many Loyalists were large landowners, wealthy merchants, or officials of the king. The Loyalists did not like British taxes or other limits on their freedom any more than the Patriots did. But they did not think that breaking away from Britain was the answer to these problems.

Some colonial families split apart when the Revolution began. Family members chose sides. Those who supported the Revolution were called **Patriots**. Those who remained loyal to Britain were known as Loyalists. For example, Benjamin Franklin was a Patriot. His son was a Loyalist.

Many Loyalists joined the British army and fought for the king. Some Loyalists moved back to Great Britain while others went to Canada or the West Indies. Those Loyalists who remained in the colonies had a hard time. Sometimes their property was taken from them. Sometimes they were humiliated or put in jail. Even so, the Loyalists as a group suffered less than dissenters in other revolutions.

This drawing illustrates Loyalists being received back into Great Britain. What rights of the Loyalists, if any, were violated by the Patriots?

Would you favor or oppose independence?

Both the Patriots and the Loyalists held strong opinions about the Revolution. Patriots and Loyalists came from all sections of American life. Native Americans were forced to choose sides in the struggle. African Americans were Loyalists as well as Patriots.

Your class can debate both sides of the issue. Work in four groups. Two groups support the revolutionary cause and two groups oppose it.

Why do you think such bitter feelings arose during the debate between the Patriots and the Loyalists?

Supporters of the Revolution
PATRIOTS

Group one. You are members of the state legislature, writers, doctors, and their friends and families. Write letters to your family or the editor of a colonial newspaper defending the actions of the Second Continental Congress. Read your letters when it is your turn to speak in the debate.

Group two. You are backcountry farmers, trappers, and schoolteachers. Draw editorial cartoons defending the American position in the conflict with Great Britain. Display your posters on your side of the debate area.

Supporters of the British
LOYALISTS

Group three. You are landowners, shipbuilders, shopkeepers, and their friends and families. Write letters to the editor of a colonial newspaper explaining why the British actions were justified. Read your letters aloud when it is your turn to speak in the debate.

Group four. Your group is composed of colonial officials such as magistrates, sheriffs, soldiers, and their friends and families. Draw editorial cartoons supporting your ideas about loyalty to England. Display your posters in your side of the debate area.

1 What were the reasons for writing the Declaration of Independence?

2 What are the four parts of the Declaration of Independence?

3 What arguments does the Declaration make in support of the colonies' independence?

4 What complaints did the colonists have against the king of Great Britain?

5 What is the purpose of government as described in the Declaration of Independence?

6 What does the Declaration say people have the right to do if a government does not protect their rights?

7 What do the following phrases from the Declaration mean?

- "all men are created equal"

- "consent of the governed"

- "self-evident"

- "unalienable rights"

ACTIVITIES

1 Rewrite the first two paragraphs of the Declaration of Independence in contemporary language. Share your revision with the class.

2 Read a novel about the Revolutionary War, such as *April Morning, Johnny Tremain, Cast Two Shadows,* or *My Brother Sam Is Dead.*

Select a character from the story. Explain his or her opinions about the Revolutionary War.

3 Play the online game *The Road to Revolution*

http://www.pbs.org/ktca/ liberty/road.html

or another online game about the American Revolution. The site is hosted by PBS.

What happened during the American Revolution? How did the government function?

LESSON PURPOSE

In this lesson, you will learn what happened during the American Revolutionary War with Britain. You will also learn about the significance of the war for the rest of the world. You will learn about the difficulties of the colonists during the war and the role played by diplomacy.

When you have finished the lesson, you should be able to explain the course of the war and how the colonial armies overcame extreme difficulties. You should also be able to explain some problems of government that Congress had to deal with during the war.

Battle of Saratoga

diplomacy

Quebec Campaign

"The Shot Heard 'Round the World"

treason

Treaty of Paris

Yorktown Surrender

How did the Revolutionary War begin, and what was its significance?

The night before fighting broke out, Paul Revere made his famous midnight ride. He warned members of the citizen militia, called Minutemen, to get ready to fight. They gathered in Lexington and Concord. The role of the citizen militia reminds us that citizens are sometimes called upon to perform service to their nation. Calling upon the citizen militia as Revere did also gives us insight into why the Founders added the Second Amendment to the Constitution. The amendment says that "a well-regulated militia being necessary to the security of a free State, the right of the people to keep and bear Arms shall not be infringed."

The Revolutionary War, which lasted for six long years, ended in victory for the former American colonists. You learned in Lesson 7 that the first shots were fired on April 19, 1775. That morning, skirmishes between American colonists and British soldiers broke out. The gunfire that opened the fighting later became known as **"the shot heard 'round the world."** People said this because news of the

How did Paul Revere's ride affect the American Revolution?

American rebellion and its demand for independence spread all over the world. Many nations eventually made the same demand of their own colonial rulers. The American Revolution changed world history. Achieving independence, however, was far more difficult than declaring it. Success often seemed impossible, but the Americans did not give up.

What did the Second Continental Congress do to direct the Revolution?

On July 4, 1776, Congress issued its formal Declaration of Independence, making a complete break from Britain. There was no turning back. The Continental Congress endured great difficulties in trying to govern during the Revolution. There were many arguments among the delegates to Congress. Because it did not have a legal charter for its existence, Congress could not force the former colonies, now independent states, to pay the costs of fighting the British. So, soldiers often went unpaid, unfed, and without uniforms.

To finance military expenses, Congress decided to issue paper money. But the paper was not backed by any precious metal. Therefore, it could not hold a steady, reliable value. Paper money did not solve the problem of lack of funds, which remained for the whole war.

Congress tried to remedy the lack of a legal basis for its existence. In November 1777, Congress passed the Articles of Confederation. It was the country's first constitution. But the states took their time in agreeing to the new frame of government. It was not until March 1, 1781, when the fighting was nearly over, that the Articles took effect. Even then, the Articles did not solve the problems of the new national government. You will learn more about the Articles of Confederation in Lesson 11.

What problems were faced by the Continental Congress?

How successful were the Americans at the beginning of the Revolutionary War?

At the beginning of the war, the Americans were not successful. They invaded Canada in the **Quebec Campaign** of 1775–76, but failed. Then in August 1776, in the Battle of Long Island, near New York City, the British defeated George Washington. But he managed to save most of his troops from capture. This occurred only two months after independence was declared.

The military situation was bleak. Washington understood how grave matters were. He tried to rally the former colonists, about a third of whom were against independence and another third were neutral, to the cause of fighting for independence by making daring raids on British positions. Near the end of December, he crossed the ice-choked Delaware River and won small battles at Trenton and Princeton, New Jersey. But prospects for the American cause were poor. The troops needed food, their pay, and equipment.

In 1777, Washington lost more encounters with the British in Pennsylvania at Germantown and Brandywine Creek. In the same year, the British tried to strangle the Revolution by cutting the colonies in two. They took control of the Hudson River, which ran through New York. But the British failed. Instead, the Americans scored a victory in the **Battle of Saratoga**. Arms and supplies secretly sent by the French government through a private arms merchant arrived in time to help the Americans. This may have been the Revolution's most important campaign. The British plan had been defeated.

What happened at Valley Forge, Pennsylvania, during the winter of 1777–78?

No one could see the importance of Saratoga until much later. In the meantime, conditions for the American army became desperate. Soldiers suffered terribly from lack of food and shelter during the winter of 1777–78 at their quarters in Valley Forge, Pennsylvania. But American spirits did not give out. Martha Washington joined her husband, sharing the hardships of a cold and bleak winter. She did what she could to assist the troops. She organized a campaign for supplies that the soldiers desperately

How did Martha Washington contribute to the success of the Revolutionary War?

needed. She was aided in her efforts by Benjamin Franklin's daughter, Sarah Franklin Bache. Together, they collected 2,200 shirts and 400 pairs of stockings for the freezing men.

During this winter in Valley Forge, Baron von Steuben, a German volunteer, gave important assistance by training the cold, ragged, half-starved soldiers. He raised their morale and helped make them into an effective fighting force. Some troops deserted, but others endured the terrible cold and hunger. The young French aristocrat and military commander, the Marquis de Lafayette, who was devoted to the American cause for independence, also spent the winter at Valley Forge. When spring arrived, the American forces, though in tatters, had endured.

What part did diplomacy play in the outcome of the war?

Events happening elsewhere, however, eventually turned the tide in the Americans' favor. Perhaps the most important event of 1778 occurred across the Atlantic in France. Congress had sent Silas Deane to France in 1776. He was successful in gaining arms and supplies as well as the services of competent military officers.

Later, however, Congress sent Benjamin Franklin to Paris, the capital of France, to seek aid. Franklin's fame as a writer and scientist preceded him. The French, who were sworn enemies of the British, admired him. For his part, Franklin showed great skill in diplomacy.

General George Washington with Lafayette at Valley Forge. What effect did the assistance of foreign nations have on the outcome of the war?

Diplomacy is the practice of carrying on formal relationships with governments of other countries. The official representatives of countries meet and discuss issues important to their governments. They work together in a peaceful manner to find solutions to common problems.

In 1778, aided by the American victory at Saratoga, Franklin secured formal treaties between France and the United States. The new alliance ensured the assistance of the French army and navy.

Making the most of his enormous popularity among the French, Franklin

Why was Benjamin Franklin successful in his diplomatic mission to France?

asked for loan after loan and was never refused. Franklin was not above hinting that the colonists might make peace with Britain, France's enemy, if the Americans did not receive what they needed. In the end, French loans, soldiers, and, especially, its navy were critical for the final victory in 1781.

What happened in the South during the war?

Little fighting took place in the Middle Atlantic region after Saratoga. In 1778–79, fighting shifted to the western frontier area, now Indiana, and to the South. Military campaigns took place in North and South Carolina and in Georgia, where Savannah fell to the British. In South Carolina, Charleston had resisted two British attacks. But in 1780 it, too, fell to the British.

Things were not going well with the American army in other parts of the former colonies. In 1780, the Americans had to endure the **treason**—the betrayal of one's country—of General Benedict Arnold when he defected to the British. Complaints about the inefficient government of Congress were voiced. Congress did not have the authority to raise money for the war from taxes. The government could only beg for funds from the states, but received little. Conditions regarding food, clothing, and pay were so poor that in January 1781, the soldiers could stand it no longer and they rebelled.

In the South, where most of the fighting was now taking place, there were great hardships. One example is that of Eliza Lucas Pinckney. She was a plantation owner famous for growing new crops to

This scene depicts the surrender of Lord Cornwallis at Yorktown on October 17, 1781. What events led the British to surrender?

avoid dependence on cotton. When war broke out, Pinckney decided not to follow her economic interests. Believing in the ideas of political liberty, she supported the Revolution. But she paid dearly for her views. The British took over her mansion, burned her crops, and killed her farm animals. By the end of the war, she was economically ruined.

How did the Revolutionary War turn in the Americans' favor and come to an end?

By the early 1780s, military matters in the South turned for the better. In 1780, American forces had defeated the British at King's Mountain, South Carolina. In the following year, American commanders forced the British army under Lord Cornwallis to leave the Carolinas and retreat to Virginia. Cornwallis soon found his armies trapped on the Yorktown Peninsula. With the French navy blocking the way, the British were unable to retreat by water.

Lafayette led American troops in containing the British on land. To the north, combined American–French forces marched south from New York to Virginia. On October 17–19, 1781, seeing that their position was hopeless, the British forces under Lord Cornwallis finally **surrendered at Yorktown**. The fighting was over. Two years later, in 1783, a formal peace treaty, known as the **Treaty of Paris**, was signed. A **treaty** is an official agreement between two or more countries. American independence was formally recognized.

1. What was the significance of the Revolutionary War for the world?

2. How did the American army stay together during the worst times of the early part of the Revolutionary War?

3. What problems did the Second Continental Congress have during the war, and how did Congress deal with them?

4. How did the Congress attempt to provide a legal basis for its authority?

5. What role did diplomacy play in the war?

6. How important was the assistance of France in the American victory?

7. What military campaigns led up to the end of Revolutionary War?

ACTIVITIES

Listed below are examples of those who played significant roles in the American Revolution during the years leading to the outbreak of fighting and during the Revolutionary War. They did so through political, diplomatic, or military leadership, or through other means. Look up at least one person in each group and find out who they were and why they are famous.

Foreign supporters who participated in significant ways in the Revolutionary War include:

John Paul Jones (English)
Marquis de Lafayette (French)
Thaddeus Kosciuszko (Polish)
Baron Friedrich von Steuben (German)

Abigail Adams	George Mason
John Adams	Robert Morris
Samuel Adams	Thomas Paine
Crispus Attucks	Eliza Lucas Pinckney
Benjamin Franklin	Molly Pitcher
Horatio Gates	Paul Revere
Nathaniel Greene	Deborah Simpson
John Hancock	Haym Solomon
Patrick Henry	Mercy Otis Warren
Agrippa Hull	George Washington
Thomas Jefferson	Martha Washington
Henry Knox	"Mad" Anthony Wayne

How did the states govern themselves after the Revolution?

LESSON PURPOSE

Shortly after the start of the Revolutionary War in 1775, many of the new states began to write their constitutions. In this lesson you will learn about these new state constitutions. You will explore the basic ideas on which the new governments were founded.

When you finish the lesson, you should be able to describe those basic ideas. You should also be able to explain the major differences between the Massachusetts constitution and the constitutions of the other states.

legislative supremacy

petition

popular sovereignty

veto

What were the basic ideas about government in the state constitutions?

After the Declaration of Independence, British government in the colonies came to an end. The colonies were free and independent states. Each state would have to create a new government.

The people wanted state governments that would protect their basic rights and promote the common good. When they began to write their state constitutions they used the ideas they had learned from political philosophy. They also used what they had learned from their own experience with colonial and British government.

The ideas they included in the state constitutions were not new. Most of the ideas had been used in the governments of the colonies. The Founders tried to design their new governments with the best ideas from the past. Their experiences with these state governments would help them design the Constitution in 1787.

These are the basic ideas that the Founders included in their state constitutions.

John Hancock was a governor of Massachusetts and a signer of the Declaration of Independence. In what ways did state constitutions limit the power of the governor?

❶ **Natural rights and higher law.** The purpose of government is to protect the rights of citizens to life, liberty, and property. Each state constitution was a higher law that everyone had to obey.

② **Social contract.** Each state made it clear that it believed that government is formed as a social contract. The people agreed to form a government to protect their natural rights.

③ **Popular sovereignty.** The term sovereign means to have the highest authority or power. **Popular sovereignty** means that the people are the highest authority. All the states adopted the idea that the people are the source of the authority of government. The people delegate their authority to government. Government gets its right to govern from the people.

④ **Representation.** Each state considered it very important that the legislature be made up of elected representatives of the people. In most states, the right to vote was limited to white men who owned property. About seventy percent of the white men in America owned enough property to be able to vote. In contrast, only about ten percent were eligible to vote in Great Britain.

⑤ **Separation of powers.** All the states used some form of separation of powers. They divided government into legislative, executive, and judicial branches.

⑥ **Checks and balances.** Although the states favored a strong legislature, the constitutions did provide for some checks. Most of the checks were within the legislatures themselves. Most legislatures had two houses. Each house could check the power of the other. The people also could check the power of the legislatures. The voters could elect new representatives to both houses if they did not like the way the government was working.

Why do you think most states required people to own property in order to be eligible to vote?

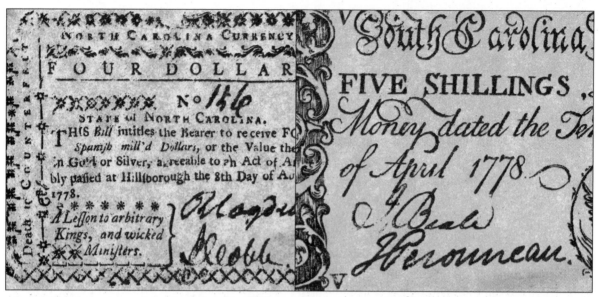

Examples of money used in North Carolina (left) and South Carolina (right) after the Revolutionary War. What problems might arise if each state could print its own paper money?

❼ Legislative supremacy. The majority of the states set up governments in which most of the power was given to the legislature. This system of government is known as **legislative supremacy**. The Founders believed that because the people elected the legislature, it was the most democratic branch of government. They were afraid of giving too much power to the executive branch. They remembered how the royal governors and the king had abused their power. So most of the state governors were given very limited power.

Despite checks on the power of the legislative branch the legislature had far greater power than the other two branches of government. Legislative supremacy led to some serious problems in most states.

- State governments did not protect the property rights of some citizens.

In these states, factions—groups of people who seek to promote their own interests—gained control of the legislature. The factions were accused of making laws that benefited themselves rather than the common good. They passed laws that canceled debts and they created paper money. These laws benefited the people who owed money and hurt those who had loaned it to them.

- The state legislatures passed laws that taxed and controlled their citizens far more than the British had done. The level of taxes during the 1780s was ten to twenty times what it had been before the Revolution.

- Many new state laws were passed which interfered with the private lives of the citizens. Laws were passed telling people what they should eat, drink, wear, and believe.

How was power distributed by the state constitutions?

Look at the two illustrations on this page and answer the questions that follow. Share the answers with the class.

❶ How was power distributed in most states?

❷ Compare the distribution of power in Massachusetts with the distribution of power in the other states. How is the distribution of power different in Massachusetts?

❸ What might be the advantages and disadvantages of giving most of the power of a government to the legislature?

❹ What might be the advantages and disadvantages of the system of government in Massachusetts?

What was important about the Massachusetts constitution?

Massachusetts was the last state to write its constitution. The citizens adopted the state constitution in 1780. The people there had learned some important lessons from the experiences of the other states. They used this knowledge in creating their state government.

Most of the other states used the idea of legislative supremacy to protect people's rights. The Massachusetts constitution, however, distributed power more evenly among the branches of government. The governor had more power and was more independent of the legislature. This was possible because the people elected the governor directly. The people expected the governor to protect their interests.

Here is how some of the powers of the governor of Massachusetts were balanced in relation to the legislature.

- The governor received a fixed salary. His salary could not be changed by the legislature.

- The governor could **veto**—refuse to sign—proposed laws put forth by the legislature. A two-thirds

This is James Bowdoin II, who, along with John Adams and Samuel Adams, drafted the Massachusetts constitution. What were the strengths and weaknesses of the Massachusetts constitution?

vote of the legislature was needed to override his veto.

- The governor could appoint officials in the executive branch. He could also appoint judges in the judicial branch.

The Massachusetts constitution also divided the people into voting groups based on their wealth. They expected that government would then more accurately represent the interests of the groups that elected them.

- Only people with a large amount of property could vote for both the governor and the legislature.

- People with slightly less property could vote for both the upper and lower houses of the legislature.

- People with the minimum amount of property could only vote for the lower house of the legislature.

The experience of writing state constitutions was a useful one to the Founders. Americans were learning what type of government worked best. The differences between the Massachusetts constitution and those that were written earlier were a result of these experiences.

Did the Massachusetts constitution contradict the idea of popular sovereignty? Why or why not?

What were the state declarations of rights?

The states did not depend solely on a system of separation of powers to protect people's rights. The first part of most state constitutions was a declaration of rights, or bill of rights. This section of the constitution listed the basic rights of citizens.

Listing the rights of the people first showed that citizens had certain basic rights that existed before the creation of the government. No constitution or government could take away these rights. Although the declarations of rights were different from state to state, they were all based on the idea that people have certain basic rights that must be protected.

What important ideas are in the Virginia Declaration of Rights?

Virginia was the first state to adopt a bill of rights. George Mason wrote most of the Virginia Declaration of Rights. Mason later was opposed to the U.S. Constitution because it did not include a bill of rights. In writing Virginia's bill of rights, Mason relied on the writing of John Locke and the ideas of republican government.

The Virginia Declaration of Rights stated that

- all power comes from and is kept by the people

- all men are by nature equally free and independent; they have certain basic rights that no social contract can take away

Why do you think most states included protections against cruel and unusual punishments in their constitutions?

- government is created for the common good, protection, and safety of the people; if a government does not serve these purposes, the people have an inalienable right to alter or abolish it

The Virginia Declaration of Rights also listed many of the rights that we enjoy today. These include the right to

- trial by jury

- protection against forced self-incrimination

- protection against cruel and unusual punishment

- freedom of the press

- free exercise of religious beliefs

What rights were protected in the other states?

Most states adopted bills of rights like Virginia's. Some states' declarations also included the idea that civic virtue was essential to preserving freedom.

The states' bills of rights were different in the rights they chose to include or leave out. Most included such political guarantees as

- the right to vote by men who met certain property qualifications

- free and frequent elections

- freedom of speech and the press

- the right to **petition** (make a formal request of) government

- no taxation without representation

All the states' bills of rights included rights for people accused of a crime.

These included the right to have

- an attorney

- a jury trial

- protection from illegal searches and seizure

- protection against forced self-incrimination

- protection from excessive bail and fines

- protection against cruel and unusual punishment

Most of the states' bills of rights expressed a fear of standing armies. The bills of rights condemned standing armies in time of peace and the quartering of soldiers in civilian homes. Many bills of rights included the right of citizens to bear arms. The Vermont bill of rights was the first to outlaw the practice of slavery.

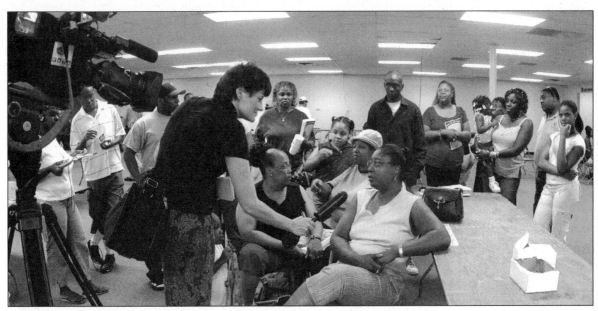

What is the importance of freedom of speech and the press?

1. What basic ideas about good government were included in the state constitutions?

2. Why did Americans believe that the legislature was the most democratic branch of government?

3. Why did some Americans distrust the executive and judicial branches of government?

4. How did the Massachusetts constitution differ from the constitutions of other states? Why was this important?

5. What was the Virginia Declaration of Rights? What rights of citizens did it include?

6. What rights did the state constitutions protect?

1. These are a few examples of the rights listed in the Maryland constitution of 1776. Examine each and write a brief explanation of what the right means and why it is important.

   - That every man hath a right to petition the Legislature, for the redress of grievances, in a peaceable and orderly manner.

   - That no...tax...ought to be set...without consent of the Legislature.

   - That no freeman ought to be taken, or imprisoned...or deprived of his life, liberty, or property, but by the judgment of his peers, or by the law of the land.

   - That the liberty of the press ought to be inviolably preserved.

2. Create a news interview set in 1780. Interview your classmates acting as representatives of the states of Massachusetts and Virginia. During the interview, the representatives should discuss the differences between their state constitutions and why they are important.

3. Find a copy of your state's constitution. What are some of the rights that your state constitution protects? How does your state constitution compare with the Virginia Declaration of Rights?

How did the Articles of Confederation organize the first national government?

LESSON PURPOSE

Our first government, the Continental Congress, drew up a constitution stating its powers. This constitution was called the Articles of Confederation. In this lesson you learn about some of the problems the Founders faced in creating our first national government. You will learn about the successes of the first national government. You also will learn about the weaknesses of government under the Articles and why some people believed that a new constitution was necessary.

When you finish this lesson, you should be able to explain how the Articles organized the national government. You should also be able to explain how the problems with the Articles caused the Founders to write a new constitution.

Articles of Confederation
national government
Northwest Ordinance
Shays' Rebellion

What are the Articles of Confederation?

Once the war against Great Britain had started, each state was like a separate nation. Each state had its own constitution and government. To the people, their state was their country.

The Founders believed that a **national government** was needed to unify the states and to conduct the war. A national government could also control trade and manage conflicts among the states. The states also needed to be united in how they related with the rest of the world.

On June 7, 1776, Richard Henry Lee introduced two proposals to the Second Continental Congress. In one, Lee proposed independence from Great Britain. In the other, Lee proposed a national government to unify the states. Both resolutions were adopted.

Our nation's first constitution was the **Articles of Confederation**. The Articles created our first national government. Congress adopted the Articles in 1777. Final approval by the states occurred in 1781, and then the Articles came into effect.

Why did the Founders believe that a national government was necessary?

What problems did the Founders face in writing the Articles of Confederation?

It was not easy to write and agree upon a constitution for the United States. The Founders had to deal with a number of difficult questions. What type of national government should they create? How much power should they give it?

The first problem the Founders faced was the people's fear of a strong national government. Americans believed that the British government had deprived people of their rights. They thought this was likely to happen with any national government that was both powerful and far away from the people. Citizens were convinced that government should be close to the people. That way the people could control their government and make certain that it did not violate their rights.

The second problem the Founders faced was the fear that some states would have more power in a national government than other states. The leaders in each state wanted to make sure that a national government would not threaten their state's interests. As a result, the most important issue was how states would vote in Congress. Would each state have one vote? Would states with greater population or wealth have more votes than the other states? Decisions in the Congress would be made by majority vote. Some leaders were afraid that the majority would use its power for its own interest at the expense of those who were in the minority.

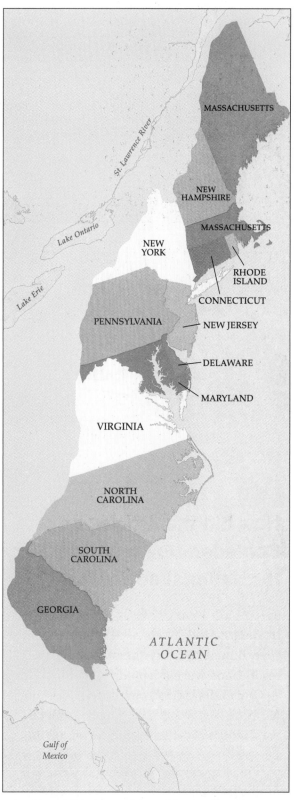

Looking at this map, why would some Founders fear that some states would have more power in a national government than others?

Why did the Founders keep the power of the national government weak?

How did the Articles of Confederation organize the national government?

The Founders did agree that the states needed a central government. Their solution to fears of a strong national government was to create a weak one. The national government under the Articles of Confederation was simply a legislature, Congress; there were no executive or judicial branches.

The states were afraid that Congress might be able to control them. So they made sure that Congress was weak and its powers limited. The Articles left most of the powers of government with the states. The national government had little power over the states and their citizens. Every action taken by Congress had to be with the consent, approval, and cooperation of the states.

To solve the problem of representation, the Articles gave each state one vote in Congress. The more populous states did not have more than one vote. The Articles also provided that on important matters, such as declaring war, nine states would have to agree. This way, the seven less populated states could not outvote the six larger states.

Why was it important that early settlers had the right to public education?

What did the national government achieve under the Articles of Confederation?

Despite a weak central government under the Articles of Confederation, the national government was responsible for a number of important achievements.

- It successfully waged the war for independence against Great Britain.
- It negotiated the peace treaty, known as the Treaty of Paris, to end the American Revolution.
- It provided that each state recognize the laws of the other states. For example, a marriage in one state would be valid in all other states. A citizen could travel freely from one state to another. Criminals who had crossed state borders could be sent back to the state in which they committed their crime.
- It passed the **Northwest Ordinance** of 1787. This was the most important law passed by Congress under the Articles. It gave people in the north-western lands the right to organize their own governments. Once they had done this, they could ask to be admitted as new states with the same rights as the original thirteen states. The law also provided for public education and forbade slavery. The western settlers were guaranteed freedom of worship, the right to trial by jury, and due process of law.

These were major accomplishments. There were serious problems with the national government, however, that led to the decision to develop a new constitution.

What problems did the country experience under the Articles of Confederation?

Governing the nation under the Articles of Confederation was difficult. Here is a list of some problems the nation experienced.

- **Congress did not have any money and it did not have the power to raise money**. Congress had no power to tax. All Congress could do was to ask the states to pay certain amounts to support the costs of the national government. The states argued about paying their fair shares of government expenses. Some states refused to pay. Congress could do nothing to force a state to pay its fair share.

- **Congress had no power over the state governments or their citizens**. State governments and individual citizens often ignored the laws

What problems did Congress face without the financial support of the states?

passed by Congress. Congress had no way to make people obey its laws. For example, at the end of the Revolutionary War Congress signed a treaty with Great Britain. In the treaty, Congress promised to respect the rights of the Loyalists and ensure that they were treated fairly. Some state governments refused to respect the treaty. Those states refused to return property they had taken away from the Loyalists. These states also refused to force payment of money owed to the Loyalists before the start of the war. Thus, the national government was unable to live up to its promise to the British.

- **Congress could not make the states live up to trade agreements with other nations.** Sometimes citizens imported goods from other countries and then refused to pay for them. This made people in foreign countries unwilling to trade with the United States. Many Americans lost money because they could not sell their goods to people in other nations.

- **Congress had no power to regulate trade among the states.** Congress had no power to make laws regulating trade among the states. States taxed goods going from one state to another. Trading often became impossible. Business slowed down and people lost their jobs.

- **Citizens thought that their property rights were threatened.** Many people believed that the states were not protecting the property rights of their citizens. Some people in the states had formed factions to promote their own interests at the expense of the common good. These factions with special interests became the majority in some state legislatures. People accused the factions of making laws to benefit themselves while ignoring the property rights of the minority. For example, they passed laws that canceled debts for those who were members of the faction and other laws that confiscated the property of people who had been Loyalists. People who were hurt by such laws argued that the states were not protecting the property of all citizens. Many people thought that a strong national government was needed to protect property rights.

Why was Shays' Rebellion important?

By 1786, many Americans were in financial trouble. Businesses failed, trade suffered, and many people were in debt. Soldiers who had fought in the Revolution still had not been paid. Congress could not control the country and people worried about what would happen.

Farmers in Massachusetts had serious economic problems. Farm prices were low, and when farmers could not pay their debts, many lost their farms and homes. Some were even put in prison. Many people claimed that the new state taxes had put them in debt. As a result, they felt that the state was not protecting their interests.

Then a dramatic series of events that became known as **Shays' Rebellion** finally convinced many Americans that it was time for a change. In an attempt to keep the state from taking their farms, local farmers under the leadership of Daniel Shays began to close down the courts where their cases were heard. The action against the courts spread to other towns and into neighboring states.

In January 1787, Shays led 2,000 rebels to Springfield, Massachusetts, to raid the federal arsenal for weapons. Shays' Rebellion frightened many property owners. People feared that the actions of the farmers might become widespread. The national government had been unable to put down the rebellion. People were asking how the country could continue to exist if it could not maintain law and order.

How did Shays' Rebellion force people to examine the weaknesses of the national government?

In January of 1786, Virginia had invited all the states to send delegates to a meeting to be held in Annapolis the following September. The purpose of the meeting was to consider trade problems. Only five states sent representatives to the Annapolis meeting. Without the other states present, the delegates who did attend the meeting were not able to accomplish much.

Everyone who was there, however, agreed that the regulation of trade could not be discussed separately from the larger political issues. The general discontent was leading to outbreaks of violence such as those led by Daniel Shays. The delegates decided to write a report for Congress. In the report, they asked for a convention of all the states.

After much debate, Congress agreed and invited the states to send delegates to a convention in Philadelphia. This meeting would be "for the sole and express purpose of revising the Articles of Confederation."

What did Daniel Shays and his followers hope to gain by their rebellion?

Is a new constitution needed?

Imagine that your state is preparing to select delegates to send to the convention in Philadelphia. Your state has to decide what position its delegates will take regarding the Articles of Confederation. A heated debate is taking place. Some people argue that the Articles are fine as they are. Some people want to make changes to the Articles. Others want to throw away the Articles and write a new constitution.

Your class will work in three groups to debate this issue.

- **Group one.** Defend the Articles of Confederation as the best way to organize the national government. You should rely on the arguments in favor of a weak national government and strong state governments. Examine the successes of the national government under the Articles. Argue that the Articles should be kept, but revised to make up for their weaknesses. Propose possible revisions.

- **Group two.** Argue to throw away the Articles and write a new constitution. Examine the arguments against a weak national government and the problems with the Articles listed in this lesson. Examine the events of Shays' Rebellion as one example of problems that might arise when there is no strong national government. Explain why you believe that the nation needs a new constitution.

- **Group three.** Organize the class debate. While the other students are preparing their arguments, you should research debate procedures. During the debate, listen to the arguments presented by the other two groups. Then decide the position of your state's delegates based on the strongest evidence presented. You may want to review other lessons to help you make your choice.

1 Why did the people in the newly independent states fear a strong national government?

2 What were the Articles of Confederation? How did the Articles organize the national government to address the fears of the people and of the states?

3 What parts of government were not included in the Articles of Confederation?

4 What did the national government achieve under the Articles of Confederation?

5 What were the weaknesses of the national government under the Articles?

6 Why was Shays' Rebellion an important event?

ACTIVITIES

1 Learn more about Shays' Rebellion. Make posters illustrating the farmers' point of view.

2 Create a short play that shows one of the problems of government under the Articles of Confederation. Perform the play for your class.

3 Learn more about the Northwest Ordinance of 1787. Explain how the ordinance provided for public education or the importance of forbidding slavery in the territories.

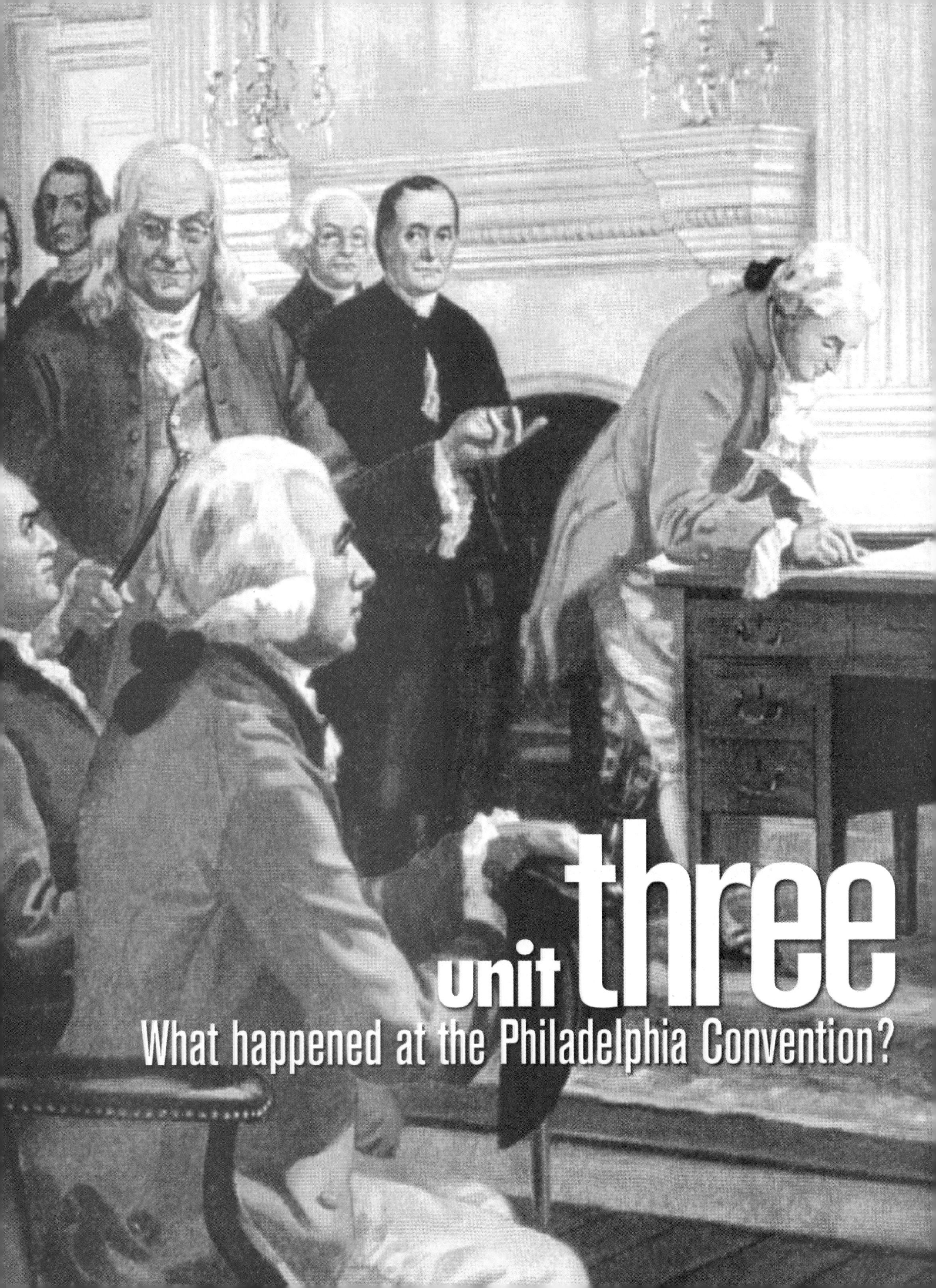

unit three

What happened at the Philadelphia Convention?

unit three

KEY CONCEPTS

electoral college

enumerated powers

equal representation

ex post facto law

general welfare clause

Great Compromise

impeach

jurisdiction

necessary and proper clause

proportional representation

writ of habeas corpus

You now are familiar with the knowledge and experiences of the Founders of our government. This unit will help you understand why the Framers, the men who created the Constitution, wrote the Constitution as they did. You will study the major problems facing the Framers and how they solved them.

When you complete this unit, you will be able to explain how the Constitution was written. You will also be able to describe some disagreements that occurred during the Philadelphia Convention and how they were solved. Finally, you will be able to explain how the Framers allocated powers to the executive and judicial branches.

Who attended the Philadelphia Convention? How was it organized?

LESSON PURPOSE

In this lesson you will learn about the Philadelphia Convention in 1787. You will learn about some of the Framers who attended the convention. You will also learn about the decisions that the Framers made at the start of the meeting.

When you finish the lesson, you should be able to explain why Congress called for the Philadelphia Convention. You also should be able to explain the decisions that the delegates made at the start of the meeting.

Who attended the Philadelphia Convention?

Congress called for a meeting to be held in Philadelphia in 1787. The members of Congress invited each state to send delegates. This important meeting is known as the **Philadelphia Convention**.

The purpose of the convention was to search for ways to improve the Articles of Confederation. At the end of the meeting, the delegates would submit a plan for Congress to approve. As far as members of Congress were concerned, the role of the delegates was advisory. But something very different was about to happen.

Fifty-five delegates attended the meeting. These delegates are called the **Framers** of the Constitution. All were men. Most were young. The average age was forty-two. Most had played important roles in the American Revolution. About three-fourths of the delegates had served in Congress. Most were leaders in their states. Some were rich; most were not, but nobody was poor.

The lives of all the Framers are worth learning about in detail. We will mention only a few.

Why is James Madison known as the "Father of the Constitution"?

James Madison. Madison of Virginia is known as the "Father of the Constitution." His influence during the convention was great. This was partly because Madison brought with him a plan for creating a stronger national government. Madison's ideas were the basis for discussing how to

George Washington refused to attend the convention at first. Why do you think his attendance at the convention was important?

structure a new government. Much of what we know about what happened at the convention is based on Madison's notes.

George Washington. Washington was probably the most respected and honored man in the country. He was convinced that a stronger national government was necessary, but he did not talk about it publicly. He did not want to become involved in politics. He preferred to return to Mount Vernon, Virginia, his home, to be a farmer. He thought that he had served enough. At first, Washington refused to attend the convention. He finally agreed. Washington was afraid that if he did not attend, people might think he had lost his faith in republican government.

Benjamin Franklin. Franklin was eighty-one years old and in poor health. He attended the convention as a delegate from the state of Pennsylvania. Franklin was one of the most respected men in America. He had a long and distinguished career as a printer, inventor, writer, revolutionary, peacemaker, and diplomat. Franklin's primary role during the convention was to encourage the delegates to cooperate with each other when they disagreed. He also supported the important compromises reached during the convention.

Gouverneur Morris. Morris was from New York. He had served in the state militia and in the New York legislature. Morris had also been a member of the Continental Congress. He was an exceptionally good speechmaker during the convention. He played an important role in writing the Constitution and prepared its final draft.

How would you organize a constitutional convention?

Imagine that the teachers and principal in your school have called for a constitutional convention for the school. They have asked each class to send delegates to the convention. A **delegate** is a person who represents other people at a meeting. In this case, the delegates represent the people of each class. The delegates are to recommend ways to improve the present school government under the school's code of conduct or constitution. Work with a partner to discuss the three questions below. Be prepared to share your ideas with the class.

1. What qualifications should a delegate have to represent your class at a constitutional convention? How should these delegates be selected?

2. What rules would you establish for the delegates to follow during the convention?

3. Would you keep the rest of the school informed about what was happening at the convention? Why or why not?

What qualifications should a student have to represent your class as a delegate?

Who did not attend the convention?

Some important Americans did not attend the Philadelphia Convention. Thomas Jefferson was in France. John Adams was in England. Both men were in Europe representing the United States.

Patrick Henry refused to attend the convention. He is quoted as saying, "I smell a rat." He was against the idea of a strong national government. Henry thought that the delegates would not work on improving the Articles of Confederation. He suspected that the delegates would instead write a new constitution that would result in a strong national government. After the convention, Patrick Henry worked hard to get the people to reject the new Constitution.

Not all segments of the American population were represented at the Philadelphia Convention. There were no women among the delegates. There were no African Americans or American Indians. Poor farmers like those who took part in Shays' Rebellion were not present either.

The Rhode Island state legislature refused to send delegates to the convention. Citizens there were fiercely independent and hostile to the idea of a new constitution.

What rules did the Framers agree to follow during the convention?

By May 25, 1787, delegates from eleven states had arrived at the convention. We call the delegates **Framers** because they framed, or shaped, and wrote the U.S. Constitution. The Framers all agreed that George Washington should preside over the meetings.

At the start of the convention, the Framers agreed on three things. They agreed they would

- not try to find ways to improve the Articles of Confederation as Congress had asked them to do. The Framers thought the problems were too serious to try to correct them. Instead, the Framers decided to write a new constitution.

Patrick Henry said he did not attend the convention because he "smelled a rat." What do you think he meant by this?

keep the record of what was said at the convention a secret for thirty years. The reason for secrecy was that the Framers wanted to develop the best constitution possible. Many feared that if their discussions were made public, the delegates would not express their opinions freely. Also, the Framers did not want people from the outside trying to influence what they were doing. Finally, the Framers wanted the new constitution to be accepted. A new constitution would have a greater chance of being approved if people did not know about the arguments that went on during the convention.

give each state one vote in the convention proceedings, no matter the size of a state's population. The reason for this decision was to gain the cooperation of the small states. Delaware, for example, had threatened to withdraw from the convention if states with large populations were given more votes than states with small populations.

What ideas about government did the Framers agree to include in the new constitution?

The Framers agreed that certain basic ideas about government should be included in the new constitution. These included the idea that

- the national government should be a constitutional government, that is, a government of limited powers

- the purpose of government should be to protect fundamental rights and promote the common good

- a strong national government was needed to protect fundamental rights

- a republican form of government of elected representatives was needed to make sure that government served the common good

- a system of separation of powers and checks and balances was needed to prevent the abuse of power

Because of their agreement on basic ideas about government, the Framers were able to write a new constitution. In less than four months they created a constitution that has lasted, with some revisions, for more than 200 years.

Why did the Framers keep the proceedings of the Philadelphia Convention secret?

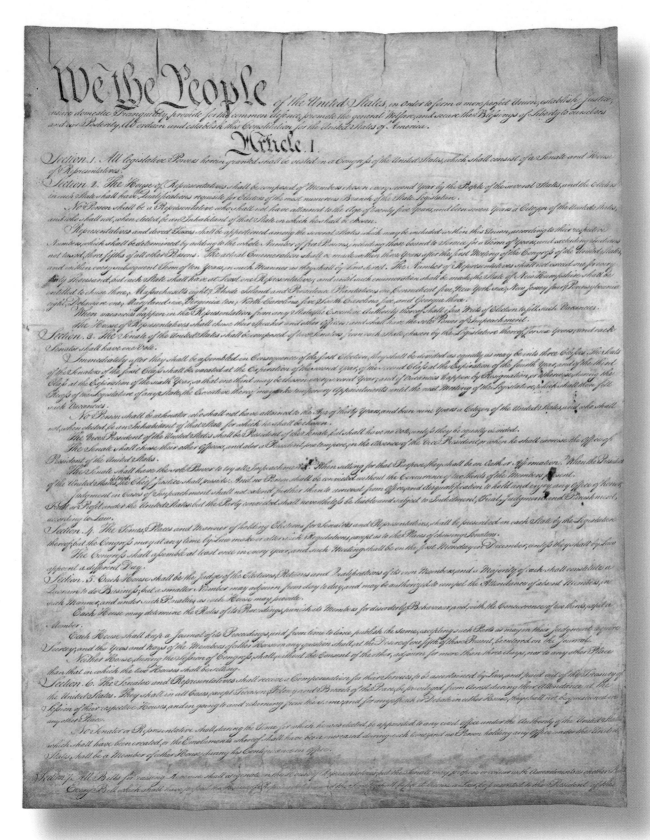

This is a reproduction of the first page of the original Constitution of the United States. Why do you think it was important to the Framers to make "We the People" so prominent on the top of the document?

1 What did Congress ask the delegates to do during the Philadelphia Convention? Did the delegates accomplish what Congress asked them to do? Explain your answer.

2 In what ways were the delegates at the Philadelphia Convention representative of the American people? In what ways were they not representative?

3 What rules did the Framers establish for the convention? What was the purpose of these rules?

4 What basic ideas about government did the Framers agree should be included in a new constitution?

ACTIVITIES

1 Find pictures of the people who attended the Philadelphia Convention. Use the pictures to create a gallery for your classroom. For each picture, write a brief biography of the Framer it represents.

2 George Washington did not want to attend the Philadelphia Convention. Conduct research to find out why Washington did not want to attend the convention, as well as why he finally changed his mind. Create a bibliography for the sources that you researched.

3 Create an editorial cartoon that expresses your opinion about whether the topics being discussed at the Philadelphia Convention should have been reported to the public during the time of the meeting.

How did the Framers solve the problem of distributing power between the state governments and the national government?

The compromises about representation and slavery reduced resistance to increasing the power of the national government. The delegates, however, still disagreed about how much power to give to each of the three branches of the national government. The problem facing the Framers was how to create a national government that was strong enough to protect the rights of the people, and yet not so strong that it would endanger those rights.

How should the Constitution be written to give power to Congress?

James Madison argued that the new Congress should keep the powers that it had under the Articles of Confederation. He also wanted Congress to make the laws that the state legislatures were prevented from making. He thought that Congress should also be given the power to reject or turn down laws made by state legislatures.

Madison's recommendations would have given the national government great power over the states and the people. To give all this power to the national government meant that the new constitution would have to be written in very general language. For example, the constitution might say, "Congress shall have the power to make all laws that are necessary."

Many of the Framers disagreed with Madison. They saw a problem with general language in the new constitution. General language could be understood to mean that government was given the power to do almost anything it wanted to do. It does not provide a good way to limit the powers of government.

Many delegates also opposed giving Congress the power to veto laws made by state legislatures. Under British rule, royal governors and Parliament had vetoed acts of the colonial legislatures. The Framers did not want to give this power to Congress.

An alternative was to write the new constitution in very specific language.

Specific language meant writing down exactly what powers Congress would have. For example, "Congress shall have the power to collect taxes." The Framers wanted a government of enumerated powers. **Enumerated powers** are powers that are specifically listed in a constitution. The problem with enumerated powers was that a constitution might leave out important powers needed by Congress to deal with unforeseen situations.

The solution was to use both general and specific language. The new constitution would give specific powers to Congress and place limitations on these powers. It would also include two general clauses that would give Congress the power to deal with unexpected situations.

What are the enumerated powers of Congress?

Article I deals with the legislative branch. Article I alone makes up more than half of the Constitution. It shows just how important the legislative branch was to the Framers.

Article I, Section 8 includes seventeen enumerated powers. Some of these powers give Congress the right to

- impose and collect taxes and duties
- borrow money
- regulate commerce with foreign nations and among the states
- coin money
- establish post offices
- declare war
- raise and support an army and navy

Should the federal government regulate postal services? Why or why not?

What are the general powers of Congress?

Article I, Section 8 also includes two general statements of power given to Congress. These are the power of Congress to

- "provide for the common Defense and general Welfare [common good] of the United States." This is called the **general welfare clause**.

- "make all Laws which shall be necessary and proper" for carrying out the other powers that the Constitution grants to Congress. This is called the **necessary and proper clause**. For example, under the enumerated powers, Congress has the power to raise and support an army. To exercise this power, it might be necessary and proper that Congress pass a law requiring citizens to serve in the armed forces.

Neither of these general clauses caused any disagreements at the convention. They did cause strong disagreements in the states about whether to approve the Constitution. Both clauses were the source of conflicts in the early years of the new government. You will learn more about these conflicts in later lessons.

What limits are there on the powers of Congress?

The Constitution includes several limits on the powers of Congress. Article I, Section 9 prohibits Congress from

- banning the slave trade before 1808

- suspending the privilege of the **writ of habeas corpus** except in

Elvis Presley was drafted into the Army in 1958. What parts of the Constitution can be used to justify the power of Congress to draft people into the armed forces?

emergencies. In Latin, habeas corpus means to "have the body." A writ of habeas corpus orders government to deliver a person it has arrested to a court of law. Government must explain why that person has been arrested and held. If government cannot show that the person has broken the law, the person must be set free.

- passing **ex post facto laws**. This is a law that makes an act a crime even though the act was legal when it took place.

- passing **bills of attainder**. This is a legislative act that declared a person guilty of violating the law and set the punishment without a court trial.

- taxing anything exported from a state

- taking money from the treasury without first passing a law to do so

- granting titles of nobility

In this way, the Framers tried to balance the need for a strong government with the need to limit its powers. Those limits were included to make sure that government did not become a threat to the people's rights.

What part of Article I, Section 8 of the Constitution gives Congress the power to conduct a space exploration program?

How do the other branches check the power of Congress?

Remember that Congress is divided into two "houses." This arrangement is a check on the power of Congress to pass laws. For example, when the House of Representatives passes a bill, it must be sent to the Senate. The bill must also pass the Senate by a majority vote before it can become law.

The executive and judicial branches also have checks, or controls, on Congress. If a bill passes in both houses of Congress, the bill must be sent to the president for approval and signature. When the president signs the bill it becomes a law.

The president may refuse to sign a bill and send it back to Congress. This is the president's power to veto a bill passed in Congress. When the president vetoes a bill, the bill can only become law if approved by a two-thirds majority in both houses of Congress.

The U.S. Supreme Court has the power to declare a law made by Congress unconstitutional. **Unconstitutional** means that the law or action is not permitted by the Constitution. The Court may say that the Constitution does not give Congress the right to pass such a law. In this case, the law can no longer be carried out or enforced. You will learn more about this power of the U.S. Supreme Court in a future lesson.

Would these bills be allowed to become law under the Constitution?

A bill is a proposed law. Members of Congress create bills and try to get a majority of both houses to vote for them.

Your class should be divided into congressional committees of about five members each. Complete the following activity and report your findings to the entire class.

Your committee wants to introduce six bills in Congress. Review the general and enumerated powers granted to Congress. For each bill in the next column identify which of these two types of powers enables Congress to pass it. Support your opinion.

Answer these two questions as part of your discussion:

- If you used only the enumerated powers of Congress to decide whether to pass a law, what problems might arise?

- If you used only the general powers of Congress to decide whether to pass a law, what problems might arise?

Bills under consideration to become laws. A law to

1 allow government to keep watch over websites on the Internet to protect children from potentially harmful material

2 allow government to draft citizens to serve in the armed forces

3 provide money to pay the expenses of the army and navy

4 allow the executive branch to conduct a space exploration program

5 allow government to impose fines as punishment for industries that pollute the air

6 require government to use tax money to provide medical assistance

1 What disagreements about the powers of Congress did the Framers have? How did they resolve these disagreements?

2 What enumerated powers does Article I, Section 8 grant to Congress?

3 What general powers does Article I, Section 8 grant to Congress? Why are these general powers necessary?

4 What limits does Article I place on the powers of Congress? Explain how these limitations protect the rights of citizens.

5 Explain some ways in which the executive and judicial branches can check the powers of Congress.

ACTIVITIES

1 Draw three illustrations. Each one should show how the limits on Congress protect the rights of citizens. Make one illustration focus on a writ of habeas corpus, one on ex post facto laws, and one on bills of attainder.

2 Article IV gives Congress power to create new states from the territories. Find out how a territory can become a state.

3 Sometimes it becomes necessary to make changes to the Constitution. This has happened twenty-seven times in the history of the United States. Read Article V in the Constitution. Explain the process for amending the Constitution.

4 Research an attempt to amend the Constitution that failed. Why did it fail? Would it be more successful today? Has the issue that the amendment was meant to correct been addressed in other ways?

How much power should be given to the executive and judicial branches?

16

LESSON PURPOSE

In this lesson you will learn about the powers that the Constitution gives to the executive and judicial branches. You will learn how the legislative and judicial branches check the power of the executive branch. You also will learn about the system that the Constitution established for electing a president.

When you finish this lesson, you should be able to explain the powers of the executive and judicial branches of government. You should also be able to explain the process for electing the president of the United States.

advice and consent

appellate jurisdiction

electoral college

impeach

jurisdiction

original jurisdiction

Twenty-second Amendment

What challenge did the Framers face in creating the executive branch?

In 1787, Americans still remembered how much trouble they had experienced with the executive branch of the British government. Americans believed that the king and his royal governors and other officials had violated their rights.

With this experience in mind, the Framers faced the problem of creating an executive branch of government. They wanted an executive branch with enough power to carry out its responsibilities yet not strong enough to overwhelm the other branches. An executive branch with too much power could endanger the rights of the people.

What powers does the Constitution give to the executive branch?

Article II of the Constitution created the executive branch. The Framers wrote Article II in more general terms than they did Article I. As a result, Article II is shorter.

What powers does Article II of the Constitution grant to the president?

138

Egyptian President Anwar Sadat, U.S. President Jimmy Carter, and Israeli Prime Minister Menachem Begin at the White House on March 26, 1979, as they completed signing of the Treaty of Peace between Egypt and Israel. Why would the Constitution require the president and the Congress to share power when negotiating treaties with other nations?

The list of powers it gives to the president is brief. These include the powers to

- carry out and enforce laws made by Congress

- make treaties with foreign nations

- appoint certain important government officials

- act as commander-in-chief of the armed forces

- veto laws passed by Congress

The president also can send and receive ambassadors to and from other countries. The president has the power to pardon people convicted of crimes against the United States.

How does the Constitution limit the powers of the executive branch?

The Constitution limits the powers of the executive branch by making it share most of its powers with Congress. Here are some examples of how this works.

- **Appointments.** The president has the power to nominate people for important jobs in government with the advice and consent of the Senate. **Advice and consent** is the term used for this process. The president also nominates people to serve in the executive and judicial branches of the national government. The Senate has the power to approve or reject the president's nominations.

- **Treaties**. The president has the power to negotiate treaties with another nation. The Senate has the power to approve or reject these treaties.

- **War**. Although the president can conduct a war as commander-in-chief, only Congress can declare war. In addition, only Congress has the power to provide money to conduct a war.

- **Veto**. The president may veto laws passed by Congress. Congress, however, may override the veto by a two-thirds vote of both houses.

The Constitution provides another important way to limit the power of the president and prevent the abuse of power. It gives the House of Representatives the power to impeach the president. To **impeach** means "to bring to trial." This means the House can accuse the president of serious crimes. The Senate then holds a trial. If the Senate finds the

Why did the Framers allow for the impeachment of presidents?

president guilty, he or she can be removed from office. While it is rarely used, impeachment is an important power that Congress has for checking the power of the executive branch.

How should the president be selected?

The Framers had given important powers to the president. It is not surprising that the Framers were concerned about how to select people to fill this position. The Framers took it for granted that George Washington would be the first president. Washington was patriotic, honest, devoted to the public good, and not interested in using power for his own advantage.

The Framers wanted a way of selecting future presidents who would be as qualified as Washington. The Framers discussed the problem for some time. They also discussed how long a president should be able to stay in office.

The Framers finally agreed that a president would serve for four years and

Why did the Framers allow presidents the power to veto laws passed by Congress?

Connecticut's electors cast their ballot during the 2004 presidential election. Do you agree with the reasoning of the Framers in their decision to establish an electoral college rather than have the people elect the president directly? Why or why not?

could be reelected any number of times. This was changed in 1951 by the **Twenty-second Amendment**. The president can now be reelected only once.

A few Framers wanted the people to elect the president directly. But James Madison thought that in such a large country the people would not know enough about the candidates to make good choices. Madison also believed that the people might not always have the wisdom to select the best person for president. Most Framers agreed with Madison.

In most states, the head of the executive branch was chosen by the state legislature. But the Framers thought that if Congress chose the executive, Congress would control the president. The result would be a weak executive branch. The Framers also thought that if the president were to be selected by the state governments, then the states would control the president. This too would result in a weak executive branch.

Either of these choices would not have helped the Framers create a stronger national government.

The method the Framers finally created for electing the president is complicated. They decided that an **electoral college** would be created once every four years to choose the president. Each state would have electors equal to the number of senators and representatives it had in Congress. Each state would decide how to select persons to serve as their electors in the college. The candidate who received a majority of votes in the electoral college would become president.

But what if no candidate got a majority of votes in the electoral college? In that case, the House of Representatives would select the president by majority vote. Each state would have one vote.

We still use the electoral college today. But it does not work the way the Framers originally planned.

What qualifications should a person have to be president?

Work with a group of three students. Examine Article II of the Constitution and review what you learned in this lesson to help you complete the chart.

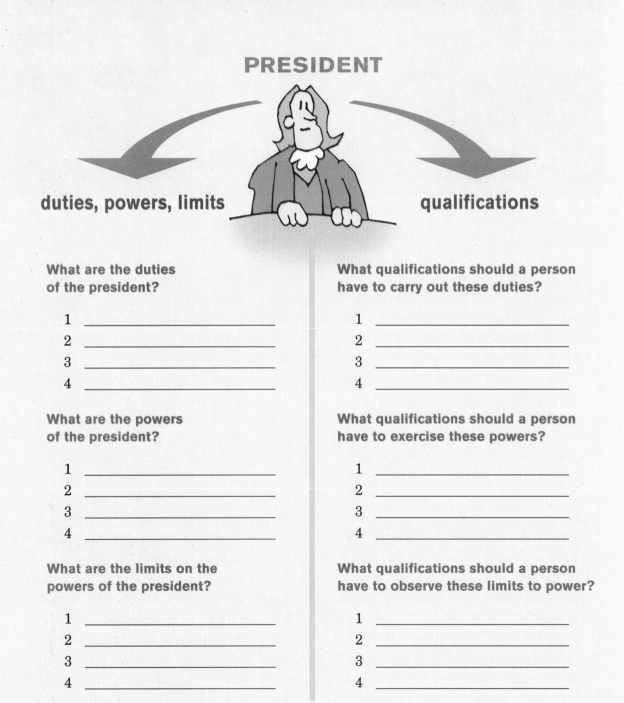

PRESIDENT

duties, powers, limits → → → **qualifications**

What are the duties of the president?

1 _____
2 _____
3 _____
4 _____

What qualifications should a person have to carry out these duties?

1 _____
2 _____
3 _____
4 _____

What are the powers of the president?

1 _____
2 _____
3 _____
4 _____

What qualifications should a person have to exercise these powers?

1 _____
2 _____
3 _____
4 _____

What are the limits on the powers of the president?

1 _____
2 _____
3 _____
4 _____

What qualifications should a person have to observe these limits to power?

1 _____
2 _____
3 _____
4 _____

What powers does the Constitution give to the judicial branch?

To complete the system of separation of powers, the Framers planned for a judicial branch. A national judiciary was needed to decide disputes between state governments and between citizens of two or more states; it was also needed for disputes between the national government and a state or a citizen.

The Framers had few problems agreeing on the powers of the judicial branch. Article III of the Constitution establishes the judicial branch. Article III includes the following ideas about a national court system.

1. Judges should be appointed, not elected. Thus, judges would be independent of politics. They could use their best judgment to decide cases and not worry about the influence of political pressures.

2. Judges should keep their positions "during good Behavior." Judges cannot be removed from office unless they are impeached. Then the judge would have to be tried and convicted of "Treason, Bribery, or other high Crimes and Misdemeanors." This means that judges should be able to make decisions without fear of losing their jobs. It also means that judges can keep their jobs for life.

3. There should be a single U.S. Supreme Court with two types of jurisdiction. **Jurisdiction** means the power or authority to hear cases and make decisions. The types of jurisdiction are original and appellate.

- The U.S. Supreme Court has original jurisdiction in cases involving a state government or an ambassador. **Original jurisdiction** means that these cases go directly to the U.S. Supreme Court. A lower court does not try these cases first.

- In all other cases, the U.S. Supreme Court has **appellate jurisdiction**. The case is tried first in a lower court. Then the decision of the lower court is appealed to the U.S. Supreme Court. The Supreme Court may decide whether to hear a case on appeal.

The Constitution clearly gave the U.S. Supreme Court the power to overrule state laws that violate the Constitution or the laws made by Congress. The power is based on the supremacy clause in Article VI. You will study the supremacy clause in Lesson 17.

The national government is supreme in those areas where the Constitution gives it the power to act. For example, suppose a state passes a law allowing factories to pollute the air. Then Congress passes a law controlling the pollution a factory can produce. The national government's laws would have to be obeyed over state laws.

Washington, Madison, and the other Framers who agreed with them got the strong national government they wanted. But the battle was not yet won. Many people in the United States were still afraid of a strong national government. They believed that it would be a threat to their rights and to their state governments.

1. What challenges did the Framers face in creating the executive branch?

2. What powers does the Constitution grant to the president?

3. Explain how the system of checks and balances limits the powers of the president. Give specific examples.

4. Explain the process for selecting a president.

5. What are the powers of the judicial branch? Why is it important that judges are appointed to office rather than elected and that they cannot be removed from office unless impeached?

6. What branch of the federal government has the power to overrule state laws that violate the U.S. Constitution?

ACTIVITIES

1. Only two presidents have faced impeachment: Andrew Johnson and William Jefferson Clinton. Richard Nixon faced the threat of impeachment, but he resigned from office. Learn more about the impeachment process and what happened with each of the three presidents listed. Share what you learned with your class.

2. Find out how electors to the electoral college are selected in your state. Share what you learned with your class.

3. Examine the Twenty-fifth Amendment to the Constitution. Draw a chart that illustrates who is next in line to become the president if a president dies while in office or otherwise cannot carry out his or her duties.

4. Learn more about John Jay and John Marshall, two justices of the U.S. Supreme Court. You can find information about these important men in your library or on the Internet.

unit four

How was the Constitution used to establish our government?

unit four

KEY CONCEPTS

Anti-Federalists

confederation

federal system

Federalists

judicial review

political parties

supremacy clause

Why is our nation's Constitution so short? The Framers wrote the Constitution as a general framework, or plan, for the new government. They left out many details because they knew that future presidents and members of Congress would add them.

In this unit, you will discover how government was organized under the Constitution. You will be able to explain the positions of the Founders who supported the Constitution and the positions of those who were against it. You will also learn about some unexpected developments that have influenced the way our nation is governed today.

How did the Constitution create a federal system of government?

17

LESSON PURPOSE

The Constitution organized government in a new way. It created a federal system of government. The Constitution gives certain powers only to the national government and certain powers only to the state governments. There are also certain powers that they share. All other powers are kept by the people.

When you finish this lesson, you should be able to explain what a federal system is. You should know how it differs from other forms of government. You should be able to explain what powers the Constitution gives to the federal government and what powers it gives to the state governments.

confederation
federal system
federalism
sovereign
supremacy clause
unitary government

How do some other nations organize their governments?

Not all nations organize government in the same way. Some nations have a unitary form of government. A **unitary government** is one in which a central government controls the state and local governments. The central government acts directly on the people. The power of state and local governments comes from the central government and it can be taken away at any time. As a result, the central government is much stronger and more powerful than the state and local governments. The United Kingdom, France, and Sweden are examples of unitary government.

Some nations have a form of government called a confederation. In a **confederation** the states are independent and have control of anything that affects their citizens and territory. In a confederation, the central government only handles those things that are of common concern. The states can withdraw from the confederation at any time. The central government acts on the states, not directly on the people. The United States under the Articles of Confederation had a confederate form of government.

This is the Swiss Bundeshaus, or Parliament. What form of government does Switzerland have? How does it differ from our form of government?

Switzerland is a modern example of a confederation.

Before the Framers created the Constitution, most nations had either a unitary or confederate form of government. The kind of government that the Framers created in our Constitution is a federal system of government.

How do these three types of government differ in their distribution of power?

What is a federal system of government?

According to the natural rights philosophy, the people have a right to create a government. The people delegate to government the right, or authority, to govern them. In return, government is responsible for protecting the people's rights to life, liberty, and property.

The Constitution begins with the words "We the People of the United States." The people have created a government and have given it the authority to govern them. Power flows upward from the people to their government. The people remain sovereign at all times. **Sovereign** means to have the highest rank of authority. The people have ultimate authority to control government.

At the time the Framers wrote the Constitution, the people in most other nations were not sovereign. Governments held authority over the people. In some countries the king was sovereign.

In a **federal system** of government, the sovereign people decide how to delegate their authority. When creating the Constitution the Framers decided to delegate the power of the people to more than one government. They delegated some powers only to the national government. They delegated other power to the state governments. Some powers, they decided, should be shared by the state and national governments. Finally, all other powers, or rights, are kept by the people.

A federal system of government may also be described as a government that is based on the principle of federalism. **Federalism** refers to the practice of dividing and sharing the powers of government between a central government and regional governments such as state governments.

What powers are delegated to the state and federal governments?

As citizens of the United States, the people delegate certain powers to the federal, or national, government. These powers are in the Constitution. They include the power to

- create post offices
- regulate interstate and foreign trade
- declare and conduct war
- create a national currency

This is President Franklin Roosevelt signing the congressional declaration of war against Japan in December 1941. Why do you think that only the federal government has the authority to engage in war?

As citizens of the various states, the people delegate certain powers to their state governments. These powers are in each state's constitution. They include the power to

- regulate trade within the state
- establish public schools
- create traffic and motor vehicle laws
- regulate marriage and divorce practices

The state and federal governments share certain powers. These include the powers to

- make their own laws
- tax the people
- borrow money
- create their own court system
- provide for the health and welfare of the people

Finally, the people have kept certain rights or powers and have not delegated them to any government. These include the right to

- believe what we wish
- form or join organizations
- select our careers and live our lives as we choose
- choose our friends
- travel where we wish to go inside or outside the country
- raise a family

What powers does the Constitution deny to the federal and state governments?

A constitutional government means that the powers of government are limited. The U.S. Constitution limits the powers of both the federal and state governments.

LIMITS ON THE POWER OF THE FEDERAL GOVERNMENT

The federal government may not

- tax exports

- spend money in a way that is not approved by law

- enact laws that favor trade in one state over the others

- exercise powers that belong to the states

- suspend the right to a writ of habeas corpus, except in a national emergency

LIMITS ON THE POWER OF THE STATE GOVERNMENTS

The state governments may not

- coin or print money

- enter into treaties with other nations

- tax imports or exports

- keep an army or navy in time of peace

- engage in war unless invaded or in immediate danger of being invaded

What powers and rights do the people keep for themselves?

LIMITS ON BOTH THE FEDERAL AND STATE GOVERNMENTS

Neither the federal nor state governments may

- deny the right to trial by jury

- enact ex post facto laws or bills of attainder

- grant titles of nobility

The Bill of Rights places other limits on federal and state governments. You will examine these in the next unit.

Do state governments or the national government have the power to do what you propose?

Work with a partner. Imagine that you want to do each of the things listed below. First, you need to decide which level of government, state or national, has the power to do what you propose. Examine each item. Decide if the power belongs to the national government, the state governments, both, or neither.

1. You want a law to help control what people can put on the Internet for children to see and read.

2. You want to increase the age at which people may buy tobacco to twenty-five.

3. You want a law that helps to control who may or may not buy and sell guns.

4. You want a law to limit driving privileges for people over eighty-five years of age.

5. You think that we no longer need a one-cent coin. You want a law to end the minting of pennies.

6. You want a law to stop the sale of sport shoes made by children who work long hours for little pay in some other countries.

7. You want a law to make it more difficult for parents of very young children to get a divorce.

8. You think that the leader of another country is not able to run the government of that country. You want a law to punish anyone who supports this leader.

9. You want a treaty that requires all nations to pass laws to clean up the air and water.

10. You want a law to raise the minimum age requirement for children to remain in school.

What part of government would negotiate treaties among nations requiring them to pass laws to clean up the air and water?

What is the supremacy clause?

There were disagreements among the Framers over what powers the federal government should have. The Framers did agree that the powers of the federal government were to be greater than the powers of the state governments. As you learned in Lesson 16, this is clearly stated in the supremacy clause of Article VI. The **supremacy clause** says,

> This Constitution, and the Laws of the United States...shall be the supreme Law of the Land.

The states cannot make laws that conflict with the Constitution or laws made by Congress.

The supremacy clause gives the courts the power to decide disagreements between the states and the federal government. It does not change the fact, however, that the Constitution limits the powers of both the federal and state governments.

What might be the advantages and disadvantages of the supremacy clause?

How has the relation between federal and state governments changed?

The Framers created a new and very complicated form of government. They could not predict exactly what powers the state and federal governments would eventually have. Early in our history, the state governments were very powerful. Today, the federal government has far more power over the state governments than most of the Framers could have imagined.

In thinking about the relationship between the federal and state governments, it is important to understand the following things:

- In spite of the increase in the power of the federal government, most of the laws that affect us directly are state or local laws. These include laws regarding education, most property, contracts, families, and criminal behavior.

- Congress makes most of the decisions about how much power is left to the states. Congress decides whether the federal or state governments should carry out certain responsibilities.

This complicated system is sometimes not as efficient as a unitary system of government. But the Framers did not see this as a disadvantage. In fact, the Framers thought that the separation of powers between the federal and state governments was one way to protect the rights of the people.

1. Explain the major differences between a unitary form of government and a confederation.

2. What is a federal system?

3. What powers does the Constitution delegate to the federal government?

4. What powers belong to the states?

5. What powers do the state and federal governments share?

6. What powers did the people keep for themselves?

7. What powers does the Constitution deny to the federal government?

8. What powers does the Constitution deny to the state governments?

9. What is the supremacy clause? Why is it important?

ACTIVITIES

1. Draw a diagram that shows how the federal system works in the United States. Your diagram should show the powers that belong to the states and powers that belong to the national government. Your diagram should also show the powers that both states and the national government share.

2. Look in a newspaper to find articles that illustrate how the federal system works. You may find articles that illustrate federal powers, state powers, and powers that both levels of government share.

3. Plan a short play. Suppose you and a few friends were in a situation like that of the Framers. You must organize a government. Explain to your classmates, the "people," what you think might be some advantages and disadvantages of a federal system of government.

- Which responsibilities and powers would you give to the national government?

- Which powers would you give to the state governments?

- Which powers would you keep for the people?

How did the people approve the new Constitution?

18

LESSON PURPOSE

In this lesson you will learn about the struggle to get the Constitution ratified. You will learn how the Framers planned to have the people decide whether or not to approve the Constitution. You will also examine the arguments made by the Anti-Federalists and the Federalists for and against the new Constitution.

When you finish the lesson, you should be able to explain why the ratification process was important. You should also be able to describe the arguments for and against approving the Constitution.

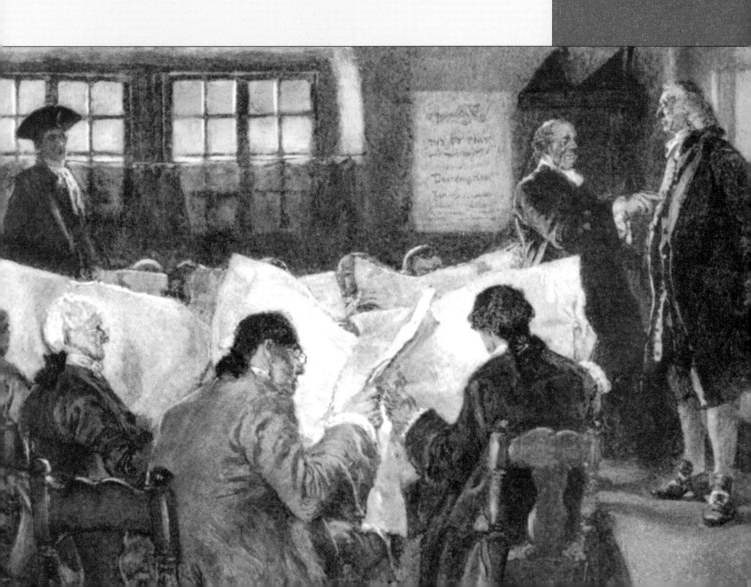

Why did the Framers want the people to ratify the Constitution?

The Framers did not believe they had created a perfect plan of government. The four months they spent creating the Constitution had been filled with disagreements. A few delegates had walked out of the convention. Some delegates refused to sign the Constitution. The great majority of Framers, however, thought they had done a good job.

After creating the Constitution, the Framers knew that they had to get it approved. James Madison was afraid that the Constitution would be rejected if either the Congress or the state legislatures were asked to ratify it. To **ratify** means to approve. To avoid rejection, Madison developed a plan. His plan was to get the voters to ratify the Constitution at special conventions to be held in each state. The delegates to these conventions would be elected by popular vote of the people for the sole purpose of approving the Constitution.

Madison based his plan on the idea in the Preamble to the Constitution. The first words in the Preamble are "We the People...do ordain and establish this

How did Madison plan to get the people to approve the new Constitution?

Constitution." The people who were to be governed by the new national government would consent to its creation and agree to obey its decisions. This was the method for establishing a government set forth in the natural rights philosophy and in the Declaration of Independence. Thus, the Framers used the idea of a social

How were people in cities far from Washington, D.C., able to participate in government?
How is it easier to participate in government now than it was in the late 1700s?

contract to get the Constitution approved. It was to be approved by an agreement among the people to create a national government.

The Framers approved Madison's plan. Article VII said that the Constitution would be in effect after it had been ratified by the conventions of nine of the thirteen states. The Framers required approval of the voters of nine states because they were afraid they would not get the approval of all thirteen.

Who were the Federalists and Anti-Federalists?

Once the Philadelphia Convention ended, the Federalists went to work. The **Federalists** were the people who supported ratifying the Constitution. The Federalists asked the states to organize their ratifying conventions as quickly as possible. They knew that their opponents had not had much time to prepare their arguments. By contrast, the supporters of the Constitution had worked on it for four months. They knew the arguments for and against it.

To explain the new Constitution to the people, Alexander Hamilton, James Madison, and John Jay wrote a series of articles for a New York newspaper supporting ratification. These collected articles are called *The Federalist*. *The Federalist* was read in other states as well. Today, *The Federalist* remains one of the most important explanations of constitutional government ever written.

The **Anti-Federalists** were the people who opposed ratifying the Constitution. Anti-Federalist leaders included George Mason, Edmund Randolph, and Elbridge Gerry. Each had attended the Philadelphia Convention but refused to sign the Constitution. Although John Hancock, Samuel Adams, and Richard Henry Lee had all signed the Declaration of Independence, they too were against ratification.

Patrick Henry had always opposed the idea of a strong national government. Henry became a leading Anti-Federalist. Mercy Otis Warren, a playwright, also was against ratification. She wrote pamphlets explaining why she did not support the Constitution.

Most Americans were very suspicious of government, but the Anti-Federalists were especially mistrustful of government in general and strong national government in particular. This mistrust was the basis of their opposition to the Constitution. They feared it had created a government the people could not control. The Anti-Federalists feared that flaws they saw in the Constitution would be a threat to their natural rights. During the ratification debates, the Anti-Federalists put up a strong fight.

Why were Anti-Federalists like Mercy Otis Warren opposed to ratification of the Constitution?

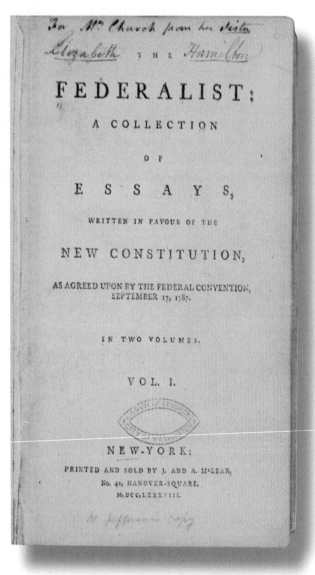

FEDERALIST:

A COLLECTION

OF

ESSAYS,

WRITTEN IN FAVOUR OF THE

NEW CONSTITUTION,

AS AGREED UPON BY THE FEDERAL CONVENTION,
SEPTEMBER 17, 1787.

IN TWO VOLUMES.

VOL. I.

NEW-YORK:

PRINTED AND SOLD BY J. AND A. M'LEAN,
No. 41, HANOVER-SQUARE.
M,DCC,LXXXVIII.

*What is The Federalist?
Who wrote it?
Why is it important?*

What issues related to the new Constitution did the people debate?

The debates in the states lasted ten months. It was an intense and sometimes bitter political struggle.

Both the Federalists and Anti-Federalists made many arguments for and against the Constitution. However,

The small republics of the ancient past eventually collapsed. How did the Federalists propose to prevent this from happening to the new nation?

the most intense arguments were about three basic issues:

- whether the Constitution would maintain republican government,

- whether the national government would have too much power, and

- whether a bill of rights was needed in the Constitution.

The chart on the next two pages will help you see both sides of the debate. The chart summarizes how the Federalists and Anti-Federalists responded to each of the three issues.

Do you think a bill of rights would cause intense debate today? Why or why not?

Does the national government have too much power?

The Constitution gives the national government too much power at the expense of the state governments. It gives government the power to tax citizens. It gives government the power to raise and keep an army during peacetime. This army could be used by government to suppress the people.

The national government will have greater power than it did under the Articles of Confederation. But its powers are limited to solving problems that face the entire nation, such as trade and defense. The recent history of the states shows that a stronger national government is needed to deal with such problems.

The supremacy clause means that all the national government's laws are superior to laws made by the states. It will only be a matter of time until the state governments are destroyed.

The Constitution provides protections for the state governments by specifically reserving certain powers for the states. This will prevent the states from being destroyed by the national government.

The necessary and proper clause is too general. It gives too much power to the national government. It is dangerous not to list all the powers of government in order to put clear limits on them.

The necessary and proper clause and general welfare clause are needed if the national government is to do the things it is responsible for doing.

The Constitution gives too much power to the executive branch of government. It will soon become a monarchy.

A strong executive branch is necessary. It is needed if the national government is to fulfill its responsibilities. Congress and the U.S. Supreme Court have checks on the use of power by the executive branch. The executive branch cannot become a monarchy.

The powers of the national government are separated and balanced among the three branches. No one branch can dominate the others. This system makes it impossible for any person or group to take complete control of government.

Does the Constitution provide for republican government?

ANTI-FEDERALISTS	FEDERALISTS
Throughout history, the only places where republican governments worked had been in small communities. There, the people had similar wealth and the same values. People who are not too rich or too poor are more likely to have civic virtue. Such people are more likely to agree on what is best for their common good. The new nation would be too large and diverse. The people will not be able to agree on their common welfare.	History has proven that selfish groups destroyed all of the small republics of the past. The civic virtue of the citizens was not enough to keep people from seeking their own interests. People did not work for the common good. A large republic where power is divided between the national and state governments is a better solution. It is also better to organize government based on checks and balances. Under such a government, it will be more difficult for special interests to work against the common good.
Free government requires the active participation of the people. The national government will be located far from where most people live. People will be unable to participate in government. As a result, the only way government will be able to rule will be with military force. The result will be a tyranny.	The national government cannot become a tyranny. The limits placed on government by the system of separation of powers and checks and balances will prevent it. Government will be so good at protecting the rights of the people that it will soon gain their loyalty and support.

Is a Bill of Rights needed for the Constitution?

ANTI-FEDERALISTS	FEDERALISTS
The Constitution does not include a bill of rights. A bill of rights is necessary to protect people against the power of the national government. There is no mention of freedom of religion, speech, press, or assembly. Since these freedoms are not in the Constitution, government is free to violate them. Americans recently fought a war to secure their fundamental rights. They do not want a constitution that places those rights in jeopardy.	A bill of rights is not needed. The Constitution is the ultimate protection for people's rights and the people are the ultimate sovereigns. The Constitution does not give government the power to deprive people of their rights. It gives government only limited power to do certain things. A bill of rights will give the impression that the people can expect protection only for the rights that are actually listed. The Constitution protects a number of rights by requiring writs of habeas corpus, and prohibiting ex post facto laws and bills of attainder.

What compromise did the Federalists finally agree to make in order to get enough support for the Constitution to be ratified?

Why did the Federalists agree to add a bill of rights to the Constitution?

A compromise was reached on the issue of a bill of rights. The Federalists made this compromise to get enough support for the Constitution so that it would be ratified. They agreed that when the first Congress was held, it would draft a bill of rights.

The argument to add a bill of rights was a victory for the Anti-Federalists. It was an important addition to the Constitution and has been of great importance in the protection of the basic rights of the American people.

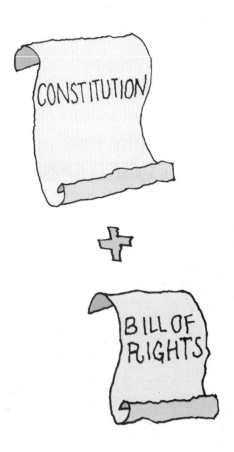

Would your class ratify the new constitution?

Imagine that your class is one of the original thirteen states. You are holding a ratifying convention to decide if your state will approve the new constitution. The students in the class are delegates to the state convention. Divide the class into two groups. One group represents the Anti-Federalists. The other group represents the Federalists.

GETTING READY FOR THE DEBATE

The debate questions are below:

- Will republican government work in such a large country?

- Does the Constitution give the national government too much power?

- Does the Constitution need to have a bill of rights?

Apply what you have learned from this text to help you prepare your arguments. You may want to divide your group into three smaller groups, so that each smaller group can prepare responses for one of the questions.

PARTICIPATING IN THE DEBATE

Before the debate begins, establish a few rules. Decide upon the amount of time each group gets to speak and how many turns each group should get.

Decide which group gets to speak first on each of the three questions.

Select one student from your group to moderate the debate. He or she should read the questions aloud to the class, call on groups to speak, and keep track of time limits.

At the end of the debate, each group should give a short summary of its arguments. Finally, everyone in the class should vote on whether or not to ratify the new constitution.

EVALUATING THE DECISION

Your class should discuss the results of the debate.

1. What do you think were the best arguments for ratifying the Constitution?

2. What were the best arguments against ratifying the Constitution?

3. What might have happened to the country if the states had not ratified the Constitution?

163

1 Why did the Framers oppose submitting the Constitution to the existing Congress or state governments for ratification?

2 What process did the Framers select for ratifying the Constitution? How did the Preamble to the Constitution help them decide on this method?

3 What arguments did the Anti-Federalists make against ratifying the Constitution?

4 How did the Federalists respond to the criticisms of the Constitution made by the Anti-Federalists?

5 The Anti-Federalists lost their battle to prevent adoption of the Constitution. Their struggle, however, permanently shaped the new Constitution. Explain how the ideas and concerns of the Anti-Federalists accomplished this. Why was this struggle important? Why is it relevant today?

6 Explain how the ratification process provided a widespread public debate about an important political decision.

1 Learn more about *The Federalist*. Find information in your library or on the Internet. Write your own Federalist paper. Read it to your class.

2 Imagine that you are an Anti-Federalist. Make a collage that illustrates your point of view about the Constitution. Include references to actual Anti-Federalist writings. Be prepared to defend your design before the class.

3 Imagine that people in 1787 drove cars like ours. Create a bumper sticker that reflects either a Federalist or Anti-Federalist point of view about the new constitution.

4 Conduct research to find information about Federalist or Anti-Federalist writers, such as Brutus and Federal Farmer.

How did Congress organize the new government?

19

LESSON PURPOSE

The U.S. Constitution is a plan for government. Once the Constitution was ratified, it was the job of the first Congress to use this plan to organize the new government. In this lesson you will read about some of the decisions made by the first Congress. You will learn how Congress organized the executive branch. You will also learn how Congress established a system of federal courts below the U.S. Supreme Court. Finally, you will learn how the Bill of Rights was added to the Constitution.

When you finish this lesson, you should be able to explain how the first Congress organized the executive and judicial branches of government. You should also be able to explain how the Bill of Rights was added to the Constitution.

appellate courts
cabinet
federal district courts
Judiciary Act of 1789
Ninth Amendment
Tenth Amendment

Who was elected the first president?

When the votes in the electoral college were counted, Washington, as expected, was elected president unanimously. John Adams of Massachusetts was elected vice president. Washington took the oath of office on April 30, 1789.

Washington did not really want to be president. He would have preferred to remain at Mount Vernon, his home, and take care of his plantation. But Washington had a strong sense of civic responsibility and felt that it was his duty to serve his country. He wrote, "when I had judged... that it was my duty to embark again on the tempestuous and uncertain Ocean of public life, I gave up all expectations of private happiness in this world." Washington knew that the Founders who were against the Constitution were afraid that it gave too much power to the president. He knew he should not do anything that added to their fears. Yet, he also knew that he had to be a strong leader.

By May of 1789 members of the new Congress of the national government were at work in New York City, the nation's temporary capital. Many people in Congress

George Washington taking the oath of office as the first president of the United States. Why was accepting the presidency so difficult for him?

were worried about how Washington would use his power. They even disagreed on what they should call the president. Some people said he should be called "His Highness, the President of the United States of America." Congress decided that because America was not a monarchy, Washington should simply be addressed as "the President of the United States."

This is a view of Federal Hall in New York City, which is where Congress first met. How did Congress help the executive branch of government deal with its responsibilities?

How did Congress and the president organize the executive branch?

The Constitution gives Congress the power to organize the executive branch. Washington could not run the executive branch alone. To help Washington fulfill his responsibilities, Congress created three departments.

- **Department of State**. Thomas Jefferson was selected to serve as Secretary of State to be responsible for the foreign relations of the nation.

- **Department of the Treasury**. Alexander Hamilton, as Secretary of the Treasury, guided the new government in money matters.

- **Department of War**. Henry Knox, as the Secretary of War, handled military affairs and defense.

In addition, Congress created the office of attorney general, whose job was to give the president legal advice. Washington appointed Edmund Randolph to this position.

Washington used these officials as advisers to help him make decisions. These officials became known as the president's **cabinet**. Today, the cabinet positions have grown from the original four to the present number of fifteen. In fact, the executive branch of the federal government has grown far beyond the expectations of the Framers.

How did Congress organize the judicial branch?

Congress set up the judicial branch of government under Article III of the Constitution. Article III provided for a U.S. Supreme Court and said that Congress could establish lower courts as needed.

In 1789, Congress passed a law that organized the court system for the new nation. This law was the **Judiciary Act of 1789**. It stated that the U.S. Supreme Court was to have a chief justice and five associate justices. Over time, Congress has increased the size of the Court to nine justices.

The lower courts that were authorized by the Judiciary Act include two kinds of courts—**federal district courts**, which hear cases involving the Constitution and federal laws, and appellate courts. **Appellate courts** handle those cases that have been tried first in district court and have been appealed. The appellate court is a higher court than a district court. But the U.S. Supreme Court is the highest court of appeals in the nation. In addition to the federal courts, each state has its own courts to rule on state laws.

How did Congress add the Bill of Rights to the Constitution?

When the Constitution was sent to the states for ratification, the Anti-Federalists opposed it. They felt that the Constitution should include a bill of rights. The Federalists claimed that

Why do you think Congress created three levels of federal courts?

What are some of the protections guaranteed by the Bill of Rights?

a bill of rights was not necessary. They said that the Constitution organized government in such a way that it would be impossible to violate people's rights. They also argued that listing individual rights might make people think that these were the only rights guaranteed by government.

Finally, a compromise was reached. The Federalists agreed that when the first Congress met, they would draft a bill of rights to add to the Constitution.

The Bill of Rights was passed by the first Congress. It contains ten amendments. The first eight amendments list basic protections already guaranteed in most state constitutions. These include:

- freedom of religion

- freedom of the press

- freedom of speech

- the rights of assembly and petition

- the right to a speedy, public trial by jury

The **Ninth Amendment** to the Constitution says that the listing of certain rights does not mean that these are the only rights the people have. Finally, the **Tenth Amendment** says that the powers not delegated to the federal government nor forbidden to the states belong to the states or to the people.

Congress proposed the Bill of Rights in 1789. It was ratified by the necessary eleven states on December 15, 1791. The Bill of Rights has proved to be very important to the protection of the basic rights of the American people. You will learn more about the Bill of Rights in the next unit.

1 The Constitution describes the organization of the executive and judicial branches only in general terms. Explain how the first Congress and the president organized the executive branch.

2 How did the first Congress organize the judicial branch?

3 What is the president's cabinet and what does it do?

4 What was the purpose of the Bill of Rights? Why was it included in our Constitution?

5 What rights are guaranteed in the Ninth and Tenth Amendments? How do these amendments differ from the other amendments in the Bill of Rights?

ACTIVITIES

1 Find out the process for amending the U.S. Constitution.

2 The idea of having one person serve as president was developed when our nation had fewer than four million people. Today we have more than 300 million people. Do you think it is still a good idea to have only one person head the executive branch? Why or why not? What alternatives can you suggest? Make a chart showing how your ideas might improve our government.

3 Visit the website of the executive branch of our national government, www.whitehouse.gov. Find a list of the fifteen cabinet positions and the functions of each. Which is the newest cabinet position? Why was it created? Write an essay explaining what you learn.

How did political parties develop?

20

LESSON PURPOSE

The new nation faced a number of problems. Differing ideas about how these problems should be resolved led to the rise of political parties. In this lesson you will learn what political parties are and how they began in American politics.

When you finish the lesson, you should be able to describe the two original political parties, their leaders, and the issues that divided them.

Why were the Framers of the Constitution against political parties?

When George Washington was elected as the first president, he received every electoral vote. One reason for this was the great respect people had for him. Another reason was that there were no political parties to run candidates against him.

The Framers were opposed to the idea of political parties. **Political parties** are groups of people who join together because they have similar views about government. The Constitution does not include rules for forming or regulating political parties.

The Framers believed that political parties were factions. As you learned in Lessons 3 and 10, a faction is usually a dissatisfied group formed within a larger group. The Framers thought that factions might fight to promote the interests of their own members. The Framers feared that the strongest faction would then control government. In such a case, government would not protect equally the rights and interests of all the people. Instead, government would promote the interests of the party in power.

What role for the federal government did Alexander Hamilton favor?

When Washington took office, the new nation faced many problems. The country was in debt and needed to create good relations with other nations. People had different ideas about how to solve these problems. As President Washington and his advisers tried to deal with the issues, disagreements arose. These disagreements eventually led to the rise of political parties.

Do you recognize these animals as symbols for contemporary political parties? Why do you suppose they adopted these symbols?

Why was the disagreement about the meaning of the words in the Constitution important?

President Washington chose Alexander Hamilton and Thomas Jefferson to be his advisers. Hamilton was the Secretary of the Treasury. Jefferson was the Secretary of State. The views of Hamilton and Jefferson about the powers of the federal government were often in conflict.

Hamilton wanted a strong federal government. He favored taking a broad view of the meaning of the words in the Constitution. The Constitution does not always use clear terms to describe the power of the federal government. Take, for example, the necessary and proper clause. What does necessary mean? Hamilton believed that necessary meant that which is needful or useful to solve a problem. He argued that the Constitution created government to solve national problems. As long as a problem was national, the federal government could and should deal with it.

On the other hand, Thomas Jefferson believed in small, local government. He favored taking a narrow view of the meaning of the words in the Constitution. To Jefferson, necessary meant "absolutely necessary." The federal government could not do whatever it wanted. Government could not exercise power just because it was convenient to do so. If government were free to define its own powers, it would threaten the liberty of the people.

The conflict about the meaning of the words in the Constitution was an important one. Hamilton would give more power to the federal government. Jefferson would limit it strictly to its enumerated powers.

The people who supported the views of Hamilton eventually became the **Federalist Party**. The people who supported Jefferson became the **Republican Party**. This is not the same Republican Party of today.

How well do you understand Jefferson's concern?

Suppose the members of your student government had the power to make whatever rules for your school they thought were "necessary and proper" for your "general welfare." What rules do you think they should make? Discuss your choices with a partner. Use the questions that follow for guidelines.

1 Who would be in a position to decide what was necessary and proper?

2 Who would decide what the general welfare was?

3 What limitations would there be on the student government's powers?

Who should decide what rules are necessary and proper for the general welfare of your class?

Why was the disagreement about the nation's economy important?

As Secretary of the Treasury, Alexander Hamilton wanted to strengthen the nation's economy. To do this, he wanted to create a strong currency. **Currency** is the form of money that a country uses.

He also wanted to encourage people to manufacture goods on a large scale. At that time, most Americans were farmers. The factories that did exist were small, family-owned businesses.

Hamilton also wanted to solve the problem of the national and state debts. Most of the debt was the result of borrowing to pay for the Revolutionary War. The federal government owed $54 million and the state governments owed about $25 million. Hamilton believed that solving the problem of the debt would strengthen the economy and would establish the public credit of the United States.

To achieve his goals, Hamilton came up with a plan to create a government bank. The bank, Hamilton said, was needed to help collect taxes, make loans to private citizens, and issue paper money. Gold and silver coins were in short supply. Paper money would increase the amount of currency available.

The problem was that the people did not trust paper money. They believed that it would not hold its value. The value of coins was based on the amount of gold or silver in the coin. Thus, the federal government would need to guarantee the value of paper money.

Hamilton advised President Washington that the necessary and proper clause gave government the power to create a bank. He argued that a bank was necessary to allow government to carry out its enumerated powers to collect taxes and regulate trade.

Why was Hamilton worried about national and state debt? Do you think the national and state debt is still something that government officials should worry about? Why or why not?

Thomas Jefferson was against the use of federal power to create a bank. He believed that the necessary and proper clause only allowed government to do those things that were absolutely necessary. Creating a bank did not pass the test.

George Washington listened to the arguments for and against the bank. He then signed the bill from Congress creating the Bank of the United States. The effect of the new law was to increase the power of the federal government. People began to take sides on whether the federal government had acted in accord with the Constitution.

Why was the disagreement about foreign affairs important?

In 1793 war broke out between France and Great Britain. This event raised the level of tension between the Federalists and the Republicans.

Thomas Jefferson wanted a close relationship with France. Many Americans had strong feelings for France. After all, the French had supported the colonies during the Revolutionary War.

During this time the British were seizing American ships on the high seas.

This building in Philadelphia was the site of the First Bank of the United States from 1795 to 1811. What were Jefferson's and Hamilton's opinions on establishing the bank?

John Jay was quoted as saying that he could travel from Boston to Philadelphia by the light of his burning effigies. Why was his treaty with the British unpopular?

Why did the war between France and Great Britain raise the level of tension between the Federalists and the Republicans?

They were searching for weapons going to France. The British also refused to leave the forts they still occupied on land that now belonged to the United States. The Republicans wanted the United States to take strong measures against the British.

Alexander Hamilton wanted a close relationship with Great Britain. Most of the colonists had come from Britain and still had links with people in that nation. In addition, the United States carried on more trade with Great Britain than it did with France. The Federalists wanted the United States to side with the British.

President Washington had sent United States Chief Justice John Jay on a mission to Great Britain. He negotiated a treaty that confirmed that the British would leave the forts they still held in the United States. They agreed to increase trade with the Americans. They did not agree to stop searching American ships for goods going to the enemy, France. The treaty was unpopular and the Republicans were greatly angered.

Washington did not want to take sides in the war between Great Britain and France. To do so, he thought, would be harmful to the United States. He declared that the American government would be neutral. When Washington left the presidency, he cautioned the new nation against entering into any permanent agreements with foreign governments.

What were the Alien and Sedition Acts?

George Washington served two terms as president. When he left office he warned the Americans about the harmful effect of political parties.

By the election of 1796, there was serious hostility between the Federalists and the Republicans. Each party wanted one of its own people to win the presidential election. John Adams, a Federalist, was elected president. Thomas Jefferson, a Republican, was elected vice president.

Jefferson and the Republicans were very critical of the way Adams ran the government. The Republicans organized their opposition. They used the newspapers to build public support for their views.

The Alien and Sedition Acts prevented the press from speaking out against the government. What limits, if any, should be placed on the people's right to criticize the government?

Adams and the Federalists in Congress were able to pass two laws called the Alien and Sedition Acts. The **Alien Act** gave the president broad powers over aliens entering the country. The **Sedition Act** made it a crime for newspaper editors, writers, or speakers to criticize the government.

The Alien and Sedition Acts outraged the Republicans. They knew that the laws were intended to silence them. Several newspaper editors and a member of Congress were fined and put in jail for writing and speaking against the government.

Why was the presidential election of 1800 important?

The election of 1800 was the first time that political parties backed candidates for president. The Federalists worked to re-elect John Adams. The Republicans supported Thomas Jefferson.

Adams and Jefferson did not campaign, the way it is done in modern elections. Instead, the parties ran the campaign, and it was a bitter one. Both parties accused each other of wishing to destroy the Constitution. The Republicans cited the Alien and Sedition Acts as proof that the Federalists were not fit to govern.

The election of 1800 was very important. Even though it had been a bitter campaign, the parties accepted the result.

Thomas Jefferson and Aaron Burr, also a Republican, tied for votes in the electoral college. So, according to the Constitution, the House of Representatives was obliged to select the winning candidate. After thirty-six ballots Jefferson was chosen.

For the first time in modern history, control of a government was transferred

State	Thomas Jefferson (Virginia)	Aaron Burr (New York)	John Adams (Massachusetts)	Charles C. Pinckney (South Carolina)	John Jay (New York)
New Hampshire			6	6	
Massachusetts			16	16	
Rhode Island			4	3	1
Connecticut			9	9	
Vermont			4	4	
New York	12	12			
New Jersey			7	7	
Pennsylvania	8	8	7	7	
Delaware			3	3	
Maryland	5	5	5	5	
Virginia	21	21			
Kentucky	4	4			
North Carolina	8	8	4	4	
Tennessee	3	3			
South Carolina	8	8			
Georgia	4	4			
	73	73	65	64	1

This is the tally of electoral votes from the election of 1800. How was the president selected when Thomas Jefferson and Aaron Burr tied for votes in the electoral college?

The following list states some ways that political parties may be useful.

- Political parties give people a way to join with others of similar interests to try to influence their government.

- People, working through their parties, can nominate candidates for public office, raise money for their candidates, and encourage people to vote for them.

- Political parties can and do get many people involved in the process of government.

- Political parties give people a choice of candidates and programs.

- The political party that is not in power can debate and criticize the party in power.

from one political party to another as the result of a democratic election. Thomas Jefferson later called it the "revolution of 1800."

Over the long term, the Federalist Party could not compete with the Republicans. Other parties arose to take its place. The modern Democratic Party claims its roots lie with the Republican Party of Thomas Jefferson. The modern Republican Party claims its roots lie with the Republican Party of Abraham Lincoln.

What is the role of political parties today?

Political parties are active today at the local, state, and national levels. Despite the fears of the Framers, they are an important part of the political system.

What might be some disadvantages of having only two political parties?

1 Why were the Framers of the Constitution against having political parties?

2 What was the disagreement over the meaning of the words in the Constitution?

3 What was the disagreement about the creation of the Bank of the United States?

4 What was the disagreement about foreign affairs?

5 What were the Alien and Sedition Acts? Why were they passed?

6 Explain how the disagreements about how to solve the new nation's problems led to the rise of political parties.

7 Why was the election of 1800 important?

1 Draw a cartoon that illustrates the disagreements between the Federalist and Republican parties.

2 Presidents and vice presidents were elected differently in 1800 than they are today. Make a chart showing what the differences are. Find out which Amendment to the Constitution was passed to correct the problems that occurred in the 1800 presidential election.

3 Use the Internet to do a research activity. Find current information about the Democratic and Republican parties. Learn what each party believes about how government should be run. Then study a policy issue that interests both parties. Create a chart that illustrates their difference of opinion over the issue.

4 Find information about the beliefs of third parties, such as the Libertarian Party, the Reform Party, or the Green Party. Write a campaign speech that explains the role of third parties in elections today. Give the speech to your classmates.

How does the U.S. Supreme Court use the power of judicial review?

21

LESSON PURPOSE

Even in our nation's earliest years, people such as Alexander Hamilton and Thomas Jefferson disagreed about exactly what the words in the Constitution mean. Who should decide which reading of the Constitution is correct? This lesson explains how the U.S. Supreme Court established its power to make such decisions. This power of the Court is called the power of judicial review. This power is not mentioned in the Constitution.

When you finish this lesson, you should be able to explain what is meant by judicial review. You should also be able to discuss how the U.S. Supreme Court established its power of judicial review in one of the most important cases in our nation's history.

judicial review
Marbury v. Madison
null and void
opinion of the Court

What is judicial review?

Judicial review is the power of the courts to decide whether laws and actions of government are allowed under the Constitution. When a court decides that a law or action is not allowed, it orders that the law or action be considered null and void. A law that is **null and void** may not be enforced. Such a law is considered unconstitutional and not acceptable as a law at all.

How does judicial review apply to laws passed by state governments?

The Framers wanted to be sure that the states obeyed the laws of the federal government. So, in Article VI of the Constitution they said that the U.S. Constitution, federal laws, and treaties are the supreme law of the land. As we discussed in Lessons 16 and 17, this is the supremacy clause. The Constitution, the laws passed by Congress, and treaties are the nation's highest laws and must be obeyed by the states. If state laws conflict with those of the federal government, the U.S. Supreme Court can order that the state laws not be enforced.

*What is the power of judicial review?
Are decisions of the Supreme Court
binding on the states?*

The U.S. Supreme Court first used its power of judicial review over state governments in 1796. After the Revolutionary War the United States signed a peace treaty with Great Britain. As part of this treaty, Americans agreed to pay all debts that they owed to British citizens. The state of Virginia passed a law that canceled all debts that its citizens owed to the British. Because this law violated the peace treaty, the Supreme Court ruled that the law could not be enforced. The citizens of Virginia would have to pay their debts.

Does the U.S. Supreme Court have the power of judicial review over acts of the federal government?

The Framers clearly meant that the U.S. Supreme Court should have the power of judicial review over acts of the state governments. The Constitution does not state that the U.S. Supreme Court has the power of judicial review over the legislative and executive branches of the federal government.

How did the U.S. Supreme Court decide the case of *Marbury v. Madison*?

The U.S. Supreme Court established its power of judicial review over the other branches of the federal government in one of the most famous cases in our history. This case, *Marbury v. Madison*, was decided in 1803.

During the last weeks that John Adams was president, he appointed a number of people to office. There had not been enough time to deliver the proper papers to all the appointees before the next president, Thomas Jefferson, took office. Without the proper papers, the appointees could not take the jobs that Adams gave them. When Jefferson did take office, he ordered his secretary of state, James Madison, not to deliver the appointments that were left.

This is a list of debts owed to the British in 1798. It was compiled by Thomas Jefferson. How did the Supreme Court use its power of judicial review to settle the matter of Virginia's British debt? Can you find where the Constitution is mentioned in this note?

Should the U.S. Supreme Court have the power of judicial review over acts of Congress?

Imagine that you must decide whether the U.S. Supreme Court should have the power of judicial review over laws passed by Congress. Work with a group of three to five students. Read the two opinions below. Consider each position and the possible results of each position. Use the Guideline Questions to help you decide which position your group would support.

OPINION 1

Give the U.S. Supreme Court the power to declare that a law passed by Congress is unconstitutional.

Possible Result Some laws, even though they were passed by a majority of representatives in Congress—people elected by citizens to represent their interests—would not be obeyed or enforced.

OPINION 2

Deny the U.S. Supreme Court the power to declare laws passed by Congress unconstitutional.

Possible Result All laws passed by a majority of representatives in Congress—people elected by citizens to represent their interests—must be obeyed or enforced.

GUIDELINE QUESTIONS

1. How is each position related to the principles of representative government and majority rule?

2. Is one position more democratic than the other? Why or why not?

3. What effect might each position have on the basic rights of the individual?

4. What effect would each position have on protecting the minority from the whims of the majority?

William Marbury. How did the court's ruling limit the powers of Congress?

One person who did not receive his appointment was William Marbury. Marbury believed that he was entitled to have the job. Marbury took his case directly to the U.S. Supreme Court because the Judiciary Act of 1789 stated he had that right.

Chief Justice John Marshall wrote the opinion for the U.S. Supreme Court. The **opinion of the Court** is the Court's decision and the reasoning behind the decision. The Court ruled that Marbury did have a right to his job. But they also said that the part of the Judiciary Act that gave Marbury the right to bring his case directly to the U.S. Supreme Court was unconstitutional.

The Constitution clearly limits the cases that can go directly to the U.S. Supreme Court without being first heard in a lower court. Marbury's case did not fit within these limits. Congress had changed the Constitution when it passed that part of the Judiciary Act. Congress by itself does not have the power to change the Constitution. So, the section of the Judiciary Act that increased the Court's power was ruled unconstitutional.

By declaring part of a law passed by Congress unconstitutional, the U.S. Supreme Court assumed the power of judicial review over the legislative and executive branches. Justice Marshall argued that the people of this nation had adopted the Constitution as the supreme law of the land and consented to be governed by its rules.

These rules include important limits on the powers of Congress. When Congress violates those limitations, it has violated the will of the people.

Marshall said that if the U.S. Supreme Court could not strike down such acts, there would be no effective way to enforce the constitutional limits on the powers of Congress. Its powers would be unlimited, and we would no longer have a constitutional government. Since the decision of *Marbury v. Madison*, the U.S. Supreme Court has exercised the power of judicial review over the federal government.

What was Chief Justice John Marshall's argument for the Supreme Court's power of judicial review?

185

1 What is judicial review?

2 How does judicial review apply to the laws passed by state governments?

3 What was the case of *Marbury v. Madison*? How did the U.S. Supreme Court decide this case?

4 Why was *Marbury v. Madison* such an important case?

5 How does judicial review protect the rights of the people?

6 How might judicial review override the will of the majority?

ACTIVITIES

1 In the history of our country, there have been several important justices on the U.S. Supreme Court. Learn more about one of the justices listed below. Share what you learned with your class.

- Oliver Wendell Holmes Jr.
- John Jay
- John Marshall
- Thurgood Marshall
- Roger B. Taney
- Earl Warren

2 Find an article in the newspaper that explains a case or constitutional issue before the U.S. Supreme Court. Be prepared to explain the article to your class.

3 With your teacher, invite an attorney or a judge to come to your classroom to discuss how our court system works. Prepare questions you want to ask the guest during the visit.

4 Almost every trial in the United States is open to the public. With your teacher, visit your local courthouse. Talk with one of the judges. Observe a trial. This will allow you to see for yourself how our justice system operates.

How does the U.S. Supreme Court determine the meaning of the words in the Constitution?

22

LESSON PURPOSE

Some parts of the Constitution are clear and easy to understand. Other parts are much more difficult. What is the best way to decide what the Constitution means? In this lesson, you will learn about some of the more common approaches the U.S. Supreme Court has used to decide what the Constitution means.

When you finish this lesson, you should be able to describe these approaches. You should also be able to give the arguments in favor of or against each of these methods.

interpret

Second Amendment

Why is it difficult to understand the meaning of some parts of the Constitution?

Deciding what the Constitution means has been a continuous process throughout our history. Even the justices of the Supreme Court sometimes disagree about the best method of deciding what the Constitution means.

Some parts are easy to understand. For example, Article II says, "The executive Power shall be vested in a President of the United States of America." This is a very specific statement about the head of the executive branch. Not all parts of the Constitution are so clear. For example, the meaning of the following statements in the Constitution is not specific:

- Congress shall have the power to make laws that are "necessary and proper" to carry out its responsibilities.

- Citizens are protected against "unreasonable searches and seizures."

- No state shall "deprive any person of life, liberty, or property without due process of law."

Sandra Day O'Connor, the first woman U.S. Supreme Court Justice. She was appointed in 1981. Who has the power to appoint Supreme Court justices? Why do you think it took so long for a woman to be appointed?

What difficulties are there in deciding the meaning of the words in the Constitution?

Work with a partner. Read the following example of language found in the Constitution.

> **EXAMPLE**
>
> **The Fourth Amendment protects citizens against "unreasonable searches and seizures."**

If you were a member of the U.S. Supreme Court, how would you decide what makes a search or seizure unreasonable?

Read the methods given below. Pick out the advantages and disadvantages of each method presented. Then, determine which method might be best for deciding the meaning of the Constitution. Be prepared to explain your opinion to the class.

1. Would you look up "unreasonable" in a dictionary to find out what it means?

2. Would you try to find out how the Framers might have explained the word "unreasonable"?

3. Would you examine the word "unreasonable" in relation to such basic ideas as natural rights and limited government?

4. Would you examine the word "unreasonable" in relation to the historical, political, and social changes that have occurred since the Constitution was written?

5. Would you rely upon previous Court rulings on "unreasonable" searches and seizures?

The Constitution only grants Congress the authority to establish an army and a navy. What argument can you make that the Constitution also grants Congress the authority to establish an air force?

How does the U.S. Supreme Court decide what the words in the Constitution mean?

When deciding constitutional cases, the justices of the U.S. Supreme Court have to interpret the Constitution. To **interpret** means to decide what the words or phrases actually mean. There are four basic methods that the U.S. Supreme Court has used to interpret the Constitution. Each method has its advantages and disadvantages.

❶ The plain meaning of the words in the Constitution
Using this method, the justices consider the literal, or plain, meanings of the words. Sometimes they study what the words meant at the time they were written.

With this method the Court bases its decisions, as closely as possible, on how the Framers meant the Constitution to be interpreted. If the meaning of the words is clear, then this is the best way to know what the Framers meant.

The problem is that at the Philadelphia Convention there was disagreement about the meaning of some words. Another problem is that some questions are not answered at all. For example, the Constitution gives Congress the power to establish an army and a navy. Does this mean that Congress does not have the power to establish an air force?

❷ The intention of the Framers
This method is based on the idea that the Constitution by itself does not always have an obvious meaning. Therefore, we should look at the intentions of the people who wrote it. Those who believe in this method say that the justices should base their decisions on how the Framers would have decided. They claim that it is the approach most faithful to the ideas in the Constitution.

The problem is that it is extremely difficult, if not impossible, to figure out what the Framers intended on some issues. There were differences of opinion among the thirty-nine Framers. How can you determine who had the correct view? This method of interpretation also gives no guidelines about types of situations that did not exist when the Constitution was written.

③ The Constitution is based on some fundamental principles of government

These principles include the natural rights philosophy, constitutionalism, and republican government. As the nation matures so does our understanding of these basic principles. This method says that the justices should make their decisions based on these basic principles and values.

④ Today's social values and needs

This method says that the justices should use today's social values in interpreting the Constitution. People who hold this view believe that the justices should not ignore the realities of our society today. Justices, they argue, should not hold back social progress by sticking to outmoded interpretations.

People opposed to methods 3 and 4 say that these approaches give the justices too much freedom to decide cases according to their own political ideas and personal beliefs. The justices can simply alter the Constitution as they please.

In deciding a case, U.S. Supreme Court justices are influenced by a number of things. They consider the literal meaning of the words in the Constitution as well as the intention of the Framers. Justices consider the basic principles of the Constitution as well as the previous decisions of the Court. The justices are also aware of the current political, social, and economic situation in the country. Finally, the justices are influenced, as is everyone, by their own personal beliefs.

The U.S. Supreme Court's decisions often raise much controversy—especially when the Court has attempted to define and protect certain basic rights. In the next unit, we will look at some of these controversies.

What are arguments for and against using today's social values and needs to interpret the Constitution?

How would you interpret what the words in the Second Amendment mean?

Senator Orrin Hatch has written: "When our ancestors forged a land 'conceived in liberty,' they did so with musket and rifle...as a nation of armed freemen...[and] they devoted one full amendment out of ten to nothing but the protection of their right to keep and bear arms against governmental interference."

Using library and Internet resources, work in small groups to answer the following questions. Share your answers with the class.

❶ In 1791, when the Second Amendment was passed, why did the nation seek to protect liberty by protecting the right to keep and bear arms? What historical background and circumstances led them to this conclusion?

❷ Do you think the Second Amendment is as important today as it was in the eighteenth century? Explain your answer.

3 In a 1998 U.S. Supreme Court case, Justice Ruth Bader Ginsburg pointed out that the text of the **Second Amendment** refers to the right to keep *and bear* arms. Since to *bear* arms means to carry them—not just to possess them—should citizens in every state be allowed to carry firearms on their person? Should they be able to keep them in vehicles? Why or why not?

4 What limitations, if any, do you think should be placed upon the right to bear arms? How would you justify your position?

1 Why is it sometimes difficult to determine the meaning of the words in the Constitution?

2 What does it mean "to interpret" the Constitution?

3 What are the four methods that justices might use to interpret the Constitution? What are the advantages and disadvantages of each method?

1 Imagine that you are a member of the United States Supreme Court. The Court has agreed to hear a case involving government agencies watching which sites citizens visit on the Internet. This technology did not exist when the Constitution was written. What method for interpreting the Constitution might you use to determine whether the practice is unconstitutional? Explain your reasons.

2 Examine the following two statements by former justices of the U.S. Supreme Court. What does each statement mean? Do you agree with these statements? Why or why not?

"We are under a Constitution, but the Constitution is what the judges say it is."

Charles Evans Hughes
Chief Justice of the United States, 1930–1941
Associate Justice of the U.S. Supreme Court, 1910–1916

"As a member of this court I am not justified in writing my opinions into the Constitution, no matter how deeply I may cherish them."

Felix Frankfurter
Associate Justice of the U.S. Supreme Court, 1939–1962

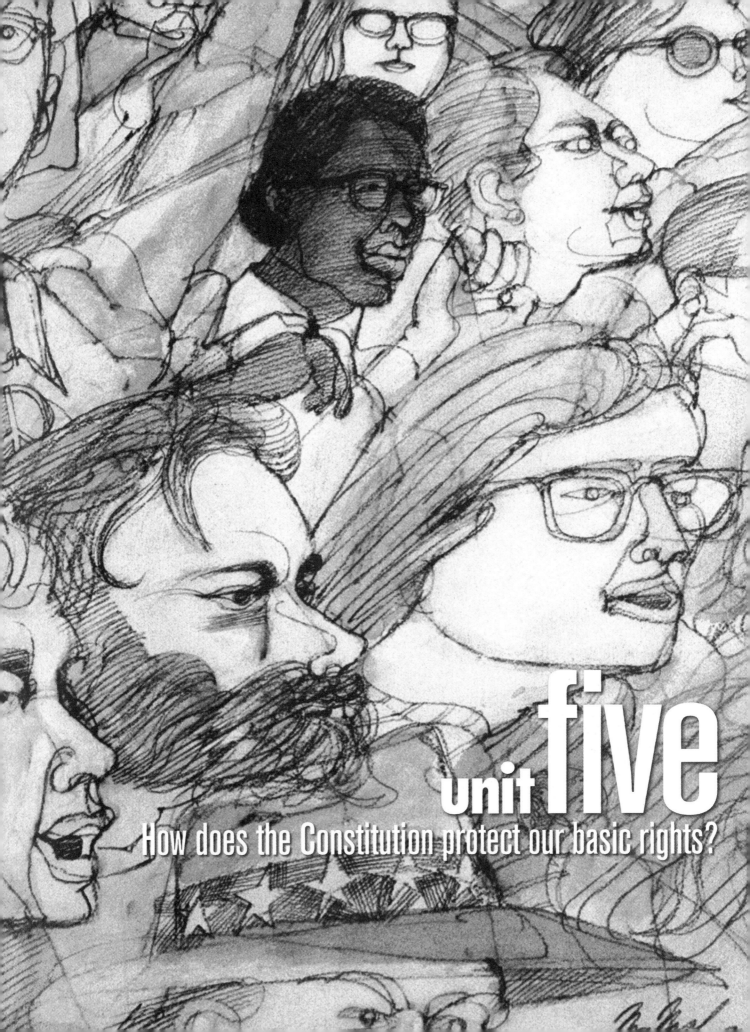

unit five
How does the Constitution protect our basic rights?

unit five

KEY CONCEPTS

due process of law

equal protection clause

establishment of religion clause

free exercise of religion clause

freedom of expression

freedom of religion

suffrage

You have learned that one of the most important purposes of government is to protect the basic rights of the people. The addition of the Bill of Rights to the Constitution was intended to achieve that purpose.

Adding the Bill of Rights, however, did not automatically guarantee these valued rights to all the people. In this unit, you will learn about five fundamental rights and how they have been extended to many people who were denied them in the past.

How does the Constitution protect freedom of expression?

23

LESSON PURPOSE

In this lesson you will learn about how the Constitution protects freedom of expression. You will also learn why freedom of expression is important to you as an individual and to the preservation and improvement of our constitutional democracy.

When you finish this lesson, you should be able to explain the importance of freedom of expression. You should also be able to describe situations in which it might be reasonable and fair to place limitations on this freedom.

abridging
assemble
First Amendment
freedom of expression
redress of grievances

What is freedom of expression?

One of the main purposes of government is to protect our freedom. The **First Amendment** to our Constitution protects our freedom of expression. This is what the First Amendment says about freedom of expression:

> Congress shall make no law... **abridging** [limiting] the freedom of speech, or of the press; or the right of the people peaceably to **assemble** [get together in one place], and to petition the government for a **redress of grievances** [to correct wrongs].

As you can see, this section of the First Amendment includes several important freedoms. **Freedom of expression** is freedom of speech, of the press, of assembly, and of petition. The right of assembly is the right to meet with others to discuss your beliefs, ideas, or feelings.

It is important to understand that the First Amendment limits the powers of Congress. It prevents Congress from placing unreasonable and unfair limits on freedom of expression. That is why the Amendment begins with the phrase, "Congress shall make no law."

What rights are the people in this photograph exercising?

How does the First Amendment protect the freedom of the press? What are some benefits of this freedom?

What are some benefits of freedom of expression?

The Founders of our nation believed that the right to hold and express one's beliefs was essential if citizens were to participate in the affairs of government. The following arguments highlight the importance of freedom of expression.

❶ Individual development and human dignity
It is important for your growth as a person to have the right to present your ideas and to consider other points of view. Your dignity as a person should be respected by allowing you the freedom to say what you think and to hear what others think.

❷ Advancement of knowledge
It is easier for new discoveries to be made when ideas can be discussed freely. Even if you disagree with someone, that person may say something that helps you test your knowledge and increase your understanding.

❸ The maintenance of representative democracy
Individual citizens participate in running our country by voting their representatives to Congress and other government officials. Citizens can also participate in making decisions about government policies. To make wise choices, you need to have good information. Free expression does not guarantee complete or accurate information, but it increases the chances of getting such information.

Should schools be allowed to place limits on freedom of expression?

When should students' freedom of expression be limited? The following is a summary of an important U.S. Supreme Court case that dealt with this question. Read and discuss the summary with a partner. Do you agree or disagree with the decision of the U.S. Supreme Court? Be prepared to share your opinions with the class.

Tinker v. Des Moines School District (1969)

This case involved a few high school students who wore black armbands to school. They were protesting American involvement in the Vietnam War. The school principal told the students to remove their armbands. The students refused and were suspended from school. The suspension was to last until they agreed to come back without the armbands. The parents took the case to court. They argued that the school was depriving the students of their right to freedom of expression.

Do you agree with the Supreme Court's decision in the Tinker *case? Why or why not?*

The school argued that they were justified in suspending the students. They said the suspension had been necessary to prevent any disturbance that could be caused by wearing the armbands.

The U.S. Supreme Court ruled that the school's action was an unnecessary limitation on freedom of expression. The Court said that a school cannot limit a student's right to freedom of expression unless the student's exercise of that right disrupts the educational process. The Court said there was "no evidence whatever of... interference...with the school's work or... with the rights of other students to be secure and to be let alone."

Justice Abe Fortas wrote the opinion for the Court. He said,

"Any word spoken, in class, in the lunchroom or on the campus, that deviates from the views of another person, may start an argument or cause a disturbance. But our Constitution says we must take this risk... and our history says that it is this sort of hazardous freedom—this kind of openness—that is the basis of our national strength and of the independence...of Americans."

The Court said that students do not give up their "constitutional rights to freedom of speech or expression at the schoolhouse gate." Freedom of expression should be protected unless it clearly violates other important rights and interests.

Should students have the same right to freedom of expression as adults? Why or why not?

Should people be allowed to demonstrate about any issue that concerns them? Why or why not?

❹ **Peaceful social change**
Freedom of expression allows you to try to influence public opinion by persuasion without feeling you have to resort to violence to make changes. Also, if you have the opportunity to express your opinions freely, you might be more willing to accept government decisions, even decisions you do not agree with.

Should there be limits to freedom of expression?

Many people believe that freedom of expression is necessary for the protection of all our individual freedoms. Does this mean there should be no limits to freedom of expression? Should you have the right to yell "Fire!" in a crowded theater when there is no fire? Such an action may cause bodily harm to others when they run to safety.

Other situations are more complicated. What if you wanted to convince other people that we should change our type of government? Should government be

What limits, if any, should there be on freedom of expression? Can you name some situations where freedom of expression might endanger people?

able to keep you from doing so? What if you are part of an unpopular group that wants to have a public demonstration in the streets? Should government be able to stop you because of the possibility of a riot?

Over the years, the courts in our country have developed guidelines to use in limiting freedom of expression. The courts use these guidelines to decide when the right to free expression interferes with other important rights and interests.

Suppose your right to freedom of expression in a particular situation

is dangerous to public safety, national security, or some other important interest. If the danger is great enough, the courts sometimes allow freedom of expression to be limited.

Also, one person's right to freedom of expression may conflict with someone else's rights. The right to a free press might conflict with someone's right to a fair trial in a court of law. For this reason, we accept limitations that are intended to protect everyone's rights.

How would you balance the rights and interests in this case?

The following U.S. Supreme Court case involves a situation about the need to balance freedom of expression with other important rights and interests. Work in groups of three to five students to complete this exercise. Each group should read the case and answer the questions that follow it. Then each group should share its answers with the class for further discussion.

Hazelwood School District v. Kuhlmeier (1988)

The journalism class in Hazelwood East High School wrote and published the high school's newspaper. In one issue of the paper, students planned to print an article about teenage pregnancy. The principal of the school thought that the story was not appropriate for younger students.

In the same issue of the paper the students also planned to run a story in which a student wrote about divorce and made negative remarks about her father. The principal said that the newspaper had not given the father a chance to respond to his daughter's remarks. The principal ordered both stories to be removed from the paper before it was printed and distributed.

1 What are the conflicting rights and interests in this case?

2 In what ways is this case similar to the *Tinker* case? In what ways is it different?

3 Examine each of the two opinions on the next page. Which opinion would you select to decide this case? Explain your reasoning.

OPINION 1

A school does not need to tolerate student speech that is inconsistent with its basic mission to educate young people. The public schools are not like the streets, parks, and other public places that are used for purposes of assembly, communicating thoughts between citizens, and discussing public questions. Accordingly, the principal had a right to regulate the contents of the school newspaper in any reasonable manner. It is this standard, rather than the decision in *Tinker*, that governs this case.

OPINION 2

The school principal removed the articles from the newspaper not because the article would interfere with school discipline. He removed the articles because he considered them inappropriate, personal, and unsuitable for student consumption. The principal's action violated the First Amendment's prohibitions against censorship of any student expression that neither disrupts class work nor denies the rights of others.

This is Robert E. Reynolds, the principal of Hazelwood East High School, with a copy of the student newspaper. Under what conditions, if any, should a principal have the right to limit what can be printed in the school newspaper?

1. How would you define freedom of expression?

2. What are the benefits of freedom of expression to the individual and to society?

3. What are some circumstances that might cause government to limit the right to freedom of expression?

4. What rights and interests are involved when limiting freedom of expression in the public schools?

1. Learn about the policies in your school district or the rules at your school that regulate how students may exercise freedom of expression. Make a computer presentation so you can share what you learned with your class.

2. Take photographs that illustrate the four parts of the right to freedom of expression. Make a collage of your photos showing the benefits of freedom of expression.

3. Suppose that an unpopular group wants to hold a demonstration in a public park in your community. Most people do not agree with the views of this group. People fear that the demonstration might become disorderly and disturb the peace. Work with a partner to create a skit. One of you should be in favor of allowing the group to hold the demonstration. The other should be opposed. Both of you should act out your views in front of the class and let them decide the issue.

4. Find a newspaper article that discusses someone exercising the right to freedom of expression in your community. Write an editorial based on the article for your school newspaper. In your essay explain the benefits of this right to you and your community.

How does the Constitution protect freedom of religion?

LESSON PURPOSE

In this lesson you will learn about freedom of religion. You will learn about the difference between religious beliefs and religious practices. You will learn why there are no limits on beliefs but some limits on religious practices. Finally, the lesson will examine issues about the relationship between religion and public education.

When you finish the lesson, you should be able to explain the importance of freedom of religion. You should be able to describe situations in which religious practices may be limited. You should also be able to explain some of the guidelines the U.S. Supreme Court has used to decide issues related to religion and the public schools.

establishment clause

free exercise clause

How does the First Amendment protect freedom of religion?

The very first part of the First Amendment says that "Congress shall make no law respecting an establishment of religion, or prohibiting the free exercise thereof." The meaning of these words in the First Amendment is explained below.

- **Establishment of religion**
  Congress may not establish, that is institute, an official religion for our country or favor any one religion over others. We call this the **establishment clause**.

- **Free exercise**
  Congress may not stop you from holding any religious beliefs you choose or having no religious beliefs at all. Government may not unfairly or unreasonably limit your right to practice any religious beliefs you wish. We call this the **free exercise clause**.

What does the "free exercise" part of the First Amendment mean?

Why did freedom of religion become an important principle in America?

Few of the early English colonies in North America permitted religious freedom. In several colonies, one religious group controlled the whole colony. Everyone living there had to follow the same religious ideas. People who disagreed were often persecuted or forced to leave the colony.

By the end of the colonial period, things had changed. For one thing, there were more religious groups, such as Baptists, Catholics, Jews, Quakers, and others. Most people's attitudes had also changed. More people practiced different religions. People became more accepting of each other's religious differences. Over time, people came to believe strongly that everyone has a right to his or her own religious beliefs.

In addition, men like Thomas Jefferson and James Madison were greatly concerned about the dangers of religious intolerance. They were well aware that throughout history, religious intolerance had often led to conflict and to the violation of individual rights. They thought religious intolerance was a danger to the community and harmful to religion.

The freedom of religion clause in the first part of the First Amendment illustrates the strong belief in America that government should not interfere with religion.

Why did some of the colonists' ideas about religious tolerance change?

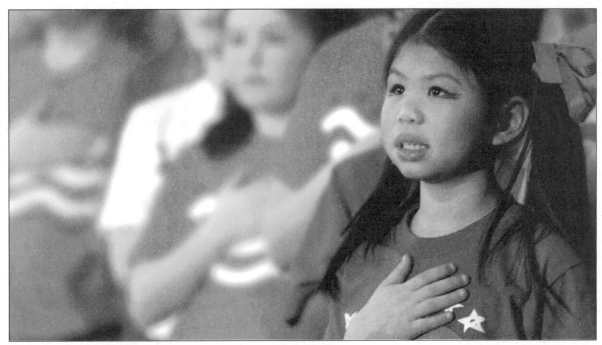

Should your government be able to require students to recite the Pledge of Allegiance if it violates their religious beliefs? Why or why not?

Why do conflicts about freedom of religion exist today?

Americans strongly believe that freedom of religion is an important right. But that does not mean that we have no disagreements about this issue today. Today's conflicts about freedom of religion focus on the following issues:

- **The establishment clause**
  This clause sets forth the idea that government is to be separated from religion.

  The meaning of the establishment clause is a continuing source of conflict among Americans. Does it mean that government may not be involved with religion in any way?

- **The free exercise clause**
  Each person has an absolute right to believe in any religion or in no religion at all. Freedom of belief is an inalienable right that cannot be interfered with by government in any way. The free exercise clause also means that your right to practice your religious beliefs is protected. But does the free exercise clause mean that all religious practices are protected? Can government prohibit a religious practice that endangers public health or safety?

Sometimes there are conflicts between the principles in the establishment and the free exercise clauses. For example, if government pays for prison chaplains, it is supporting religion. On the other hand, to prohibit government from doing this would interfere with the right of prisoners to practice their religion.

Disagreements like these about the relationship between government and religion have caused a number of important cases to be brought before the U.S. Supreme Court. In each case, the Supreme Court has had to decide how the freedom of religion clauses of the First Amendment should be interpreted.

Can government limit your right to practice your religious beliefs?

In certain cases government can limit the way you practice your religious beliefs. The U.S. Supreme Court has ruled that certain religious practices may be forbidden without violating constitutional rights. The Court has said that religious practices may be limited if they are contrary to public morals, endanger health, or harm the common good.

U.S. Supreme Court decisions have said that religious practices involving polygamy—being married to more than one person at the same time—may be forbidden. Government can also require that children be vaccinated against certain contagious diseases before being admitted to public school. They may require vaccination even if it violates a family's religious beliefs.

Under what conditions, if any, should the government be able to control the practice of religious beliefs?

How can we decide issues about religion in the public schools?

At the time the Constitution was written, public schools as we know them did not exist. Children who attended school usually received a great deal of religious training. In fact, their parents expected the schools to give religious instruction.

There has been growing disagreement about whether religious teaching should be supported in public schools. During the past seventy years especially, the U.S. Supreme Court has heard many cases dealing with this subject. Some questions the Court has tried to answer are

- should tax money be used to support religious schools?

- should public schools be allowed to provide periods of time when students can attend special classes to receive religious instruction from their own minister, priest, or rabbi?

- should public schools be allowed to require students to take part in prayers or read the Bible during regular school hours?

The establishment clause requires that government be neutral toward religion. Government cannot support one type of religion over another type, nor can it support religion over nonreligion.

The courts follow guidelines when deciding whether government is complying with the establishment clause. They look at three factors.

1 The courts examine whether government is actively endorsing religion.

2 The courts examine whether government is compelling people to participate in religious activities or to accept religious beliefs.

3 The courts examine whether government is providing special treatment to one type of religion that it is not providing to other types of religion.

If government fails any one of these factors, it is in violation of the establishment clause. In a recent case, for example, the U.S. Supreme Court ruled that a high school could not require its students to participate in a prayer at their graduation ceremony. The Court concluded that the high school, by requiring the prayer, was endorsing religion and compelling the students to participate in the prayer.

Under what conditions, if any, should a student be allowed to recite a prayer at a public school's graduation ceremony?

212

How would you decide these issues concerning religion in public schools?

Work in groups of three to five. Read each of the four situations. Use the guidelines discussed in the previous section to decide whether the laws and actions described should be declared unconstitutional. Be prepared to explain your decisions to the class.

1 Your state passes a law allowing your public school principal to post the Ten Commandments in every classroom.

2 Your state passes a law that gives parents who send their children to religious schools a tax deduction for tuition, transportation, and educational materials.

3 Your state allows your public school's algebra teacher to spend part of his class day at a church school, giving instruction to students having difficulty with math.

4 There is an unused classroom at your public school. The student council requests permission to use it after school hours for voluntary prayer meetings. The principal refuses to make the classroom available.

How do the courts determine whether government is complying with the establishment clause?

1. What is the establishment clause?

2. What is the free exercise clause?

3. Why was freedom of religion an important principle in early America?

4. What conflicts exist over the freedom of religion clauses in the First Amendment? Give examples of each.

5. Can government limit your right to freedom of belief? Why or why not?

6. Can government limit your right to practice your religious beliefs? If so, under what circumstances?

7. What conflicts exist between freedom of religion and public education?

ACTIVITIES

1. Some people have suggested adding an amendment to the Constitution that would allow public schools to set aside time for voluntary prayer. Use the Internet or your school library to find more information about this proposal. Then decide if you would support such an amendment. Write a brief essay explaining why or why not.

2. Thomas Jefferson and James Madison had strong opinions about the separation of church and state. Write an essay comparing and contrasting your opinions on this issue with those of Jefferson and Madison.

3. Make an illustration in the style you think might be found in eighteenth-century schoolbooks. In your drawing show your understanding of the establishment clause.

How has the right to vote expanded since the Constitution was adopted?

LESSON PURPOSE

The Constitution originally left it up to the state governments to decide who should have the right to vote. In the early years of our nation the states limited the right to vote to white men who owned property. In 1789 white males who did not own property, members of certain religious groups, freedmen, Native Americans, slaves, and women were not allowed to vote.

In this lesson you will learn about how the right to vote has been expanded in the last two hundred years to achieve a basic ideal of our representative democracy—the constitutional right of all adult citizens to vote.

When you finish this lesson you should be able to explain how voting rights were extended by changes in state voting laws, amendments to the Constitution, acts of Congress, and decisions of the U.S. Supreme Court.

civil rights movement

Civil War Amendments

grandfather clause

literacy test

poll tax

register

suffrage

Voting Rights Act

Thirteenth Amendment

Fourteenth Amendment

Fifteenth Amendment

Nineteenth Amendment

Twenty-fourth Amendment

Twenty-sixth Amendment

How was the right of suffrage extended before the Civil War?

The colonial limits on who could vote did not change much during the early years of the new nation. Many colonies only allowed white men who owned property and belonged to a particular religious group to vote.

After the Revolution, an increasing number of people objected to these limits on voting rights. States began to do away with property and religious restrictions. In addition, new states joining the Union placed fewer limitations on suffrage. **Suffrage** means the right to vote. In the early 1800s, for example, six new Western states gave the vote to all adult white males.

Although the states took steps before the Civil War to extend suffrage to more people, change was not easy. For example, as late as 1842 in Rhode Island, only men with property were allowed to vote. This situation caused an armed rebellion. The rebellion failed. But the following year Rhode Island adopted a new state constitution that gave voting rights to all male citizens who paid a tax of at least one dollar a year.

What criteria should be used to determine who should be eligible to vote?

Before the Civil War, a large part of the population—including African American men and all women—still could not vote. In the remaining sections of the lesson, you will learn how these groups, Native Americans, and others gained the right to vote.

How did African American men gain the right to vote?

Although many black men fought in the Revolutionary War, the right to vote was not extended to African Americans. In 1860 only six of the thirty-four states allowed freedmen to vote.

After the Civil War, the states approved the Thirteenth, Fourteenth, and Fifteenth Amendments to the Constitution. These amendments are known as the **Civil War Amendments**. The **Thirteenth Amendment** abolished slavery. The **Fourteenth Amendment** granted full citizenship to African Americans. The **Fifteenth Amendment** guaranteed the right to vote to men regardless of their "race, color, or previous condition of servitude."

Adding these Civil War Amendments to the Constitution was only the start of an effort to guarantee voting rights to African Americans. Many people in the Southern states did not want black people to vote or hold public office. Some states passed laws that made it impossible for African Americans to vote. Some examples of these laws follow on the next page.

What problems were the Fourteenth and Fifteenth Amendments intended to solve?

- **Literacy tests**

  A **literacy test** requires that a person prove that he or she is able to read and write. Some states required all men to pass these tests before being allowed to vote. Because most African American men had been denied an education they could not pass the test. Often the people who gave the test behaved unfairly. They made it impossible for even educated African American men to pass the test.

- **Grandfather clause**

  Some states had voting laws with wording that we call **grandfather clauses**. A grandfather clause said that a person had the right to vote only if his grandfather had had the right to vote. Few African American men could qualify. Their grandfathers had been slaves and had been denied the right to vote.

- **Poll tax**

  A **poll tax** is a fee that a person must pay in order to vote. Some states charged all people a poll tax. Since most former slaves were very poor, they could not afford to pay the tax and, therefore, could not vote.

People fought to get these state laws changed, but it took a long time. In 1915, the U.S. Supreme Court said that grandfather clauses were unconstitutional. Some states, however, continued to use literacy tests and poll taxes until the 1960s in order to keep African Americans from voting.

In the 1950s, more and more people began to demand that the federal government protect the right of African Americans to vote. People of all races worked together to change unfair state laws. People gave speeches and marched in the streets. These actions became known as the **civil rights movement**.

What was unfair about these voting requirements?

What was the poll tax? Why was it used?

As a result of the civil rights movement, the **Twenty-fourth Amendment** was added to the Constitution in 1964. The amendment says that the right to vote in national elections shall not be denied because a person fails to pay a poll tax or any other tax. The U.S. Supreme Court later said that the Twenty-fourth Amendment also applied to state elections.

Congress passed a law called the **Voting Rights Act** in 1965. The law protected the right to vote for all citizens. The law forced the states to obey the Constitution. It made it clear that the right to vote could not be denied because of a person's color.

How did women gain the right to vote?

In 1848, a convention was held at Seneca Falls, New York, that launched a national movement by women to win the right to vote. Although suffrage for women had many supporters among men, the battle was a difficult one. In those days it was common to believe that women should not participate in government. This idea made it harder for women to achieve their goal.

In 1876, Susan B. Anthony led a delegation of women to Philadelphia to celebrate the one-hundred-year anniversary of the

Why do you think women did not gain the vote until 1920?

How did Native Americans gain the right to vote?

American Indians governed themselves by their own tribal laws, treaties with the United States government, and by special laws passed by Congress. These laws did not recognize American Indians to be citizens of the United States. As a result, they did not have the right to vote.

The first attempt to grant Native Americans citizenship came in 1887 when Congress passed the Dawes Act. The Dawes Act granted a tract of land and citizenship to those who were willing to give up their allegiance to their tribe. The law was strongly resented by most tribes.

Finally, Congress passed a law in 1924 called the Indian Citizenship Act. This law fully recognized Indians as citizens of the United States. The law also gave Indians the right to vote in federal elections.

Declaration of Independence. While there, the women publicly protested their lack of suffrage by reading the Women's Declaration of Rights.

Gaining the right to vote for women was a long, slow process. The earliest gains were made in the western part of the country. The territory of Wyoming granted women the right to vote in 1869. By 1900, Colorado, Utah, and Idaho had followed Wyoming's lead.

It was not until 1912 that the movement to give women the right to vote gained national recognition. Presidential candidate Theodore Roosevelt's Bull Moose Progressive Party supported the movement. In 1913 women were granted the right to vote in the territory of Alaska.

In 1920, the states ratified the **Nineteenth Amendment** to the Constitution, which gave women the vote. One hundred and thirty years after the signing of the Constitution, women had finally gained the right to vote.

President Calvin Coolidge with a group of Osage Indians after the signing of the Indian Citizenship Act of 1924. What rights were realized by Native Americans with the passage of this law?

How did eighteen-year-olds gain the right to vote?

In the 1960s and 1970s, the government drafted thousands of young men to fight in the Vietnam War. Many of these young men were too young to vote. They did not have a voice in the elections for government officials responsible for deciding America's role in that war. The voting requirement at that time was twenty-one years of age.

Congress passed a law in 1970 lowering the voting age to eighteen. The U.S. Supreme Court then ruled that Congress could only regulate federal elections. At that time, only four states allowed eighteen-

What is the relationship between who is allowed to vote and how democratic a country is?

year-olds to vote. Following the Court's decision, steps were taken to amend the Constitution so that suffrage would be extended to eighteen-year-olds in both state and federal elections.

In 1971, the **Twenty-sixth Amendment** was added to the Constitution. The amendment grants the right to vote to any citizen who is eighteen years of age or older.

What are voting requirements today?

The states, although limited by the Constitution and the federal Voting Rights Act, still make some decisions regarding voting rights. All states have laws saying only citizens have the right to vote, although the Constitution does not require this. Every state requires that persons must live in the state for a period of time before they can vote, and all states except North Dakota require citizens to register

Why should people who are old enough to serve in the armed forces also have the right to vote?

Why do you suppose older Americans vote more frequently than younger Americans?

before voting. To **register** to vote means to have your name added to a list. Voters are required to register to ensure that they are qualified to vote and to keep people from voting more than once.

Throughout our history we have used our Constitution to achieve nearly universal adult suffrage. Today, almost every American of voting age has the right to vote. This has made the United States one of the most democratic nations on earth. Americans can use the power of the ballot box to choose more public officials at more levels of government than can voters in any other democracy.

As the right to vote has expanded, though, the willingness of American citizens to participate has decreased. In recent years there has been a steady decline in voter turnout for elections.

The United States now ranks eleventh among the world's democracies in the percentage of eligible voters who exercise the right to vote.

Many people worry about the unwillingness of so many Americans to use this most fundamental right and duty of citizenship. They fear that not voting may reflect a growing feeling of being disconnected from government. However, if the United States is to be a country that is truly of, by, and for the people, it is essential that the people exercise their right to vote competently and responsibly. Responsible voting is essential to democracy.

What suggestions do you have for increasing participation in elections today?

Generally, better-off and better-educated citizens use their right to vote to a much greater extent than do poor or uneducated citizens. Voter turnout is also related to age. Older Americans are almost twice as likely to vote than are young Americans.

Work in groups of three to five to discuss the following questions. Share your opinions with the class.

❶ Why do you think that older Americans might be more interested in government policies than younger Americans?

❷ What political issues motivate younger citizens to get involved with public life? Give examples.

❸ Some countries increased voter participation by holding elections on Sundays. What other methods can you suggest to increase voter turnout?

❹ In some countries voter participation is mandatory. What effect might this have on elections? Do you think this is a good way to increase citizen participation in elections?

Do you think something should be done to increase voter turnout? Why or why not?

1 What were some of the restrictions on voting rights that kept various groups of people from voting?

2 Explain how each of the following groups of people gained the right to vote.

- African Americans
- eighteen-year-olds
- Native Americans
- women

3 What amendments were added to the Constitution so that more people would have the right to vote?

4 What laws did Congress pass to protect the constitutional right of citizens to vote?

5 What actions did citizens take to expand the right to vote to most Americans?

ACTIVITIES

1 With help from your teacher, invite someone from the League of Women Voters to come to your class to discuss elections in your state. Prepare questions to ask your guest during the visit.

2 Use the Internet to find information about the requirements for voting in your state. Obtain a copy of a voter registration form and a sample ballot from a recent election. Your community library, county clerk, or registrar's office should be able to help you. Share the information you find with your class.

3 Follow a political campaign in your community or state. Learn about the candidates. Keep articles from the newspaper. Keep a journal where you record your impression about the election process.

4 Write a story that shows how one person's vote can determine the outcome of an election. Share your story with the class.

How does the Constitution safeguard the right to equal protection of the law?

LESSON PURPOSE

In this lesson you will be introduced to one of the most important parts of the Fourteenth Amendment to the Constitution—the equal protection clause.

When you finish this lesson, you should be able to explain the purpose of the equal protection clause. You should also be able to describe some of the steps that Congress, the executive branch, the U.S. Supreme Court, and citizens have taken to end unfair discrimination in our nation.

boycott
Civil Rights Act of 1964
equal protection clause
Jim Crow laws
segregation
separate but equal

How did the Constitution end unfair treatment of citizens by government?

Although the Thirteenth Amendment abolished slavery in 1865, it did not end unfair treatment of African Americans by government. Many states in the South passed laws that discriminated against black people. State and local laws required that public facilities such as restrooms, theaters, and parks have separate areas for black people and white people.

Congress adopted the Fourteenth Amendment in 1868. The **equal protection clause** is stated in Section 1 of the amendment. It is the most important constitutional protection that the people have against unfair discrimination by state and local governments. The equal protection clause says that

no State shall...deny to any person within its jurisdiction the equal protection of the laws.

At the time it was ratified, this clause was intended to prevent discrimination against African Americans and guarantee them the rights that go along with citizenship.

Why did the passage of the Thirteenth Amendment fail to end unfair treatment of African Americans?

Are these situations unfair treatment by government?

With a partner, read each of the following situations.
Explain to the class why each is or is not unfair government treatment.

1 In your state there is a law that says students belonging to a certain race must go to schools that are separate from those that other students attend.

2 Your city has a regulation requiring people with particular religious beliefs to live in a special section of town.

3 Your state has a law that says people must marry within their own race.

4 Your city fire department will not hire women as firefighters.

5 You and a friend of the opposite sex work for the state. You both do the same jobs. Yet you are each paid at a different rate.

Under what conditions, if any, would it be fair to pay people at a different rate for doing the same work? Explain your reasoning.

The Fourteenth Amendment did not by itself prevent discrimination, however. The states continued to pass laws requiring African Americans to go to separate schools and to use separate public facilities. These laws came to be called **Jim Crow laws**. The states claimed that such laws did not violate the equal protection clause because the separate schools and facilities for blacks were equal to those provided for whites. This is known as the **separate but equal** argument. The U.S. Supreme Court considered this argument in two famous cases: *Plessy v. Ferguson* (1896) and *Brown v. Board of Education* (1954).

How did the U.S. Supreme Court interpret the equal protection clause in two separate cases?

CASE ONE
Plessy v. Ferguson (1896)

The state of Louisiana passed a law requiring railroad companies to provide separate, similar cars for white passengers and black passengers. A group of African American leaders decided to challenge the law.

In what ways did Jim Crow laws violate the equal protection clause?

Homer Plessy bought a railroad ticket and took a seat in a car set aside for whites. Plessy was arrested when he refused to move. The Louisiana state court found him guilty of violating state law. Plessy took his case to the U.S. Supreme Court, arguing that the Louisiana law violated the equal protection clause.

The Supreme Court ruled against Plessy. The Court said that separating the races did not mean that one race was inferior to the other. Because the state law required the facilities to be separate but equal, the Supreme Court said there was no discrimination.

The decision in this case, *Plessy v. Ferguson* (1896), allowed states to practice **segregation**, separation of the races, for almost sixty years. Then, in the case of *Brown v. Board of Education* (1954), the U.S. Supreme Court changed its interpretation of the equal protection clause.

CASE TWO

Brown v. Board of Education (1954)

Linda Brown was a seven-year-old child who lived five blocks from an elementary school. Linda was forced to attend a school for African American children twenty-one blocks away from her home. Linda's parents, along with twelve other parents, brought a lawsuit against the school board of Topeka, Kansas, saying their children had been deprived of equal protection of the law.

One of the lawyers for the parents was Thurgood Marshall, an attorney for the National Association for the Advancement of Colored People. Marshall later became the first African American justice of the U.S. Supreme Court. He argued that segregated schools could not be equal.

This time the Court agreed. It said that placing African American children in schools separate from white children denied them the equal protection of the laws guaranteed by the Fourteenth Amendment. The Court said,

> To separate [children]...solely because of their race generates [causes] a feeling of inferiority... that may affect their hearts and minds in a way unlikely ever to be undone.

These are the lawyers for the Brown family and the other families: George E.C. Hayes, left, Thurgood Marshall, center, and James M. Nabrit Jr. What was their argument before the Supreme Court? How did the Court rule in this case?

How did Congress, the executive branch, and citizens work to end unfair discrimination by government?

The Court's decision in *Brown v. Board of Education* was the first important step in ending school segregation. Although the *Brown* case was a turning point in the fight against discrimination, it dealt only with segregated schools. The Court decision by itself did not end discrimination. Many states resisted the Court's order to integrate their schools. As late as 1957, the governor of Arkansas tried to stop black students from entering a

What means did leaders of the civil rights movement use to obtain their goals?

Who is Rosa Parks? Why did African Americans begin a boycott of buses in Montgomery, Alabama, in 1955?

white high school in Little Rock. In response, President Dwight Eisenhower ordered federal troops to escort the students and enforce the law.

The civil rights movement started in the 1950s. It was a time when many people of both races worked to end unfair treatment by government. People marched in the streets. They wrote letters to Congress asking for stronger laws. They held boycotts. A **boycott** means that they refused to buy from or deal with stores and companies that practiced racial discrimination.

One of the earliest boycotts began in 1955. Rosa Parks was a working woman who lived in Montgomery, Alabama. She was on her way home one day when the bus she was riding became crowded. Parks refused to give up her seat to a

What democratic ideals were expressed by Martin Luther King Jr. in his "I Have a Dream" speech?

white man. She was arrested for violating a city law. The African American community boycotted the city buses until the city changed the law. The boycott lasted more than a year.

In August of 1963, thousands of Americans marched in Washington, D.C. They wanted to show their support for the civil rights movement. Dr. Martin Luther King Jr. was an important civil rights leader. It was here that Dr. King gave his famous "I Have a Dream" speech. King told the crowd, "I have a dream that my four little children will one day live in a nation where they will not be judged by the color of their skin, but by the content of their character." One day, he hoped, all people would join hands and be "free at last."

In 1964, Congress passed the Civil Rights Act. The **Civil Rights Act of 1964** ended segregation in public places such as restaurants and hotels. The law also said that employers could not discriminate against people because of their race, national origin, religion, or gender.

When African Americans won these civil rights after years of struggle, other groups began to call for equal protection. Women, disabled people, older people, and other groups worked to get laws passed guaranteeing their right to equal protection of the laws. In response to their efforts, Congress and state legislatures have passed laws prohibiting unfair discrimination against these groups.

1 What was the purpose of the Thirteenth and Fourteenth Amendments to the Constitution?

2 What is the meaning of the equal protection clause? Why is this clause important?

3 What did the U.S. Supreme Court decide in the *Plessy v. Ferguson* case? What effects did the decision have on the lives of African Americans?

4 What did the U.S. Supreme Court decide in the *Brown v. Board of Education* case? Why was this an important decision?

5 What actions did ordinary citizens take to help end unfair discrimination?

6 What laws did Congress pass to help end unfair discrimination?

7 What actions did the executive branch take to help end unfair discrimination?

1 Research information about Martin Luther King Jr. Read his *Letter from Birmingham City Jail*. What kinds of inspiration did he have for his ideas about nonviolence? Share what you learned with the class.

2 "Equal treatment" continues to be an important issue in the United States today. Find information about issues of equality that organized groups are seeking to address today. Explain what these issues are in a report to your class.

3 Create a timeline of historical events in the struggle to gain equal protection by various groups in America. Each student should research one event to include in a classroom poster commemorating the struggle for equal rights.

How does the Constitution protect the right to due process of law?

LESSON PURPOSE

In this lesson we will look at another part of the Constitution that is concerned with fairness. This is the idea of due process of law. The due process clause is intended to guarantee that government will use fair procedures when gathering information and making decisions that affect our rights to life, liberty, or property.

When you finish this lesson you should be able to explain in general terms what due process means. You should also be able to explain how due process applies to the rights of juveniles who are accused of breaking the law.

due process
Fifth Amendment
procedure

What is due process of law?

It is difficult to define due process of law exactly. We may say that **due process** is the right to be treated fairly by government. There are two important ways this meaning is applied.

1 Due process means that the **procedures**, or methods used to conduct hearings and to apply and enforce the law, must be fair and reasonable. All branches of the federal and state governments must use fair procedures when they are carrying out their responsibilities.

2 Due process also means that the **content** of laws that legislatures pass must be fair and reasonable. Congress and the state legislatures cannot pass laws that place unfair or unreasonable limitations on people's rights to life, liberty, or property.

The ideas of due process can be found in the body of the Constitution and several amendments. The Fifth and Fourteenth Amendments specifically use the term due process of law.

In what way does due process limit the powers of government?

The Fifth Amendment does not mention state governments. Therefore, this amendment applies only to actions of the federal government.

What rights do you think you should have if you were to be accused of breaking the law?

The **Fifth Amendment** says

> *No Person shall...be deprived of life, liberty, or property, without due process of law.*

The Fourteenth Amendment includes actions by the states. The Fourteenth Amendment says

> *nor shall any State deprive any person of life, liberty, or property, without due process of law.*

In the remainder of this lesson we focus on the first meaning of due process: members of all branches of government must use fair procedures when fulfilling their responsibilities.

We will concentrate on the rights of persons suspected or accused of crimes. We examine the procedures that were followed in a situation that led to a famous U.S. Supreme Court case called *In re Gault* (1967). This case concerns the treatment of a juvenile accused of a crime.

What are fair procedures?

Work with a group of three to five students to complete the following exercise.

❶ Read the summary of the *Gault* case.

❷ Make a list of unfair procedures used by government officials in the case.

❸ Read the Fifth, Sixth, and Eighth Amendments to the Constitution. Identify the parts of each Amendment that apply to this case.

❹ Evaluate the facts, then take and defend a position on how the U.S. Supreme Court should have dealt with *In re Gault*.

In re Gault (1967)

Gerald Gault was fifteen years old. On the morning of June 8, 1964, the sheriff of Gila County, Arizona, arrested Gerald and a friend, Ronald Lewis. The sheriff took the boys to the Children's Detention Home.

The boys were accused of telephoning a neighbor, Mrs. Cook, and saying offensive and obscene things to her. Mrs. Cook had then called the sheriff.

While the boys were in detention, Officer Flagg, a deputy probation officer, questioned them. The boys admitted making the calls. Each boy blamed the other.

At the time that Gerald was arrested, his parents were at work. The sheriff who arrested the boys did not tell the parents that Gerald was being taken to a detention home. No one from the sheriff's office called the Gault home.

When Gerald's mother arrived home that evening, she sent her older son to look for Gerald. At the home of Ronald Lewis, he learned that Gerald was being held in the detention home.

Mrs. Gault went to the detention home and Officer Flagg explained why the sheriff had arrested her son. Officer Flagg informed Mrs. Gault that there would be a hearing in juvenile court the next afternoon.

Gerald, his mother, Officer Flagg, and the judge were the only ones at the hearing. Mrs. Cook was not present. During the hearing, no one was asked to swear to tell the truth. No record was made of what was said. No lawyers were present.

At later hearings, the judge, Mrs. Gault, and Officer Flagg agreed on some things that were said at the first hearing but disagreed about others. They agreed that the judge had asked Gerald about the telephone call. They disagreed about what Gerald answered.

His mother remembered that Gerald said he had dialed Mrs. Cook's number and then handed the telephone to Ronald. Officer Flagg said that Gerald had admitted making one insulting remark.

Two or three days later, Officer Flagg drove Gerald home. On that day, Gerald's mother received a note from the court that was written on plain paper. The note said, "Mrs. Gault, Judge McGhee has set Monday, June 15, 1964 at 11 A.M. as the date for further hearings on Gerald's delinquency."

On June 15, the Gaults appeared in court. Mrs. Gault had requested that Mrs. Cook be present but she did not attend. The judge, who had not spoken with Mrs. Cook, said that it was not necessary that Mrs. Cook be in court. Again, no one was asked to swear to tell the truth and no record was made of this hearing.

During the hearing, Officer Flagg handed the judge a report saying that Gerald had made insulting phone calls. The Gaults had never seen the report.

In the end, the judge ruled that Gerald was guilty of violating a state law that said that a person who "in the presence or hearing of any woman or child...uses vulgar, abusive, or obscene language, is guilty of a misdemeanor." The judge sentenced Gerald to the State Industrial School for juvenile delinquents until he reached age 21.

If Gerald had been 18, he would have been tried in a regular criminal court. There, the maximum penalty for making "vulgar, abusive, or obscene" calls would have been a $5 to $50 fine or not more than two months' imprisonment.

The Gaults appealed the case and it eventually reached the U.S. Supreme Court. Gault's lawyers argued that

the procedure used in Gerald's case had denied him due process under the Fourteenth Amendment. Attorneys for the state argued that the informal proceedings under the juvenile court system were intended to help juveniles, rather than treat them as regular criminals. They said that this system would be undermined if the Court gave young offenders all the specific guarantees in the Bill of Rights.

What conflicts might arise over protecting the rights of an individual and protecting society?

How can the rights of the individual and the rights of society conflict?

Problems of due process involve two government responsibilities. These responsibilities are to

1. protect the rights of an individual who may have broken the law

2. protect everyone else from people who break the law and endanger the lives, liberty, or property of others

These responsibilities sometimes conflict. Balancing them is a difficult job. It is the duty of government and the courts to balance these responsibilities.

Protecting the individual from unfair treatment by government is among the most important protections of our constitutional democracy.

We have discussed due process of law as it applies to the rights of someone accused of a crime. It is important to remember that the right to due process means the right to be treated fairly by all the agencies of government, not just the courts and law enforcement.

Due process of law has been called the "primary and indispensable [necessary] foundation of individual freedom" because it protects the individual from government wrongdoing. Due process applies to local school board hearings, to congressional hearings, and to hearings of the administrative agencies of your state and federal governments.

How might the right to due process of law protect the individual?

1. Where in the Constitution will you find the two due process clauses? In what way are the two clauses different?

2. What is the meaning of due process?

3. Why do you think the guarantee of due process is so important?

4. Why must all agencies of government protect the individual's right to due process of law?

ACTIVITIES

1. With a partner, videotape an interview with your school principal or a member of your school board. Ask them about the policy in your school district regarding due process rights of students. Show the tape to your class and explain what you learned.

2. With a partner search the Constitution to see how many references each of you can find to elements related to fair procedures and due process of law. Combine your lists and share them with the class.

3. Draw a picture or a poster. On one side of your picture illustrate a situation in which a due process right is being violated. On the other side illustrate the same situation but with the due process right being protected.

4. With your teacher's help, invite a police officer to your class to discuss how the police have to protect due process rights when they suspect that someone has committed a crime. Prepare questions to ask your guest during the visit.

unit SIX
What are the responsibilities of citizens?

unit SIX

KEY CONCEPTS

citizen

international law

nation-state

naturalized citizen

legal permanent resident

You have studied the basic ideas of our constitutional democracy. You have learned about our government's responsibility to protect the basic rights of the people and promote the common welfare. This unit deals with a question of equal or greater importance: what is the role of the citizen?

This book will not answer this question for you. The answer is one you must arrive at yourself. This unit raises some important ideas that you might find useful in deciding what your responsibilities as a citizen are.

What is the relationship of the United States to other nations in the world?

LESSON PURPOSE

In this lesson you will learn some ways in which countries interact with one another. You will also learn how the ideas about government in the Declaration of Independence and in the U.S. Constitution and Bill of Rights have influenced other countries.

When you finish this lesson, you should be able to explain how countries in the world interact with one another. You should be able to explain how American ideas about freedom and government have influenced people in other countries.

What are nation-states?

There are many countries in the world. A country is also called a **nation-state**. The government of a nation-state claims the authority to govern the people who live within its territory.

The government of a nation-state also makes and carries out agreements with other nation-states. Today there are more than 200 nation-states in the world. Some are tiny countries such as Monaco and Singapore. Others are very large countries such as China and Russia.

Who has authority over nation-states?

At the international level, there is no organization with formal political power comparable to that of the nation-state. There is no international government that has authority over the world's nation-states. That is why each nation-state is said to be sovereign. By sovereign we mean that a country has the right to be free from outside interference within its boundaries.

Nation-states often agree to cooperate with each other. For example, letters

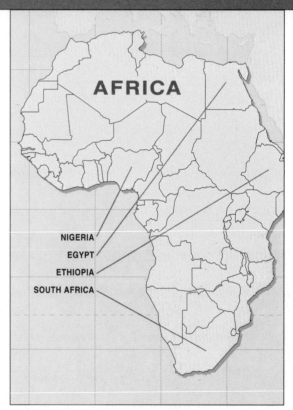

What is government's role in the nation-state?
What are some examples of nation-states?

mailed in one country arrive at their destination in another country. Telephone services function worldwide. Airplanes take off from one country and land in another. Nations trade goods and services daily. These few examples show that countries can live in peace and cooperate in their means of dealing with each other.

In what ways might nation-states agree to cooperate with each other?

What is international law?

One thing that makes interactions among countries possible is a system of international law. **International law** consists of those rules that regulate how countries behave toward one another. International law is usually made by treaties that nation-states make among themselves.

It is up to each nation-state to enforce its treaties. For example, Article VI of the U.S. Constitution says, among other things,

> This Constitution, and the Laws of the United States...and all treaties made under the Authority of the United States, shall be the supreme law of the Land.

This means that all treaties that the United States makes with other nations become part of our national laws, and they have to be enforced by the federal government.

There is no international police organization to enforce international law. This does not mean that it is impossible to make nations live up to their responsibilities to each other. Some nations use economic, political, or military pressure to keep other nations in line.

How do nations of the world interact with each other?

Today, the nations of the world are increasingly dependent on each other. Nations have many ways of interacting. Here are some common examples:

- **Cultural, science, and business exchanges**
  People travel all over the world. People living in different countries share ideas. Doctors, scientists, educators, and business people from many countries meet to share advances in their fields. Students and teachers live with families in

other countries to learn their language and to learn about their culture. Artists show their work in the museums of other countries.

- **Humanitarian aid**
  The term **humanitarian** means to show concern for the pain and suffering of others. During natural disasters such as floods and earthquakes, countries help the victims in other countries by giving humanitarian aid. Countries send medicine, food, and shelter to suffering people. Individuals and organizations also respond to natural disasters.

- **Trade**
  Countries buy and sell factory goods, farm products, and services to one another.

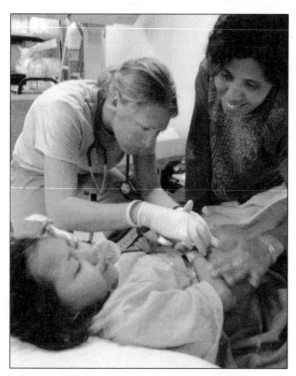

Do you think nations have a responsibility to provide humanitarian aid to the people of other nations? Why or why not?

- **Diplomacy**
  As you learned in Lesson 9, the term diplomacy means the practice of carrying on formal relationships with governments of other countries. The official representatives of countries meet and discuss issues important to their governments. They work together in a peaceful manner to find solutions to common problems.

- **Treaties and agreements**
  Countries make treaties and agreements. They agree to promote trade among themselves. They agree to do certain things to protect the environment. Some agree to help each other in time of war.

- **Military force**
  When two or more countries cannot solve their disagreements peacefully, they sometimes threaten to use military force. Sometimes, the disagreement results in a war.

What international organizations promote interaction among nations?

There is no single organization in the world that has the power to force countries to settle conflicts peacefully. There are some organizations that help countries reach agreements without going to war. The most important worldwide organization is the United Nations. A treaty signed in 1945, after World War II, created the United Nations. The purposes of the **United Nations,** according to its charter, are to maintain international peace and security; develop friendly

What is the United Nations? What does the United Nations do?

relations among nations; cooperate in solving international economic, social, cultural, and humanitarian problems; and promote respect for human rights and fundamental freedoms. Most nations of the world are members of the United Nations.

There are also regional treaty organizations that promote interaction among nations. These organizations deal with regional matters. The Organization of American States (OAS) promotes peace and security among all member nations in the Americas. Other examples of regional organizations are the League of Arab States and the Association of Southeast Asian Nations (ASEAN).

Many international organizations are not under direct government control. These are nongovernmental organizations, often

called NGOs. Some of these organizations provide humanitarian aid, for example, the International Federation of Red Cross and Red Crescent Societies. Others, such as Amnesty International, address human rights concerns.

What powers does the U.S. Constitution give to government to deal with other nations?

Each branch of the U.S. government has certain powers that come from the Constitution. The Constitution gives each branch the following powers to deal with other countries.

- **Congress**

  Congress has the power to regulate commerce with other countries and with the Indian tribes, declare war, approve treaties, approve ambassadors, raise and support armies, and punish piracies and crimes committed on the high seas.

- **President**

  The president has the power to make treaties and to name ambassadors, with the approval of Congress. The president is also the commander-in-chief of the military forces.

- **U.S. Supreme Court**

  The U.S. Supreme Court has the power to hear all cases affecting ambassadors; cases in which the United States is a party; and cases involving a foreign state, its citizens or subjects.

How have other countries influenced the United States?

Many of the ideas about government that you have studied started in other countries. The Founders learned about government from studying the histories of ancient Greece and Rome. From the Greeks and Romans, they learned about republican government, civic virtue, and the common good.

The European philosophers also had a great influence on the Founders. The theories of Baron de Montesquieu of France influenced their thinking about the separation of powers. The writings of John Locke of Great Britain guided their thinking about natural rights.

What do you think citizens of the United States gain from relationships with other countries? What do you think citizens in other countries gain from their relationships with us?

Colonial Americans also enjoyed the rights of Englishmen. Among these are the right to trial by jury, the right to be secure in one's home, and the right to express one's views about taxes through representatives in government.

How have the Declaration of Independence and the U.S. Constitution and Bill of Rights influenced other countries?

The United States has given many things to the world—advanced medical and industrial technology and the personal computer to name a few. The discoveries

How have democratic ideals from the United States influenced the people of other nations?

and inventions that we as a nation have shared with the world are important, but not as valuable or as lasting as the democratic ideals expressed in the Declaration of Independence and the U.S. Constitution and Bill of Rights. Some of these democratic ideals are listed below.

1. Power comes from the people and the people are the ultimate source of the authority of their government.

2. People in government are the servants of the people, not the masters of the people.

3. All people are political equals. No person's vote counts more than another's.

4. The people delegate their powers to their government. They consent to be governed only so long as those in power fulfill their responsibilities. They can take back those powers and change their government.

5. The purpose of government is to protect the people's rights to life, liberty, and property, and to promote the common good.

6. A nation's constitution should be approved by the people and serve as a higher law that everyone must obey, including the people and those serving in their government.

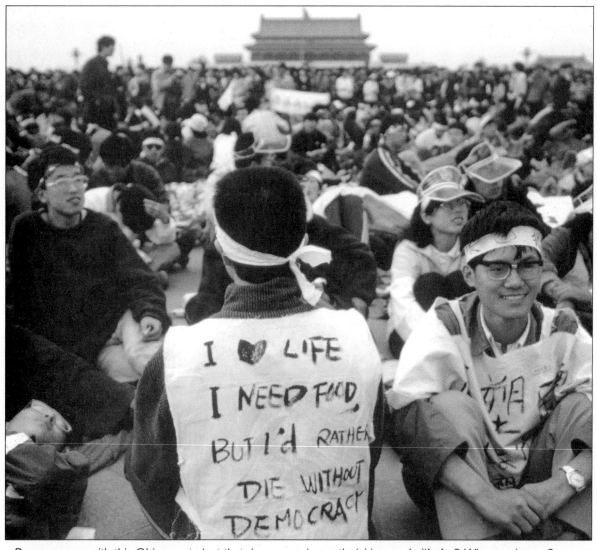

Do you agree with this Chinese student that democracy is worth risking one's life for? Why or why not?

7 A nation's constitution should include a list of the rights of the people.

During the nineteenth and twentieth centuries, the American ideal of self-government spread around the world. People from many countries read and studied the ideas in the Declaration of Independence and in the U.S. Constitution and Bill of Rights. These documents influenced other countries to adopt similar ideas about government.

The American Revolution gave hope to many people in Europe and Latin America who wanted to promote democratic change in their own countries. The French Constitution of 1791 included many ideas from the United States. The Declaration of Independence and the U.S. Constitution and Bill of Rights also inspired Latin American leaders. In more recent years, when students in the People's Republic of China demonstrated for more freedoms from their government, they carried copies of the Declaration of Independence.

How do countries influence each other?

Work with a partner to discuss the following questions.
Be prepared to share your ideas with the class.

❶ What events in the United States today might affect other people or countries of the world? Explain how.

❷ What events in the world today might affect U.S. citizens? Explain how.

❸ What do U.S. citizens gain from our relationships with other countries of the world? What do citizens in other countries gain from their relationships with the United States?

❹ Why is it important that countries be able to have a free exchange of ideas?

1 What is a nation-state?

2 List some ways in which countries interact with each other.

3 What powers does the U.S. Constitution give the national government to deal with other countries?

4 List some ideas in the Declaration of Independence and the U.S. Constitution and Bill of Rights that have influenced government in other countries.

1 Learn more about the United Nations. Why and how was the United Nations established? What does the United Nations do? Share what you learned with your class.

2 Suppose you make a telephone call to a friend or relative in Mexico or in France. Suppose you send a letter to China using a stamp from the United States. Learn about international agreements that make it possible for your telephone call or letter to reach its destination. Find information about the Universal Postal Union or the International Telecommunications Union.

3 Choose one of the following countries: China, Colombia, Egypt, France, Indonesia, Israel, Mexico, Nigeria, Panama, Russia, Saudi Arabia, or Vietnam. Learn about the country's relationship with the United States in the past and today. Share what you learned with your class.

4 Find an article of clothing or other item around your home. Examine the label. Where was the item made? What international agreements exist that regulate how such items are traded on world markets? Identify some items that are manufactured in your state and exported to other countries.

5 The State Department is the cabinet position in charge of conducting our relations with other nations in the world. Who is the current Secretary of State? Explain some of his or her responsibilities. Write a brief biography of this person.

What are the rights and responsibilities of citizenship?

LESSON PURPOSE

In this lesson you will examine the meaning of citizenship and how one becomes a citizen of the United States. You will examine the rights of citizens as well as the responsibilities that accompany our citizenship in this nation. Finally, you will develop positions on what a citizen might do when he or she thinks that a law is unjust.

When you finish this lesson, you should be able to explain the meaning of citizenship and how one becomes a citizen of the United States. You should also be able to explain some of the rights of citizens and the responsibilities that accompany those rights.

citizen

civic responsibilities

economic rights

legal permanent resident

naturalized citizen

personal rights

personal responsibilities

political rights

What does it mean to be a citizen?

A **citizen** is a person who is a legal member of a self-governing community, such as a nation or state. In the United States, there are no degrees or classes of citizenship. In this country, citizenship does not depend on a person's race, gender, or ethnic origin. Every citizen is a full member of the political community.

A citizen is one person among equals. Each citizen possesses equal rights under the law. In addition, our rights as citizens come with certain responsibilities. It is also important to remember that under our federal system, Americans are citizens of both their state and the United States.

How does a person become a citizen of the United States?

Every person born in the United States is a citizen of this country. A person born in another country to parents who are citizens of the United States is also a citizen of this country.

A **legal permanent resident** is someone who is not a citizen of the United States

What is a citizen? Should some citizens have more rights than others? Why or why not?

but who is legally permitted to live here. Legal permanent residents enjoy most of the rights of citizens and like citizens

Should a person born in the United States automatically become a citizen? Why or why not?

they must obey the laws and pay their taxes. They have the same rights to due process as citizens.

Legal permanent residents are not full members of the political community because there are some rights that are reserved for citizens. Only citizens may vote in national elections, hold public office, or serve on juries.

In most cases, legal permanent residents can become citizens. An adult permanent resident may apply for citizenship after living in the United States legally for five years. Before becoming a citizen, the person must pass a test to show that he or she understands the history and Constitution of the United States. The person must be of good moral character and demonstrate the ability to communicate in English. A person who gets his or her citizenship in this way is a **naturalized citizen**. The minor child of a naturalized citizen becomes a citizen of the United States when the parents do.

What are the rights of citizens?

There are three categories of rights that are important to democracy and to American citizens. These are personal rights, political rights, and economic rights.

Personal rights are those rights that allow a person to do as he or she wishes so long as those actions are consistent with the public order and do not interfere with the rights of others. The following are some personal rights:

- freedom to associate with whomever one pleases
- freedom of conscience and religion
- freedom of expression for creativity
- freedom to have children
- freedom to live where one chooses
- freedom to have privacy
- freedom to travel

Political rights are those rights that allow citizens to participate in the political process. Without these rights, democracy could not exist. The following are political rights:

- due process of law and fair procedures

- equal protection under the law

- freedom to examine the conduct of public officials

- freedom of expression for political purposes

- freedom of political association and assembly

- freedom to seek and hold public office

- freedom to serve on juries

- freedom to vote in free, fair, and regular elections

Economic rights are those rights needed to earn a living and to acquire and transfer property or to produce goods and services. The following are economic rights:

- freedom to acquire, use, and sell or give away property

- freedom to choose one's work

- freedom to enter into lawful contracts

- freedom to establish and operate a business

- freedom to join professional associations and labor unions

It is important to remember that it is reasonable and fair to place limits on most rights; they are not absolute. Most people argue that the only right that cannot be limited is freedom of belief. All other rights can be limited in certain situations. For example, you learned in an earlier lesson that freedom of expression

can be limited if and when it seriously harms or endangers others.

Some rights may be limited when they conflict with other rights or with other important values and interests. For example, the right to own and use property can conflict with our interest in having a safe and healthy environment.

What responsibilities accompany the basic rights of citizens?

With the rights of citizens of the United States come certain responsibilities. Citizens do not always agree on their responsibilities. Some responsibilities that Americans have agreed upon over the years are listed below.

Personal responsibilities are obligations that each person assumes individually. The following are examples of personal responsibilities:

- accepting the consequences of one's actions

- adhering to moral principles

- behaving in a civil manner

- considering the rights and interests of others

- supporting one's family

- taking care of one's self

Civic responsibilities are obligations that each person has to society. The following are examples of civic responsibilities:

- being informed about public issues

- voting and deciding how to vote

- keeping watch over political

What are some examples of your responsibilities as a citizen of the United States?

leaders and governmental agencies and taking appropriate action if they do not follow constitutional principles

- obeying the laws

- participating in civic groups

- paying taxes

- respecting the rights of others

- serving as a juror

- serving in the armed forces

Citizens must not only be aware of their rights. They must also learn to use their rights responsibly. Fulfilling personal and civic responsibilities is a necessity in a self-governing, free, and just society.

Must you obey a law you think is unjust?

When laws or governmental actions conflict with a citizen's views of what is right and wrong, the citizen faces a difficult decision. In our system of government, you have a right to try to have laws changed. There are many ways that you and others can work to change laws that you think are unjust. Until you get them changed, however, you are held responsible for obeying the laws.

Suppose a law requires you to do something you believe is wrong. Must you obey the law? Some people argue that since no government is perfect, a citizen's responsibility to obey the law has limits. In their view, if a law is unjust, the citizen has no responsibility to obey it.

Deciding to disobey a law is a serious step. Disobeying the law has consequences that the citizen must be prepared to accept. Such consequences might include paying fines and even going to jail.

Throughout history, many citizens have accepted the consequences of disobeying the law. In the 1800s the famous American philosopher Henry David Thoreau chose to go to jail rather than pay a tax to support slavery and the Mexican-American War. In the 1950s and 1960s, Dr. Martin Luther King Jr. and others chose to go to jail to protest racial segregation laws. During the Vietnam War, many young men burned their draft cards and refused to serve in the armed forces because they believed the war was unjust.

Why did Henry David Thoreau (above) and Dr. Martin Luther King Jr. (below) practice civil disobedience? What should a citizen consider before deciding to disobey the law?

What are your responsibilities as a citizen?

You have learned a great deal about our nation's government from studying this book. You also have learned about some of the rights and responsibilities of citizenship. You and all citizens will be faced with difficult decisions about your role in a democratic society.

What commitment are you willing to make to the basic principles of our government? How will you decide which of your rights, desires, or interests may have to take second place to your responsibility to the common good? It is your responsibility as a citizen to make these difficult decisions.

What responsibilities of citizens are portrayed in this picture?

What decision would you make?

Work in groups of three to five. Read the story, then work through each of the six steps that follow it. The step-by-step procedure can help you make a good decision. Finally, decide what you think Gail should do. Explain and defend your answer before the class.

A NEW SCHOOL POLICY

Gail was worried. Five of her friends were going to take part in a protest during the last period of school the next day. They were planning to demonstrate against the new school policy prohibiting the wearing of T-shirts with controversial slogans. Like her friends, Gail believed that this situation was unfair to the students. She believed that the T-shirts were legal and not vulgar or offensive. She felt strongly that this policy should be changed.

Gail was worried about what would happen if she joined the picket line. She worried that she might be suspended from school. If this happened it might affect her chances of being accepted by a college. She was also afraid that she might be arrested, especially if the demonstration got out of hand. An arrest on her record could keep her from getting a good job.

On the other hand, she wanted to show her views and help change what she thought was an unjust situation. What should Gail do?

1. What rights do you think Gail has in this situation?

2. What responsibilities accompany these rights?

3. What are some alternative actions that Gail might take to solve her problem or reach a decision?

4. List the advantages and disadvantages of each alternative.

5. Decide what you think should be done, considering the advantages and disadvantages of the alternatives.

6. Be prepared to explain the reasons for your decision and how that decision reflects the basic principles of our government.

After each group has presented its decision, you may wish to discuss the plans presented by the groups and vote to adopt the plan the majority favors. Or, discuss how the procedure above could be used in other situations in which citizens have to make difficult decisions.

Would you protest against a school policy that you thought was unfair, even at the risk of being suspended? Why or why not?

1. What does the term citizen mean?

2. Who is a citizen of the United States?

3. How can noncitizens acquire citizenship in this country?

4. What are the personal, political, and economic rights of citizens?

5. What responsibilities accompany our basic rights?

6. What are some consequences to consider when deciding whether to challenge a law that you think is unjust?

ACTIVITIES

1. Write a short essay in which you describe the qualities of good citizens in a constitutional democracy. Explain why you think these qualities are necessary.

2. Debate the following questions with groups of three or four students.

   - What should a person do when he or she thinks that a law is unjust? Give examples to support your opinion.

   - Suppose you cannot agree on what is in the common good. Should you pursue your own interests or still try to consider the interests of others? Explain your answer and provide examples.

3. Learn more about resident aliens in the United States. Use the Internet to do some research. In what regions of the country do a majority of resident aliens live? What motivates resident aliens to want to live in the United States?

4. Learn more about individuals who have become naturalized citizens of the United States. Here is a list of people you might want to research in your library or on the Internet.

   - Madeleine Albright
   - Albert Einstein
   - Marcus Garvey
   - Andrew S. Grove
   - Henry Kissinger
   - Chien-Shiung Wu

5. Develop a poster that illustrates the rights of citizens and the responsibilities that those rights carry.

6. Does modern technology make the right to privacy easier or harder to protect? Write a report to share with your class that deals with the issues of privacy today.

How might citizens participate in civic affairs?

LESSON PURPOSE

In this lesson you will learn about one of the most important rights of citizenship. This is the right to participate in governing our nation. In this lesson the different ways you might participate in your government and in voluntary organizations outside of government will be discussed. The lesson also suggests things to consider when deciding whether you should participate.

When you finish the lesson, you should be able to support your views on whether, and to what extent, a citizen should participate in government and in voluntary organizations.

civic life

civic participation

constitutional principle

influence

monitor

political action

social action

What role should citizens have in government?

As you learned in the last lesson, in the United States each citizen is a full and equal member of the political community. Each citizen has certain basic rights and responsibilities. You also learned that government and citizens are both responsible for protecting the rights of individuals. Both are also responsible for promoting the common good.

Citizens have other vital roles in our government. One important role that citizens fulfill is to monitor the decisions and actions of government. To **monitor** means to keep watch over something. Citizens monitor government to be informed about what the government is doing in their name. They also monitor government to ensure that it serves the purposes for which it was created.

Another important role of citizens is to attempt to influence the decisions and actions of government. To **influence** means to have an effect on or to cause changes in something. It is the right of citizens to try to influence the decisions and actions of government that affect our lives.

From where do you get the right to influence your government?

In a sense, citizenship is an office of government. Some people might say that it is the highest office of government because citizens are the source of government's authority. Like any other office, citizenship carries important responsibilities.

Civic participation means taking part in formal political processes and taking part in community activities outside of government. Millions of Americans participate in thousands of voluntary organizations and associations. These organizations seek to improve the life of the community in many different ways. Some benefit the poor, sick, or old people. Other organizations are concerned with the environment, health care, or the needs of children. They deal with many other community problems and issues.

Participating in these organizations gives community members the means to deal with community issues. It also allows them to participate in the way the organizations are run.

Government must deal with some matters such as arresting lawbreakers or establishing rules for building safety. There are other issues where government works with voluntary organizations to solve community problems. In other cases, voluntary organizations act by themselves to address community issues.

How much participation in government should citizens be willing to contribute?

Some citizens do not participate in government. They do not vote or take part in other ways. Some people, however, believe that citizens have a responsibility to participate.

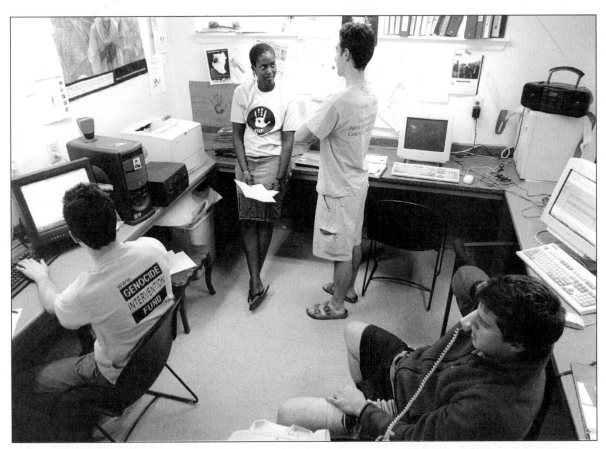

What might be the advantages or disadvantages of joining volunteer organizations to influence government?

How would you respond to a poorly fixed bike from the bike shop? Would you respond in a similar way to something the government had done poorly?

Deciding whether to participate in government and how much time to spend is important. To make good decisions, you must think about such things as

1. the purposes of government

2. how important your rights are to you

3. how satisfied you are with the way government is working

An example might help.

If you took your bike in for repairs, you would make sure that the shop repaired bicycles, not cars or toasters. Then when you claimed your bike, you would check it to make sure that they did what you had hired them to do.

If you thought they did a good job but your bike broke the next week, you might bring it back, but you would check or monitor their work more closely.

Suppose the shop wanted to do more repairs than those you requested. You would want to participate in making that decision. If you were denied the right to participate in the decision, you might be very upset, especially when you got the bill.

If the shop did a poor job on the repairs again, you would not go back nor would you recommend them to your friends. You might call various agencies to complain or you might even try to force them out of the bike repair business.

The same is true of government. We should make sure that the people we elect are capable of doing the job we are choosing them for. Once they get the job, we should monitor them to make sure they are doing their job of representing us correctly. If they do a good job, we might not watch them as closely. If they do a bad job, we might check them more closely and might even decide to replace them. Because our officials make decisions that affect us, we are entitled to participate in those decisions.

Of course, not all jobs have to be accomplished by government. Americans are famous for doing many things for themselves. We organize groups to accomplish any number of things. These include building neighborhood swimming pools, discussing foreign policy issues, or improving our communities in hundreds of ways. Participating in these activities is also civic participation.

Some citizens mostly participate in formal governmental processes. Others participate mostly in volunteer groups. Many citizens take part in both forms of civic activity. Americans realize how important civic participation is. When civic participation declines, our democracy declines. It is not just others who are responsible for the civic health of our democracy. We are all responsible.

What are some of the ways citizens can monitor the decisions and actions of government?

How might citizens participate in their government?

Civic life is the public life of citizens. Civic life is different, but not necessarily separate, from private or personal life. In our personal life, we concern ourselves with our particular interests, such as getting an education or having a good job. Our civic life, on the other hand, is concerned with our own interests as well as the common affairs and interests of our community and nation.

Civic life includes the things that we do to carry out our responsibilities and roles as citizens. One example of this is monitoring and influencing the decisions of government. Sometimes our actions can be both personal and civic. These include being a decision-maker or being a participant in nongovernmental organizations. For example, we might

- direct the activities or policies of organizations and associations. These could include voting for leaders or holding a leadership position yourself.

- take part in an organization's meetings and community activities such as rallies, fundraising, or writing, or handing out pamphlets and articles.

What are some examples of civic life?

Should citizens participate in their government?

One way to understand the role of citizens in government is to think about the basic principles of our Constitution. In this case, we are discussing constitutional principles. A **constitutional principle** is an essential idea that we as a nation believe about good government. These are principles that you have learned during your study of this text.

Work with a partner. Read aloud each of the basic principles of government listed below. Then respond to the three questions.

CONSTITUTIONAL PRINCIPLES

- common good
- consent of the governed
- constitutional government
- individual rights
- popular sovereignty
- representative government

❶ What is the meaning of each basic principle of government listed?

❷ What do each of these principles imply about the role of citizens in their government?

❸ What actions might citizens take to fulfill the roles of citizens that you have identified?

How might participating in government help us achieve our personal goals?

As individuals, we have personal goals that we would like to achieve, and that is one reason we participate in government.

Sometimes our personal goals are linked to the common good. A personal goal might be to get a good education. It is also in the common good that communities provide good schools so that everyone in the community can get a good education and be able to contribute to the community. Everyone should have the opportunity to realize that goal.

Suppose that you have four personal goals. They are to

- live in a safe and orderly neighborhood

- get a good education

- live in a healthy environment

- feel that you are a full member of your community and not an outsider

DISCUSS THESE QUESTIONS WITH A PARTNER

❶ Why are these goals important to you?

❷ How might these personal goals be related to the common good? In other words, how might your achievement of these goals help make our country better?

❸ How might your participation in government help you attain these goals for yourself and the community?

❹ How might your participation in civic life help you attain goals for yourself and the community?

How can we determine what serves the common good?

What are the advantages and disadvantages of participation in civic life?

In small groups read the list of ways in which citizens can participate in political and other forms of civic action. Then discuss the three questions at the end. Share your responses with your class.

WAYS CITIZENS CAN PARTICIPATE

- looking for information about government officials and activities in newspapers, magazines, the Internet, and reference materials and judging its accuracy

- voting in local, state, and national elections

- participating in political discussions

- signing a petition

- writing letters to elected representatives

- contributing money to a political party or candidate

- attending meetings to gain information, discuss issues, or lend support

- campaigning for a candidate

- lobbying for laws that are of special interest to you

- taking part in marches, boycotts, sit-ins, or other forms of protest

- serving as a juror

- running for public office

- holding public office

- serving the country through military or other service

- joining independent civic groups and attending meetings

- holding office in and giving financial support to independent civic groups

- taking part in solving public problems by joining voluntary groups, independent of or in cooperation with government

- discussing civic problems and issues informally with friends and neighbors

- becoming informed by reading, watching television programs, or doing Internet research about public problems by yourself or with others

1. What are the advantages and disadvantages of each form of participation given?

2. Are all these forms of participation equally important in protecting our basic rights and the common good? Why or why not?

3. In which of these activities are you most likely to participate?

What is political action and what is social action?

There are two general ways that citizens can address problems in the community through participation in civic life. They are social action and political action.

Political action comes in two forms: formal and informal.

- Formal political action means voting in elections, petitioning government officials, seeking and holding public office, and similar activities.

- Informal political action means face-to-face meetings with public officials, writing to newspapers stating your opinion on issues, conducting email or telephone campaigns, attending marches and demonstrations, and similar activities.

There is a wide range of political actions that citizens can engage in when attempting to influence the actions of government. These actions are relevant at local, state, and national levels.

To help solve a crime problem you might meet with government officials requesting that they provide more police services to protect your neighborhood. In dealing with poverty, you might create a government program such as a food bank to feed the hungry. Then you might work to get government to adopt and pay for the program.

Social action means that individuals and groups solve community problems without relying on government to do it

for them. If you are dealing with crime in your neighborhood, you might form a neighborhood watch group. If you are dealing with poverty, you might work in a food bank organized by a charitable organization.

Why should I participate in the affairs of my community?

Participation in government is in our self-interest. The amount of time spent participating will probably depend on how well we think our elected officials are doing. When everything is going well, we might spend less time. If we are pleased with government, we might vote and do little else. When we are concerned

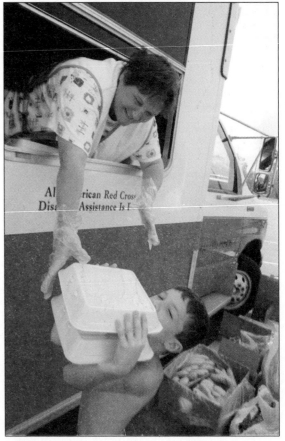

What are some examples of social action?

that government is not meeting our needs or is violating our rights, we might spend more time. If we are dissatisfied, we might engage in a variety of types of action.

Citizens must actively participate in the civic life of their community and nation if they want their voices heard. Citizenship in a democracy is more than a legal status. Democratic citizenship is a way of life that guides our relationships with other people and with government.

Democracy can exist only if it lives in the minds and hearts of its citizens. Citizens should do more than say they are committed to democracy. They should demonstrate their commitment by their participation. It is up to each citizen to determine the level and nature of her or his participation in the civic life of the community and nation.

At the end of the Constitutional Convention, Mrs. Samuel Powell asked Benjamin Franklin "Well, Doctor, what have we got, a Republic or a Monarchy?" Franklin replied, "A Republic, if you can keep it."

From the notes of James McHenry, delegate from Maryland

1. How is political action different from social action?

2. Why are both political and social action necessary?

3. How is citizen participation in political action related to the purposes of our government?

4. Explain why participating in government is in our self-interest.

1. Make a poster that demonstrates the different ways that citizens can participate in government. Take your own photos or use photographs from newspapers and magazines to illustrate each idea on your poster.

2. Use the Internet to find information about political action groups in your community that work to monitor and influence the decisions and actions of government.

3. Use the Internet to find information about social action groups in your community that work to address local community problems.

4. Monitor the newspaper in your community for one week. Look for articles that describe citizens participating in local, state, or national government.

5. Justice Louis Brandeis of the U.S. Supreme Court wrote, "The only title in our democracy superior to that of President is the title of citizen." Do you think that Justice Brandeis was correct? Write a short essay explaining your opinion.

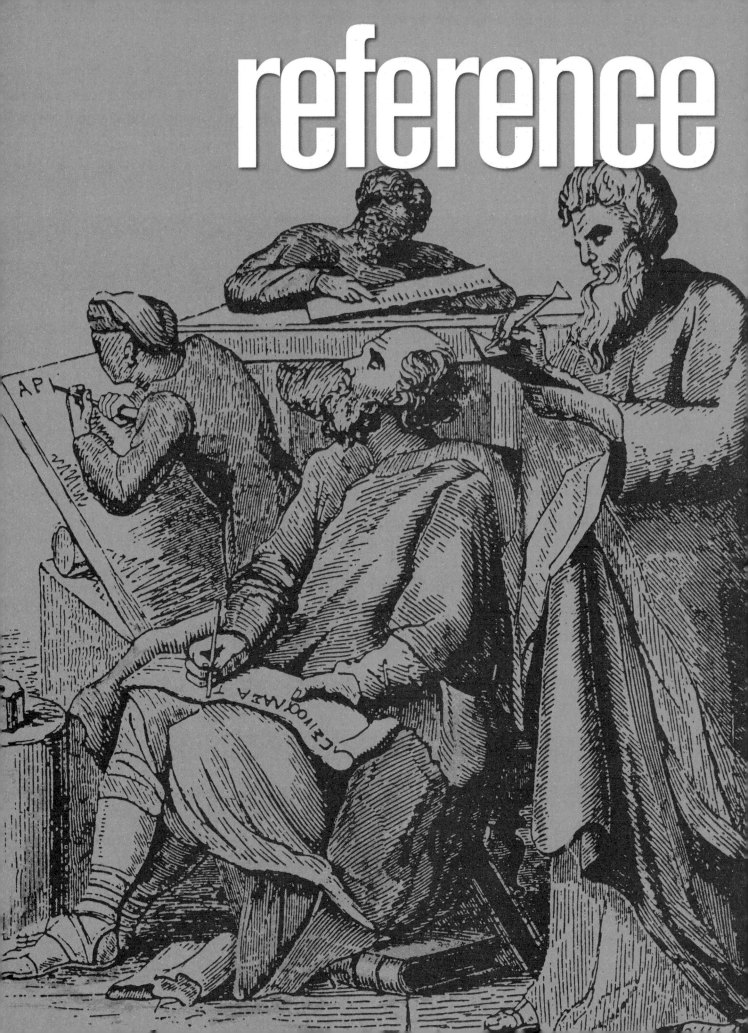

reference

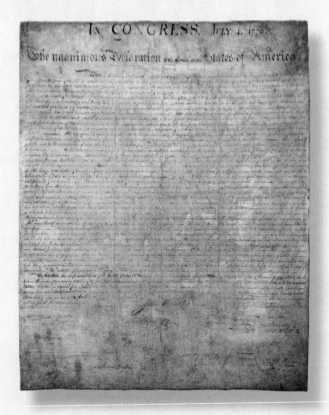

**In CONGRESS,
July 4, 1776.
The unanimous
Declaration of the
thirteen united
States of America,**

WHEN in the Course of human Events, it becomes necessary for one People to dissolve the Political Bands which have connected them with another, and to assume among the Powers of the Earth, the separate and equal Station to which the Laws of Nature and of Nature's God entitle them, a decent Respect to the Opinions of Mankind requires that they should declare the causes which impel them to the Separation.

We hold these Truths to be self-evident, that all Men are created equal, that they are endowed by their Creator with certain unalienable Rights, that among these are Life, Liberty, and the Pursuit of Happiness—That to secure these Rights, Governments are instituted among Men, deriving their just Powers from the Consent of the Governed, that whenever any Form of Government becomes destructive of these Ends it is the Right of the People to alter or to abolish it, and to institute new Government, laying its Foundation on such Principles, and organizing its Powers in such Form, as to them shall seem most likely to effect their Safety and Happiness. Prudence, indeed, will dictate that Governments long established should not be changed for light and transient Causes; and accordingly all Experience hath shewn, that Mankind are more disposed to suffer, while Evils are sufferable, than to right themselves by abolishing the Forms to which they are accustomed. But when a long Train of Abuses and Usurpations, pursuing invariably the same Object, evinces a Design to reduce them under absolute Despotism, it is their Right, it is their Duty, to throw off such Government, and to provide new Guards for their future Security. Such has been the patient Sufferance of these Colonies; and such is now the Necessity which constrains them to alter their former Systems of Government. The History of the present King of Great-Britain is a History of repeated Injuries and Usurpations, all having in direct Object the Establishment of an absolute Tyranny over these States. To prove this, let Facts be submitted to a candid World.

He has refused his Assent to Laws, the most wholesome and necessary for the public Good.

He has forbidden his Governors to pass Laws of immediate and pressing Importance, unless suspended in their Operation till his Assent should be obtained; and when so suspended, he has utterly neglected to attend to them.

He has refused to pass other Laws for the Accommodation of large Districts of People, unless those People would relinquish the Right of Representation in the Legislature, a Right inestimable to them, and formidable to Tyrants only.

He has called together Legislative Bodies at Places unusual, uncomfortable, and distant from the Depository of their public Records, for the sole Purpose of fatiguing them into Compliance with his Measures.

He has dissolved Representative Houses repeatedly, for opposing with manly Firmness his Invasions on the Rights of the People.

He has refused for a long Time, after such Dissolutions, to cause others to be elected; whereby the Legislative Powers, incapable of Annihilation, have returned to the People at large for their exercise; the State remaining in the mean time exposed to all the Dangers of Invasions from without, and Convulsions within.

He has endeavored to prevent the Population of these States; for that Purpose obstructing the Laws for Naturalization of Foreigners; refusing to pass others to encourage their Migrations hither, and raising the Conditions of new Appropriations of Lands.

He has obstructed the Administration of Justice, by refusing his Assent to Laws for establishing Judiciary Powers.

He has made Judges dependent on his Will alone, for the Tenure of their Offices, and the Amount and Payment of their Salaries.

He has erected a Multitude of new Offices, and sent hither Swarms of Officers to harass our People and eat out their Substance.

He has kept among us, in Times of Peace, Standing Armies, without the consent of our Legislatures.

He has affected to render the Military independent of and superior to the Civil Power.

He has combined with others to subject us to a Jurisdiction foreign to our Constitution, and unacknowledged by our Laws; giving his Assent to their Acts of pretended Legislation:

For quartering large Bodies of Armed Troops among us:

For protecting them, by a mock Trial, from Punishment for any Murders which they should commit on the Inhabitants of these States:

For cutting off our Trade with all Parts of the World:

For imposing Taxes on us without our Consent:

For depriving us, in many Cases, of the Benefits of Trial by Jury:

For transporting us beyond Seas to be tried for pretended Offenses:

For abolishing the free System of English Laws in a neighbouring Province, establishing therein an Arbitrary Government, and enlarging its Boundaries, so as to render it at once an Example and fit Instrument for introducing the same absolute Rule into these Colonies:

For taking away our Charters, abolishing our most valuable Laws, and altering fundamentally the Forms of our Governments:

For suspending our own Legislatures, and declaring themselves invested with Power to legislate for us in all Cases whatsoever.

He has abdicated Government here, by declaring us out of his Protection and waging War against us.

He has plundered our Seas, ravaged our Coasts, burnt our Towns, and destroyed the Lives of our People.

He is, at this Time, transporting large Armies of foreign Mercenaries to compleat the Works of Death, Desolation, and Tyranny, already begun with circumstances of Cruelty and Perfidy, scarcely paralleled in the most barbarous Ages, and totally unworthy the Head of a civilized Nation.

He has constrained our fellow Citizens taken Captive on the high Seas to bear Arms against their Country, to become the Executioners of their Friends and Brethren, or to fall themselves by their Hands.

He has excited domestic Insurrections amongst us, and has endeavoured to bring on the Inhabitants of our Frontiers, the merciless Indian Savages, whose known Rule of Warfare, is an undistinguished Destruction, of all Ages, Sexes and Conditions.

In every stage of these Oppressions we have Petitioned for Redress in the most humble Terms: Our repeated Petitions have been answered only by repeated Injury. A Prince, whose Character is thus marked by every act which may define a Tyrant, is unfit to be the Ruler of a free People.

Nor have we been wanting in Attentions to our British Brethren. We have warned them from Time to Time of Attempts by their Legislature to extend an unwarrantable Jurisdiction over us. We have reminded them of the Circumstances of our Emigration and Settlement here. We have appealed to their native Justice and Magnanimity, and we have conjured them by the Ties of our common Kindred to disavow these Usurpations, which, would inevitably interrupt our Connections and Correspondence. They too have been deaf to the Voice of Justice and of Consanguinity. We must, therefore, acquiesce in the Necessity, which denounces our Separation, and hold them, as we hold the rest of Mankind, Enemies in War, in Peace, Friends.

We, therefore, the Representatives of the UNITED STATES OF AMERICA, in GENERAL CONGRESS, Assembled, appealing to the Supreme Judge of the World for the Rectitude of our Intentions, do, in the Name, and by Authority of the good People of these Colonies, solemnly Publish and Declare, That these United Colonies are, and of Right ought to be, FREE AND INDEPENDENT STATES; that they are absolved from all Allegiance to the British Crown, and that all political Connection between them and the State of Great Britain, is and ought to be totally dissolved; and that as FREE AND INDEPENDENT STATES, they have full Power to levy War, conclude Peace, contract Alliances, establish Commerce, and to do all other Acts and Things which INDEPENDENT STATES may of right do. And for the support of this Declaration, with a firm Reliance on the Protection of divine Providence, we mutually pledge to each other our Lives, our Fortunes, and our sacred Honor.

Signed by ORDER and
in BEHALF of the CONGRESS,

JOHN HANCOCK, PRESIDENT.

New-Hampshire

Josiah Bartlett,
Wm. Whipple,
Matthew Thornton.

Massachusetts-Bay

Saml. Adams,
John Adams,
Robt. Treat Paine,
Elbridge Gerry.

Rhode-Island and Providence, &c.

Step. Hopkins,
William Ellery.

Connecticut

Roger Sherman,
Saml. Huntington,
Wm. Williams,
Oliver Wolcott.

New-York

Wm. Floyd,
Phil. Livingston,
Frans. Lewis,
Lewis Morris.

New-Jersey

Richd. Stockton,
Jno. Witherspoon,
Fras. Hopkinson,
John Hart,
Abra. Clark.

Pennsylvania

Robt. Morris,
Benjamin Rush,
Benja. Franklin,
John Morton,
Geo. Clymer,
Jas. Smith,
Geo. Taylor,
James Wilson,
Geo. Ross.

Delaware

Casar Rodney,
Geo. Read,
(Tho M·Kean.)

Maryland

Samuel Chase,
Wm. Paca,
Thos. Stone,
Charles Carroll,
of Carrollton.

Virginia

George Wythe,
Richard Henry Lee,
Ths. Jefferson,
Benja. Harrison,
Thos. Nelson, jr.,
Francis Lightfoot Lee,
Carter Braxton.

North-Carolina

Wm. Hooper,
Joseph Hewes,
John Penn.

South-Carolina

Edward Rutledge,
Thos. Heyward, junr.,
Thomas Lynch, junr.,
Arthur Middleton.

Georgia

Button Gwinnett,
Lyman Hall,
Geo. Walton.

PREAMBLE

We the People of the United States, in Order to form a more perfect Union, establish Justice, insure domestic tranquility, provide for the common defense, promote the general Welfare, and secure the Blessings of Liberty to ourselves and our Posterity, do ordain and establish this Constitution for the United States of America.

ARTICLE I

The Legislative Branch

Section 1

All legislative Powers herein granted shall be vested in a Congress of the United States, which shall consist of a Senate and House of Representatives.

Section 2

House of Representatives: Organization and Power of Impeachment

1. The House of Representatives shall be composed of Members chosen every second Year by the People of the several States, and the Electors in each State shall have the Qualifications requisite for Electors of the most numerous Branch of the State Legislature.

2. No Person shall be a Representative who shall not have attained to the Age of twenty five Years, and been seven Years a Citizen of the United States, and who shall not, when elected, be an Inhabitant of that State in which he shall be chosen.

3. [Representatives and direct Taxes shall be apportioned among the several States which may be included within this Union, according to their respective Numbers, which shall be determined by adding to the whole Number of free Persons, including those bound to Service for a Term of Years, and excluding Indians not taxed, three fifths of all other Persons.]* The actual Enumeration shall be made within three Years after the first Meeting of the Congress of the United States, and within every subsequent Term of ten Years, in such Manner as they shall by Law direct. The number of Representatives shall not exceed one for every thirty Thousand, but each State shall have at Least one Representative; and until such enumeration shall be made, the State of New Hampshire shall be entitled to choose three, Massachusetts eight, Rhode Island and Providence Plantations one, Connecticut five, New York six, New Jersey four, Pennsylvania eight, Delaware one, Maryland six, Virginia ten, North Carolina five, South Carolina five, and Georgia three.

4. When vacancies happen in the Representation from any State, the Executive Authority thereof shall issue Writs of Election to fill such Vacancies.

5. The House of Representatives shall choose their Speaker and other Officers; and shall have the sole Power of Impeachment.

Section 3

The Senate, Organization and Powers to Try Cases of Impeachment

1. The Senate of the United States shall be composed of two Senators from each State, chosen [by the Legislature thereof,]** for six Years; and each Senator shall have one Vote.

2. Immediately after they shall be assembled in Consequence of the first Election, they shall be divided as equally as may be into three Classes. The seats of the Senators of the first Class shall be vacated at the Expiration of the second Year, of the second Class at the Expiration of the fourth Year, and of the third Class at the Expiration of the sixth Year, so that one third may be chosen every second Year; [and if Vacancies happen by Resignation, or otherwise, during the Recess of the Legislature of any State, the Executive thereof may make temporary Appointments until the next Meeting of the Legislature, which shall then fill such Vacancies.]**

3. No Person shall be a Senator who shall not have attained to the Age of thirty Years, and been nine Years a Citizen of the United States, and who shall not, when elected, be an Inhabitant of that State for which he shall be chosen.

4. The Vice President of the United States shall be President of the Senate, but shall have no Vote, unless they be equally divided.

*Changed by Section 2 of the Fourteenth Amendment

**Changed by the Seventeenth Amendment

5. The Senate shall choose their other officers, and also a President pro tempore, in the Absence of the Vice President, or when he shall exercise the Office of President of the United States.

6. The Senate shall have the sole Power to try all Impeachments. When sitting for that Purpose, they shall be on Oath or Affirmation. When the President of the United States is tried, the Chief Justice shall preside; And no person shall be convicted without the Concurrence of two thirds of the Members present.

7. Judgment in Cases of Impeachment shall not extend further than to removal from Office, and disqualification to hold and enjoy any Office of honor, Trust or Profit under the United States; but the Party convicted shall nevertheless be liable and subject to Indictment, Trial, Judgment and Punishment, according to Law.

Section 4

Elections and Meeting of Congress

1. The Times, Places and Manner of holding Elections for Senators and Representatives shall be prescribed in each State by the Legislature thereof; but the Congress may at any time by Law make or alter such Regulations, except as to the Places of choosing Senators.

2. The Congress shall assemble at least once in every Year, and such Meeting shall be [on the first Monday in December,]* unless they shall by Law appoint a different Day.

Section 5

Congress's Rules of Procedure, Powers, Quorum, Journals, Meetings, Adjournments

1. Each House shall be the Judge of the Elections, Returns and Qualifications of its own Members, and a Majority of each shall constitute a Quorum to do Business; but a smaller Number may adjourn from day to day, and may be authorized to compel the Attendance of absent Members, in such Manner, and under such Penalties as each House may provide.

2. Each House may determine the Rules of its Proceedings, punish its members for disorderly Behavior, and, with the Concurrence of two thirds, expel a Member.

3. Each House shall keep a Journal of its Proceedings, and from time to time publish the same, excepting such Parts as may in their Judgement require Secrecy; and the Yeas and Nays of the Members of either House on any question shall, at the Desire of one fifth of those Present, be entered on the Journal.

4. Neither House, during the Session of Congress, shall, without the Consent of the other, adjourn for more than three days, nor to any other Place than that in which the two Houses shall be sitting.

*Changed by Section 2 of the Twentieth Amendment

Section 6

Pay, Privileges, Limitations

1. The Senators and Representatives shall receive a Compensation for their Services, to be ascertained by Law, and paid out of the Treasury of the United States. They shall in all cases, except Treason, Felony and Breach of the Peace, be privileged from Arrest during their Attendance at the Session of their respective Houses, and in going to and returning from the same; and for any Speech or Debate in either House, they shall not be questioned in any other Place.

2. No Senator or Representative shall, during the Time for which he was elected, be appointed to any civil Office under the Authority of the United States, which shall have been created, or the Emoluments whereof shall have been increased during such time; and no Person holding any Office under the United States, shall be a Member of either House during his Continuance in Office.

Section 7

Procedure in Passing Bills, President's Veto Power

1. All Bills for raising Revenue shall originate in the House of Representatives; but the Senate may propose or concur with Amendments as on other Bills.

2. Every Bill which shall have passed the House of Representatives and the Senate, shall, before it becomes a Law, be presented to the President of the United States; if he approves he shall sign it, but if not he shall return it, with his Objections, to that House in which it shall have originated, who shall enter the Objections at large on their Journal, and proceed to reconsider it. If after such Reconsideration two thirds of that House shall agree to pass the Bill, it shall be sent, together with the Objections, to the other House, by which it shall likewise be reconsidered, and if approved by two thirds of that House, it shall become a Law. But in all such Cases the Votes of both Houses shall be determined by Yeas and Nays, and the Names of the Persons voting for and against the Bill shall be entered on the Journal of each House respectively. If any Bill shall not be returned by the President within ten Days (Sundays excepted) after it shall have been presented to him, the Same shall be a Law, in like Manner as if he had signed it, unless the Congress by their Adjournment prevent its Return, in which Case it shall not be a Law.

3. Every Order, Resolution, or Vote to which the Concurrence of the Senate and House of Representatives may be necessary (except on a question of Adjournment) shall be presented to the President of the United States; and before the Same shall take Effect, shall be approved by him, or being disapproved by him, shall be repassed by two thirds of the Senate and House of Representatives, according to the Rules and Limitations prescribed in the Case of a Bill.

Section 8

Powers Delegated to Congress

The Congress shall have Power

1. To lay and collect Taxes, Duties, Imposts and Excises, to pay the Debts and provide for the common Defense and general Welfare of the United States; but all Duties, Imposts and Excises shall be uniform throughout the United States;

2. To borrow Money on the credit of the United States;

3. To regulate Commerce with foreign Nations, and among the several States, and with the Indian Tribes;

4. To establish a uniform Rule of Naturalization, and uniform Laws on the subject of Bankruptcies throughout the United States;

5. To coin Money, regulate the Value thereof, and of foreign Coin, and fix the Standard of Weights and Measures;

6. To provide for the Punishment of counterfeiting the Securities and current Coin of the United States;

7. To establish Post Offices and post Roads;

8. To promote the Progress of Science and useful Arts, by securing for limited Times to Authors and Inventors the exclusive Right to their respective Writings and Discoveries;

9. To constitute Tribunals inferior to the Supreme Court;

10. To define and punish Piracies and Felonies committed on the high Seas, and Offenses against the Law of Nations;

11. To declare War, grant Letters of Marque and Reprisal, and make Rules concerning Captures on Land and Water;

12. To raise and support Armies, but no Appropriation of Money to that Use shall be for a longer Term than two Years;

13. To provide and maintain a Navy;

14. To make Rules for the Government and Regulation of the land and naval Forces;

15. To provide for calling forth the Militia to execute the Laws of the Union, suppress Insurrections and repel Invasions;

16. To provide for organizing, arming, and disciplining the Militia, and for governing such Part of them as may be employed in the Service of the United States, reserving to the States respectively, the Appointment of the Officers, and the Authority of training the Militia according to the discipline prescribed by Congress;

17. To exercise exclusive Legislation in all Cases whatsoever, over such District (not exceeding ten Miles square) as may, by Session of particular States, and the Acceptance of Congress, become the Seat of the Government of the United States, and to exercise like Authority over all Places purchased by the

Consent of the Legislature of the State in which the Same shall be, for the Erection of Forts, Magazines, Arsenals, dock-Yards and other needful Buildings;—and

18. To make all Laws which shall be necessary and proper for carrying into Execution the foregoing Powers, and all other Powers vested by this Constitution in the Government of the United States, or in any Department or Officer thereof.

Section 9

Powers Denied to Congress

1. The Migration or Importation of such Persons as any of the States now existing shall think proper to admit, shall not be prohibited by the Congress prior to the Year one thousand eight hundred and eight, but a Tax or duty may be imposed on such Importation, not exceeding ten dollars for each Person.

2. The Privilege of the Writ of Habeas Corpus shall not be suspended, unless when in Cases of Rebellion or Invasion the public Safety may require it.

3. No Bill of Attainder or ex post facto Law shall be passed.

4. [No Capitation, or other direct, Tax shall be laid, unless in Proportion to the Census or Enumeration herein before directed to be taken.]*

5. No Tax or Duty shall be laid on Articles exported from any State.

6. No Preference shall be given by any Regulation of Commerce or Revenue to the Ports of one State over those of another; nor shall Vessels bound to, or from, one State, be obliged to enter, clear, or pay Duties in another.

7. No Money shall be drawn from the Treasury, but in Consequence of Appropriations made by Law; and a regular Statement and Account of the Receipts and Expenditures of all public Money shall be published from time to time.

8. No Title of Nobility shall be granted by the United States: And no Person holding any Office of Profit or Trust under them, shall, without the Consent of the Congress, accept of any present, Emolument, Office, or Title, of any kind whatever, from any King, Prince, or foreign State.

Section 10

Restrictions on States' Powers

1. No State shall enter into any Treaty, Alliance, or Confederation; grant Letters of Marque and Reprisal; coin Money; emit Bills of Credit; make any Thing but gold and silver Coin a Tender in Payment of Debts; pass any Bill of Attainder, ex post facto Law, or Law impairing the Obligation of Contracts, or grant any Title of Nobility.

2. No State shall, without the Consent of the Congress, lay any Imposts or Duties on Imports or Exports, except what may be absolutely necessary for executing its inspection Laws:

*Changed by the Sixteenth Amendment

and the net Produce of all Duties and Imposts, laid by any State on Imports or Exports, shall be for the Use of the Treasury of the United States; and all such Laws shall be subject to the Revision and Control of the Congress.

3. No State shall, without the Consent of Congress, lay any Duty of Tonnage, keep Troops, or Ships of War in time of Peace, enter into any Agreement or Compact with another State, or with a foreign Power, or engage in War, unless actually invaded, or in such imminent Danger as will not admit of delay.

ARTICLE II

The Executive Branch

Section 1

President and Vice President: Election, Qualifications, and Oath

1. The executive Power shall be vested in a President of the United States of America. He shall hold his Office during the term of four Years, and, together with the Vice President, chosen for the same Term, be elected, as follows.

2. Each State shall appoint, in such Manner as the Legislature thereof may direct, a Number of Electors, equal to the whole Number of Senators and Representatives to which the State may be entitled in the Congress: but no Senator or Representative, or Person holding an Office of Trust or Profit under the United States, shall be appointed an Elector.

3. [The Electors shall meet in their respective states, and vote by Ballot for two Persons, of whom one at least shall not be an Inhabitant of the same State with themselves. And they shall make a List of all the Persons voted for, and of the Number of Votes for each; which List they shall sign and certify, and transmit sealed to the Seat of the Government of the United States, directed to the President of the Senate. The President of the Senate shall, in the Presence of the Senate and House of Representatives, open all the Certificates, and the Votes shall then be counted. The Person having the greatest Number of Votes shall be the President, if such Number be a Majority of the whole Number of Electors appointed; and if there be more than one who have such Majority, and have an equal Number of Votes, then the House of Representatives shall immediately choose by Ballot one of them for President; and if no Person have a Majority, then from the five highest on the List the said House shall in like manner choose the President. But in choosing the President, the Votes shall be taken by States, the Representation from each State having one Vote; A quorum for this Purpose shall consist of a Member or Members from two thirds of the States, and a Majority of all the States shall be necessary to a Choice. In every Case, after the Choice of the President, the Person having the greatest Number of Votes of the Electors shall be the Vice President. But if

there should remain two or more who have equal Votes, the Senate shall choose from them by Ballot the Vice President.]*

4. The Congress may determine the Time of choosing the Electors, and the day on which they shall give their Votes; which Day shall be the same throughout the United States.

5. No Person except a natural born Citizen, or a Citizen of the United States at the time of the Adoption of this Constitution, shall be eligible to the Office of the President; neither shall any person be eligible to that Office who shall not have attained to the Age of thirty five Years, and been fourteen Years a Resident within the United States.

6. [In Case of the Removal of the President from Office, or of his Death, Resignation, or Inability to discharge the Powers and Duties of the said Office, the Same shall devolve on the Vice President, and the Congress may by Law provide for the Case of Removal Death, Resignation or Inability, both of the President and Vice President, declaring what Officer shall then act as President, and such Officer shall act accordingly, until the Disability be removed, or a President shall be elected.]**

7. The President shall, at stated Times, receive for his Services, a Compensation, which shall neither be increased nor diminished during the Period for which he shall have been elected, and he shall not receive within that Period any other Emolument from the United States, or any of them.

8. Before he enter the Execution of his Office, he shall take the following Oath or Affirmation:—"I do solemnly swear (or affirm) that I will faithfully execute the Office of President of the United States, and will to the best of my Ability, preserve, protect, and defend the Constitution of the United States."

Section 2

Powers of the President

1. The President shall be Commander in Chief of the Army and Navy of the United States, and of the Militia of the several States, when called into the actual Service of the United States; he may require the Opinion, in writing, of the principal Officer in each of the executive Departments, upon any Subject relating to the Duties of their respective Offices, and he shall have Power to grant Reprieves and Pardons for Offenses against the United States, except in Cases of Impeachment.

2. He shall have Power, by and with the Advice and Consent of the Senate, to make Treaties, provided two thirds of the Senators present concur; and he shall nominate, and by and with the Advice and Consent of the Senate, shall appoint Ambassadors, other public Ministers and Consuls, Judges of the supreme Court, and all other Officers of the United States, whose Appointments are not herein otherwise provided for, and which shall be

*Changed by the Twelfth Amendment
**Changed by the Twenty-fifth Amendment

established by Law: but the Congress may by Law vest the Appointment of such inferior Officers, as they think proper, in the President alone, in the Courts of Law, or in the Heads of Departments.

3. The President shall have Power to fill up all Vacancies that may happen during the Recess of the Senate, by granting Commissions which shall expire at the End of their next Session.

Section 3

Duties of the President

He shall from time to time give to the Congress Information of the State of the Union, and recommend to their Consideration such Measures as he shall judge necessary and expedient; he may, on extraordinary Occasions, convene both Houses, or either of them, and in Case of Disagreement between them, with Respect to the Time of Adjournment, he may adjourn them to such Time as he shall think proper; he shall receive Ambassadors and other public Ministers; he shall take Care that the Laws be faithfully executed, and shall Commission all the Officers of the United States.

Section 4

Impeachment and Removal from Office for Crimes

The President, Vice President and all civil Officers of the United States, shall be removed from Office on Impeachment for, and Conviction of, Treason, Bribery, or other high Crimes and Misdemeanors.

ARTICLE III

The Judicial Branch

Section 1

Federal Courts, Tenure of Office

The judicial Power of the United States, shall be vested in one supreme Court, and in such inferior Courts as the Congress may from time to time ordain and establish. The Judges, both of the supreme and inferior Courts, shall hold their Offices during good Behavior, and shall, at stated Times, receive for their Services a Compensation, which shall not be diminished during their Continuance in Office.

Section 2

Jurisdiction of Federal Courts

1. The judicial Power shall extend to all Cases, in Law and Equity, arising under this Constitution, the Laws of the United States, and Treaties made, or which shall be made, under their Authority;—to all Cases affecting Ambassadors, other public Ministers and Consuls; —to all Cases of admiralty and maritime Jurisdiction;—to Controversies to which the United States shall be a Party;—to Controversies between two or more States; [between a State and Citizens of another State;]* between Citizens of different States;—between Citizens of the same State claiming Lands under Grants of different States;—[and between a State, or the Citizens thereof, and foreign States, Citizens or Subjects.]*

*Changed by the Eleventh Amendment

2. In all Cases affecting Ambassadors, other public Ministers and Consuls, and those in which a State shall be Party, the supreme Court shall have original Jurisdiction. In all the other Cases before mentioned, the supreme Court shall have appellate Jurisdiction, both as to Law and Fact, with such Exceptions, and under such Regulations as the Congress shall make.

3. The Trial of all Crimes, except in Cases of Impeachment, shall be by Jury; and such Trial shall be held in the State where said Crimes shall have been committed; but when not committed within any State, the Trial shall be at such Place or Places as the Congress may by Law have directed.

Section 3

Treason: Conviction Of and Punishment For

1. Treason against the United States shall consist only in levying War against them, or in adhering to their Enemies, giving them Aid and Comfort. No Person shall be convicted of Treason unless on the Testimony of two Witnesses to the same overt Act, or on Confession in open Court.

2. The Congress shall have Power to declare the Punishment of Treason, but no Attainder of Treason shall work Corruption of Blood, or Forfeiture except during the Life of the Person attainted.

ARTICLE IV

Relations among the States

Section 1

Full Faith and Credit

Full Faith and Credit shall be given in each State to the public Acts, Records, and judicial Proceedings of every other State; And the Congress may by general Laws prescribe the manner in which such Acts, Records and Proceedings shall be proved, and the Effect thereof.

Section 2

Rights of State Citizens; Right of Extradition

1. The Citizens of each State shall be entitled to all Privileges and Immunities of Citizens in the several States.

2. A Person charged in any State with Treason, Felony, or other Crime, who shall flee from Justice, and be found in another State, shall on Demand of the executive Authority of the State from which he fled, be delivered up, to be removed to the State having Jurisdiction of the Crime.

3. [No person held to Service or Labour in one State, under the Laws thereof, escaping into another, shall, in Consequence of any Law or Regulation therein, be discharged from such Service or Labour, but shall be delivered up on Claim of the Party to whom such Service or Labour may be due.]*

*Changed by the Thirteenth Amendment

Section 3

Admission of New States

1. New States may be admitted by the Congress into this Union; but no new State shall be formed or erected within the Jurisdiction of any other State; nor any State be formed by the Junction of two or more States, or parts of States, without the Consent of the Legislatures of the States concerned as well as of the Congress.

2. The Congress shall have Power to dispose of and make all needful Rules and Regulations respecting the territory or other Property belonging to the United States; and nothing in this Constitution shall be so construed as to Prejudice any Claims of the United States, or of any particular State.

Section 4

Republican Government Guaranteed

The United States shall guarantee to every State in this Union a Republican Form of Government, and shall protect each of them against Invasion; and on Application of the Legislature, or of the Executive (when the Legislature cannot be convened) against domestic Violence.

ARTICLE V

Amendment Procedures

The Congress, whenever two thirds of both Houses shall deem it necessary, shall propose Amendments to this Constitution, or, on the Application of the Legislatures of two thirds of the several States, shall call a Convention for proposing Amendments, which, in either Case, shall be valid to all Intents and Purposes, as Part of this Constitution, when ratified by the Legislatures of three fourths of the several States, or by Conventions in three fourths thereof, as the one or the other Mode of Ratification may be proposed by the Congress; Provided that no Amendment which may be made prior to the Year One thousand eight hundred and eight shall in any Manner affect the first and fourth Clauses in the Ninth Section of the first Article; and that no State, without its Consent, shall be deprived of its equal Suffrage in the Senate.

ARTICLE VI

Supremacy of the Constitution and Federal Laws

1. All debts contracted and Engagements entered into, before the Adoption of this Constitution, shall be as valid against the United States under this Constitution, as under the Confederation.

2. This Constitution, and the Laws of the United States which shall be made in Pursuance thereof; and all Treaties made, or which shall be

made, under the Authority of the United States, shall be the supreme Law of the Land; and the Judges in every State shall be bound thereby, any Thing in the Constitution or Laws of any State to the Contrary notwithstanding.

3. The Senators and Representatives before mentioned, and the Members of the several State Legislatures, and all executive and judicial Officers, both of the United States and of the several States, shall be bound by Oath or Affirmation, to support this Constitution; but no religious Test shall ever be required as a Qualification to any Office or public Trust under the United States.

ARTICLE VII
Ratification

The Ratification of the Conventions of nine States, shall be sufficient for the Establishment of this Constitution between the States so ratifying the Same.

Done in Convention by the unanimous consent of the States present the seventeenth day of September in the year of our Lord one thousand seven hundred and eighty seven and of the Independence of the United States of America the Twelfth. In witness whereof we have hereunto subscribed our Names,

President and deputy from Virginia

George Washington

New-Hampshire

John Langdon
Nicholas Gilman

Massachusetts

Nathaniel Gorham
Rufus King

Connecticut

William Samuel Johnson
Roger Sherman

New York

Alexander Hamilton

New Jersey

William Livingston
David Brearley
William Paterson
Jonathan Dayton

Pennsylvania

Benjamin Franklin
Thomas Mifflin
Robert Morris
George Clymer
Thomas Fitzsimons
Jared Ingersoll
James Wilson
Gouverneur Morris

Delaware

George Read
Gunning Bedford, Jr.
John Dickinson
Richard Bassett
Jacob Broom

Maryland

James McHenry
Daniel of St. Tho. Jenifer
Daniel Carroll

Virginia

John Blair
James Madison, Jr.

North Carolina

William Blount
Richard Dobbs Spaight
Hugh Williamson

South Carolina

John Rutledge
Charles Cotesworth Pinckney
Charles Pinckney
Pierce Butler

Georgia

William Few
Abraham Baldwin

Attest:

William Jackson, Secretary

The Constitution was adopted in
Philadelphia on September 17, 1787,
by the Constitutional Convention
and was declared ratified
on July 2, 1788.

AMENDMENT I

Congress shall make no law respecting an establishment of religion, or prohibiting the free exercise thereof; or abridging the freedom of speech, or of the press; or the right of the people peaceably to assemble, and to petition the Government for a redress of grievances.

AMENDMENT II

A well regulated Militia, being necessary to the security of a free State, the right of the people to keep and bear Arms, shall not be infringed.

AMENDMENT III

No Soldier shall, in time of peace be quartered in any house, without the consent of the Owner, nor in time of war, but in a manner to be prescribed by law.

AMENDMENT IV

The right of the people to be secure in their persons, houses, papers, and effects, against unreasonable searches and seizures, shall not be violated, and no Warrants shall issue, but upon probable cause, supported by Oath or affirmation, and particularly describing the place to be searched, and the persons or things to be seized.

AMENDMENT V

No person shall be held to answer for a capital, or otherwise infamous crime, unless on a presentment or indictment of a Grand Jury, except in cases arising in the land or naval forces, or in the Militia, when in actual service in time of War or public danger; nor shall any person be subject for the same offence to be twice put in jeopardy of life or limb; nor shall be compelled in any criminal case to be a witness against himself, nor be deprived of life, liberty, or property, without due process of law; nor shall private property be taken for public use, without just compensation.

AMENDMENT VI

In all criminal prosecutions, the accused shall enjoy the right to a speedy and public trial, by an impartial jury of the State and district wherein the crime shall have been committed, which district shall have been previously ascertained by law, and to be informed of the nature and cause of the accusation; to be confronted with the witnesses against him; to have compulsory process for obtaining witnesses in his favor, and to have the Assistance of Counsel for his defence.

AMENDMENT VII

In Suits at common law, where the value in controversy shall exceed twenty dollars, the right of trial by jury shall be preserved, and no fact tried by a jury, shall be otherwise re-examined in any Court of the United States, than according to the rules of the common law.

AMENDMENT VIII

Excessive bail shall not be required, nor excessive fines imposed, nor cruel and unusual punishments inflicted.

AMENDMENT IX

The enumeration in the Constitution, of certain rights, shall not be construed to deny or disparage others retained by the people.

AMENDMENT X

The powers not delegated to the United States by the Constitution, nor prohibited by it to the States, are reserved to the States respectively, or to the people. [The first ten amendments were ratified December 15, 1791.]

AMENDMENT XI

The Judicial power of the United States shall not be construed to extend to any suit in law or equity, commenced or prosecuted against one of the United States by Citizens of another State, or by Citizens or Subjects of any Foreign State. [Ratified February 1795.]

AMENDMENT XII

The Electors shall meet in their respective states and vote by ballot for President and Vice-President, one of whom, at least, shall not be an inhabitant of the same state with themselves; they shall name in their ballots the person voted for as President, and in distinct ballots the person voted for as Vice-President, and they shall make distinct lists of all persons voted for as President, and of all persons voted for as Vice-President, and of the number of votes for each, which lists they shall sign and certify, and transmit sealed to the seat of the government of the United States, directed to the President of the Senate;—the President of the Senate shall, in the presence of the Senate and House of Representatives, open all the certificates and the votes shall then be counted;— The person having the greatest number of votes for President, shall be the President, if such number be a majority of the whole number of Electors appointed; and if no person have such majority, then from the persons having the highest numbers not exceeding three on the list of those voted for as President, the House of Representatives shall choose immediately by ballot, the President. But in choosing the President, the votes shall be taken by states, the representation from each state having one vote; a quorum for this purpose shall consist of a member or members from two-thirds of the states, and a majority of all the states shall be necessary to a choice. [And if the House of Representatives shall not choose a President whenever the right of choice shall devolve upon them, before the fourth day of March next following, then the Vice-President shall act as President, as in the case of the death or other constitutional disability of the President.—]* The person having the greatest number of votes as Vice-President, shall be the Vice-President, if such number be a majority of the whole number of Electors appointed, and if no person have a majority, then from the two highest numbers on the list, the Senate shall choose the Vice-President; a quorum for the purpose shall consist of two-thirds of the whole number of Senators, and a majority of

*Superseded by Section 3 of the Twentieth Amendment

the whole number shall be necessary to a choice. But no person constitutionally ineligible to the office of President shall be eligible to that of Vice-President of the United States. [Ratified June 1804.]

AMENDMENT XIII

Section 1

Neither slavery nor involuntary servitude, except as a punishment for crime whereof the party shall have been duly convicted, shall exist within the United States, or any place subject to their jurisdiction.

Section 2

Congress shall have power to enforce this article by appropriate legislation. [Ratified December 1865.]

AMENDMENT XIV

Section 1

All persons born or naturalized in the United States and subject to the jurisdiction thereof, are citizens of the United States, and of the State wherein they reside. No State shall make or enforce any law which shall abridge the privileges or immunities of citizens of the United States; nor shall any State deprive any person of life, liberty, or property, without due process of law; nor deny to any person within its jurisdiction the equal protection of the laws.

Section 2

Representatives shall be apportioned among the several States according to their respective numbers, counting the whole number of persons in each State, excluding Indians not taxed. But when the right to vote at any election for the choice of electors for President and Vice-President of the United States, Representatives in Congress, the Executive and Judicial officers of a State, or the members of the Legislature thereof, is denied to any of the male inhabitants of such State, being twenty-one years of age,* and citizens of the United States, or in any way abridged, except for participation in rebellion, or other crime, the basis of representation therein shall be reduced in the proportion which the number of such male citizens shall bear to the whole number of male citizens twenty-one years of age in such State.

Section 3

No person shall be a Senator or Representative in Congress, or elector of President and Vice-President, or hold any office, civil or military, under the United States, or under any State, who, having previously taken an oath, as a member of Congress, or as an officer of the United States, or as a member of any State legislature, or as an executive or judicial officer of any State, to support the Constitution of the United States, shall have engaged in insurrection or rebellion against the same, or given aid or comfort to the enemies thereof. But Congress may by a vote of two-thirds of each House, remove such disability.

*Changed by Section 1 of the Twenty-sixth Amendment

Section 4

The validity of the public debt of the United States, authorized by law, including debts incurred for payment of pensions and bounties for services in suppressing insurrection or rebellion, shall not be questioned. But neither the United States nor any State shall assume or pay any debt or obligation incurred in aid of insurrection or rebellion against the United States, or any claim for the loss or emancipation of any slave; but all such debts, obligations and claims shall be held illegal and void.

Section 5

The Congress shall have the power to enforce, by appropriate legislation, the provisions of this article. [Ratified July 1868.]

AMENDMENT XV

Section 1

The right of citizens of the United States to vote shall not be denied or abridged by the United States or by any State on account of race, color, or previous condition of servitude.

Section 2

The Congress shall have the power to enforce this article by appropriate legislation. [Ratified February 1870.]

AMENDMENT XVI

The Congress shall have power to lay and collect taxes on incomes, from whatever source derived, without apportionment among the several States, and without regard to any census or enumeration. [Ratified February 1913.]

AMENDMENT XVII

The Senate of the United States shall be composed of two Senators from each State, elected by the people thereof, for six years; and each Senator shall have one vote. The electors in each State shall have the qualifications requisite for electors of the most numerous branch of the State legislatures. When vacancies happen in the representation of any State in the Senate, the executive authority of such State shall issue writs of election to fill such vacancies: *Provided*, That the legislature of any State may empower the executive thereof to make temporary appointments until the people fill the vacancies by election as the legislature may direct. This amendment shall not be so construed as to affect the election or term of any Senator chosen before it becomes valid as part of the Constitution. [Ratified April 1913.]

AMENDMENT XVIII

Section 1

After one year from the ratification of this article the manufacture, sale, or transportation of intoxicating liquors within, the importation thereof into, or the exportation thereof from the United States and all territory subject to the jurisdiction thereof for beverage purposes is hereby prohibited.

Section 2

The Congress and the several States shall have concurrent power to enforce this article by appropriate legislation.

Section 3

This article shall be inoperative unless it shall have been ratified as an amendment to the Constitution by the legislatures of the several States, as provided in the Constitution, within seven years from the date of the submission hereof to the States by the Congress. [Ratified January 1919.]*

AMENDMENT XIX

The right of citizens of the United States to vote shall not be denied or abridged by the United States or by any State on account of sex. Congress shall have power to enforce this article by appropriate legislation. [Ratified August 1920.]

AMENDMENT XX

Section 1

The terms of the President and the Vice President shall end at noon on the 20th day of January, and the terms of Senators and Representatives at noon on the 3d day of January, of the years in which such terms would have ended if this article had not been ratified; and the terms of their successors shall then begin.

Section 2

The Congress shall assemble at least once in every year, and such meeting shall begin at noon on the 3rd day of January, unless they shall by law appoint a different day.

Section 3

If, at the time fixed for the beginning of the term of the President, the President elect shall have died, the Vice President elect shall become President. If a President shall not have been chosen before the time fixed for the beginning of his term, or if the President elect shall have failed to qualify, then the Vice President elect shall act as President until a President shall have qualified; and the Congress may by law provide for the case wherein neither a President elect nor a Vice President elect shall have qualified, declaring who shall then act as President, or the manner in which one who is to act shall be selected, and such person shall act accordingly until a President or Vice President shall have qualified.

Section 4

The Congress may by law provide for the case of the death of any of the persons for whom the House of Representatives may choose a President whenever the right of choice shall have devolved upon them, and for the case of the death of any of the persons from whom the Senate may choose a Vice President whenever the right of choice shall have devolved upon them.

Section 5

Sections 1 and 2 shall take effect on the 15th day of October following the ratification of this article.

*Repealed by the Twenty-first Amendment

Section 6

This article shall be inoperative unless it shall have been ratified as an amendment to the Constitution by the legislatures of three-fourths of the several States within seven years from the date of its submission. [Ratified January 1933.]

AMENDMENT XXI

Section 1

The eighteenth article of amendment to the Constitution of the United States is hereby repealed.

Section 2

The transportation or importation into any State, Territory, or Possession of the United States for delivery or use therein of intoxicating liquors, in violation of the laws thereof, is hereby prohibited.

Section 3

This article shall be inoperative unless it shall have been ratified as an amendment to the Constitution by conventions in the several States, as provided in the Constitution, within seven years from the date of the submission hereof to the States by the Congress. [Ratified December 1933.]

AMENDMENT XXII

Section 1

No person shall be elected to the office of the President more than twice, and no person who has held the office of President, or acted as President, for more than two years of a term to which some other person was elected President shall be elected to the office of the President more than once. But this Article shall not apply to any person holding the office of President when this Article was proposed by the Congress, and shall not prevent any person who may be holding the office of President, or acting as President, during the term within which this Article becomes operative from holding the office of President or acting as President during the remainder of such term.

Section 2

This article shall be inoperative unless it shall have been ratified as an amendment to the Constitution by the legislatures of three-fourths of the several States within seven years from the date of its submission to the States by the Congress. [Ratified February 1951.]

AMENDMENT XXIII

Section 1

The District constituting the seat of Government of the United States shall appoint in such manner as the Congress may direct: A number of electors of President and Vice President equal to the whole number of Senators and Representatives in Congress to which the District would be entitled if it were a State, but in no event more than the least populous State; they shall be in addition to those appointed by the States, but they shall be considered, for the purposes of the election of President and Vice President, to be electors appointed by a State; and they shall meet in the District and perform such duties as provided by the twelfth article of amendment.

Section 2

The Congress shall have power to enforce this article by appropriate legislation. [Ratified March 1961.]

AMENDMENT XXIV

Section 1

The right of citizens of the United States to vote in any primary or other election for President or Vice President, for electors for President or Vice President, or for Senator or Representative in Congress, shall not be denied or abridged by the United States or any State by reason of failure to pay any poll tax or other tax.

Section 2

The Congress shall have power to enforce this article by appropriate legislation. [Ratified January 1964.]

AMENDMENT XXV

Section 1

In case of the removal of the President from office or of his death or resignation, the Vice President shall become President.

Section 2

Whenever there is a vacancy in the office of the Vice President, the President shall nominate a Vice President who shall take office upon confirmation by a majority vote of both Houses of Congress.

Section 3

Whenever the President transmits to the President pro tempore of the Senate and the Speaker of the House of Representatives his written declaration that he is unable to discharge the powers and duties of his office, and until he transmits to them a written declaration to the contrary, such powers and duties shall be discharged by the Vice President as Acting President.

Section 4

Whenever the Vice President and a majority of either the principal officers of the executive departments or of such other body as Congress may by law provide, transmit to the President pro tempore of the Senate and the Speaker of the House of Representatives their written declaration that the President is unable to discharge the powers and duties of his office, the Vice President shall immediately assume the powers and duties of the office as Acting President.

Thereafter, when the President transmits to the President pro tempore of the Senate and the Speaker of the House of Representatives his written declaration that no inability exists, he shall resume the powers and duties of his office unless the Vice President and a majority of either the principal officers of the executive department or of such other body as Congress may by law provide, transmit within four days to the President pro tempore of the Senate and the Speaker of the House of Representatives their written declaration that the President is unable to discharge the powers and duties of his office. Thereupon Congress shall decide the issue, assembling within forty-eight hours for that purpose if not in session. If the Congress, within twenty-one days after receipt of the latter written declaration, or, if Congress is not in session, within twenty-one days after Congress is required to assemble, determines by two-thirds vote of both Houses that the President is unable to discharge the powers and duties of his office, the Vice President shall continue to discharge the same as Acting President; otherwise, the President shall resume the powers and duties of his office. [Ratified February 1967.]

AMENDMENT XXVI

Section 1

The right of citizens of the United States, who are eighteen years of age or older, to vote shall not be denied or abridged by the United States or by any State on account of age.

Section 2

The Congress shall have power to enforce this article by appropriate legislation. [Ratified July 1971.]

AMENDMENT XXVII

No law, varying the compensation for the services of the Senators or Representatives, shall take effect, until an election of Representatives shall have intervened. [Ratified May 1992.]

abolish To formally put an end to.

abridging Limiting or reducing.

advice and consent The right of the U.S. Senate, granted in Article II of the Constitution, to review treaties and major presidential appointments. Two-thirds vote of senators is required for treaties and a simple majority for appointments.

alien A foreign-born resident.

Alien and Sedition Acts Laws passed during President John Adams' administration that made it a crime for editors, writers, or speakers to criticize the government and its Federalist policies.

allegiance (1) Loyalty to a government, ruler, or nation. (2) Loyalty to a person, social group, or cause.

amendment A change in or addition to a legal document.

American Revolution The war fought by the American colonists to gain their independence from Great Britain. It took place from 1775 to 1783.

Amnesty International An international nongovernmental organization that advocates the protection of human rights.

Anti-Federalists People who were against ratification of the Constitution because they thought it gave too much power to the federal government and did not protect the political rights of the people.

appeal The bringing of a court case from a lower court to a higher court in an attempt to have the lower court's decision reversed or for other reasons.

appellate court A judicial body that hears appeals from a lower court.

appellate jurisdiction The legal authority of a court to hear appeals from a lower court.

aristocrats People of the highest class of society who held inherited titles. They were often part of the ruling class in government.

Article I The part of the Constitution that describes the legislative branch of the government and its powers.

Article II The part of the Constitution that describes the executive branch of the government and its powers.

Article III The part of the Constitution that describes the judicial branch of the government and its powers.

Article IV The part of the Constitution that deals with the relationship between the states and the federal government and states' relationships with each other.

Article V The part of the Constitution that describes the process for amending the Constitution.

Article VI The part of the Constitution that deals with debts and contracts that were entered into before adoption of the Constitution; the supremacy of the Constitution; and the requirement of an oath of office for executive, legislative, and judicial officials. It prohibits the institution of a religious test for officeholders.

Article VII The part of the Constitution that describes the requirement for ratification of the Constitution.

Articles of Confederation The first constitution of the United States, created to form a perpetual union and a firm league of friendship among the thirteen original states. It was adopted by the Second Continental Congress on November 10, 1777, and sent to the states for ratification. It came into force on March 1, 1781, and served as the nation's constitution until 1789, when the U.S. Constitution replaced it. The Articles provided for a weak central government.

assembly, right of The right or legal claims that allow a person to meet with others to discuss one's beliefs, ideas, or feelings.

association An organized group of people joined together for a common purpose.

Association of Southeast Asian Nations (ASEAN) "The Association represents the collective will of the ten member nations to work together to secure peace, freedom, and prosperity for their peoples." (ASEAN Declaration 1967)

autocratic government Government in which a single ruler or group has unlimited power.

avarice An excessive desire for money; greed.

bail Money or other security given to obtain a person's release from custody, which is forfeited if the person subsequently fails to appear before the court for trial.

bailiff (1) An officer who carries out legal orders, makes arrests, keeps order in court, or serves as a messenger and doorkeeper. (2) (chiefly British) A local official who has some judicial powers.

balance of power The division of governmental powers among different persons or institutions in such a way that no one individual or group can dominate or control the exercise of power by others.

basic rights Fundamental rights such as life, liberty, and property.

Battle of Saratoga (1777) An important battle of the Revolutionary War that lasted from June to October 1777, when the British surrendered in Saratoga, New York. The American victory prevented the British from splitting the colonies in two, increased American morale, and encouraged the French to sign a treaty with the Americans.

bill A proposed law given to the legislature for approval.

bill of attainder An act of the legislature that inflicts punishment on an individual or group without a judicial trial.

Bill of Rights The first ten amendments to the Constitution. It lists basic rights of the people that the federal government may not interfere with and must protect.

Boston Massacre (1770) On March 5, 1770, a mob of colonists harassed British soldiers guarding the tax collector's office in Boston. The soldiers opened fire, killing five Bostonians.

Boston Tea Party (1773) An act of rebellion against British authority, and in particular in response to the Tea Act, in which a band of colonists boarded ships in Boston Harbor and destroyed thousands of dollars worth of tea by throwing it overboard.

boycott To refuse to buy from or deal with a store or company as an act of protest.

***Brown v. Board of Education of Topeka* (1954)** The U.S. Supreme Court case in which the Court declared that "separate but equal" educational facilities are inherently unequal and therefore a violation of the equal protection of the laws guaranteed by the Fourteenth Amendment.

cabinet The advisors to the president who are the heads of the departments of the executive branch.

charter A written document from a government or ruler that grants certain rights to an individual, group, organization, or to people in general. In colonial times, a charter granted land to a person or a company along with the right to start a colony on that land.

chattel Personal property that can be moved from place to place.

checks and balances The distribution and balancing of power among different branches of government so that no one branch is able to dominate the others.

chief justice The head of a court. The Chief Justice of the United States is the highest ranking judicial official in the nation and is the head of the U.S. Supreme Court.

citizen A person who is a legal member of a nation, country, or other self-governing community.

civic (1) Related to citizens or citizenship. (2) Related to the public affairs of a city or country.

civic life The public life of citizens; that which is concerned with a citizen's own interests and the common affairs and interests of his or her community and nation.

civic participation Taking part in formal political processes and community activities outside of government.

civic virtue The dedication of citizens to the common welfare of their community or country, even at the cost of their individual interests.

civil Related to citizens, particularly the relationship between citizens and government.

civil disobedience The refusal to obey laws one regards as unjust.

civil rights Fundamental rights belonging to every member of a society.

Civil Rights Act of 1964 This law ended segregation in public places including restaurants, movie theaters, and hotels. The law also said that employers could not unfairly discriminate against people because of their race, national origin, religion, or gender.

civil rights movement A social movement in the United States during the 1950s and 1960s, in which people organized to demand equal rights for African Americans and other minorities. People worked together to change unfair laws. They gave speeches, marched in the streets, and participated in boycotts.

Civil War The war between the Northern and Southern states. It took place from 1861 to 1865.

Civil War Amendments The Thirteenth, Fourteenth, and Fifteenth Amendments to the U.S. Constitution ratified after the Civil War. The Thirteenth Amendment abolished slavery. The Fourteenth Amendment granted full citizenship to African Americans. The Fifteenth Amendment guaranteed the right to vote to men regardless of their "race, color, or previous condition of servitude."

commander-in-chief Highest leader of the military forces. According to the Constitution, the president is the commander-in-chief of the nation's armed forces.

commerce The buying and selling of goods, particularly on a large scale.

committees of correspondence Committees that began as voluntary associations and were eventually established by most of the colonial governments. Their mission was to make sure that each colony knew about events and opinions in the other colonies. They helped to unite the people against the British.

common good The good of the community as a whole.

common law The body of unwritten law developed in England from judicial decisions based on custom and earlier judicial decisions, which constitutes the basis of the English legal system and became part of American law.

compromise A way to settle differences by each side giving up some of its claims or demands and agreeing to a common solution.

confederation A form of political organization in which the sovereign states combine for certain specified purposes such as defense. Member states can leave a confederation at any time. The United States was a confederation from 1776 to 1789.

Congress The national legislature of the United States. Congress has two parts, also called houses: the Senate and the House of Representatives.

consent To agree and accept something, approve of something, or allow something to take place.

consent of the governed The expressed agreement by the people to obey the laws and the government they create.

constable A public official with limited police and judicial powers.

constitution A set of customs, traditions, rules, and laws that set forth the way a government is organized and operated.

Constitution, United States The supreme law of the United States that provides the framework for the government. The Constitution outlines the nation's institutions of government and the most important rights of the people. The document was created in 1787 during the Philadelphia Convention. The government created by the Constitution took effect on March 4, 1789.

Constitutional Convention See Philadelphia Convention.

constitutional government A government in which the powers of the ruler or rulers are limited by a constitution.

constitutional principle An essential idea contained in the Constitution. For example, the idea that no branch of government should have a monopoly on power.

contract A binding agreement between two or more persons.

covenant A binding agreement made by two or more persons or parties. The original idea of a covenant was an agreement made in the sight of God. The Mayflower Compact was such a covenant.

cruel and unusual punishment A criminal sanction or penalty that is not in accord with the moral standards of a humane and compassionate society. Such punishments are prohibited by the Eighth Amendment.

currency Any form of money used in a nation.

custom (1) An accepted practice or way of behaving that is followed by tradition. (2) A tax on goods entering a country.

Daughters of Liberty An organization formed by women prior to the American Revolution. They got together to protest treatment of the colonies by their British rulers. They helped make the boycott of British trade effective by making their own materials instead of using British imports.

Dawes Act (1887) An act of Congress that granted American citizenship and small parcels of land to American Indians who would give up allegiance to their tribe, their historical traditions, and ways of life. The law was devastating to Indian cultural traditions and forced many Indians into farming.

Declaration of Independence A proclamation that listed the basic principles of democratic government, stated the colonists' grievances against the king, and gave reasons why the colonists were free from British rule. It was signed by the members of Congress on July 4, 1776.

Declaratory Act (1766) A British law that reaffirmed the right of Parliament to pass laws for the colonies in "all cases whatsoever." The purpose of the law was to remind the colonists that the authority of the king and Parliament was superior to colonial governments.

delegate (1) (noun) A person chosen to act for or represent others. (2) (verb) To entrust someone to represent your interests.

democracy A form of government in which political power is exercised by all citizens, either directly or through their elected representatives.

dictator A head of government who has unlimited power.

dictatorial government A political system in which the ruler or rulers has unlimited power and which denies peoples' fundamental rights.

diplomacy The practice of carrying on formal relationships with governments of other countries.

direct democracy A type of government in which the people themselves meet and make the laws that they decide are needed.

discrimination Unfair treatment of people based on such things as their race, religion, or gender.

district court The court of original jurisdiction for most federal cases. This is the only federal court that holds trials in which juries and witnesses are used. Each state has at least one district court.

diverse (1) Of different kinds, types, or forms. (2) People of many different races, cultures, and ethnic groups.

domestic tranquility As used in the Preamble, this phrase means peaceful conditions within our country.

due process of law A requirement, stated in the Fifth and Fourteenth Amendments, that treatment by state and federal governments that involves life, liberty, or property of individuals be reasonable, fair, and follow known rules and procedures.

duty A tax on goods that are either imported or exported.

economic rights Rights essential to citizens that allow them to earn a living, to acquire and transfer property, and to produce, buy, and sell goods and services in open and free markets.

Eighth Amendment An amendment to the Constitution that bans excessive bail or fines and cruel and unusual punishment.

elector (1) One of the 538 members of the electoral college chosen by the political parties in a state. (2) Any qualified voter.

electoral college The group of presidential electors who cast the official votes for president and vice president after a presidential election. Each state has a number of electors equal to the total of its members in the Senate and House of Representatives.

English Bill of Rights An act passed by Parliament in 1689 that limited the power of the monarch. This document established Parliament as the most powerful branch of the English government.

enumerated powers Those rights and responsibilities of the U.S. government specifically provided for and listed in the Constitution.

equal protection clause Section 1 of the Fourteenth Amendment, which has been used to prevent states from treating individuals unfairly because of their race, national origin, citizenship status, or gender. It prohibits laws that unreasonably and unfairly favor some groups over others; it states that laws may not arbitrarily discriminate against persons.

equal protection of the law See equal protection clause.

equal representation The idea that each state should have the same number of representatives in Congress. The number of representatives in the Senate is based on equal representation.

establishment clause The part of the First Amendment that says the government cannot declare an official religion.

ex post facto law A law that makes an act a crime that was not a crime when the act was committed, that increases the penalty for a crime after it was committed, or that changes the rules of evidence to make conviction easier. Ex post facto laws are forbidden by Article I of the Constitution.

excise A tax on goods produced within a certain country imposed by that country's government.

executive branch The branch of government that carries out the laws made by the legislative branch.

executive power The authority to carry out and enforce the law.

faction (1) A small group within a larger group. (2) According to James Madison, a group that seeks to promote its own special interests at the expense of the common good.

federal courts The courts of the national government that deal with problems between states, with the Constitution, and with laws made by Congress.

federal government Another name for our national government.

federalism or **federal system** A form of government in which power is divided and shared between a central government and state and local governments.

Federalist, The A series of letters to the editor written in 1787–88 by Alexander Hamilton, James Madison, and John Jay, urging the adoption of the Constitution and supporting the need for a strong national government.

Federalists Advocates for ratification of the Constitution and for a strong centralized government; they flourished as a political party in the 1790s under the leadership of Alexander Hamilton. The party disappeared from national politics in 1816.

feudalism A system of social, economic, and political organizations in which a politically weak king or queen shared power with the nobility. The nobility required work and services from the common people in return for allowing them to live on and make use of the noble's land and benefit from the noble's protection.

Fifteenth Amendment An amendment to the Constitution, ratified after the Civil War in 1870, that forbids the denial of voting rights to any person based on race, color, or whether that person was previously a slave.

Fifth Amendment An amendment to the Constitution that states that no person will have their life, liberty, or property taken away by the federal government without due process of law. This amendment protects your right to be treated fairly by the federal government.

First Amendment An amendment to the Constitution that protects freedom of expression and the right of assembly.

First Continental Congress The body of colonial delegates who convened to represent the interests of the colonists and protest British rule. The First Continental Congress met in 1774 and drafted a Declaration of Rights.

Founders The political leaders of the thirteen original colonies. They were key figures in the establishment of the United States of America.

Fourteenth Amendment An amendment to the Constitution that states that no person—including people who are not citizens—will have their life, liberty, or property taken away by state or local governments without due process of law. This amendment protects a citizen's right to be treated fairly by his or her state and local governments. It also defines a citizen as anyone born or naturalized in the United States. It was one of the Civil War amendments.

Fourth Amendment An amendment to the U.S. Constitution that protects citizens from unreasonable searches and seizures and requires that warrants be issued only for "probable cause."

Framers The delegates to the Philadelphia Convention of 1787. They are the group of men who composed the United States Constitution.

free exercise clause The part of the First Amendment that says the government may not stop anyone from holding any religious beliefs they choose and may not unfairly or unreasonably limit anyone's right to practice their religious beliefs.

freedom of assembly The right to meet with others to discuss one's own beliefs, ideas, or feelings.

freedom of belief or conscience The right to freedom from being coerced to believe in something that you do not believe.

freedom of expression The right to make known one's attitudes, emotions, thoughts, feelings, etc., as protected by the First Amendment.

freedom of the press The right to read and write whatever you wish, as well as the right to publish your ideas without government interference.

freedom of religion The right to hold whatever religious beliefs you wish and the right to practice your beliefs without unfair or unreasonable interference from the government.

French Constitution of 1791 A constitution adopted during the French Revolution that established a constitutional monarchy in France. Power was concentrated in the legislative assembly and the power of the king was limited.

fugitive slave clause Article IV, Section 2, Clause 3 of the Constitution, which stated that slaves who escaped must be returned to their owners. It was later abolished by the Thirteenth Amendment.

general welfare What is best for most of the people.

general welfare clause Article I, Section 8, Clause 1 of the Constitution that authorizes Congress to provide for the common defense of the country and for the common good, described as the "general Welfare."

George III King of Great Britain during the American Revolution.

government The people and institutions with authority to make and enforce laws and manage disputes about laws.

grandfather clause A law that stated that a citizen could vote only if his grandfather had been allowed to vote. The law made it impossible for African Americans to vote because their grandfathers had not been allowed to vote.

Great Compromise This was a plan accepted at the Philadelphia Convention that called for Congress to have two houses. In the Senate representation of the states would be equal, with each state having two senators. The House of Representatives would use proportional representation of the states, and therefore, the number of representatives from each state would be determined by its population. Also called the Connecticut Compromise.

habeas corpus See writ of habeas corpus.

Hazelwood School District v. Kuhlmeier **(1988)**
A Supreme Court ruling that students' First
Amendment rights were not violated when their
principal deleted two articles from the school's
newspaper. The Court distinguished between
speech that occurs in a public forum and speech
that occurs "in school-sponsored expressive
activities...related to legitimate pedagogical
[teaching] concerns."

hearing A meeting in which citizens give their
views to public officials.

higher law As used in describing a legal
system, this term refers to the superiority
of one set of laws over another. For example, the
Constitution is a higher law than any federal or
state law. In the natural rights philosophy, it
means that natural law and divine law are
superior to laws made by human beings.

House of Representatives One part or house
of Congress. Often referred to simply as
"the House." Each state may send a number
of representatives based on its population.

human rights Basic rights and freedoms said
to belong to all people everywhere.

humanitarian To have compassion and show
concern for the pain and suffering of others.

I Have a Dream **speech** A speech delivered
by Martin Luther King Jr. at the Lincoln
Memorial in Washington, D.C., on August 28,
1963, during a civil rights march. King spoke
against segregation and the unequal treatment of African Americans. Also known as
the "March on Washington" speech.

ideal A standard of perfection that serves
as a model for imitation.

impeach To bring to trial a public official
accused of committing a crime or engaging
in misconduct while in office.

impost A tax or customs duty.

In re Gault **(1967)** A Supreme Court ruling
that the due process rights of Gerald Gault,
a minor accused of making rude telephone
calls, had been violated.

inalienable rights Fundamental rights that
every person has that cannot be taken away
by government. This phrase was used in the
Virginia Declaration of Rights and the
Declaration of Independence. Sometimes
spelled unalienable rights.

indentured servant A person who voluntarily
sold his or her labor for a set period of time
in return for the cost of coming to America.
The most important source of labor in the
colonies in the seventeenth century and
for a large part of the eighteenth century.

independence Self-rule; not ruled by
another country.

Indian Citizenship Act (1924) An act of
Congress that recognized all American
Indians as citizens of the United States
and granted them the right to vote in
federal elections.

individual rights Specific rights that belong
to each person, such as those listed in the
Bill of Rights, rather than general rights.

international law Rules, usually the result of
treaties, that regulate how countries behave
toward one another.

International Red Cross and Red Crescent
Two international humanitarian organizations
that provide assistance to victims of war and
natural disasters. There are 181 Red Cross
and Red Crescent societies throughout the
world. Red Cross societies operate out of
countries with majority Christian populations;
Red Crescent societies operate out of countries
with majority Muslim populations.

International Telecommunications Union
An agency of the United Nations dedicated
to improving and coordinating international
efforts related to telecommunications. Also
known as the ITU.

Jim Crow laws Laws common in the South from 1877 until the 1950s that required African Americans to use separate schools and other public facilities and that prevented them from exercising the right to vote.

judicial branch The branch of government that interprets and applies the laws and settles disputes.

judicial review The power of the courts to declare laws and actions of the local, state, or national government invalid if they contradict the Constitution.

Judiciary Act of 1789 A law passed by the first Congress to establish the federal court system. The act determined the organization and jurisdiction of the courts.

jurisdiction The power or authority to hear cases and make decisions.

justice (1) Fair treatment according to law. (2) A member of the Supreme Court.

law A rule established by government or other source of authority to regulate people's conduct or activities. In the United States a bill that is passed by the legislature and is signed by the executive, or which is passed over his or her veto, becomes a law.

law of nature In natural rights philosophy, the law of nature would prevail in the absence of man-made law and contains standards of justice that apply to all people.

legal permanent resident A person who is not a citizen, but who legally lives in the United States. Legal permanent residents enjoy most of the rights of citizens. They have the same right to due process of law as citizens, they must pay taxes, and they may serve in the military.

legislative branch The branch of government that makes the laws.

legislative supremacy A system of government in which the legislative branch has ultimate power.

legislature A group of officials in government who have the authority to make and change laws.

Letter from Birmingham City Jail A letter written to fellow clergymen by Martin Luther King Jr. in Birmingham, Alabama, on April 16, 1963, after his arrest for violating a state court order against participating in protests. In his letter, King explains the reasons for his involvement in the civil rights movement and for his belief in nonviolent methods of protest.

liberty, right to The right to be free. Some examples of liberties are the rights to believe what you wish, to read what you want, to speak freely, and to travel wherever you want to go.

life, right to The right to live without fear of being injured or killed by others or by government.

limited government In natural rights philosophy, a system restricted to protecting natural rights that does not interfere with other aspects of life.

limits Restrictions or boundaries on governmental power.

literacy test A test that requires people to prove that they are able to read and write. Until 1964, these tests were used in various states throughout the country to keep minorities from voting.

lobby To represent a group in trying to influence legislatures.

Loyalists Colonists who opposed American independence and remained loyal to Great Britain during the American Revolution.

magistrate A lower-level judicial officer, usually elected in urban areas, who handles traffic violations, minor criminal offenses, and civil suits involving small amounts of money.

Magna Carta This document, also known as the Great Charter, was agreed to by King John of England in 1215 at the demand of his barons. The Magna Carta granted certain civil rights and liberties to English nobles, such as the right to a jury of one's peers and the guarantee against loss of life, liberty, or property, except in accordance with law. In doing so, it also limited the power of the monarch. The document is a landmark in the history of limited constitutional government.

majority rule A principle of democracy that asserts that the greater number of citizens in any political unit should select officials and determine policies.

Marbury v. Madison (1803) A landmark case in which the Supreme Court, for the first time in American history, struck down an act of Congress as unconstitutional, establishing the Court's power of constitutional judicial review.

Massachusetts Body of Liberties (1641) The first American document to describe the rights of individuals.

Massachusetts constitution A state constitution ratified by Massachusetts voters in 1780. It is the oldest written constitution still in use in the world today.

Mayflower Compact An agreement to form a political body signed in 1620 by all adult males aboard the Mayflower before the ship landed in Plymouth, Massachusetts. The signers agreed to submit to "just and equal Laws" put into effect under the compact.

misdemeanor A minor criminal offense that is less serious than a felony, a major offense. The punishment for a misdemeanor is a fine or imprisonment for up to one year.

monarchy A form of government in which political power is held by a single ruler such as a king or queen.

monitor To keep watch over something.

National Association for the Advancement of Colored People An interracial interest group founded in 1909 to advocate the rights of African Americans, primarily through legal and political action. Also called the NAACP.

national government The organization having central political authority in a nation. The representative unit of political organization.

nation-state The modern nation or country as the typical unit of political organization in the world.

natural law A higher, unchanging set of rules that govern human relations believed by the Founders to have come from "Nature and Nature's God" (from the Declaration of Independence).

natural rights A doctrine that human beings have basic rights, such as those to life, liberty, and property in a state of nature and that people create governments to protect those rights.

naturalized citizens People who are born elsewhere but pass a citizenship test on the Constitution and the history of the United States and swear an oath of loyalty to their new country.

necessary and proper clause Article I, Section 8, Clause 18 of the Constitution that gives Congress the power to make all laws that are "necessary and proper" to carry out the powers specifically delegated to it by the Constitution. It is also known as the elastic clause.

New Jersey Plan The plan presented at the Philadelphia Convention that called for a one-house national legislature with each state having equal representation. The New Jersey Plan followed the framework of the Articles of Confederation and favored a weak national government.

Nineteenth Amendment Added to the Constitution in 1920, it gave women the right to vote.

Ninth Amendment This amendment states, in effect, that the Bill of Rights is only a partial listing of the rights of the people.

nongovernmental organization An organization independent of direct governmental control that exists to perform humanitarian or educational services or to affect public policy. Also called an NGO.

Northwest Ordinance (1787) An important law passed by Congress under the Articles of Confederation. The law prohibited slavery in the Northwest Territory and provided for settling the western lands and the admission and organization of new states.

null and void Of no legal or binding force; invalid.

opinion of the Court A written explanation of the Supreme Court's decision in a particular case and its reasoning behind the decision.

ordinance A municipal statute or regulation.

Organization of American States A regional organization composed of North, South, and Central American nations. It was formed in 1948 to promote economic, political, military, and cultural cooperation among its members.

original jurisdiction The legal authority of a court to be the first to hear a case.

override To pass a bill after it has been vetoed. Congress may override the president's veto by a two-thirds vote of both houses.

Parliament The British legislature, which consists of two houses: the House of Lords, representing the nobility, most of whose appointments are no longer hereditary, and the House of Commons, representing the people.

participation Taking part in or sharing in the activities of a group, organization, or system.

Patriots Those Americans who supported the war for independence against Great Britain.

peer A person of equal standing or rank.

persecute To harass or cause suffering to a person or group because of such things as their beliefs or principles.

petition, right to The legal claim that allows a person to ask his or her government to correct things that he or she thinks are wrong or to do things he or she believes are needed.

Petition of Rights (1628) A statute that limited the English monarch's power to tax people without the consent of Parliament and guaranteed certain rights to English subjects.

Philadelphia Convention The meeting held in Philadelphia from May to September 1787 at which the Constitution was written. Also called the Constitutional Convention.

plantation A large farm usually located in the Southern states.

Plessy v. Ferguson **(1896)** The case in which the Supreme Court ruled that "separate but equal" public facilities for blacks and whites were permissible under the Constitution.

political action Any organized attempt to influence the political process, from lobbying legislators to seeking the election or defeat of particular candidates.

political parties Any organization that seeks to achieve political power by electing members to public office so that their political philosophies can be reflected in public policies.

political philosophy A set of ideas about government and politics.

political rights All rights of a citizen in a free society that are clearly expressed and guaranteed by the Constitution and implied by natural laws.

politics A process by which people with different opinions and interests reach decisions without the use of violence.

poll tax A tax that voters in many states were required to pay in order to exercise their right to vote. These barriers were used until 1964 to prevent African Americans from voting.

popular sovereignty The natural rights concept that ultimate political authority rests with the people.

population The number of people living in an area.

Preamble The introduction to the Constitution. It states that the people establish the government and lists the purposes of the government.

press (1) Newspapers, magazines, television, and other news media. (2) The reporters and people who produce them.

principle A general statement of moral or political belief.

privacy, right to The right or legal claim that allows a person to be free from intrusion by government officials into areas of one's life that are of no concern to government.

private domain Areas of a person's life that are not subject to governmental interference.

procedure The methods or steps taken to accomplish something.

Proclamation of 1763 A British law that banned settlement in certain western lands to reduce tensions between the colonists and Native Americans. The law was unpopular among American frontiersmen and traders.

property, right to The right or legal claim that allows a person to own things and to transfer them to others. Your labor or work is also your property.

proportional representation The electoral system in which the number of representatives for a state is based on the number of people who live in that state. Proportional representation is used to determine the number of each state's representatives serving in the House of Representatives.

Quartering Act (1765) Also known as the Mutiny Act, this British law authorized colonial governors to requisition certain buildings for the housing, or "quartering," of British troops.

Quebec Campaign (1775–76) A military expedition that was an attempt by the Americans to protect the American north and persuade the Canadians to join their rebellion against Britain. American forces invaded Canada and captured Montreal in late 1774. The British forced the Americans to retreat in the spring of 1776.

ratification Formal approval of the Constitution by the ratifying conventions held in each state.

ratify To confirm and approve.

ratifying conventions Meetings held in the states to approve the Constitution.

Red Cross See International Red Cross and Red Crescent.

redress of grievances Correction of complaints. The First Amendment protects the right to petition the government to obtain a remedy for a claimed wrong.

regenerate To revive, renew, or give new life to.

register To enroll one's name officially as a requirement for voting.

representative A person elected to act and speak for others.

representative democracy A system of government in which the people elect officials to make and administer laws for their country.

representative government A system for ruling in which elected representatives are chosen by the people to act on their behalf.

republic A nation that has a government in which power is held by the people who elect representatives to manage the government for them for the sake of the common good.

republican government A system for ruling in which power is held by the people who are eligible to elect representatives to run the government for the common good. The term does not refer to a political party.

Republican Party The first political organization formed in opposition to the Federalist Party by the supporters of Thomas Jefferson. It evolved into the Democratic Party in 1828 and has no connection to the present-day Republican Party.

republicanism A form of government in which the supreme political power resides in the people who are qualified to vote; governance is carried out by representatives who are responsible to the people. Republicanism requires the citizenry and public officials to be devoted to the common good.

rights of Englishmen Basic legal claims established over time, that all subjects of the English monarch were understood to have. They included the right not to be kept in prison without a trial and the right to trial by jury.

rule of law The principle that both those who govern and those who are governed must obey the law and are subject to the same laws. This principle is contrasted to the "rule of men," in which those in power make up the rules as they please.

Second Amendment Part of the Bill of Rights added to the Constitution in 1791. The Amendment says "A well-regulated militia, being necessary to the security of a free State, the right of the people to keep and bear Arms, shall not be infringed."

Second Continental Congress The body of delegates representing the colonies that met in 1775 shortly after the start of the Revolutionary War. They organized the Continental Army, called on the colonies to send troops, selected George Washington to lead the army, and appointed a committee to draft the Declaration of Independence.

segregation The separation or isolation of a race, class, or ethnic group from the rest of society.

self-evident Easy for anyone to see; obvious.

self-incrimination, right against The Fifth Amendment guarantees that one cannot be forced to give testimony that could subject oneself to prosecution.

self-interest One's personal concern.

self-sufficient Able to provide for most of one's own needs.

Senate One of the two houses of Congress. Each state is represented by two members in the Senate.

separate but equal The argument, once upheld by the Supreme Court but later reversed, that different public facilities for blacks and whites were constitutional if the facilities were of equal quality.

separation of church and state A basic principle of American government that no one religion should be favored by government over other religions. Nor should government interfere with one's right to practice or not practice religious beliefs. This metaphor was used in 1802 by President Thomas Jefferson to explain his understanding of the protection of religious freedom afforded by the Constitution.

separation of powers The division of powers among the different branches of government. In the United States, powers are divided among the legislative, executive, and judicial branches.

serf In feudal times peasants were also known as serfs. They farmed the land and were not free to leave the area in which they worked.

Shays' Rebellion An armed revolt by Massachusetts farmers in 1786–87 who sought relief from debts and foreclosures of mortgages. Led by Daniel Shays, the group prevented judges from hearing mortgage foreclosure cases and attempted to capture an arsenal.

"the shot heard 'round the world" A line in a poem by Ralph Waldo Emerson describing the effect of the outbreak of the American Revolution in April 1775. The American Revolution and its principles became extremely influential around the world. It was the first of many rebellions by countries against their colonial rulers.

sit-in Nonviolent demonstration in which persons protesting certain conditions sit down in an appropriate place and refuse to move until their demands are considered or met.

Sixth Amendment An Amendment that guarantees the rights to a "fair and speedy" trial by jury in criminal cases, to be informed of the nature of the charges in the case, to call witnesses, and to have the assistance of a lawyer.

slave A person whose human rights are denied and who is forced to work for another person without compensation.

slave trade The commercial practice of forcibly taking people from their homes in Africa and selling them into slavery in the new world.

social action Attempts by groups or individuals to change society using a variety of means.

social contract An agreement among the people to set up a government and obey its laws. The theory was developed by the natural rights philosopher John Locke to explain the origin of legitimate government.

Sons of Liberty An organization created in 1765 in every colony to express opposition to the Stamp Act. A popular goal of the organization was to force stamp distributors throughout the colonies to resign.

sovereign A person or group having the highest authority or power in a country or state.

speech, freedom of The right to express your beliefs, ideas, or feelings.

Stamp Act (1765) A British law that required the payment of a tax through the purchase of stamps for documents such as newspapers, magazines, and legal and commercial papers of all kinds.

state of nature The basis of natural rights philosophy; a state of nature is the condition of people living in a situation without man-made government, rules, or laws.

subject Someone who owes allegiance to a government or ruler.

suffrage The right to vote.

Sugar Act of 1764 A British law designed to stop smuggling of goods into and out of the colonies. The law gave the British navy greater power to search colonial ships.

supremacy clause Article VI, Section 2 of the Constitution, which states that the Constitution, laws passed by Congress, and treaties of the United States "shall be the supreme Law of the Land" and binding on the states.

tariff A tax on imported or exported goods or a list or system that describes such taxes.

Tea Act (1773) The British law that granted the East India Company a monopoly on the importation of tea into the colonies, thus eliminating the profits of colonial importers and shopkeepers.

Tenth Amendment This Amendment holds that the "powers not delegated to the United States by the Constitution, nor prohibited by it to the States, are reserved to the States respectively, or the people." The Tenth Amendment embodies the principle of federalism, which reserves for the states the residue of powers not granted to the federal government or withheld from the states, and the principle of popular sovereignty, which reserves other rights to the people.

Thirteenth Amendment This Amendment abolished slavery. It was adopted after the Civil War in 1865.

three-fifths clause Article I, Section 2, Clause 3 of the U.S. Constitution, later eliminated by the Fourteenth Amendment. The clause provided that each slave should be counted as three-fifths of a person in determining the number of representatives a state might send to the House of Representatives. It also determined the amount of direct taxes Congress may levy on a state.

***Tinker v. Des Moines School District* (1969)** A Supreme Court case in which the Court ruled that schools cannot limit a student's right to freedom of expression unless the student's exercise of that right disrupts the educational process.

tract An area of land or water.

treason Betrayal of one's country, especially by giving aid to an enemy in wartime or by plotting to overthrow the government. Treason is carefully defined in the Constitution to ensure that government cannot abuse its powers against dissenters.

Treaty of Paris The agreement signed on September 3, 1783, between Great Britain and the United States that ended the Revolutionary War. With the treaty, Great Britain recognized the independence of the United States. Also called the Peace of Paris.

Twenty-fifth Amendment The Amendment that describes who becomes president if the president dies, is removed from office, resigns, or can no longer perform presidential duties. It also describes how the office of vice president is to be filled if a vacancy occurs.

Twenty-fourth Amendment The Amendment adopted in 1964 that forbids the levying of a poll tax or any other tax on eligible voters in elections for federal officials, including the president, vice president, and members of Congress.

Twenty-second Amendment The Amendment that prohibits any person from being elected president more than twice.

Twenty-sixth Amendment The Amendment adopted in 1971 that says a state cannot deny someone the right to vote if they have reached the age of 18 and are otherwise eligible to vote. Although eighteen-year-olds had already been accorded the vote in national elections by the Voting Rights Act of 1970, the Twenty-sixth Amendment assured them the vote in all elections.

tyranny A government in which a single ruler possesses and abuses absolute power.

unalienable rights See inalienable rights.

unconstitutional Not allowed by the Constitution; illegal; contradicts the Constitution.

unitary government A centralized form of government in which states or local governments exercise only those powers delegated to them by the central or national government.

United Nations An international organization created in 1945 to maintain peace through the collective security of its members.

United States Supreme Court The highest court in the United States. See Article III, Section 1 of the Constitution.

Universal Postal Union An agency of the United Nations dedicated to improving postal services throughout the world. Also called the UPU.

vassal In feudal times, a person granted the use of land by a feudal lord, in return for which he rendered military or other service.

veto The right of a branch of government to reject a bill that has been passed in an effort to delay or prevent its enactment. Under the U.S. Constitution it is the power of the president to refuse to sign a bill passed by Congress, thereby preventing it from becoming a law. The president's veto may be overridden by a two-thirds vote of both the Senate and House of Representatives.

Virginia Declaration of Rights The first state declaration of rights, which served as a model for other state declarations of rights and the Bill of Rights and influenced the Declaration of Independence. It was adopted on June 12, 1776.

Virginia Plan The plan presented at the Philadelphia Convention that provided for a national government composed of three branches. It proposed a Congress of two houses, both of which would be based on proportional representation. The Virginia Plan favored a strong national government.

Voting Rights Act (1965) The act further protected the right to vote for all U.S. citizens. It forced the states to obey the Constitution. It made it clear that the right to vote could not be denied because of a person's color or race.

writ of habeas corpus A court order directing that a prisoner be brought to court before a judge to determine if the detention of the person is lawful. From the Latin term meaning, "you shall/should have the body."

writs of assistance Documents giving a governmental authority the power to search and seize property without restrictions.

Yorktown Surrender The final military act that ended the Revolutionary War. In October 1781, American and French forces blocked a British escape from the Yorktown Peninsula in Virginia. On October 17–19, 1781, the British forces under Lord Cornwallis surrendered at Yorktown to the American army under George Washington.

Tea Act (1773) 61, 64

Tenth Amendment, (def.) 169, **170**

Thirteenth Amendment (def.) 217, 226, **232**

Thoreau, Henry David 258

three-fifths clause (def.) 126

Tinker v. Des Moines School District 200–01, **204–05**

trade
American colonies and, 60–61, 64, **66**, 71
Articles of Confederation and, 94, 117, 130
ban on British, 64–65
Declaration of Independence and, 71
Federalists and, **160**
government and, 94, 99, 150–51, **160**
Hamilton and, 175
international, 99, 126, 177, 244, 246, **252**
New Jersey Plan and, 117
North–South conflict and, 122–24, 126
Shays' Rebellion and, 99–100
slave, 126, 133
treaty with British and, 177
See also tariffs

treason (def.) 80, 143

treaty (def.) 81, 98, **139–40, 151–2,** 177
during war between France and
Great Britain, 176–177, 182–83
to create United Nations, 246–47

Treaty of Paris (def.) 81, 97

Twenty-fifth Amendment 144

Twenty-fourth Amendment (def.) 219

Twenty-second Amendment (def.) 141

Twenty-sixth Amendment (def.) 221

Two Treatises of Government 14

unalienable rights *See* inalienable,
(unalienable) rights

unitary government (def.) 148, **153–154**

United Nations (def.) 246, 247, **252**

Valley Forge 78–79

Vermont bill of rights 91

veto (def.) 88, 89, 131, 134, 139–40

Virginia
American Revolution and, 81
colonies' first elected legislature in, 58
debts to the British and, 182–83
Declaration of Rights, 90–91, **92**
home of Jefferson, Madison,
and Washington, 107
in Mayflower Compact, **20**
population of colonial, **115**

Virginia Plan (def.) 116, 117–**118**, **120**

von Steuben, Friedrich 79, **82**

voting rights *See* suffrage

Voting Rights Act (1965) (def.) 219, 221

Warren, Mercy Otis 11, **82**, 158

Washington, George
American Revolution and, 65, 78–79, **82**
civic virtue and, **30**
as first president, 140, 166–67, 172, 175–78
as Founder, 11
Philadelphia Convention and, 107, 109, **112**

Washington, Martha 78, **82**

William the Conqueror 51, **56**

women
in colonies, 7, **12**, 64
discrimination against, 10, 227
equal protection and, 231
Philadelphia Convention and, 109
suffrage for, 10, 215–16, 219–20, **224**
See also Daughters of Liberty

Women's Declaration of Rights 219, 220

writ of habeas corpus (def.) 133, **136**, 151, 161

writs of assistance (def.) 61

Yorktown Surrender 81

Cover

Frank Blackwell Mayer, *The Continentals*, Prints and Photographs Division, Library of Congress, PGA-Mayer-Continentals (C size)

Front Matter

Page i, Jacob Lawrence, *The 1920's...The Migrants Arrive and Cast Their Ballots*, The Collection of The Newark Museum, Kent Bicentennial Portfolio, Gift of Lorillard, 1975; vii, Warren Burger, Supreme Court Historical Society; viii, Rotunda for the Charters of Freedom, National Archives and Records Administration.

Unit One

Page xiii, Benjamin West, *The American Peace Commissioners*, Treaty of Paris, 1783, detail, left to right: John Adams, Benjamin Franklin, Henry Laurens, and William Temple Franklin, The Granger Collection, New York.

Lesson One

Page 3, A New England kitchen of the American Revolutionary War period, The Granger Collection, New York; Terms to Understand: 4, 14, 22, 32, 42, 50, 58, 68, 76, 84, 94, 106, 114, 122, 130, 138, 148, 156, 166, 172, 182, 188, 198, 208, 216, 226, 234, 244, 254, 264, Bostonians reading news of the Stamp Act in August 1765, The Granger Collection, New York; 4, *His Most Sacred Majesty George III, King of Great Britain & c.*, Prints and Photographs Division, Library of Congress, LC-USZ62-7819; 5, *Crates Ligneain Quapifces Vftulant, from A Briefe and True Report of the New Found Land of Virginia in 1590*, The Mariner's Museum, Newport News, VA; 6, Edward Hicks, *The Residence of David Twining*, detail, Art Resource, NY; 7, AP/WIDE WORLD PHOTOS/The Daily Commercial, Christian Fuchs; 11, Eliphalet Frazer Andrews, copy of George Peter Alexander Healy, after Gilbert Stuart, *John Adams*, U.S. Senate Collection.

Lesson Two

Page 13, Cornelia Adele Strong Fassett, *The Florida Case Before the Electoral Commission*, U.S. Senate Collection; 14, H. Garnier, *J. Locke*, Prints and Photographs Division, Library of Congress, LC-USZ62-59655; 16, John Locke, *Two Treatises of Government*, Library of Congress; 17, Carol Guenzi Agents/Index Stock Imagery.

Lesson Three

Page 21, Cicero pronouncing his first oration against Cataline in the Roman Senate in 64 B.C., after the mural by C. Maccari, The Granger Collection, New York; 22, Cesare Maccari, Mural at Palazzo Madama, Rome, Francesco Venturi/CORBIS; 23, AP/WIDE WORLD PHOTOS/John Duricka; 24, AP/WIDE WORLD PHOTOS/Eric Risberg; 28, Campaign poster for William McKinley, Prints and Photographs Division, Library of Congress, LC-USZC4-1329; 29, AP/WIDE WORLD PHOTOS/Harry Hamburg.

Lesson Four

Page 31, Bettmann/CORBIS; 32, Allegorical Virginia Constitution ratification poster, 1987, after John Singleton Copley's *Watson and the Shark*, Courtesy of Picture History; 34, *Temple of Liberty*, detail from 1876 campaign broadside, Photographs Division, Library of Congress, LC-USZ62-91368.

Lesson Five

Page 41, Hans Holbein, *Henry VIII, King of England*, detail, Prints and Photographs Division, Library of Congress, LC-USZC4-8327; 42, Julius Caesar regaining the loyalty of mutinous soldiers of the 10th legion in the Campus Martius at Rome, 47 B.C., The Granger Collection, New York; 43 (l), Alexander Hamilton, Prints and Photographs Division, Library of Congress, LC-USZ62-91098; 43 (c), Antoine Maurin, *Benjamin Franklin: Peint D'Après Nature pour la Famille*, Prints and Photographs Division, Library of Congress, LC-USZ62-21488; 43 (r), Dominic W. Boudet, *George Mason*, The Granger Collection, New York; 45, U.S. Supreme Court, Hisham F. Ibrahim/Volume 74: U.S. Landmarks and Travel 2/Getty Images.

Unit Two

Page 47, *Evacuation of New York by the British*, November 25, 1783, Prints and Photographs Division, Library of Congress, LC-USZC4-1306.

Lesson Six

Page 49, AP/WORLD WIDE PHOTOS/Michael Stephens/WPA POOL; 50, Elizabeth Canning sentenced for perjury in 1754 at the Session's House of the Old Bailey, London, The Granger Collection, New York; 52, *King John Signing the Great Charter*, illustration from *Cassell's Ilustrated History of England*, London, 1903, from Wikipedia, "John of England"; 55, Photo by Dave Gatley/ FEMA News Photo.

Lesson Seven

Page 57, *John Malcolm, British Commissioner Tarred and Feathered, Jan. 25. 1774.*, Picture Collection, The Branch Libraries, The New York Public Library, Astor, Lenox and Tilden Foundations; 58, Charter deed from Charles II to James, the Duke of York, for Delaware, March 22, 1682, Delaware Public Archives; 59, Tompkins Harrison Matteson, *Founding of Maryland*, Courtesy of the Maryland Commission on Artistic Property of the Maryland State Archives; 63 (l), Oliver Pelton, *James Otis*, Prints and Photographs Division, Library of Congress, LC-USZ62-102561; 63 (r), *William Bradford, 1755–1795*, reproduction of painting by Bass Otis after St. Memin, Prints and Photographs Division, Library of Congress, LC-USZ6-830; 64, Boston Massacre, 1770, Crispus Attucks in center foreground, The Granger Collection, New York; 65, Allyn Cox, *The First Continental Congress, 1774*, Architect of the Capitol.

Lesson Eight

Page 67, *The Rebels of '76*, Prints and Photographs Division, Library of Congress, LC-USZC4-2485; 68, J.L.G. Ferris, *Writing the Declaration of Independence, 1776,* Prints and Photographs Division, Library of Congress, LC-USZC4-9904; 69, Declaration of Independence, National Archives and Records Administration; 70, Pendelton's Lithography, *Thomas Jefferson*, Prints and Photographs Division, Library of Congress, LC-USZ62-117117; 72, Benjamin West, *Reception of the American Loyalists in England*, Picture Collection, The Branch Libraries, The New York Public Library, Astor, Lenox and Tilden Foundations; 73, Colonial boys mocking a Loyalist, The Granger Collection, New York.

Lesson Nine

Page 75, *British Soldiers During a Reenactment of the Battle of Lexington,* © Franklin McMahon/CORBIS; 76, Paul Revere's ride from Boston to Lexington, April 18, 1775, The Granger Collection, New York; 78, Martha Washington visits George Washington at headquarters, Morristown, Picture Collection, The Branch Libraries, The New York Public Library, Astor, Lenox and Tilden Foundations; 79, General George Washington with Lafayette at Valley Forge, 1777, The Granger Collection, New York; 80, Anton Hohenstein, *Franklin's Reception at the Court of France, 1778*, Prints and Photographs Division, Library of Congress, LC-USZC4-623; 81, British surrender at Yorktown, October 19, 1781, after Arthur Burdett Frost, The Granger Collection, New York.

Lesson Ten

Page 83, James B. Marston, *Old State House*, © Burnstein Collection/CORBIS; 84, John Hancock, by unidentified artist after John Singleton Copley, Collection of The New-York Historical Society, accession number 1945.84; 85, E. Percy Moran, *The Concord Stage*, Prints and Photographs Division, Library of Congress, LC-USZC4-4972; 86 (l), North Carolina banknote, 1778, The Granger Collection, New York; 86 (r), South Carolina banknote, 1778, The Granger Collection, New York; 88, Robert Feke, *Portrait of James Bowdoin II*, Bowdoin College Museum of Art, Brunswick, Maine, Bequest of Mrs. Sarah Bowdoin Dearborn; 90, *The Pillory*, The Granger Collection, New York; 91, Liz Roll/FEMA.

Lesson Eleven

Page 93, Articles of Confederation, National Archives and Records Administration; 94, Howard Pyle, Carpenter's Hall, Philadelphia, The Granger Collection, New York; 95, *American Colonies, 1777*, by Mapping Specialists, www.mappingspecialists.com, © 2006 Center for Civic Education; 97, Howard Pyle, A colonial schoolmaster and his pupils, Pennsylvania, The Granger Collection, New York.

Unit Three

Page 103, Henry Hintermeister, *The Foundation of American Government*, detail, Prints and Photographs Division, Library of Congress, LC-USZ62-950.

Lesson Twelve

Page 105, Junius Brutus Stearns, *George Washington as Statesman at the Constitutional Convention*, The Granger Collection, New York; 106, John Vanderlyn, *James Madison*, White House Historical Association (White House Collection); 107, Howard Chandler Christy, *Scene at the Signing of the Constitution of the United States*, U.S. Capitol Historical Society; 108 (l), Photograph by Martin Lenders for the U.S. Census Bureau, Public Information Office (PIO); 108 (cl), Photograph by Lloyd Wolf for the U.S. Census Bureau, Public Information Office (PIO); 108 (cr), Photograph by Lloyd Wolf for the U.S. Census Bureau, Public Information Office (PIO); 108 (r), Photograph by Michael Newell for the U.S. Census Bureau, Public Information Office (PIO); 111, First page of the U.S. Constitution, National Archives and Records Administration.

Lesson Thirteen

Page 113, U.S. Senate, 109th Congress (2006), U.S. Senate Historical Office; 114, © 2006 Jupiterimages Corporation; 115, *Population of American Colonies, 1790*, by Mapping Specialists, www.mappingspecialists.com, © 2006 Center for Civic Education; 118, Department of Defense photo by Master Sgt. Ken Hammond; 119, AP/WORLD WIDE PHOTOS/Joe Marquette.

Lesson Fourteen

Page 121, Currier & Ives, *A Cotton Plantation on the Mississippi*, Prints and Photographs Division, Library of Congress, LC-USZC2-3367; 122, Earle Wilton Richardson, *Employment of Negroes in Agriculture*, detail, Smithsonian American Art Museum, Washington, D.C./Art Resource, NY; 123, Fitz Hugh Lane, *The Fort and Ten Pound Island, Gloucester, 1848*, detail, The Newark Museum/Art Resource, NY; 125, *A Slave-Coffle Passing the Capitol*, Prints and Photographs Division, Library of Congress, LC-USZ62-2574; 126, John Singleton Copley, *Paul Revere*, The Granger Collection, New York; 127, James E. Taylor, *The Primary Causes of War—The Negro and Cotton*, Picture Collection, The Branch Libraries, The New York Public Library, Astor, Lenox and Tilden Foundations.

Lesson Fifteen

Page 129, © CORBIS; 130, AP/WIDE WORLD PHOTOS/Danny Johnston; 132, Photo by Vance Harris, USPS; 133, © Bettmann/CORBIS; 134, Courtesy NASA.

Lesson Sixteen

Page 137, William Philpott/Reuters; 138, George Bush Presidential Library; 139, AP/WIDE WORLD PHOTOS/Bob Daugherty; 141, AP/WIDE WORLD PHOTOS/Bob Child.

Unit Four

Page 145, © 2006 Jupiterimages Corporation.

Lesson Seventeen

Page 147, © 2006 Visions of America, LLC; 148, © Wolfgang Kaehler/CORBIS; 150, Prints and Photographs Division, Library of Congress, LC-USZ62-128756; 151, © 2006 Jupiterimages Corporation; 152, Robert Kaufmann/FEMA.

Lesson Eighteen

Page 155, *In the Reading Room of an 18th Century New York Coffee House*, after Howard Pyle, The Granger Collection, New York; 156, *Along the Waterfront in Old New York*, after Howard Pyle, The Granger Collection, New York; 157, Howard Pyle, Women at the polls in New Jersey ca. 1790–1807, The Granger Collection, New York; 158 (l), *Mrs. James Warren (Mercy Otis)*, John Singleton Copley, © Museum of Fine Arts, Boston, Massachusetts, Bridgeman Art Library International Ltd., London/New York; 158 (r), First edition of *The Federalist*, 1788, Rare Books and Special Collections Division, Library of Congress; 159 (t), School of Giovanni Paolo Panini, *Capricci of Classical Ruins with the Arch of Septimus Severus, Trajan's Column, and the Maison Carree, with Philosophers Discoursing and Figures Strolling*, © Christie's Images/CORBIS; 159 (b), Bill of Rights, Library of Congress, American Memory, Printed Ephemera Collection, Portfolio 244, Folder 44.

Lesson Nineteen

Page 165, J.L.G. Ferris, *Washington's Inauguration at Philadelphia*, Prints and Photographs Division, Library of Congress, LC-USZC4-12011; 166, George Washington's inauguration, The Granger Collection, New York; 167, George Holland, *A View of the Federal Hall of the City of New York, As Appeared in the Year 1797; with the Adjacent Buildings Thereto*, Prints and Photographs Division, Library of Congress, LC-USZCN4-180; 169, AP/WORLD WIDE PHOTO/Chitose Suzuki.

Lesson Twenty

Page 171, Franklin McMahon, *Flag Sales*, © Franklin McMahon/CORBIS; 172, John Trumbull, *Portrait of Alexander Hamilton*, detail, National Portrait Gallery, Smithsonian Institution/Art Resource, NY; 173, Reza Estakhrian/Getty Images; 174, Patrick Clark/Photodisc Green/Getty Images; 175, Peter Morgan/Reuters; 176 (l), Prints and Photographs Division, Library of Congress, HABS, PA, 51-PHILA, 235-6; 176 (r), John Jay burned in effigy, 1794, The Granger Collection, New York; 177, Thomas Sutherland, after Thomas Whitcombe, *Capture of l'Immortalité*, © Stapleton Collection/ CORBIS; 179 (l), Tally of electoral votes for the 1800 presidential election, February 11, 1801, Records of the United States Senate, National Archives; 179 (r), AP/WORLD WIDE PHOTO/Las Cruces Sun-News, Norm Dettlaff.

Lesson Twenty-One

Page 181, Franklin McMahon, *Supreme Court Hears Nixon Case*, © Franklin McMahon/CORBIS; 182, © 2006 Visions of America, LLC; 183, List of American debts owed to the British compiled in 1798 by Thomas Jefferson, Prints and Photographs Division, Library of Congress, Thomas Jefferson Papers Series 1, General Correspondence, 1651-1827; 185 (l), James Peale, *William Marbury*, The Maryland Historical Society, Baltimore, Maryland; 186 (r), *John Marshall*, detail, National Portrait Gallery, James Reid Lambdin, after James Inman, Smithsonian Institution/Art Resource, NY.

Lesson Twenty-Two

Page 187, "West Façade of the Supreme Court Building, 1993," Photograph by Franz Jantzen, Supreme Court of the United States; 188, © CORBIS; 190, NASA Dryden Flight Research Center Photo Collection; 191, Mark Wallheiser/Reuters.

Unit Five

Page 195, Franklin McMahon, *1971 Anti-War Protest*, © Franklin McMahon/CORBIS.

Lesson Twenty-Three

Page 197, Arthur Segal, *The Speaker, 1912*, detail, Erich Lessing/Art Resource, NY; 198, © Jeffrey Markowitz/CORBIS SYGMA; 199, Win McNamee/Reuters; 200, © Betmann/CORBIS; 202, AP/WORLD WIDE PHOTOS/Al Grillo; 205, © Betmann/CORBIS.

Lesson Twenty-Four

Page 207, AP/WORLD WIDE PHOTOS/Reed Saxon; 208, Detail of *Freedom of Worship* by Norman Rockwell, Printed by permission of the Norman Rockwell Family Agency, Copyright © 1943 the Norman Rockwell Family Entities, Norman Rockwell Art Collection Trust, Norman Rockwell Museum, Stockbridge, Massachusetts; 209, Mary Dyer led to execution on Boston Common, June 1, 1660, The Granger Collection, New York; 210, CJ GUNTHER/EPA/LANDOV; 211, Tami Chappell/Reuters; 212, © 2006 JupiterImages Corporation; 213, AP/WORLD WIDE PHOTOS/ Chambersburg Public Opinion, Christopher Shatzer.

Lesson Twenty-Five

Page 215, SHAWN THEW/EPA/LANDOV; 216, Gordon Grant, *Giddap!*, detail, Prints and Photographs Division, Library of Congress, LC-USZC2-

1184; 217, Thomas Kelly, *The Fifteenth Amendment, Celebrated May 19th 1870*, Prints and Photographs Division, Library of Congress, LC-USZC4-2399; 219, Theodor Geisel (Dr. Seuss), *Democracy's Turnstile*, published originally in *PM*, October 12, 1942, courtesy of Mandeville Special Collections Library, University of California, San Diego, copyright holder unknown; 220 (l), Prints & Photographs Division, Library of Congress, LC-USZ62-75334; 220 (r), Prints & Photographs Division, Library of Congress, LC-USZ62-111409; 221 (l) U.S. Air Force photo by Airman Basic Stacey Jeanpaul; 221 (r), AP/WORLD WIDE PHOTOS/Dave Martin; 222, AP/WORLD WIDE PHOTOS/Kuni; 223, AP/WORLD WIDE PHOTOS/Paul Connors.

Lesson Twenty-Six

Page 225, © Bettmann/CORBIS, 226; *Scene in the House on the Passage of the Proposition to Amend the Constitution, January 31, 1865*, Prints & Photographs Division, Library of Congress, LC-USZ62-127599; 227, AP/WORLD WIDE PHOTOS/ Toby Talbot; 228, Ted Streshinsky/CORBIS; 229, AP/WORLD WIDE PHOTOS; 230 (l), AP/WORLD WIDE PHOTOS/Gene Herrick; 230 (r), Prints & Photographs Division, Library of Congress, LC-DIG-ppmsca-03130; 231, AP/WORLD WIDE PHOTOS.

Lesson Twenty-Seven

Pages 233, 234, 235, 239 (l), William Fritsch/Brand X Pictures; 239 (r), © Bettmann/CORBIS.

Unit Six

Page 241, Evan Vucci/epa/Corbis.

Lesson Twenty-Eight

Page 243, AP/WORLD WIDE PHOTOS/J. Scott Applewhite; 244, © 2006 Center for Civic Education; 245, George Bush Presidential Library; 246, Department of Defense photo by Petty Officer 3rd Class Rebecca J. Moat, U.S. Navy; 247, UN photo; 248, U.S. Air Force photo by Tech. Sgt. Brian Davidson; 249, © European Community, 2005; 250, Peter Turnley/CORBIS.

Lesson Twenty-Nine

Page 253, AP/WIDE WORLD PHOTOS/Steven Senne; 254, Photo Courtesy of the Indian Health Service/ U.S. Department of Health and Human Services; 255, Mel Yates/Photodisc Red/Getty Images; 257, James Montgomery Flagg, *I Want You for U.S. Army: Nearest Recruiting Station*, Prints & Photographs Division, Library of Congress, LC-USZC4-3859; 258 (t), Prints & Photographs Division, Library of Congress, LC-USZ61-361; 258 (b), ©Bettmann/CORBIS; 259, AP/WORLD WIDE PHOTOS/ Scott Applewhite; 261, © 2006 Center for Civic Education.

Lesson Thirty

Page 263, CJ GUNTHER/EPA/LANDOV; 264, AP/WORLD WIDE PHOTOS/Steve Cannon; 265, AP/WORLD WIDE PHOTOS/Coke Whitworth; 267, AP/WORLD WIDE PHOTOS/Doug Dreyer; 270, United States Environmental Protection Agency Great Lakes National Program office, photo by David Riecks; 272, Jocelyn Augustino/FEMA.

Reference

Page 275, Scribes in ancient Greece, The Granger Collection, New York; 276, Declaration of Independence, National Archives and Records Administration; 280, U.S. Constitution, National Archives and Records Administration.

QUICKFIND COLOR KEY